Lecture Notes in Artificial Intelligence 2569

Subseries of Lecture Notes in Computer Science
Edited by J. G. Carbonell and J. Siekmann

Lecture Notes in Computer Science
Edited by G. Goos, J. Hartmanis, and J. van Leeuwen

Springer
Berlin
Heidelberg
New York
Barcelona
Hong Kong
London
Milan
Paris
Tokyo

Dimitris Karagiannis   Ulrich Reimer

Practical Aspects of Knowledge Management

4th International Conference, PAKM 2002
Vienna, Austria, December 2-3, 2002
Proceedings

Series Editors

Jaime G. Carbonell, Carnegie Mellon University, Pittsburgh, PA, USA
Jörg Siekmann, University of Saarland, Saarbrücken, Germany

Volume Editors

Dimitris Karagiannis
University of Vienna
Department of Knowledge Engineering
Brünner Str. 72, 1210 Vienna, Austria
E-mail: dk@dke.univie.ac.at

Ulrich Reimer
Business Operation Systems
Esslenstr. 3, 8280 Kreuzlingen, Switzerland
E-mail: Ulrich.Reimer@bauer-partner.com

Cataloging-in-Publication Data applied for

A catalog record for this book is available from the Library of Congress.

Bibliographic information published by Die Deutsche Bibliothek
Die Deutsche Bibliothek lists this publication in the Deutsche Nationalbibliografie; detailed bibliographic data is available in the Internet at <http://dnb.ddb.de>.

CR Subject Classification (1998): I.2, H.2.8, H.3, H.4, H.5, K.4

ISSN 0302-9743
ISBN 3-540-00314-2 Springer-Verlag Berlin Heidelberg New York

Springer-Verlag Berlin Heidelberg New York
a member of BertelsmannSpringer Science+Business Media GmbH

http://www.springer.de

Printed in Germany

Typesetting: Camera-ready by author, data conversion by PTP Berlin, Stefan Sossna e.K.
Printed on acid-free paper SPIN: 10872247 06/3142 5 4 3 2 1 0

Preface

This book contains the papers presented at the 4th International Conference on Practical Aspects of Knowledge Management organized by the Department of Knowledge Management, Institute of Informatics and Business Informatics, University of Vienna. The event took place on 2002, December 2–3 in Vienna, Austria.

The PAKM conference series is a forum for people to share their views, to exchange ideas, to develop new insights, and to envision completely new kinds of solutions to knowledge management problems, because to succeed in the accelerating pace of the "Internet age," organizations will be obliged to efficiently leverage their most valuable and underleveraged resource: the intellectual capital of their highly educated, skilled, and experienced employees. Thus next-generation business solutions must be focussed on supporting the creation of value by adding knowledge-rich components as integral parts in the work process. The authors, who work at the leading edge of knowledge management, have pursued integrated approaches which consider both the technological side, and the business side, and the organizational and cultural issues.

We hope the papers, covering a broad range of knowledge management topics, will be valuable, at the same extent, for researchers and practitioners developing knowledge management approaches and applications.

It was a real joy seeing the visibility of the conference increase and noting that knowledge management researchers and practitioners from all over the world submitted papers. This year, 90 papers and case studies were submitted, from which 55 were accepted.

We would like to thank all those involved in organizing the conference. We want to thank the international program committee for its excellent, yet laborious, job in reviewing all submitted papers. The high quality of the conference is a reflection of the quality of the submitted papers and the quality of the reviewing process.

Dimitris Karagiannis
Ulrich Reimer

Chairs, International Program Committee, Reviewers

Co-chairs:
Dimitris Karagiannis, University of Vienna, Austria
Ulrich Reimer, Swiss Life, Switzerland

Members:
Irma Becerra-Fernandez, Florida International University, USA
V. Richard Benjamins, iSOCO, Intelligent Software Components S.A., Spain
Rose Dieng, INRIA, France
Juan Manuel Dodero, iSOCO, Intelligent Software Components S.A., Spain
Joaquim Filipe, Escola Superior Tecnologia, Setubal, Portugal
Norbert Gronau, University of Oldenburg, Germany
Udo Hahn, University of Freiburg, Germany
Knut Hinkelmann, FH Solothurn, Switzerland
Werner Hoffmann, Österreichisches Controller-Institut, Austria
Gerold Jasch, IBM Central Europe Region, Austria
Manfred Jeusfeld, Tilburg University, The Netherlands
Ann Macintosh, Napier University, UK
Frank Maurer, University of Calgary, Canada
Hermann Maurer, Technical University, Graz, Austria
Heinz-Juergen Mueller, University of Cooperative Education, Mannheim, Germany
Brian (Bo) Newman, Founder, The Knowledge Management Forum, USA
Dan O'Leary, University of Southern California, USA
Bodo Rieger, University of Osnabrueck, Germany
Roy Rajkumar, Cranfield University, UK
Beat Schmid, University of St. Gallen, Switzerland
Heinz Schmidt, Philips Austria, Austria
Ulrich Schmidt, PricewaterhouseCoopers Unternehmensberatung GmbH, Germany
Steffen Staab, University of Karlsruhe, Germany
Rudi Studer, University of Karlsruhe, Germany
Ulrich Thiel, GMD-IPSI, Germany
A Min Tjoa, Technical University of Vienna, Austria
Klaus Tochtermann, Know-Center, Graz, Austria
Eric Tsui, Computer Sciences Corporation, Australia
Rosina Weber, Drexel University, USA
Karl M. Wiig, Knowledge Research Institute, USA
Michael Wolf, UBS, Switzerland

Additional Reviewers:

Holger Brocks, GMD-IPSI, Germany
Chaomei Chen, Drexel University, USA
Libo Chen, GMD-IPSI, Germany
Susan Clemmons, Florida International University, USA
Thomas Grimm, IBM Austria, Austria
Klaus Hammermüller, IBM Knowledge & Content Management, Austria
Kenneth Henry, Florida International University, USA
Helmut Hnojsky, IBM Austria, Austria
Randy Kaplan, Drexel University, USA
Gerald Jäschke, GMD-IPSI, Germany
Marcello L'Abbate, GMD-IPSI, Germany
Yair Levy, Florida International University, USA
Grigori Melnik, University of Calgary, Canada
Frank Mickeler, University of St. Gallen, Switzerland
Claudia Niedereé, GMD-IPSI, Germany
Simeon Simoff, University of Technology, Sydney, Australia
Ljiljana Stojanovic, University of Karlsruhe, Germany
Nenad Stojanovic, University of Karlsruhe, Germany
York Sure, University of Karlsruhe, Germany
Andreas Witschi, PricewaterhouseCoopers Consulting, Switzerland

Table of Contents

Invited Talk

Practical Aspects of Knowledge Management in Industry

Angelika Mittelmann

voest-alpine Stahl GmbH
angelika.mittelmann@voest.co.at

Abstract. After a short introduction into the problem area of knowledge management and some basic definitions of key terms a holistic process model – the K2BE® Roadmap – is introduced as apractical guideline for the implementation of knowledge management. The four sections and phases of the K2BE® Roadmap are described shortly. Its actual application in an industrial environment is discussed in more detail. Starting with a general view of the ongoing project two action domains the launch of communities of practice, the application of Story Telling in a major project -are depicted. At last the core lessons learned are outlined.

D. Karagiannis and U. Reimer (Eds.): PAKM 2002, LNAI 2569, p. 1, 2002.

KMap: Providing Orientation for Practitioners When Introducing Knowledge Management

Stefanie Lindstaedt[1], Markus Strohmaier[1], Herwig Rollett[1], Janez Hrastnik[1], Karin Bruhnsen[2], Georg Droschl[3], and Markus Gerold[4]

[1]Know-Center, Graz, Austria
{slind, mstrohm, hrollett, jhrastnik}@know-center.at
http://www.know-center.at
[2]Gosch Consulting, Graz, Austria
kbruhnsen@gosch.com
http://www.gosch.com
[3]Hyperwave, Graz, Austria
gdroschl@hyperwave.com
http://www.hyperwave.com
[4]Leykam Medien AG, Graz, Austria
markus.gerold@leykam.com
http://www.leykam.com

Abstract. One of the first question each knowledge management project faces is: Which concrete activities are referred to under the name of knowledge management and how do they relate to each other? To help answer this question and to provide guidance when introducing knowledge management we have developed KMap. KMap is an environment which supports a practitioner in the interactive exploration of a map of knowledge management activities. The interaction helps trigger interesting questions crucial to the exploration of the solution space and makes hidden argumentation lines visible. KMap is not a new theory of knowledge management but a pragmatic "object to think with" and is currently in use in two case studies.

1 Introduction

In recent years knowledge management has gained importance in the business world. For more and more managers it is now a priority to introduce knowledge management into their organizations. They have heard a lot about knowledge management, its benefits, and especially the technology and believe that this knowledge-oriented perspective will help solve many of the reoccurring communication and information problems they face. More than that, they often enough expect something magical to occur to their organization at the moment they introduce knowledge management. Maybe hidden treasures will be found which will raise the profits or at least the organization will become highly efficient over night? These expectations are not surprising since the field is highly interdisciplinary, drawing from very different disciplines such as organizational development, business sciences, psychology, all the way to computer science – and the solutions offered are typically rather fragmented.

D. Karagiannis and U. Reimer (Eds.): PAKM 2002, LNAI 2569, pp. 2–13, 2002.

People in general feel overwhelmed by the broadness of the topic, do not know how to communicate the value of knowledge management to their superiors, and do not know where to start. In our experience this confusion expresses itself through the following three questions which typically arise at the beginning of any knowledge management project:

1. Which concrete activities are referred to under the name of knowledge management and how do they relate to each other?
2. How can top management be convinced that knowledge management activities are instrumental to reach business goals?
3. How can knowledge management be introduced effectively into an organization?

While a lot of research has been conducted to design new knowledge management theories [1,2,3], methods [4,5], systems [6,7], etc. little has been published on how to address a broad range of pragmatic, down to earth problems and questions involved in introducing knowledge management into an organization. This paper aims at helping to close this gap and provide answers to the three questions above by giving pragmatic guidance to practitioners.

The work reported in this paper rests on our long-year experience as knowledge management researchers and consultants. We have introduced knowledge management into a number of very different organizations ranging from large automobile companies, over medium sized governmental institutions, to small consulting companies – even into our own firm. We have captured and documented the experiences we have gained throughout the different projects and have condensed them into KMap (Knowledge Management Map) – a tool which helps to interactively explore the possibilities of knowledge management and "serves as an object to think with" [8] during the early phase of introduction.

In the following we first illustrate a typical knowledge management introduction process and explain which role KMap can play within this process. Section 3 explains why we chose concrete knowledge management activities as the focus of our work. The KMap structure is then introduced in Section 4 and in Section 5 we explain the features of KMap on usage scenarios illustrating corresponding to the introduction process of Section 2. Finally, in Section 6 you find the conclusion and outlook of future work.

2 Introduction Process of Knowledge Management

Typically a project for the introduction of knowledge management follows four phases:

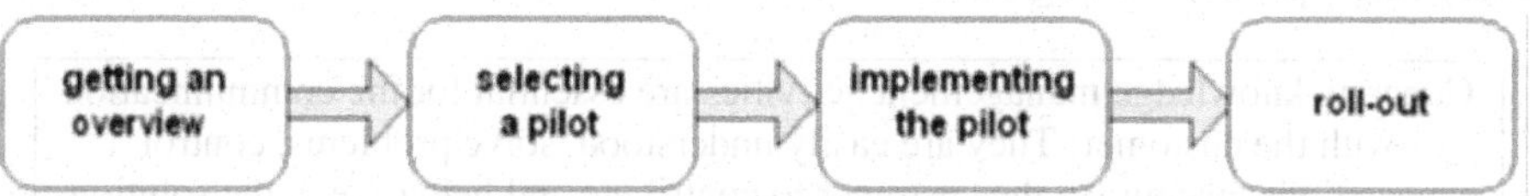

KMap is intended to be used within the first two phases of the introduction process in order to provide an overview, to clarify the relationships between possible knowledge management activities, to improve the communication to the practitioners, and most importantly to help select concrete knowledge management activities to be introduced. In the later phases of implementation and roll-out, KMap serves as a crystallization point for documenting experiences, success stories, and return on investment (ROI) measures. Feeding the obtained experiences back into the tool ensures a living artefact whose value to the user will grow over time.

3 Focus on Knowledge Management Activities

In our work we have found that by arranging our thinking around concrete knowledge management activities – the ones which are applicable within a given situation – we are able to communicate effectively and efficiently with our customers. A business goal or problem typically can be addressed by introducing one or a number of interconnected knowledge management activities, a success story can illustrate the effectiveness of a knowledge management activity, and ROI measures only make sense in the context of a concrete activity and the corresponding business goal which it is supposed to achieve.

So what is a knowledge management activity? We consider activities which range from human-oriented approaches such as skills management, to organization-oriented activities such as establishing knowledge management roles and process-oriented such as business process modelling, to technology support such as groupware systems. Applying these activities to an organization they all support knowledge management in some way or another. However, many of them could also be used to achieve very different goals and might already be used within the organization – but in a different context. Knowledge management activities are concrete enough to provide a basis for an interesting discussion and to ask intelligent questions but they are also general enough to leave sufficient room for interpretation and adaptation to a specific situation.

By talking about concrete knowledge management activities we are able to communicate better with our customers and to give them a "hands on" feeling on what can be done to solve their problems. But most importantly, by making knowledge management concrete and viable we are able to control expectations. The side effect is that people also become disenchanted with knowledge management and realize how much work they themselves have to contribute in order to make it a success. Suddenly knowledge management is not perceived anymore as something which is introduced by consultants and consumed by employees, but something which is owned by the organization and which can only be of benefit if it is of benefit to every single person working there.

> Concrete knowledge management activities are essential for the communication with the customer: They are easily understood, solve problems, control expectations, encourage the customer to contribute and help to own the solution.

4 KMap

Building KMap we started out by collecting about 130 typical knowledge management activities ranging from human- and organization-oriented approaches to technology support. Over time this collection developed into a systematic graph and later was implemented in an interactive environment. The name KMap refers to the union of the graph and its environment, together providing a map of knowledge management.

Obviously any collection of knowledge management activities can never be complete. A user will always be able to come up with new activities which are not included or she will find relationships between activities which are not represented. However, this is not a bug but a feature. By providing a reasonable large number of activities and bringing them in relationship to each other we are able to provide an overview to the user, enable her to explore the possible solution space, and help her to come up with new ideas which can be easily added to the collection.

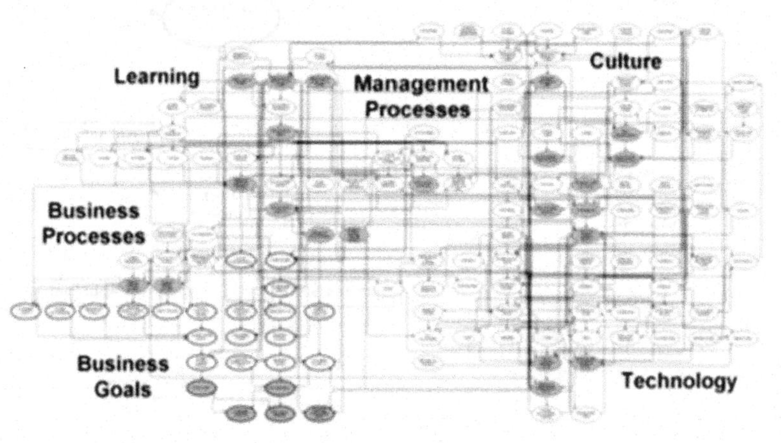

Fig. 1. KMap

KMap consists of six large areas (business goals, process-, learning-, culture- and technology-oriented knowledge management activities) in order to group the provided KMap elements into coarse clusters. The geometric position of knowledge management activities is determined by means of their relationship to one of the five knowledge management activity areas and their relationships among each other. The sixth area contains business goals.

The interactive environment of KMap allows for effective filtering, visualization, extension, modification, customisation, and personalization of information. In addition to knowledge management activities, KMap contains a number of success stories and ROI considerations. Currently we are using KMap within two case studies.

As indicated in Section 2 the experiences gained will in turn flow back into KMap and enrich it even further.

KMap Structure

KMap consists of the following main elements:

- business goals
- knowledge management activities
- success stories
- ROI approaches

Elements in KMap are interconnected via directed lines that express "X supports Y" relationships between two elements and are called a*rgumentation lines* since they can be used to support argumentation of knowledge management activities.

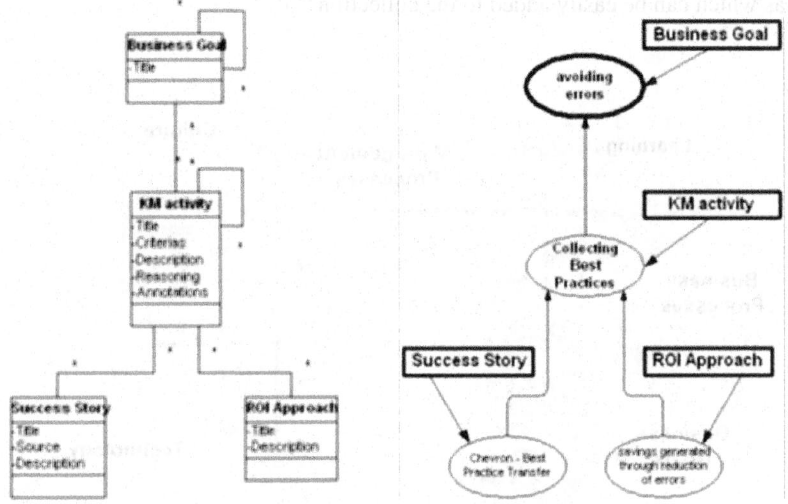

Fig. 2. UML diagram and corresponding KMap structure

The UML diagram on the left of Figure 2 describes the structure of and relationships between these main elements. The graph on the right shows the concrete representation used in KMap. In the interactive version of KMap, thick lines indicate business goals while ROI approaches and success stories are color coded.
To distinguish between different abstraction levels in KMap, two types of elements exist: Abstract elements provide a conceptual summarization of contributing elements (along argumentation lines to reduce complexity and to enable easy navigation) while regular elements describe concrete knowledge management activities or business goals.

Knowledge Management Activities

Knowledge management activities are activities that contribute to the overall goal of introducing knowledge management into an organization (for instance "Communities of Practice", "Portals", and "Knowledge Maps"). For each activity a generalized description and pointers to further reading are provided, and a classification along organization- and activity-specific criteria is suggested.

The following set of criteria is available for each of the provided knowledge management activities:

- *Number of employees*
  to classify knowledge management activities which are most useful in e.g. larger organizations
- *Attitude of the employees concerning knowledge management*
  to classify knowledge management activities which are not appropriate e.g. for employees with a negative attitude concerning knowledge management
- *Initial time of implementing the knowledge management activity*
  to classify knowledge management activities which e.g. can be implemented very quickly in an organization
- *Potential decision level for the knowledge management activity*
  to classify knowledge management activities which e.g. need the top-management's commitment
- *Costs of implementing the knowledge management activity*
  to classify e.g. very costly knowledge management activities
- *Focus of the knowledge management activities*
  to classify knowledge management activities which e.g. primarily have effects on an organization's culture

These criteria enable the classification and structuring of activities and allow for effective filtering in the interactive environment. To provide a clear description of the reasons that led to a certain classification of a knowledge management activity, a text field for rationale is provided. Additionally, each of the knowledge management activities can be annotated.

Through information hiding, all of this additional information described above is only available "on demand"; that is the user has to click on an element in KMap and after that, a separate browser window appears containing the requested information. (see Figure 3)

Business Goals
Business goals (like "Company Growth", "Reduction of Expenses" or "Improvement of Customer satisfaction") are described via descriptive names. Because the value of potential knowledge management projects strongly depends on how much they contribute to organizational business goals, knowledge management activities are related to business goals via argumentation lines.

Success Stories
Success stories (from companies like Chevron, McKinsey, and Sun) consist of textual descriptions and references to the sources of the success stories. Because success stories document successful knowledge management implementations, they contain experiences and best practices and thus are important to be included in KMap.

ROI Approaches

ROI approaches (like “Reduction of travel expenses”, “Reduction of education costs” or “Reduction of maintenance costs”) provide a textual description of measures that allow for effective calculation of ROIs for certain activities. ROI approaches take the financial aspects of knowledge management projects in account and thus are important in planning stages of knowledge management projects.

By default both success stories and ROI approaches are not visible in KMap, their visibility is controlled separately. Also, success stories and ROI approaches are related to knowledge management activities (via a n:n relationship) *and* vice versa, thus enabling navigational aid (through Hypertext links) from knowledge management activity descriptions (displayed in the browser window) to related success stories and back to other related knowledge management activity descriptions.

5 KMap Implementation

KMap itself is an example of how complexity in a broad problem domain can effectively be reduced with the support of technology. KMap builds on an authoring and representation tool for complex graphics (Microsoft Visio ®) and uses its development environment to fulfil the KMap system requirements. KMap is visualized through graphical elements and connections which are located on static geometric positions even when they get greyed-out by the provided filtering mechanism. This ensures that users do not get lost in the complexity of the provided information or loose orientation after filtering knowledge management activities and thus reduces the cognitive burden. Detailed element descriptions are provided via generated HTML pages that can be accessed through KMap.

Although KMap comes with a large set of already structured, classified and described elements, it also focuses on the support of easy modification. The interactive environment aids in extending and altering both the structure and the content of KMap through an intuitive graphical interface. Thus, KMap can be tailored to specific needs of a variety of potential users and ensures personalization of the provided knowledge.

6 KMap Application Scenarios

In this section three scenarios are introduced that demonstrate the typical usage and potential benefits of KMap.

Scenario 1: “Providing orientation in the broad field of knowledge management”

The Case: Bill is a manager who wants to implement knowledge management activities in his division. Because he is new to the field of knowledge management he needs to get a quick overview of potential knowledge management activities and how they can be implemented effectively. Also, he needs to get a deeper understanding of how certain activities depend on each other and where to find further information.

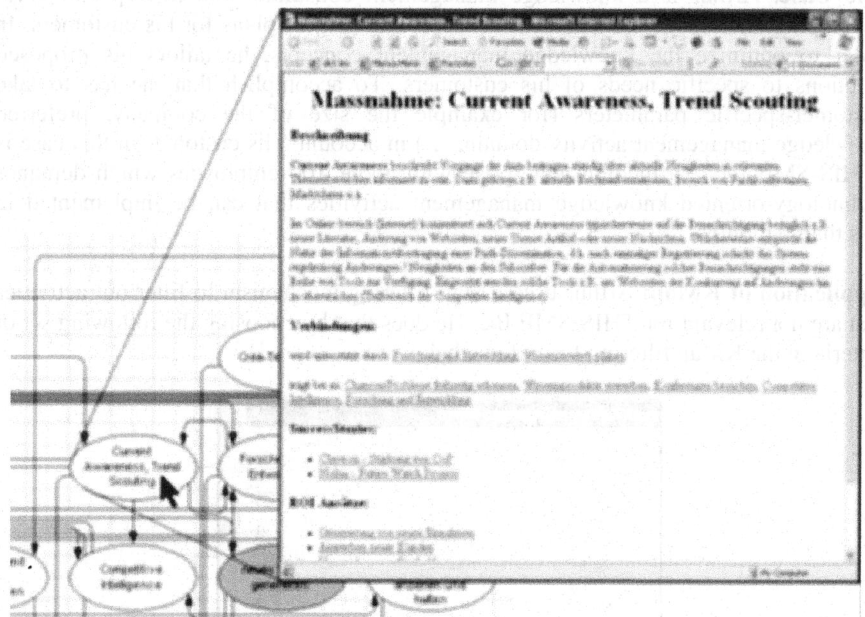

Fig. 3. Details of a knowledge management activity description. After clicking on elements in KMap, a browser window appears containing: the knowledge management activity's textual description, assigned criteria, links to other KMap elements (such as business goals, knowledge management activities, success stories, ROI approaches), reasoning concerning the assigned criteria and annotations.

Application of KMap: Because of the coarse positioning of the KMap elements in six large areas, Bill is able to quickly get an overview over the main domains involved in knowledge management. By focussing on the provided abstract elements of KMap, Bill recognizes basic concepts of knowledge management. One concept that grasps Bill's attention is "Early recognition of opportunities and threats". To learn more about this concept, Bill follows the provided argumentation lines to more concrete knowledge management activities (e.g. "Current Awareness and Trend Scouting") and thus he understands various relationships between concepts and activities involved. Now Bill wants to read more details about certain activities. By clicking on "Current Awareness and Trend Scouting", he gets more background information on this specific knowledge management activity as well as links to related success stories that contain experiences and best practices (see Figure 3).

Benefits of using KMap: In this scenario, KMap supports knowledge management practitioners in getting an overview of a large set of knowledge management activities and thus aids practitioners in building mental models of involved relationships and dependencies.

Scenario 2: "Supporting the planning stage of knowledge management projects"

The Case: Arthur is a knowledge management consultant and is responsible for developing knowledge management concepts and project plans for his customers. In order to optimize the knowledge management concepts, he tailors his proposed solutions to specific needs of his customers. To accomplish that, he has to take customer-specific parameters (for example the size of the company, preferred knowledge management activity domain, …) in account. His customer in this case is "THIS-SME Inc.", a medium enterprise with about 100 employees which demands technology-oriented knowledge management activities that can be implemented in less than 6 months.

Application of KMap: Arthur uses KMap filtering mechanism to filter out activities that are not relevant for THIS-SME Inc. He does that by choosing the following set of criteria in the KMap filtering form down below.

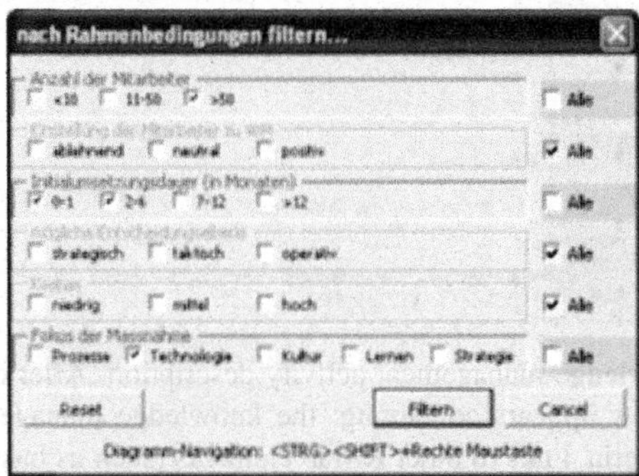

Fig. 4. The filtering form that enables filtering of knowledge management activities based on organization- and activity-centric criteria.

After filtering, KMap now only visualizes knowledge management activities (and relations between them and business goals) that are potentially suitable for THIS-SME Inc.; knowledge management activities that do not fit these criteria are greyed out.

Subsequently, Arthur matches the business goals of THIS-SME Inc. to the provided KMap business goals. By following the argumentation lines that link to the remaining knowledge management activities, he can effectively work out a customer-centric knowledge management project plan that includes a set of appropriate knowledge management activities which contribute to THIS-SME Inc.'s business goals. Related success stories support Arthur with successful examples which can act as templates for his concepts.

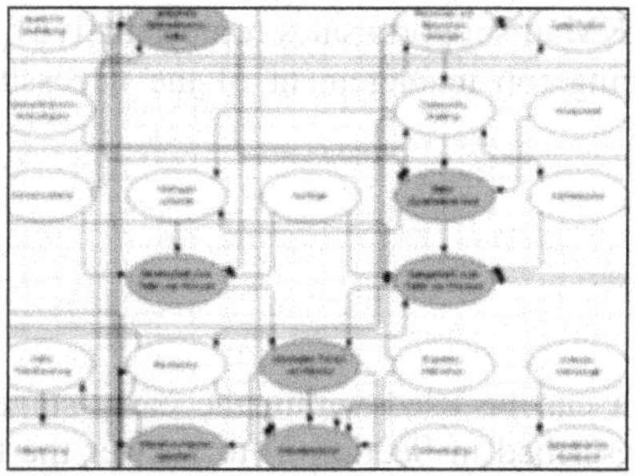

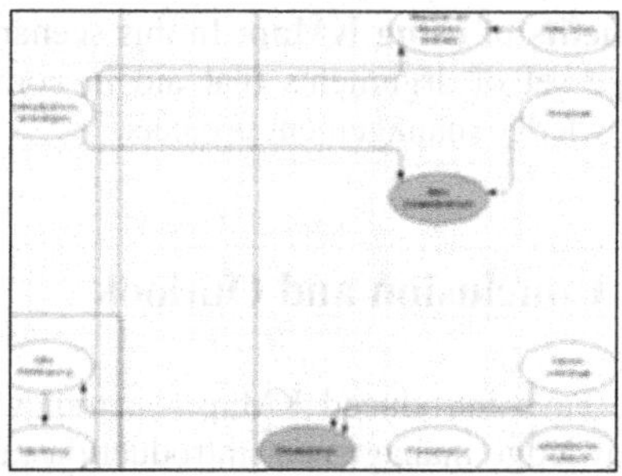

Fig. 5. An example of filtering KMap: On the left, KMap is in an unfiltered condition while on the right side, non-appropriate knowledge management activities are greyed out by the filtering mechanism and thus, the set of potential knowledge management activities is reduced.

Benefits of using KMap: This scenario demonstrates how KMap can effectively be utilized to provide guidance in the introduction stage of a knowledge management project by supporting the development of concepts which are tailored to specific needs of an organization.

Scenario 3: "Supporting knowledge management practitioners in convincing (top) management of the necessity of knowledge management projects"

The Case: Kris is a sales representative of a company which sells groupware systems. In order to sell his products, he has to convince the customer's top management, division managers and technical staff. Also, he has to find and introduce knowledge management activities that complement his products.

Application of KMap: Kris browses KMap for groupware-related knowledge management activities. In order to convince top management, he follows the provided links from the "Groupware" knowledge management activity to related ROI approaches (e.g. "reduction of communication costs"). Based on that, Kris can work out a set of arguments that focus on financial aspects of introducing groupware, which is appropriate for convincing top management. When talking to division managers, Kris uses KMap to find success stories which aid in demonstrating potential benefits. Thus, Kris can draw up a picture of the future that describes how groupware can increase effectiveness of work in a division. Also, through argumentation lines, Kris finds related knowledge management activities like "community building" that are necessary in order to successfully implement the new groupware system. These arguments are suitable to use when talking to division managers. When talking to technicians, KMap aids Kris in keeping an overview over various technical concepts of knowledge management. This enables him to be well prepared for a broad range of discussions with customers that cover aspects of knowledge management that are not addressed by his product.

Benefits of using KMap: In this scenario, KMap supports sales representatives via a large set of arguments that aid in convincing top management of the necessity of knowledge management projects.

7 Conclusion and Outlook

We have introduced KMap – a tool which can be used within the early stages of knowledge management introduction (as described in Section 2) to answer the three questions typically asked in each knowledge management project (as described in Section 1):

1. KMap offers a collection of over 130 concrete knowledge management activities to the user and allows an interactive exploration of the field. The rich content and context of KMap enables a practitioner to gain an overview of the complex, interdisciplinary field in a short time.
2. KMap visualizes argumentation lines which start from concrete business goals and lead to knowledge management activities which could be applied to reach this goal. These argumentation lines serve to trigger important questions, open the mind to different solutions and thus help a practitioner to design his/her thread of argumentation in support of knowledge management.
3. KMap provides success stories and ROI approaches for the knowledge management activities. This information enables a practitioner to judge the introduction context of the activity and helps her to set up efficient evaluation processes to measure the benefits.

This paper also provides additional guidance to the practitioner by illustrating a typical knowledge management introduction process and by explaining which role KMap can play within this process.

Future Functionality
During the use of KMap in different projects, two additional technical features emerged and will be implemented soon:

- *Spotlight-filtering* allows to visualize the n-neighbourhood (based on the connections between elements) of a certain knowledge management activity or business goal. This can further reduce complexity in cases where users of KMap are only interested in a single knowledge management activity and its related KMap elements (neighbours).
- V*isualising changes* made to a KMap is necessary to compare multiple instances (created through extension or customization) of KMaps.

In addition, we consider customizing or personalizing the names of the knowledge management activities to the vocabulary of the organization in which it is in use. In the application projects it has become obvious that the adjustment of the vocabulary can significantly increase the acceptance of the tool.

Acknowledgements. The Know-Center is a Competence Center funded within the Austrian Competence Center program K plus under the auspices of the Austrian Ministry of Transport, Innovation and Technology (www.kplus.at).

References

[1] Probst, G., Raub, S., Romhardt, K.: Wissen managen: Wie Unternehmen ihre wertvollste Ressource optimal nutzen, FAZ Verlag, Gabler, Frankfurt am Main, Wiesbaden, third edition, (1999)

[2] Nonaka, I., Takeuchi, H.: A dynamic theory of organizational knowledge creation, Organizational Science, 5(1) (1994)

[3] Davenport, T. H., Prusak, L.: Working Knowledge: How Organizations Manage What They Know, Harvard Business School Press, Boston, MA (1998)

[4] Dixon, N. M.: Common Knowledge: How Companies Thrive by Sharing What They Know. Harvard Business School Press, Boston, MA (2000)

[5] Bukowitz, W. R., Williams, R. L.: Knowledge Management Fieldbook, Financial Times/Prentice Hall, London, revised edition (2000)

[6] Gentsch, P.: Wissen managen mit moderner Informationstechnologie: Strategien, Werkzeuge, Praxisbeispiele. Gabler, Wiesbaden (1999)

[7] Borghoff, U. M., Pareschi, R.: Information technology for knowledge management, Journal of Universal Computer Science, 3(8) (1997) 835-842

[8] Fischer, G., Ostwald, J.: Knowledge Management - Problems, Promises, Realities and Challenges, IEEE Intelligent Systems, Vol. 16, No. 1, January/February (2001) 60–72

Knowledge Maps of Knowledge Management Tools – Information Visualization with BibTechMon

Margit Noll[1], Doris Fröhlich[2], and Edgar Schiebel[1]

[1] Department for Technology Management, ARC Seibersdorf research GmbH, 2444 Seibersdorf
margit.noll@arcs.ac.at

[2] Business Area Monitoring, Energy and Drive Technologies, ARC arsenal research, 1030 Vienna,
doris.froehlich@arsenal.ac.at

Abstract. Companies, R&D-departments or managers are confronted with an increasing amount of information which has to be analysed corresponding to their importance and applicability for the company and the current question. For this purpose information from internal or external sources like internal documents, patent information, literature quotations or internet information has to be identified, surveyed, read, distributed and used. Especially the search for relevant information and the decision about their applicability gets more and more time-consuming. In order to reduce the efforts for structuring and sorting information the Department of Technology Management of the ARC Seibersdorf research GmbH has developed the software tool BibTechMon for structuring, visualising and analysing large amounts of information. Several thousands of documents available from external or in-house databases or from internet can be worked up with the software BibTechMon. The advantage of this method is based on the possibility of content-based structuring of the information, the identification of subtopics, the visualisation of the contents, of structure and connections of the information and the subtopics. Application fields are widespread – from patent management, technology monitoring or analysis of internal documents up to competitive analysis of companies and products and identification of co-operation behaviour of persons or institutions. Therefore BibTechMon allows the mapping of information to support internal communication, information retrieval and strategic decision support. Due to its different fields of application in the context of knowledge management, BibTechMon is part of a fast growing number of software tools designed to support knowledge management. The exploding amount of software products on that sector make it rather impossible to get a sufficient overview or to select the appropriate tool for a given question. In order to support the analysis and classification of software tools for knowledge management a survey was performed and analysed with BibTechMon. Using this example the possibilities of our method will be demonstrated as well as an overview over the results of our survey will be given.

D. Karagiannis and U. Reimer (Eds.): PAKM 2002, LNAI 2569, pp. 14–27, 2002.

1 Introduction

In the last years information and knowledge has gained new importance for enterpreneurial activities. This development is mainly based on the facts that due to the new technologies access to information is available immediately and rather unrestricted and that the efficient use of these information allows the establishment of a significant competitive advantage. Awareness has increased that the efficient use of knowledge and the avoidance of errors improves the business performance by reducing costs and enhancing customer satisfaction. The awareness of the consequences of not-using existing knowledge or information has increased the efforts of consciously handling it. But due to the fast increase of information available rather immediately via internet or other media new strategies have to be set up for handling such amount of information.

Many different models have been developed in the last years for describing the process and the importance of knowledge management. The perspective of knowledge management can be focusing on the processes of organisational learning [1, 2], on the knowledge creation process [3, 4] as well as a management based description [5]. All of those models are concerned with different aspects of knowledge management. Some of them have a knowledge based perspective which concentrates on a personalization strategy and others refer to a more information based perspective which focuses on the codification of knowledge.

Also in practise manifold types of knowledge management can be found. The spectrum reaches from the development of expert systems, the improvement of communication processes or the institutionalising of organisational learning up to document management, the improvement of knowledge transfer, storage and utilisation. Each of these topics requires different strategies, the involvement of different experts and departments in the organisation as well as different supporting tools.

Based on these different aspects of knowledge and information management many software tools have been developed in the last years. Many software products are described with the term knowledge management tool for marketing purpose but do not support the knowledge or information management process substantially. Therefore it is rather difficult to identify those software products which focus on knowledge management. On the other hand the subjects of knowledge management tools are widespread. Among others the objectives are the support of e-learning, workflow, data- and text mining, document management, information search and retrieval or groupware solutions. This exploding amount of software products for knowledge or information management make it rather impossible to get a sufficient overview or to select the appropriate tool for a given question. Some surveys have been performed which are based on a more or less comprehensive selection of software products.

Most of those surveys are concerned with the classification and structuring of knowledge management tools [6] – [8]. The University of Washington [8] published a comprehensive summary of knowledge management tools in order to give information about the objectives of the tools, the costs, the return on investment and the potential impact on customers. Föcker [6] structures the tools corresponding to the knowledge management cycle published by Probst et al. [5] and gives examples for software products supporting the processes of knowledge identification, documentation, administration and organisation. Böhmann et al. [7] used the four modes of knowledge creation identified by Nonaka [3] for their classification. By considering external and internal knowledge this analysis does not only focus on products for document management but furthermore takes into account tools for organisational or learning processes.

The results of the studies show that in many cases it is rather difficult to classify the software tools. Depending on the theoretical model used or the perspective of the structuring person the classifications vary. In order to perform a comprehensive and objective survey on knowledge management tools which allows the consideration of as many product information as available a new method of information analysis was applied. One way of structuring and classification of information is by using bibliometrics. Bibliometric methods allow the content-based structuring of objects due to identification of the relation between these objects and visualising the results of structuring [9] – [12]. In other words bibliometrics want to measure and visualise the content of (text-) information. Bibliometric methods were developed for the monitoring of technological developments but in the last years they are going far beyond this field of application. At the Department of Technology Management of the ARC Seibersdorf research GmbH the bibliometric method BibTechMon has been developed which allows the structuring, visualisation and the analysis of large amounts of information [13]. This method was applied for structuring, classification and visualisation of knowledge management tools in order to get an objective overview over some hundreds of software products labelled with the term knowledge management and to identify those companies and products with similar content and objectives.

2 Basics of Bibliometric Analysis

One of the limiting requirements for the information handling process is no longer the storage capacity in databases but the time required for information search and analysis. The discrimination of relevant and irrelevant information is one of the most time consuming parts in information search. Therefore the appropriate structuring and classification of information is one of the crucial points in information storage and retrieval. The use of hierarchical structures of information comes to an end by the necessity of handling and surveying thousands of documents. Therefore new ways of information analysis have to be found in order to manage those large amounts of information.

Bibliometric methods have been developed for analysis of specific fields of technology or for identification of experts and institutions leading in technology by surveying literature and patent information from databases [14, 15]. Relations between technological developments, different fields of application and leading experts can be determined. Upcoming technologies can be identified or trend analysis of future developments can be performed. Therefore the bibliometric analysis is applicable for strategic decision support as well as for the daily work [16]. In the context of knowledge management several other fields of applications have been identified like

- competitive analysis of companies, products and fields of activity,
- analysis of the co-operation behaviour of institutions and persons
- patent analysis and management [14] as well as
- structuring of documents and information for knowledge management [17].

Bibliometric methods are tools for structuring information which are mainly stored in databases. The structuring is based on the calculation and visualisation of relations between objects like key-words, publications, authors, institutions, products or companies. The structuring process is performed by calculating indicators for the relation between those objects. For calculation of the indicators several models can be applied [10].

3 Visualization of Information Using BibTechMon

The bibliometric method developed at the Department of Technology Management applies the co-word analysis [13]. This method is based on the calculation of the co-occurencies of words, that is the common occurency of words or groups of words in documents [18] – [21]. The basis for structuring documents and information are therefore words that represent the content of the documents [22].

Before calculating the co-occurencies the words describing the content – the so called key-terms – have to be identified. While literature quotations are described by key-terms, patents, internet information or other documents usually do not have any descriptive terms. Therefore the software BibTechMon contains an automatic key-term generation module which allows the computer based automated generation of the relevant key-terms [23]. Those key-terms are the input for the co-word analysis. The co-occurencies of the key-terms are calculated. The more often two key-terms are used together in documents the stronger is the relation between them and the stronger is the common context in which they occur. Using those co-occurencies, indicators can be determined which give the intensity of the relation of any two key-terms identified. Through this procedure a network of relations is determined which is based on the content of the documents. Since the result of those calculations is a large matrix of numbers the analysis would be rather difficult. In order to allow an easy interpretation of the results the relations based on the indicators are transferred into graphical information and so called knowledge maps are generated.

Beside the visualisation of the content (= key-terms) of the documents, further analysis of the co-operation behaviour of institutions or companies, the identification of experts or product cluster or the comparison of companies and their fields of activity can be of great importance. By using institutions, personnel data, products, companies, patent numbers or documents as objects being related to each other instead of the key-terms several different knowledge maps can be determined based on the same stock of information.

As an example the knowledge map of knowledge management tools is given below in figure 1. It can be seen that the network consists of circles which represent the objects (in this case key-terms) and lines which show the intensity of the individual relation between two objects. The size of the circles represents the total frequency of the key-term occurency in the stock of data. This means that a large circle represents a high absolute frequency of appearance of a term while a small corresponds to a small frequency. Due to the indicator used those objects with a high frequency are positioned in the centre of the map while those with a low frequency find their position at the periphery. Important is furthermore the position of the objects compared to each other. Objects which are positioned close to each other form subtopics and clusters because they occur in similar contexts. The absolute position of the objects in the north or east of the knowledge map is of smaller importance because the knowledge map is invariant to translation and rotation.

In order to facilitate the interpretation and analysis of the map, a statistical cluster analysis is performed in addition which allows the identification of the subtopics. This information is visualised by colouring the objects as it is shown in figure 1.

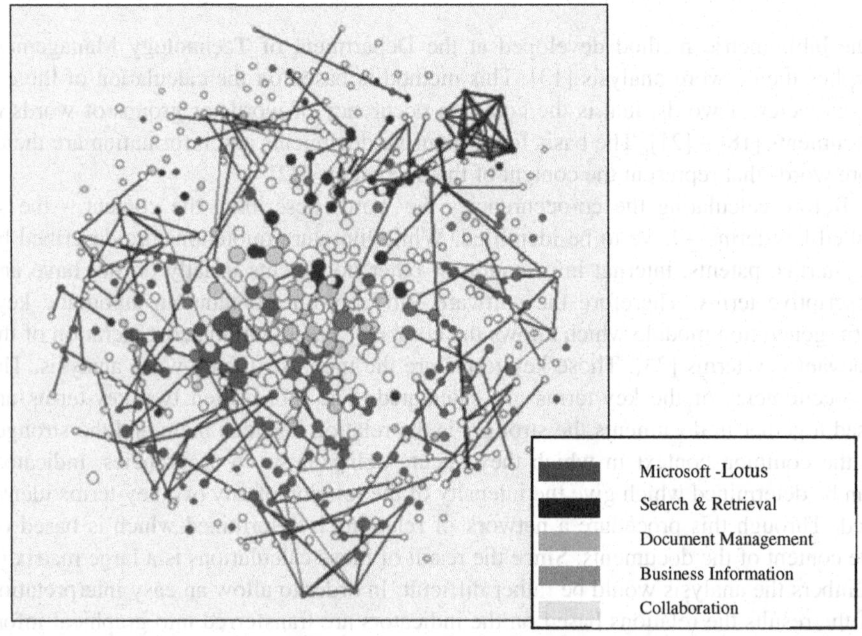

Fig. 1. Knowledge map of key-terms of knowledge management software products. The circles correspond to the key-terms identified, the size of the circles to the total frequency of the terms in the stock of data and lines to the intensity of the individual relation between two objects.

4 Survey on Knowledge Management Tools

Due to the fact that the bibliometric tool BibTechMon can support different processes in the context of knowledge management our interest in an overview over different knowledge management tools has increased. Therefore we decided to apply Bib-

TechMon for structuring and visualising as much information about knowledge management tools as available.
In August 2000 a database query was performed in the databases SOFT (Softbase: Reviews, Companies & Products) and CMPT (Computer Database) using the search string „knowledge management + software + tool". 293 documents were identified fitting on that search string. A database was built up containing those articles and – if available – further relevant information like author, institution, source of publication, company name, product name, etc.

4.1 Key-Term Map

The abstracts and, if available, the full text of the documents were analysed with BibTechMon – the key-terms were generated, the co-occurencies and the indicators were calculated and the key-terms and their relations visualised. The result of the key-term map is given in figure 1. The basic description of the map is given above. As can be seen the topics *Microsoft-Lotus*, *document management*, *business information*, *search & retrieval* and *collaboration* were identified, each of them consisting of several subtopics.

A first information can be obtained by looking at the map. What can be seen at first glance is that the topic *search & retrieval* is a very strong cluster and rather separated from the other topics due to specific terms used in that cluster. Search tools are used in many other software tools nevertheless the development of search technologies and methods are very specialised. Also the topic *Microsoft – Lotus* is a strong cluster lying near to the centre based on the dominance of the terms Microsoft and Lotus. Many other tools are focused on integration into and compatibility with those systems. Furthermore the overlapping of the cluster *collaboration* with nearly every other cluster is significant. This is based on the fact that the networking of teams or different working locations respectively the consideration of management or social aspects play a central role in knowledge management. These first results seem to be obvious for experts. Nevertheless they are indicating that – without reading any of the documents – an overview over a large amount of information is possible within short time and a structure is determined which supports more detailed analysis.

Using the interactive software it is possible to navigate through the map. Figure 2 gives a zoomed view of the topic *Microsoft-Lotus*. All terms corresponding to that topic are labelled. For a detailed and structured analysis of the map access to the information lying behind the network can be used. By selecting one or more key-terms access to the full text information of the database is possible. This allows a detailed analysis of the topics.

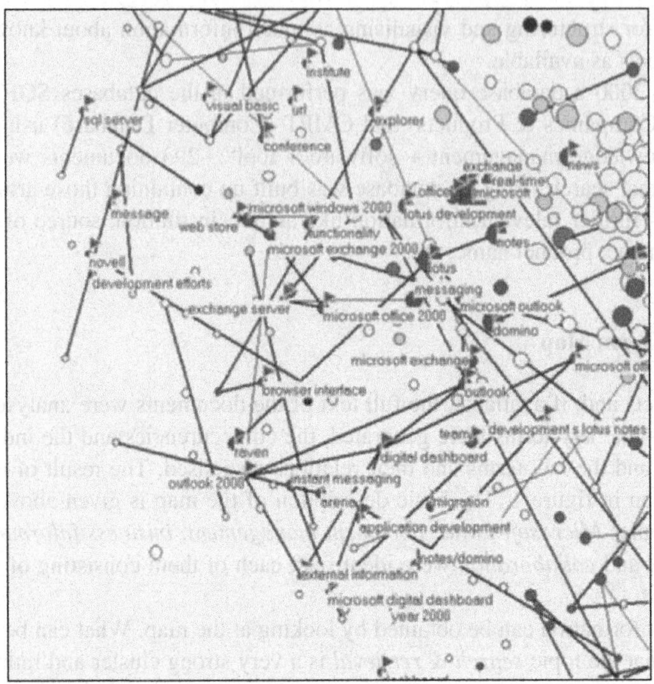

Fig. 2. Zoomed view of the topic *Microsoft-Lotus* with the corresponding terms.

4.2 Analysis of the Key-Term Map

This section gives an overview over the topics identified in the key-word map and a short description of the relevant products and technologies.

Looking at the topic *Microsoft-Lotus* several modules supporting knowledge management developed by Microsoft respectively Lotus are discussed and compared. In the context of knowledge management especially the Microsoft modules Microsoft Exchange and Digital Dashboard are discussed. On the other hand Lotus is developing from groupware solutions to knowledge management. The knowledge management tools from Lotus, like Raven, deal mainly with knowledge generation and distribution. Furthermore some studies are concerned with the comparison of Microsoft and Lotus products for knowledge management.

One of the central aspects of information and knowledge management is the search for relevant information (topic *search & retrieval*). Dataware Technologies, Excalibur, Fulcrum or Verity are only some of the companies concerned with the development of new technologies and methods for searching and filtering of information. Search algorithms were not only developed for text analysis but also for video sequences. These search technologies are in many cases integrated in knowledge management systems. These systems consist of databases, search functions and analyses modules. Different knowledge management systems were developed from KnowledgeX, Grapevine Technologies, Sovereign Hill Software, or Wincite Systems. The result of several studies is that Wincite is one of the best software solutions in that context although the expeditures of integration are rather high. Further products are from Intraspect Software, Datachannel, or Backweb Technologies.

Document management tend to optimise the administration of documents and the support of searching and filing. For that purpose the documents and their content are combined with metadata like key-words, authors, names of customers or companies or further relevant information. Some of the products support the version documentation, access control and security. Products for document management were developed from Documentum, Excalibur Technologies, Interleaf, Novasoft Systems, World Software, Xerox, Open Text, or PC Docs. A further aspect discussed in that context is the increasing importance of artificial intelligence for document management, data or text mining or information search. Also for learning processes, intelligent filtering of web pages or for application of XML for the representation of knowledge artificial intelligence-tools are of importance.

In the context of *business information* portals play a central role. "Corporate portals" are company-internal web-pages which allow the integration of and the access to information from the whole company. The advantage of such portals lies in the combination of structured information from databases and unstructured information, like documents or emails, in one information system. Provider of such solutions are beside others Oracle, Autonomy and Plumtree Software. Due to the fact that those portals integrate all company departments and topics the customising of such systems require high efforts.

In order to get access to business information several products based on databases have been developed, like DB2 from IBM, Java from Sun Microsystems, Microsoft Excel and the SQL Server 7.0. In combination with corporate portals relevant business information is available in short time. Especially for internationally operating organisations the SAP tools allow access to business information and international networking using a web-based portal.

The networking of companies and the customer support are one of the central aspects of knowledge management. Therefore several software developers are concerned with the support of the sales department, the customer support or the linkage of companies. Enterprise relationship management tools want to connect business processes, workflow and knowledge management as well as the sales department with hotlines, notifications, news-systems and web information. Databases containing customer information are combined with other databases and information relevant for sales and customer support. Relevant products are available from Nortel Networks, Customersoft, Ima, Molloy Group or Royalblue, etc.

Last but not least the topic *collaboration* focuses on the employees as well as the co-operation of teams and organisations. The implementation of software tools requires not only technical skills but also the establishment of an adequate infrastructure, management chances and consideration of social aspects. Individual and organisational learning processes have to be established and supported as well as multidisciplinary knowledge management teams. For supporting the networking of different local separated organisation units or teams several tools have been developed, like Docsfulcrum, Intraspect Knowledge Server or Insight. Most of them can be used for gathering and pooling information and building up a „collective memory".

4.3 Product Map

A different view on the survey which focuses on the products themselves is based on the product map. Figure 3 shows the structuring of the products and technologies based on the key-terms describing them. Therefore the product map allows the identification of similar products corresponding to their product description.

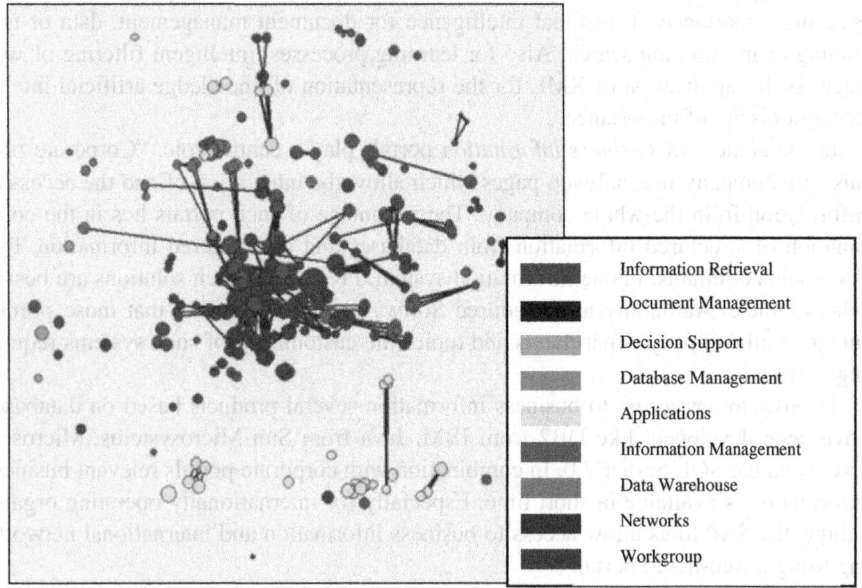

Fig. 3. Product map of knowledge management products. The structuring is based on the key-terms, that means that those products with a strong relation and proximity have similar content.

For example in the cluster *information retrieval* the terms Verity, Lotus Raven, Wincite, Grapevine, KnowledgeX Enterprise, Themescape, Smartpatent, Altavista, Inquery, internet search engines, Livelink, Lexis-Nexis Universe, Seagate, push technology and several more can be found. Although these products may use different technologies all of the terms are connected in some way or the other with the topic *information retrieval.*

That tells me that – for example – *push technology* is one of the technologies for information retrieval and that it will be used in some of the products contained in that cluster. Nevertheless the information which products apply push technology is still missing. For that analysis the relations lying behind the map can be used. For one or more selected terms all relating objects can be identified at once. Figure 4 gives as an example the co-star of all terms relating to the selected term *push technology*. It can be seen that the relations do not only exist within the cluster *information retrieval* but also to the topic *network*. In addition to the graphical presentation also a ranking of the co-terms can be obtained (lower side of figure 4). The relating terms are given with decreasing relation intensity. Relevant terms with a strong relation to push technology are e.g. Agent Server, internet, Channelmanager, Intraspect, KnowledgeX, Altavista, etc. The results of that analysis are on one hand information about relevant tools corresponding with the term *push technology* and on the other hand information about correlating technologies.

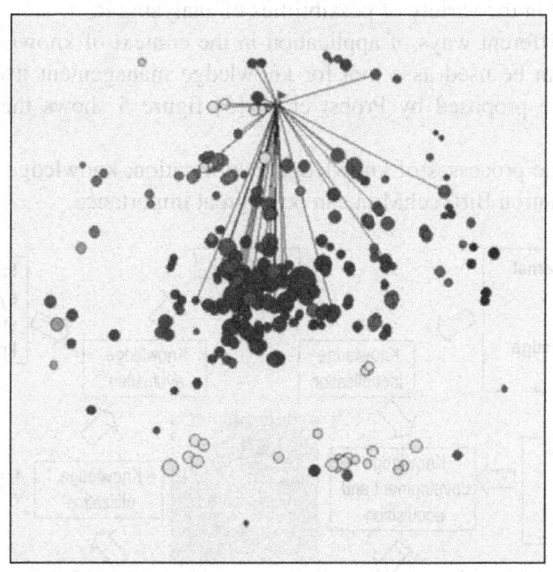

check	freq	sum of	max of	term	theme
☐	8	0.222	0.222	agent server	networks
☐	14	0.214	0.214	internet	information retrieval
☐	3	0.200	0.200	channelmanager 2.0	networks
☐	3	0.200	0.200	intraspect 2.0	networks
☐	3	0.200	0.200	knowledgex 1.0	networks
☐	3	0.200	0.200	workflow	networks
☐	4	0.167	0.167	bongo	networks
☐	4	0.167	0.167	libraries	information retrieval
☐	4	0.167	0.167	solaris	networks
☐	5	0.143	0.143	ca-unicenter tng software	applications
☐	5	0.143	0.143	dr-link	information retrieval
☐	5	0.143	0.143	k.store	information retrieval
☐	5	0.143	0.143	lexis-nexis universe	information retrieval

Fig. 4. Co-star (up) and ranking of the co-terms (down) for the term push technology.

5 Discussion

The results of our automated structuring fit very well to the results of other studies which were structured „by hand". For example the University of Washington [8] identified the categories *managing documents*, *database management*, *search engines*, *customer relationship management*, *help desk/service desk tools*, *tools for managing employee information* as well as *content providers* and *portal builders*.

The advantage of our method compared with traditional information analysis tools lies in the objective and automated way of structuring and visualising the information and furthermore in the variety of possibilities of analysing it.

Due to the different ways of application in the context of knowledge management BibTechMon can be used as a tool for knowledge management itself. Based on the knowledge cycle proposed by Probst et al. [5] figure 5 shows the contributions of BibTechMon.

Especially for the processes of knowledge identification, knowledge acquisition, utilisation and evaluation BibTechMon can be of great importance.

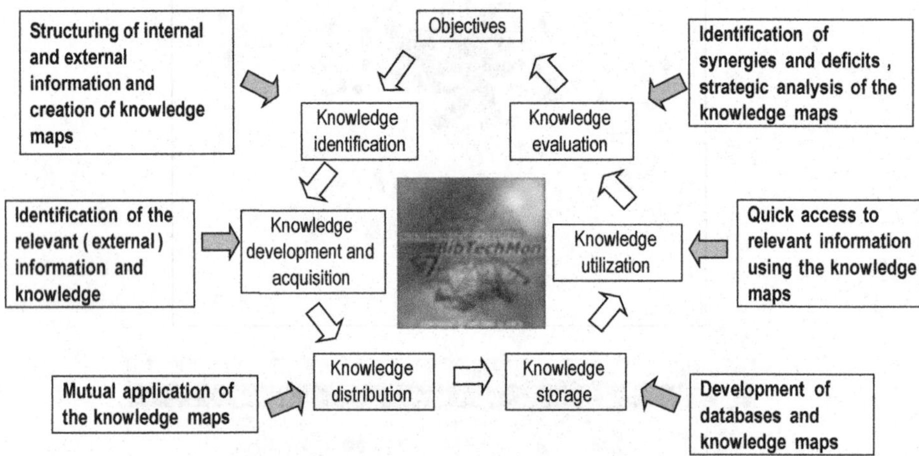

Fig. 5. The knowledge management process as defined by Probst et al. [5] and different contributions of BibTechMon to support the process.

5.1 Knowledge Identification

Knowledge maps are widely used for knowledge identification. Nevertheless in most cases the knowledge respectively the information has to be structured by hand. Relations between different stocks of information have to be identified or the key-words have to be generated by the users themselves. That means that a very subjective view of the knowledge is the result. The generation of an objective knowledge map which is not based on the knowledge and interpretation of people allow new ways in information analysis. Synergies, overlappings or deficits can be identified easily. Fields of applications are beside others the analysis of project reports or other internal documents, the analysis of the internal or external co-operation behaviour of departments or people as well as skill networks of the employees for optimised team assorting. Therefore those knowledge maps can be used for strategic analysis of the existing knowledge as well as for daily business.

5.2 Knowledge Acquisition

Also in the process of knowledge acquisition BibTechMon can play a central role. The integration of large amounts of information allow a comprehensive survey of external information. Especially in the context of technological monitoring or competitive analysis the consideration of large stocks of information is of importance. Due to the flexible use of BibTechMon the identification of leading experts or institutions is possible as well as the analysis of co-operation behaviour of persons or departments.

5.3 Knowledge Utilization

An intuitive and easy access to information is of great importance for the use of existing information and knowledge especially due to the increasing amount of information available. In many cases many documents have to be read and analysed in order to identify the relevant one. The visual representation and structuring makes access to information much easier. Compared to hierarchically structured information the two-dimensional map gives a better overview over the existing or selected information which can be of great help especially for non-experts.

A further advantage for knowledge utilisation is the use of the relations between the key-terms for information retrieval as given above. For one or more selected key-terms the identification of all those key-terms which have a relation to the selected ones is possible. Using these relations the identification of synonyms is possible which is not the case with other search algorithms. Having identified relevant key-terms and topics access to the corresponding documents is possible as discussed before.

5.4 Knowledge Evaluation

For evaluation of the existing knowledge one has to define the knowledge objectives. Based on that objectives decisions have to be drawn which information is important, missing or no longer of relevance. Also for that purpose knowledge maps give assistance based on the aggregation and objective structuring of information.

6 Conclusions

The bibliometric method BibTechMon was described as a tool for information management. It allows the structuring, visualisation and analysis of large amounts of information and supports therefore new ways in information handling and analysis. As an example of the functionalities and applicabilities BibTechMon was used for structuring and classification of knowledge management tools. Based on software product descriptions available in databases knowledge maps were calculated which give an overview over hundreds of software products branded with the label *knowledge management*. Several knowledge maps were generated based on 293 product descriptions, like the key-term map and the product map. The topics identified in the key-term map were a *Microsoft-Lotus* cluster and the clusters *search & retrieval, business information, collaboration* and *document management*. These results fit very well to results obtained in other studies on knowledge management tools.

The advantage of our method compared with the traditional and hierarchical way of information analysis and structuring lies in the objective and automated way of analysing the information, in the amount of documents which can be considered at once and in the manifold possibilities of analysing and visualising information.

Fields of applications of this method are the survey of technologies, the analysis of co-operation behaviour of institutions or persons, the identification of experts, competitive analysis of companies, the analysis of product clusters, the structuring of internal or external documentation for knowledge management or the support of patent management. Summarising it can be stated that the method supports the development and analysis of a comprising knowledge base.

References

1. Senge, P.: The Fifth Discipline. Doubleday Books, 1st edition, (1994)
2. Kim D.H.: The Link between Individual and Organisational Learning. Sloan Management Review, Fall 1993, 37-50.
3. Nonaka, I. A Dynamic Theory of Organizational Knowledge Creation, Organization Science, Vol. 5, No. 1 (1994) 14-37
4. Krogh, G., Ichijo, K., Nonaka, I. Enabling Knowledge Creation. Oxford University Press Inc., USA, (2000)
5. Probst, G., Raub, St., Romhardt, K. Wissen managen – Wie Unternehmen Ihre wertvollste Ressource managen. Dr. Th. Gabler Verlag (1999)
6. Föcker, E. (2001) Die Werkzeuge des Wissensmanagements. Wissensmanagement, Vol March/April (2001), http://www.wissensmanagement.net/online/archiv/2001/03_0401/ wissensmanagment_ software.htm.
7. Böhmann, T., Krcmar, H.: Werkzeuge für das Wissensmanagements. Report Wissensmanagement. Ed.: C.H. Antoni, T. Sommerlatte (1999)
8. University of Washington: Knowledge Management Tools, (2000) http://courses.washington.edu/~hs590a/modules/39/kmtools39.html

9. Van Raan, A.F.J.: Handbook of Quantitative Studies of Science and Technology, Elsevier Science Publishers B.V., Amsterdam (1998)
10. Van Raan, A.F.J.: Advanced bibliometric methods to assess research performance and scientific development: basic principles and recent practical applications. Research Evaluation, Vol 3, No 3 (1992) 151–166
11. Glänzel W., Kretschmer H.: Special issue on bibliometrics, informatics and scientometrics: Part 1. Research Evaluation, Vol 3 (1992) 122
12. Glänzel W., Kretschmer H. Special issue on bibliometrics, informetrics and scientometrics: Part 2. Research Evaluation, Vol 3 (1993) 1
13. Kopcsa, A., Schiebel, E. Science and Technology Mapping: A New Iteration Model for Representing Multidimensional Relationsships. Journal of the American Society for Information Science JASIS, Vol 49, No 1 (1998) 7–17.
14. Noll, M.: Patentmanagment with BibTechMon, Proceedings Epidos Conference, Vienna, October (2000)
15. Noll, M., Schiebel, E.: Bibliometric Analysis for Knowledge Monitoring, Proc. R&D Management Conference, Manchester, July (2000)
16. Grupp, H., Reiss Th., Schmoch, U.: Knowledge interface of technology and science - Developing tools for strategic R&D-management. FhG – ISI report to the Volkswagen Foundation, Karlsruhe (1990)
17. Noll, M., Kopcsa, A., Seidler, G.: Getting Knowledge from a Picture, Proc. 10th International Forum on Technology Management, Vienna, November. (2000)
18. Callon, M., Courtial, J.P., Turner, W.A., Bauin S.: From Translations to Problematic Networks: an Introduction to Co-Word Analysis. Social Sciences Information, Vol 22 (1983) 191–235
19. Kostoff R.: Co-Word Analysis. Kluwer Academic Publishers, (1993) 63–78
20. Rip, A., Courtial, P.: Co-Word Maps of Biotechnology: An Example of cognitive Scientometrics. Scientometrics, Vol 6 (1984)
21. Turner, W.A., Chartron, G., Laville, F., Michelet, B.: Packaging Information for Peer Review: New Co-Word Analysis Techniques. Handbook of Quantitative Studies of Science and Technology, North-Holland (1988) 291–323,
22. Leyersdorf, K.: Words and Co-Words as Indiciators of Intellectual Organizations, Research Policy, Vol 18 (1989) 209–223
23. Widhalm, C., Kopsca, A., Schiebel, E., Müller, H.G., Balling, N.: Conceptual Development of a Text Import and Automatic Indexing Procedure. ARC report OEFZS–S-0051 (1999) (confidential)

Implementing KM Solutions in a Public Research Institution: The CNRS Case

Gérard Lelièvre and Jacques Souillot

CNRS, Direction des Etudes et des Programmes, Mission Ressources et Compétences Technologiques (UPS2274),
1 Place Aristide Briand, 92195 Meudon Cedex, France
{gerard.lelievre, jacques.souillot}@cnrs-dir.fr
http://www.cnrs.fr/RT

Abstract. The "Mission des Ressources et Compétences Technologiques" (MRCT), of the "Centre National de la Recherche Scientifique" (CNRS), is a small unit in charge of optimising the technological potential of the institution. One of its main objectives is to provide the CNRS scientific research teams with the best technological conditions that can be hoped for on the basis of the tools, competencies, structures, funds that are available throughout the institution. Redistributing, or even sharing, elements of all natures, whatever the situation, is always a task demanding heavy efforts in the public sector. The MRCT has developed a soft approach to make things evolve as smoothly as possible and take into account the reactivity of the knowledge eco-system it is inviting to transform. Extra carefulness, and realism, has driven the MRCT team to implement its KM approach by impregnation, that is via its competencies networks.

1 Prologue

People's business at the CNRS (Centre National de la Recherche Scientifique) is to produce knowledge. In such a context, where every individual has a highly idiosyncratic view of what knowledge is, how it works, how it is used, what it is for, developing schemes for its management is a somewhat perilous task.

What then of optimising the management of knowledge at the CNRS to produce "more" knowledge? It will be understood that there is no simple, no clear-cut solution, but a number of measures which, by being combined in different ways and implemented in a variety of frameworks, open up new opportunities, new perspectives.

The size of the CNRS itself, the biggest (public) research institution in France (and in Europe), constitutes a given of fundamental importance. The national centre for scientific research is not just one laboratory or a dozen but an administration directly responsible for (according to May 2002 figures) 1,153 laboratories. Its strictly CNRS labelled researchers add up to over 10,500 and the number of its engineers and technicians reaches 10,000. Through its various contracts with other French research institutions, of which national universities, the CNRS is in fact in charge, at least

D. Karagiannis and U. Reimer (Eds.): PAKM 2002, LNAI 2569, pp. 28-36, 2002.

partially, of 64,000 people altogether (researchers, engineers, technicians, administrative staff and PhD students included).

Those first figures can make it quite clear that we are dealing here with a huge entity which can be highly complex and of a great heterogeneity. Organisational chaos is avoided through the divide into 8 department directions, each one dealing with a relatively homogeneous set of scientific fields (e.g., chemical sciences, humanities and social sciences). The CNRS central administration is also relieved of some weight thanks to a kind of decentralisation (but not devolution) in the form of regional structures (called "Délégations régionales"); there are 18 of them covering the whole of France – though more than 45% of the CNRS laboratories concentrate in the Paris region or Ile-de-France (representing 5 "délégations"!).

Indeed complexity calls for an ever increasing set of solutions, and along the years quite a few have been put into action to tackle, for example, specific CNRS management issues:

- CNRS research and universities
- the CNRS and industr-y (-ies)
- the CNRS and foreign exchanges and co-operations
- and so on.

2 Where Does the MRCT Stand then?

There is no KM department as such, however, at the CNRS, although obviously Scientific Directions may have their own implementation of KM approaches. And who would take any kind of responsibility in this field within such a complex structure [1]? Well, no doubt, only those who dare speak to you today for a start –and the other MRCT members (making it a total of 4)–, plus a few of their colleagues and, hopefully, a growing number of researchers.

The acronym MRCT stands for "Mission Ressources et Compétences Technologiques". The declared objectives of this unit are to promote examples of best practice, give laboratories some help to ensure the tuning of prototype technological items (machines, methods, "experimental devices"), foster the duplication of those which can be used in other laboratories, encourage the adaptation of some which can have new applications in other disciplines, support the creation of centres of excellence as resource units on the basis of medium size technological platforms. Knowledge capitalisation [2], as can be expected, is far from being neglected and remains a fundamental.

A strong emphasis is laid, at the MRCT, on cross-disciplinarity, transfer of technological knowledge and know-how, fast acquisition of technological novelties and inherent skills. Technological wake, whether external or internal, is a key factor in the overall process. What is at stake is innovation, that is the creation, production of knowledge, here, at the CNRS. Technologies are but a means to carry out research [3], ultimately they will enable scientific teams to make "discoveries". Consequently they certainly have to be made as efficient and as effective as can be to comply with research requirements (this is called "customer's satisfaction" in the industrial sector!).

So one could say, to a certain extent, that, more or less directly, the MRCT participates in the implementation of KM strategies, at least at the technological level. Besides it also summons quite a few KM tools and techniques to achieve its goals.

3 Making Things Simple, but Not too Simple (A. Einstein)

Before the scope of the MRCT's ambitions one might feel a bit bewildered, especially since the CNRS is a permanently growing "encyclopaedia", containing so exotic disciplines that their taxonomies are completely foreign to the layman (e.g., tribology, mesoscopic quantum optics). The KM specialists will have understood that the role of the MRCT is not to provide "everything" ready made for the engineers and researchers, but to enable them to get access to what they need: information, technologies, funding, staff, partnership... As a facilitator the MRCT helps whole populations of the CNRS organise themselves together, structure their common activities (KM based activities, for the major part), share their resources.

As was said above, solutions are multifarious; at the same time, having to deal with publics of various interests, the MRCT has to offer a wide range of responses to suit them best, taking into account as many parameters as possible [4], and maintain in the process a high degree of motivation and stimulation so as to exacerbate people's creativity.

The first basic step consists in bringing researchers and engineers to spend time reflecting on the information and knowledge they deal with everyday, and give more value to that activity, which they have to perceive at least as an intellectual investment (but it is not always easy to explain what intangibles are, and make it clear that the long term is not tomorrow).

4 Networking

And that is where we introduce the notion of networks: competencies, technological, thematic networks –for engineers and researchers–, strategy networks –for management staff. The network background is a very favourable framework to keep people involved, interested, through interaction, discussion, sharing of experience, etc. [5]. It makes it possible to ensure a significant adoption of bottom of the line KM habits –provided the members set themselves solid and realistic objectives, and that they be somehow "formally" bound to work regularly at reaching their targets.

It will be noticed that the MRCT does not use the more widely spread denomination: "communities of practice" (CoPs). The feeling of "community" at the CNRS resides in the fact of belonging to the CNRS, of belonging to the sphere of research. Referring to a group of people inside the CNRS as a community would be to "singularise" them (and could be depreciative) and give them too strong an identity *vis à vis* the rest of the CNRS population. Secondly people are already categorised in quite a number of ways and shapes within the CNRS, from an administrative point of view. They will not be told they belong to something else, i.e., a new subset (in which they have to fit), but they will agree they participate in something like a *network* (which has a less reductive dimension, and is implicitly open).

On the other hand the word "network" sounds less emotionally loaded and essentially more active than the word "community". It also acknowledges the transient nature of human and professional relationships, the predominance of change, uncertainty, non-finiteness, complexity in our environment. Moreover it conveys a sense of required adaptability, which is the key factor to any evolution, a measure of a system's potential future. *This could also be the expression of a South-European sensibility though!*

As for the second term of the "CoP" denomination, that is the word "practice", it will surprise nobody if it is refuted as an extension of "community" or "network" at the CNRS. One should bear it in mind that we are evolving in the realm of research. Here the word "practice" evokes aspects which seem too close to repetitive processes, too far away from innovative, original "improvisation". The "French touch", on top of that, calls for a more self-esteem enhancing notion: that of *competencies*. This is particularly relevant in our field of activity since the word "competencies" is largely permeated with the notion of learning, training, of permanent growth, as regards knowledge and know-how.

As a conclusion on the community/network opposition, or distinction, let us recapitulate the points the MRCT insists on.

Community. The word "community" could convey the notion of standardisation since a community adopts common societal and ritual traits or routines. It is self-centred. Its social dimensions take more importance than its cognitive tools and objectives. This causes emotional "noise" and cognitive "silence". In particular it can dictate attitudes of "no controversy". What is looked for is "harmony", systematic "agreement" (inside the community).

Network. The network reaches higher degrees of interactivity. The flows of interaction take many directions, are more varied, there are more of them and they are more active. It leaves much less room to "friendly" noise and essentially more space for discussion and controversy. What the network is to favour is creativity, or at least the growth of its knowledge capital.

	CoPs	**Networks**
Exchanges:	standardisation	interactivity
	• ritual traits or routines	• flows of interaction
	• self-centered	• many directions
	• emotional noise	• less "friendly" noise
Knowledge contents:	cognitive silence	creativity
	• harmony	• space for discussion
	• no controversy	• space for controversy
Results:	systematic agreement	growth of knowledge capital

4.1 How Are They Run?

There is not a one and only way of running a network (this is something which can perturb an institution: realising that things can be different from one place to another). Further more each network develops its own personality. One of the main influences on the shape of a network is its group of people who take the responsibility to start it and formalise its objectives, its programme of actions. In a not so favourable case, so to say (but this is a kind of value judgement, my apologies!), it tends to be a "one person governing body". There again it can reach very positive results, but it is somewhat counterproductive to concentrate all responsibilities on one individual's qualities, competencies, leadership, charisma, authority [6], when your ultimate aim is to empower a collective entity based on sharing, co-operating, collaborating, ensuring the growing of each and every of its members! This first shape of "governance" is avoided.

Most of the networks the MRCT works with (it is part of its missions to start interdisciplinary networks, that is cross-departmental ones, enable them to develop, give them the information and communication tools such virtual "gatherings" of people require, help them acquire the needed methodologies...) will adopt a collective decision making body, generally called "the Steering Committee". A steering committee will consist of a number of active persons making proposals and sharing the work it involves or delegating to more competent, more experienced colleagues. They can create specific workshops with their colleagues, outside the steering committee, and will report (at least they should) to the steering committee, who is in charge of the overall strategy of the network.

Another type of network governance is present in what more advanced groups call "the co-ordination group" (sometimes "bureau de coordination"). Terminology, again, one has to admit, cannot be *that* neutral. Knowledge is collective. It is recorded in individuals' brains. The addition of those records will be the state of the art of the knowledge in a particular domain (without emphasising the fact that the whole is more than the sum total of its parts!). Therefore some networks understand an action requires the stimulation of specific nodes of the network. That means locating the appropriate nodes, reinforcing, intensifying the flow of information, communication between those nodes, while irrigating the whole network with quasi-permanent reporting on those actions so as to guarantee immediate diffusion, thus common culture growing. Transparency, trust, build up to a high level, making the network run and compute like a farm of PCs.

But in fact networks come in all shades of grey as would be expected, there is no strict divide between them, their project teams do not belong to one definite category either. The two sketchy typologies that have been reviewed above only show trends, they are not meant to be caricatures. What has to be taken into account is that we (MRCT people) feel more comfortable with our modelling, our analogies, in relation to our work as facilitators and catalysis agents –keeping in mind that we evolve in a region of the public sector which is prone to avoiding (1) shows of enthusiasm for forceful operational structures and (2) serene acceptance of strong hierarchies.

As a consequence the functioning of the MRCT in relation to the various networks it is linked with cannot be dependent on the subordination of the networks objectives to those of the Mission [7]. This implies making permanent efforts for modulating adequate adaptive tactics, acquiring, maintaining long term perspectives on how a specific network may develop, what its next project will be, that is anticipating.

There exist types of networks other than those associated with the MRCT. To some extent they might play similar roles. However one must recall that the MRCT deals with cross-department networks, that no singular CNRS Scientific Department could cope with, especially when advanced cross-disciplinary technologies are concerned. Also the absence of a formal hierarchy in the structures it helps organise is a very strong encouragement to move fast forward at different levels and in various directions.

4.2 Networks and Computer Technologies

As was evoked earlier the MRCT does not provide the networks with what they are not asking for. It leads them, when thought relevant, to feel that they have a need, that they could start a new project. At the same time, the number of networks increasing permanently, the new networks have a tendency to adopt immediately what has successfully been experimented by their older peers.

Typically today a new network will start directly with its discussion list, its forum, and its web-site. Dynamic pages are now quite fashionable with them, and data-bases have to be part of all their projects: directories, inventories of technological equipment, of competencies. This also applies to the follow up of the training courses and summer schools they design with the help of the Training units of the Human Resources Department, in conjunction with the MRCT. Their technological documents are to be made available for downloading via a library section of the network web-site [8].

When they have reached that point the networks generally become aware they are dealing with a wealth of information and that it is worth much more than they had figured in the beginning. They will then think of allowing different levels of access to the various sections of their web-sites. Conceivably the information they deal with can be quite sensitive and confidential, and it is not infrequent in research projects to be submitted to restrictions of publication.

Consequently the intranet technology is gaining more and more favour with the networks. Until now two of the networks associated with the MRCT have chosen that option: the "electronics network" and the "mechanics network". Concerning the web-site of the electronics network there would appear to prevail a gimmicky appetite for passwords and restricted areas, which lessen the interest of the wider public for their digital show. The mechanics web-site offers a wider space of consultation for the non-members and this understandably looks more attractive. Ultimately the number of members of that network has increased rapidly, reaching 800 (engineers and technicians, plus a number of researchers). Besides the site offers more hyperlinks targeting on web-sites outside the CNRS. It even points to on-line training courses (from a technical college) for CAD software.

Whatever the case what comes out is the fact that the networks are quite aware of their needs for training: their on-line libraries are perceived as learning resources as well as treasures of descriptions of technical processes, reference data-bases. Indeed the networks have started to prepare the foundations for their own e-learning activities. They are all the more motivated to keep on developing that new branch of their web resources since they realise that their data-bases are manifold and can be used for knowledge capitalisation, verifications, validations, quality control, making sure of not re-inventing something already dealt with, storing examples of good practice.

Exploiting data-bases thoroughly can stimulate creativity, innovation, but it is also an asset for life-long learning and permanent updating of knowledge. Moreover people get very keen on participating in data-base projects and using their outputs since the tools and resources will have been designed and collected by themselves or their peers.

5 The MRCT's KM Approach and ICTs

For quite some time the MRCT has had a very close look at ICTs implementations within the CNRS [9]. It has taken part in a number of commissions, and made the most of it to lobby for more recognition of the KM aspects involved. It has also led an in-depth work of advocacy for getting equipped whole populations of technicians.

One example, which is a clear illustration of it, is that of the mechanics CAD software. First the MRCT, heavily shouldered by the mechanics network, carried out an enquiry on the use of Computer Aided Design or Drawing (CAD) in the CNRS laboratories. Results showed that a dozen CAD software products were in use. Some mechanics engineers and technicians had none in their laboratories, some even had no computers! After some serious benchmarking a CAD software solution was selected and very favourable prices were negotiated for it with the software providers. That encouraged a lot of laboratories to acquire the aforesaid software. Those who had never had one got financial help from the MRCT, a measure meant to give more momentum to the action. The laboratories who had not equipped their mechanics with computers were heavily subsidised so as to ensure a healthy harmonisation of the use of the CAD software in each and every laboratory.

Since there are no technology decisional bodies at the CNRS this shows the significant role the MRCT played on that occasion. Also it establishes quite clearly that the MRCT's action is transverse to all scientific departments. Above all it strongly confirms that supporting collective entities' projects has more effect than asking its parts to even simply "follow recommendations". Calling on and linking people's intelligence and knowledge is more productive than squeezing them into formatted boxes [10].

But the effect of the CAD software saga did not stop there. The mechanics network realised that facing a huge demand concerning the software, they had to express their needs and their views on how to master the situation, with the support of the MRCT. They then made proposals to the Human Resources Department and handed them their book of requirements. Their training plan received approbation from the HRD, especially since their solution was to be cheaper than that of the software providers!

Another step forward was made when the network decided they would ensure the software hot-line themselves at regional levels: they had representatives with high competencies in relation to CAD in general and that piece of software in particular. Other discussions had to be led with the laboratory directors whose mechanics engineers were to be the hot-line or resource persons in their district. Today, with the spreading all over CNRS laboratories of the software (around 200 licences) and with the growing number of CAD competent mechanics engineers and technicians, the network has started designing its intranet CAD library. The logic of it all was to bring them there!

For some sections of the CNRS population the MRCT has worked well: standardising software, rationalising the use of resources (money, competencies, training), modernising practices and tools, it has accomplished its mission [11]. What the MRCT and others see as perhaps more meaningful and encouraging is the fact that all this was achieved thanks to the collective entity, i.e., the mechanics network –the MRCT being there as a strategy and methodology adviser, as a "coach".

6 Other Examples

Some less dramatic results are obtained in other KM-ICTs sub-domains since they address smaller groups of people (at present): data-mining, knowledge-discovery, scientific and technological wake, quality and project management… More has to be done to increase the influence of KM projects at the CNRS, and more KM projects have to develop and produce significant outputs. The MRCT hopes the CNRS is to amplify its efforts in that direction.

7 Conclusion

Little could be said at the CNRS in favour of implementing monolithic architectures. The tacit principles of freedom of the researcher, of his laboratory, already require the decisional CNRS bodies to associate, far too often, the scientists to "all" the actions, projects, commissions that take place at the highest levels of the management of the institution. The MRCT's approach offers an alternative.

Allowing for less rigidity and more trust is the price of innovation; the return on investment, in the less productive cases, is an environment conducive to a climate of higher motivation and greater efficiency. And with a little bit more luck it equates to an overall conversion to knowledge management approaches [12], bringing in its trail wagonloads of fundamental revisions which help reshape our research technology strategies, and subsequently, all being well, increase the potential of success of scientific research at the CNRS.

References

1. Le Moigne, J.-L., Morin, E.: L'Intelligence de la Complexité. L'Harmattan, Paris (1999)
2. Ballay, J.F.: Capitaliser et transmettre les savoir-faire de l'entreprise. Eyrolles, Paris (1997)
3. Briot, R., Lelièvre, G.: Le potentiel technologique du CNRS (1999). In CNRS, Direction de la Stratégie et des Programmes, Publications. *Site de la Direction de la Stratégie et des Programmes*, [On-line]. Available HTTP: http://www.cnrs.fr/DEP/doc/potentech.pdf (cited August 01, 2002)
4. Malhotra, Y.: Knowledge Management, Knowledge Organizations and Knowledge Workers: A View from the Front Lines (1998). [On-line]. Available HTTP: http://www.brint.com/interview/maeil.htm (cited August 01, 2002)

5. Legris, J.-R.: Note de réflexion sur le concept de réseau. In Journal du METL - CEDIP (April 1999). *Site du Réseau d'Information Compétences et Formation*, [On-line]. Available HTTP: http://www.3ct.com/ridf/ (cited August 01, 2002)
6. Bartlett, C.A., Ghoshal, S.: Changing the Role of the Top Management: Beyond Systems to People. Harvard Business Review (May-June 1995), 132–142
7. BULLETIN OFFICIEL du CNRS: Décision n° 000340DCAJ du 17 mai 2000 portant création de la mission des ressources et compétences technologiques. "Art. 6. – Réseaux thématiques, technologiques et professionnels". In CNRS, Bulletin Officiel. *Site de la Direction des Systèmes d'Information*, [On-line]. Available HTTP: http://www.dsi.cnrs.fr/bo/2000/07-00/246-bo0700-dec000340dcaj.htm (cited August 01, 2002)
8. Pomian, J.: Mémoire d'entreprise : techniques et outils de la gestion du savoir. Sapienta, Paris (1996)
9. Lelièvre, G., Souillot, J.: Knowledge Management at the CNRS. Proceedings of the 2001 International Seminar on the Management of Industrial and Corporate Knowledge (ISMICK'01). Université Technologique de Compiègne (October 2001). Available HTTP: http://www.hds.utc.fr/~barthes/ISMICK01/papers/IS01-Lelievre.pdf (cited August 01, 2002)
10. Suurla, R., Markkula, M., Mustajärvi, O.: Developing and Implementing KM in the Parliament of Finland. Oy Edita Ab, Helsinki, Finland (2002). [On-line] Available HTTP: http://www.knowledgeboard.com/library/km_finnish_parliament.pdf (cited August 01, 2002)
11. Ermine, J.-L.: La gestion des connaissances, un levier de l'intelligence économique. Revue d'intelligence économique, n°4, (avril 1999)
12. Davenport, T.H.: Think Tank: The Future of Knowledge Management. CIO, (December 15, 1995)

Knowledge Management in Enterprises: A Research Agenda

Konstantinos Ergazakis[1], Konstantinos Karnezis[2], Konstantinos Metaxiotis[3], and Ioannis Psarras[4]

[1] Msc. Electrical & Computer Engineer, National Technical University of Athens, Institute of Communications & Computer Systems, Zografou 15773, Athens, Greece
kergaz@epu.ntua.gr

[2] Msc. Electrical & Computer Engineer, National Technical University of Athens, Institute of Communications & Computer Systems, Zografou 15773, Athens, Greece
kkarnez@epu.ntua.gr

[3] Dr. Electrical & Computer Engineer, National Technical University of Athens, Institute of Communications & Computer Systems, Zografou 15773, Athens, Greece
kmetax@epu.ntua.gr

[4] Professor, National Technical University of Athens, Institute of Communications & Computer Systems, Zografou 15773, Athens, Greece
john@epu.ntua.gr

Abstract. Knowledge Management is an emerging area, which is gaining interest by both enterprises and academics. The effective implementation of a KM strategy is considering as a "must" and as a precondition of success for contemporary enterprises, as they enter the era of the knowledge economy. However, the field of Knowledge Management has been slow in formulating a universally accepted methodology, due to the many pending issues that have to be addressed. This paper attempts to propose a novel taxonomy for Knowledge Management research by co instantaneously presenting the current status with some major themes of Knowledge Management research. The discussion presented on these issues should be of value to researchers and practitioners.

1 Introduction

Knowledge Management (KM) is the process of creating value from the intangible assets of an enterprise. It deals with how best to leverage knowledge internally in the enterprise and externally to the customers and stakeholders. Knowledge is considered as a valuable asset that must be managed, and the essence of KM is to provide strategies to get the right knowledge to the right people at the right time and in the right format [1-6].

During the past years, KM has become a major issue of discussion in the business literature. It is a common belief that by leveraging knowledge, an enterprise can stay competitive in the more globally oriented market of today. The KM software and services market is exhibiting strong growth as more companies begin to understand

D. Karagiannis and U. Reimer (Eds.): PAKM 2002, LNAI 2569, pp. 37-48, 2002.

how to apply KM practices for the improvement of enterprise value. The majority of today's companies are using KM programmes and almost all say they will increase these efforts over the next five years, according to a study by the Conference Board[1]. This study is based on a Conference Board survey, sponsored by PriceWaterhouse Coopers, of 150 top executives of 96 leading companies (83% U.S., 14% Europe, 3% Asia/Pacific). Eighty-two percent of the surveyed companies said that are involved in KM activities.

It must also be noted that KM is an important issue as well for smaller businesses. Much of the recent interest in KM and its potential leverage has come from the examples of multinational corporations. Research [7] shows that while there are many reports highlighting the success of KM efforts in large companies, there are clearly many methods for achieving success is smaller companies as well.

It is clear that KM is an emerging field that has commanded support and attention from the industrial and academic community. Many large, medium and small-scale enterprises are now engaging in KM in order to gain a competitive advantage in the market place.

Many researchers have presented methodologies and frameworks for implementing KM. However, frameworks do not provide sufficient detail for the execution of KM initiatives. In addition, existing methods do not adequately address all of the requirements for effective KM [8]. There is a lack of a universally accepted methodology for KM as well as of a universal set of terms, vocabulary, concepts and standards in the KM community.

In this context, the need for a new research agenda has never been more urgent. The fact that KM is the major theme in academic conferences reflects the dire need for structured and targeted research in this rapidly emerging field. This research will address many of the pending issues, like the above mentioned, and it will create the necessary conditions for the creation of a common language and understanding on this field.

Based on a comprehensive review of much of what has been written so far about KM, Figure 1 illustrates the major streams of KM research. The main goal of this paper is, by reviewing available studies and exploring future research avenues, to present a new agenda to support the research on the KM phenomenon in order to address the different critical issues.

2 Technology and KM

A brief review of the available literature about KM reveals that most of the emphasis so far has been on KM frameworks, approaches and methodologies [9-14]. Undoubtedly, there is need for concerted efforts towards the direction of formulating a

[1] Source:
http://www.pwcglobal.com/extweb/ncpressrelease.nsf/DocID/ID3F52FB40278395852568A9006527BA
http://www.ebusinessisbusiness.com/pdf/ExecOutlook2000.pdf

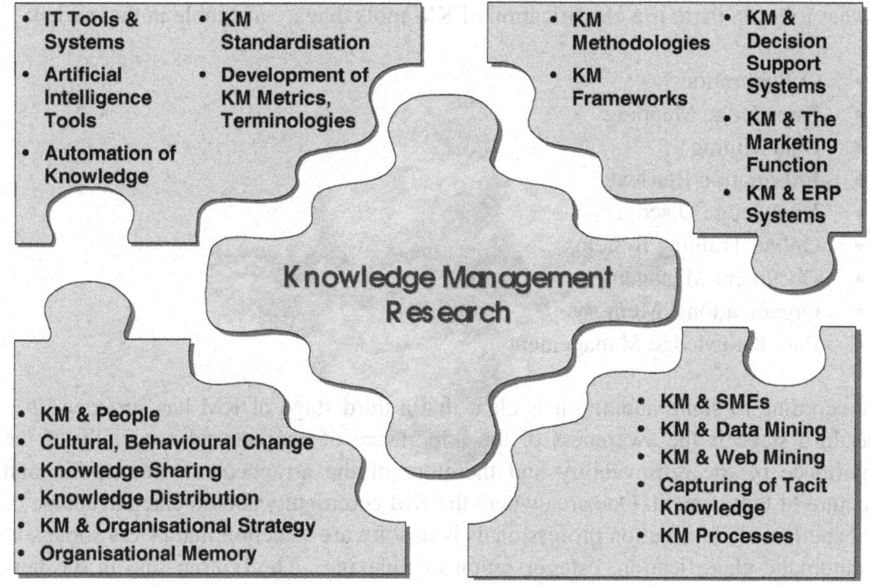

Fig. 1. Major Streams of KM Research

generally accepted, comprehensive framework for KM. [15]. However, the role of technology in this effort should not be underestimated. This is reflected by the fact that according to recent studies (April 2002) the technologies used to support KM initiatives are evolving rapidly [16]. In addition, according to the results of a pilot survey that was sent to European firms [17], the group "KM and Technologies" received the highest level of support from respondents as current or needed areas of training investment. Finally, according to another study (through contacts to the FTSE 100 listed companies) [18] the emphasis of KM projects is in IT (intranet, MIS, extranet etc.). This result, according to the authors conducted the research, emphasises their view that a greater focus is necessary in these areas.
In this framework, we present some critical issues relating to IT Tools and Systems that support the KM function as well as the theme of Artificial Intelligence.

2.1 IT Tools & Systems

The IT systems involved in the process of KM should fulfill, to a greater or lesser extent, two technical characteristics [19]:

- Facilitate collaborative work among the users involved in the process of KM.
- Establish a robust structure for administering the information on which the knowledge to be managed is based.

In what follows, there is a classification of KM tools that are available in the market:

- Collaboration
- Knowledge Mapping
- Data Mining
- Information Retrieval
- Knowledge Discovery
- Online Training Systems
- Document Management
- Organizational Memory
- Pure Knowledge Management

According to some authors, it is clear that a third stage of KM has surfaced [20]. The third stage is the awareness of the importance of content and especially of the importance of the retrievability and therefore of the arrangement, description and structure of that content. One area where the KM community should take advantage of the expertise of information professionals is in software selection that offers some sort of automatic classification, categorization or indexing.. The bottom line in the new third stage of KM is that information professionals need to make their skills known to the KM community, and the KM community needs to seek out information professionals and bring them more into the KM fold. If that does not happen, there will be a lot of needless reinvention of the taxonomic wheel.

The great majority of the KM tools on the market are server-based enterprise systems and in this way, they are often designed top-down, centralized, inflexible and slow to respond to change. There is a lack of research into KM tools for individuals and server-less KM tools/systems [21].

According to a report of an IST project [22] that it describes recommendations for the IST 6th FP, focusing on the future of research and technological development (RTD) in the European KM domain, it is highly recommendable to specifically combine efforts for developing fundamental, cross-functional technologies, applications and the interface with the human user. For example, *3G mobile communications* will be one of crucial drivers for supporting KM. Besides 3G applications, the further development of *intelligent KM systems* is also very important in combination with the goal of the *automation of knowledge*. Moreover, research should investigate: the improvement of human computer interface design & methods; network effects, emergent properties and behaviours from dense ubiquitous connectivity (focusing on the co-evolution of networked systems and knowledge flows) etc. The output of this research will be the advancement of crucial technologies and applications, aiming at quick access to the needed knowledge, at the right time and the right place.

2.2 Artificial Intelligence

Artificial Intelligence (AI) is considered to be of particular interest within the framework of technology's role in KM. AI does not substitute human intelligence, but it can provide a mechanism to support and enable an organization's KM processes. It can be used to enhance KM and its knowledge conversion processes: tacit to tacit knowledge sharing, tacit to explicit knowledge conversion, explicit knowledge leveraging and explicit to tacit knowledge conversion [23]. In this way, AI is capable of manipulating raw data and to produce higher-order information and thus, contribute to the development and leveraging of knowledge in new and effective ways. The main categories of AI that can play a supportive role in the KM process are Expert Systems (ES), Artificial Neural Networks (ANN) and Intelligent Agents and Case-Based Reasoning (CBR). Each category offers some advantages but they have also some limitations in terms of their capacity to support the KM process. In what follows, we briefly present these limitations, which, according to the authors, constitute major topics for future research:

Expert Systems. The classical rule-based ES rely on assumptions of certainty and rationality, which are oriented towards solutions based on best choice between clearly available alternatives [24]. On the other side, KM assumes a world based on uncertainty and subjective belief (reflected also by the concept of tacit knowledge). The use of fuzzy logic in ES could be a possible solution to this conflict. Another issue is that there are many difficulties in the maintenance and updating of the knowledge base of an ES [25]. Finally, ES can not learn automatically by experience.

Artificial Neural Networks. ANN need their inputs to be presented in numeric form so that they can be subjected to the learned weighting algorithms. This is in contrast to ES, Intelligent Agents and CBR, which accept symbolic inputs. If such inputs can be presented in appropriate form, neural nets may have much to offer.

Intelligent Agents. The study of intelligent agents has become one of the most important fields in Distributed Artificial Intelligence [26-28]. Intelligent Agents can be used to help in the search and retrieval methods of knowledge in KM systems as well as to assist in combining knowledge and thus leading to the creation of new knowledge. Future research should measure accurately the importance of the factors that affect intelligent agents and the use of technical tools and attempt to incorporate significant differences between internal and external intelligent agents, relating them to an integrated utilisation of organizational resources [29].

Case-Based Reasoning. CBR performs operations based on raw data (past cases and associated solutions) rather than on stored explicit facts and rules [30-31]. CBR systems can be particularly appropriate in domains where theory is acknowledged to be weak and case influences and interactions are poorly understood. Nevertheless, they do not necessarily overcome the problems inherently associated with the "knowledge bottleneck" phenomenon as presented in knowledge engineering.

The creation of hybrid systems comprising combinations of rule-based expert systems and Neural Networks may offer access to embedded knowledge coupled with an ability to function in the partial absence of certain data.

3 Various KM Issues

3.1 KM Standardisation

Standardisation in general is quite a complex venture that is mostly discussed very deeply. In fact, the relevance of standardisation can be discussed from a number of perspectives. Taking the analogy from other sectors like IT or automotive industry, we can acknowledge that method or process standardisation has lead to large benefits from all kind of perspectives (e.g. organisation, financial, production, etc.). Compared to this relatively hard driven subjects, the domain of KM consists of more soft and holistic oriented objects. For standardization of KM, which is a relatively young discipline and deals with quite 'soft' objects, a number of arguments are speaking in its favour. The most important are the following [32]:

- The activity itself will lead to transparency, bringing all involved institutions and bodies together and thereby achieve a common understanding and common terminology through the process itself.
- Standardised KM aspects (like common approaches to KM processes, knowledge technologies, knowledge based human resources, KM strategies, etc.) will bring the benefits of KM development to a broader circle of users.
- Moreover, from a KM expert point of view, standardised KM approaches will allow the experts to use a validated world-wide common terminology. According to this, communication in this field will be easier and can start from a higher common platform.
- Finally, standardized KM elements like a common KM framework will be used in further research and education environments.

The European KM Forum has carried out several workshops and interviews in order to collect opinion of European KM experts about the most relevant issues for standardisation. It was identified that a common KM *framework*, a common KM *terminology*, and a common KM *implementation approaches* were considered as the most pertinent elements. Figure 2 shows a mind-map detailing the most relevant areas for standardization, as decided by the participants of a workshop [33].

The need for a common KM framework was rated highest (24 points), while the definition of a common implementation methodology was seen as being second most important (23 points). The definition of a common KM terminology was given third priority (16 points). The European KM Forum considers KM standardisation to be a holistic process involving a spectrum of standards on different levels for specific components of KM. In the first step of this process, the most appropriate and relevant areas for standardization should be extracted and collated in a systematic, structured way in order to develop a common terminology, based on common experiences and leading to a degree of commonality in how these issues are approached in future. This builds the KM framework. From this framework, further guidelines and standards can be built for other components of the discipline. With this set of solutions, different organisations with various knowledge needs should be able to solve their specific KM problems.

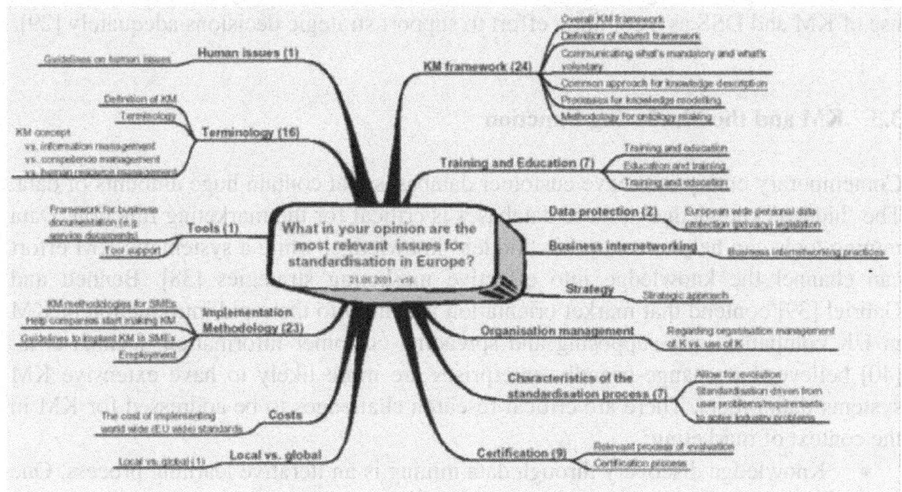

Fig. 2. The most relevant issues for standardisation

In order to develop a solid starting point for any attempt to pursue standardization, it is necessary to define a comprehensive framework that describes each major aspect of KM, as it is understood by academics and practitioners.

3.2 KM and Decision Support Systems

In the decision-making process, decision makers combine different types of data (e.g. internal data and external data) and knowledge (both tacit and explicit knowledge) available in various forms in the organisation. The decision-making process itself results in improved understanding of the problem and the process, and generates new knowledge. Despite such interdependencies, the research in the fields of Decision Support Systems (DSS) and KM systems has not adequately considered the integration of such systems. This integration is expected to enhance the quality of support provided by the system to decision makers and also to help in building up organizational memory and knowledge bases [14].

It is true that, as the enterprises increase in scope, the greater their ramifications for broad spectrums of societies and cultures become. More effective ways must be found to support the vast array of knowledge that will be required in these highly interconnected, wicked situations of the future [34]. In this way, enterprises employ systems whose purpose is to capture critical knowledge, placing it in databases and allowing the access of those intelligent agents who may profit from that knowledge. There are already examples of methods in which the decision-makers use knowledge-based tools for the externalization of tacit models [35-37]. In this manner, is much more possible to improve the decision-making process. Future research on the link between strategic management and IT should examine carefully the evolution of the use of KM and DSS as a common effort to support strategic decisions adequately [29].

3.3 KM and the Marketing Function

Contemporary enterprises have customer databases that contain huge amounts of data. The 'hidden' knowledge in these databases is critical for the marketing function. Data mining tools can help uncover this 'hidden' knowledge, while a systematic KM effort can channel the knowledge into effective marketing strategies [38]. Bennett and Gabriel [39] contend that market orientation is central to the rapid introduction of KM in UK companies, pre-supposing and spreading customer information. Dennis et al. [40] believe that change-friendly enterprises are more likely to have extensive KM systems than others. There are critical research challenges to be addressed for KM in the context of marketing:

- Knowledge discovery through data mining is an iterative learning process. One of the research challenges is to make this process more structured and thus improve the productivity of the data mining efforts.
- A second challenge is the management of knowledge that is distributed across supply chain partners. The key research issues are the development of appropriate inter-organisational KM models, protection of knowledge rights and distribution of knowledge benefits among partners.
- Finally, another important issue is "Web Mining". The Web is an important source of customer data. However, the distributed nature of the knowledge in the Web, make it a challenge to collect and effectively manage the knowledge that can be useful in the marketing function of an enterprise.

3.4 KM and People

Any KM initiative that is driven purely by technology, without a corresponding change in the culture of the organisation, is certain to eventually fail. Too often, companies implement state-of-the-art technology and then discover that culture and behavior are slow to change. The success of KM initiatives depends equally to the active involvement of everyone throughout the organization as well as to their consistency with the organisation's broader business strategy and culture. Technologies and social systems are equally important in KM [41-42].

Companies which follow the KM programme with clear objectives and approaches and which they manage to coordinate their social relations and technologies, tend to be more successful, whereas some other companies which implement a KM initiative with focus on IT, in order to reap some quick benefits without having focus on human side and a long-term strategy, fail [43-44]. It is clear that any proposed methodology /

framework for KM should take under account the fact that KM is not only about technology and that people and process play a major role.

Since the returns from the KM are not instant and take a long time, any KM initiative requires strong support and commitment from top management, especially in the first few years [45-46]. In addition, enterprises that recognize and use their employees' steadily growing wealth of tacit knowledge to solve problems and achieve goals, have a major competitive advantage. The improvement of the procedure in which enterprises acquire and share tacit and explicit knowledge is very important. Supportive, interactive learning environments built on trust, openness and collective ownership definitely encourage knowledge acquisition and sharing [47]

3.5 KM and SME's

The field of small and medium-sized companies gets little or no attention in the research done into KM [48]. This finding is similar to that of the historical development of most emergent management philosophies of recent times, which have started in large organizations; for example, total quality management (TQM) [49-50], reengineering [51] balanced scorecards, etc. Unquestionably, these companies need KM just as much as the giant enterprises [52].

There are a plethora of KM tools on the market. While most tools seem to be targeted at the large companies, there is no shortage of software that is suitable, or can be adapted to, any smaller-sized company. The SME sector would appear to need to develop their understanding of KM further as a key business driver rather than as a resource-intensive additional initiative [53].

4 Conclusion

This paper has presented a taxonomy of research, which is believed to be covering the major issues in KM field. The conclusion is that much still needs to be done. There is not a universally accepted standard methodology for KM and consequently a general understanding of how to undertake comprehensive and systematic KM within an organisation. This methodology will help any enterprise to manage knowledge effectively, to tie it properly to its strategy, tactics, and daily operations as well as to recognize that people and their behaviours, contribute much more to the enterprise success than conventional assets. On the other side, the development of new, intelligent IT tools that will support any KM initiative is of great importance.

Several themes have been discussed in this paper, and future work will continue to survey the different issues related to KM. It is expected that the current and future work will provide researchers and practitioners with a good reference to research and practice in this emerging field.

References

1. Nonaka, I.: The knowledge-creating company. Harvard Business Review, Vol. 69 (1991) pp. 96-104.
2. Wiig, K.: Knowledge management foundations: Thinking about thinking-how people and organizations create, represent and use knowledge. Arlington, TX: Schema Press, (1993)
3. Wilkins, J., Van Wegen, B., De Hoog, R.: Understanding and valuing knowledge assets: Overview and method. Expert Systems With Applications, Vol. 13 (1997) pp. 55-72
4. Wiig, K.: Knowledge Management: Where did it come from and where will it go? Expert Systems With Applications, Vol. 13 No. 1 (1997) pp. 1-14
5. Davenport, T., Prusak, L.: Working Knowledge: Managing What Your Organisation Knows, Harvard Business School Press, Boston, MA (1998)
6. Milton, N., Shadbolt, N., Cottman, H., Hammersley, M.: Towards a knowledge technology for knowledge management. International Journal Human-Computer Studies, Vol. 51 (1999) pp. 615-641
7. Wickert, A., Herschel, R.: Knowledge-management issues for smaller businesses. Journal of Knowledge Management, Vol. 5, No 4 (2001) pp. 329-337
8. Rubenstein-Montano, B., Liebowitz, J., Buchwalter, J., McCaw, D., Newman, B., Rebeck, K.: SMARTvision: a knowledge-management methodology. Journal of Knowledge Management, Vol. 5, No 4 (2001) pp. 300-310
9. Nonaka, I.: A dynamic theory of organizational knowledge creation. Organization Science, Vol. 5. (1994)
10. Holsapple, C., Joshi, K.: Knowledge management: a three-fold framework. Kentucky Initiative for Knowledge Management, paper No. 104 (1997)
11. Wiig, K., de Hoog, R., van der Spek, R.: Supporting knowledge management: a selection of methods and techniques. Expert Systems with Applications, Vol. 13 No.1 (1997)
12. Basu, A.: Perspectives on operations research in data and knowledge management. European Journal of Operational Research, Vol. 111 (1998) pp. 1-14.
13. Levett, G., Guenov, M.: A methodology for knowledge management implementation. Journal of Knowledge Management, Vol. 4, No. 3 (2000) pp. 258-269
14. Bolloju, N., Khalifa, M., Turban, E.: Integrating knowledge management into enterprise environments for the next generation decision support. Decision Support Systems, Vol. 33 (2002) pp. 163-176.
15. Rubenstein-Montano, B., Liebowitz, J., Buchwalter, J., McCaw, D., Newman, B., Rebeck, K.: A systems thinking framework for knowledge management. Decision Support Systems Vol. 31 (2001)
16. IDC: Knowledge Management Study, *eINFORM*, Vol. 3, Issue 8 (2002)
17. Chauvel, D., Despres, C.: Knowledge Management and the Management Development Function in European Business. Working Paper No 01-04-2002, The European Center for Knowledge Management (2002)
18. Longbottom D., Chourides, P.: Climbing new heights: Conquering K2. Article on Knowledge Management Magazine (17-06-2001)
19. Cobos R., Esquivel, J.A., Alaman, X.: IT tools for KM: A study of the current situation. Upgrade, Vol. III, No. 1 (2002)
20. Koenig, M.: The Third Stage of KM Emerges. KMWorld, Vol. 11, Issue 3 (2002)
21. Tsui, E.: Technologies for Personal and Peer-to-Peer (P2P) Knowledge Management. Research Paper, Computer Sciences Corporation, North Sydney, Australia (2002)
22. European KM Forum, Working Paper, IST Project No 2000-26393 (2002)
23. Nemati, R., Steiger, D., Iyer, L., Herschel, R.: Knowledge warehouse: and architectural integration of knowledge management, decision support, artificial intelligence and data warehousing. Decision Support Systems, Vol. 33 (2002)

24. Fowler, A.: The role of AI-based technology in support of the knowledge management value activity cycle. Journal of Strategic Information Systems, Vol. 9, (2000) pp. 107-128
25. Prusak, L.: The eleven deadliest sins of knowledge management. Butterworth-Heinemann, Boston (1998)
26. Murch, R., Johnson, T.: Intelligent Software Agents, Prentice Hall, Canada (1998)
27. Wagner, G.: Foundations of Knowledge Systems: With Applications to Databases and Agents, Kluwer Academic Publishers (1998)
28. Bradshaw, R., Carpenter, J., Cranfill, R., Jeffers, R., Poblete, L., Robinson, T., Sun, A., Gawdiak, Y., Bichindaritz, I., Sullivan, K.: Roles for agent technology in knowledge management: examples from applications in aerospace and medicine, White Paper, Boeing Information and Support Services, Seattle, WA. (1998)
29. Carneiro, A.: The role of intelligent resources in knowledge management, Journal of Knowledge Management, Vol. 5, No. 4 (2001) pp. 358-367
30. Allen, B.P.: Case based reasoning: business applications. Communications of the ACM 37 (1994) pp. 40-44
31. Cunningham, P., Bonano, A.: Knowledge engineering issues in developing a case-based reasoning application. Knowledge Based Systems 12 (1999) pp. 371-379
32. Weber, F., Wunram, M., Kemp, J., Pudlatz, M., Bredehorst, B.: Standardisation in Knowledge Management – Towards a Common KM Framework in Europe. Proceedings of UNICOM Seminar "Towards Common Approaches & Standards in KM", 27 February, 2002, London
33. Weber, Frithjof, Kemp, Jeroen: Common Approaches and Standardisation in KM. European KM Forum Workshop Report from a Workshop at the European Commission's IST Key Action II Concertation Meeting, Brussels, 14 June 2001
34. Courtney, J.: Decision making and knowledge management in inquiring organizations: toward a new decision-making paradigm for DSS. Decision Support Systems, Vol. 31 (2001) pp. 17-38
35. Bhargava, H.K., Krishnan, R.: Computer-aided model construction. Decision Support Systems, Vol. 19 (1997), pp. 193-214
36. Raghunathan, S., Krishnan, R., May, J.H.: MODFORM: a knowledge-based tool to support the modeling process. Information Systems Research Vol. 4 (1993), pp. 331-358
37. Tseng, S.: Diverse reasoning in automated model formulation, Decision Support Systems, Vol. 20 (1997), pp. 357-383
38. Shaw, M.J., Subramaniam, C., Woo Tan, G., Welge, M.E.: Knowledge management and data mining for marketing. Decision Support Systems Vol. 31 (2001) pp. 127-137
39. Bennett, R., Gabriel, H.: Organisational factors and knowledge management within large marketing departments: an empirical study. Journal of Knowledge Management, Vol. 3, No. 3 (1999) pp. 212-15
40. Dennis, C., Marsland, D., Cockett, T.: Data mining for shopping centers – customer knowledge management framework. Journal of Knowledge Management, Vol. 5, No. 4 (2001) pp. 368-374
41. Bhatt, G.: Knowledge management in organizations: examining the interaction between technologies, techniques, and people. Journal of knowledge Management. Vol. 5, No. 1 (2001) pp.: 68-75
42. McDermott, R., O'Dell, C.: Overcoming cultural barriers to sharing knowledge. Journal of knowledge Management. Vol. 5, No. 1 (2001) pp.: 76-85
43. Avora, R.: Implementing KM – a balanced score card approach. Journal of Knowledge Management. Vol. 6, No. 3 (2002) pp.: 240-249
44. Bhatt, G.: Managing knowledge through people. Knowledge and Process Management: Journal ob business transformation, Vol. 5, No. 3 (1998) pp.: 167-171

45. Soliman, F., Spooner, K.: Strategies for implementing knowledge management: role of human resources management. Journal of Knowledge Management. Vol. 4, No. 4 (2000) pp.: 337-345
46. Soliman, F., Innes, C., Spooner, K.: Managing the human resources' knowledge. Proceedings of the Seventh Annual Conference of the International Employment Relations Association, Lincoln University, Christchurch, New Zealand (13-16 July, 1999) pp.: 497-510
47. McAdam, R., Reid, R.: SME and large organization perceptions of knowledge management: comparisons and contrasts. Journal of Knowledge Management. Vol. 5, No. 3 (2001) pp.: 231-241
48. Beijerse, R.: Knowledge management in small and medium-sized companies: knowledge management for entrepreneurs. Journal of Knowledge Management. Vol. 4, No. 2 (2000) pp.: 162-179
49. Wilkinson, A., Willmott, H.: Making quality critical: new perspectives on organisational change. Routledge, London (1994)
50. Kanji, G., Asher, G.: Total quality management process: a systematic approach. Journal of Total Quality Management, Vol. 4 (1993)
51. McAdam, R., Donaghy, J.: Business process reengineering in the public sector: a study of staff perceptions and critical success factors. Journal of Business Process Management, Vol. 5, No. 1 (1999) pp.: 33-49
52. Hylton, A.: Small Companies Also Need Knowledge Management. Hylton Associates (2000)
53. Smith, E.: The role of tacit and explicit knowledge in the workplace. Journal of Knowledge Management. Vol. 5, No. 4 (2001) pp.: 311-321

Spatial Subgroup Discovery Applied to the Analysis of Vegetation Data

Michael May and Lemonia Ragia

Fraunhofer Institute for Autonomous Intelligent Systems
Knowledge Discovery Team
Schloss Birlinghoven, D-53754 Sankt Augustin, Germany
Tel.: +49-+2241-14-2039, Fax-2072
{michael.may, lemonia.ragia}@ais.fraunhofer.de

Abstract. We explore the application of Spatial Data Mining, the partially automated search for hidden patterns in georeferenced databases, to the analysis of ecological data. A version of the subgroup mining algorithm is described that searches for deviation patterns directly in a spatial database, automatically incorporating spatial information stored in a GIS into the hypothesis space of a data mining search. We discuss results obtained on a multi-relational biodiversity data set recorded in Niger. Vegetation records are georeferenced and associated with a set of environmental parameters. Further data provide information on climate, soil conditions, and location of spatial objects like rivers, streets and cities. The subgroup mining finds dependencies of a plant species on other species, on local parameters and non-local environmental parameters.

Keywords: Data Mining, Spatial Analysis, Geographic Information Systems, Vegetation Ecology, Subgroup Discovery

1 Introduction

In the past, biodiversity data were spread around in museum or university collections, and public, or even private, archives. No standards existed for storing the data, and many of the data did not exist in digital format. This is going to change. There are now several initiatives for collecting biodiversity data and making them accessible in databases over the internet. The upcoming *Global Biodiversity Information Facility* (www.gbif.org) will possibly provide a type of world-wide coordination. This will result in a vast amount of biodiversity data residing in numerous distributed databases. To cope with this data flood, new computational methods are needed. Data mining provides such methods.

Data mining is the partially automated search for hidden patterns in typically large and multi-dimensional databases. Data mining techniques have been developed in areas such as machine learning, statistics and database theory (Fayyad et al. 1996, Klösgen and May 2002). This paper explores the application of *spatial data mining*, the partially automated search for hidden patterns in *georeferenced* databases, to the analysis of biodiversity data.

D. Karagiannis and U. Reimer (Eds.): PAKM 2002, LNAI 2569, pp. 49-61, 2002.

We focus on a special type of data: vegetation records. Vegetation ecologists have collected huge amounts of vegetation records (also known as *phytosociological relevès*), which serve collectively as a main empirical foundation for vegetation ecology. Vegetation records contain information about which plants occur together at a certain site. They are the basis for classifying plant communities and are used for determining ecological conditions favourable for the existence of a community. They are of practical importance in various fields, e.g. environmental impact studies, landscape-, agricultural- and forestry-planning.

Vegetation records were traditionally analyzed by manipulating and rewriting the tables by hand (Dierschke 1994). Even for a table consisting of just several dozens relevés, this is a laborious task. It is interesting to note that computers were applied as early as 1960 for the task of clustering plant communities, i.e. numeric taxonomy (Williams and Lambert 1960). Many such tools have been developed in the meantime (Dierschke 1994). Data mining is not intended to replace those methods, but to complement them.

The vegetation records are georeferenced and often associated with a set of environmental parameters, e.g. soil conditions. Yet plant growth is influenced not only by local conditions, but also by larger spatial configurations such as being close to a river, being far from the sea, being in a mountainous region, and so on. Such knowledge about spatial relations between objects is traditionally encoded in geographical maps, and, in the last decades, increasingly stored in digital format, using Geographic Information Systems (GIS). The question we explore in this paper is: *How can the spatial information implicit in the data be utilized for a data mining search in an automated way*?

The challenge arises from the fact that standard data mining algorithms represent data in a matrix (single table) containing only atomic values. Yet geographic information as represented in modern GIS is typically stored in multiple relations, allowing for complex values, e.g. points, lines and polygons, to represent spatial objects.

In this paper we focus on spatial patterns from the perspective of the subgroup mining paradigm. Subgroup Mining (Klösgen 1996, Klösgen and May 2002) is used to analyse dependencies between a target variable and a large number of explanatory variables. In the present case this is the dependency of the occurrence of plant species (target variable) on other species and ecological parameters. Interesting subgroups are searched that show some type of deviation, e.g. subgroups with an overproportionally high target share for a value of a discrete target variable, or a high mean for a continuous target variable.

We describe a method that automatically incorporates spatial information stored in a GIS into the hypothesis space of a data mining search. Spatial subgroups are represented using an object-relational query language by embedding part of the search algorithm in a spatial database (SDBS). Thus the data mining and the visualization in a Geographic Information System (GIS) share the same data.

Subgroup mining methods have been first extended for multirelational data by (Wrobel 1997). Our approach allows flexible link conditions, an extended definition of multirelational subgroups including numeric targets, spatial predicates, and is database integrated.

In the paper (Malerba and Lisi 2001) apply an ILP approach for discovering association rules between spatial objects using first order logic both for data and subgroup description language. They operate on a deductive relational database (based on Datalog) that extracts data from a spatial database. This transformation includes the pre-calculation of all spatial predicates. Also the logic-based approach cannot handle numeric attributes and needs discretizations of numerical attributes of (spatial) objects. On the other side, the expressive power of Datalog allows to specify prior knowledge, e.g. in the form of rules or hierarchies. Thus their hypothesis language is in this respect more powerful than the hypothesis language used here.

Ester et al. (Ester et al.1999) define neigborhood graphs and neighborhood indices as novel data structures useful for speeding up spatial queries, and show how several data mining methods can be built upon them. Koperski et al. (1996) propose a two-level search for association rules, that first calculates coarse spatial approximations and performs more precise calculations to the result set of the first step.

Several approaches to extend SQL to support mining operations have been proposed, e.g. to derive sufficient statistics minimizing the number of scans (Graefe et al. 1998). Especially for association rules, a framework has been proposed to integrate the query for association rules in database queries (Imielinski et al. 2000). For association rules, also various architectures for coupling mining with relational database systems have been examined (Sarawagi et al. 2000). However, database integration for subgroup mining has not been investigated before. Several applications of data mining to biodiversity data are reported in the literature (Moraczweski et al. 1995, Kirsten et al. 1998, Mannila et al. 1998)

The paper is organized as follows: First we discuss the general issues of representing spatial data suitable for data mining. Next we describe a data mining algorithm suitable for analyzing these data: the spatial subgroup mining algorithm. Then we focus on the application to a multi-relational data set collected in Niger that combines vegetation records, data on climate and soil conditions, and location of spatial objects like rivers, streets and cities.

2 Methods

2.1 Representation of Spatial Data and of Spatial Subgroups

Representation of spatial data

Most modern Geographic Information Systems use an underlying Database Management System for data storage and retrieval. While both purely relational and object-oriented approaches exist, a hybrid approach based on object-relational databases is becoming increasingly popular. Its main features are:

- A *spatial data base S* is a set of relations $R_1,...,R_n$ such that each relation R_i in *S* has a geometry attribute G_i or an attribute A_i such that R_i can be linked (joined) to a relation R_k in *S* having a geometry attribute G_k.
- A *geometry attribute* G_i consists of ordered sets of *x-y*-coordinates defining points, lines, or polygons.

- Different types of spatial objects (e.g. streets, buildings) are organized in different relations R_i, called *geographical layers*. Each layer can have its own set of attributes $A_1,..., A_n$, called *thematic data*, and at most one geometry attribute G_i.

This representation extends a purely relational scheme since the geometry attribute is non-atomic. One of its strengths is that a query can combine spatial information with attribute data describing objects located in space.

For querying multirelational spatial data a spatial database adds an operation called the *spatial join*. A spatial join links two relations each having a geometry attribute based on distance or topological relations (*disjoint, meet, overlap, covers, covered by, contains, equal, inside*) (Egenhofer 1991). Special purpose index structures e.g. KD-trees or Quadtrees are used for supporting efficiently spatial joins.

Pre-processing vs. dynamic approaches

A GIS representation is a *multi-relational* description using non-atomic data types (the geometry) and applying operations from computational geometry to compute the relation between spatial objects. Since most machine learning approaches rely on single-relational data with atomic data types only, they are not directly applicable to this type of representation. To apply them, a possibility is to pre-process the data and to join relevant variables from secondary tables to a single target table with atomic values only. The resulting table can be analysed using standard methods like decision trees or regression. While this approach may often be practical, it simply sidesteps the challenges posed by multi-object-relational datasets (Klösgen and May 2002).

Instead, our approach to spatial data mining relies on using a Spatial Database without transformation and pre-processing. Tables are dynamically joined. Variables are selected during the central search process of a data mining algorithm, and inclusion depends on intermediate results of the process. Expensive spatial joins are performed only for the part of the hypothesis space that is really explored during search.

Spatial subgroups

Subgroups are subsets of analysis objects described by selection expressions of a query language, e.g. simple conjunctional attributive selections, or multirelational selections joining several tables. *Spatial subgroups* are described by a spatial query language that includes operations on the spatial references of objects. A spatial subgroup, for instance, consists of the vegetation records which are close to a river. A spatial predicate, e.g. *minimum distance*, operates on the coordinates of the spatially referenced objects *vegetation records* and *rivers*.

Hypothesis Language

The *domain* is an object-relational database schema $S = \{R_1, ..., R_n\}$ where each R_i can have at most one geometry attribute G_i. Multirelational subgroups are represented by a concept set $C = \{C_i\}$, where each C_i consists of a set of conjunctive attribute-value-pairs $\{C_i.A_1=v_1,..., C_i.A_n=v_n\}$ from a relation in S, a set of links $L=\{L_i\}$ between two concepts C_j, C_k in C via their attributes A_m, A_k, where the link has the form $C_i.A_m$ θ,

$C_k.A_m$, and θ can be '=', a distance or topological predicate (*disjoint, meet, equal, inside, contains, covered by, covers, overlap, interacts*).

For example, the subgroup

sites with medium distance from a river, many plants of indigofera strobilifera and having soil type Ql1l-1

is represented as

C={ *{records.river_distance=medium, records.indigofera strobilifera=3}, {soil.type='Ql1l-1a'}}*

L={{spatially_interacts(records.geometry, soil.geometry)}}

Multirelational subgroups have first been described in (Wrobel 1997) in an Inductive Logic Programming (ILP) setting. Our hypothesis language is more powerful due to numeric target variables and spatial links. Moreover, all combinations of numeric and nominal variables in the independent and dependent variables are permitted in the problem description (table 1). Numeric independent variables are discretised on the fly. This increases applicability of subgroup mining.

Table 1. All combinations of numeric and nominal variables are permitted

	Numeric Target	Nominal Target
Numeric input variables	yes	yes
Nominal input variables	yes	yes
Mixed numeric/nominal	yes	yes

Representation of spatial subgroups in query languages

Our approach is based on an *object-relational* representation. The formulation of queries depends on non-atomic data-types for the geometry, spatial operators based on computational geometry, grouping and aggregation. For calculating spatial relationships, we use the spatial extension of *Oracle Spatial* (similar solutions exist for other major commercial databases). For database integration, it is necessary to express a multirelational subgroup as defined above as a query of a database system. The result of the query is a table representing the extension of the subgroup description.

The space of subgroups to be explored within a search depends on the specification of a relation graph which includes tables (object classes) and links. For spatial links the system can automatically identify geometry attributes by which spatial objects are linked, since there is at most one such attribute. A relation graph constrains the multi-relational hypothesis space in a similar way as attribute selection constrains it for single relations.

2.2 Database Integrated Spatial Subgroup Mining

Subgroup mining search

The basic subgroup mining algorithm will only be summarized here. Different subgroup patterns (e.g. for continuous or discrete target variables), search strategies and quality functions are described in (Klösgen 1996). The search is arranged as an iterated *general to specific generate and test procedure.* In each iteration, a number of parent subgroups is expanded in all possible ways, the resulting specialized subgroups are evaluated, and the subgroups are selected that are used as parent subgroups for the next iteration step, until a prespecified iteration depth is achieved or no further significant subgroup can be found. There is a natural partial ordering of subgroup descriptions. According to the partial ordering, a specialization of a subgroup either includes a further selector to any of the concepts of the description or introduces an additional link to a further table.

The statistical significance of a subgroup is evaluated by a quality function. As a standard quality function, subgroup mining uses the classical binomial test to verify if the target share is significantly different in a subgroup:

$$\frac{p-p_0}{\sqrt{p_0(1-p_0)}}\sqrt{n}\sqrt{\frac{N}{N-n}} \qquad (1)$$

This quality function based on comparing the target group share in the subgroup (p) with the share in its complementary subset balances four criteria: size of subgroup (n), relative size of subgroup with respect to total population size (N), difference of the target shares (p-p_0), and the level of the target share in the total population (p_0). The quality function is symmetric with respect to the complementary subgroup. It is equivalent to the χ^2-test of dependence between subgroup S and target group T, and the correlation coefficient for the (binary) subgroup and target group variables. For continuous target variables and the deviating mean pattern, the quality function is similar, using mean and variance instead of share p and binary case variance $p_0(1$-$p_0)$.

Evaluation of contingency tables

To evaluate a subgroup description, a contingency table is statistically analyzed (tab 2). It is computed for the extension of the subgroup description in the target object class. To get these numbers, a multirelational query is forwarded to the database. Contingency tables must be calculated in an efficient way for the very many subgroups evaluated during a search task.

Table 2. Contingency table for target indigofera strobilifera = 3 vs. soil.type=Ql11-1a.

		Target		
		indigofera strobilifera=3	¬ indigofera strobilifera=3	
Subgroup	soil.type='Ql11-1a'	15	20	35
	¬ soil.type='Ql11-1a'	5	90	95
		20	110	130

We use a two-layer implementation, where evaluation of contingency tables is done in SQL, while the search manager is implemented in Java. A sufficient statistics approach is applied by which a single query provides the aggregates that are sufficient to evaluate the whole set of successor subgroups. In the data server layer, within one pass over the database all contingency tables are calculated that are needed for a next search level. Thus a next population of hypotheses is treated concurrently to optimize data access and aggregation needed by these hypotheses. The search manager receives only aggregated data from the database so that network traffic is reduced.

3 Application

The application has been developed within the IST-SPIN!-project, that integrates a variety of spatial analysis tools into a spatial data mining platform based on Enterprise Java Beans (May 2000, May and Savinov 2001). For our application we used spatial data collected in Niger in West Africa. This data is part of the *Atlas of Natural and Agronomic Resources of Niger and Benin*, which is a result of the project *Adapted Farming in West Africa* funded by the *Deutsche Forschungsgemeinschaft* DFG (German Research Foundation) and carried on by the University of Hohenheim (www.uni-hohenheim.de/~atlas308). The Atlas includes a wealth of data related to the natural resources and to the economic environment of Niger. We transformed and imported the original data into a 'biodiversity data warehouse' using an Oracle Spatial Database, which provides the engine for the spatial analysis.

The basic object of analysis is a data set containing 132 vegetation records describing individual sites. Each record contains information which plants occur at a site. The abundance of a plant is recorded on a so-called Barkman scale (Dierschke 1994), which includes numeric and non-numeric attributes. For our purposes we transformed these measurements to the van der Maarel's scale (Dierschke 1994) which involves only numbers from 1 to 9. Local ecological parameters are the age of fallow, the total cover in the field, the herb layer and shrub layer.

Secondary tables provide information on terrain and soil components. The terrain components give a description with parameters such as surface form, surface drainage, slope form, length and lithology. The soil components give a description of erosion degree and rootable depth. Also available is a table giving the rainfall in mm for a region. Using other thematic layers describing rivers, cities, we also extracted geographical parameters such as the minimum distance of a site from a river and from a village, which can be calculated from a GIS-representation.

In our biodiversity data warehouse, this information is distributed over many tables. The tables describe the properties of different types of object. The sites where the vegetation is recorded are the basic objects of analysis. Secondary objects are rivers, streets, cities, villages, geologically homogenous regions, climatic regions. There is no way to link these objects using a traditional join of a relational database. But these objects stand in various spatial relations to each other, e.g. a site is in a certain climatic zone, has a certain minimum distance to the next river, etc. For a human, these spatial relations are easily understood when visualized on a map (see fig. 2). For the computer, this information is extracted using a *spatial join* which, for example, calculates the climatic region in which a given site is located. Thus the climatic region becomes an additional property of the primary object of analysis, the vegetation record.

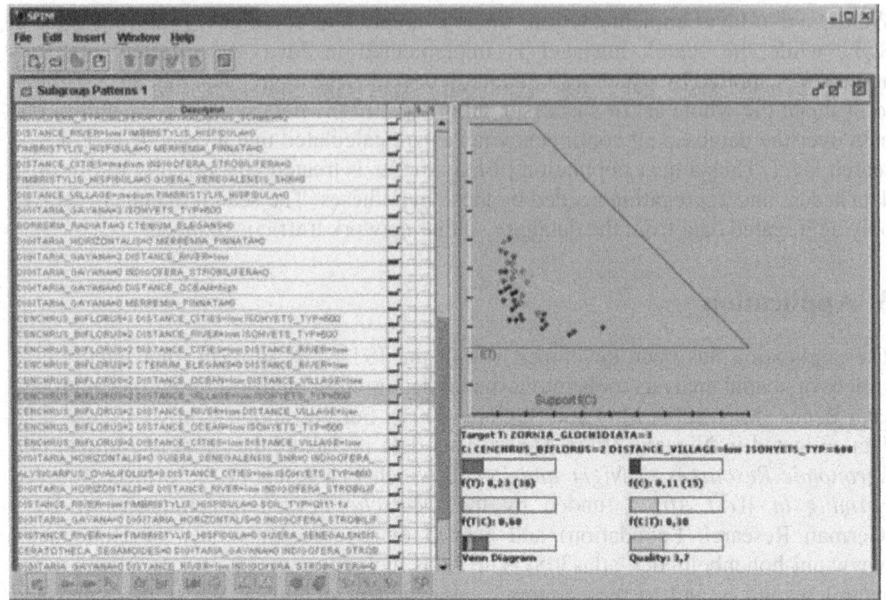

Fig. 1. Overview on subgroups found showing the subgroup description (left). Bottom right side shows a detail view for the overlap of the concept *C* (e.g. cenchurus biflorus=2) and the target attribute *T* (zornia glochidiata=3). The window on the right top plots p(*T*|*C*) against p(*C*) for the subgroup selected on the left and shows *isolines* as theoretically discussed by Klösgen (1996).

The basic task is to examine the conditions that are favorable for the existence of a plant species. Such conditions can be grouped into different categories:

1. co-occurrences with other plant species;
2. dependence on local ecological conditions, e.g. soil type or rainfall;
3. dependence on non-local conditions, e.g. distance to a river or to the sea.

Spatial subgroup discovery helps to find dependencies by searching the hypothesis space, which contains all three types of attributes, for interesting deviation patterns with respect to the target attribute.

As an example, assume we are interested in vegetation records with a value of 3 for the species *Zornia Glochidiata*. (The value of three means that there are many such plants in this area). The target attribute *T* is then *zornia glochidiata is 3*. The subgroup mining search is executed specifying a maximum search depth, and certain threshold values such as a minimum coverage for a concept *C* and a given minimum confidence *P*(*T* | *C*), and the number of hypotheses to be returned on each level of search. Results are visualized both in abstract and geographical space (fig 2, 3). A pattern found in the search is that the *abundance of zornia glochidiata= 3* is overproportionally high for sites satisfying a concept C which is: *abundance of cenchurus biflorus= 2, being far away from villages and having a rainfall of 600mm*. There is a sharp increase in the conditional probability p(*T*|*C*) with respect to p(*T*), which increases from 0.23 to 0.6.

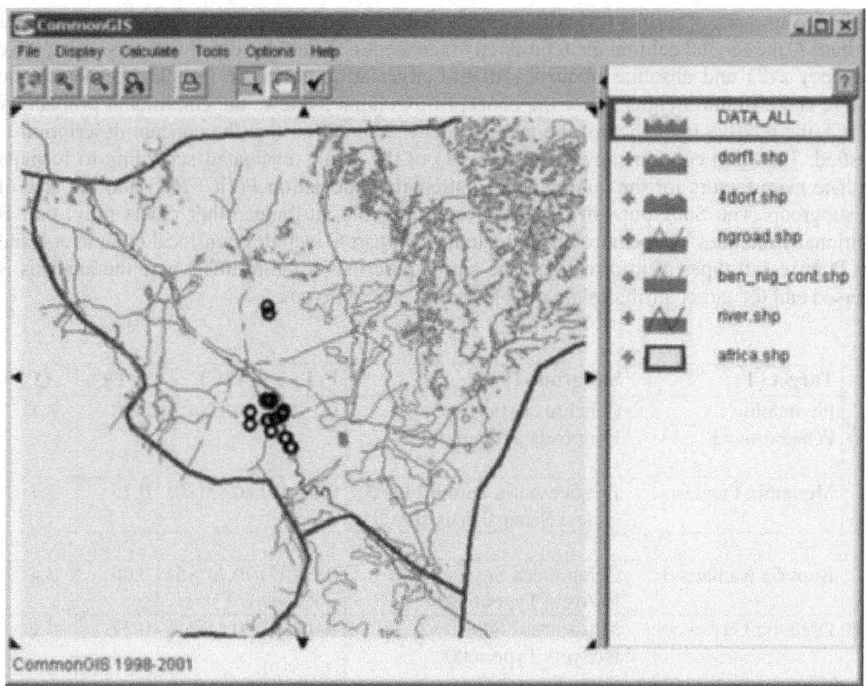

Fig. 2. Vegetation records satisfying the subgroup description *C* (cenchrus biflorus 2, distance from village low and isohyet type 600) are highlighted with a thicker black line. The vegetation records are displayed in a lighter color (yellow). The villages (orange colour), the river (blue) the streets (brown) and the topography (green) are also displayed.

The way data mining results are presented to the user is essential for their appropriate interpretation. We use a combination of cartographic and non-cartographic displays linked together through simultaneous dynamic highlighting of the corresponding parts. The user navigates in the list of subgroups (fig. 1), which are dynamically highlighted in the map window (fig. 2). As a mapping tool, the SPIN!-platform integrates the CommonGIS system (Andrienko et al. 1999) whose strengths lies in the dynamic manipulation of spatial statistical data. Figure 1 and 2 show an example for a plant species, where the subgroup discovery method reports a co-occurrence relation between two plant species together with geographical parameters and rainfall.

Table 3 summarizes some results of the data mining run. Part A of table 3 shows how the occurrence of a plant depends on the co-occurrence of other plants. This type of problem is also familiar from association rule analysis. An advantage of subgroup discovery is that the results are more focused since the target attribute (the plant of interest) is kept fixed and much fewer results are produced. Part B shows the dependence on the co-occurrence of other plants and on local conditions like rainfall and soil type. Note that both soil type and rainfall are described in secondary tables and have to be included using a spatial join, which the subgroup mining can perform dynamically during its search. Part C shows the dependence on non-local conditions like distance to a river, and part D (maybe the most interesting) mixes all types of information.

Table 3. Summary of results for spatial subgroup discovery. The first column shows the target attribute *T*, the second column the (conjunctive) concept *C*. The third column shows the relative frequency *P(T)* and absolute frequency of the target attribute in the sample, the fourth the relative and absolute frequency for the concept *C*. Column 5 shows the conditional probability *P(T|C)*, the relative frequency of the target under the condition that the concept description is satisfied. The sixth column shows the quality Q of the results evaluated according to formula (1). The main factors for the quality are the strength of deviation *P(T|C)-P(T)* and the size of the subgroup. The Subgroups in part A have as possible attributes other plants only, part B additionally includes local environmental parameters, part C includes non-local parameters, and part D mixes all types of information. The part E describes some results where the analysis is reversed and the target attributes are not plants, but e.g. soil types.

	Target (T)	**Subgroup (C)**	**P(T)**	**P(C)**	**P(T|C)**	**Q**
A	Phyllanthus Pentandrus=3	Cenchrus Biflorus=3, Eragrostis Tremula=3	0.15(20)	0.12(16)	0.50	4.1
A	Merremia Pinata=3	Jacquemontia Tamnifolia=3, Guiera Senegalensis shr.=9	0.37(49)	0.15(20)	0.75	3.1
B	Borreria Radiata=3,	Ceratotheca Sesamoides=3 Isohyets Type=600	0.25(33)	0.11(15)	0.60	3.4
B	Digitaria Gayana=8	Mitracarpus Scaber=2, Isohyets Type=600, Soter Type=cc2	0.07(9)	0.11(15)	0.27	3.2
B	Ipomoea Vagans=3	Borreria Stachydea=3, Soil Type=Ql1	0.14(18)	0.11(14)	0.43	3.3
C	Mitracarpus Scaber=3	Village Distance=medium, Jacquemontia Tamnifolia=3	0.24(32)	0.14(18)	0.56	3.3
C	Andropogon Gayanus=3	River Distance=low, Merremia Pinnata=2	0.09(12)	0.17(22)	0.27	3.2
C	Alysicarpus Ovalifolius=9	River Distance=low, Village Distance=high	0.14(18)	0.11(14)	0.43	3.4
D	Zornia Glochidiada=3	Cenchrus Biflorus=2, Village Distance=low, Isohyets Type=600	0.23(30)	0.11(15)	0.60	3.7
D	Ctenium Elegans=3	Isohyets Type=600, Soil Type=Ql1, Soter Type=cc2	0.17(23)	0.21(28)	0.36	2.9
E	Soter Type=cc2	River Distance=low Merremia Pinnata=3	0.57(75)	0.34(45)	0.84	4.6
E	River Distance=medium	Alysicarpus Ovalifolius=3, Soil Type=Ql1-1a	0.05(7)	0.12(16)	0.25	3.8
E	Soil Type=Ql1-1a	Guiera Senegalensis Shr=9, Isohyets type=500	0.30(39)	0.13(17)	0.94	6.3

4 Concluding Remarks

In contrast to approaches to Spatial Data Mining export and pre-process the data from a SDBS, effectively converting it into a non-spatial representation. Our dynamic approach embraces the full complexity and richness of the spatial domain. This results in significant improvements for all stages of the knowledge discovery cycle:

- *Data Access*: Subgroup Mining is partially embedded in a spatial database, where analysis is performed. No data transformation is necessary and the same data is used for analysis and mapping in a GIS. This is important for the applicability of the system since pre-processing of spatial data is error-prone and complex.
- *Pre-processing and analysis*: The system handles both numeric and nominal target attributes. For numeric explanatory variables on-the-fly discretisation is performed. Spatial and non-spatial joins are executed dynamically.
- *Post-processing and Interpretation*: Similar subgroups are clustered according to degree of overlap of instances to identify multicolinearities. A Bayesian network between subgroups can be inferred to support causal analysis.
- *Visualisation*. The subgroup mining module is dynamically linked to a GIS, so that spatial subgroups are visualized on a map. This allows the user to bring in background knowledge into the exploratory process, to perform several forms of interactive sensitivity analysis and to explore the relation to further variables and spatial features.

A problem is still the computational cost of spatial joins, resulting in long processing time for complex hypothesis spaces. We currently investigate various caching techniques, so that intermediate results can be re-used.

By integrating analysis, pre- and post-processing and visualization, the system should be especially valuable in an exploratory stage of a biological investigation, where the investigator is exploring the data looking for fruitful initial hypotheses. The user does not need to know the quite complex machinery for performing spatial joins, since this is done dynamically by the system. When assessing the potential for generalizing results or when validating hypotheses, some caution is in order. The data collected for the *Atlas of Natural and Agronomic Resources of Niger* come from various original sources and the procedures for preparing the data were often very complex, introducing various possibilities for error. Moreover, the data have not necessarily been collected for the purpose of a statistical investigation. Thus the vegetation records certainly do not form a complete representative sample for the vegetation in Niger. For this reasons, initial hypotheses formed with the help of subgroup mining have to be validated by other means. Here, the tight integration of data mining with a GIS visualization is highly valuable, since it allows the analyst to bring in all sorts of background domain knowledge.

We described a new method for spatial analysis using the subgroup mining method and reported first experiments on a set of vegetation data collected in Niger . Integration of data mining in an object-relational spatial database allows the dynamic extraction of spatial information from a GIS for the data mining search. This results in deviation patterns that describe spatial configurations of objects and take into account both local (plant species, soil type, rainfall) and non-local features (distance to a river). The system is especially useful in the exploratory stage of a biological investigation, where initial hypotheses are formed. The link between the data mining and a GIS allows the user to bring his spatial and non-spatial background knowledge into the analysis.

Acknowledgments. Work was partly funded by the European Commission under IST-1999-10563 SPIN! – Spatial Mining for Data of Public Interest. We would like to thank Dr. Ludger Herrmann from the Institute of Soil Science and Land Evaluation (310) Univ. Hohenheim, Stuttgart (Germany) for making available the data and Dr. Alexander Wezel for his help.

References

1. **Andrienko, G., Andrienko, N,** 1999. Interactive Maps for Visual Data Exploration, International Journal of Geographical Information Science 13(5), 355-374
2. **Dierschke, H.** 1994: Pflanzensoziologie. Stuttgart, Ulmer (in German)
3. **Egenhofer, M. J.**, 1991. Reasoning about Binary Topological Relations, Proc. 2nd Int. Symp. on Large Spatial Databases, Zürich, Switzerland, 143-160
4. **Ester, M. , Frommelt, A., Kriegel, H.P, Sander, J.,** 1999. Spatial Data Mining: Database Primitives, Algorithms and Efficient DBMS Support, in: Data Mining and Knowledge Discovery, 2
5. **Fayyad, U., G. Piatetsky-Shapiro, Uthurusamy, R. (eds.)** 1996: Advances in Knowledge Discovery and Data Mining. Menlo Park, AAAI Press
6. **Graefe, G. , Fayyad, U., Chaudhuri, S,** 1998. On the efficient gathering of sufficient statistics for classification from large SQL databases. Proc. of the 4th Intern. Conf. on Knowledge Discovery and Data Mining, Menlo Park: AAAI Press, 204-208
7. IST-10536-SPIN!-project web site, http://www.ccg.leeds.ac.uk/spin/
8. **Imielinski, T., Virmani, A.,** 2000. A Query Language for Database Mining. Data Mining and Knowledge Discovery, Vol. 3, Nr. 4, 373–408
9. **Kirsten, M., Wrobel, S., Dahmen, F.W., Dahmen, H.C,** 1998: Einsatz von Data Mining-Techniken zur Analyse ökologischer Standort- und Pflanzendaten. KI 2/98, 39-42
10. **Klösgen, W.,** 1996. Explora: A Multipattern and Multistrategy Discovery Assistant. Advances in Knowledge Discovery and Data Mining, eds. U. Fayyad, G. Piatetsky-Shapiro, P. Smyth, and R. Uthurusamy, Cambridge, MA: MIT Press, 249–271, 1996
11. **Klösgen, W.,** 2002. Causal Subgroup Mining. to apear.
12. **Klösgen, W., May, M.,** 2002. Subgroup Mining Integrated in an Object-Relational Spatial Database, to appear.
13. **Klösgen, W., W., Zytkow, J. (eds.),** 2002., Handbook of Data Mining and Knowledge Discovery, Oxford University Press, New York
14. **Koperski, K., Adhikary, J., Han, J.,** 1996. Spatial Data Mining, Progress and Challenges, Vancouver, Canada, Technical Report
15. **Malerba, D., Lisi, F.,** 2001. Discovering Associations between Spatial Objects: An ILP Application. Proc. ILP 2001, eds. Rouveirol, C., Sebag, M., Berlin: Springer, 156-163
16. **Mannila, H., Toivonen, H., Korhola, A.; Olander, H.,** 1998: Learning, Mining, or Modeling? A Case study from Paleoecology. In: Arikawa, S., Motoda, H. (eds.): Discovery Science. Proceedings from the First International Conference, Fukuoka, Japan, Lecture Notes in Artificial Intelligence 1532. Berlin, Springer, 12-24

17. **May, M..** Spatial Knowledge Discovery, 2000. The SPIN! System. Proc. of the 6th EC-GIS Workshop, Lyon, ed. Fullerton, K., JRC, Ispra
18. **May, M., Savinov, A.,** 2001. An Architecture for the SPIN! Spatial Data Mining Platform, Proc. New Techniques and Technologies for Statistics, NTTS 2001, 467-472, Eurostat
19. **Moraczewski, I.R. , Zembowicz, R., Zytkow J. M.,** 1995: Geobotanical Database Exploration. in: Valdes-Perez (ed.) AAAI Spring Symposium "Systematic Methods of Discovery" Stanford University. CA (AAAI-Press), 76-80
20. **Sarawagi, S., Thomas, S., Agrawal, R.,** 2000. Integrating Association Rule Mining with Relational Database Systems. Data Mining and Knowledge Discovery, 4, 89-125
21. **Wrobel, S.,** 1997. An Algorithm for Multi-relational Discovery of Subgroups. In Proc. of First PKDD, eds. Komorowski, J., Zytkow, J., Berlin:Springer, 78-87
22. **Williams, W.T. , Lambert, J. M.** 1960: Multivariate Methods in Plant Ecology II. The use of an electronic digital computer for association analysis. J. Ecology 47, 689-710

Knowledge Management Case-Toolkit for the Support of ERP Modelling and Optimal Adaptation Procedure

Kostas Karnezis[1], Kostas Ergazakis[2], Kostas Metaxiotis[3], Dimitris Askounis[4], and John Psarras[5]

[1] MSc. Electrical & Computer Eng.
National Technical University Of Athens. Institute of Communication & Computer Systems
[2] MSc. Electrical & Computer Eng.
National Technical University Of Athens. Institute of Communication & Computer Systems
[3] Dr. Electrical & Computer Eng.
National Technical University Of Athens. Institute of Communication & Computer Systems
[4] Dr. Electrical & Computer Eng.
National Technical University Of Athens. Institute of Communication & Computer Systems
[5] Assistant Professor Mechanical Eng.
National Technical University Of Athens. Institute of Communication & Computer Systems

Abstract. One of the most difficult works in the world of ERP systems is proven to be their installation and customization to fulfil the needs of the customer. With the great development of Knowledge Management in the last decade a new era has begun; the era of capturing, storing and managing effectively ERP Consultants' knowledge in order to rapidly build customized enterprise systems, which in other times would take months to model and develop. This paper presents such a case, where IT and Knowledge Management power are used in order to surpass the difficulties of this ERP field. The authors describe an advanced generic Case-Toolkit, which is able to support the complicated process of Modelling and optimal adaptation (MOA) of an ERP system to the needs of an enterprise. This tool-kit aims to be used by the ERP consultants in two ways. The first is to analyse, categorise and store the business processes and the second is to use the business processes that are created for presale reasons.

1 Introduction

The 21st century finds the enterprises confronted with new challenges. In today's fiercely competitive business environment, in order to produce goods tailored to customer requirements and provide faster deliveries, an enterprise must be closely linked to both suppliers and customers. We observe that the business environment is altered radically and the way of enterprises' operation is modernized by the use of modern

D. Karagiannis and U. Reimer (Eds.): PAKM 2002, LNAI 2569, pp. 62-74, 2002.

and advanced information systems. Indeed, the evolution of Information technology, the enlargement of the use of Internet, the spreading of electronic trade, creates, for all the enterprises and specifically for the small and medium ones a difficult path but simultaneously a big occasion as well. Information Technology and Business Process re-engineering, used in conjunction with each other, have emerged as important tools, which give organizations the leading edge. Especially the last five years have seen an explosion in the implementation of Enterprise Resource Planning (ERP) systems [1-8]. The ERP solutions seek to streamline and integrate operation processes and information flows in the company to synergise the resources of an organization. The disparate transaction systems are replaced by a single, integrated system that embodies the tight interdependencies among a firm's functional units. The integration of business processes through technologically advanced systems, like ERP systems, is necessary for a company that aims at the immediate adaptation to the new conditions of global competition. According to scientific research, companies, which have adopted an ERP system since 1998, have achieved an annual rate of growth of 10% [9-10]. Generally the complete installation of an ERP system and the start of its use include basically modelling, optimal adaptation to the needs of the enterprise and installation and operation of all the sub-systems in the respective departments of the enterprise. The successful installation of an ERP system is a very difficult and important IT work.

On the other hand, knowledge management (KM) is today the subject of much literature, discussion, planning and some action [11-14]. Most of the emphasis in the literature so far has been on KM frameworks, approaches and not on the use of KM in ERP systems [15-20]. Although there is a recognition that knowledge is a key business asset, organizations are still in the early stages of understanding the implications of KM, while a fair percentage of senior managers believe that KM may just be embellished information management and business process reengineering (BPR) efforts; many BPR efforts have been failures, so there is a concern that KM may fall victim to the same perils.

In the following sections it will be shown in which way and at which extent Knowledge Management can help in the complex process of Modelling and optimal adaptation (MOA) of an ERP system to the needs of an enterprise.

2 The Process of Modelling & Optimal Adaptation of ERP System

The process of Modelling and Optimal Adaptation (MOA) of an ERP system is a process particularly time-consuming and complicated. The difficulty of this process is directly linked with the complicated structure, nature and concept of the ERP system itself. The proper installation and operation of such a system requires the Modelling and adaptation of existing systems of the company as well as business processes reengineering (BPR), so that the smooth and effective operation of the whole IT system is ensured, according to the real requirements and needs of the customer [21-24].

The methodological analysis of the business processes requires experienced and specialized personnel from the supplier of the ERP. It is also obvious that the cooperation and contribution of the customer are essential for the proper and effective configuration and adaptation of the provided platform. This work is of significant investment in time and resources both for the customer (company) and the supplier of the ERP (software house). It must also be ensured that the exploitation of the advantages and benefits of the ERP system from the customer will be optimal.

For this reason, it would be very helpful if a supportive IT tool-kit existed, which would support methodologically and functionally the whole process of M.O.A of an ERP system. We should always keep in mind that the whole project of installation or customisation of an ERP system today is relied on the role of ERP Consultants. They are highly experienced persons but are few and also very expensive. It would be very important for an ERP company to try to store their knowledge about business processes so that other experts, not so specialised, can use it and learn from it.

In this context, the Case-Toolkit could store ERP Consultants' knowledge on the enterprise models but also technical knowledge on the adaptation of an ERP system to business processes, as well as it could also offer an advanced environment for modelling the business processes of the enterprise. In the following sections such a Case-Toolkit is presented. It is stressed that the tool-kit has been designed in such a way so that it will be generic and can be used by consultants for any ERP system.

3 The Technical Characteristics of the Proposed Case-Toolkit

The proposed Case-Toolkit has been designed and developed in a conceptual framework (Figure 1), which gives particular focus on the achievement of specific technical characteristics, which ensure the viability, and the high added value of system. These characteristics are the following:

- ✓ Interfacing - Interoperability
- ✓ Possibility of direct interconnection of the completed Case-Toolkit with the ERP for the achievement of semi-automated adaptation of system in the requirements and structures of the enterprise
- ✓ Architecture of an open system (open systems architecture) for the scalability and adaptability in dynamically altered needs but also its adaptation according to the internal requirements that are set by the ERP
- ✓ Increased possibilities of use in different environments and fields of application and extension depending on the requirements (adaptability - expandability).
- ✓ Support of multiprocessing via suitable layout in sub systems (modularity).
- ✓ Friendly and functional environment of communication with the user.

4 The Proposed Knowledge Management Case-Toolkit

The aim of the proposed toolkit is the best possible (optimal) Modelling of operations and processes of the enterprise in combination with the essential adaptation and parameterization of the ERP, targeting at the creation of more efficient enterprise model that will lead to the most optimal ERP operation. This will be done by providing an appropriate choice of models from the KM Database. The toolkit offers an integrated and visual description, which represents the structures of the enterprise and its operations with the highest possible precision. This description substantially provides the entry points of parameterization and adaptation of the ERP system for installation in a specific enterprise.

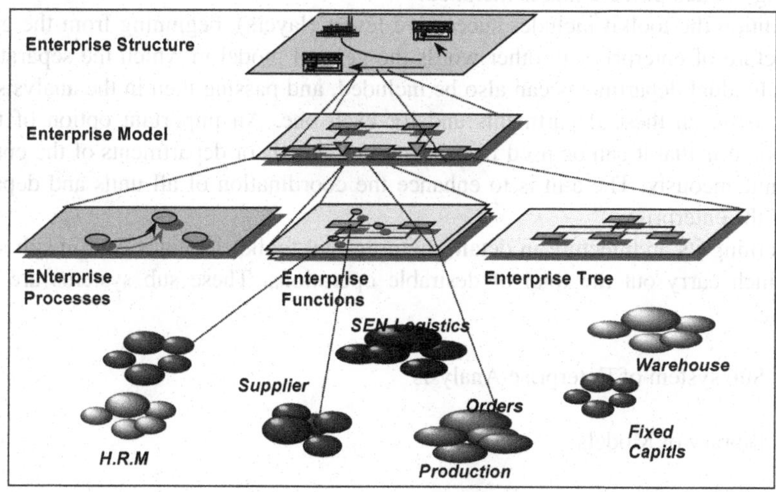

Fig. 1. The Conceptual Framework

The toolkit creates the theoretical structure of the informative system, providing the programmers who will undertake the adaptation of ERP system with the informational skeleton that they will use. The general way of operation of the proposed Case-Toolkit is illustrated in the following Figure 2.

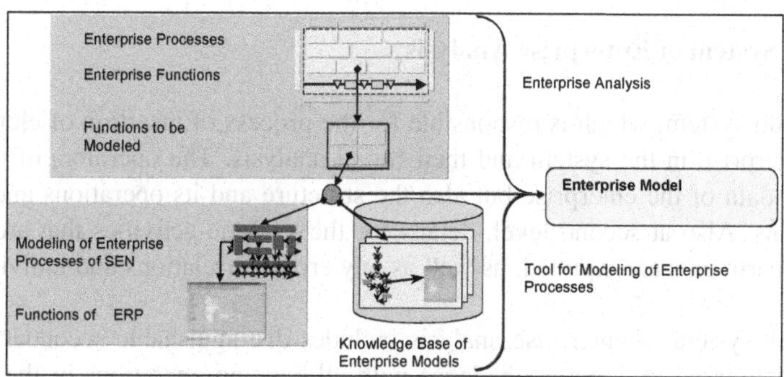

Fig. 2. The Case -Toolkit Operation

It includes, in the Knowledge Base, many best practice' models of enterprises (templates), structures or internal processes, which have resulted from already applied cases and success stories. It is planned that in near future, libraries of documentation, directives and advice, as well as useful guidelines for the persons in charge of the completion of work of analysis and Modelling of the enterprise will be incorporated in the system. In this way the enterprise structure will be approached in a multifaceted and multileveled way, beginning from the general operation and leading to the detailed Modelling of each process that is included.

In addition the toolkit includes successive levels (layers), beginning from the general structure of enterprise, in other words the general model in which the separation of the individual departments can also be included, and passing then in the analysis of relations between these departments and for each one. An important option of this Case-Toolkit is that it can be used from many individuals or departments of the enterprise simultaneously. The aim is to enhance the coordination of all units and departments of the enterprise.

Concerning its architecture in detail, the proposed toolkit includes certain sub systems, which carry out the total of desirable operations. These sub systems are the following:

- Sub system of Enterprise Analysis
- Library of Models
- Knowledge Base
- Sub system of Adaptation to ERP
- Sub system of Communication with the User

4.1 Sub System of Enterprise Analysis

It is the sub system, which is responsible for the process of insertion of elements/data of the enterprise in the system and their initial analysis. The operators of the system insert the data of the enterprise but also the structure and its operations and potential connections. Also at second level, details for the analytic activities that are executed by the departments are inputted, as well as any cross-correlations and individual processes.

The sub system of enterprise analysis includes distinguishable secondary sub systems, which come in direct equivalence with all existing operations of the enterprise that can be incorporated in the ERP System (Economic Management, Commercial Management, Management of Deposits, Planning and Control of Reserves, Management of Capitals, Maintenance of Equipment, Administration of Production). With the proportional use of these sub systems, the tool of Modelling accepts all the data of the enterprise and analyzes the relations and their dependences. The exported elements of this sub system are:

a) Users: Diagrams of Structure of the enterprise (Organizational Diagram), Diagrams of Operations & Activities (Business Process Diagrams), Diagrams of Entities-cross-correlation (ERD).

b) System: Primary elements, which are stored in the Knowledge Base of the system; Analysis of data of the enterprise to be inserted in the sub system of modelling.

4.2 Library of Models

It is a sub system that includes models (templates) for enterprises, departments, operations and structures. The library of models is constantly renewed ("self-learning") with the repetition of the use of the Case-Toolkit in different and other types of enterprises. The models that are included in the library are used by the sub system of modelling, which will be analyzed in the following sections. The library is directly linked with the Knowledge Base and many parameters and information are stored there.

4.3 Knowledge Base

It is the sub system, which constitutes the conjunctive point between all the other sub systems of the Case-Toolkit. In the Knowledge Base, all the elements, both from the insertion of data of the enterprise, and the process of analysis, Modelling and adaptation are stored. Respectively, each sub system of the Case-Toolkit uses all the necessary elements from the Knowledge Base in order to carry out its operations. Through the Knowledge Base the sub systems are constantly interlinked, exchanging data.

4.4 Sub System of Adaptation to ERP

The sub system of adaptation undertakes the creation and the calculation of parameters that should be imported in the ERP system, so that its "optimal" adaptation is ensured, based on the needs and structures of the enterprise. Accepting feedback from the sub system of modelling, using the stored data in the database as well as combining appropriate models, the sub system of adaptation produces the values of parameters precisely as they should be given to the ERP in the process of adaptation.

4.5 Sub System of Communication with the User

The aim of this particular sub system is to play the role of the basic interface during the insertion of elements and data of the enterprise, as well as during the whole operation of the toolkit and the provision of outputs. This sub system includes two components: the first one concerns the central management of analysis and modelling while the second one the big distance access to the system. The particular characteristics of this sub system are presented in detail in the following section.

5 Communication with the User

The visible part of the Case-Toolkit, which is basically, the "Sub system of Communication with the User" is made up by the following two components:

- Design component (Knowledge Import)
- Web component. (Knowledge Presentation)

These two components, which are constantly interlinked through the common sub-systems of the Case-Toolkit that they use, are the front end of the whole system.

Only the Design Team has the right to use the first one and everyone in the company can use that second. The database of the system which is connected to the Web Presentation Module has different read rights for the users. Thus, a user can see only the processes and objects that the group that he belongs is allowed to see.

5.1 The Design Component

The design component provides the user with design capabilities in order to represent, store and manage the knowledge related to business/enterprise processes and functions in diagram form. These diagrams, which are flowchart-like, are designed by the ERP Consultants and, through the system's functions, are stored in the system's database.

The design component is implemented in Microsoft Visio, a well-known design program. With the use of ready to use templates and stencils, which are previously created, the user can create new models or update older models/diagrams, keeping in this way the Knowledge Base always updated. It helps the ERP Consultants to "illustrate" their knowledge in a diagram form, using many parameters, but also is a powerful navigation and administration tool for all the models/diagrams that are previously stored. Through the constant link with the Knowledge Base of the enterprise models, it transparently organizes the models/diagram, while the ERP Consultants deal only with their creation and/or their update.

The design component as well as the web component, which is described in the next section, is designed in a way that can work in a network environment. In this way many groups of ERP Consultants can work in parallel and exchange information easily. It is presumed that the system will be used by a team of consultants. In case different experts have different opinions about a model about a same business process, the whole team must chose one. Of course the two models can coexist as variants and can be used in different cases.

5.2 Web Component

The aim of the web component is to present the models/diagrams which are previously designed, in the Internet or in a local network. This component through the Knowl-

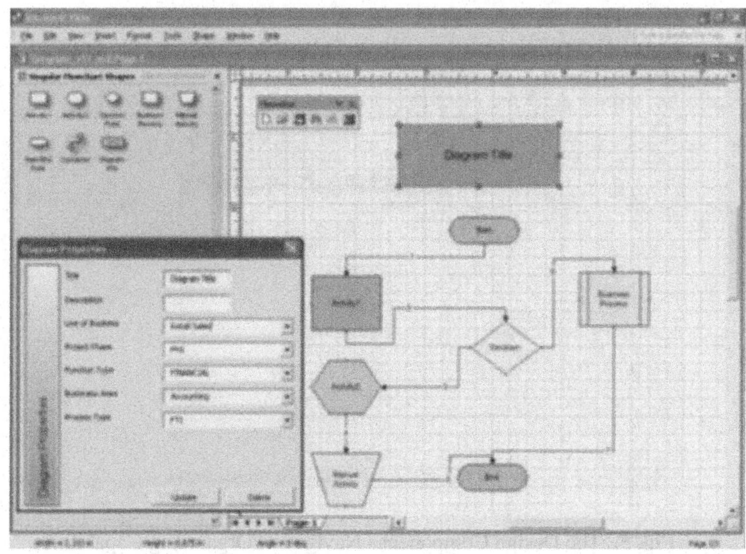

Fig. 3. The Design Component -Insertion of Knowledge

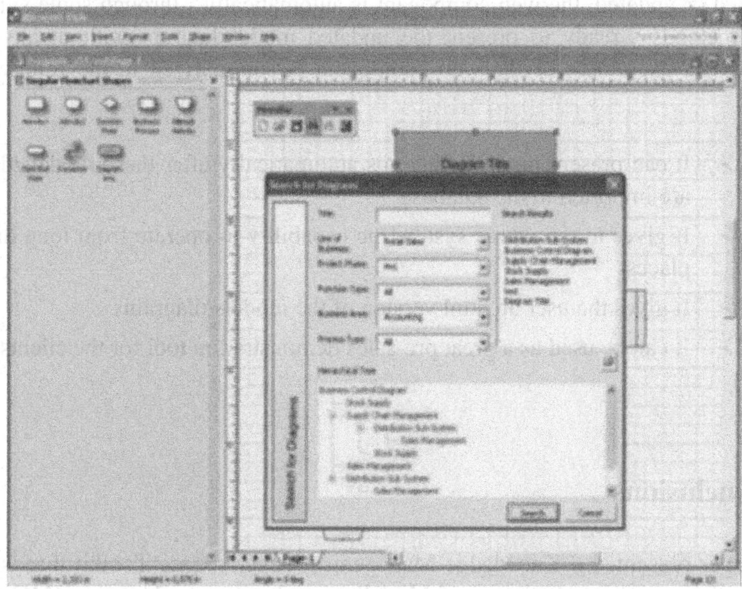

Fig. 4. The Design Component - Search Capabilities

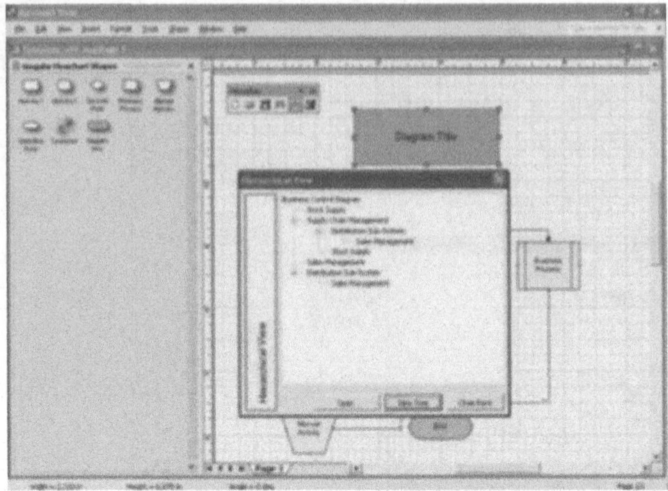

Fig. 5. The Design Component - Navigation/Organizing Capabilities

edge Base is constantly connected with the design component. When a model/diagram is created or updated, the web component is automatically - through some synchronization methods - ready to present the updated model/diagram without any further actions. The usefulness of the web component is summarized in the following key points:

- It can present models/diagrams automatically after these models/diagrams are imported to the database
- It gives to the whole system the capability to operate from long distanced places
- It gives the user an html version of the models/diagrams
- It can be used as a great pre-sales demonstration tool for the clients

6 Conclusions

This paper presented a Knowledge Management generic Case-Toolkit that is able to support the complicated process of Modelling and optimal adaptation (MOA) of an ERP system to the needs of an enterprise. The design of this Case-Toolkit was based on a practical methodology, which translated some conceptual ideas of Knowledge Management into an advanced application.

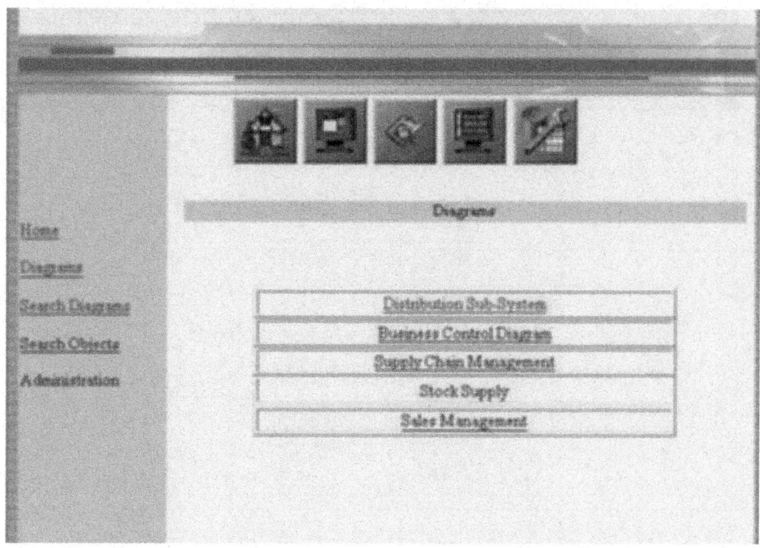

Fig. 6. The Web Component - Business Diagram View

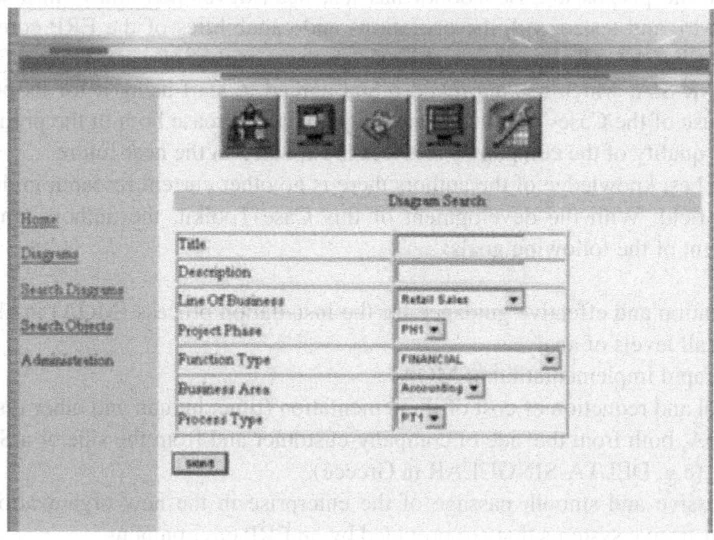

Fig. 7. The Web Component - Search Form

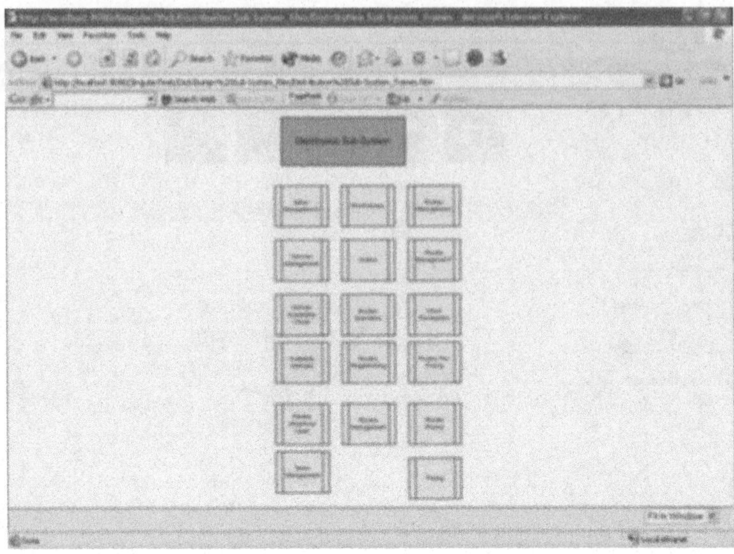

Fig. 8. Web Component -Html representation of a model/diagram stored in the systems database

As such, the proposed Case-Toolkit has just been developed and is now about to connected to, and tested with the operations and capabilities of the ERP commercial package "SINGULAR Enterprise (SEn)" of the Greek Software House DELTA-SINGULAR S.A, which has approved it and agreed to start using it for its products. With the use of the Case-Toolkit by the company, an increase both in the productivity and in the quality of the company's services is expected in the near future.

To the best knowledge of the authors there is no other current research in this technological field. With the development of this Case-Toolkit, the authors aim at the achievement of the following goals:

- ✓ Facilitation and effective guidance for the installation process (MOA) in all stages and in all levels of analysis.
- ✓ More rapid implementation of MOA.
- ✓ Control and reduction of cost of implementation (time, human and other resources) of MOA, both from the side of company-customer and from the side of a Software House (e.g. DELTA-SINGULAR in Greece).
- ✓ Progressive and smooth passage of the enterprise in the new organizational and administrative systems that are provided by an ERP environment.
- ✓ Optimal adaptation of processes and structures of the enterprise in an ERP environment.

References

[1] Pawlowski, S. and M-C Boudreau et al.: *"Constraints and Flexibility in Enterprise Systems: A Dialectic of System and Job."*, Americas Conference on Information Systems, August 13-15 1999, Milwaukee, WI.

[2] Chung, SH. and CA. Synder: *"ERP Initiation – A Historical Perspective."*, Americas Conference on Information Systems, August 13-15 1999, Milwaukee, WI.

[3] Markus, ML. and Tanis C.: *"The Enterprise systems experience – from adoption to success"*, Framing the Domains of IT Research: Glimpsing the Future through the Past, RW Zmud, ed. Inc., Cincinnati, OH: Pinnaflex Educational Resources (2000).

[4] Davenport, TH.: *"Mission Critical: Realizing the Promise of Enterprise Systems."*, Boston, MA, Harvard Business School Press (2000).

[5] Laudon, KC. and JP. Laudon: *"Management Information Systems: Organization and Technology in the Networked Enterprise."*, Upper Saddle River, NJ, Prentice Hall (2000).

[6] Soh, C. and SS. Kien and J. Tay-Yap: "Cultural fits and misfits: Is ERP a universal solution?", *Communications of the ACM*, Vol. 43 (2000), pp. 47-51

[7] Kennerley, M. and Neely Andy: "Enterprise resource planning: analyzing the impact", *Integrated Manufacturing Systems*, Vol. 12, Issue 2 (2001), pp.103-113.

[8] Metaxiotis, K., Psarras, J. and Ergazakis, K.: "Production Scheduling in ERP Systems: An AI-based Approach to Face the Gap", *Business Process Management Journal* (under publication in 2003).

[9] Laughlin, S.: "An ERP Game Plan", *Journal of Business Strategy*, pp. 32-35 (1999).

[10] Rosemann, M.: *"ERP Software: "Characteristics and Consequences"*, 7th European Conference on Information Systems -ECIS '99, Copenhagen, Denmark, June 1999.

[11] Wiig, K.: *"Knowledge management foundations: Thinking about thinking-how people and organizations create, represent and use knowledge"*, Arlington, TX: Schema Press (1993).

[12] Wilkins, J., Van Wegen, B., and De Hoog, R.: "Understanding and valuing knowledge assets: Overview and method", *Expert Systems With Applications*, Vol. 13 (1997), pp. 55-72.

[13] Davenport, T., DeLong, D. and Beers, M.: "Successful knowledge management projects", *Sloan Management Review*, Vol. 39 No. 2 (1998), pp. 43-57.

[14] Leonard, D.: *"Wellsprings of Knowledge – Building and Sustaining the Sources of Innovation"*, Harvard Business School Press, Boston, MA (1999).

[15] Rosemann, M. (2000), *"Structuring and Modeling Knowledge in the Context of Enterprise Resource Planning"*, 4th Pacific Asia Conference on Information Systems -PACIS 2000, Hong-Kong, June 2000.

[16] Van Stijn, E. and Wensley, A. (2001), "Organizational memory and the completeness of process modelling in ERP systems: Some concerns, methods and directions for future research", *Business Process Management Journal*, Vol. 7 No. 3, pp. 181-194.

[17] Bolloju, N., Khalifa, M. and Turban, E.: "Integrating knowledge management into enterprise environments for the next generation decision support", Decision Support Systems, Vol. 33 (2002), pp. 163-176.

[18] Gable, G., Scott, J. and Davenport, T. (1998), "Cooperative ERP Life-cycle Knowledge Management", *Proceedings of the Ninth Australasian Conference on Information Systems*, Sydney, Australia, pp. 227-240.

[19] Chan, R. (1999), "Knowledge management for implementing ERP in SMEs", *SAPPHIRE '99*, pp. 21-39.

[20] Malhotra, Y. (2001), "Knowledge Management and Business Model Innovation", Idea Group Publishing, London, UK.

[21] Maull, R., Weaver, A., Childe, S., Smar, P and Bennett, J.: "Current issues in business process re-engineering", *International Journal of Operations & Production Management*, Vol. 15 No. 11 (1995), pp. 37-52.

[22] Archer, R., and Bowker, P.: "BPR consulting: an evaluation of the methods employed", *Business Process Management Journal*, Vol. 1 No. 2 (1995), pp. 28-46.

[23] Soliman, F.: "Optimum level of process mapping and least cost business process re-engineering", *International Journal of Operations & Production Management*, Vol. 18 No. 9-10 (1998), pp. 810-816.

[24] Koch, C.: "BPR and ERP: realising a vision of process with IT", *Business Process Management Journal*, Vol. 7 No. 3 (2001), pp. 258-265.

Readiness to Adopt Data Mining Technologies: An Exploratory Study of Telecommunication Employees in Malaysia

Noornina Dahlan, T. Ramayah, and Looi Lai Mei

School of Management, Universiti Sains Malaysia, 11800 Penang, Malaysia
{Nina, Ramayah}@usm.my
Komag USA (M) Sdn, Malaysia
LM.Looi@komag.com

Abstract. This paper addresses the readiness of telecommunication employees in adopting data mining technologies. In addition, the paper highlights the relationship between employee data mining readiness and the clarity of the business strategy, users' skills and experience, data-driven culture, and data quality. The investigations reveal an encouraging degree of readiness by the employees to embrace data mining and the findings also show high levels of optimism and innovativeness. The implications here are two-fold: first, the employees are optimistic that data mining can improve efficiency as well as allow greater flexibility and control at work. Second, the employees' innovativeness suggests their willingness to accept new technologies and to continuously acquire the necessary skills. Additionally, the employees are highly motivated to adopt and respond to data mining efforts when it is clearly defined in the business strategy.

1 Introduction

Business organizations worldwide constantly face numerous forms of organizational, managerial, technological, and social challenges brought about by contemporary and globalization issues ranging from business process re-engineering, to the demands of the Internet and Web-based applications. As in all profit-driven ventures, businesses must attract and retain high-volume as well as high-value customers [1].

Fig. 1 depicts the business models of many businesses that have now shifted from product-driven to customer-driven strategies. In order to implement customer-driven strategy, it may be necessary for business organizations to acquire a thorough understanding of customer information [2]. In particular, organizations must intelligently dissect data (customer information) and translate it into formal explicit knowledge that is subsequently used to enhance customer satisfaction [3]. Additionally, this practice of utilizing, sharing, and using intellectual capital (data, information, knowledge) to gain competitive advantage and customer commitment refers to knowledge management' [4], which utilises the necessary tools to transform data into knowledge [5]. Moreover, knowledge management is also responsible for improving efficiency and innovation, and for enabling faster and more effective decision-making [6].

D. Karagiannis and U. Reimer (Eds.): PAKM 2002, LNAI 2569, pp. 75-86, 2002.

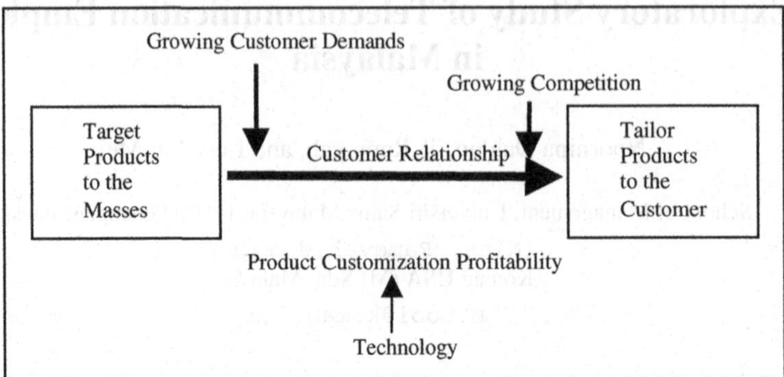

Fig. 1. Customer-Driven Strategy (Source: Anonymous [1998] - Data Warehousing for the telecommunications industry, Informix Corporation)

Data mining' technologies are deemed critical to the successful adoption and implementation of knowledge management. For example, data mining extract previously unknown and actionable information from large consolidated databases to identify trends and patterns to support strategic and tactical decision-making [7]. Fig. 2 depicts data mining as a major component of the Knowledge Discovery Database process that enhances knowledge-driven decision-making and forecasts the effects [8].

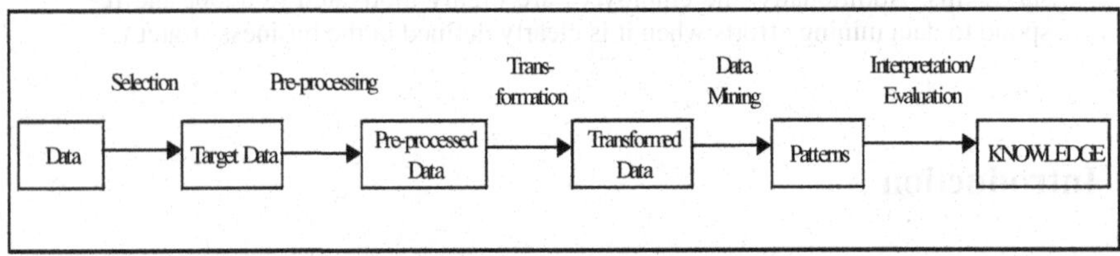

Fig. 2. Knowledge Discovery Database Process

Beyond personal attitudes towards the job and organization, employees' perception of readiness for change reflects the organization's ability to implement the change [9]. Similarly, users' readiness reflects positive attempts by the change agents to influence the beliefs, attitudes, intentions, and behaviour of the change participants [10].

This paper presents a study that attempts to address the employees' data mining readiness (DMR). In particular, the focus is on the telecommunication employees' readiness to adopt data mining technologies at work.

DMR, although is an individual-level construct, requires a consideration of the organizational context. In addition, there is a need to study primary success factors that must be present in order to build organizational capabilities for transforming data into knowledge, and then into business results [11]. The Technology Readiness Index's scores answer questions on technology strategies and on customer-technology link [12]. In addition, the Data Mining Readiness Index (DMRI) is used to gain a better understanding of the employees' DMR; whereby a higher score displays an inclination to more effective data mining-support roles.

This study therefore examines the DMRI of the employees and the contextual variables (organization, cultural and strategic) that contribute to the employees' DMR.

Based on a survey of 106 telecommunication employees, this study empirically provide some preliminary new insights into the propensity of the employees to accept and use data mining technologies for accomplishing their tasks at work, and to identify the organizational factors that can significantly influence employees' readiness. The findings from the study can therefore be used to choose the best options by planning and implementing the appropriate efforts to create and enhance readiness -that can then be used to make employees more prepared for new challenges notably in highly competitive industry such as telecommunication.

2 Data Mining Readiness

The new information revolution can be viewed as creating competitive advantage by providing organizations with new ways to outperform their rivals' [13]. Knowledge can thus be regarded as being of critical importance to business and competitive advantage is gained from what an organization (or its employees) knows and the speed with which this knowledge is put to use [14]. Similarly, an organization's performance depends on the ability of managers to turn the knowledge resources into value-creating activities [15]. Decision support systems, executive information systems, online analytical processing, and data mining are tools designed to help organization leverage transaction data. These knowledge discovery tools are considered as technological innovations.

Innovation can be defined as an idea, practice or material artifact perceived to be new by the relevant unit of adoption' [16]. The innovation presents potential adopters with new means of solving problems and exploiting opportunities. In addition, change in management techniques and organizational structures may be directly related and even precedes successful technological innovations [17]. Since data mining is considered as a technological innovation, it is therefore appropriate to refer to technological innovation theories for this study. Subsequently, the employees' DMR is reviewed using the concepts of change management, organization readiness model, technology acceptance model, and building an analytical capability model.

2.1 Change Management

Most organizational change is triggered by the need to respond to new challenges or opportunities due to external environment or anticipation of the need to cope with potential future problems. Five broad headings are proposed for the forces of changes; changing technology, knowledge explosion, rapid product obsolescence, changing nature of workforce, and quality of work life [18]. Therefore, the adoption of technological innovation involves large-scale organization change. The change management is the process of continually renewing the organization's direction, structure, and capabilities to serve the ever-changing needs of the market place, the organization, and its employees [19].

In order to make the change process work, the following must take place at the organizational level: people must clearly understand the purpose of the change required; new performance requirements must be clearly stated and understood by the employees; roles and responsibilities must be updated to reflect new performance demands;

the organization must have constant supply of timely and useful information; core processes must be aligned with organizational goals; and the organization's culture must be reshaped in ways that motivate all its employees [19].

Additionally, management of change must include the creation of an environment in which the people involved in the change are encouraged to open themselves to new ideas and concepts; thereby overcoming any resistance to change [20].

Creating readiness involves proactive attempts by a change agent to influence the beliefs, attitudes, intentions, and behaviour of change participants [21]. Individuals usually have preconceived notions about the extent to which the organization is ready to make the desired change [22], and some may react differently to the same message. For example, the ‛innovators' are likely to respond positively to programmes for fundamental change (using different mental processes and requiring new skills) while the ‛adaptors' may respond more positively to programmes for incremental change (needing minor modifications in thought patterns and fine tuning existing skills) [23].

2.2 Technology Acceptance Model (TAM)

Recent findings suggest that Information Technology adoption literature focuses on acceptance models relating perceptions and beliefs to attitudes, behavioural intention and technology usage. [24].

Additionally, ‛sense making' refers to the cyclical process of taking action, extracting information from that action, and incorporating information from that action into the mental framework that guides further action. Hence, if technology adoption is a form of sense making then it should have the following characteristics: it should be influenced by initial and evolving mental frameworks; users should have initial perception and understanding about the technology; these perceptions and understandings should be subject to change based upon stimuli (information) that the user receives; and the mental frameworks should be changed because of the incorporation of the stimuli [24].

Based on the social psychology Theory of Reasoned Action (TRA) [25, 26], Davis et al. present the Technology Acceptance Model (TAM) as a linear representation of a portion of the sense making process [27].

Essentially, TAM suggests that two specific behavioural beliefs (perceived usefulness and perceived ease-of-use) affect individual's behavioural intention to use the technology. Perceived usefulness captures the extent to which a potential adopter views the technology as offering value over alternative ways of performing the same task; while ease of use encapsulates the degree to which a potential adopter views the usage of the target to be relatively free of effort.

In a nutshell, an innovation perceived to be easier to use and less complex has a higher likelihood of being accepted and used by potential users [27]. Nevertheless, people may also conduct certain behaviour even if they do not have a positive attitude towards the behaviour [28].

2.3 Building Analytical Capability Model

The analytical capability model can be used to study the transformation of transaction data into knowledge, and the findings are based on three major elements namely:

context, transformation and outcomes [11]. Context includes the strategic, skill-related, organizational, cultural, technological, and data factors that must be present for an analytic effort to succeed. These are prerequisites of success though they are continually refined and affected by other elements. The transformation element is where data is actually analyzed and used to make business decisions. The outcomes are the changes that result from the analysis and decision-making. These changes involve behaviours, processes, programmes, and financial conditions.

2.4 Data Mining in the Telecommunication Industry

The telecommunication industry is fast evolving as it faces various contemporary and globalization issues ranging from deregulations and consolidation, to the challenges of the Internet and e-commerce. Further, this industry leads in terms of the amount of data collected for its business. Since it costs close to ten times more to acquire a new customer than to retain an existing one, telecommunication companies should invest in data mining tools to equip themselves for churn management [35], and they need to strategically position themselves to grab a larger slice of the growing pie. Thus, they should focus on developing and maintaining committed customer relationships.

Competition is getting more intense as network operators compete for subscribers, who demand superior network coverage and delivery, innovative data services, excellent customer relationship, and competitive pricing. Data mining is able to identify the potential niche market segments and where opportunities exist to cross sell. It is also able to identify customer likelihood of learning the service using the classification and prediction techniques. Data mining too provides more information and discovery of customer value, which are useful for customer retention.

2.5 Employees' Data Mining Readiness

The Technology Readiness Index (TRI) uses four dimensions that are reliable and are good predictors of technology-related attitudes and behaviours of customers namely: optimism and innovativeness (both are drivers of technology readiness), discomforts and insecurity (both are inhibitors) [12]. Optimism is a belief that technology offers increased control and efficiency, while discomforts are perceived lack of control. Innovativeness pinpoints to technology pioneer and leader, while insecurity reveals distrust of technology and skepticism about its ability to work properly. As TRI is used to assess customers' attitude to computer-based technology, it is therefore important in designing, implementing, and managing employee-technology link.

This study has adapted the items in the four dimensions to access the DMRI. In the context of employees' readiness, the contextual variables are measured in terms of the clarity of the business strategy, users' skills and experience, data-driven culture, and data quality.

3 Research Model and Hypotheses

This study aims to understand the contextual factors in the telecommunication organizations that influence employees' DMRI. The theoretical framework is adapted from the Model for Building an Analytical Capability [11], which states that the more analytically capable the individual, the higher the readiness.

Fig. 3 illustrates the dependent variable (employees' DMR) and the independent variables (business strategy, users' skills and experience, data-driven culture, and data quality).

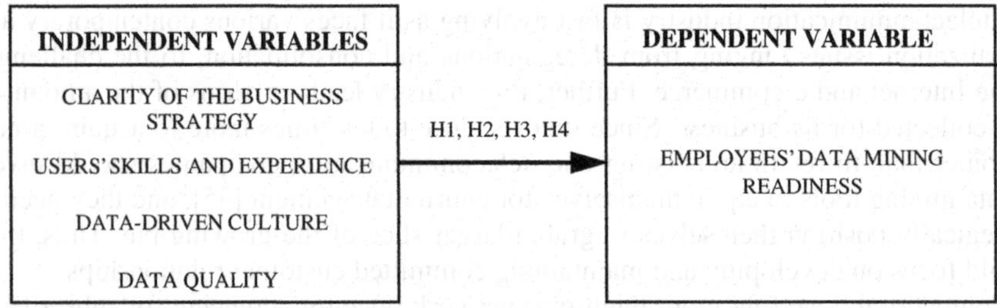

Fig. 3. Theoretical Framework

3.1 Clarity of the Business Strategy

Clarity of the business strategy requires the top management to convey a clear definition of the purpose for change, to continually improve, and to align the core processes with organizational goals [19]. Additionally, change must be top-down to provide vision and create structure and it must also be bottom-up to encourage participation and support. The clearer and more detailed the business strategy, the more obvious what data and analytical capabilities the organization requires. Thus, the first hypothesis:

- H_1: The clearer the business strategy's definition, the higher the employees' DMR

3.2 Users' Skills and Experience

Users' skills and experience is accounted by the level and structure of skills needed to support data analysis capabilities [11]. For example, twothirds of companies experience major challenges in recruiting, developing, and retaining highly skilled people with analytic capabilities. As for the requisite skills that are aligned to the business strategy, four dimensions are proposed: technology management skills, business functional skills, interpersonal skills, and technical skills [29]. There is empirical evidence that techno-savvy employees are likely to use more innovations [30], and there is a positive link between computing technology experience and outcomes such as affinity towards computers and computing skill [31]. Thus, the second hypothesis:

- H_2: The better the users' skills and experience in analytic capabilities, the higher the employees' DMR

3.3 Data-Driven Culture

A CEO's characteristic that plays an active role in the allocation of resources is crucial to the organisation's technological direction [30]. For example, sixty-two percent of the managers responding in an informal survey indicate that organizational and cultural factors are the greatest barriers to the returns on system investments [11]. A major concern is creating a data-driven culture that requires for the logistics and systems' support to be part of strategic policy [32]. As culture dictates acceptance of all organizational change, issues such as policies and practices dictate individual's actions and interactions within a culture [33]. Any large-scale change should involve the reshaping of the organizational culture in ways that will motivate its employees to care for the business as their own [19]. For example, in investigating the impact of organizational resources on innovation adoption, adaptors and innovators are identified as the two extreme ends of the innovativeness continuum [23].

To ensure successful analytical capability, the entire organization needs to value data-based analysis and to adopt a data-driven culture. Thus, the third hypothesis:

- H_3: The higher the data-driven culture, the higher the employees' DMR

3.4 Data Quality

The quality of the data used for data mining-related activities is crucial to successful data mining because quality data must be organized into an accessible and extendible data warehouse. The data must be of the right age and richness (depth) for the task [34]. Without good quality data, data mining loses its central function of providing managers with meaningful patterns and trends. In other words, the dynamic nature of business data affects the quality of information retrieved. The technology underlying analytic processes includes the hardware and software used in the data capture, cleaning, extractions, and analysis, as well as the networking and infrastructure capabilities needed to transfer data and provide end-user access [11].

As a result, the technological infrastructure conducive for an analytic capability to succeed is critical to get the data-driven organization to the goal of converting data-to-knowledge-to-results. Thus, the fourth hypothesis:

- H_4: The better the data quality, the higher the employees' DMR

4 Research Methodology

Data is collected using e-mail questionnaire. The questionnaires are mailed to selected employees working in the telecommunications industry. The questionnaires contain multiple measurement items relating to each of the constructs in the theoretical framework. For the independent variables (the contextual factors of the organisation namely: clarity of the business strategy, users' skills and experience, data-driven culture, and data quality), these are based on reviews of relevant literature [11, 22, 30]. For the dependent variable (employees' DMR), it is adapted from Parasuraman's Technology Readiness Index [12].

5 Findings

A total of 245 questionnaires are distributed and 115 responses received. Of these, 9 have missing critical data and are excluded for data analysis. A factor analysis with Varimax rotation is conducted and the results are presented in Tables 1 and 2. For the independent variables, twenty-four items are used and a four factor solution emerged. Five items are dropped due to low inter-item correlation and low factor loadings of less than 0.4. Table 1 show that the four distinct factors together explain a cumulative variance of 66.27%, which provides support for further interpretation.

Table 1. Result of Factor Analysis on the independent variables

Independent Variables	Factors			
	1	2	3	4
Clarity of Business Strategy				
BizStra Q2	.073	.145	**.712**	.328
BizStra Q3	.131	.116	**.820**	.120
BizStra Q4	.299	.258	**.734**	-0.022
BizStra Q9	.428	-0.0002	**.550**	.328
User's Skills & Experience				
Skills & Exp Q1	.212	**.562**	.136	.040
Skills & Exp Q2	.053	**.808**	.077	-0.165
Skills & Exp Q3	.095	**.767**	.076	.224
Skills & Exp Q4	.045	**.852**	.017	.160
Skills & Exp Q5	.101	**.787**	.106	-0.087
Skills & Exp Q6	.139	**.715**	.157	.120
Data-driven Culture				
Culture Q4	**.601**	.274	.362	.197
Culture Q8	**.699**	.119	.182	.164
Culture Q9	**.660**	.109	.094	.370
Culture Q10	**.839**	.217	.036	.206
Culture Q11	**.845**	.129	.101	.230
Culture Q12	**.750**	-0.049	.220	.073
Data Quality				
Data Quality Q3	.359	.074	.242	**.783**
Data Quality Q4	.388	.016	.196	**.766**
Data Quality Q7	.202	.087	.122	**.801**
No of items included for analysis	6 of 10	6 of 7	4 of 4	3 of 3
Variance %	20.851	19.449	12.799	13.174
Cummulative Percentage	20.851	40.300	53.099	66.273
Eigenvalue	3.962	3.695	2.432	2.503
Reliability (Cronbach alpha value)	.885	.859	.785	.862
Mean value	3.593	3.165	3.875	3.593
Standard deviation	.689	.702	.537	.689

For the dependent variable, a two factor solution emerged. Three items are dropped due to low inter-item correlation and low factor loading of less than 0.4. As shown in Table 2 the two factors together explain a cumulative variance of 52.68 percent of the total variance.

Table 2. Result of Factor Analysis on the dependent variables

Dependent Variables	Factors	
	Optimism	Innovativeness
Optimism		
OPT Q1	**.626**	.245
OPT Q4	**.686**	-0.077
OPT Q6	**.650**	.245
OPT Q7	**.707**	.192
OPT Q8	**.833**	-0.013
OPT Q9	**.732**	.088
Innovativeness		
INN Q1	.129	**.661**
INN Q6	.330	**.582**
INN Q7	-0.116	**.802**
No of items included for analysis	6 of 6	3 of 4
Variance %	35.039	17.647
Cummulative Percentage	35.039	52.686
Eigenvalue	3.153	1.588
Reliability (Cronbach alpha value)	.811	.502
Mean value	3.915	3.280
Standard deviation	.498	.519

The DMRI shows a mean of 3.60 and standard deviation of 0.4. Thus, telecommunication employees are reasonably ready to accept data mining. The mean of optimism and innovativeness are 3.92 and 3.28 respectively. High optimism implies confidence in better control and efficiency at work, while high innovativeness implies leadership tendency, and eager to try and use newly-introduced technology such as, data mining. The optimism mean of 3.92 and standard deviation of 0.5 suggest that the employees are confident of data mining, while the innovativeness mean of 3.28 and standard deviation of 0.5 suggest that the employees are inclined to accept data mining technology. As these two factors are the driving forces of DMR, the higher the optimism and innovativeness, the higher the employees' DMR.

To test the hypotheses generated, three separate regression analyses are performed; first using the DMRI composite score, then separately with the two extracted factors. The results are presented in Table 3. For Model 1, the R-square implies that 19.3% of the variances in employees' DMR are significantly explained by the four independent variables. The findings reveal that Clarity of Business Strategy is the only significant predictor of DMR at $t=3.368$, $p<0.01$. Therefore, only H_1 is accepted; suggesting that the clearer the definition of the business strategy, the higher the employees' DMR.

Since DMRI is an average of the scores of the two components, the following is supplementary to the main regression model by testing the two components individually with the four independent variables to determine possible relationships.

For Model 2, 20.3% of the variances in employees' innovativeness are significantly explained by the four independent variables. Users' Skills and Experience is directly related to employees' innovativeness at $t=2.125$, $p<0.05$. Thus, the analytically skilled and experienced an employee, the higher the inclination to be innovative. For model 3, 17.8% of the variances in employees' optimism are explained by the four independent variables. The findings reveal that Clarity of Business Strategy is directly related to employees' optimism at $t=4.323$, $p<0.05$.

Table 3. Result of regression analysis

Independent Variables	Model 1	Model 2	Model 3
Clarity of Business Strategy	0.393**	0.096	0.510**
Users' Skills and Experience	0.101	0.199*	0.001
Data-Driven Culture	-0.024	0.234	-0.214
Data Quality	0.088	0.066	0.005
R^2	0.193	0.203	0.178
Adjusted R^2	0.160	0.172	0.146
F value	5.962**	6.436**	5.476**
Durbin Watson	1.526	1.616	1.791

** $p < 0.01$; * $p < 0.05$
Model 1: Dependent variable=DMR
Model 2: Dependent variable=Innovativeness
Model 3: Dependent variable=Optimism

6 Discussion

This study aims to assess the readiness of telecommunication employees to embrace data mining technology. Overall, the findings reveal encouraging degree of readiness, with high levels of optimism and innovativeness. The implications are that these employees are ready to adopt data mining, and they are also optimistic that the new technology increases efficiency, flexibility, and control. The employees' innovativeness implies pioneer qualities. Thus, they are willing to accept new technologies, and they are also ready to acquire the necessary skills as a continuous improvement effort.

Interestingly, this study also discovers that optimism is directly related to Clarity of Business Strategy; implicating that if the technology-optimistic employees believe that the technology-driven strategy can satisfy their personal needs, they will be more mentally ready to accept change. Further, the findings learn that innovativeness is directly related to Skills and Experience; suggesting that prior experience, knowledge and skills on new technologies can enhance the employee's ability to accept change.

A recent study on bank employees reveals that the higher the Users' Skills and Experience and Data-Driven Culture, the higher the employees' DMR [36]. In contrast, only H_1 is accepted in this study involving telecommunication employees; suggesting that the clearer and well-defined the business strategy, the higher the readiness in technology adoption and greater ability to understand requirements such as data and analytical capabilities required in technology adoption. Although the other three hypotheses are not supported, for argument's sakes, data quality and data-driven culture are already established in the telecommunication industry; they are therefore not drivers of readiness. Additionally, user's skill is directly related to innovativeness, which is already a prevailing requirement in the acceptance of a new technology.

Finally, this study shows that optimism and innovativeness are the key drivers to data mining readiness. It is therefore vital for the telecommunication organizations to strategize their business plans, which could enhance technology-optimism and technology-innovativeness in their employees. Importantly, business strategies should be initiated top-down so that bottom-up propagation could be implemented across the organization, once the employees are ready to accept the change.

7 Conclusion

Technology readiness assessment is a relatively new construct that is fast becoming very important and useful with tremendous growth for technology-based products and services. With its original intent to be used for customers' technology readiness, it is now used for internal customers' technology readiness. The findings suggest that its adaptation to a technology-based application such as data mining is acceptable because it is able to provide an understanding of the employees' data mining readiness in the telecommunication industry. This will enable the industry to put this information into perspective and to subsequently use it to gain competitive advantage.

References

1. Faltys, J.: Rules-Based Software for Telecommunications Targeted Marketing. Data Mining Direct. (2000) 20-23
2. Day, G.S.: Managing Market Relationships. Journal of the Academy of Marketing Science, 28(1). (2000) 24-30
3. Choo, C.W.: The Knowing Organization - How Organisations Use Information to Construct Meaning, Create Knowledge, and Make Decisions. International Journal of Information Management, 16(5). (1996) 329-340
4. Zorn, P.E., Emanoil, M., Marshall, L. and Panek, M.: Mining Meets the Web. Online, 23(5). (1999). 16-28
5. Shoemaker, M.E.: A Framework for Examining IT-Enabled Market Relationships. Journal of Personal Selling and Sales Management, 28(1). (2001). 24-30
6. Barth, S.: ID Check. Customer Relationship Management, (June). (2000). 113-114
7. Piatersky-Shapiro, G. and Frawley, W. (ed.): Knowledge Discovery in Databases. AAAI Press /MIT Press (1991)
8. Fayyad, U.M., Gregory, P.S., Padhraic, S. and Ramasamy, U.: Advances in Knowledge Discovery and Data Mining. AAAI Press (1996)
9. Kotter, J.P.: Leading Change: Why Transformation Efforts Fail. Harvard Business Review, 73(2). (1995). 59-67
10. Jansen, K.J.: The Emerging Dynamics of Change - Resistance, Readiness and Momentum. Human Resource Planning, 23(2). (2000). 53-55
11. Davenport, T.H., Harris, J.G., Russell, J.E.A., De Long, D.W., and Jacobson, A.L.: Data to Knowledge to Results - Building an Analytic Capability. California Management Review, 43(2). (2001). 117-138
12. Parasuraman, A.: Technology Readiness Index (TRI): A Multiple-Item Scale to Measure Readiness to Embrace New Technologies. Journal of Service Research, 2(4). (2000). 307-320
13. Porter, M.E. and Millar, V.E.: How Information Gives You Competitive Advantage. Harvard Business Review, 63(4). (1985). 149-60
14. Cohen, D.: Towards A Knowledge Context. Report on the first annual U.C. Berkeley Forum on Knowledge and Firm, California Management Review, 40(3). (1998). 22-39
15. Von Krogh, G.: Care in Knowledge Creation. California Management Review, 40(3). (1998). 133-153
16. Zaltman, G., Duncan, R.B. and Holbeck, J.: Innovation and Organization. New York: Wiley & Sons (1973)
17. Damanpour, F., Szabat, F. and Evans, W.: The Relationship between Types of Innovation and Organizational Performance. Journal of Management Studies. (1989). 587-601
18. Mullins, L.J.: Management and Organisational Behaviour. Pittman Publishing (1996)

19. Moran, J. and Avergun, A.: Creating Lasting Change. TQM Magazine, 9(2). (1997) 146-151
20. Hassan, M.M.: Effects of Change Management on Implementation of Total Productive Maintenance. MBA thesis, School of Management, Universiti Sains Malaysia, Penang (2000)
21. Armenakis, A.A., Harris, S.G. and Mossholder, K.W.: Creating Readiness for Organizational Change. Human Relations, 46. (1993) 681-703
22. Eby, L.T., Adams, D.M., Russell, J.E.A. and Gaby, S.H.: Perceptions of Organizational Readiness for Change - Factors Related to Employees; Reactions to the Implementation of Team Based Selling. Human Relations, 53(3). (2000) 419-442
23. Kirton, M.J: Adaptor and Innovators in Organizations. Human Relations, 3. (1980) 213-224
24. Pereira, R.E.: An Adopter-Centered Approach to Understanding Adoption of Innovations, European. Journal of Innovation Management, 5(1). (2002) 40-49
25. Ajzen, I. and Fishbein, M.: Attitude-Behaviour Relations - A Theoretical Analysis and Review of Empirical Research. Psychological Bulletin, 84. (1977) 888-918
26. Ajzen, I. and Fishbein, M.: Understanding Attitudes and Predicting Social Behaviour. NJ: Prentice-Hall (1980)
27. Davis, F., Bagozzi, R. and Warshaw, P.: User Acceptance of Computer Technology - A Comparison of Two Theoretical Models. Management Science, 35(8), (1989) 982-1003
28. Venkatesh, V. and Davis, F.D.: A Model of the Antecedents of Perceived Ease of Use: Development and Test. Decision Sciences, 27(3). (1996) 451-481
29. Bryd, T.A. and Turner, D.E.: An Exploratory Analysis of the Value of the Skills of IT Personnel - Their Relationship to IS Infrastructure and Competitive Advantage. Decision Sciences, 32(1). (2001) 21-54
30. Thong, Y.L.: An Integrated Model of Information Systems Adoption in Small Businesses. Journal of Management Information Systems, 15(4). (1999) 187-214
31. Aggarwal, R. and Prasad, J.: Are Individual Differences Germane to the Acceptance of New Information Technologies? Decision Sciences, 30(2). (1999) 361-391
32. Schneider, B. and Bowen, D.E.: The Service Organization: Human Resources Management Is Crucial. Organizational Dynamics, 21. (1993) 39-52
33. McNabb, D.E. and Sepic, F.T.: Culture, Climate and Total Quality Management: Measuring Readiness for Change. Public Productivity & Management Review, 18(4). (1995) 369-385
34. Baker, S. and Baker, K.: Mind over Matter. Journal of Business Strategy, (July/August). (1998) 22-26
35. Peters, R.: Data Warehousing in the Telecommunications Services Industry. DM Review. (2000) 25-29
36. Dahlan, N., Ramayah, T., and Koay, A.H.: Data Mining in the Banking Industry –An Exploratory Study. In the Proceedings of the International Conference 2002 –Internet Economy and Business. 17 to 18th, September, 2002, Kuala Lumpur, Malaysia.

Creating Incentive-Driven Tasks to Improve Knowledge Management in Sales Chain Relationships

Flavia Morello

Department of Information Systems
Faculty of Information Technology
University of Technology, Sydney
AUSTRALIA
flavia@it.uts.edu.au

Abstract. This paper looks at a business solution that has been designed to improve product knowledge in a company's supply chain by creating incentive-driven tasks to strengthen knowledge and communication links between members of the sales chain. Nonaka's theory of organizational knowledge creation is applied to this practical business solution in an effort to create a model for improving knowledge management strategy in the sales chain.

There is a large amount of research on transaction management in the supply chain however this paper focuses on the management of industry and product knowledge in the supply chain. Many manufacturing companies rely on their sales chain to disseminate product and industry knowledge to the consumer yet there are few strategies designed to ensure that members of the sales chain develop this knowledge in the first place.

This paper suggests ways of improving relationships along the sales chain by encouraging knowledge sharing and strengthening communication links along the chain by offering members of the chain rewards/incentives for their efforts. The tasks are incentive-driven, meaning that the people who are assigned the tasks will be rewarded for completing the tasks. The tasks are designed to encourage communication between the company and its supply chain members and ensure that knowledge is disseminated through the sales chain to the consumer. This paper also looks at technical solutions, using Internet-based knowledge management applications to support the knowledge sharing tasks and manage the rewards associated with them.

1 Introduction

This paper looks at ways to improve communication across the organizations involved in the sales process by creating incentive-driven tasks that encourage inter-organizational communication. More specifically, this paper looks at the people involved in the sales process of a company's value chain and how they can be encouraged to share knowledge and strengthen their communication links with the use of incentive-driven tasks designed to close knowledge gaps and strengthen inter-organizational relationships.

D. Karagiannis and U. Reimer (Eds.): PAKM 2002, LNAI 2569, pp. 87-96, 2002.

The tasks are incentive-driven, meaning that the people who are assigned the tasks will be rewarded for completing the tasks. The tasks are designed to encourage communication between the company and its supply chain members and ensure that knowledge is disseminated through the sales chain to the consumer.

The technical solution that supports these tasks is designed to capture all the information relating to the tasks. As these tasks are designed to capture and distribute knowledge, the technical solution becomes a knowledge management system. Communication is emphasised as a tool to create and distribute the knowledge in the tasks by ensuring that there is more interpersonal contact between members of the sales chain. Communication can be in the form of training seminars, visits, emails or phone calls.

2 The Sales Chain

A company's sales chain is comprised of sales representatives, distributors, distributor outlet owners and distributor sales staff, and the consumer. Generally speaking, the only people in the sales chain who are employed by the manufacturer are the sales representatives. The sales representatives are required to communicate product information and industry knowledge with the distributors, distributor outlet owners and distributor sales staff, who are then required to pass this knowledge on to the consumer. Figure 1 illustrates the roles people have in the sales chain and shows the breakdown of those involved in the distribution channel.

2.1 The Distribution Channel

There are may people involved in the sales chain, especially the distributor channel, so it is difficult to ensure that everyone in the sales chain has the latest knowledge and it is also difficult to ensure that members of the sales chain communicate regularly with company representatives and other members of the sales chain. Distributor knowledge and their direct contact with consumers can influence consumers more than the manufacturer can [1], therefore ensuring that distributor knowledge is current and accurate is essential to a company's competitiveness as improvement to the links in the sales chain improves the company's efficiency and thus competitive advantage [2]. By the same token, distributors are also able to gain better knowledge of a manufacturer's consumers as they have a direct relationship to the consumer. If this knowledge is harnessed and returned to the manufacturer then they are able to build a better profile of their consumers.

2.2 Knowledge & Communication Gaps

Figure 1 shows that there are a lot of avenues for communication in the sales chain but there are few strategies in place to ensure that these avenues of communication are being utilised or optimised. The lighter communication links in Figure 1 are rarely established yet have the most potential as they are closer to the consumer. The knowledge management solution in this paper promotes and rewards communication and knowledge exchange along these communication channels.

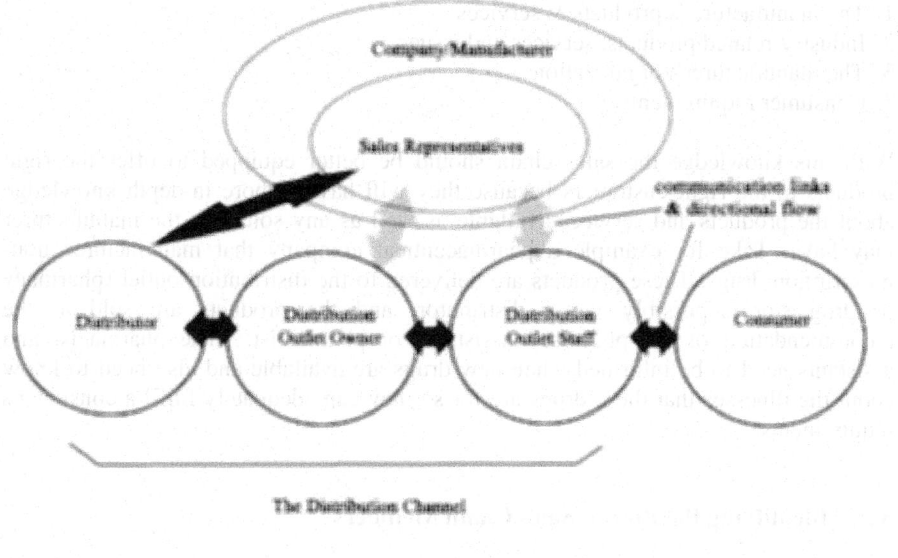

Fig. 1. The Sales Chain

3 Communication in the Sales Chain

Usually the sales representative communicates with one member of the distributor channel. For the company to communicate to the consumer via the distribution channel the company must rely on people outside their own company, this means relying on inter-organizational communication links. Members of a company's sales channel may also be performing the same role for a company's competitors, which means that communication links between the distribution channel and the manufacturer need to be as strong or stronger than their competitors. If the people in the distribution channel have no incentive for selling the manufacturer's product over a competitor's product then the sales and communication of products may rely heavily on the interpersonal relationship established between the sales representative and the distributor [3]. Similarly, if the sales representative has no incentive for sharing company information with the distributor, that is, they are only rewarded for sales but not for service, then regular communication between distributors and manufacturers may be irregular.

3.1 Advantages of Improving Knowledge & Communication in the Sales Chain

Communication in the sales chain and across the distribution channel needs to be strengthened such that people in the sales chain have comprehensive and just-in-time knowledge of:

1. The manufacturer's products & services
2. Industry-related products, services and issues
3. The manufacturer's organization
4. Consumer requirements

With this knowledge the sales chain should be better equipped to offer the right products to the right customers because they will have a more in-depth knowledge about the products and services available as well as any solutions the manufacturer may have. Take for example a pharmaceutical company that manufactures non-prescription drugs. These products are delivered to the distribution outlet (pharmacy or drug store), possibly via a distributor, and the products are sold at the recommendation of the pharmacy assistants or pharmacist. The pharmacist and assistants need to be informed when new drugs are available and also need to know about the illnesses that these drugs are for so they can adequately fulfil a consumer's requirements.

3.2 Identifying the Role of Sales Chain Members

The distribution outlet staff interacts directly with consumers giving them first hand knowledge of consumer behaviour such as buying trends, attitudes and requirements. If this knowledge is filtered back to the manufacturer it will complete the communication cycle and provide valuable consumer feedback which can be used to improve products so they are more suited to consumer needs. Again, in the case of the pharmaceutical company, knowledge regarding the demographics and behaviour of their consumers, or their competitor's consumers can help determine whether issues ranging from the appropriateness of product packaging to problems with product side effects need to be addressed.

This transfer of information can strengthen the role of the sales chain such that the distribution channel acts as an expert in the manufacturer's field rather than a third party operator. It emphasises that both the distributors and the manufacturer can benefit from each other's knowledge so a solution should look at a multi-directional exchange of knowledge across organizations.

4 Incentive-Driven Tasks

To improve communication in the sales chain the distribution channel must have an incentive for improving their industry and product knowledge and for sharing their consumer knowledge with a manufacturer. This paper presents the solution of implementing incentive-driven tasks to improve inter-organizational knowledge and communication.

At this point it is important to define the link between communication and knowledge. The aim of these tasks is to improve inter-organizational knowledge, however, in order to improve inter-organizational knowledge the communication between organizations must be established to facilitate the exchange.

4.1 Rewarding Knowledge Exchange

The strategy is to create tasks that encourage people to exchange information and reward them for successfully completing the assigned tasks. For example, a pharmacy assistant may be asked to participate in a training seminar organised by a pharmaceutical company and presented by their sales representatives. This event has three aims:

1. To open a communication channel between the distributors and the manufacturer's sales representatives.
2. To improve the product and industry knowledge of the distributors.
3. To give the distributors an opportunity to give their feedback to the sales representatives.

Every member of the sales chain needs to be rewarded for participating in any task that stimulates knowledge exchange or creation. One approach to rewarding people is an incentive scheme where people are rewarded with some kind of "reward points" similar to frequent flyer mileage points used by airlines and credit card companies. People are given points for each task they complete and they are then able to trade these points in for some sort of prize. Incentive schemes are useful because the have a longer duration than giving an instant prize and they give the people in the scheme the ability to work towards a prize of a certain value. The right incentives can also encourage task participation where inter personal relationships are initially weak [4]. Using incentives that do not provide an instant reward encourage people to commit themselves to the long-term tasks of knowledge sharing rather than engaging in a one off task. In the example mentioned above, the sales representatives would get points for conducting a training seminar for their distributors, and the distributors would get points for attending the seminar and training other members of the distribution chain. Additional tasks can also be assigned, such as getting the distributors to complete a product-related questionnaire as a follow up to the seminar, to ensure that they understood the seminar and to reinforce the objectives of the training.

Tasks can also be used to capture consumer information. For example, distribution staff can be given a questionnaire regarding their customers, again being rewarded for their efforts with reward points. The tasks should be aimed at knowledge exchange and communication, and the information gathered from these tasks could be used to help identify any knowledge or communication gaps that need to be addressed. This is can be done by ensuring that the tasks encourage feedback from the sales chain and invite suggestions for improvement.

4.2 Creating Incentive-Driven Tasks

The knowledge exchanged using incentive-driven tasks is designed to add value to each person and their role in the sales chain which in turn adds value to the organization's knowledge. To ensure that the tasks are appropriate and effective, gaps in organizational knowledge need to be identified so that an appropriate strategy can be put in place. The tasks need to be dynamic in nature and are themselves a product of the organizational knowledge gathered and created from their implementation.

Nonaka's Theory of Organizational Knowledge Creation

The process that best describes the task creation process is Nonaka's theory of organizational knowledge creation [5]. Nonaka divides the knowledge creation process into four stages socialisation, externalisation, combination and internalisation. Nonaka explains that social interaction such as sharing experience, or *socialisation* creates tacit knowledge. This knowledge is then transformed into a more communicable form, or is *externalised* into explicit knowledge. Frameworks for this explicit knowledge are created from other forms of explicit knowledge and thus new knowledge is created from the *combination* of explicit knowledge. This explicit knowledge is then transferred to other members of the organization who absorb or *internalise* this information turning it into tacit knowledge. This cycle continues as organizational knowledge evolves. Figure 2 illustrates how incentive-driven tasks are created in relation to Nonaka's theory.

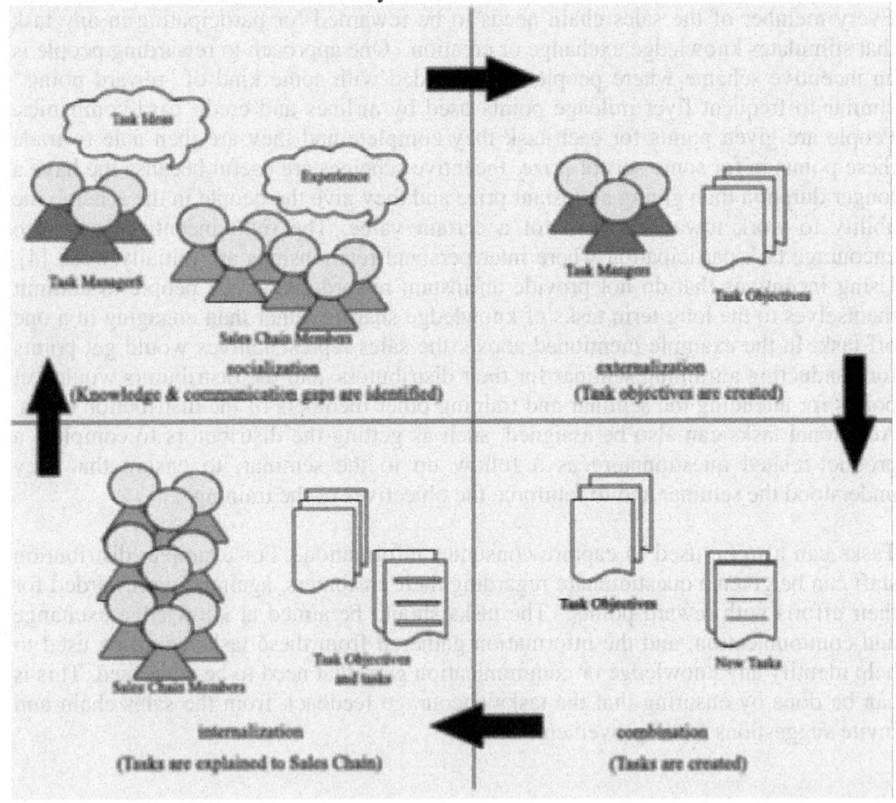

Fig. 2. The Task Creation Process

Applying Nonaka's Theory to the Task Creation Process

Before tasks can be identified and addressed, a sales chain knowledge management team needs to be established so they can manage the incentive-driven tasks. In the initial stages of incentive-driven task creation, the knowledge management team

(Task Managers) are assigned to manage the creation and maintenance of any information relating to the incentive-driven tasks.

Improving the Company's Knowledge of Their Sales Chain to Identify Communication & Knowledge Gaps
The Task Managers socialise with members of the sales chain in an effort to identify communication and knowledge gaps in the sales chain. For example, they may try to find out what the members of the distribution channel know about their products or about certain industry-related issues. In the case of the pharmaceutical company they may ask all the members of the distribution channel questions to determine the extent of their knowledge about a certain health condition.

Defining Knowledge & Communication Issues & Objectives
Once these gaps have been established the Task Managers create a set of task objectives or strategies designed to solve the communication and knowledge gaps they have identified. This externalisation sees the newly created tacit knowledge put into an explicit form. Again, the pharmaceutical company may determine inconsistencies in people's knowledge of a certain illness and the possible remedies. They can determine where these inconsistencies lie and what they would like members of the sales chain to know.

Creating a Solution to Implement Knowledge & Communication Objectives
Once the task objectives have been determined, the Task Managers use a framework of task types, such as paper based tasks, training seminars, and so on, to create tasks that will address the task's objectives. These tasks will also address the individual requirements of the different roles in the sales chain. For example, the tasks assigned to a sales representative are different to those assigned to a distributor. In the pharmaceutical company example, the sales representative's task is to conduct a training seminar, whilst the distributor's task is to attend the training seminar. This stage of the task creation process is reflective of Nonaka's combination stage where explicit knowledge is created from explicit knowledge.

Implementing the Solution
Once the incentive-driven tasks are established, the tasks are explained to the people in the distribution channel who are given task information kits explaining the tasks they are required to undertake, it benefits for them including details of the rewards they will receive for successfully completing the tasks. In this phase the task details are internalised as participants learn about the tasks and express their tacit knowledge by undertaking the tasks. The feedback and results gained from the implementation of the tasks are externalisations of this implicit knowledge.

The Dynamic Nature of Knowledge Creation
The cycle continues when the knowledge gained from the tasks is shared with the Task Managers along with any feedback the distribution channel may have in terms of task implementation. For example, the distributors may complain about the length of the seminars or request a written task instead. Similarly, the sales representative may

wish to have greater control over the training topics or request that their next task be a follow up visit to training participants. This feedback is discussed as are any newly identifiable knowledge or communication gaps regarding industry or company news (for example, there could be a shortage of a product, or the company has just merged with a competitor, etc). This information is used to create the objectives for the next set of tasks (externalised). These new objectives are compared to the results and feedback from the first set of tasks, and then a new set of tasks is created taking into account all the knowledge that has been documented to date (combination). These new tasks are then internalised as they are explained, disseminated and performed by the distribution channel.

Tasks as Knowledge Management Tools

The tasks are used as a tool for creating knowledge. Actively ensuring that Nonaka's theory of knowledge creation is used in the process of creating tasks helps ensure that the tasks are adding to the company's organizational knowledge and that the knowledge that is gained from performing the tasks is adding the maximum possible value. The dynamic nature of the creation of tasks also empowers the participants such that their feedback can help them gain knowledge that they feel is valuable while strengthening the communication channels in the sales chain.

5 Technical Support for Incentive-Driven Tasks

There are enormous amounts of information that can be captured for each task at each stage of the task creation process described above. The information that can be captured and codified includes task objectives, task instructions, task results and task feedback.

5.1 Documentation for Task Creation

By documenting the task objectives and instructions, the Task Managers can create library of tasks that can be re-used for similar problems or objectives. The feedback and task responses can also be used to rate the effectiveness of the tasks in relation to their objectives.

Shared workspaces as described by Hawryszkiewycz [6] can be used to store and share any documents related to the creation of task objectives as this is an effective method for harnessing the tacit nature of the knowledge used to create strategies and tasks.

5.2 Information Management

As the tasks also emphasise the importance of communication links, a customer relationship profile of all members of the sales chain can be established to help filter the information gathered in the incentive-driven tasks. A web-based application which allows everyone involved in the tasks the ability to complete written tasks online, or attend web-based seminars, would help with the knowledge management and would reduce the data entry requirements. Such an application would also mean faster responses to tasks, which tightens and refines the knowledge creation cycles for new tasks.

5.3 Multi User System

To avoid excessive data management administration, the web-based has an interface that allows sales chain members to enter their own data regarding tasks and personal information. A more sophisticated solution would create a cascade-effect for data management and maintenance. For example, sales representatives are given access to records regarding their distributors, distribution outlets and distribution outlet staff and they are required to maintain all information related to those records. Again, this may be a task that they are assigned so that they are rewarded for their efforts with reward points.

Usually keeping such information relevant is an enormous job, especially when trying to keep track of distributors and distributor outlet staff. However, the Task Managers need to have relevant and current details of the people in the sales chain, if these details are not current then the person is not likely to get their tasks, points or prize for their points. This incentive usually ensures that the database of people in the distribution channel is accurate and self-maintained. This part of the web application is a cross between a bank account and online store. A task participant should be able log on to the site and view their reward point balance as well as a break down of their points. There should also be information regarding their task objectives, task instructions, relevant task forms, and a news page with the latest task information and reminders. An online catalogue of reward items could be available along with a facility to trade points for reward items online. Where possible, tasks could be available to complete online, this may even include FTP facilities where items such as distribution outlet photos may be uploaded and stored. Finally, participants should always have access to an online feedback form and/or task evaluation form.

5.4 Data Analysis & Integration

Data collected from and about members in the sales chain is invaluable but only if it is used as more than just assigning reward points. This data needs to be collated and analysed so that it can provide information that can contribute to the company's organizational knowledge and help establish knowledge and communication gaps as well as providing possible insights into the behaviour and attitudes of the sales chain members.

The distribution channel has long been the subject of concern for adding value to a company by improving delivery speed and improving retail stock levels [7]. If this information can be combined with product and industry knowledge, companies will be one step closer to integrating their systems from the aspects of transaction support as well as knowledge management support.

6 Conclusion

The sales chain can be crucial to a company's success [7] as they are in close contact with the consumer and are assumed to have vast and accurate product and industry knowledge. They are required to disseminate company and industry knowledge to the consumer yet there is little incentive for them to gain or distribute such knowledge. With the implementation of incentive-driven tasks a company can improve the knowledge of the sales chain and leverage their competitiveness [2]. These tasks can be successfully implemented by using Nonaka's theory of organizational knowledge creation to design the knowledge-creating tasks. Using this process ensures that the tasks are used as tools to create and distribute the organization's knowledge to all members of its sales chain. By implementing a technical solution to help manage sales chain knowledge, the company can improve their knowledge management systems and make them accessible to relevant members of the company's sales chain.

References

1. Stern, L.W. and B.A. Weitz, *The revolution in distribution: Challenges and opportunities.* Long Range Planning, 1997. **Vol. 30**(Issue 6): p. 823.
2. Porter, M.E., *The competitive advantage of nations.* 1990, London: Macmillan.
3. Kumar, K. and H.G. van Dissel, *Sustainable collaboration: Managing conflict and cooperation in interorganizational systems.* MIS Quarterly, 1996. **20**(3): p. 96.
4. Murry, J.P. and J.B. Heide, *Managing promotion program participation within.* Journal of Marketing, 1998. **62**(1): p. 58.
5. Nonaka, I., *A Dynamic Theory of Knowledge Creation.* Organization Science, 1994. **5**(1): p. 14-37.
6. Hawryszkiewycz, I. *Developing the Infrastructure for Knowledge Based Enterprises.* in *International Conference on Enterprise Information Systems (ICEIS).* 2001. Setubal, Portugal: Springer-Verlag.
7. Weitz, B.A. and S.D. Jap, *Relationship marketing and distribution channels.* Journal of the Academy of Marketing Science, 1995. **23**(4): p. 305.

Employing the Unified Process for Developing a Web-Based Application – A Case-Study

Renate Motschnig-Pitrik

University of Vienna
Department of Computer Science and Business Informatics
Rathausstrasse 19/9
A-1010 Vienna, Austria
Tel. +43 (1) 4277-38415
renate.motschnig@univie.ac.at

Abstract. This paper describes the author's experience in applying the Unified Process (UP) to a mid-sized web-based application in cooperation with a small multi-media agency. The peculiarities of the project, which make it an optimal test-bed for exploration, are the project's non-time critical nature, its modest size, the curiosity and openness of all collaborators, and the author's opportunity to accompany the project from a first, vague idea up to the initial operation, and maintenance phase. Rather than documenting each step of the UP, the paper focuses on selected steps and artifacts, discusses the strong and the weak points of the UP as perceived in the concrete project and tries to draw some generalized hypotheses. The paper further touches some key issues of a situational project management style. The case study encourages the use of a tailored version of the UP, given essential preconditions concerning the project and the project team are being met.

1 Introduction

The Unified Process (UP) is a recent, powerful software development process incorporating mature, proven techniques and the best practices covering the whole software development life cycle. First officially released in 1999, the Unified Process [5] was designed to optimally support software development with the UML (Unified Modeling Language [15]) such that notation and process complement one another. Since then the UP has successfully been applied to major projects predominantly in large organizations [6]. It is characterized by being use-case driven, architecture-centric, iterative and incremental. These features, in the author's view, make it a good candidate for supporting any innovative project needing to be adaptable to the changing needs of its dynamic environment.

This paper is written to share the author's experience in applying the UP for developing a medium-sized, non-time-critical, extendible web-application in a small team. Major design decisions, tailoring steps, required extensions, and insights gained will be addressed and communicated by means of tracking a concrete project, called UniKid. The purpose of this paper is not to drive the reader through every detail of the UP. Rather, it is to give a glimpse on what it can mean to apply the UP in a mid-sized

D. Karagiannis and U. Reimer (Eds.): PAKM 2002, LNAI 2569, pp. 97-113, 2002.

web-project and thus to help in deciding whether to employ the UP in some concrete project situation. In this spirit we address questions like: Is it justified to use the UP in a development team with just 4 people? How difficult is it to learn to use this process and will it really be effective? What insights can be gained from a first attempt? What support can one expect from this process and what has to be decided and worked out separately? Since success in a project is a multi-facetted, complex issue, I am by no means sure in how far my largely positive experience can be generalized. Nevertheless, I do hope to communicate some arguments that convinced me that following a mature process in a flexible and situation-driven way can largely benefit even web-applications of modest size. Individual issues contributing to this hypothesis will be presented throughout the paper.

We proceed chronologically covering the whole process but focus on those steps and decisions the author perceived as most relevant, such as initial considerations, a two step bidding process, allocating sufficient effort to the early phases, gathering early user feedback, synchronizing content- and graphical design issues, having the use-case model drive the test process, and employing an adaptable project management style. Special emphasis will further be given to the features identified as particularly supportive, such as the consideration and mitigation of risks, the identification of actors and use-cases encompassing a clear account and delimitation of content, and clarity about the non-functional requirements. Equally, tasks and documents needed in web-based applications but completely missing form the UP are discussed. Fortunately it will turn out that complementing the process and its workers (i.e. roles of collaboration) is easier than extending the UML for issues like graphic layout and navigation design [1], [13]. The final Section summarizes the strengths and some weaknesses of the UP as viewed from the author's experience in the particular process instance. From this we try to derive some general hypotheses on the applicability of the UP based on project characteristics and team issues. Questions for further research conclude the case study.

2 Getting Started: The Topic, Initial Steps, and the First Iteration of the Inception Phase

2.1 Genesis

As the representative of the University of Vienna in a working group on child-care in the context of universities, the author realized that important information was spread across the heads of several individuals and brochures at different places. Consistent, coherent, complete information, however, was missing and hard to acquire. Thus the author – a software engineer – couldn't help but suggest a web-based information system be built in order to provide information around the clock and, at the same time, provide a medium for contacts, communication, and any initiatives for self-help. Soon thereafter the author was asked to submit a project to develop such a system. Building a social web-application sounded like a fascinating enterprise, in particular, if it could be combined with some experimentation in web-development techniques and a time schedule giving room for such experimentation.

In the very beginning it was by no means clear that the project would be developed following the UP. Only when assembling the proposal, thereby identifying actors, functions, and delimiting the system's scope, the author recognized that several activities match the first iteration of the UP's inception phase. Thus, the first steps seemed to pop up intuitively for someone being used to work with the UML (Unified Modeling Language) [15] in the course of small OO-development projects. In other words, the UP more or less suggested itself by offering support for activities that were deemed essential. But would a team be found who is willing to follow the UP and would this be effective, even if no OO code was ever to be written in this project?

2.2 UniKid – Studying/Working with Kids

The whole discussion of the project's conduct would be superficial without stating the scope and the goals of the project. Since they have not until the operation phase, we refer to the (english version of the) introductory text of the web-application:

"Do you see yourself in the need of coordinating lectures with urgently seeing the pediatrician, combining exams with changing diapers, or preparing exciting lectures concurrently with good-night stories? If so, we encourage you to continue exploring this web-application that has been designed to make your challenging life a little easier. UniKid aims to supply studying and working parents with all kinds of information they may find useful in order to help them save time. Focusing on child-care, UniKid provides contact addresses of university-related and other child-care institutions and persons whom to contact for further information. Particularly, UniKid also supports parents by offering the capability of initiating contacts for reasons of mutual help, in particular with baby-sitting and child care (see the "Parent2Parent" page). Also, UniKid offers a platform for discussion of all topics regarding kids in the context of universities."

2.3 Initial Considerations

The core idea being born, the author looked for similar applications on the web but, except for some loose information pages, flee markets, online baby-sitting ads, etc. nothing could be found. This meant that the application was fairly innovative. In any case, some good estimate on the whole project was needed, but the author had hardly any data or experience to hold on. Furthermore, there were hard risks that could lead to a complete failure after construction, such as having nobody to maintain the system. These observations as well as the clearly perceived complexity of the system convinced the author that having a two-step bidding process is the only meaningful and responsible way to proceed. Planning for putting together a detailed concept thereby addressing initial risks and developing a plan on how to proceed felt right and feasible. Striving for a smooth transition to later phases let UML and the UP come into the process, although it was by no means clear which part - if any - OO programming would play.

Revealing the two-step strategy to the ministry left the prospective promoters with clear disappointment. They should pay (even only a very modest sum for about one person month) for a concept – and what if the project wouldn't proceed then? Only after intense personal reassurance where the author tried to make clear that she would withdraw only if irresolvable problems popped up, and that the concept would be the only serious way to learn and to estimate the effort, they gave in. Using UP terminology, we will refer to the work in putting together the proposal for the concept phase (i.e. the very first document in the whole project) as the first iteration of the inception phase. The work to be done to elaborate that proposal for the detailed concept in order to arrive at a viable proposal for all aspects of the conceived web-application will be allocated to the second iteration of the inception phase.

Table 1. Deliverables of the Inception Phase [5]

Deliverable	*1. Iteration*	*2. Iteration*
Feature list	started	Refined
First version of a business or domain Model	existed to some degree	reflected in glossary
First cut of Use-Case Model	done	Refined
First cut of Analysis Model	-	Done
First cut of Design Model	-	very rudimentary
optionally: Implementation/Test model	-	test of use-cases planned
First version of supplementary requirements	done	Continued
First draft of candidate architecture description with views of individual models	-	concept for software - and content architecture
Optional: proof-of-concept prototype	-	only for DB-module
Initial risk list	done	Updated
Use-Case ranking list	-	two priorities assigned
Beginnings of a plan for the entire project	very rudimentary	Done
First draft of business case	for first phase only	Done
Time schedule, duration	1.5 days	6 weeks

2.4 The Inception Phase in General

The initial proposal that served as the basis for the approval of the construction of the concept--conceived of as the first iteration of the inception phase in UP terminology--had a table of contents that results directly from concatenating the individual deliverables listed in the column called "1. Iteration" as given in Table 1. It was complemented by an introductory part explaining the topic, motivation, goals, scope of the project along with the strategy chosen for construction. It took approximately 1.5 days to complete, compared to 6 weeks for the second iteration, where we worked part-time in a team of three people including the author in a role that comes closest to that of a coordinator (team, ministry, university). While Table 1 provides an overview of the deliverables of the Inception Phase, below we discuss selected processes and artifacts in more detail.

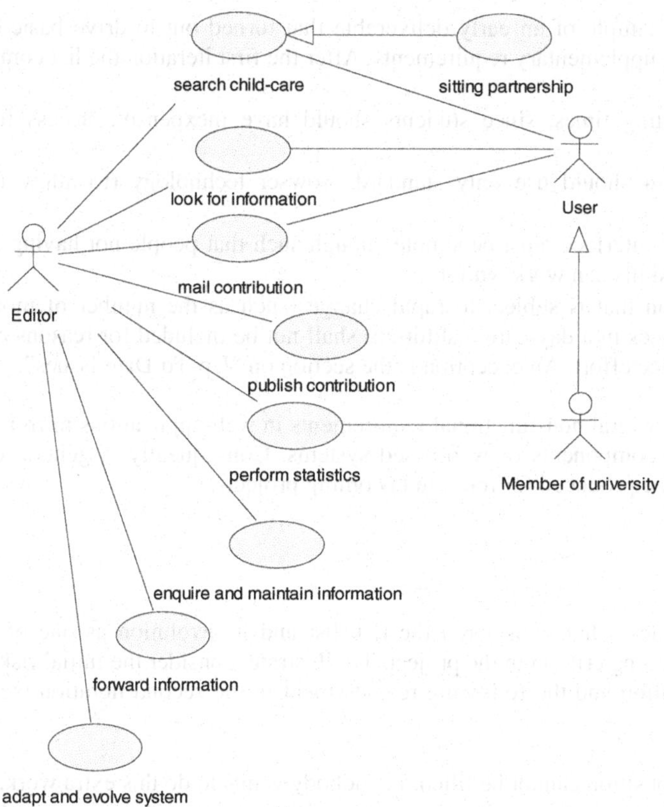

Fig. 1. Use-Case overview from the first iteration of the inception phase

2.5 Initial Use-Case Overview

In order to survey the functionality of the proposed system a very coarse grained use-case diagram as sketched in Figure 1 has been designed and individual use-cases have been briefly but systematically described following the proposal by Schneider and Winters [16]. They were conceived as very useful on at least three occasions:

- They clarified the need for the provision of individual interfaces for individual actors such as members of the university, occasional users, and the editor.
- They provided a breakdown of the basic functionality of the system to be detailed later.
- They were used to derive test cases for the black-box part of the test process [5].

2.6 Supplementary Requirements

As a further sample of an early deliverable that turned out to drive basic decisions consider the supplementary requirements. After the first iteration the list comprised:

- Short loading times, since students should have inexpensive access from their homes.
- The system should use only standard browser technology (to allow for broad usability).
- The editor interface must be simple enough such that people not having advanced technical skills can work with it.
- Information that is subject to rapid change (such as the number of momentarily vacant places in a day-care institution) shall not be included for reasons of modest maintenance effort. An exception is the section on "Up-To-Date Issues".

Note that several non-functional requirements in web-applications mirror attributes of particular components of web-based systems. Consequently, a generic check-list could easily be produced for reuse in upcoming projects.

2.7 Risks

Personally, the author considered the risk list and its evolution as one of the most important guiding criteria in the project. To illustrate, consider the initial risk list from the first iteration and the following reassessment in the second iteration (see Section 3):

- Editorial position cannot be filled, i.e. nobody wants to do this extra work.
- The universities' computing centre is not willing to host the system and no other sponsor can be found.
- Student organizations consider the system to mean competition rather than support.
- Legal problems, e.g. warranty, may pop up in the case of accidents with sitters that were mediated by a system hosted by the university.
- Information already on the Internet does not justify the development of a further system.

2.8 Planning

The project idea document – the deliverable of the first iteration of the inception phase – was concluded with a detailed plan encompassing the activities of the next iteration and a gross plan for further phases. It required a two-step bidding process, arguing on the foremost importance of mitigating the risks identified so far, and suggesting the basic content architecture, the technical variants for service modules, the interlinking, and editing.

3 The Second Iteration in the Inception Phase and Situational Project Management

3.1 General Issues and the Team

The goal of this iteration was to set up the first, as realistic as possible proposal of the web-application in terms of its contents, its basic structure, the services it should provide on the one hand and the process, the team, and the budget for its completion on the other hand. Besides the author, two people worked on the concept: An expert on web-technology and a PhD student researching content issues. In one of our first meetings we agreed to name our project "UniKid". We met once a week for 3 hours during a period of 6 weeks. While an overview of the deliverables of this iteration is given in Tables 1 and 2, below we turn to selected issues for further discussion.

3.2 Addressing Risks

Fortunately, all these risks could be mitigated early in the second iteration by means of contacting responsible positions. The author felt relieved having found a home for the new application and being promised a person who would maintain it as part of her job description. Finally, detailed search on the internet revealed some general web-sites and -applications to link to for general issues but no web-presence of a comprehensive site with university related child care themes. Suddenly a new risk came to our minds: would there be sufficient interest in and accesses to the system to justify its construction? We suggested two means to deal with this risk: First, public relations efforts were devised to promote the system. Second, in order to gain further reassurance or a warning, a shortened form of the concept document including a user interface prototype for the parent2parent service was emailed for feedback to all university staff and major student groups.

3.3 Supplementary Requirements

During the second iteration non-functional requirements were added, such as:

- The skills necessary for the editor interface must be learnable within less than one day for a person with basic knowledge of word-processing.
- The editor interface is to be constructed such that more than one person can work with it.
- Maintenance effort should be held low. Only information being central to the topic shall be explicitly included. Other information is to be interlinked.
- If successful, the system should be adapted for other university cities in Austria.
- The system's look and feel should emphasize systematic organization of services.

3.4 Detailing the Most Important Use-Case

Sitting Partnership from Figure 1. One novel variant of child-care to be supported in UniKid is the Parent2Parent service. Its goal is to support mutual help in baby-sitting between families such that contacts between parents are established in order to arrange taking terms in sitting for children. The respective use-case overview diagram is shown in Figure 2 and is intended to illustrate the level of description chosen for the architecturally most important use case. Further, a first cut of the analysis model has been designed which, for space limitation is not shown in this paper. Also, a web-user-interface prototype for the Parent2Parent service has been designed to be available for evaluation by prospective users.

3.5 What Is a Use-Case in a Web-Based System?

In general we tried to identify all use-cases for UniKid, getting into interesting arguments on what a use-case is in a web-based system. While discussing several options we settled at the definition that every actor that causes interaction with the system, even if he/she only looks up information encoded in HTML, executes a use-case. This is mainly because the respective information needs to be provided and also be navigable in a way that seems intuitive to the human actor.

3.6 Technical Alternatives and First Cut on System Structure

The technical expert produced a document that discussed technical alternatives regarding the following issues: storage and retrieval of ads, authorization, referring to foreign content, and the technology for the editor interface. While the final decisions were postponed to the elaboration phase, the team discussed preliminary preferences and found the supplementary requirements a valuable aid in the decision process. The first proposal on the system architecture, as depicted in Figure 3 (further discussed in Section 4) was produced.

3.7 Content Structure

In devising the structure we followed the strategy to keep issues that change fast, such as addresses, local and also to localize information that differs regionally, in order to ease adaptability for other regions. Furthermore, in cases of doubt, we made the structure more explicit rather than collapsing issues since we felt that later integration might prove easier than finding structures in complex, convoluted material. In a nutshell, structuring guidelines from object-oriented technology proved helpful for logically structuring the content. Localization of regional information proved particularly effective during the adaptation of the system during operation and maintenance.

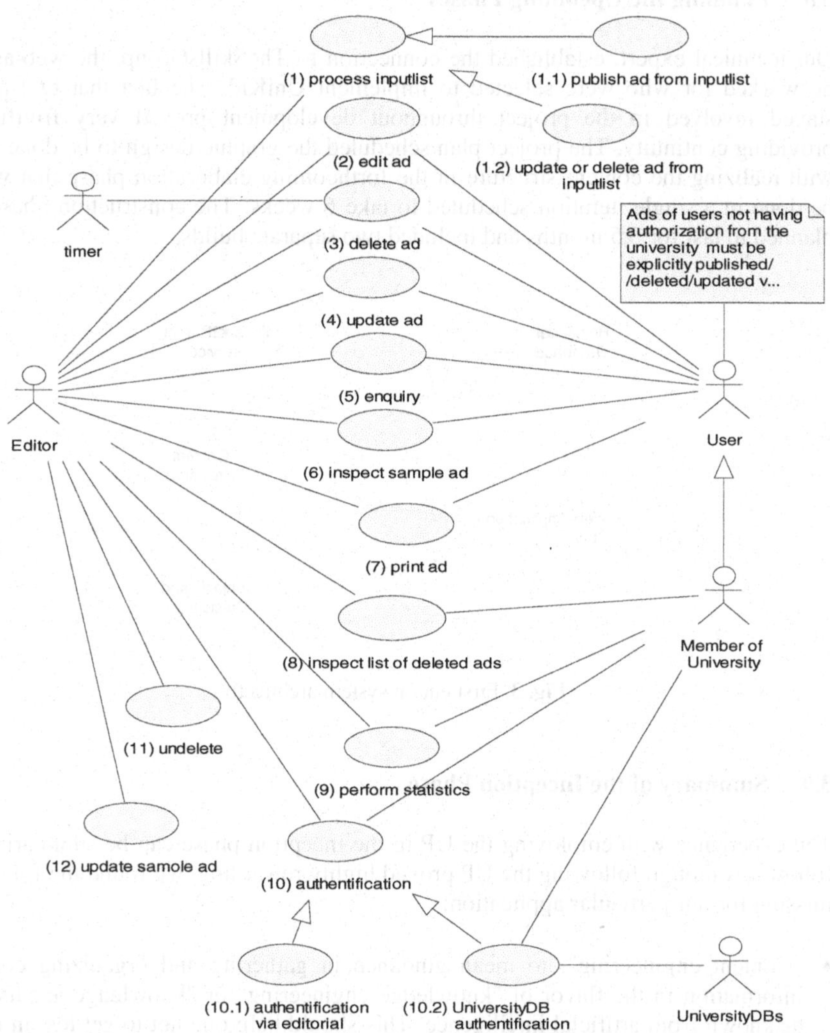

Fig. 2. Detailing the most important use-case called sitting partnership or the Parent2Parent module

3.8 Planning the Upcoming Phases

Our technical expert, established the connection to TheSkillsGroup, the web-agency he worked for who were selected to implement UniKid. The fact that two people stayed involved in the project throughout development proved very fruitful for providing continuity. The project plan scheduled the graphic design to be done along with realizing the content structure in the forthcoming elaboration phase that was to be done in a single iteration scheduled to take 6 weeks. The construction phase was planned to last for 3,5 months and included two separate builds.

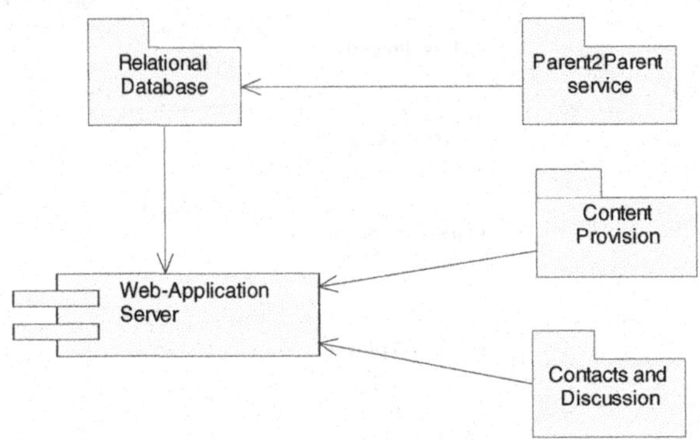

Fig. 3. First cut on system architecture

3.9 Summary of the Inception Phase

The experience with employing the UP in the inception phase can be summarized as follows. Although following the UP proved highly rewarding, we found the following missing for our particular application:

- "Content engineering", to mean guidance in gathering and organizing content-information in the flavor of "knowledge engineering" or "knowledge acquisition" as known from artificial intelligence. This should help one not to get lost in multi-medial oceans of contents.
- Generic consideration of non-functional requirements that are particularly relevant for web-applications.
- Strategy to navigation and links as a gross architectural issue.
- Regard to graphic design as one component or at least gross idea waiting for elaboration in the next phase. The provision of a first impression of the look and feel of an application should be addressed. This last observation is fully shared and resolved in the literature [17].

As a consequence, Table 2 proposes some activities and corresponding deliverables that we propose to complement the UP and indicates at which iteration respective issues had been tackled in the case study. In the literature [17], the last field of Table 2 is also referred to as "creative design brief".

Table 2. Complements to deliverables for the Inception Phase of web-applications that primarily publish information

Activity / Deliverable	*1. Iteration*	*2. Iteration*
Initial collection of content material	started	continued, organized in a physical folder along topics
Analysis of information available on the internet	discussed	documented systematically
Initial documentation of relevant links	listing only	done in brief to be complemented
Initial ideas on graphic layout and user unterface	-	discussed, documented in notes

Some *key observations* and *insights* we gained are paraphrased as follows:

- Innovative projects profit from a two-step bidding process.
- The topic needs a clear direction and clear delimitation from the very first beginning. Considering prospective users and their needs in the form of use cases significantly reduces overhead.
- The consideration of risks from the very first beginning proves crucial to initiating the project. Several important risks appear to be non-technical by their nature and need to be mitigated almost at once.
- In web applications, a tendency to a shift in emphasis towards a strong inception phase can be perceived. We conjecture that it is partly due to the fact that in web application the software tends to be less complex and components can often be reused effectively.
- The feedback we received from sending out the concept to prospective clients provided valuable comments, and helped to make design decisions later in the project. Thus, early involvement of prospective users can warmly be suggested as in classical software development.

4 Elaboration

4.1 The New Team and Process

While our web-technology expert and the author stayed with the team, the editorial was taken over by a new team member and a graphics expert, being the web-agencies managing partner, joined the team. An open discussion brought us to the conclusion that most advantages could be gained if the web agencies managing partner and the author acted as managing partners in the project with the former coordinating members of his company and the author coordinating the process and all contacts with the university. We clearly distributed our responsibilities and made only the best experience with this form of cooperative leadership. The managing partner appreciated the idea to try to pursue the UP, in particular, as the author offered to explain it and to cooperate in adopting it to the agencies' own process in the context of our needs.

4.2 Content Architecture and Graphics

In one of the first sessions with the new team, the graphics expert illustrated overlaps of subtopics in the content list of the previous phase and we tried out various criteria on the organization of the material. From the start on, about 4 of 12 topics stayed stable, the others were constantly renamed and reorganized according to different criteria. The author truly experienced how important intuitive naming was and how the number of sections would have an influence on the graphic organization of the start page and on the whole navigation structure. After intense discussion the team converged to a proposal that was appreciated by all team members: The graphics expert suggested to introduce a section called "Info-Safari" and to arrange all links to general information to individual tracks of the safari, such as "track for fathers" "track for health", etc. (see http://www.univie.ac.at/unikid/infosafari/index.html), basically a form of guided tour with intersections. This helped to reduce the number of sections on the highest level to 8 and to clearly localize portions of content that primarily referenced other web sites. In the upcoming sessions, the graphics expert presented his proposals for the home page and we iterated to agreement on individual page structures. Then, weekly sessions focused on individual sections of content as well as on user-interface and navigation design in the Parent2Parent module. While a gross sketch of the deliverables is given in Table 3, aspects we found missing from the UP are summarized in Table 4.

4.3 User Interaction and Navigation Design

Attempts to specify user-interaction in the Parent2Parent module via activity diagrams turned out to be complex and highly time consuming. The resulting diagrams were too complex to provide an overview but still usable as specifications for the implementation and for testing individual access paths. Techniques described in the literature were found effective for selected issues: Purely static reach ability can be modeled employing the "Full Navigation Map" [17] or, as in our case, Conallen's extensions to static structure diagrams [3]. Cases where navigation follows a predefined pattern are well served by the UML extensions proposed in [2] that help to simplify the visualization of the access structure. In more complex cases, textual specifications called specification cards [4] were tried to describe navigation paths. In general, however, all cases in which the navigation target depended on the user's role and on the session history led to diagrams that were rather convoluted and not at all transparent to provide guidance for the user. Hence, we conjecture that distributing the complexity by means of modeling contexts and views [12], [10], [11] in order to be able to capture differences among individual user roles and tasks would simplify the resulting diagrams to a considerable degree.

Consequently, since current techniques did not really prove effective to completely cover our needs for navigation design, our implementors used story-board-like, interlinked sketches with miniature icons for pages, buttons, etc. in order to specify navigation. The author could only agree that these intuitive sketches provide useful information and thinks about ways to incorporate them into UML.

Table 3. Deliverables of the Elaboration Phase according to [5]

Deliverable	*Handling of deliverable*
Preferably a complete business (or domain) model which describes the context of the system	not further refined
New version of all models (complete between 10% - 80%): use-case analysis design deployment, implementation	 done, also activity diagrams done for Parent2Parent package partly, for complex use-cases-
Executable architectural baseline	basic, high-level navigation
Architecture description	done wrt. system- and content structure
Updated risk list	done, no new risks found
Project plan for the construction and transition phases	refined
Completed business case	done as one of the first tasks
Time schedule, duration	6 weeks

4.4 Selecting Technical Variants

The only aspect that did not follow the proposal from the inception phase (see Section 3) was the choice of the database system. Due to strict security policy, the computing centre supported only ORACLE databases and PERL to be addressed via the standard port. This was the main reason to use ORACLE .

Table 4. Complements to deliverables of the UP's Elaboration Phase for web-applications

Deliverable or aspect:	*The way it was dealt with:*
concept and specification of graphic layout	done and presented as prototype
user interaction and navigation design	specified in class diagrams and in story-board-like diagrams
page structure view	done as skeletons in HTML
prototype of user interface (or its update)	done and tested briefly
concept for information update (e.g. html-editor, web-editor, etc.)	decided
means of interconnection with other web-sites	decided
strategy for authorization	specified in activity diagrams

4.5 Summary of Elaboration Phase

Some versatile *observations* resulting from the team's experience with applying the UP in the Elaboration Phase are as follows:

- Non-functional requirements were found to drive the choice of technical variants.
- Initial content delimitation proved extremely important for decision support.
- State charts were found useful for the specification of client-server interactions.
- Openness to content restructuring has been found essential to improvement.
- Intuitive wording of concepts has been found essential for usability.
- The five elements: content structure, wording, page structure, functionality and graphic concept are highly interdependent and need to be synchronized iteratively and incrementally for optimal fit. They should be conceived as being part of the concept of architecture in web-based systems and as such a basis for further deepening.

5 Construction, Stepwise Transition, and First Experiences with Maintenance

5.1 Construction

After the basic page structures have been designed during elaboration, construction meant to fill them with content. Concurrently, the database has been constructed except for the editor's interface that was scheduled for the second built. Also, the Info-Safaris proved to be quite independent from the rest such as to be realized in the second built. Due to the fact that PEARL is not an object-oriented language, the use of class-diagrams in the design model was kept optional. Nevertheless, some class diagrams with web-extensions were drawn to specify reach ability in the Parent2Parent module. Further, state-transition diagrams for the more sophisticated CGI-scripts helped to gain overview over the numerous states in the advertisement submission process.

5.2 Testing

Although the use-case model was the leading artifact for performing black-box tests [5], the class diagram with navigation paths (see section 4) proved more fine-grained to track all technically possible navigation paths and point to incomplete navigations or inconsistent naming of navigation targets. For example, "to start" was ambiguously used to get to the start of a topic or to the home page.

5.3 Transition

The launching of the project was delayed for a couple of weeks because we underestimated the effort for the detailed testing of the Parent2Parent module. Due to the numerous options provided by the Parent2Parent service, the correction of errors took longer than expected. Interestingly, it was precisely this module whose user-interaction and navigation had been defined only semi-formally (see Section 4).

5.4 Maintenance

The first weeks of operation brought several requests for updates of information and links. This shows that in a period of about 4 months (between content-gathering and release) information on the topic changed to a considerable but easily manageable degree. The Transition Phase in Vienna meant the beginning of the adaptation of UniKid for Graz, Austria's second largest city. About three months later, the adapted version of UniKid became operational there. The current spread of UniKid to other Austrian cities inspires the exploration of several organizational issues such as the coordination of real as well as virtual strategies to support working/studying parents.

6 Summary, Discussion, and Further Work

Summarizing, undoubtedly all three characteristics of the UP, namely its use-case driven, architecture centric, and iterative and incremental nature, were found highly useful in the case study although the first two needed a special interpretation for the development of web-based systems. A use-case is interpreted to mean any meaningful interaction of an actor with the system, including queries on categories of information. Likewise, the term architecture subsumed the system architecture as well as the content architecture and the page structure.

Foremost, the vital role that is ascribed to identifying and mitigating risks has not only been appreciated but also successfully applied in the case study. Also, the consideration of supplementary requirements and the addressing of project management issues have been found essential. We would not have been able to follow the UP if it did not allow for a loose handling of the number of iterations and the degree of completion of all artifacts and workflows. In a small team with no severe time pressure, this freedom, in the author's view, led to a fairy optimal degree of the utilization of guidance and freedom as offered by the powerful and yet highly flexible process. Some features we had to complement for developing a web application were the organization of content gathering and structure, the graphic layout, navigation design, suitable wording of concepts, page structure and the integration of structural, functional, content and graphic issues, including the timing of these integrative steps, primarily throughout the elaboration phase. Thus, the case study showed that in order to provide guidance in web development, the UP needs adaptation along numerous dimensions only some of which are discussed in the literature [17], [3], [4], [2].

Regarding project management, we appreciated cooperating in a small project team under the managing partnership between the web-agencies' manager (coinciding with the graphics expert) and the author. A technical expert and an editorial position complemented the team from elaboration on. The fact that two core members stayed on the team from inception to transition was essential to ensure continuity between the phases even though the organizational context changed from university to commerce. The project's modest size and non-time-critical nature both were essential factors in the bi-directional transfer of knowledge and skills.

Being fully aware of the limitations of generalizing from a single case, we return to the questions posed in the introduction and try to give some tentative responses. Whereas the degree of support and the individual insights gained from employing the UP have been attributed to individual phases and discussed throughout the paper, in this place we respond to the question on whether applying the UP with small teams and projects is justified. We conjecture that the answer is yes the more of the following factors are found to be true in a particular setting:

- High quality requirements are posed on the project and/or the process;
- The application is to be long-lived and potentially also extendable, distributable;
- The organization and the project team are experienced in following some disciplined process and motivated to challenge/improve their process;
- An experienced team member has at least good theoretical knowledge of the UP;

- Most team members have fair knowledge and skills in applying the UML;
- The time for development is not critical in order to allow for some experimentation with new techniques;

Ongoing research addresses the use of contexts [12], [11] to web-design in general and to navigation structures in particular. We are also in the process of experimenting with and adapting various requirements engineering techniques [8] for web-based systems. Further case-studies are needed to assess the factors for a successful application of the UP to web-based systems as well as for pointing to its appropriate tailoring and extension. If this work has inspired further exploration of the power of a mature and open-ended software development process, it has served its purpose well.

References

1. Baresi L., Garzotto F., Paolini P.: From Web Sites to Web Applications: New issues for Conceptual Modeling. In: Liddle S., W. et al. (eds.): Conceptual Modeling for E-Business and the Web, LNCS no 1921, Springer (2000) 89 - 100
2. Baresi L., Garzotto F., Paolini P.: Extending UML for Modeling Web Applications; Proc. of the 34th Hawaii Conf. on System Sciences, Decision Technologies for Mngmt. track; Maiu, USA (Jan. 2001)
3. Conallen J.: Building Web-Applications with UML; Addison-Wesley (2000)
4. Güell N., Schwabe D., Vilain P.: Modeling Interactions and Navigation in Web Applications; Proc. of the WWW and Conceptual Modeling'00 Workshop; LNCS #1921 (2000)
5. Jacobson I., Booch G., Rumbaugh J.: The Unified Software Development Process; Addison-Wesley, Object Technology Series (1999)
6. Kruchten P.: The Rational Unified Process - An Introduction; Addison-Wesley (1999)
7. Kruchten P.: From Waterfall to Iterative Lifecycle: A taugh transition for project managers; ROSE Architect, 2(3), Rational (Spring 2000) 57 - 63
8. Loucopoulos P., Karakostas V.: System Requirements Engineering; McGraw-Hill Book Company Europe (1995)
9. Motschnig-Pitrik R., Kaasboll J.: Part-Whole Relationship Categories and Their Application in Object-Oriented Analysis; IEEE KDE 11(5) (Sept./Oct. 1999) 779-797
10. Motschnig-Pitrik R.: A Generic Framework for the Modeling of Contexts and its Applications; Data & Knowledge Engineering 32 (2000) 145-180
11. Motschnig-Pitrik R.: The Viewpoint Abstraction in Object-Oriented Analysis and the UML; ER'2000; Proc. of the 19th Internat. Conf. on Conceptual Modeling, Laender A., H., F., Liddle S., W., Storey V., C., editors, Lecture Notes in Computer Science 1920, Springer, Salt Lake City, Utah, USA (October 2000) 543 - 557
12. Mylopoulos J., Motschnig-Pitrik R.: Partitioning Information Bases with Contexts; Proc. of the 3rd International Conference on Cooperative Information Systems, Vienna (May 1995)
13. Rossi G., Schwabe D., Lyardet F.: Abstraction and Reuse Mechanisms in Web Application Models. In: Liddle S., W. et al. (eds.): Conceptual Modeling for E-Business and the Web, , LNCS no 1921, Springer (2000) 76 - 88

14. Royce W.: Software Project Management; Addison-Wesley (1998)
15. Rumbaugh J., Jacobson I., Booch G.: The Unified Modeling Language Reference Manual; Addison-Wesley, (1999)
16. Schneider G., Winters J., P.: Applying Use Cases - A Practical Guide; Addison-Wesley (1998)
17. Ward S., Kroll P.: Building Web Solutions with the Rational Unified Process: Unifying the Creative Design Process and the Software Engineering Process; http://www.rational.com/products/rup/prodinfo/whitepapers/dynamic.jtmpl?doc_key=10105

Enhancing Experience Management and Process Learning with Moderated Discourses: The indiGo Approach

Angi Voss[2], Klaus-Dieter Althoff[1], Ulrike Becker-Kornstaedt[1], Björn Decker[1], Andreas Klotz[2], Edda Leopold[2], and Jörg Rech[1]

[1] Fraunhofer IESE, Sauerwiesen 6, D-67661 Kaiserslautern, althoff@iese.fraunhofer.de
[2] Fraunhofer AIS, Schloss Birlinghoven, D-53754 Sankt Augustin, angi.voss@fraunhofer.de
http://www.ais.fraunhofer.de/MS/projects/indigo/htdocs/index.html

Abstract. The indiGo project aims at improving process knowledge by successive consolidation of feedback, ranging from private annotation, through structured communication in communities of practice, to improved process models and lessons learned. It develops a methodology and integrates previously independent software for process modeling, moderated discourses, experience management and text mining. Both will be evaluated in case studies.

1 Introduction

The business process models of organizations operating in innovative, knowledge-intensive or service-oriented markets are one of their major knowledge assets and a competitive advantage. However, these models need to be constantly evaluated and hardened in the business of those organizations and enhanced by further knowledge to make them operable.

The approach of the project indiGo (Integrative Software Engineering using Discourse-Supporting Groupware) is to support this evaluation and enhancement offering members of an organization to engage in discourses about the process models and their execution (communities of practice) and by presenting process-related lessons learned fitting to the current project context. On the organizational level, finished discourses will be analyzed and summarized to improve process models (process learning) and create new lessons learned (learning from experience).

To achieve these objectives, indiGo will develop an integrated, comprehensive set of methods and a technical infrastructure as a joint effort of two Fraunhofer Institutes: Fraunhofer IESE (Institute for Experimental Software Engineering) in Kaiserslautern and Fraunhofer AIS (Autonomous Intelligent Systems) in Sankt Augustin. The German Bundesministerium für Bildung und Forschung BMBF supports the project.

D. Karagiannis and U. Reimer (Eds.): PAKM 2002, LNAI 2569, pp. 114-125, 2002.

2 The Framework

Let us introduce the ideas with a fictitious example. Assume Ms. Legrelle, a team leader in the organization, has to compose an offer for a subcontract from a small start-up. The process model for the acquisition of industrial projects has a subprocess devoted to the contract. It suggests that the payment scheme should not be too fine-grained in order to minimize administrative overhead. Ms. Legrelle feels uncomfortable with this guideline. The year before she had had a subcontract with another start-up, Orion, which got bankrupt, so that the last payment was lost for her team although they had completed the work. Ms. Legrelle prefers to design the new offer with a frequent payment schedule, at the cost of more overhead in the administrative unit.

Clearly, Ms. Legrelle would not like to modify the organization's process model (1) for industrial project acquisition on her own - it is not her job and her view may be too subjective. She would probably agree that her experience with the Orion project be recorded as a lesson to be learned, but even so, she would hardly take the trouble to fill in the required form to create an "official" case (2). Rather, she would like to suggest her exception from the guideline to her colleagues, backed up by the example of Orion, and wait for their responses (3). Whatever the conclusion, she would probably add it as a personal note (4) to the guideline in the respective subprocess.

2.1 Knowledge Compaction, Usage, and Construction

indiGo takes into account all four kinds of knowledge occurring in the example and supports them as successive stages in a process of knowledge compaction (aggregation, condensation, summarization, or classification). Figure 1 arranges the four knowledge categories on one layer and embeds it into layers of knowledge usage and knowledge construction.

Knowledge compaction is a process of decontextualization (a) and formalization (b) with the goal of decreasing modification times (c) as well as increasing lifetime (d) and obligingness (e); and of course more obliging knowledge should be more visible (f). As indicators of knowledge compaction (a-f) are correlated, and they exhibit a clear progression from private annotations to group discussions, to stored cases, to an organization's process models. Private annotations are highly contextualized, informal, secret, and non-binding, they have a short lifetime and can be updated often, while process models are highly decontextualized, formal, public, and obliging, they have a long lifetime and are updated infrequently.

The central issue in knowledge usage is how to offer the right knowledge at the right time. As the domain of indiGo is dominated by process models, they should form the backbone for knowledge delivery. While applying (instantiating) a particular process model, members of the organization should find - a mouse click away - supplementary knowledge in associated cases that are dynamically retrieved with regard to the users' current project context. The supplementary knowledge is provided through associated discussions in the users' groups and in their private annotations.

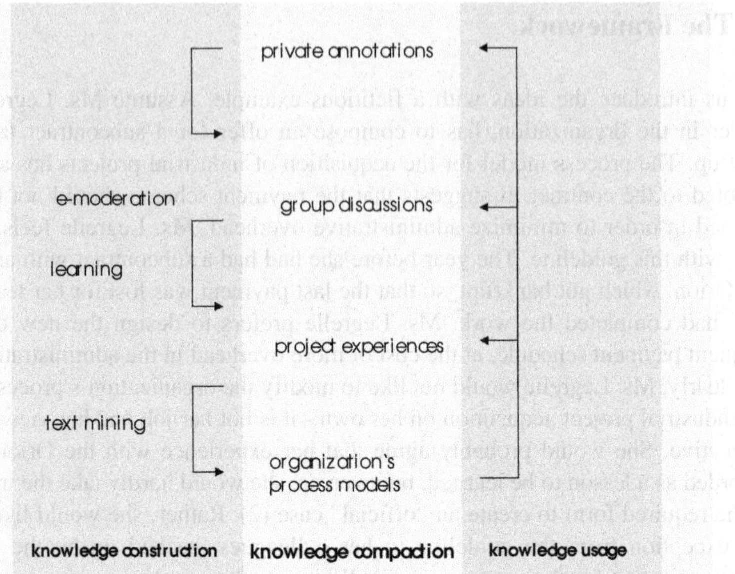

Fig. 1. Layers of knowledge compaction, usage and creation for process-centered applications

If no relevant knowledge is available, the users have encountered a gap in the knowledge. If they know a solution themselves, they may write a quick private note and attach it to the current part of the process model. Otherwise, they may raise the problem in one of their discussion groups. Other users may be able to help, possibly they had been confronted with a similar problem formerly and had written a private note to remember the solution. Then they may bring this note into the group discussion.

Either way, if a new solution turns up and stands its test, it may be added as a new case to the experience base. The process model would be adapted periodically as substantial feedback is accumulated from the discussions and the new experiences. Again, contributing new bits of knowledge should be a matter of very few mouse clicks.

To extract knowledge from a discussion for the experience base, the indiGo system will be enhanced by text mining tools, and the experience base should offer analytic tools that cluster, categorize, or differentiate the cases as input for improving the process models.

On the one hand, indiGo is more comprehensive than approaches to experience management like [1], [2], [3], [4], [5], because it bridges the gap between informal, communication-oriented knowledge and formal, organization-oriented knowledge and provides a socio-technical solution that covers individual knowledge usage as well as social knowledge creation. On the other hand, indiGo is more focused than comprehensive approaches to organizational learning like ENRICH [6].

3 The Software Platform

The indiGo technical platform integrates two independent types of systems for a completely new service. While one system acts as a source for documents, like descriptions of business process models, the other acts as a source for related information, like private annotations, public comments or lessons and examples from an experience base. The business process model repository CoIN-IQ acts as the document source, related information is provided by the groupware Zeno or the experience management system CoIN-EF [7]. Figure 2 shows a split screen of indigo with CoIN-IQ at the top and Zeno at the bottom.

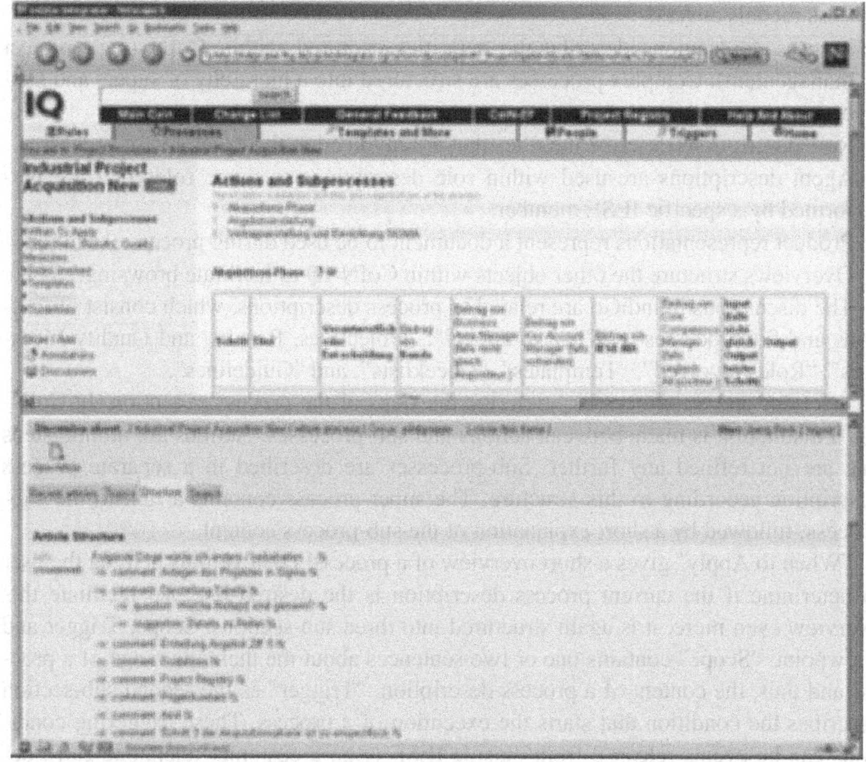

Fig. 2. Split View with CoIN-IQ at the top and a related discussion in Zeno beneath

3.1 CoIN-IQ

CoIN-IQ is IESE's business process model repository [8]. The process modeling technique of CoIN-IQ is structured text, which is due to several reasons: Zero effort training, straightforward modeling, and perpetuation in industrial strength applications. Zero effort has to be spent on training, since any IESE member can read structured text without previous training. Furthermore, straightforward modeling means that any IESE members can model processes using structured text, if supported by guidelines and the CoIN team. This aspect is additionally fortified by the experience in scientific publishing of most IESE members. In addition, the experience made with the Electronic Process Guide (EPG) [9] showed that web-based process descriptions are a feasible way of distributing process knowledge within creative environments such as software business. In particular, changes to web-based process models can be communicated much quicker than paper-based process models, thus enabling quick integration of experience.

The topics currently covered range from core processes (e.g., project set-up and execution) to support processes (e.g., using the IESE information research service) to research focused processes (e.g., performing Ph.D. work at IESE). Conceptually, the process models covers:

- Process descriptions describe the activities captured within CoIN (e.g., project management). Complex processes are structured into a hierarchy of super- and sub-processes.
- Role descriptions describe the roles that are involved in the execution of processes.
- Agent descriptions are used within role descriptions to name roles that are performed by a specific IESE member.
- Product representations represent a document to be used during process execution.
- Overviews structure the other objects within CoIN-IQ to facilitate browsing.

The discussions in indiGo are related to process descriptions, which consist of "Actions and Subprocesses", "When to apply?", "Objectives, Results, and Quality Measures", "Roles involved", "Templates", "Checklists", and "Guidelines".

"Actions and Subprocesses" describe the steps of the process execution. In CoIN-IQ, a distinction is made between actions and sub-processes. Actions are atomic steps that are not refined any further. Sub-processes are described in a separate process description according to this structure. The super-process contains a link to the sub-process, followed by a short explanation of the sub-process content.

"When to Apply" gives a short overview of a process' context, thus helping the user to determine if the current process description is the desired one. To facilitate this overview even more, it is again structured into three sub-sections: Scope, Trigger and Viewpoint. "Scope" contains one or two sentences about the thematic range of a process and thus, the content of a process description. "Trigger" as the second sub-section describes the condition that starts the execution of a process. These triggering conditions can be events released from outside IESE (e.g., a customer telephone call), dependencies with other process executions (e.g., start or finish of a process) or dependencies from product states (e.g., a deliverable is about to be finished). "Viewpoint" contains the role from whose view the process is described.

"Objectives, Results and Quality Measures" is information intended to guide the execution of a process. The difference between the three sub-sections is the increasing degree of quantification of quality information. "Objectives" are general objectives of the process. "Results" are tangible outcomes of the process (e.g., meeting minutes). "Quality Measures" describe properties of such results (e.g., the number of pages of the meeting minutes should range between 10 and 20) or the process itself (e.g., the effort spent on preparing a meeting should not exceed one person day).

"Roles involved" provides an overview of the roles involved in the process and links the Role Descriptions. An experienced user can quickly find the Role Descriptions that are distributed within the "Actions and Subprocesses" and "Guidelines" Section.

"Templates" lists the products referenced by the process description. This overview is intended to support IESE members, who are accustomed to the process and just need quick access to artifacts.

"Checklists" is also intended for the experienced user. It summarizes important steps and results of the Process Description.

"Guidelines" give hints for performing a process, like "do's and don'ts" or frequently asked questions about a process. Furthermore, frequently used variances of a process are modeled as guidelines. This reduces the number of similar process descriptions and lowers the effort to maintain the process description. Each guideline has a "speaking headline" in the form of a question or statement, followed by explanatory text.

3.2 Zeno

Zeno is an e-participation platform (www.e-partizipation.org) [10] which. addresses a broad spectrum of discourses in the knowledge society: participatory problem solving, consensus building [11] , mediated conflict resolution [12], teaching, and consulting. The new Zeno focuses on e-discourses and supports e-moderators in turning discussions into discourses, elaborating the argumentation, and carving out rationales.

Zeno distinguishes three kinds of objects: Sections to tailor the settings for an e-discourse, articles as units of a communication (contributions), and links as directed relations between articles or even sections.

Moderators specify the readers, authors, and co-editors of the section, its discourse grammar, a style sheet to control the presentation, and plugged-in functionality (for mapping, awareness, polling, etc).

An article has a title, usually a note (plain text or html), and possibly document attachments. From its author it may get a label to indicate its pragmatic (or ontological) role in the discourse (e.g. issue, option, criterion, argument, decision, summary, question, comment), and it may receive an additional qualifier from the moderator (e.g. green, yellow, red cards). Articles may be selected (and deselected) as topics and may be ranked to influence their ordering. An article may have temporal references (to be displayed on a timeline), keywords (to be searched together with the title and note), and attributes related to its visibility and accessibility.

Links between articles or sections may be labeled to express relations, such as refers-to, responds-to, justifies, questions, generalizes, suggests, pro, contra) so that complex networks (or hyperthreads) can be built. Links between Zeno articles and sections are visible at both end points and can be traversed in both directions. They are automatically maintained by Zeno, so moderators may edit, copy, and move groups of articles with their links.

Zeno links may also point to external web resources; they are used for document references in indiGo and for spatial references (to be displayed on a map) in KogiPlan (www.kogiplan.de).

Users are received on a personal home page. Here they can bookmark and subscribe sections in order to be notified of their latest contributions. Each section offers different views: The latest articles, the topics, the complete article structure, a sorted list of articles as a result of a full-text search, the hierarchy of subsections, or the timeline. Authors may create or respond to articles in a section, and moderators may edit, move and copy articles, change links and assign labels, and manipulate sections. Users and groups are administered through an address book.

Zeno can be accessed from any regular web browser without any local installations. The Zeno server is implemented on top of open source products: tomcat as web server and servlet runner, velocity for templates in the user interface, Java for the kernel, and MySQL for the data base. Zeno itself is available as open source (http://zeno.berlios.de/).

3.3 Integration

Figure 3 shows the components of the indiGo platform as planned for the final version. This paper focuses on the version presented at CeBIT 2002, which comprises an integrator, CoIN-IQ, and Zeno.

The integrator acts as a middleware between the document and information source. CoIN-IQ, as the document source, hosts the business process models that can be supported by the information from the second system. Zeno, as the information source, manages annotations and discussions about the business process models from CoIN-IQ.

The integrator is the glue between a document server like CoIN-IQ and a server for related information like Zeno. It provides an integrated view upon a document and related information. Based on Perl the integrator is a CGI script that offers three fundamental functions that are called either by CoIN-IQ or Zeno:

- *Discuss*: This function creates a split view upon a document and related information. In the current indiGo context this is a view on the specific business process model from CoIN-IQ in the upper part and beneath the appropriate discussion from Zeno.
- *Annotate*: Analogous to the previous function, the integrator creates a split view upon a business process model and a personal annotation for the current user.
- *Destroy*: To work with only one system this function collapses the split view of indiGo to a single frame. This is particularly helpful if the user wants to turn off the discussions from Zeno or if he switches into another discourse in Zeno that is not
- related to business processes.

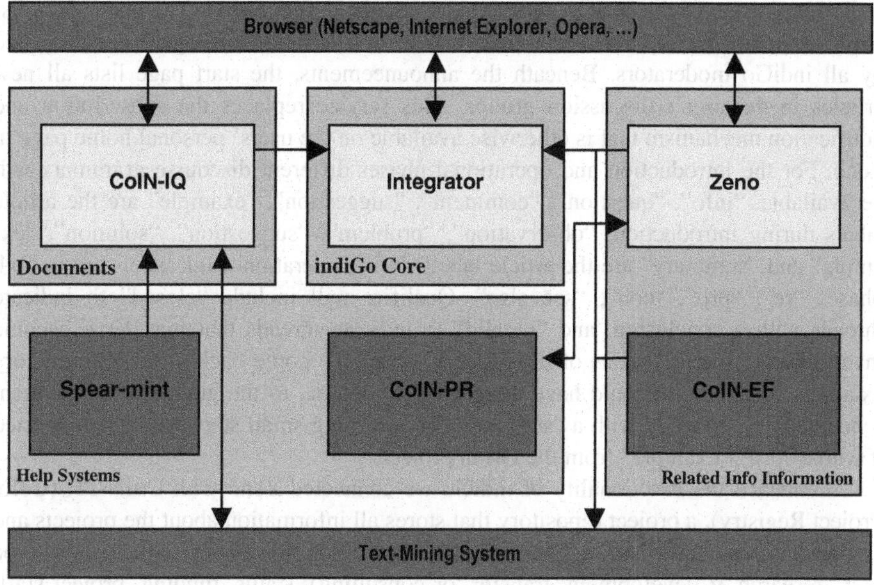

Fig. 3. Information flow in the indiGo platform (upper level presented at CeBIT 2002)

In the indiGo platform, CoIN-IQ's start page is automatically generated by Zeno from articles in a special section for announcements. Other modifications of CoIN-IQ for indiGo concern the insertion of buttons for private annotations, group discussions, and lessons learned. The buttons are displayed or hidden at the user's discretion. Buttons are inserted for entire processes and for all process elements. Internally, each process and element is identified by a unique number for the indiGo integrator and the other components; this number will not change even if the process model is reorganized.

The structure and ordering of CoIN-IQ's process models and their elements is reflected in Zeno by the hierarchies of sections and their ranking. The mapping between these structures is accomplished through Zeno links, the names of which encode identifiers for the process model and element.

Moderators first create entries for users and groups in the address book. Next, to generate a section for discussing a process, the moderators click on the "discussion" button of the process or any of its elements and then select a group as readers and writers for the discussion. Subsections for discussing process elements are created on demand, when users click on the associated processes and selects the discussion group. The subsections inherit the discourse grammar of their super-section and are restricted to the selected group as authors.

When a user clicks on an "annotation" button for the first time, a personal section is created. This section and its subsections can only be accessed by this user with all rights of a moderator. Subsections for processes and their elements are again created on demand, when the user clicks on the corresponding "annotation" buttons.

The start page of the indiGo system is automatically generated. The upper part displays announcements. These are articles in a section called “StartPage” , can be edited by all indiGo moderators. Beneath the announcements, the start page lists all new articles in the user’s discussion groups. This service replaces the subscription and notification mechanism that is otherwise available on the users’ personal home page in Zeno. For the introduction and operational phases different discourse grammars will be available. “info”, “question”, “comment”, “suggestion”, “example” are the article labels during introduction, “observation”, “problem”, “suggestion”, “solution”, “example” and “summary” are the article labels during operation. Link labels are in both phases “re”, “pro”, “con”, “see also”. Qualifier will include “closed” to indicate threads with a conclusion, and “invalid” to indicate threads that may have become invalid due to modifications of the process model. To come back to the introductory example, Ms Legrelle could have attached a “problem” to the guideline on payment schedules, “re”sponded with a “suggestion” concerning small start-ups, and supported it with a ”pro” “example” from the Orion project.

To enhance the functionality of indiGo we connected Zeno with CoIN-PR (CoIN Project Registry), a project repository that stores all information about the projects and associated users. Information about the projects include, for example, the project type (e.g., research & development, transfer, or consulting), status, funding, project staff, project manager, or the list of participating partners.

CoIN-PR delivers information about a specific user’s current projects, which is used to index contributions in Zeno with a project context and to construct queries for CoIN-EF. Beside commenting the business process models, the user will have the opportunity to recall context-specific lessons learned from CoIN-EF. To support and enhance the various roles in indiGo text-mining tools will be applied to analyze the discussions in order to detect new, previously unknown or hidden information for moderators and other roles, especially with the goal to extend or improve the lessons learned and the process models.

Based on standard internet technology indiGo is a truly distributed system. While Zeno is hosted on a web server at Fraunhofer AiS in Sankt Augustin, Germany, the CoIN system family is located at and maintained by Fraunhofer IESE in Kaiserslautern, Germany.

4 Conclusion and Outlook

indiGo aims at supporting all kinds of knowledge that have been identified as being import for process learning, namely process models (with their associated templates), experiences from instantiating process models in concrete projects, discussions about processes in closed or open groups, and private annotations of process models. Thus, with indiGo, any concerned organization member can make private annotations for a newly introduced, or changed, business process model. Staff can decide which of the issues that attracted their attention should be discussed within a selected group of people.

This paper focused on the technical infrastructure of indiGo, as presented at CeBIT 2002. It enables the organization of various process-related annotations and moderated discussion groups based on a customizable discourse grammar.

How an organization can accomplish process learning using the indiGo platform is the core of the indiGo methodology. In [13] the methodology is described in more detail and more references to related work is provided. It is itself phrased as a set of process models. The self-description of the indiGo methodology through indiGo process models offers the opportunity to 'bootstrap' indiGo, that is, to apply indiGo to itself. First, it allows having a test run of both the methodology and the technical infrastructure during the introduction of indiGo. Furthermore, since the persons involved in the indiGo introduction directly perform and experience this approach, it will be their prime interest to resolve occurring difficulties. Therefore, the members of the organization can rely on a tested infrastructure and a consolidated team to support them in the roll-out phase.

In April 2002, the indiGo case study has been started, carried out at Fraunhofer IESE in Kaiserslautern, Germany. New project and research processes will be introduced for the whole institute. We expect very valuable feedback for all the described indiGo methods and technologies.

In parallel, work on the software platform is progressing with specified but not yet implemented features. For instance, if a process model is modified or reorganized, the corresponding annotations and discussions should automatically be marked for revalidation or be reorganized accordingly. Next, the components indicated in Figure 2 will be integrated, starting with CoIN-EF.

indiGo's e-moderation method guarantees that discussions are carried out in a structured and goal-oriented manner. This helps to identify valuable experiences, which then are represented as semi-formal cases, and stored in the experience base. Using case-based reasoning, these experiences are then available for both process improvement/change and process execution.

As soon as discussions will become available from the case study, text mining experiments can begin [14], [15]. For that purpose, the discussions in Zeno will be exported in GXL, an XML dialect for graph structures. Private annotations remain private and will not be subject to text mining.

Beyond the current project we consider the possibility to extend the indiGo approach to applications where process models do not play such a central ("backbone") role. Although a platform for organizational learning should eventually cover all knowledge categories treated in indiGo, the first steps to organizational learning need not necessarily involve process models. Maybe, an organization would first like to invest into an experience base or into a communication platform, and add process models only later. The challenging research question here is, to which degree indiGo's methods and technologies can still be applied or easily tailored to such an organization's needs.

References

1. Althoff, K.-D., Feldmann, R. & Müller, W. (eds.) (2001). *Advances in Learning Software Organizations.* Springer Verlag, LNCS 2176, September 2001.
2. Althoff, K.-D., Decker, B., Hartkopf, S., Jedlitschka, A., Nick, M. & Rech, J. (2001). Experience Management: The Fraunhofer IESE Experience Factory. In P. Perner (ed.), Proc. Industrial Conference Data Mining, Leipzig, 24.-25. Juli 2001, Institut für Bildverarbeitung und angewandte Informatik
3. Tautz, C. (2000). *Customizing Software Engineering Experience Management Systems to Organizational Needs.* Doctoral Dissertation, Department of Computer Science, University of Kaiserslautern, Germany.
4. Bergmann, R. (2001). Experience management - foundations, development methodology, and internet-based applications. Postdoctoral thesis, Department of Computer Science, University of Kaiserslautern.
5. Minor, M. & Staab, S. (eds.) (2002). 1st German Workshop on Experience management – Sharing Experiences about the Sharing of Experience, Berlin, March 7-8, 2002, Lecture Notes in Informatics, Gesellschaft für Informatik (Bonn).
6. Mulholland, P., Domingue, J., Zdrahal, Z., and Hatala, M. (2000). Supporting organisational Learning: An Overview of the ENRICH Approach. *Journal of Information Services and Use*, 20 (1) 9-23.
7. Althoff, K.-D.; Birk, A.; Hartkopf, S.; Müller, W.; Nick, M.; Surmann, D. Tautz, C.: Managing Software Engineering Experience for Comprehensive Reuse; Proceedings of the Eleventh Conference on Software Engineering and Knowledge Engineering, Kaiserslautern, Germany, June 1999; Knowledge Systems Institute; Skokie, Illinois, USA; 1999.
8. Decker, B. & Jedlitschka, A. (2001). The Integrated Corporate Information Network iCoIN: A Comprehensive Web-Based Experience Factory. In *Althoff, Feldmann & Müller (2001)*, 192-206.
9. Ulrike Becker-Kornstaedt, Dirk Hamann, Ralf Kempkens, Peter Rösch, Martin Verlage, Richard Webby, and Jörg Zettel. Support for the Process Engineer: The Spearmint Approach to Software Process Definition and Process Guidance. In Proceedings of the 11th Conference on Advanced Information Systems Engineering (CAISE '99), Heidelberg, Germany, June 1999. Lecture Notes on Computer Science, Springer-Verlag.
10. Voss, A. (to appear (2002)): „Zeno – Software für Online-Diskurse in der Mediation". In Online-Mediation. Theorie und Praxis computer-unterstützter Konfliktmittlung(Eds, Märker, O. and Trenél, M.) Sigma, Berlin.
11. Voss, A., Roeder, S. and Wacker, U. (to appear (2002)): „IT-support for mediation in decision making - A role playing experiment". In Online-Mediation. Theorie und Praxis computer-unterstützter Konfliktmittlung.(Eds, Märker, O. and Trenél, M.) Sigma, Berlin.
12. Märker, O., Hagedorn, H., Trénel, M. and Gordon, T. F. 2002 'Internet-based Citizen Participation in the City of Esslingen. Relevance - Moderation - Software', in M. Schrenk (ed) CORP 2002 - "Who plans Europe's future?" Wien: Selbstverlag des Instituts für EDV-gestützte Methoden in Architektur und Raumplanung der Technischen Universität Wien.
13. Althoff, K.-D., Becker-Kornstaedt, U., Decker, B., Klotz, A., Leopold, E., Rech, J., Voss, A. "The indigo project: enhancement of experience management and process learning with moderated discourses". In Data mining in marketing and medicine (Ed. P. Perner), Springer Verlag, LNCS.

14. Kindermann, Jörg & Diederich, Joachim & Leopold, Edda & Paaß, Gerhard (2002): *Identifying the Author of a Text with Support Vector Machines*; accepted at *Applied Intelligence.*
15. Leopold, Edda & Kindermann, Jörg (2002): *Text Categorization with Support Vector Machines. How to Represent Texts in Input Space?;* in: *Machine Learning* 46, 423 - 444.

Decisio-Epistheme: An Integrated Environment to Geographic Decision-Making

Manuel de Castro[1], Jonice Oliveira[1], Julia Strauch[2], and Jano M. Souza[1,3]

[1]COPPE/UFRJ – Computer Science Department, Graduate School of Engineering, COPPE/UFRJ, PO Box 68513. ZIP Code: 21945-970, Rio de Janeiro, RJ, Brazil.
{manuel, jonice, jano}@cos.ufrj.br

[2]EMBRAPA/ Solos – Brazilian Agricultural Research Corporation
Rua Jardim Botânico, 1024. ZIP Code: 22460-000, Rio de Janeiro, RJ, Brazil.
julia@cnps.embrapa.br

[3]IM/UFRJ – Mathematics Institute, Federal University of Rio de Janeiro, PO Box 68511. ZIP Code: 21945-970, Rio de Janeiro, RJ, Brazil.

Abstract. Collaborative decision-making in geographic-driven management projects often face problems as: difficulties of manage spatial data as a component of the process, lack of coordination of the different areas involved in the process, difficulties of knowledge access, badly defined decision processes, and absence of an appropriate tool that manages spatial data in a collaborative approach. Decisio-Epistheme is an integrated web-based environment that uses workflow, knowledge management and decision support tools to ease collaborative decision processes that deal with spatial data. In our approach, the collaborative decision process is treated as a form of knowledge creation because its definition and related activities are complementary to the process of externalization, internalization, combination and socialization of knowledge. The system is being applied in an agro-meteorological project, with the purpose of improving the results at the Brazilian agro-business.

Keywords: Decision Support, Knowledge Management, CSCW, Knowledge Awareness, Geographic Information System, Workflow.

1 Introduction

In a geographic data-driven business project, data from different sources are aggregated in such a way that an objective is reached, i.e., the choice of the best plantation for a certain region, antennas´localization for mobile phone systems or a logistics study. Moreover, because of the large amount of data, its different formats and quality levels, the decision process becomes more difficult.

The collaborative decision-making based on geographic data inherits group activities problems, i.e., the emphasis given to social activities, failure to define the problem before the judgment, elimination of the creativity due to established hierarchies, etc. As an addition to these problems we may also find the meeting time,

D. Karagiannis and U. Reimer (Eds.): PAKM 2002, LNAI 2569, pp. 126-136, 2002.

disorganization, absence of objectives or agenda, non-conclusion of the solution, absence of individual leadership during a meeting, lack of efficiency in the decision-making and the redundancy of solutions. Besides, this kind of activity generally involves teams of different areas, as cartographers, geologists and business managers. So, there is the need for an environment to integrate people with different expertise, giving them support to cooperate, providing the necessary knowledge to make the right decisions, avoiding these problems.

Moreover, there are difficulties in making a collaborative decision using spatial data, because coordinates, areas and maps can be used by specialists in different contexts, making harder the association of the different knowledge that this map represents in a geo-referenced manner.

Another key tool to the decision process is the correct use of information and data. The excess of information is a real problem in this context because it makes the decision maker spend a large amount of time searching for what information is relevant, not finding the appropriate information in a large result set or losing the focus of the domain. However, the lack of information also makes the decision process harder because the decision maker may not have sufficient knowledge to evaluate the problem adequately, what can possibly lead to an incorrect decision.

The Knowledge Management (KM) of explicit or tacit knowledge is important in the decision process. Previous cases, expert opinions, best practices and explicit knowledge found in technical reports, books and documents, help in decision making. They provide ways for the decision maker to enrich and support the goal or criteria chosen, and enable learning in the context that will hold the decision.

In this paper, we show our integrated environment that uses knowledge management as a support to collaborative decision-making, allowing the use of this kind of information as a key support to the entire process. This environment also brings cooperative work features and process management tools that help group interaction, enabling a well-defined group decision process. In section two, we present the environment's architecture and its development modules; in section three, we show the implemented parts of the environment applied to an agro-meteorological business project at Embrapa[1]; in section four, we expose our final considerations and future work.

2 Decisio-Epithesme Environment

Some proposals are found in literature to support spatial analysis in-group, as for example the system AR/GIS [FABER et al., 1997], GEO-WASA [MEDEIROS et al., 1996], SDSS [JABLONSKI et al., 1997] and SPeCS [Medeiros et al. 2000], among others. But only the SPeCS proposal integrates workflow and Electronic Meeting Systems (EMS) [Nunamaker, J. F. et al 1991] functionalities to the GIS environment

[1] Embrapa: Brazilian Agricultural Research Corporation

to support collaborative discussion in the decision process, emphasizing the coordination aspects of the meeting and the relevance of spatial data.

In the SPeCS architecture, the workflow tool guarantees the logic of the process with their standards and the efficient management of the information flow, allowing the teams to have all the necessary resources. It manages and supports the decision process, assuring that the tasks are executed by the right teams, within the proper time limits and supporting individual task execution. The EMS tool has extensions to allow individual textual observation entries, statistical graphics and several assorted geographical forms, with visualization of all existing alternatives, supporting spatial components interfaces that let manipulate, collaboratively, geographic data.

We propose an extension of the SPeCS approach, integrating the role of knowledge management in the decision process. Concomitantly, we propose some modifications in the electronic meeting system that permits an efficient usage of the knowledge base and spatial data manipulation, better individual organization tools, collaborative multiple criteria analysis support and a framework that helps the creation of a decision process that involves spatial data in business management.

Decision Support Systems (DSS) [Turban 2001] and Knowledge Management Systems (KMS) [Probst et al, 2000] are complementary, and some DSS processes are very similar to KMS processes. According to Nonaka and Tacheuchiś Theory [Nonaka, Takeuchi 1995], knowledge creation is a process that has four phases: externalization, combination, internalization and socialization, showed in Fig. 1. There are two kinds of knowledge, tacit and explicit, and each phase from Nonaka and Tacheuchiś Theory corresponds to a transition of a kind of knowledge into another. The knowledge externalization (tacit → explicit knowledge) is similar to the process of decision modeling, which involves elicitation of the problem-solving knowledge from the decision maker and its representation. In the combination (explicit → explicit knowledge), where an explicit knowledge will be re-used in a different context or will generate a new explicit knowledge, we found similarities to the model integration in DSS. Knowledge internalization (explicit → tacit knowledge) corresponds to the adoption and learning by use of explicit organizational knowledge by individuals. It can be compared to building DSS using elicited decision models. Another analogy is the socialization (tacit → tacit knowledge), where sharing information pertaining to decisions made by different decision makers, as such information reflects the tacit models followed by these decision makers (e.g., through group discussions) can be exchanged [Bolloju et al. 2002].

Our environment can be used in all phases of the decision process: the decision planning, choice, implementation and feedback phases. In the decision planning, the problem definition and classification, objectives, individual tasks, relevant data, relevant knowledge, and the decision process are defined. In the choice phase, the decision is taken. After the decision is already taken, it is time to implement the changes, what is called the implementation phase. Then, with the changes already made and the results in mind, the feedback phase has the role of storing their success.

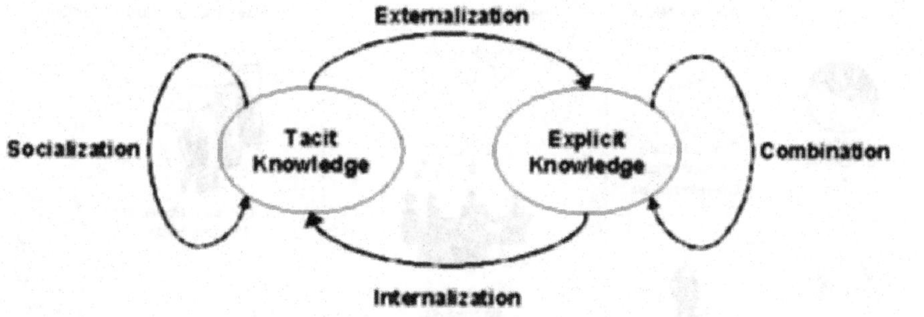

Fig. 1. Knowledge Creation Processes (adapted from [Nonaka, Takeuchi 1995])

When any of these phases are carried out in a collaborative way, they can be divided into three parts where the knowledge management can be a useful tool, illustrated in Fig. 2 and detailed above.

In the first part, the decision maker acquires new knowledge to better understand the context of the meeting, called Knowledge Acquisition. After that, the decision maker organizes the knowledge, data, maps and any kind of information that could be used in the meeting, which we call Personal Knowledge Organization. Then, each participant can suggest the important points that should be talked about in the meeting, as a Meeting Guideline. Sometimes, individual knowledge should be disseminated to the other participants, or Individual Knowledge Dissemination.

In the second part, the electronic meeting is conducted and the participants can access collaboratively spatial data. In this phase, the environment can supply knowledge that is necessary during the decision.

In the third part, when the decision is made, the knowledge created during the meeting is stored in the knowledge base for future access. The description of the decision process, the main ideas with keywords that synthesize them, the next goals and the workflow to be executed is stored in the knowledge base. A log of the electronic meeting is filtered, and the main topics of the conversation are a way to get the decision history.

After the goals are implemented, the decision makers store practical results of the solution and evaluate the quality of the decision. This can help measure the quality of the decision process and choices in future decisions.

The Decisio-Ephisteme provides tools that support the activities of this three-part process. The system is divided into two modules. The Decisio Module treats the cooperative and decision support tools, personal organization, meeting guideline and process definition/execution tools. The Epistheme Module implements a knowledge base with support to knowledge acquisition, storage and distribution activities, enabling the dynamic creation, maintenance and easy access of the knowledge inherent to the decision process. Both modules are adapted to manipulate spatial data.

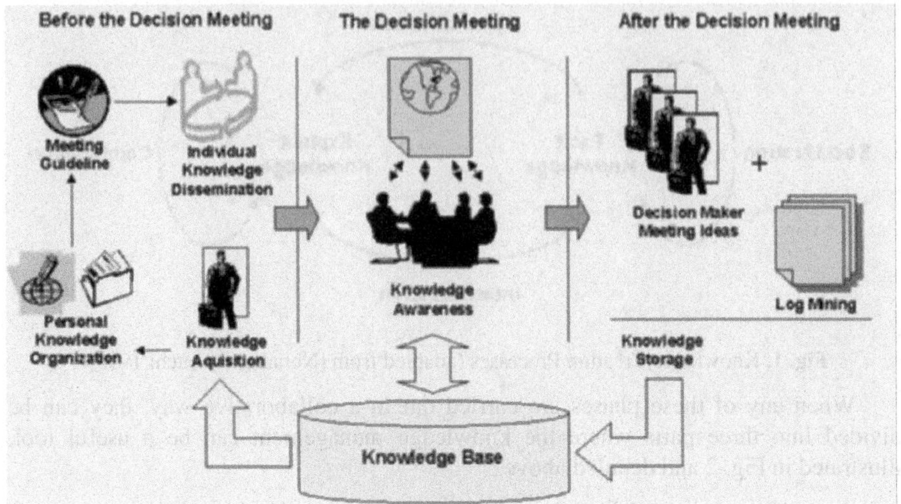

Fig. 2. Decisio-Epistheme Environment

2.1 The Decisio Module

The Decisio Module components are illustrated in Fig. 3. The whole decision process is defined and executed by a workflow tool that controls user access and role, the documents needed in each decision task and the process flow. The decision planning toolbox has the personal organization and meeting guideline tools to help each decision maker in his work of planning the decision meeting. A brainstorming tool is provided for idea generation in the group. A collaborative multiple criteria tool is provided to help on the decision tree definition and analysis with qualitative and quantitative constraints. A voting tool with different types of voting systems can be used to solve conflicts. Meeting participants can construct a rank of the alternatives to help the consensus decision. Finally, a decision feedback tool can be used to evaluate the result of the chosen decision.

In the next sub-items, each toolbox will be detailed.

Workflow

The workflow system is divided into two main parts: definition and execution. In the first one the decision process, team and individual tasks, data and documents to be manipulated and the necessary tools are defined. In the second, the tasks are executed chronologically, as was previously defined by each responsible team or individual.

Decision Planning

The decision planning tools are simple applications that permit individual data and knowledge organization, diffusion and meeting guideline planning.

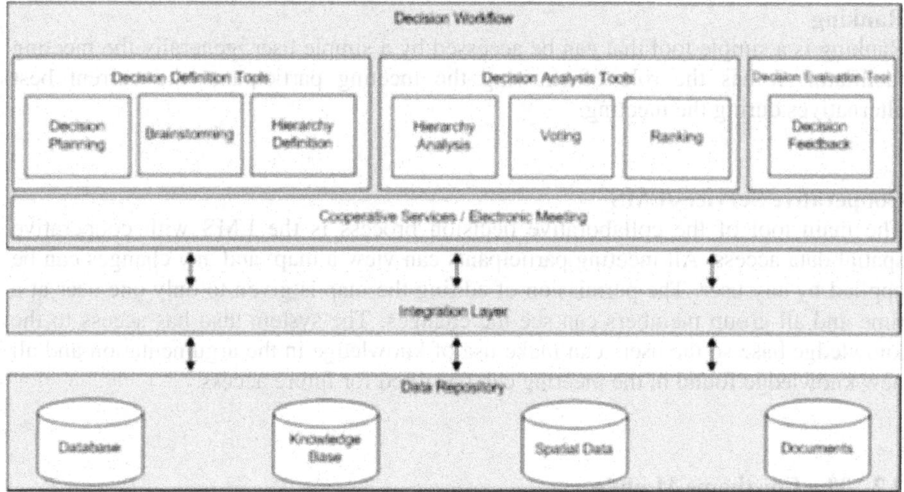

Fig. 3. The Decisio Module

Brainstorming

An electronic brainstorm, where participants, anonymously or not, work rapidly in generating a free flow of ideas, can be used for idea or possible alternative generation.

Hierarchy Definition / Analysis

The hierarchy definition tool can be used to build decision trees collaboratively, with its criteria and alternatives. In the Hierarchy analysis tool, participants of the meeting evaluate the hierarchy of criteria and alternatives with the application of the Analytic Hierarchy Process (AHP) [Saaty, T. L., 1995]. The results can be evaluated online, as criteria and alternatives weights are assigned. The outcome of the analysis points out the best choices of the group opinion, which does not imply that this is the group's choice. It is just an aid to reach the best consensus choice in a faster way.

Voting

A voting tool is provided to solve conflicts in the group decision. The different kinds of voting methods available are:

- The Majority Criterion: Any candidate receiving a majority of first place votes should be the winner.
- The Condorcet Criterion: A candidate who wins head-to-head confrontations with all other candidates should be the winner.
- The Monotonicity Criterion: If an election is held and a winner is declared, this winning candidate should remain the winner in any revote in which all preference changes are in favor of the winner of the original election.

Ranking
Ranking is a simple tool that can be accessed by a simple user, generally the meeting facilitator. It has the role of showing the meeting participants the current best alternatives during the meeting.

Cooperative Services/EMS
The main tool of the collaborative decision process is the EMS with cooperative spatial data access. All meeting participants can view a map, and any changes can be applied by any user. The permission of editing the map is given to only one user at a time and all group members can see the changes. The system also has access to the knowledge base so the users can make use of knowledge in the argumentation and all new knowledge found in the meeting can be stored for future access.

2.2 The Epistheme Module

The activities in knowledge management enable the dynamic creation and maintenance of decision models, in this way, enhancing the decision support process [Bolloju et al. 2002]. Epistheme's proposal is to be a proactive system, that is, a system capable of taking initiatives according to the user's profile and area, as well as, reactive, responding to the requests and changes in the environment, making it possible for the acquisition, dissemination and creation of knowledge. In this way it will supply, in the right time, certain new and relevant knowledge to help decision makers in their tasks. The architecture supports the creation of an effective learning environment for all those involved, bringing distributed knowledge together into a single and accessible system. In order to reach this objective, Epistheme will be composed of modules for knowledge acquisition, identification, integration, validation and creation according to the architecture shown in Fig. 4.

Knowledge Acquisition
This module has the purpose of capturing knowledge through the interaction of Epistheme with people or other computational systems and storing it in structured form. This acquisition can be done in an automatic manner, using the concept of "Data Webhousing". Following and capturing the tracks of a user, through the analysis of logs, we can get to know his profile, the data pattern that he usually obtains, and his usual flow of information. With this, it becomes easier to make more relevant information available in a much quicker manner.

A Best and Worst Practices Center, where experts can make available a successful or a not successful decision-making, becomes useful for greater knowledge exchange between decision makers. It's worth emphasizing that in a decision-making process, errors are also important sources of information and an unsuccessful case should be stored and documented so that future errors are avoided.

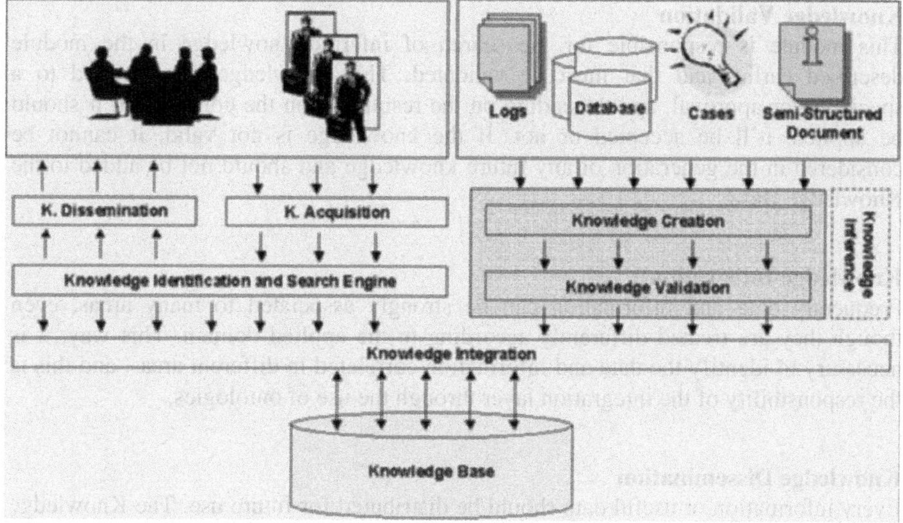

Fig. 4. The Epistheme Module

Knowledge Identification

The identification of the organizational knowledge starts with the recognition of the necessary knowledge for the tasks execution, who executes them (the actors), the importance of each task and the possible problems when: i) the activity is not executed, and ii) when there is loss of knowledge, in other words, when some actor is moved away from his activity. After the knowledge necessary is associated to the activity to be performed, this module even helps the knowledge administrator, indicating possible actors in the team when the actor responsible for the activity is moved. This module is also composed of tools to find relevant information or specialists on the subject, put knowledge in context and categorize information. In this module we have the filters, in which searches can be made on keywords or metadata of the databases.

Knowledge Creation

To accomplish the creation of knowledge a component is necessary to supply the creation and integration of rules and cases for the generation of a new piece of knowledge. This component includes a rule generator, responsible for translating certain knowledge into a group of rules, a sub-module for Case Based Reasoning, capable of identifying the same or similar cases accomplished in the past, and an inference machine, which is a sub-component that generates new conclusions based on already existent knowledge. A specialist in the validation module shall verify these conclusions.

Knowledge Validation

This module is responsible for the search of inferred knowledge in the module described earlier and that must be validated. This knowledge is submitted to a specialist for approval, and depending on the result and on the context that it should be applied, it'll be accepted or not. If the knowledge is not valid, it cannot be considered in the generation of any future knowledge and should not be added to the Knowledge Base.

Knowledge Integration

Frequently data and information can be strongly associated to many areas, even though they are treated differently according to the applied domain. This way, it is necessary to identify the data and information correlated in different areas, and this is the responsibility of the integration layer through the use of ontologies.

Knowledge Dissemination

Every information or useful data should be distributed for future use. The Knowledge Dissemination Module has the purpose of distributing the knowledge acquired, using for this e-mail, FAQs, discussion forums, chats, audio and videoconference.

2.3 Decisio-Epistheme: The Integration

The integration can be done in the following parts:

- Before the decision meeting, each participant does an internalization process when searching for knowledge. In the Individual Knowledge Dissemination the externalization and internalization processes occur, because a tacit to tacit exchange is made using an explicit translation.
- In the decision meeting externalization, internalization and socialization processes occur because the tacit knowledge can be transformed into explicit knowledge or into another piece of tacit knowledge.
- After the decision meeting, an externalization process occurs when decision makers store the knowledge acquired during the decision process. Log mining is done to obtain the knowledge generated in the electronic meeting, representing the combination process.

3 Case Study: Agromet – A Natural Resource Management Project

Decisio-Epistheme is being developed in the Agromet Project [Souza et al. 2002], a Knowledge Management System applied to agro-meteorological zoning projects in a partnership between COPPE/UFRJ and Embrapa.

The main goal of an agro-meteorological zoning study is to discover the potential of an area towards a certain kind of culture, aiming at the harmony between production and environmental preservation, affecting directly productivity and final crop quality.

The project aims at improving methods, procedures and techniques for the dissemination of agro-meteorological information, development of agro-meteorological adaptation strategies to climate variability and climate change and the promotion of a better understanding of the interactions between climate and biological diversity.

Decisio-Epistheme tools have the important roles of providing an easy to use and intuitive user interface to facilitate collaborative decision-making with a high support of knowledge management for the Agromet Project. The system is being implemented in a web-based environment because users can be geographically distributed.

In Figure 5, two screenshots of the first prototype developed in Java are shown. The left-hand screen is the EMS with integrated cooperative spatial data manipulation. The right-hand screen is the Best and Worst Practices Center where cases can be obtained by a Brazilian region, state, or city.

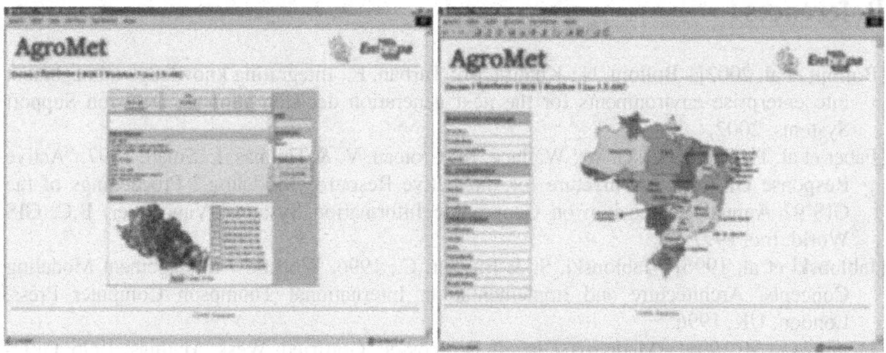

Fig. 5. Electronic Meeting and Practices Center

4 Final Considerations

The Decisio-Epistheme environment brings a new approach into the business process, aggregating KMS, collaborative DSS and spatial data in a web-based application.

The focus of the proposed environment is the use, manipulation and capture of knowledge in collaborative decision processes in which spatial data represents the main information source to the decision making. The main difficulties in making the decision using spatial data is that coordinates, areas and maps can be used in different contexts by different specialists, what difficult the association of the different types of knowledge that they represent in a georeferenced way.

Our proposal includes the use of a workflow system to define and manage the decision process, an EMS integrated with spatial data edition/visualization to ease the communication between decision makers and free access to a KMS. The KMS permits the capture of specialists' knowledge during and after the decision process, the suppliment of the decision maker with the adequate knowledge to help in the decision making, the awareness of the necessary knowledge along the entire process and knowledge generation from the already obtained knowledge.

Our approach proposes the use of the collaborative decision process as a form knowledge acquisition and utilization, integrating DSS and KMS. This integration allows the better understanding of the knowledge kinds that are manipulated in this context, implying that its capitation and use can be increased, making the business process more efficient and productive.

The prototype is being used in Agromet project, a Brazilian agro-meteorological knowledge management project demonstrating the premises of this paper and opening new perspectives in studying the collaborative interaction among users in a GIS environment and the knowledge management related to this activity.

Acknowledgment. This work is being developed with financial support from CNPq and CAPES. The authors thank Lucietta Martorano from Embrapa for the support provided, and Carlete Marques for helping in building the text.

References

[Bolloju et al. 2002] - Bolloju, N.; Khalifa, M.; Turban, E., Integrating knowledge management into enterprise environments for the next generation decision support, Decision Support Systems, 2002

[Faber et al. 1997] - Faber, G. W.; Wallace, K.; Croteau, V. & Thomas, L. Small, 1997. "Active Response GIS: An Architecture for Interactive Resource Modeling." Proceedings of the GIS'97 Annual Symposium on Geographic Information Systems. Vancouver, B.C, GIS World, Inc, 1997

[Jablonski et al. 1996] - Jablonski, S. & Bussler, C., 1996. Workflow Management Modeling Concepts, Architecture and Implementation. International Thompson Computer Press, London, UK, 1996.

[Medeiros et al. 1996] - Medeiros, Claudia B.; Vossen, Gottfried; Wesk, Mathias, 1996. GEO-WASA - Combining GIS Technology with Workflow Management. 1-23p. February, 1996.

[Medeiros et al. 2000] - Medeiros, S., Souza, J.M., Strauch, J., Pinto, G., Specs - A Spatial Decision Support Collaborative System for Environment Design, Proceedings of CSCWD 2000, Hong Kong, December, 2000.

[Medeiros et al. 2001] - Medeiros, S.P. J., Strauch, J.C.M., Souza, J.M., Pinto, G.R.B.; "Coordination aspects in a Spatial group Decision Support Collaborative System"; Proceedings of 15th Annual Symposium On Applied Computing, ACM SAC 2001, April, 2001 - Las Vegas.

[Nonaka, Takeuchi 1995] - Nonaka, I.; Takeuchi, H., The Knowledge-Creating Company: How Japanese Companies Create the Dynamics of Innovation, Oxford Univ. Press, 1995

[Nunamaker, J. F. et al 1991] - Nunamaker, J. F., Dennis, A. R. et al, Electronic Meeting Systems to Support Group Work, Communication of the ACM, Vol. 34, No 7, July, 1991

[Probst et al, 2000] – Probst, G., Raub S. et al, Managing Knowledge: Building Blocks for Success, John Wiley & Sons, 2000

[Saaty, T. L. 1995] – Decision Making for Leaders: The Analytic Hierarchy Process for Decisions in a Complex World, revised ed. Pittsburg, PA: RWS Publishers, 1995

[Souza et al. 2002] - Souza, J.M., Strauch, J.C., Martorano, L., Cardoso, L.F., et al. -Agromet: Gestã do Conhecimento em Agrometeorologia – Technical Report # ES-581/2002, July 2002.

[Turban 2001] – Turban, E., Aronson, J. E., Decision Support Systems and Intelligent Systems, 6th Edn, Prentice Hall, New Jersey, 2001

The General Motors Variation-Reduction Adviser: An Example of Grassroots Knowledge Management Development

Alexander P. Morgan[1], John A. Cafeo[2], Diane I. Gibbons[1], Ronald M. Lesperance[1], Gulcin H. Sengir[1], and Andrea M. Simon[3]

[1] General Motors R&D Center, Mail Code 480-106-359, Manufacturing Systems Research Laboratory, 30500 Mound Rd., Warren, MI 48090-9055,
{alexander.p.morgan, ronald.m.lesperance, diane.gibbons, gulcin.h.sengir}@gm.com

[2] General Motors R&D Center, Mail Code 480-106-256, Vehicle Analysis and Dynamics Laboratory, 30500 Mound Rd., Warren, MI 48090-9055,
john.a.cafeo@gm.com

[3] General Motors R&D Center, Mail Code 480-106-390, Electronics and Controls Integration Laboratory, 30500 Mound Rd., Warren, MI 48090-9055
andrea.m.simon@gm.com

Abstract. One approach to developing knowledge management systems is to seed the system in key communities of practice and then encourage its customization and spread throughout the enterprise by local ("grassroots") initiative. This has the benefit of worker buy-in and adaptation of the local systems to their workflows. The concept is that, in exchange for some loss of control and standardization, the grassroots systems will be used and appreciated and will grow into an enterprise-wide system. In this paper, we discuss this approach and how it is emerging in General Motors' Variation-Reduction Adviser, a manufacturing knowledge-sharing and lessons-learned system.

1 Introduction

It is natural that knowledge management (KM) has often been conceptualized in broad "enterprise-wide" sweeps, big systems having big impacts. Management looks for significant return on investment, and KM systems, like other information technology systems, are often framed in terms of big up-front investments, significant support infrastructure, and centralized control. However, there have been enough failures of this approach to suggest a search for alternatives. The grassroots approach is one alternative. It features less centralized control and a weak form of standardization, combined with intense user feedback and customization. Its advantages include user buy-in and blending with existing workflows. General Motors' Variation-Reduction Adviser (V-R Adviser) provides an example of grassroots KM development. We include a brief overview of the V-R Adviser's evolution to date, with reference to the grassroots aspects of the project. (More details are given in [2, 6].)

D. Karagiannis and U. Reimer (Eds.): PAKM 2002, LNAI 2569, pp. 137-143, 2002.

A key aspect of the grassroots vision is that "spontaneous sharing" of the system is emergent from its success at key seed communities of practice (CoP's) in the enterprise. This is occurring with the GM system. Here, we purposely evoke the concept of "emergent behavior" in the sense of agents, derived from biological systems. For example, the following is a nice summary of the concept: "Naturally occurring multi-agent systems exhibit remarkable problem-solving capabilities, even in the absence of centralized planning. These systems exhibit complex, *emergent behavior* that is robust with respect to the failure of individual agents. Such systems are usually characterized by the interaction of a large number of simple agents that sense and change their environment locally" [9, abstract, our italics]. Grassroots KM depends on an emergent sharing behavior in lieu of centralized control.

In the next section, we will develop the concept of grassroots KM development. In section 3, we will turn to the V-R Adviser: what it is, how it has evolved, its current status. The final section provides a summary and some conclusions.

2 Grassroots KM Development

Here is the essence of the grassroots approach to building a KM system:

1. Start at a few seed locations, the local CoP's.
2. For each seed CoP, choose a liaison person from the KM system development team to spend time with the CoP, to develop trust and a good working relationship.
3. Adapt and customize the system and its user interface to gain strong user enthusiasm at these seed CoP's.
4. There will be an emergent, spontaneous sharing of the adapted system with "nearby" CoP's, which is supported by further local customizations.
5. Eventually, the whole target global CoP (the ensemble of the local CoP's) is using the system, whose local versions link well enough to enable global sharing.

Let us consider these points further.

The grassroots approach is well-supported by KM development principles in the literature. For example, consider the following four quotations:

- Undertake "bite-sized" and sharply targeted KM initiatives with clear benefit expectations that cumulatively build to implement the KM vision [10, p. 4].
- Divide the implementation into a series of nonoverlapping increments, each of which enables measurable business benefits and improvements, even if no further increments are implemented [7, p. 384].
- Historically, communities of practice have evolved; no one has consciously created them. They resist "management" as we generally think of it; instead they require value-driven leadership by members [5, p. 57].

- New technologies are almost never perfect when they are initially introduced. … The interface itself should be user customizable to a fairly high degree [7, p. 388].

There are many ways to realize these (and similar) principles. In the "grassroots" approach, we envision an archipelago of related but relatively independent communities of practice, perhaps logically forming a single super community but working fairly independently at the start. The assembly centers of a large manufacturer might be an example. In one community (an "island" in the archipelago), we set up a prototype KM system, expecting to adapt and adjust to local feedback and giving as much local control over the system to the users as is possible, at least by being extremely responsive. Time passes and the system may have gained new features and it may have lost some features; it surely has a rather different user interface than it did when introduced. However, guided by centralized technical assistance, the changes don't affect the core functionality of the (envisioned) global system. We try to reach the (critical) point where *the users will brag about their new system*, and then others will want to try it. In any case, when the system seems to be relatively stable and functional, it is introduced into more communities. Whatever local adaptations occur, the different communities can share their knowledge with each other. Hopefully, the "haves" will brag, and the "have-nots" will want to be included. In time, the whole archipelago is using the "same" KM system, with many local flavors, but still basically compatible. The grassroots approach follows the "incremental development with incremental benefits" principles noted in the quotes from KM literature above.

In KM, there can be sometimes a tendency to create a pre-ordained infrastructure, and then blame the workers if it is not enthusiastically adopted. "KM needs a technological infrastructure, but … workers need to have the discipline to use the infrastructure" [3]. In the grassroots conception, users buy into the system, both because they helped create it and also because it really did adapt to their needs and preferences. There is a loss of centralized control, as the original design is modified, customized, and localized, but knowledge is always messy and never quite neatly captured. Here, if all goes according to plan, the system becomes an integral and unavoidable part of the workflows, with the incentives for its use inherent in its implementation process. Each local system has its own integrity and benefits, so that the overall process is seen to be incrementally worthwhile and robust. In the grassroots vision, the most enthusiastic users begin the process, the least enthusiastic will wait until after everybody else signs on. The system will be proving its worth long before the skeptics are (or need to be) converted.

A key for facilitating the grassroots approach is the liaison to the seed CoP's created by assigning specific team members to specific CoP's. These individuals serve the same function for the KM development process that nurses serve in patient care. Nurses develop sympathetic relationships with patients, gain patient trust, help doctors and patients communicate, and are strong patient advocates within the medical establishment. In the same way, the KM liaison people establish sympathetic relationships with key members of the CoP's. They take time to understand the workflow and the pressures that drive the work. Thus, these individuals build trust and a good working relationship between the KM team and the CoP's. They act as advocates for the CoP's during KM team meetings. They are able to interpret what is needed by the CoP in terms that the KM team can address. Although domain understanding is a part of any KM project, this intimate and time-consuming contact between the KM team and the CoP's is fundamental to the grassroots KM development process.

3 The General Motors Variation-Reduction Adviser

The V-R Adviser began as a "pure" case-based reasoning (CBR) project [4] and evolved into a knowledge management system, with an emphasis on capturing lessons learned and knowledge sharing, much as described in [1]. See also [8] for a presentation of KM as CBR. Here we describe the context and functionality of the V-R Adviser, a brief history of its development so far, and its current status.

3.1 Dimensional Control in a Vehicle Assembly Center

A basic vehicle body (the frame) is measured in meters but must meet its nominal tolerances to within a few millimeters. Otherwise, difficult-to-diagnose-and-cure problems arise in the final build, such as wind noise, water leaks, and a host of "fit and finish" issues. Typically, stamped sheet metal is welded together to make the frame, then parts and paint are added to complete the finished vehicle. The basic frame, however, is the critical part of the build for *dimensional integrity*. Minute deviations in the tooling which holds the metal for welding, or in the thickness of the metal, or in the wear on the weld-gun tips, or in many other process elements, can significantly affect dimensional control. When a problem is detected "downstream" in the process, it can be very challenging to discover quickly the source of the problem and find a cure. Working with measurements at various stages of the process, as well as other information about the build, a *Dimensional Management* (DM) team hypothesizes cause from effect to create a short list of most likely problems, makes visual inspections to refine the list, and makes process adjustments to solve the problem. Sometimes the problem is directly observed and fixed, sometimes a "cause" is inferred from a "fix" suggested by the list, and sometimes problems are not solved.

The members of the DM Team generally know the process very well. This knowledge tends to be very specific, is sometimes documented in process documents but often is not, and involves a great deal of three-dimensional intuitive reasoning, as well as experience with the basic materials and machines that make up the process. Because the DM team members can consider questions such as "If the tooling in a particular station is defective in a particular way, what particular problems will this cause later in the process?" one might be led to consider a rule-based approach to capturing this knowledge. However, there are several key aspects that suggest "cases" rather than "rules." The most important is coverage; that is, it is difficult to imagine a complete set of rules for such a high-dimensional problem space. A related issue is capturing the three-dimensional and the pictorial nature of the knowledge; that is, part of the reason the problem space is so high-dimensional is that the knowledge and reasoning process are expressed in terms of three-dimensional structures. In a case-based system, we can evoke the powerful ability of expert humans to interpret and use such knowledge. The reasoning doesn't have to be "automated." In their own problem-solving process, the DM team members work from previous experiences in a way that strongly suggests a case-based approach. Only the most trivial problems are solved via pure "if-then" reasoning.

General Motors has about 60 assembly centers worldwide. They operate independently on a day-to-day basis. The V-R Adviser's purpose is to improve communication and memory both within plants and between plants on quality-related problem solving.

3.2 The V-R Adviser

The V-R Adviser was originally proposed as a standard diagnostic CBR system combined with a lessons-learned database, in which lessons were to be captured as cases [2, 6]. The cases were to be strongly structured via templates and a domain-specific ontology, which would also be used in an ontology-based similarity-search capability. These ideas evolved as we began to work with our Flint Assembly Center partners. Flint suggested a number of changes and extensions, to make the system fit in better with current work habits. A yearlong interactive design evolution resulted, yielding significant changes in our prototype. We briefly describe these changes here, which will illustrate the extent to which our partners engaged with us in the project and the extent to which our initial ideas were forced to adapt. The initial and current versions have many features in common, but there is a strong difference in emphasis. (There were many "intermediate" versions, but we will simplify the story here for clarity and brevity.)

In this comparison of the features of the two versions, we will call the initial version v.1 and the current version v.2.

- For v.1, the long-term memory (lessons-learned archive) is separate from the short-term memory (message log). For v.2, no *formal* distinction is made between short- and long-term knowledge.
- For the v.1 archive, the core knowledge is templated with pull-down menus of standard concepts, and free text is allowed as an annotation. For v.2, the core knowledge is free text, with templated knowledge used as an annotation.
- For the v.1 long-term memory, the basic unit of text knowledge is comprised of observations, but these are grouped into cases to complete a lesson learned (solved problem). Each observation is essentially one sentence. For v.2, the basic unit of text knowledge also consists of observations, but these can be any number of sentences, since they are simply unrestricted blocks of text. Observations can be linked into cases, but a single observation can be a case, also.

Informally, a case contains symptoms, fault descriptions, and actions to fix the faults. This structure is more explicit in v.1 than v.2, but considerable flexibility is provided in both versions.

- For both versions, attachments to observations are allowed, and these consist of graphical objects (digital photos, statistical graphs, video clips, parts drawings) and certain text items (Shim Log reports and tables created in Microsoft Word or Excel).
- For both versions, the templated part of the knowledge is based on an ontology of domain-specific concept words, which are used as the basis of similarity search.
- For v.2, there is a strong function of integration of various knowledge sources not anticipated in the original concept. That is, observations with their annotations provide a convenient way to gather together and "remember" a great variety of information that is typically used by the DM team but not previously integrated.

The users like the spontaneity of knowledge entry in v.2. The drawback is that lessons are mixed indiscriminately with messages, and extracting the essence of the archival knowledge will require further processing, either human or machine. Also, since the text is not formatted, the same lesson might be written in many ways and with many individualized abbreviations. On the other hand, with this group of knowledge authors, it may be the best that can be done. We have incorporated as much templated knowledge as we thought would be accepted, in the annotations of the free-text observations and in the captions for the attachments. These preserve a good deal of the original intent of templated knowledge.

3.3 Emergent Spontaneous Sharing

The V-R Adviser has one striking quality: its users are proud and boastful owners of their new system. So the maintenance engineers at Flint (a separate group from the dimensional engineers) wanted to try it, and they were given a copy. Some of the functionality doesn't make sense for them (e.g., the body-location identifiers), so they are simply ignoring that part and have begun to use the system. The V-R Adviser was mentioned in a body manager's video conference, and now several other plants want to try it. They are already suggesting changes.

This process of spontaneous sharing (and adaptation) is facilitated by the "lightness" of the implementation, meaning it is easy to install, adapt, and maintain. It is written in Microsoft Visual Basic, linked to a Microsoft Access database. Since the platforms in the plants are all running Microsoft operating systems, it is relatively easy to distribute copies of the system to interested communities and to integrate with existing tools running on the same platforms. Although we anticipate (perhaps) changing some of this in a final production version, we will work to preserve the flexibility and adaptability of the system.

4 Summary and Conclusions

We have formulated a concept of "grassroots knowledge management development" to capture the idea of knowledge management which is strongly customized to local communities of practice and whose roll-out plan is guided by the spontaneous spread of local enthusiasm. In this concept, a strong sense of local pride and satisfaction is allowed to create an emergent sharing of the system from a core of one or more local CoP's to others, eventually covering the global CoP. A certain loss of centralized control is counterbalanced by strong buy-in from the users, while global compatibility is maintained through centralized technical support, which still allows customized user interfaces. We offered as an example General Motors' V-R Adviser, whose development is following this pattern. We will continue to encourage this process, even as the system hardens into a production product. It remains to be seen if the current lightness and adaptability can be maintained. Although we expect some "hardening," the essence of the grassroots approach is in the initial proof of concept and user acceptance, which has already been confirmed.

References

1. Bartlmae, K., Riemenschneider, M.: Case Based Reasoning for Knowledge Management in KDD-Projects. In: U. Reimer (ed.): Proc. of the Third Int. Conf. On Practical Aspects of Knowledge Management (PAKM2000), Basel, Switzerland, (Oct. 30-31, 2000) 2-1– 2-10
2. Cafeo, J. A., Gibbons, D. I., Lesperance, R. M., Morgan, A. P., Sengir, G. H., Simon, A. M.: Capturing Lessons Learned for Variation Reduction in an Automotive Assembly Plant. Proceedings of the Fourteenth International Florida Artificial Intelligence Research Society Conference. AAAI Press, Menlo Park, California (2001) 89-92
3. I.T. Works' Resource Site on Knowledge Management, www.itworks.be/knowledge management/index.html (July 19, 2002)
4. Leake, D. (ed.): Case-Based Reasoning: Experiences, Lessons, and Future Directions. AAAI Press, Menlo Park, California and The MIT Press, Cambridge, Massachusetts (1996)
5. Liedtka, J. M., Haskins, M. E., Rosenblum, J. W., Weber, J.: The Generative Cycle: Linking Knowledge and Relationships. Sloan Management Review (Fall 1997) 47–58
6. Morgan, A. P., Cafeo, J. A., Gibbons, D. I., Lesperance, R. M., Sengir, G. H., Simon, A. M.: CBR for Dimensional Management in a Manufacturing Plant. Proceedings of the 4th International Conference on Case-Based Reasoning. ICCBR 2001. Vancouver, BC, Canada (2001) 597-610
7. Tiwana, A.: The Knowledge Management Toolkit: Practical Techniques for Building a Knowledge Management System, Prentice Hall PTR, Upper Saddle River, NJ (2000)
8. Watson, Ian (ed): Applying Knowledge Management: Techniques for Building Corporate Memories, Morgan Kaufman, New York (to appear in 2002)
9. White, T., Pagurek, B.: Emergent Behavior and Mobile Agents. In Proceedings of the Workshop on Mobile Agents in Coordination and Cooperation, Autonomous Agents 99, Seattle (May 1–5, 1999); also available at http://www.sce.carleton.ca/ researchers/tony /index. html
10. Wiig, K. M.: Perspectives on Introducing Enterprise Knowledge Management. In: U. Reimer (ed.): Proc. of the 2nd Int. Conf. On Practical Aspects of Knowledge Management (PAKM98), Basel, Switzerland (Oct. 29-30, 1998), 1– 10

From Speech Acts to Multi-agent Systems: The MAYBE Method

Sophie Gouardères[1], Guy Gouardères[1], and Philippe Delpy[2]

[1]LIUPPA, Université de Pau et des Pays de l'Adour - Département informatique - BP1155 - 64013 - Pau cedex – France
sophie.gouarderes@univ-pau.fr
gouarde@larrun.univ-pau.fr
[2]CENTRE HOSPITALIER DE LA COTE BASQUE, UMR 5823- 13, Avenue de l'Interne J. Loëb - 64100 Bayonne

Abstract. This paper describes a method of multi-agent analysis and design for reactive, real-time information systems, relating to complex and risks applications in medicine. According to specific needs in emergency healthcare units : spatio-temporal deployment of heterogeneous tasks, non-determinism of actors and self-organization in an unpredictable and/or disrupted environment, we propose MAYBE - Multi-Agent Yield-Based Engineering. MAYBE is a solution that makes possible for the agents to evolve and adapt by instantiation in different contexts. This paper details the various stages of the methodology applied to an emergency case, in parallel with the computerization of the process. It also compares the issues with other current work.

1 Introduction

Distributed and cognitive multi-agent systems are used in various fields, notably that of Health Care, as an aid to decision making for the different steps to train emergency staffs to the risk prevention process[1]. In these systems, four orders of difficulty are encountered : the modeling itself, the syntax and conventions used for representation, the calculation aspect of the resolution, the traceability of the training session and validation of the results.

Until now, effective, user-friendly and versatile models of interactions between human agents and artifact entities have only partially integrated formal approaches such as planning, scheduling and constraint satisfaction throughout the development, utilization and maintenance cycle of intelligent interfaces [1].

Current so-called "intelligent" multi-agent systems are evolving towards a more self-organized, collective intelligence in terms of autonomous and deliberative agents [2].

This paper proposes a complete methodological approach that responds to these criteria for the design and implementation of more "cognitive" Multi-Agent Systems,

---

[1] To : 1-Identify, 2-Understand, 3-Estimate, 4-Prevent, 5-Manage/Master/Back up

D. Karagiannis and U. Reimer (Eds.): PAKM 2002, LNAI 2569, pp. 144-155, 2002.

more capable of adapting to emerging crisis situations (in terms of resources) or individual and / or collective dysfunctions. We have already had the opportunity to evaluate the effectiveness of flexible and cognitive MAS in the fields of aeronautics [3] and e-learning [4]. Likewise, the premises of the method presented here were drawn from these studies [5].

One question to be resolved is whether we can develop software for long life training in the hospital context, based on actors of the type described above, which is both highly reliable and sufficiently versatile to adapt to situations of dysfunction or even crisis.

2 Problematics

Multi-Agent Systems are a highly appropriate tool for the real-time management of the constantly modified activities of a complex process, such as the emergency room chain. In this case, they are an indispensable information system, within the global clinical situation, for studying competition, cooperation, and conflict resolution phenomena in highly unpredictable, high-risk situations for training.

Different crisis situation scenarios have highlighted the following needs :

- distribution : the tasks, resources, organization and know-how are distributed among human actors, services, jobs etc. Communication is therefore transmitted via various media and handles different ontologies ;
- competition : at any moment tasks may be carried out in parallel, generating all kinds of conflicts ;
- non-determinism : the patient, the care provider, etc. are living beings who produce unexpected events ;
- self-organization : in an unpredictable and/or disrupted world, the system's response must be flexible ; even if the protocols are strictly regulated, many decisions must be negotiated as a result of limited resources
- intensive communication : everything must be dispatched to the right place and the right person with maximum efficiency.

For these reasons, the software agents designed using MAYBE are based on the concepts of flexible determinism, rational agents and the emergence of flexible cooperation models.

In the evolution that we propose, we have the same concepts of goals, roles, activities, tasks, and models of communication and coordination. We introduce two new paradigms that are of great importance for more open environments : a. delayed assignment of goals, roles, and tasks in order to allow them to be achieved ; b. needs analysis, based on observation of the progressive constraint satisfaction steps that occur in the real process (including the time factor).

Needs are expressed as "naturally" as possible in speech acts, based on the expressions of the actors so that even they are active in the process. Any modification to a situation, (change of actor, discourse, context, etc.) is indexed by a trigger (a signal triggered by an event). Each "speech act" is situated with respect to triggers that dynamically punctuate the process in rhythm with the performatives. Each end of sequence specifies a goal attained through the sub-goals of the activities that make it up.

At this stage, we should progressively start to declare the primitives used to model the steps in a functional environment.

Next, each transaction is formally specified in terms of roles and the interactions between roles using task grammars to satisfy the internal consistency and completeness constraints. Each role, provided with a goal and a planned set of tasks, now prefigures something that will become an agent.

But this formal specification is not rigid ; each task can at any time be rewritten in the declared functional environment (like the communication model (multithread) and the coordination model (logical programming)). This characteristic will make it possible to cause the agents to evolve and adapt by instantiation in different contexts [5]. We call this approach MAYBE - Multi-Agent Yield-Based Engineering.

3 The Agent Design Methods

The two paradigms described above (emergent modeling and delayed autonomous distribution) modify the methods for designing and implementing agents. To explain the evolution required in the agent design methods, we decided to place our approach in relation to some well-known frames of reference : a. Analysing Agent Interaction [6], b. GAIA [7] and c. MASE [8]. These three methods support high-level abstraction (design meta-entities) in a descending approach that allows for evolutive, step-by-step structuring to facilitate the re-use and flexible maintenance of the agents.

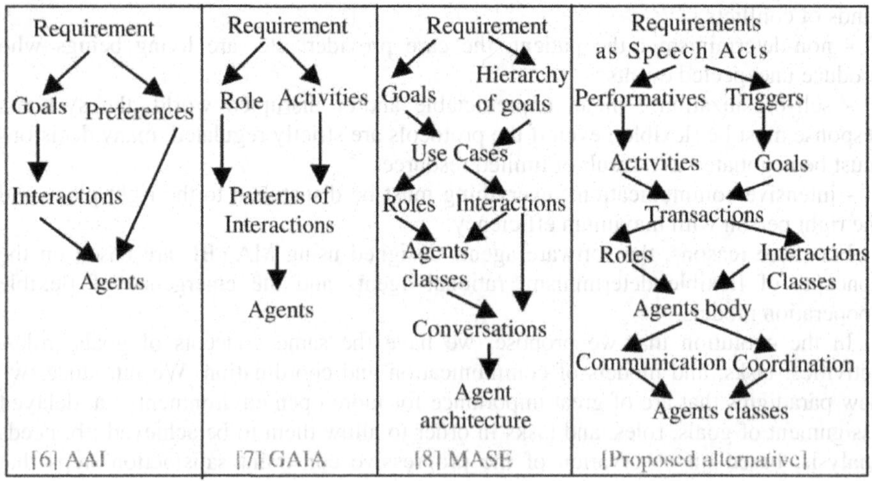

Fig. 1. Respective approaches of the AAI, GAIA, MASE and MAYBE methods

3.1 From Dialogue Acts to Transactions between Agents

To model our method, we used speech acts. The fundamental idea in speech act theory is that a speech act can be considered to be a combination of acts or locutionary, illocutionary and perlocutionary forces. For "performative" utterances, in addition to the locutionary act, speech act theory also enumerates acts that are performed in speaking (illocutionary acts) and as a result of what is said (perlocutionary acts). Austin classifies these "performative" acts into five categories : verdictives (judgment), exercitives (sanctioning a behavior), commissives (commitment), behabitives (congratulations), expositives (clarifications). These primitives become more operational in K. Allan's vocabulary [9] : statements, expressives, invitationals, authoratitives.

For the example illustrating the reception of a patient into the emergency room chain in a hospital [10], we have used the simplified approach proposed by K. Allan [9] :

In this emergency room chain in a hospital, at a given moment, a "dialogue" takes place between the Reception-Orientation Nurse (RON) (r) and the patient P (p) to assign him or her a place for care : a bed or an examination room.

According to Ferber and others, the RON and P roles, attributed to the actors a priori (the ARG solution : Actor-Role-Goal), makes it possible to define two agents : RON and P whose contact will result in RON assigning P to Bed(i) at instant t_i. If the contact takes place at instant $t_i+\Delta t$, then this will not be Bed(i) but Bed (j), such that it satisfies both the goals of IAO, P, and the service (system).

In reality, if the RON is already assigned to a sick patient, a doctor D (r), who is still available may assign the patient to a bed. In the ARG system, the roles of the D and the RON must be exchanged ; at the same time he or she assigns the patient to a bed, the doctor begins the diagnosis, or even the medical care ! This case poses the tricky problem of "merging agents", because there are so many actors and even more patients, and time and space are not extendable from one end of the emergency room chain to the other.

We therefore chose to consider that the assignment of patient P is the result of a meeting between actors, actions or acts in the real world. This meeting leads to a change of context that can be detected in space and time, and that can be identified by a dialogue to which a goal is assigned, which will be attained by a transaction between agents.

Table 1. Example of a speech act.

Receive, assertion and inter-actors (Allan 1998 -99)	
Description	Patient receives as *p*
Pre-condition	Identification : Receiver r accepts *p as* patient
Elocutive Intention	Reflexive dialog confirms r as receiver and p as patient in C_{rp} context

To define these agents, an analysis of the different activities must be performed, not based on the roles attributed a priori to the actors in the real world, but based on the internal and external events that punctuate the process in terms of "dialogues" between these actors. This dialogue is represented by a speech act (see table 1).

To represent the reception of a patient, we formalized the constraints and rules in the following manner :
Concepts : *Speech act*

$A = \{a_i\}$ with $i = 1..n$, set of activities (patient-exam, treatment-suggest …)
$P = \{p_j\}$ with $j = 1..m$, set of constraints (free-box, free-doctor…
$T = \{t_k\}$ with $k = 1..p$, temporal context (t1, t2…)

Axioms :

For constraints on activities (2-to-2) :

$a_i + a_{i+1}$ => execute the two activities sequentially
$a_i \cdot a_{i+1}$ => execute the a_i activity and then the a_{i+1} activity
$a_i \mid a_{i+1}$ => execute the 2 activities in parallel (patient-exam | diagnostic-establish)

For temporal constraints on the set of activities :

$t_k + t_{k+1}$ => execute the two set of activities sequentially (t1 + t2)
$t_k \cdot t_{k+1}$ => execute the set of t_k time activities and then the set of t_{k+1} time activities
$t_k \mid t_{k+1}$ => execute the two set of t_k and t_{k+1} time activities in parallel

Rules :

R1 : [at, before, time] *time* if p_j execute $\Sigma\, a_i$ with $i = 1..n$. (present t2 patient-exam)
R2 : for each a_i execute $\Sigma\, t_k$ with $k = 1..p$. (patient-exam, diagnostic-establish, treatment-suggest)

3.2 The Model

The method we propose consists of 7 steps, presented in the diagram below. These steps have been formalized in Scheme in order to automate the method.

The first step is manual and consists in analyzing the dialogues of the process to be studied in order to bring out all the triggers, activities and goals. It is based on interviews that are interpreted as dialogue acts between real actors. This progressively enables the performatives and their triggers to be extracted from an analysis of the interactions between the actors (human or artifactual). From this highly abstract division, the following steps use a succession of appropriate formalisms (GOMS, ETAG) to select the goals and define the tasks, integrating the spatio-temporal constraints from an individual and a collective point of view.

Two models of coordination and communication defines, the acquaintancy rules and their evolutions in function of the context. The following steps in the method structure the architecture by refinement and coordination according to various models and methods (formal or semi- formal grammars). These steps are explained in detail later in this paper.

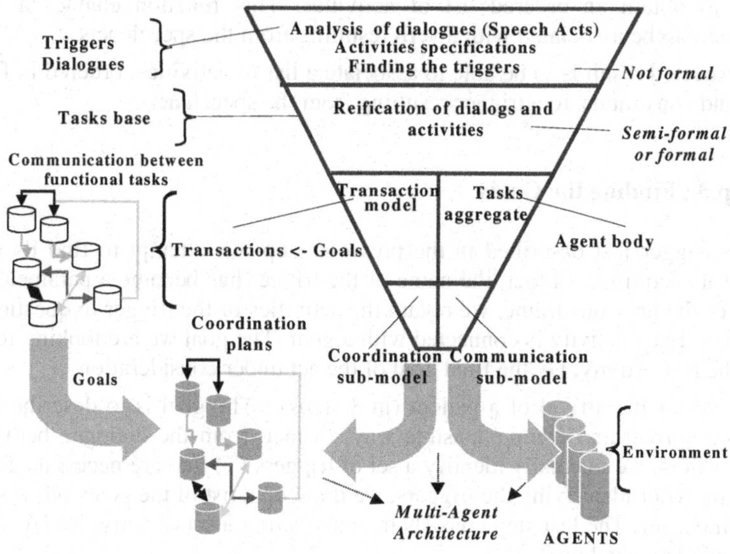

Fig. 2. General synopsis of the approach

4 A Formalization of the Steps for Automating MAYBE

We shall now return to the 7 steps in the MAYBE method. In this paper, we shall limit ourselves to providing an example result for each step in order to improve readability. This example deals with the reception of a patient into the emergency room chain of a hospital.

4.1 Step 1 & 2 : Definition of the Environment in Scheme and Next Finding the Triggers

The starting point is to account for the exchange between the components of the system, using the dialogue acts approach, which provides the dialogues and triggers. In the first step, based on speech acts, we pick-up parts of dialogue rather than goals that could lead directly to the agents. But the frame of dialogues obtained is continuous and does not include any notion of time. Finding the triggers provides the timing of the illocutionary acts and makes it possible to classify them using the temporal references given by Allan. The system of triggers thus sequences the speech acts.

In order to find the triggers, we defined a function called frame_trigger. This function takes as its parameters the verb resulting from the speech acts, the concepts (in other words the whole set of activities, constraints, and temporal contexts), the axioms that enable the concepts to be linked two by two, and the rules that make it possible to obtain an ordered list of activities. This function enables a specific environment to be associated with a verb resulting from the speech acts.

The expected result is to be able to associate a list of activities, ordered in function of time and constraints, to a trigger resulting from the speech acts.

4.2 Step 3 : Finding the Goals

From the trigger just described in the previous step, we attempt to find its goal by means of its activities. In fact, the name of the trigger has become a parameter. With the help of the previous frame, we obtain the activities of the trigger in question as an ordered list. Each activity is connected with a goal. The goal we are looking for is the goal of the last activity, i.e. the final goal of the act under consideration.

Example for the arrival of a patient (in 3 steps) : The goal is to describe the real world in a correct and comprehensible way. In fact, from the dialogue between the different actors, we manually identify a set of triggers (T) that are necessary for using the system. After identifying the triggers, we draw up a list of the goals (G) associated with each trigger. The last step consists in constructing a set of activities (A) for each trigger and associated goal.

To find the goals, we opted for a matrix representation, where the columns represent the activities Ai of the dialogue, which may or may not be set off by a trigger, and where each line entry of the matrix (corresponding to trigger T_i) is associated with a goal "G_k" by an activity vector $< A_{1,\dots} A_m>$ of this matrix (cf. table 2).

Table 2. Example of matrix to find goals.

	A1	A2	A3	A4	A5	A6	Goals
T1	1	1	0	0	0	0	G1
T2	0	1	0	0	0	0	G1
T3	0	0	1	0	0	0	G2
T4	0	0	0	1	1	1	G3

4.3 Step 4 : Reification of the Dialogues and Activities

In this step, we "reify" the dialogues and activities identified above into sequences of tasks. This step is necessary for finding the articulations between the activities in order to avoid modeling too many agents. Without this step, we would have one agent per speech act, which would lead to rigid assignment of roles to agents and, in the long run, to conflict resolution problems.

This step takes place in two stages : a semi-formal specification of activities by means of a task analysis method, which makes it possible to describe the activities resulting from the dialogues as a sequential set of tasks, and a formal specification of the methods by means of a task grammar (<events, tasks> grammar) which makes it possible to describe the graph of tasks by class of triggers and for each class of entry points in the graph of tasks (functional and formal reorganization of tasks).

The goal of the first part of this step is to obtain a finer decomposition into tasks of the activities associated with a trigger resulting from the speech acts. As for the second part, the result obtained is a detailed and formal description of each method (task) associated with the events that triggered the task. The formalization of the tasks is thus reduced by one level of granularity.

We have chosen an example using GOMS [11] for the semi-formal specification and ETAG [12] for the formal specification.

GOMS Specification. Once the goals have been extracted, the GOMS method enables these goals to be formalized by means of scripts and scenarios. The objective is to describe the sequence of steps required to attain the goal. Each vector of the first matrix provides a scenario.

This step is also formalized by means of a matrix. The lines represent the set of methods (M) required to accomplish the activities. The columns represent the set of scenarios. Each vector is associated with a selection rule (SR).

When a patient is admitted, procedures vary depending on whether or not the patient is known to the emergency room service, which gives us the following selection rule :

```
SR1 : Selection rule to accomplish goal "admission of a patient"
  If new patient then accomplish goal "admission of a new patient"
  If old patient then accomplish goal "admission of an old patient"
  Return with goal accomplished
```

According to these rule, we found some script :

```
S1 : method for goal "admission of a new patient"
      step 1 : social allowances (M1)
      step 2 : visual allowances (M2)
      step 3 : method for goal : "create file" (M3)
      step 4 : box attribution (M4)
      step 5 : validation (M5)
      step 6 : return goal accomplished (M6)
S2 : method for goal "admission of an old patient"
      step 1 : social allowances (M1)
      step 2 : visual allowances (M2)
      step 3 : display old file (M7)
      step 4 : modify file date if necessary  (M8)
      step 5 : box attribution (M4)
      step 6 : validation (M5)
      step 7 : return goal accomplished (M6)
S3 : method for goal "create file"
      step 1 : label attribution (M9)
      step 2 : whereabouts keyboard (M10)
```

```
step 3 : read letter of the doctor (M11)
step 4 : usual doctor keyboard (M12)
step 5 : validation (M5)
step 6 : return goal accomplished (M6)
```

So we can establish the matrix (cf table 3).

Table 3. Example of matrix for GOMS specification.

	M1	M2	M3	M4	M5	M6	M7	M8	M9	M10	M11	M12	SR
S1	1	1	1	1	1	1	0	0	0	0	0	0	SR1
S2	1	1	0	1	1	1	1	1	0	0	0	0	SR1
S3	0	0	0	0	1	1	0	0	1	1	1	1	

ETAG Specification. The objective is, on the one hand, to construct the set of tasks "Entries" required to execute the methods of each step and, on the other hand, to extract the set of resources (objects, states, events). These tasks and resources are defined according to the ETAG grammar and provide the details of each method in the second matrix.

This step is also formalized by means of a matrix. The lines represent the methods and the columns describe the objects, states, and events of the tasks. The following example only models one part of the final matrix for the M3 and M4 methods.

In ETAG, we have :

```
Type (object = box )
Value set : occupied | free
End object

Type (object = patient)
Value set : new | old
End object

Entry 1 :
(task > file creation), (event > patient), (object >
patient = *P), (object > file = *F)
t1(event > new patient), (object > patient = p), (object
file = f)
      "create the medical file of a new patient"

Entry 2 :
(task > box attribution), (event > patient), (object >
patient = *P), (object > box  = *B)
t2(event > patient), (object > patient = p), (object >
box = "free")
      "attribute a box to a patient"
```

Table 4. Example of matrix for ETAG specification.

	Object	States	Events	Entry : task
M3	< file >	< >	(event > patient)	< Entry 1 >
M4	< box >	< occupied, free>	(event > patient)	< Entry 2 >

4.4 Step 5 : Finding the Transactions

The design of these interaction classes could be decomposed into two phases :

1) Top-Down Analysis : reasoning on the basis of the <states, events> component of M under the constraint of planning the tasks using Colored Petri Nets, for instance [7]

2) Bottom-up Analysis : reasoning only on the basis of the Entries obtained under the constraint of the <states, events> transitions associated by selecting representative examples : for instance, a Galois lattice would be used as the indexing structure according to the principles used in IGLUE [1].

In the MAYBE method, the associations between Entries and <states, events> are already placed in the matrix (Step 4) based on the GOMS/ETAG articulation and, in addition, this matrix directly provides the selection rules for individuals. In fact, the expected results have already been attained through the complex and costly combination in the previous approach.

4.5 Step 6 : Coordination and Communication Models

The representation of interactions between agents (human or artificial) is a central problem in the structuring of multi-agent architectures. These two models are a necessary requirement in any multi-agent system for coordinating the agents. The communication model represents the synchronous and asynchronous relationships between the agents (model situating the agent in its environment), whereas the coordination model is essential for avoiding conflicts between the agents involved in a transaction (model situating the agent in a transaction).

Coordination Sub-model. The problem consists in sharing the allocation of resources in accordance with the "stream" mode of the STROBE (STReam Object Environment) model [13]. For this model, we define a set of Scheme predicates of the following type : use?, product?, produce?, is_used?, is_shared?. The application on which we tested the method (the emergency service of the hospital) did not require a sophisticated real-time coordination model, because the procedures are defined by the hospital's protocols.

Communication Sub-model. We use the STROBE model to list the communication protocols between the different entities "1-to-1," and thus add a collective dimension to each agent. This model checks that the communication between two potential agents A and B, as defined in step 5, takes place according to the REPL (Read, Evaluate, Print, Listen) cycle in Stream mode

For example, one can be note that the assignment of a variable (allocation of a bed) that is private to B, but accessible to both A and C may cause either A or C to perceive B as behaving unexpectedly (or incorrectly) when, for example, isolation rules are broken due to adverse events.

4.6 Step 7 : Conflict Resolution

The above remarks concerning adverse events do not imply that cooperation patterns are wrong or not fully completed, but that this open scheme for communicating between agents substantially shifts the focus of any realistic client-server scenario to a double integration : the Human in the loop, and different theoretical, experimental and applicative approaches are considered to be complementary resources for solving complex problems in a usable way.

Unfortunately, clinical performance may deviate from the ideal and, even if all physicians involved in acute or emergency care can be expected to perform practical procedures, we need to differentiate active errors (which are those that immediately precede an adverse event) from, for example, latent errors (which are factors inherent in a system). For this reason, we use a set of predicates (use?, is_used?, product?, produce?, is_shared?) as defined above for the coordination model in step 6. Nevertheless, this approach may be insufficient for a field that has weaker or more informal procedures.

When these 7 steps are completed, the final multi-agent system is made up of the library of agents validated in step 6, in accordance with the architecture derived from the coordination model in step 5.

5 Conclusion

We consider the essential result of the MAYBE method to be the interactive concurrent bottom-up analyses, based on multiple points of view between different agents. Our approach offers flexibility, which stems from the fact that agents can be modified and are autonomous, in contrast with other more integrated and rigid methodologies, based on agents defined in advance in terms of their roles.

MAYBE uses a series of models in "cascade" to go from an abstract representation of the problems to a formal one of the directly programmable agent. But, these various models lead to a real complexity of the method. This is why we wanted to automate the process. So, the used formalisms are transparent for the user. The method's use is easy and the complexity of the models is hidden as a black box for the user.

In term of implementation, a first prototype (a simulator) was developed to test the method within the emergency room chain of the "centre hospitalier côte basque", situated in Bayonne. We used an Agent Building Environment (ABE) of IBM but it was too poor in terms of inference and adaptation according to rules. So an implementation of the MAYBE framework in Scheme using Jaskemal multi-agent platform is currently in progress [14].

References

1. M. Burstein, G. Ferguson and J. Allen Integrating, Agent-based Mixed-initiative Control with an Existing Multi-agent Planning System, in *the Proceedings of the 2000 International Conference on Multi-agent Systems* (ICMAS) (July 2000).
2. D. Kinny, M. Georgeff and A. Rao, A methodology and modelling technique for systems of BDI agents. in :W. van de Velve and J. W. Perram eds, *Agent Breaking Away : proceeding of the seventh european workshop on modelling autonomous agents in a multi-agent world*, Lecture Notes in Artificial Intelligence #1038, (Springer-Verlag, Berlin, Germany, 1996) 56-71.
3. G. Gouardères, A. Minko and L. Richard, Cooperative Agents to Track Learner's Cognitive Gaps, actes du congrès *5th International Conference on Intelligent Tutoring Systems'2000* (Montréal, Canada), Lecture Notes in Computer Sciences #1839,(Springer ed, 2000), 443-453.
4. C. Frasson, L. Martin, G. Gouardères and E. Aimeur, LANCA : a distance Learning Architecture based on Networked Cognitive Agents. *4° International Conference on Intelligent Tutoring Systems -ITS'98-* (San Antonio, USA, 1998), Lecture Notes in Computer Sciences 1452, (Springer Verlag) 142-151.
5. H. Kriaa and G. Gouardères, Revisable Analysis and Design by Actors Interaction : Emergency Case Study, in R. Kowalczyk, S.W. Loke, N.E. Reed, G. Graham eds. : *Advances in Artificial Intelligence*. Lecture Notes in Artificial Intelligence #2112, (Springer ed., 2001), 259-269.
6. S. Miles, M. Joy and M. Luck, Designing Agent-Oriented Systems by Analysing Agent Interactions. In P. Ciancarini and M. Wooldridge editors, *Agent-Oriented Software Engineering*, Lecture Notes in Computer Science, (Springer-Verlag 1957, 2001), 171-183.
7. G. Wagner, Toward Agent-Oriented Information Systems. Technical report, Institute for Information, University of Leipzig, March 1999. AOIS
8. M. Wood and S. A. DeLoach. An Overview of the Multiagent Systems Engineering Methodology. *The First International Workshop on Agent-Oriented Software Engineering (AOSE-2000)*, (Limerick, Ireland, 2000).
9. K. Allan, Speech act theory -- an overview. *Concise Encyclopedia of Grammatical Categories* in E. K. Brown & J. Miller eds, (Oxford : Elsevier Science, 1999).
10. Kendall, E. A., "Patterns of Agent Analysis and Design," in *Handbook of Agent Technology*, J. Bradshaw, Ed., AAAI Press/ MIT Press, 2000.
11. S.K. Card, T.P. Moran and A. Newell, *The Psychology of Human-Computer Interaction.* (Lawrence Erlbaum Ass., Hillsdale, New Jersey, 1983).
12. G. De Haan, ETAG-based Design : User Interface Design as Mental Model Specification. In : Palanque and Benyon eds. *Critical Issues in User Interface Systems Engineering*. (Springer Verlag, London, 1996), 81-92.
13. S. A. Cerri, Shifting the focus from control to communication : the STReams OBjects Environments model of communicating agents, in J. Padget Eds, *Collaboration between human and artificial societies* vol. 1624, LNAI, (Berlin, Heidelberg, New York : Springer-Verlag, 1999), 71-101.
14. S.A. Cerri, V. Loia, and D. Maraschi, Jaskemal : a language for Java agents interacting in Scheme, Presented *at Workshop on Interaction Agents*, (L'Acquila, Italy).

Design Issues for Agent-Based Resource Locator Systems

Gary Wills, Harith Alani, Ronald Ashri, Richard Crowder, Yannis Kalfoglou, and Sanghee Kim

Intelligence Agents Multimedia Group
Department of Electronics and Computer Science,
University of Southampton,
Southampton SO17 1BJ,
UK
{gbw,ha,ra00r,rmc,y.kalfoglou,sk98r}@ecs.soton.ac.uk

Abstract. While knowledge is viewed by many as an asset, it is often difficult to locate particular items within a large electronic corpus. This paper presents an agent based framework for the location of resources to resolve a specific query, and considers the associated design issue. Aspects of the work presented complements current research into both expertise finders and recommender systems. The essential issues for the proposed design are scalability, together with the ability to learn and adapt to changing resources. As knowledge is often implicit within electronic resources, and therefore difficult to locate, we have proposed the use of ontologies, to extract the semantics and infer meaning to obtain the results required. We explore the use of communities of practice, applying ontology-based networks, and e-mail message exchanges to aid the resource discovery process.

1 Introduction

Many organisations view knowledge as an asset, though this knowledge is buried within the corporate memory, with much of the understanding and constraints surrounding the knowledge being held tacitly by people within the organisation [23]. It is not uncommon in some multi-site organisations to repeat work already undertaken elsewhere in the organisation, then try to discover if it has been carried out at a different location [7]. In addition, people do not always stay in the same location; they move into different task locations, disciplines or other organisations, and the changes in technologies may make a field of expertise irrelevant.

Organisations capitalise on their best practices through improvements in sharing knowledge, which can lead to a higher level of productivity and competency. The development of best practices is linked with the process of learning from experiences, which is initiated by individuals and are shared through communication. One of the most effective methods of transferring knowledge, within organisations, is to involve individuals in cross-functional teams, as individuals naturally apply their expertise in different task contexts [2]. However, many organisations find difficulty in maximising the benefits when the individuals are moved or are reluctant to contribute [3].

D. Karagiannis and U. Reimer (Eds.): PAKM 2002, LNAI 2569, pp. 156–167, 2002.

This paper focuses on design issues surrounding an agent-based resource locator for use within organisations. The system's response to a particular query directs the user to the most appropriate set of resources. For example, if the query is of a *who knows about*... type it will direct the user to a person, while a *why does this occur* ... query may direct the user to a document describing the process. The system combines features of both expertise and expert finders together with that of recommender systems, but has fundamental differences:

- An expert or expertise finder system will locate an expert who has the special knowledge or skill that causes that person to be regarded as an authority on a specific topic. The quality of the answer will depend on the explicit knowledge being used for the search, in some cases this is not peer reviewed, but supplied by the experts themselves or as the result of a consultancy exercise. Expertise systems range from centrally held database of personnel skills [6], searching a limited range of personally selected documents [17] to systems that use real-time information held within the corporate system [29];
- A recommender system is an extension of the basic expertise finder approach, where the results will be modified by feedback provided by previous users, as to the quality and validity of the recommendations [25].

In our view, a resource locator looks across **all** the information repositories of the organisation, and if needed outside the organisation, to locate the most suitable resources to resolve a specific query. As in some recommender systems the results of the query will be personalised to the user, for example by job function or status. In order to address the perceived problems of expertise finders and recommended system it was considered that a different design philosophy was required, to provide access to an organisation's tacit and implicit knowledge to give the optimum answer to a query. Consider the following scenario:

> "An engineer has to resolve a specific problem regarding a product test failure. By examining the data it is clear that reference must be made to a set of standards and their interpretation. The query *tell me about this standard*, will result in the standard itself, while a query *asking for interpretation* will result in identifying company's expert in this field, together with interpretative document from the standard's body and professional institutions."

In order to return the knowledge required by the engineer, the following steps are required:

- Refine the query;
- Search and retrieve information from the organisation's electronic resources;
- Search and retrieve other resources across the Internet, if required to resolve the query;
- Interpret the retrieved results, and
- Present the results in an appropriate manner.

2 Related Work

Our work complements related research into expert finder and recommender systems. A full listing is impractical, and space prevent us from a detailed comparison but we cite representative works as to highlight the research in these areas.

In the context of managing user profiles we point to attempts that have been made to infer user profiles from analyzing patterns of access to documents, for example the *InfoFinder* system described in [16]. Most of these approaches try to deduce user interests by employing empirical methods, as in Kanfer et al, [11]. However, the *MyPlanet* system deliberately imposes an ontology-driven structure to the user profile which enables the system to reason about it using semantically rich relations as specified in the underlying ontology, [10].

In the Java Programming domain, Vivacqua and Lieberman presented a system that models users' programming skills by reading source code files, and analysing what classes, libraries or methods are used and how often [28]. They then compare these to the overall usage for the remaining users, to determine their levels of expertise for specific topics (e.g., methods).

Kanfer and colleagues have used an agent based system to recommend people from within the user's own social network [11]. Their work emphasizes the social nature of communication, and that people prefer to contact people they know or are acquainted with, when asking for help. This work is supported by the study undertaken by McDonald and colleagues in which the social, cognitive and information aspects of the system play a key role [18]. The authors observed that in the social context of any expertise finder systems, the user has two problems to solve, expert identification and expertise selection.

Social and collaborative networks had been the focus of much research on finding people. For example the *Referral Web* project at AT&T [13], focused on the creation of social networks from the co-existence of names on the Web and use these models to locate experts and referral paths. However, it is not possible to infer the type of relations with this approach. Newman [21], investigated searching for scientists in collaboration networks, built mainly from document co-authorships. He argues that true collaboration networks are based on the affiliations of people and their memberships to clubs, teams, and organisations.

The *Expert Finder* and *XpertNet* projects at MITRE [17] aim to provide an online search facility for searching for experts within the organisation. *Expert Finder* identifies experts in certain topics by searching a database of a variety of documents authored and submitted by employees. In this system a person is considered to be an expert in a certain field if their name is associated with many documents about a specific subject. The type of association with these documents and the type of employee (e.g., researcher, administrative staff) indicates the degree of expertise. *XpertNet* constructs social networks from projects, publications, and technical interactions, and applies statistical clustering techniques and social network analysis to bring together people with similar skills and interests. Experts are rated according to their network connectivity with relevant projects, documents, and other related experts.

In the *FindUR* project [19], the means for knowledge-enhanced search by using ontologies were investigated. McGuinness describes a tool, deployed at AT&T, which uses ontologies to improve search from the perspectives of recall and precision as well as ease of query formation. Their tool is mainly targeted to the Information Retrieval research area and aims to improve search engines technology. They provide means for updating the topic sets used to categorize information. In addition to the use of ontologies, the *FindUR* team also used the notion of 'evidence phrases' to uncover hidden information related to a given topic. For example, the company *Vocaltec* could be an evidence for the topic *Internet telephony*. The *MyPlanet* system however, elaborates this approach and use *cue phrases* which are used both as an evidence and an abstraction of a given topic. A similar system, *OntoSeek*, is presented in [9]. It deploys *content matching* techniques to support content-based access to the Web. As in the *FindUR* project, the target was the Information Retrieval area with the aim of improving recall and precision and the focus was two specific classes of information repositories: yellow pages and product catalogues. Their underlying mechanism uses conceptual graphs to represent queries and resources descriptions. However these graphs are not constructed automatically. The *OntoSeek* team developed a semi-automatic approach in which the user has to verify the links between different nodes in the graph via a designated user-interface.

Other uses of ontologies in this area include skills management as discussed in [27]where *OntoProper* is discussed. It is an ontology-based approach for skills management. The authors tackle two problems: find the approximate matches and maintaining skill data. They use a decision theory method, Multiple Attribute Decision Making (MADM), also known as non-compensatory and compensatory methods to tackle the problem of approximate matching of skills. To maintain skill data, they use an ontology on users' profiles and skills.

Agent-based approaches to expert finder systems have been used in the past. Sol and Sierra describe *NetExpert* in [26] where the search for experts is conducted on the Web using a multi-agent approach with similarity measures used for analysing experts' profiles. The *Agent Amplified Communication (AAC)* relies on e-mail communication to construct a referral chain which is a kind of communication channel that a user refers to in order to obtain needed information [12]. A user profile is built as the user provides his/her interests in terms of a list of keywords. When a help-seeking query is submitted, *AAC* firstly looks up a list of contact name addresses available for each user. However if there is no good match, it generates a list of possible referrals using email records and the contact addresses.

Finally, a survey of AI-based expert-finding systems is given by Becerra-Fernandez in [4]. The author elaborates on the requirements for building such systems in large organisations in [3] where a prototype system, *ExpertSeeker*, is presented.

3 Design Issues

In designing resource locator systems, which rely on gathering a wide range of information across different locations within and outside organisations and making this accessible, a number of issues have to be addressed:

- The system should continuously update information about individual resources while these are resources are created, revised, or eliminated as users or other resources make use of them;

- The system should take into account the different perspectives of resource providers as well as users, such that it will provide only required information to relevant users;
- The system should keep a balance between enabling the discovery of information in distributed environments and ensuring the provision of a resource locator that collects and combines such information in order to provide an appropriate user interaction.

All these requirements lead to a system design that is complex and needs to take into account interactions between subsystems that change over time. Our implementation is based on an agent-based approach since it demonstrates a number of features which can support the above requirements. Firstly, in order to deal with distributed and heterogeneous resources, it is necessary to reduce effort and time needed for combining and maintaining such resources. By decomposing such sources into configurable components that can be easily incorporated or eliminated and treating them as individual agents, it is possible to build a scalable system. As such, we can capitalise on similarity between information sources which operate in a similar context while still allowing unique features to be captured. Secondly, in order to build a centralised resource locator without adding much workload to users, a learning capability that automatically allows changes in resources to be tracked is necessary and as reported in [20] study, an agent-based approach is suitable where an prompt adaptation is crucial.

The architecture presented in this paper is dependent on ontologies to retrieve and infer all necessary information when searching and locating resources.

Ontologies can provide systems with classifications of topics, people roles, events, and all sorts of activities that could be relevant to locating resources within or across organisations. Information about the user, for example, can help personalising the expert search to those with similar roles or job categories as the user, or to those that are within short social paths to the user to encourage response [13]. The hierarchy of topics can be used to narrow down or broaden a query if too many or too few results are found respectively. Furthermore, ontology relations can be valued differently when searching for resources, thus gaining more control on the process and obtaining well tuned results.

Social networks have shown to have an important role in people finder applications [13, 21]. In our approach we intend to treat the ontology and its assertions themselves as a social network and analyse it to infer a variety of information, such as hub and authoritative people, communities of practice, shortest paths, etc. (see section 4.1 on implementation).

4 System Framework

The block diagram of the proposed framework is shown in Figure 1, each block represents an agent or group of agents.

The goals of the *User Interface agent* are to communicate the question to a query refinement agent, inform the personalisation agent who asked the question and present the answers to the person who asked the question. As the user may be at a terminal or in a mobile situation, the *User Interface agent* would be responsible for delivering the answer in an appropriate manner. The type of user interface could range from a simple command-line input to range of mobile devices (for instance PDAs), [24]. This will

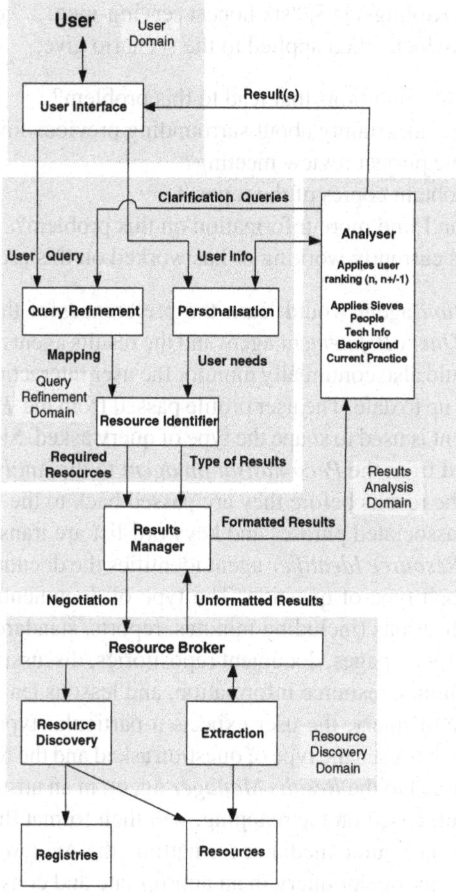

Fig. 1. An agent based framework for resource location.

allow the engineer in the scenario to use the system in the office, on a factory floor or at a remote location.

The goal of the *Query Refinement* agent is to identify the main components of the question and compose an appropriate query. It would be difficult to process any natural language request from the user unless it could be refined into a format that an agent-based system could understand. The processes used include stemming, removal of stop-lists, and the use of contexts by means of synonyms, thesaurus, or hyponyms. The result is a list of phrases and keywords and the query focus. The knowledge needs of the user are derived from their user profiles. In the case of our engineer scenario this will be based on current responsibilities, project allocation and other management information. At this stage, there is no limit to the types of query that could be asked by the user or the type of interfaces that could be used. The type of questions that users would typically ask can be grouped under Kipling's [15] "six honest serving-men..." of *What, Why, When, How, Where* and *Who*,which when applied to the scenario give:

- **What**: What are the conditions that lead to this problem?
- **Why**: Why is there uncertainty about surrounding previous findings?
- **When**: When is the project review meeting?
- **How**: How can I obtain copies of the report?
- **Where**: Where can I find more information on this problem?
- **Who**: Who else is currently working or has worked on this problem?

The *Personalisation* agent would learn the preferences of the user and pass this information onto the *Query Refinement* agent and the results agents. In addition, the Personalisation agent would also continually monitor the user interaction with the system to keep the user's profile up to date. The user profile passed from the *Personalisation* to the *Query Refinement* agent is used to shape the type of query asked. Similarly, the user profile information passed from the *Personalisation agent* to the *Analyser* would influence the filters applied to the results before they are passed back to the user. Once the query has been refined, the associated phrases and keyword-list are transferred to a *Resource Identifier* agent. The *Resource Identifier* agent identifies the documentary types that are required to support each type of question. The type of documentary sources required typically include publications (including minutes, reports, standards, handbooks, CAD models), departmental Web pages, document repositories, discussion groups, telephone directories, E-mails, human resource information, and lessons learnt log.

Based on the type of query, the user expects a particular type of answer, Table 1 shows typical mapping between the type of question asked and the form of the reply. This information is then passed to the *Results Manager* agent, in an unstructured format. The *Results Manager* agent, based on the mapping, will then format the result accordingly. Hence, irrespective of the source media or formatting, the *Analyser* agents will receive the information from a particular query in an appropriate and consistent format.

Table 1. Mapping the type of questions to resources and results required.

Query Type	Resources	Result Required
How	Information	Document or Information
When	Time, Name, Information	Time
Where	Name, Information	Place
Who	Name, Appellation, Information	Person
What	Focus of Query, Complement (constraints)	Answer
Why	Focus of Query (motive), Complement	Answer and Document/Information

The *Analyser* agent will then decide to:

- Pass the results onto the *User Interface* agent.
- If there is a compound query, wait until all the answers are received.
- Ask for a further query to be made, by sending a query to the *Query Refinement* agent.

The *Analyser* agent will do more than just sieve the result; for instance, it may run a statistical analysis of the results to check the probability of reliable data and the level of trust associated with the information. The sieves are used to rank the results, for instance if people are returned, it will suggest people that are in the same location or department at the top of the list. The order that the sieves are applied depends on the user profiles and user information needs. Table 2 shows the type of sieves to be applied in relation to the documentary sources. There are additional heuristics when the results are related to people. That is, since people tend to feel less threatened when asking questions of colleagues, the positions in organisational hierarchy can be exploited.

Table 2. List of sieves (filters) applied to results.

People	Information	Background	Best Practice
Location	Relevance	Relevance	Relevance
Site	Date of Origin		Date of Origin
Status			Context (project)

The resources can be external to the system and could be in any location on the intranet or internet, hence the requirement for a *Resource Discovery* agent that will query a number of documentary sources. In addition to the *Extraction* agent, it is necessary to have a separate agent that would locate new or changed resources. For each of the specific resource type there is a corresponding agent, that will understand how to integrate, analyse and extract the knowledge from the resource.

4.1 Implementation

We have already developed a set of systems offering specific services which realise parts of the proposed resource locator system. Some of these implementations are described below:

ONTOCOPI. One of the tools that can support a resource locator system is ONTOCOPI [1], a community of practice (CoP) identifier that applies Ontology-based Network Analysis (ONA) [22] to uncover the most related cluster of entities to a specific person or object. ONTOCOPI will form part of the "Resource Identifier" agent in Figure 1. The tool analyses the relations between ontology assertions to calculate their relatedness. The user can control the selection of relations and their relative importance, and the range of the CoP to be identified.

In a similar way to finding CoPs, ONA can be used to search for resources by analysing the ontology assertions around the subject of interest. For example when the requirement is to locate an expert in Knowledge Management (KM), ONA algorithm spreads its activation starting from the assertion that represents the subject of KM until the search limit is reached (maximum number of links to be traversed). This crawl takes into account the type of relations being traversed to reflect their different impact on the judgement of expertise, so for example a relation between a person and a project on KM can be valued higher than a relation between a person and a KM workshop that he attended. Hubs and authoritative people can be identified by ONA and used to measure the level of expertise. At the end of this search, a list of people and objects will be produced, ranked according to their degree of relativity to the specific query topic, estimated from the amount and type of semantic paths between each entity in the network and the query object.

The temporal dimension can be an important one when searching for current resources. ONA can be tuned to work within a time limit, where time-related assertions can be filtered accordingly. For example, a document published in 1980 about KM may be less accounted for or disregarded when searching for current experts in this subject.

ONTOCOPI can also be used to find close alternatives to a specific resources if the later is unreachable for any particular reason. The top people in the CoP list will most likely be working on the same areas, and hence may all be consulted.

EMNLP. One of the potential information resources that "Resource Discovery" agent, in Figure 1, can exploit is e-mail messages exchanged within companies across different organisational departmental groups and outside organisations. Among other types of content, messages which carry task discussion, action decisions or business rules are particularly important in organisational task analysis. Since contextual information is inherently included in exchanged messages, for example, the names of communicators or time information, it enables the extracted user information to be easily attached to context-specific properties which are important in creating expertise models. EMNLP is an example of expertise modeling based on e-mail communication [14]. EMNLP examines the application of NLP (Natural Language Processing) technique and user modeling to the development of expertise modeling based on e-mail communication. It captures the different levels of expertise reflected in exchanged e-mail messages, and makes use of such expertise in facilitating a correct ranking of experts. Its linguistic perspective regards the exchanged messages as the realization of verbal communication among users based on the following assumption that user expertise is best extracted by focusing on the sentence where users' viewpoints are explicitly expressed. In addition, the names and structures of e-mail folders can also be used for discovering user interests with regard to message content. Its supporting assumption is that folder names tend to show the information needs of given users since they associate meaningful concepts to the names as described in [5]. This implies that users whose tasks are similar might have the same name folders in common. The analysis of the patterns concerning with e-mail access can also play a role in mining social interaction among a group of users. User studies reported both by [8] and [30], for example, reveal that organisational roles are slightly co-related with respective user behaviour, e.g. users may be more receptive of information authorised by their bosses than those from secretaries.

5 Conclusions

Many of the current approaches to resource location have focused on locating experts. Those systems that are designed solely to return a person or persons, together with their current location. Various approaches have been published to provide this service; some have relied on management and social aspects of a community, while others methods have tried to infer expertise, from local resources or self published material.

In practice, we realised that people want more from their knowledge system than to just locate a person. We have taken a holistic knowledge management approach, in the design of an agent based framework for resource location. We did not focus on any particular implementation, and intended to design a generalised agent based approach to location of resources in an organisation and on the World-Wide-Web in response to a specific query.

The requirement of an agent-based resource locator to harness knowledge from a wide range of disparate systems, which may reside in different operating environments and administration domains, lead to the proposed framework detailed in this paper. In the approach we have taken, scalability, and the ability to learn and adapt to changing resources are essential, hence the multi-agent approach taken. The abstraction of goal-directed agents and multi-agent systems is especially suited to the area of resource location.

While the agent framework allows us to deal with the issues of accessing knowledge in many different environments, it alone will not be enough to obtain the answer the user requires. The knowledge is often implicitly held in electronic resources, hence the requirement for the ontologies, to extract the semantics and infer the results required.

Many of the agents shown in the block diagram (Figure 1) will require further detailed design. At which stage experiments to find the advantages or disadvantages of a particular statistical technique or the exact heuristic to be used.

Acknowledgements. This work is supported under the Advanced Knowledge Technologies (AKT) Interdisciplinary Research Collaboration (IRC), which is sponsored by the UK Engineering and Physical Sciences Research Council under grant number GR/N15764/01. The AKT IRC comprises the Universities of Aberdeen, Edinburgh, Sheffield, Southampton and the Open University. The views and conclusions contained herein are those of the authors and should not be interpreted as necessarily representing official policies or endorsements, either expressed or implied, of the EPSRC or any other member of the AKT IRC.

References

1. H. Alani, K. O'Hara and N. Shadbolt. ONTOCOPI: Methods and tools for identifying communities of practice *Proceedings of 2002 World Computer Congress, Intelligent Information Processing Stream, Montreal* 2002
2. L. Argote. *Organizational Learning: Creating, Retaining and Transferring Knowledge.* Kluwer Academic Publishers, 1999. ISBN: 0-7923-8420-2.
3. I. Becerra-Fernandez. Facilitating the online search of experts at NASA using expert seeker people-finder. In I. Becerra-Fernandez, editor, *Proceedings of the 3rd International Conference on Practical Aspects of Knowledge Management (PAKM2000), Basel, Switzerland,* October 2000.
4. I. Becerra-Fernandez. The role of artificial intelligence technologies in the implementation of people-finder knowledge management systems. In S. Staab and D. O'Leary, editors, *Proceedings of the Bringing Knowledge to Business Processes Workshop, AAAI Spring Symposium Series, Menlo Park, CA, USA*, March 2000.

5. G.C. Bowker and S.L. Start. *Sorting Things Out: Classification and its consequences.* The MIT Press, England, 2000.
6. T. Davenport and L. Prusak. *Working Knowledge: How Organizations Manage What They Know.* Harvard Business School Press, MA,USA, 1998.
7. D. DeRoure, W. Hall, S. Reich, G. Hill, A. Pikrakis, and M. Stairmand. Memoir - an open distributed framework for enhanced navigation of distributed information. *Information Processing and Management*, 37:53–74, 2001.
8. N. Ducheneaut and V. Bellotti. E-mail as habitat: An exploration of embedded personal information management. *ACM Interactions*, pages 30–38, October 2001.
9. N. Guarino, C. Masolo, and G. Vetere. OntoSeek: Content-Based Access to the Web. *IEEE Intelligent Systems*, 14(3):70–80, May 1999.
10. Y. Kalfoglou, J. Domingue, E. Motta, M. Vargas-Vera, and S. Buckingham-Shum. MyPlanet: an ontology-driven Web-based personalised news service. In *Proceedings of the IJCAI'01 workshop on Ontologies and Information Sharing, Seattle, USA*, August 2001.
11. A. Kanfer, J. Sweet, and A. Schlosser. Humanizing the net: Social navigation with a "know-who" e-mail agent. In *Proceedings of the 3rd Conference on Human Factors and the Web, Denver, CO, USA*, 1997.
12. H. Kautz, B. Selman, and A. Milewski. Agent amplified communication. In *Proceedings of the 13th National Conference on Artificial Intelligence (AAAI'96),USA*, pages 3–9, August 1996.
13. H. Kautz, B. Selman, and M. Shah. The hidden web. *AI Magazine*, 27(36), 1997.
14. S. Kim, W. Hall, and A. Keane. Natural language processing for expertise modelling in e-mail communication. In *Proceedings of the 3rd International Conference on Intelligent Data Engineering and Automated Learning, Manchester, England*, 2002.
15. R. Kipling. "keep six honest..." a poem in the Elephant's Child. In *Just So Stories*, 1902.
16. B. Krulwich and C. Burkley. The InfoFinder Agent: Learning User Interests through Heuristic Phrase Extraction. *IEEE Intelligent Systems*, 12(5):22–27, 1997.
17. M. Maybury, R. Damore, and D. House. Awareness of organizational expertise. Technical report, MITRE, October 2000.
18. D.W. McDonald and M.S. Ackerman. Just talk to me: A field study of expertise location. In *Proceedings of the 1998 ACM Conference on Computer Supported Cooperative Work (CSCW)*, pages 14–18, 1998.
19. L.D. McGuinness. Ontological Issues for Knowledge-Enhanced Search. In N. Guarino, editor, *Proceedings of the 1st International Conference on Formal Ontology in Information Systems(FOIS'98), Trento, Italy*, pages 302–316. IOS Press, June 1998.
20. P. Maes Agents that Reduce Work and Information Overload In *Software Agents* ed. B Jeffrey, 1997
21. M. Newman. Who is the best connected scientist? a study of scientific coauthorship networks. *Physics Review*, E64, 2001.
22. K. O'Hara, H. Alani, and N. Shadbolt. Identifying Communities of Practice: Analysing Ontologies as Networks to Support Community Recognition *Proceedings of the World Computer Congress*, 2002
23. D. O'Leary. How knowledge reuse informs effective system design and implementation. *IEEE Intelligent Systems*, 16(1):44–49, January 2001.
24. G. Power, R. Damper, W. Hall. and G. Wills Realism and Naturalness in a Conversational Multi-Modal Interface In *Proceedings of the IDS02, ISCA Tutorial and Research Workshop on Multi-Modal Dialogue in Mobile Environments Kloster Irsee, Germany*, June 17 - 19, 2002
25. P. Resnick and H.R. Varian. Recommender systems. *Communications of the ACM*, 40(3):56–58, March 1997.

26. R. Sol and J. Serra. Netexpert: A multiagent system for expertise location. In *Proceedings of the IJCAI-01 Workshop on Knowledge Management and Organizational Memories, Seattle, USA*, August 2001.
27. Y. Sure, A. Maedche, and S. Staab. Leveraging Corporate Skill Knowledge - From ProPer to OntoProPer. In *Proceedings of the 3rd International Conference on Practical Aspects of Knowledge Management(PAKM2000), Basel, Switzerland*, October 2000.
28. A. Vivacqua and H. Lieberman. Agents to assist in finding help. In *Proceedings of the 2000 ACM Conference on HCI, The Hague, Netherlands*, pages 65–72, April 2000.
29. M. Weal, G. Hughes, D. Millard, and L. Moreau. Open hypermedia as a navigational interface to ontological information spaces. In *Proceedings of the 20th ACM Conference on Hypertext and Hypermedia (HT'01), Aarchus, Denmank*, pages 227–236, August 2001.
30. E. Williams. E-mail and the effect of future developments. *First Monday*, 4(8), 1999.

Analysis of Clustering Algorithms for Web-Based Search

Sven Meyer zu Eissen and Benno Stein

Paderborn University
Department of Computer Science
D-33095 Paderborn, Germany
{smze,stein}@upb.de

Abstract. Automatic document categorization plays a key role in the development of future interfaces for Web-based search. Clustering algorithms are considered as a technology that is capable of mastering this "ad-hoc" categorization task.

This paper presents results of a comprehensive analysis of clustering algorithms in connection with document categorization. The contributions relate to exemplar-based, hierarchical, and density-based clustering algorithms. In particular, we contrast ideal and real clustering settings and present runtime results that are based on efficient implementations of the investigated algorithms.

Keywords. Document Categorization, Clustering, Clustering Quality Measures, Information Retrieval

1 Web-Based Search and Clustering

The Internet provides a huge collection of documents, and its use as a source of information is obvious and became very popular. As pointed out and analyzed by Dennis et al. there is a plethora of Web search technology, which can broadly be classified into four categories [4]:

(1) *Unassisted Keyword Search.* One or more search terms are entered and the search engine returns a ranked list of document summaries. Representatives: Google (`www.google.com`) or AltaVista (`www.altavista.com`).
(2) *Assisted Keyword Search.* The search engine produces suggestions based on the user's initial query. Representative: Vivisimo (`www.vivisimo.com`).
(3) *Directory-based Search.* Here, the information space is divided into a hierarchy of categories, where the user navigates from broad to specific classes. Representative: Yahoo! (`www.yahoo.com`).
(4) *Query-by-Example.* The user selects an interesting document snippet, which is then used as the basis of a new query.

In our working group we concentrate on developing smart interfaces for Web-based search. We think that the ideal search interface should model the search process within three phases: (a) An initialization phase according to the plain unassisted keyword search paradigm, (b) a categorization phase similar to the directory-based search paradigm, and (c) a refinement phase that may combine aspects from assisted keyword search and

D. Karagiannis and U. Reimer (Eds.): PAKM 2002, LNAI 2569, pp. 168–178, 2002.

the query-by-example paradigm. Our realization of this process pursues a meta search strategy similar to that of Vivisimo; i. e., it employs existing search technology within the initialization phase.

The outlined ideal search process is the result of the following observations:

Existing search engines do an excellent and convenient job. They organize up to billions of documents which can be searched quickly for keywords, and, the plain keyword search forms the starting point for the majority of users. However, while this strategy works fine for the experienced human information miner, the typical user is faced either with an empty result list or with a list containing thousands of hits. The former situation is the result of misspelling or contradictory Boolean query formulation; it can be addressed with a syntactic analysis. The latter situation lacks a meaningful specification of context—it requires a semantic analysis, which can be provided by means of category narrowing. In this connection some search engines use a human-maintained predefined topic hierarchy with about 20 top-level categories like sports, art, music etc. Such static hierarchies are unsatisfactory within two respects: They require a considerable human maintenance effort, and, for special topics (example: "sound card driver") the categories constitute an unnecessary browsing overhead which defers the search process. A powerful focusing assistance must be based onto a query-specific—say: ad-hoc—categorization of the delivered documents.

1.1 Contributions of the Paper

This paper focuses on ad-hoc categorization. Ad-hoc categorization comes along with two major challenges: Efficiency and nescience. Efficiency means that category formation must be performed at minimum detention, while nescience means that the category formation process is unsupervised: Except for experimental evaluation purposes, no predefined categorization scheme is given from which classification knowledge can be acquainted.

The paper in hand provides results of an analysis of clustering algorithms in connection with automatic document categorization. In particular, our contributions are threefold:

(1) The categorization performance of exemplar-based, hierarchical, and density-based clustering algorithms is shown within an idealized scenario. Such a scenario is characterized by the fact that no parameters of the clustering algorithm need to be estimated but the optimum values are chosen by a global analysis.
(2) In a realistic scenario, internal clustering quality measures are necessary to estimate cluster numbers, agglomeration thresholds, or neighborhood densities. From the various number of internal measures we have chosen approved ones and analyze the degradation of categorization performance compared to the optimum values.
(3) Several runtime issues are presented. They relate to both the algorithmic properties of the investigated algorithms and the difference when switching from an idealized to a realistic scenario.

Altogether, our analysis shall help to answer the question whether the investigated clustering technology is suited to master the pretentious job of ad-hoc categorization.

2 Document Representation, Clustering, and Quality Measures

The statistical method of variance analysis is used to verify whether a classification of given objects by means of nominal features is reflected in significant differences of depending metric features. Clustering can be considered as some kind of inverse operation: It tries to identify groups within an object set such that elements of different groups show significant differences with respect to their metric features.

Clustering algorithms operate on object similarities, which, in turn, are computed from abstract descriptions of the objects. Each such description is a vector $\mathbf{d}$ of numbers comprising values of essential object features. This section outlines the necessary concepts in connection with text documents: A suited object description, a related similarity measure, an overview of clustering algorithms, and—in particular, clustering quality measures for the analysis of an algorithm's categorization performance.

2.1 Document Representation

A common representation model for documents is the vector space model, where each document is represented in the term space, which roughly corresponds to the union of the m words that occur in a document collection [17,11]. In this term space, common words are filtered out by means of a stop word list, words that are unique in the collection are omitted, and stemming is applied to reduce words towards a canonical form. The document collection $D = \{d_1, \ldots, d_n\}$ can then be described by means of vectors $\mathbf{d}_j = (w_{j1}, \ldots, w_{jm})$, where w_{ji} designates a weight of term t_i in document d_j. Widely accepted variants for the choice of w_{ji} are the following.

(1) The term frequency $tf(d_j, t_i)$ denotes the frequency of term i in document j. Defining the weights w_{ji} as $tf(d_j, t_i)$ implies that terms that are used more frequently are rated more important.
(2) The inverse document frequency is defined as $idf(t_i) := \log(\frac{n}{df(t_i)})$, where n is the total number of documents in the collection and $df(t_i)$ is the number of documents which contain the term t_i. The hypothesis is that terms that occur rarely in a document collection are of highly discriminative power. Defining $w_{ji} := tf(d_j, t_i) \cdot idf(t_i)$ combines the hypothesis with Point (1) and has shown to improve the retrieval performance [20]. Note that the representation of a single document requires knowledge of the whole collection if *idf* is used.

2.2 Document Similarity

Clustering exploits knowledge about the similarity among the objects to be clustered. The similarity φ of two documents, d_1, d_2, is computed as a function of the distance between the corresponding term vectors $\mathbf{d_1}$ and $\mathbf{d_2}$. There exist various measures for similarity computation, from which the cosine-measure proved to be the most successful for document comparison. It is defined as follows.

$$\varphi(d_1, d_2) = \frac{\langle \mathbf{d_1}, \mathbf{d_2} \rangle}{||\mathbf{d_1}|| \cdot ||\mathbf{d_2}||},$$

where $\langle \mathbf{d}_1, \mathbf{d}_2 \rangle = \mathbf{d}_1^T \mathbf{d}_2$ denotes the scalar product, and $||\mathbf{d}||$ the Euclidean length. It calculates the cosine of the angle between two documents in $\mathbf{R}^m$. Note that a distance measure can easily be derived from φ by subtracting the similarity value from 1.

2.3 Clustering Algorithms

Let D be a set of objects. A clustering $\mathcal{C} = \{C \mid C \subseteq D\}$ of D is a division of D into sets for which the following conditions hold: $\bigcup_{C_i \in \mathcal{C}} C_i = D$, and $\forall C_i, C_j \in \mathcal{C}: C_i \cap C_{j \neq i} = \emptyset$.

Clustering algorithms, which generate a clustering $\mathcal{C}$, are distinguished with respect to their algorithmic properties. The following overview cannot be complete but outlines the most important classes along with the worst-case runtime behavior of prominent representatives. Again, n designates the number of documents in a given collection.

Iterative Algorithms. Iterative algorithms strive for a successive improvement of an existing clustering and can be further classified into exemplar-based and commutation-based approaches. These approaches need information with regard to the expected cluster number, k. Representatives: k-Means, k-Medoid, Kohonen, Fuzzy-k-Means [15,9,10, 24]. The runtime of these methods is $\mathcal{O}(nkl)$, where l designates the number of necessary iterations to achieve convergence.

Hierarchical Algorithms. Hierarchical algorithms create a tree of node subsets by successively merging (agglomerative approach) or subdividing (divisive approach) the objects. In order to obtain a unique clustering, a second step is necessary that prunes this tree at adequate places. Representatives: k-nearest-neighbor, linkage, Ward, or Min-cut methods [6,21,7,13,23]. Usually, these methods construct a complete similarity graph, which results in $\mathcal{O}(n^2)$ runtime.

Density-based Algorithms. Density-based algorithms try to separate a similarity graph into subgraphs of high connectivity values. In the ideal case they can determine the cluster number k automatically and detect clusters of arbitrary shape and size. Representatives: DBSCAN, MAJORCLUST, CHAMELEON [22,5,8]. The runtime of these algorithms cannot be stated uniquely since it depends on diverse constraints. Typically, it is in magnitude of hierarchical algorithms, $\mathcal{O}(n^2)$, or higher.

Meta-Search Algorithms. Meta-search algorithms treat clustering as an optimization problem where a given goal criterion is to be minimized or maximized [1,18,19,18]. Though this approach offers maximum flexibility, only less can be stated respecting its runtime.

2.4 Clustering Quality Measures

Many clustering algorithms do not return a definite clustering but a set of clusterings from which the best one has to be chosen. In particular, uniqueness within exemplar-based algorithms requires information about the cluster number, uniqueness within hierarchical algorithms requires an agglomeration threshold, or, within density-based algorithms, uniqueness requires a threshold for interpreting the neighborhood graph. If we had a measure to assess the quality of a clustering, the ambiguity could be mastered by simply computing several candidate clusterings and choosing the best one with respect to that measure. Note, however, that this is not a runtime problem in first place, but a problem of defining a suited quality measure.

Clustering quality measures evaluate the validity of a clustering and can be grouped into two categories: external and internal[1]. The following paragraphs introduce two clustering quality measures that are used within our experiments.

External Measures. External clustering quality measures use statistical tests to quantify how well a clustering matches the underlying structure of the data. In our context, the underlying structure is the known categorization of a document collection D as provided by a human editor. A broadly accepted external measure is the F-Measure, which combines the precision and recall ideas from information retrieval [12].

Let D represent the set of documents and let $\mathcal{C} = \{C_1, \ldots, C_k\}$ be a clustering of D. Moreover, let $\mathcal{C}^* = \{C_1^*, \ldots, C_l^*\}$ designate the human reference classification. Then the recall of cluster j with respect to class i, $rec(i,j)$, is defined as $|C_j \cap C_i^*|/|C_i^*|$. The precision of cluster j with respect to class i, $prec(i,j)$, is defined as $|C_j \cap C_i^*|/|C_j|$. The F-Measure combines both values as follows:

$$F_{i,j} = \frac{2 \cdot prec(i,j) \cdot rec(i,j)}{prec(i,j) + rec(i,j)}$$

Based on this formula, the overall F-Measure of a clustering is:

$$F = \sum_{i=1}^{l} \frac{|C_i^*|}{|V|} \cdot \max_{j=1,\ldots,k} \{F_{i,j}\}$$

A perfect clustering matches the given categories exactly and leads to an F-Measure value of 1.

Internal Measures. In absence of an external judgment, internal clustering quality measures must be used to quantify the validity of a clustering. Bezdek et al. present a thorough analysis of several internal measures, and, in this paper we rely on a measure from the Dunn Index family, which came off well in Bezdek et al.'s experiments [3,2].

Let $\mathcal{C} = \{C_1, \ldots, C_k\}$ be a clustering, $\delta : \mathcal{C} \times \mathcal{C} \to \mathbf{R}_0^+$ be a cluster-to-cluster distance measure, and $\Delta : \mathcal{C} \to \mathbf{R}_0^+$ be a cluster diameter measure. Then all measures $d : \mathcal{C} \to \mathbf{R}_0^+$ of the form

$$d(\mathcal{C}) = \frac{\min_{i \neq j}\{\delta(C_i, C_j)\}}{\max_{1 \leq l \leq k}\{\Delta(C_l)\}}$$

are called Dunn Indices. Of course there are numerous choices for δ and Δ, and Bezdek et al. experienced that the combination of

$$\delta(C_i, C_j) = \frac{1}{|C_i||C_j|} \sum_{x \in C_i, y \in C_j} \psi(x,y) \quad \text{and} \quad \Delta(C_i) = 2\left(\frac{\sum_{x \in C_i} \psi(x, c_i)}{|C_i|}\right)$$

[1] Several authors also define relative clustering qualtity measures, which can be derived from internal measures by evaluating different clusterings and comparing their scores [9].

gave reliable results for several data sets from different domains. Here, ψ denotes a distance measure between the objects to be clustered, and c_i is the centroid of cluster C_i. Since we use the cosine similarity φ as similarity measure, we set $\psi = 1 - \varphi$.

Remarks. As mentioned at the outset, the use of external and internal measures corresponds to an idealized and realistic experimental scenario respectively: During ad-hoc categorization, only very little is known a-priori about the underlying structure of a document collection.

3 Experimental Setting and Results

The experiments have been conducted with samples of the Reuters-21578 text document database [14]. In this database a considerable part of the documents is assigned to more than one category. To uniquely measure the classification performance, only single-topic documents are considered within our samples comprising 1000 documents from exactly 10 classes each. To account for biased a-priory probabilities in the class distribution of Reuters-21578, the investigated test sets are constructed as uniformly distributed.

The generation of a sample requires some preprocessing effort that should not be underestimated. It includes the reading and parsing of the documents, the elimination of stop words according to standard stop word lists, the application of Porter's stemming algorithm [16], the computation of term frequencies, the creation of compressed index vectors, etc. Table 1 shows exemplary the runtime of important preprocessing steps, compression ratios, and term reduction ratios for different sample sizes.

Table 1. Runtime and impact of selected preprocessing steps, depending on the size of the investigated sample.

# Documents in sample	# Classes in sample	Indexing time	Compression time	Compression ratio	# Terms (raw)	# Terms (reduced)	Term reduction
400	10	1.80s	0.23s	98.6%	6010	4153	31%
800	10	2.88s	0.64s	99.0%	8370	5725	32%
1000	10	3.40s	0.89s	99.1%	9192	6277	32%

The plots at the end of this section present the results of the categorization performance experiments. In particular, the following three variates are combined:

(1) *Cluster Algorithm.* "k-Means" versus "Single-Link" versus "MajorClust".

The algorithms are applied within a wide range of their respective parameters while paying attention to their special properties and strengths. More precisely: For k-Means all k-values between $1, \ldots, 20$ are considered. For Single-Link, clusterings at different agglomeration levels are considered. For MajorClust, the threshold for edge weights is successively advanced within 20 steps, from 0 to 1.

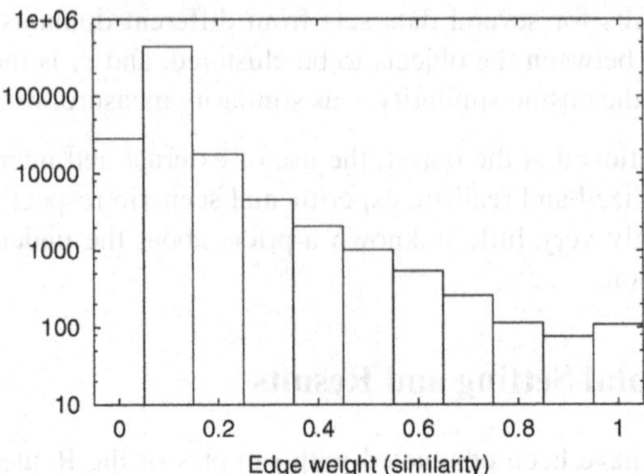

Fig. 1. Distribution of edge weights in a completely connected graph with thousand nodes; nodes correspond to documents, edge weights correspond to similarities. Observe the logarithmic scale.

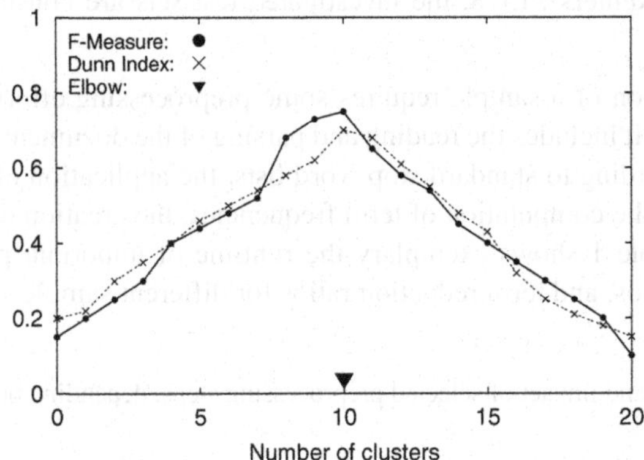

Fig. 2. Fictitious curves of a consistent k-Means and perfect clustering quality measures: If the true number of classes is 10, and if the clustering algorithm behaves in a consistent manner, then the F-Measure values will follow the shape of a wedge with the maximum at $k = 10$. The values of a perfect Dunn Index will follow the F-Measure more or less, and the perfect elbow criterion indicates $k = 10$ as the optimum cluster number.

The standard versions of Single-Link and MajorClust operate on a completely connected distance or similarity graph. It is interesting—not only for experts in the field of clustering—how these edge weights are distributed in our samples (cf. Figure 1). Of course, the creation of the graph imposes a severe performance burden, which can also be seen in the overview of Table 2.

(2) *Document Representation.* "tf" versus "$tf \cdot idf$".

The categorization performance of the three clustering algorithms is tested with both document representations.

(3) *Scenario.* "Idealized" versus "Realistic".
In the idealized scenario, the best clustering of an algorithm is determined by means of the F-Measure. In the realistic scenario, the internal measures Dunn Index and variance drop (elbow criterion) are used to evaluate the clustering quality. To get an idea of the prediction quality, the variations in the F-Measure and the Dunn Index are plotted over the variation in selected parameters of the clustering algorithms. Remember that for both measures holds that larger values indicate better categorization performance. Figures 2 exemplifies a fictitious comparison for k-Means with variation in k, the cluster number parameter.

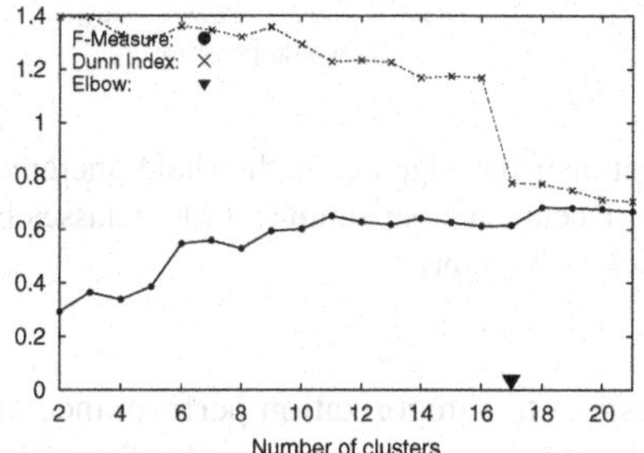

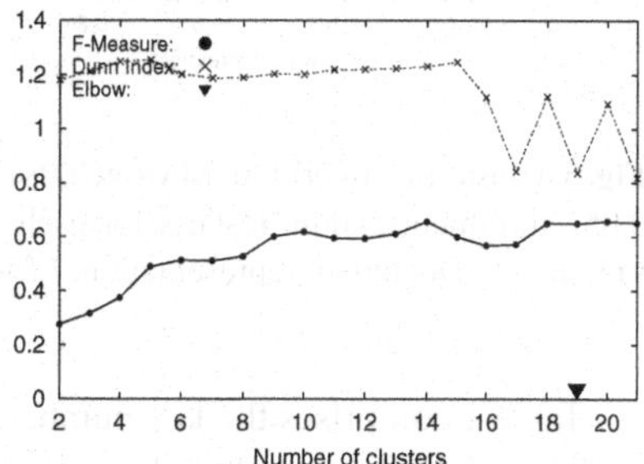

Fig. 3. Clustering algorithm: k-Means with variation in the cluster number k and three random restarts for each k. Documents per sample: 1000. Classes per sample: 10. Document representation: tf (left) and $tf \cdot idf$ (right).

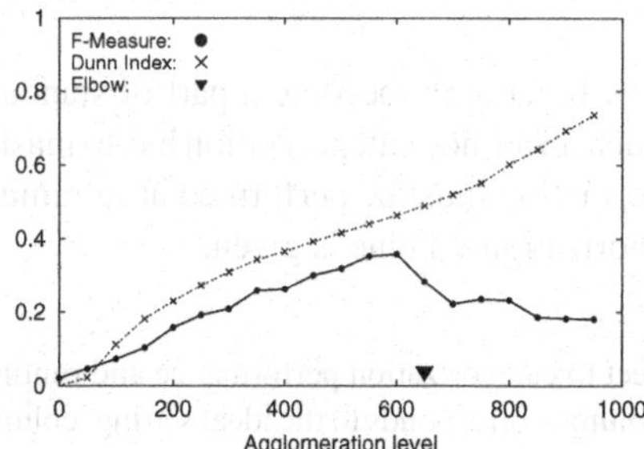

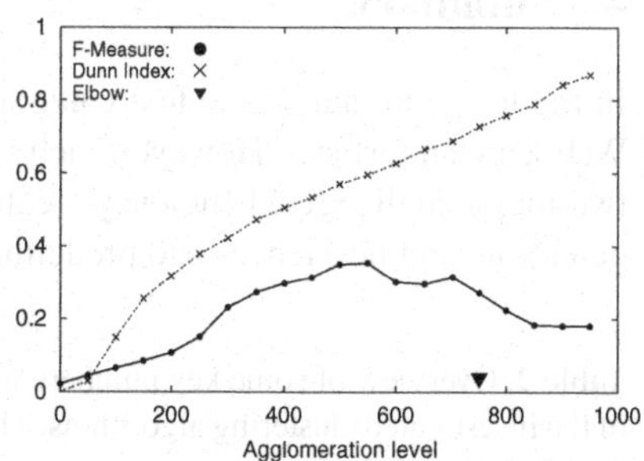

Fig. 4. Clustering algorithm: Single-Link with variation in the agglomeration level (increment 50). Documents per sample: 1000. Classes per sample: 10. Document representation: tf (left) and $tf \cdot idf$ (right).

3.1 Categorization Results

The six plots in the Figures 3-5 show the categorization performance of k-Means, Single-Link, and MajorClust (in this order). The plots on the left-hand side and right-hand side comprise the experiments with the document representation "tf" and "$tf \cdot idf$" respectively.

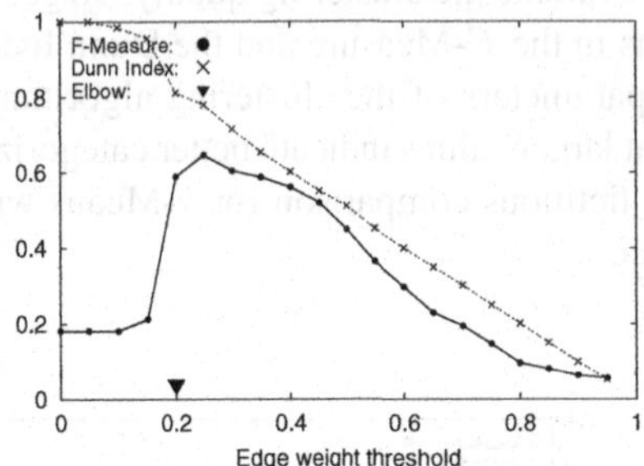

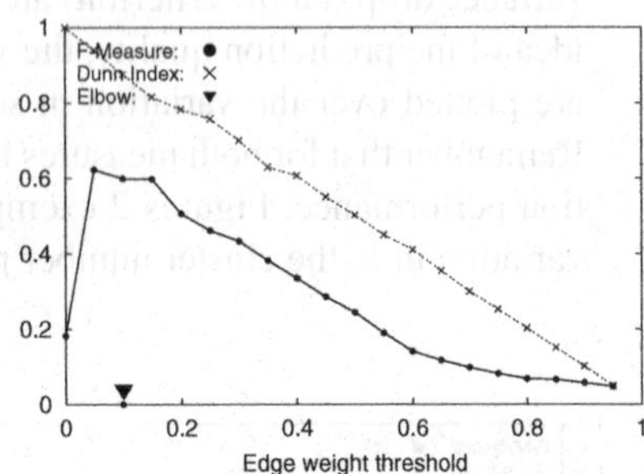

Fig. 5. Clustering algorithm: MAJORCLUST with variation in the edge weight threshold (increment 0.05) and three random restarts for each threshold. Documents per sample: 1000. Classes per sample: 10. Document representation: tf (left) and $tf \cdot idf$ (right).

Table 2 comprises the key numbers with respect to categorization performance and runtime of the investigated clustering algorithms. The experiments were performed on a Pentium IV 1.7GHz. In this connection it should be noted that our text processing and classification environment is implemented in Java—but has been developed in the face of efficiency. Among others we developed tailored classes for symbol processing, efficient vector updating, and compressed term vectors.

4 Summary

In the long run, automatic text categorization will certainly become a part of standard Web search interfaces. However, each kind of such an ad-hoc categorization has to master two major challenges: Efficiency—category formation must be performed at minimum detention, and nescience—no predefined categorization scheme is given.

Table 2. Overview of some key numbers with respect to categorization performance and runtime of the investigated clustering algorithms. The first column corresponds to the ideal setting, column 2 and 3 to the realistic setting.

	F-Measure Values			Runtime		
	Maximum	according to Dunn Index	according to elbow criterion	Preprocessing	Graph creation	Clustering
k-Means	0.68	0.29	0.61	4.29s	–	2.33s
Single-Link	0.36	0.18	0.28	4.29s	5.78s	1.58s
MAJORCLUST	0.65	0.18	0.58	4.29s	5.78s	2.38s

Clustering algorithms are considered as a technology that is capable of mastering the challenges, and this paper provides selected results of a comprehensive analysis. We compare the categorization performance of exemplar-based (k-Means), hierarchical (Single-Link), and density-based (MAJORCLUST) clustering algorithms. The main result of the experiments can be comprised as follows.

Aside from the Single-Link algorithm, the categorization performance on samples (size: 1000, classes: 10) drawn from the Reuters-21578 text database achieves acceptable values—especially in an ideal scenario, where an external cluster performance measure is given. Even in a realistic scenario, reasonable F-Measure values can be realized. Here, a crucial role comes up to the internal clustering quality measure, which can completely ruin smart clustering technology. The presented results give an example: The celebrated Dunn Index performs worse than a simple variance-based elbow criterion.

References

1. Thomas Bailey and John Cowles. Cluster Definition by the Optimization of Simple Measures. *IEEE Transactions on Pattern Analysis and Machine Intelligence*, September 1983.
2. J. C. Bezdek, W. Q. Li, Y. Attikiouzel, and M. Windham. A Geometric Approach to Cluster Validity for Normal Mixtures. *Soft Computing 1*, September 1997.
3. J. C. Bezdek and N. R. Pal. Cluster Validation with Generalized Dunn's Indices. In N. Kasabov and G. Coghill, editors, *Proceedings of the 2nd international two-stream conference on ANNES*, pages 190–193, Piscataway, NJ, 1995. IEEE Press.
4. Simon Dennis, Peter Bruza, and Robert McArthur. Web searching: A process-oriented experimental study of three interactive search paradigms. *JASIST*, 53(2):120–133, 2002.
5. M. Ester, H.-P. Kriegel, J. Sander, and X. Xu. A Density-Based Algorithm for Discovering Clusters in Large Spatial Databases with Noise. In *Proceedings of the 2nd International Conference on Knowledge Discovery and Data Mining (KDD96)*, 1996.
6. Zubrzchi] K. Florek, J. Lukaszewiez, J. Perkal, H. Steinhaus, and S. Zubrzchi. Sur la liason et la division des points d'un ensemble fini. *Colloquium Methematicum*, 2, 1951.
7. S.C. Johnson. Hierarchical clustering schemes. *Psychometrika*, 32, 1967.
8. G. Karypis, E.-H. Han, and V. Kumar. Chameleon: A hierarchical clustering algorithm using dynamic modeling. Technical Report Paper No. 432, University of Minnesota, Minneapolis, 1999.
9. Leonard Kaufman and Peter J. Rousseuw. *Finding Groups in Data.* Wiley, 1990.
10. T. Kohonen. *Self Organization and Assoziative Memory.* Springer, 1990.
11. Gerald Kowalsky. *Information Retrieval Systems—Theory and Implementation.* Kluwer Academic, 1997.
12. Bjornar Larsen and Chinatsu Aone. Fast and Effective Text Mining Using Linear-time Document Clustering. In *Proceedings of the KDD-99 Workshop San Diego USA*, San Diego, CA, USA, 1999.
13. Thomas Lengauer. *Combinatorical algorithms for integrated circuit layout.* Applicable Theory in Computer Science. Teubner-Wiley, 1990.
14. David D. Lewis. Reuters-21578 Text Categorization Test Collection. `http://www.research.att.com/~lewis`, 1994.
15. J. B. MacQueen. Some Methods for Classification and Analysis of Multivariate Observations. In *Proceedings of the Fifth Berkeley Symposium on Mathematical Statistics and Probability*, pages 281–297, 1967.
16. M.F. Porter. An algorithm for suffix stripping. *Program*, 14(3):130–137, 1980.

17. C. J. van Rijsbergen. *Information Retrieval.* Buttersworth, London, 1979.
18. Tom Roxborough and Arunabha. Graph Clustering using Multiway Ratio Cut. In Stephen North, editor, *Graph Drawing*, Lecture Notes in Computer Science, Springer, 1996.
19. Reinhard Sablowski and Arne Frick. Automatic Graph Clustering. In Stephan North, editor, *Graph Drawing*, Lecture Notes in Computer Science, Springer, 1996.
20. G. Salton. *Automatic Text Processing: The Transformation, Analysis and Retrieval of Information by Computer.* Addison-Wesley, 1988.
21. P.H.A. Sneath. The application of computers to taxonomy. *J. Gen. Microbiol.*, 17, 1957.
22. Benno Stein and Oliver Niggemann. *25. Workshop on Graph Theory*, chapter On the Nature of Structure and its Identification. Lecture Notes on Computer Science, LNCS. Springer, Ascona, Italy, July 1999.
23. Zhenyu Wu and Richard Leahy. An optimal graph theoretic approach to data clustering: Theory and its application to image segmentation. *IEEE Transactions on Pattern Analysis and Machine Intelligence*, November 1993.
24. J. T. Yan and P. Y. Hsiao. A fuzzy clustering algorithm for graph bisection. *Information Processing Letters*, 52, 1994.

An Agent Based Approach to Finding Expertise

Richard Crowder, Gareth Hughes, and Wendy Hall

IAM Group
Department of Electronics and Computer Science
University of Southampton
Southampton
{rmc, gvh, wh}@ecs.soton.ac.uk

Abstract. In many organisations people need to locate colleagues with knowledge and information to resolve a problem. Computer based systems that assist users with finding such expertise are increasingly important to organizations and scientific communities. In this paper we discuss the development of an agent based expertise finder (EF) suitable for use within an academic research environment. A key feature of this work is that the EF returns both recommended contacts and supporting documentation. The EF bases its results on information held within the organisation, for example publications, human resource records and not on CVs or user maintained records. The recommendations are presented to the user with due regard to the social context, and are supported by the documents used to make the recommendation. The technology used allows the development of distributed, interchangeable agents that use real time data to find expertise. It is our intention to use this approach within manufacturing and other knowledge intensive organisations.

1 Introduction

In the course of most activities, people face problems that they cannot solve alone. Their natural response is to study past experiences and re-use previously acquired knowledge, either from their own experiences or from resources within their organisation. Goa et al, [7] estimated that 90% of industrial design activity is based on variant design, while in a redesign activity 70% of the information is re-used from previous solutions [9]. For many problems, access to documentation through hypermedia or similar systems may give adequate solutions [6]. However to solve many problems people need to have specific expertise, that will allow the problem to be resolved. In this paper, the term expertise assumes the embodiment of knowledge and skills within individuals. This definition distinguishes expertise from an expert. An individual may have different levels of expertise about different topics. Expertise can be topical or procedural and is arranged and valued within the organisation. In some cases expertise can be captured from a person and used to populate a database. This works very well when the problem is restricted to a very specific domain, for example robot maintenance, [2]. However for many problems the required expertise can only be accessed through a social network.

D. Karagiannis and U. Reimer (Eds.): PAKM 2002, LNAI 2569, pp. 179–188, 2002.

To solve a specific problem people want to quickly find other people with the required expertise. In many organisations, key personnel (managers, senior employees, information concierges [10]) will facilitate the contacts. Recommender systems are one approach to automate this process, by augmenting and assisting the natural expertise-locating behavior within an organisation. A recommender system that suggests people who have some expertise with a problem holds the promise to provide, in a small way, a service similar to these key personnel. Expertise recommender systems can also reduce the load on people in these roles and provide alternative recommendations when these people are unavailable.

In the recommendations provided by the expertise finder (EF), trust is important, this can be achieved by showing why people were not recommended or why a document was not considered so important. A document might seem relevant based on a full text search but is actually twenty years old, an important factor in some situations, but not in others. The provision of evidence for its decisions in the form of a list of documents and other data is considered a key EF output. This approach contrasts with a number of reported systems where web based information is used to provide the recommendation, [3, 4, 5]. Answer Garden 2 [1] has an explicit expertise-location engine and provided computer-mediated communications mechanisms to find others with a range of expertise, though the mechanisms were not very elaborate. A different approach was taken by McDonnald [10] who used software developed by employees to identify their expertise in various aspects of software development.

2 Problem Definition and Context

When attempting to find an answer to a problem people will tend to use the social network around them. It is natural to first ask people nearby if they know the answer or if they can recommend someone else who may know the answer. Thus a chain of connections are made utilising the experienced members of an organisation. As people are now being moved around organisations at a faster rate and organisations are becoming increasingly distributed this model starts to fail. There may be no social connection between specially separated groups even though they work on similar problems. Our system attempts to alleviate this by using the company's own resources to recommend people to contact. It does not replace the social network but attempts to speed up the connection making process.

The work reported in this paper presents details of an Expertise Finder system, which is summarised in Fig. 1. The problem that is being addressed is summarised in Fig. 1(a), how does a person located in Site A, locate the best expertise to solve a specific problem? The person's local network will only extend to within the site, and therefore expertise in other sites can not accessed. It should be remembered that sites can share common problems, but not necessarily be easily accessible to each other. For example within the academic community, a question on robotics could easily draw on expertise from either a Department of Mechanical Engineering or a Department of Cognitive Physiology. While the sites may not form a cohesive social network, they do share common sets of resources, including e-mail, phone books, publication and report repositories, Fig. 1(b). In our approach to EF systems, these information repositories are used to identify the required expert, Fig 1(c).

3 How Do We Identify an Expert?

In an academic organisation an expert will be the person who has the most publications, largest number of grants, and extensive experience either with the current or similar organisation. In addition they will tend to hold senior posts. These people are subject experts not skills experts.

However when a person wishes to contact an expert, there are additional social factors that need to be taken into account. Without these factors, the single expert will be swamped with queries for everyone ranging from Undergraduates to Vice-Chancellors. The appropriate person depends on the query and the users requirements, typically the peer-to-peer approach is considered best in the first instance, however the person requiring the expertise needs to be free to make a valued judgement as whom to approach. It is for this reason we make available all the sources used for the recommendation available for review.

As discussed by McDonald [11] the details matter in successful expertise location. The heuristics used to select the expert are bound to the organisational environment. Systems that augment expertise locating must be capable of handling large number of details that depend on the specific context and problem.

4 Implementation of the Expertise Finder

The Expertise Finder system is designed to mimic the reality of an organisation in terms of its social structures and information infrastructure. The implementation of the Expertise Finder consists of a number of DIM (Distributed Information Management) Agents operating within SoFAR (Southampton Framework for Agent Research) [12]. SoFAR was developed at the University of Southampton as an agent framework designed to address the problems of distributed information management. On each occasion that the EF system is deployed the sources of data available to be used and their structures will be different. There will be commonalities due to the use of standards such as being able to access a database using standard query language or the use of protocols such as LDAP. There will still be subtle differences that require the customisation of the system. Therefore it is apparent that the high level steps that any system should take to identify an expert will be unique on each occasion.

In order to communicate with each other agents use a shared understanding of a domain called an ontology. Ontologies are a conceptualisation of a domain into a form which can be understood both by humans and computers. A well known definition is an ontology is an explicit specification of a conceptualisation. [8]. Ontologies provide a mechanism to allow communication and interaction about a real world domain. They remove ambiguity from language through careful

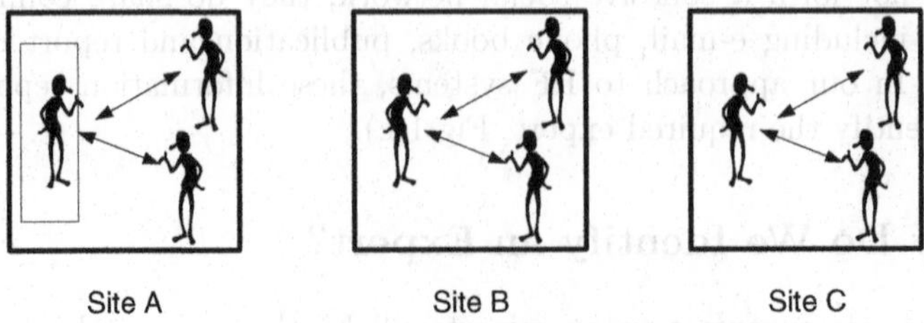

(a) Local social network independent of each other

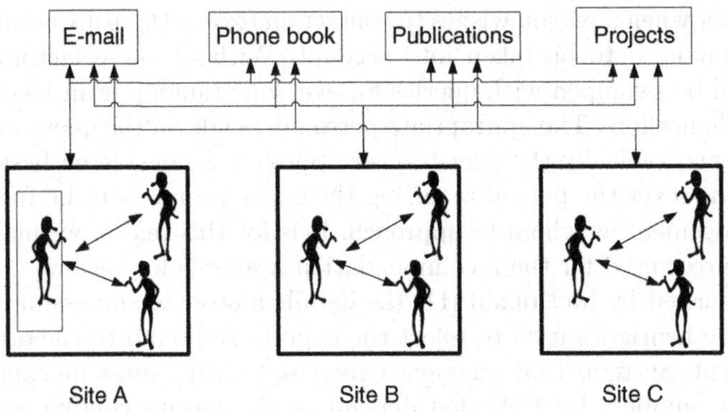

(b) Local groups are known to organisation wide electronic resources

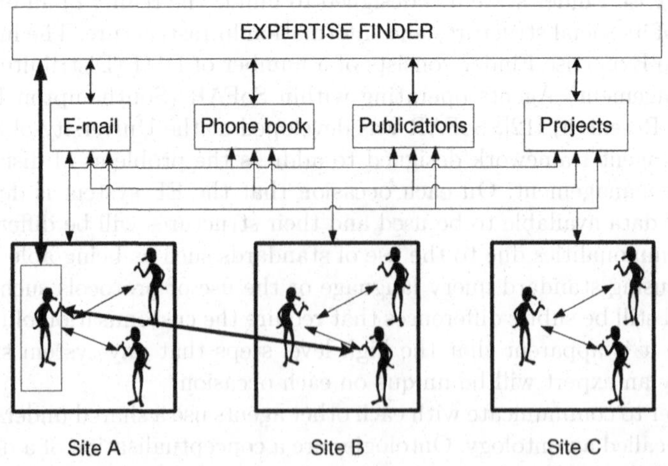

(c) Expertise Finder finds people-to-people links regardless of location

Fig. 1. Overview of the Expertise Finder

design. Pragmatically it allows us to concentrate on high level concepts rather than spend time on the implementation details such as communications and data representation. It therefore follows that the design of the ontology is crucial to the project and careful work is required to correctly understand and map the real world situation into the ontological vocabulary. Further technical details of how ontologies are implemented and used in the SoFAR framework can be found in [12]. The ontologies used in this work were designed previously within the IAM group but extended for this application. They represent the activities and people in our research group. A detailed explanation of their design and implementation can be found in [13].

The EF system consists of a main agent, the EF Agent, which uses a set of simpler `Source Agents` in some algorithm to determine a list of people and documents to recommend to a user. The EF agent builds an answer as XML before transforming that to HTML for delivery to the user via the Web server agent. The use of XML allows the EF Agent to be reused in other systems and its results transformed as required. Figure 2 shows the overall architecture of the system. In it we show all of the agents we have at our disposal but here we concentrate on the core interactions between those outlined in solid.

Source Agents (the Academic Publications and Directory Services agents) are designed to represent sources of information and data within the organisation. These can range from the simple, an agent that understands the data stored in the internal phone book, to more complex knowledge such as an agent interface to a publications database. In the diagram we include examples of some of the ontological predicates the agents support. For instance the Directory Services agent can answer queries about the location of people or return all of the people with a certain phone number.

The EF application is based on a previous agent application, the Dynamic CV [13]. This application used the notion of query recipes to dynamically construct a Curriculum Vitae or other page about a person. For instance for the CV query, a general information page about a person, it would find and use agents to obtain telephone number, office location, and email address. The answers were combined into a Web page in which links to new queries were automatically added and thus a user could navigate around the information space. Figure 3 shows the result of a CV query.

The key weakness of the Dynamic CV application was that the main agent would gather information from Source Agents following the instructions of a query template. It would extract the data and place it onto the Web page with no understanding of the results. The EF Agent is a total redesign of this system with the express intention of not only supporting the types of query performed by Dynamic CV but also to perform complex interactions with Source Agents in order to build towards a final answer. In order to do this the Source Agents have been radically improved and the services they provide have been expanded considerably.

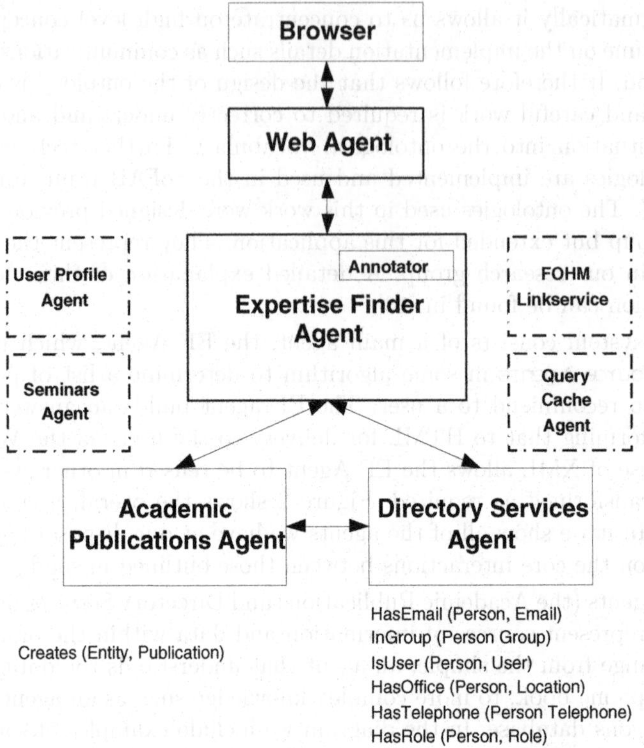

Fig. 2. Expertise Finder architecture. Typical predicates used are given below the respective agents

5 Running the System

The current application of the EF is used to find people using the scientific publication repository within the authors' Department. The goal being to aid people to find experts on a topic amongst the people in the Department. A user enters a query on a research subject into a Web search page. This query is given to the EF Agent by the Web Agent. The EF Agent first asks the Publications Agent to find publications using the search terms. The Publications Agent takes the query terms from the Predicate and uses them to form an SQL query. The query is run on the department publications database. The publication database lists authors by a list of full names and a corresponding parallel list of full email addresses. Hence some understanding of this and some data translation must be performed. The Publications Agent uses the Directory Services to help identify authors. It then uses the results of the query to build new Creates Predicates and return them to the EF Agent. The EF Agent will maintain a record of their details, saving duplication of queries, and begin to count the number of times the

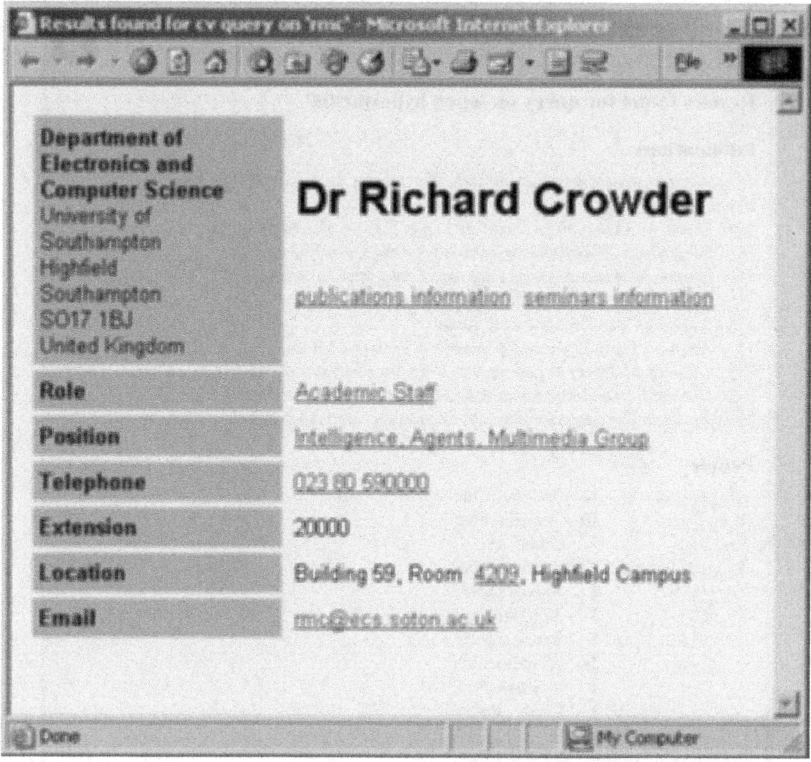

Fig. 3. The Dynamic CV agent system found agents to fill in query templates. There was no attempt to understand or use the information that is returned.

person appears in the returned publications. The EF Agent will also maintain a list of people not identified.

The final results page is made up of the returned publications, the list of found authors with a count of their occurrences and their status within the department. The list of unknown authors is also returned to allow users to decide for themselves the usefulness of such information. In the context of this application this list consists of people who have left the department or external collaborators, and are less useful to the user.

6 Discussion

The results page, Fig 4, gives a list of papers followed by a list of people together with the number of times that person's name appears in the publications list, together with their status within the department. For brevity the results have been condensed in the illustration. The system also lists names that could not be matched by the Directory Services agent so the user understands more about the reasoning for the final answer.

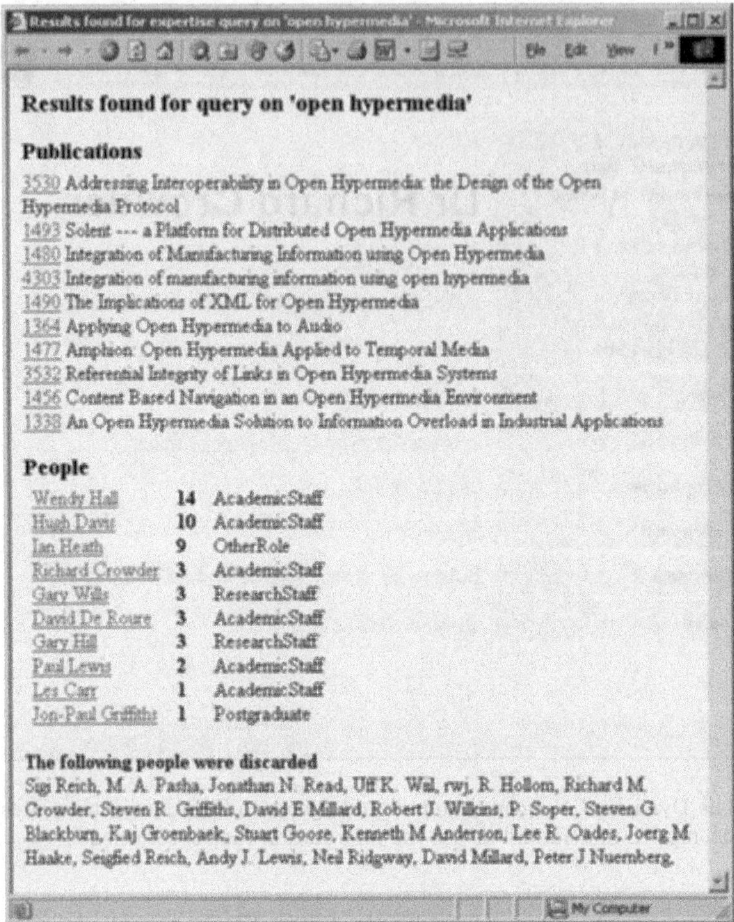

Fig. 4. The results of the prototype EF, the first ten publications used to rank the experts are given unranked at the top of the page.

Our prototype procedure to find an expert is simple but effective and the results show that it gives a fair indication of who would be a good person to contact. The resultant list of experts relates well to our knowledge of the group and individuals' profiles. The system invariably finds more senior members of staff and less of the PhD students and researchers because they tend to leave after a shorter period of time and have fewer publications. It is quite likely that the contacted person would be able to quickly point the enquirer to a specialist or less senior member of staff to help with the answer. However an important social connection has been made regardless of the location of the member of staff. If the EF system provides just that one connection saving valuable time then it has been useful. The documents returned in this example are not presented with any great intelligence or ranking and the search is crude but effective. The agent approach means that a new query method or publications database can be added without disturbing the rest of the system. Currently the system does not take account of the profile of the user making the query. However we have the majority of the components required to build a user profile agent in order to add this factor into the equation.

The procedure involved in this system seems to be simple at first glance but the complexities of implementation have taught us many lessons. The agents are not as independent of each other as was planned. The complex interactions between the source agents and the large amounts of error checking they need to do are a classic example of writing systems to deal with real life data. Also if one of the underlying data sources changed significantly then it may not be able to support some part of the ontology and hence the EF Agent will need to be modified. This demonstrates that where complex queries and interactions between component systems are required there will be more brittleness in the design. This applies equally to an agent based system as it does to one based on some other black box design such as RMI or Web Services.

7 Conclusion

Significant progress has been made in the development of our Expert Finder and its associated agents. The use of peer reviewed document and not an individual's own documentation gives our approach to EF results in a high degree of trust to the recommendations. We are currently considering the use of this system within industry, using technical reports and similar controlled documentation. By the use of corporate data resource we will maximise trust, and minimise possible confidentiality issues. The latter issue will be address by using only information supplied to the organisation as part of a persons employment. We are proposing to undertake the development of additional agents to refine the system including integrating other information sources for example, skills databases and captured design rational, and we will also undertake further evaluation using exemplar information resources.

References

1. M. Ackerman and D. McDonald. Answer garden 2: Merging organisational memory with collaberative help. In *Proceedings of ACM 1998 Conference on Computer Supported Cooperative Work, CSCW 96*, pages 97–105. ACM, New York, 1996.
2. E. Auriol, R. M. Crowder, R. J. McKendrick, R. Rowe, and T. Knudsen. Integrating case-based reasoning and hypermedia documentation: An application for the diagnosis of a welding robot at Odense steel shipyard. In *Proceeding of the International Conference on Case-Based Reasoning (ICCBR'99)*. 1999.
3. I. Becerra-Fernandez. The role of artificial intelligence technologies in the implementation of people-finder knowledge management systems. In *Proceedings of the 2000 American Association for Artificial Intelligence Spring Workshop*. AAAI, March 2000.

4. K. Bollacker, S. Lawrence-S, and C. Giles. Citeseer: an autonomous web agent for automatic retrieval and identification of interesting publications. In K. Sycara and M. Wooldridge, editors, *Proceedings of the Second International Conference on Autonomous Agents*, pages 116–23. ACM, 1998.
5. P. Chandrasekaran and A. Joshi. An expertise recommender using web mining. In *Proceedings of AAAI 14th Annual International Florida Artificial Intelligence Research Symposium.* 2001.
6. R. Crowder, G. Wills, I. Heath, and W. Hall. Hypermedia information management: A new paradigm. In *3rd International Conference on Managing Innovation in Manufacture*, pages 329–34, University of Nottingham, 1998.
7. Y. Goa, I. Zeid, and T. Bardez. Charcteristics of an effective design plan to support re-use in case-based mechanical design. *Knowledge based systems*, 10:337–50, 1998.
8. Thomas R. Gruber. Toward principles for the design of ontologies used for knowledge sharing. Technical Report KSL-93-04, Knowledge Systems Laboratory, Stanford University, August 1993.
9. D. Khadilkar and L. Stauffer. An experimental evaluation of design information reuse during conceptual design. *Journal of Engineering Design*, 7(4):331–9, 1996.
10. D. McDonald and M. Ackerman. Just talk to me: a field study of expertise location. In *Proceedings of ACM 1998 Conference on Computer Supported Cooperative Work, CSCW 98*, pages 315–24. ACM, New York, 1998.
11. D. McDonald and M. Ackerman. Expertise recommender: a flexible recommendation system and architecture. In *ACM 2000 Conference on Computer Supported Cooperative Work*, pages 231–40. ACM, New York, December 2000.
12. L. Moreau, N. Gibbins, D. DeRoure, S. El-Beltagy, W. Hall, G. Hughes, D. Joyce, S. Kim, D. Michaelides, D. Millard, S. Reich, R. Tansley, and M. Weal. SoFAR with DIM agents: An agent framework for distributed information management. In *Proceedings of PAAM00.* Manchester UK, 2000.
13. M. Weal, G. Hughes, D. Millard, and L. Moreau. Open hypermedia as a navigational interface to ontological information. In H. Davis, Y Douglas, and D Durand, editors, *Proceedings of Hypertext'01*, pages 227–36. ACM, 2001.

OntoWeb – A Semantic Web Community Portal

Peter Spyns[2], Daniel Oberle[1], Raphael Volz[1,3], Jijuan Zheng[2], Mustafa Jarrar[2], York Sure[1], Rudi Studer[1,3], and Robert Meersman[2]

[1] Institute AIFB, University of Karlsruhe, D-76128 Karlsruhe, Germany
lastname@aifb.uni-karlsruhe.de

[2] STAR Lab, Vrije Universiteit Brussels,
Pleinlaan 2 Gebouw G-10, B-1050 Brussel
first.lastname@vub.ac.be

[3] FZI – Research Center for Information Technologies
Haid-und-Neu-Strasse 10-14, D-76131 Karlsruhe, Germany
lastname@fzi.de

Abstract. This paper describes a semantic portal through which knowledge can be gathered, stored, secured and accessed by members of a certain community. In particular, this portal takes into account companies and research institutes participating in the E.U. funded thematic network called OntoWeb. Ontology-based annotation of information is a prerequisite in order to offer the possibility of knowledge retrieval and extraction. The usage of well-defined semantics allows for the knowledge exchange between different OntoWeb community members. Thus, members are able to publish annotated information on the web, which is then crawled by a syndicator and stored in the portal's knowledge base. The backbone of the portal architecture consists of a knowledge base in which the ontology and the instances are stored and maintained. In addition, ontology-boosted query mechanisms and presentation facilities are provided.

1 Introduction

Although an ubiquitous and overwhelming amount of information is available at a snap of one's fingers, knowledge is not so easily retrievable. For knowledge is the result of an information processing activity. Knowledge has become a valuable asset for companies and institutions (or so-called communities in general) to such a degree that specific mechanisms have been put into place for the provision of high quality knowledge. Storing and aggregating knowledge may be one important aspect; accessing and finding appropriate knowledge is just as important. After all, how can one benefit from the knowledge available if one cannot find and retrieve it? In this paper, work in progress on a semantic portal[1] is described through which knowledge can be gathered, stored, secured and accessed by members of a certain community (c.q. companies and research institutes working in the field of the Semantic Web and participating in the E.U. funded thematic network called OntoWeb [4]). It is an open community, i.e. new members can join at any time. The positive effects of the existence of such a portal are multiple. Only the most

[1] The portal with its current test content can be accessed on http://ontoweb.aifb.uni-karlsruhe.de or http://starpc14.vub.ac.be:8000/OntoWeb/Browse/index.html.

D. Karagiannis and U. Reimer (Eds.): PAKM 2002, LNAI 2569, pp. 189–200, 2002.

important ones will be mentioned. At a first stage, the portal serves as an inventory of knowledge available in the community. In the case of an Internet portal, knowledge has been made available outside of the organization of the original producer or owner. E.g., members of the community get a good overview of the skills and profiles of the various community members. In the case of an intranet, it may stimulate the communication between departments of a same company and support the local (technology) innovation management process.

Turning information into knowledge that suits the above mentioned situation, requires a shared conceptualization of the domain in question. In the present OntoWeb case, the domain spans a conceptualization of the OntoWeb organization (e.g., companies, research institutions, special interest groups etc.), of various kinds of documents (e.g., meeting minutes, deliverables, papers etc.), of events and their organizations (e.g., conferences, workshops, internal meetings etc.), of scientific results and material (e.g., cases, programs, etc.), and so forth. A formal version of such a shared conceptualization is commonly called an ontology [15]. When relating specific terms to concepts, a controlled vocabulary or some other common terminological framework can be created.

Ontology-based annotation of the community information is a prerequisite in order to offer the possibility of knowledge retrieval and extraction (also known as conceptual or intelligent search — cf. [12] as an example). The usage of well-defined semantics allows for the knowledge exchange between different OntoWeb community members. Members can publish annotated information on the web, which is then crawled by a syndicator and stored in the portal knowledge base.

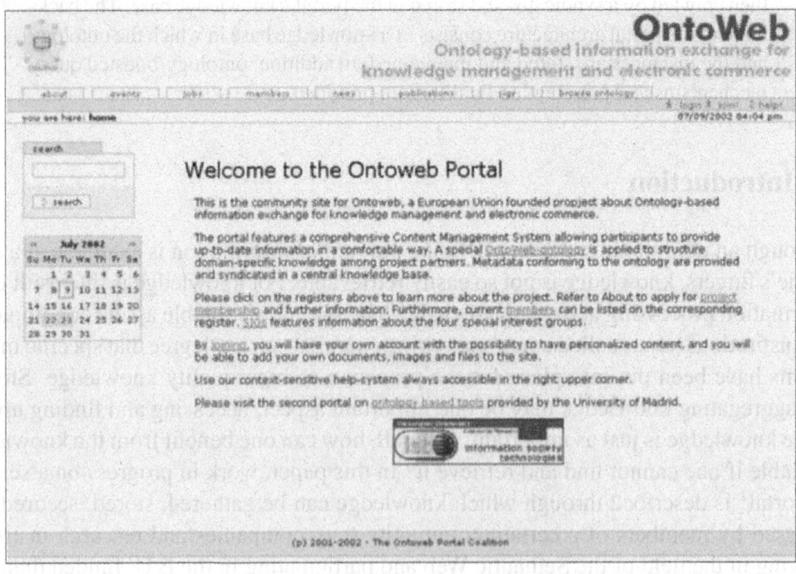

Fig. 1. www.ontoweb.org - the OntoWeb portal

The paper is structured as follows: In section 2, we describe how information is semantically annotated on-site, crawled and subsequently aggregated (or syndicated) into a common database (cf. 2.1). An alternative is that the community members upload annotated information themselves. Therefore, we define a model for a publication workflow in subsection 2.2 and discuss the integration in the portal in 3. Section 3 deals with how the content (or community knowledge) can be accessed. By pointing and clicking, a user can browse the concepts of the ontology and the related instances (cf. subsection 3.1). He/She can enter one or more search terms in a query box (cf. subsection 3.2) or a form (cf. subsection 3.2). A short overview of related work is presented in section 4 before the future work on the OntoWeb semantic portal is sketched in section 5. Finally, section 6 contains some concluding remarks.

2 Content Provision

Basically, there are two ways of providing content to the OntoWeb portal. First, there is the syndication mechanism, automatically gathering metadata from participating sites. Second, the portal allows for content provision itself. Both possibilities are discussed in subsections 2.1 and 2.2, respectively.

2.1 Content Syndication

The portal allows centralized access to distributed information that has been provided by participants on their own sites. To facilitate this, participants can enrich resources located outside of the portal with metadata according to the shared OntoWeb ontology. This annotation process can be supported semi-automatically by the Ontomat Annotizer tool [10] for instance.

As depicted in Figure 2, syndicating information from participants is done by replicating their metadata. The information finds its way in the so-called DOGMA Server [11] which exploits a relational DBMS for storing and can be queried by users (cf. section 3 for a detailed discussion). Within the portal, authenticated users may generate content objects on their behalf (cf. subsection 2.2). As we use Zope[2] as underlying technology, such objects are stored in its respective database (so-called ZODB). Besides, metadata, both conforming to Dublin Core [17] as well as to the Ontoweb ontology, are generated for all the portal's objects. This can be achieved easily as all metadata are stored within Zope's own database. When adding new content to the portal, users have the possibility to supply metadata accordingly.

2.2 Content Objects

We acknowledge the fact that some members might not be able to publish data on the web on their own due to corporate restrictions or other reasons. Therefore OntoWeb participants' staff members are provided with a personal space to create and manage content for the portal. To facilitate this, the portal includes a fully-fledged content management system. Additionally, all content created within the portal is automatically associated with the predefined OntoWeb design to achieve an integrated visual experience with a consistent appearance. In the personal space people can provide the following types of content:

[2] cf. http://www.zope.org

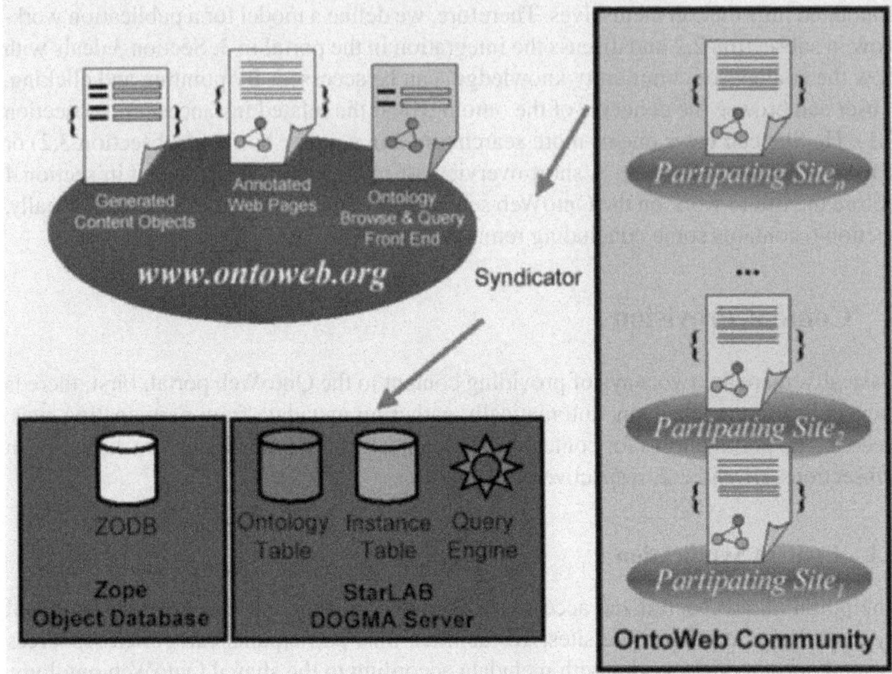

Fig. 2. Content Syndication

- HTML-documents
- arbitrary files and folders
- selected predefined content types based on ontological concepts: Publications, News, Events, Scientific Events, Jobs, etc.

If a member chooses to create new content based on the predefined content types, appropriate metadata is automatically generated. Second, all content is associated with standard Dublin Core metadata to keep track of publishing information such as date of creation, last modification, authorship and subject classification.

Process Model for Publishing Workflows. As mentioned in section 1, OntoWeb is an open community posing additional constraints since data that is (re)published through the portal could be provided by arbitrary people. In order to guarantee quality of data in such an environment, an additional model regulating the publishing process is required, which prevents foreseeable misuses. To support this requirement the established portal architecture was extended with a workflow component which regulates the publishing process. In the following we will begin with introducing the concept of a publishing workflow in general. Afterwards we explain how we instantiated this generic component in OntoWeb.

A publishing workflow is the series of interactions that should happen to complete the task of publishing data. Business organizations have many kinds of workflow. Our notion of workflow is centered around tasks. Workflows consist of several tasks and several transitions between these tasks. Additionally, workflows have the following characteristics: (i) they might involve several people, (ii) they might take a long time, (iii) they vary significantly in organizations and in the computer applications supporting these organizations respectively, (iv) sometimes information must be kept across states, and last but not least, (v) the communication between people must be supported in order to facilitate decision making. Thus, a workflow component must be customizable. It must support the assignment of tasks to (possibly multiple) individual users. In our architecture these users are grouped into roles. Tasks are represented within a workflow as a set of transitions which cause state changes. Each object in the system is assigned a state, which corresponds to the current position within the workflow and can be used to determine the possible transitions that can validly be applied to the object. This state is persistent supporting the second characteristic mentioned above. Due to the individuality of workflows within organizations and applications we propose a generic component that supports the creation and customization of several workflows. In fact, each concept in the ontology, which – as you might recall – is used to capture structured data within a portal, can be assigned a different workflow with different states, transitions and task assignments. As mentioned above, sometimes data is required to be kept across states[3]. To model this behavior, the state machine underlying our workflow model needs to keep information that "remembers" the past veto. Thus, variables are attached to objects and used to provide persistent information that transcends states. Within our approach, variables also serve the purpose of establishing a simple form of communication between the involved parties. Thus, each transition can attach comments to support the decision made by future actors. Also metadata like the time and initiator of a transition is kept within the system.

Workflows in OntoWeb. Figure 3 depicts the default workflow within OntoWeb. There are three states: private, pending, and published. In the private state the respective object is only visible to the user himself, the pending state makes it visible to reviewers. In the published state, a given object is visible to all (possibly anonymous) users of the portal. If a user creates a new object[4], it is in private state. If the user has either a reviewer or a manager role the published state is immediately available through the publish transition. For normal users such a transition is not available. Instead, the object can only be sent for a review leading to the pending state. In the pending state either managers or reviewers can force the transition into the published state (by applying the transition "publish") or retract the object leading back to the private state. The reject transition deletes the object completely. When an object is in the private state, only the user who created it and users with manager roles can view and change it. Once an object is in published state, the modification by the user who created it resets the object into pending state,

[3] For example, envision the process of passing bills in legislature, a bill might be allowed to be revised and resubmitted once it is vetoed, but only if it has been vetoed once. If it is vetoed a second time, it is rejected forever.

[4] Currently only within the portal, the content syndicated from other OntoWeb member web sites and within the databases is "trusted". We assume that this kind of data already went through some kind of review.

thus the modification must be reviewed again. This does not apply to modifications by site managers.

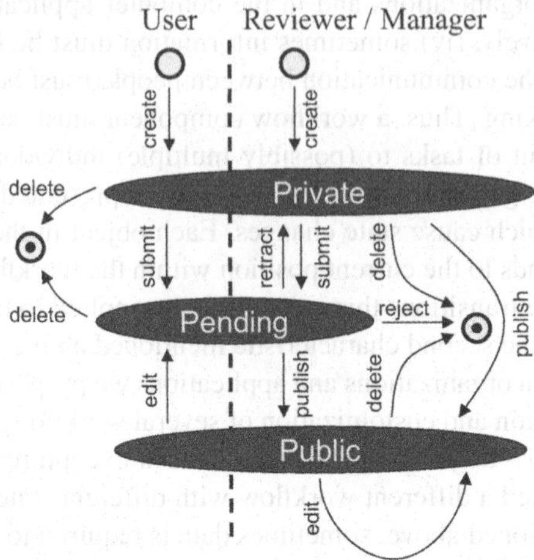

Fig. 3. OntoWeb Publishing workflow

3 Content Accessing

The hypothesis is that using an ontology results in an improved query refinement compared with a conventional keyword-based search. A (partial) validation of this hypothesis can be found in [9]. The browse and query facility has been developed as a highly generic system that offers exploration of the available information at the conceptual level. The semantic relationships are exploited to navigate through the application domain. As it concerns a shared "mental map", users are able to locate and find the desired information more rapidly. The main distinctions made when presenting the information to a user are between the sub- and superconcepts and the literal and non-literal properties of the different concepts. Currently, the user interface is work in progress.

3.1 Browsing

When browsing the semantic portal one can distinguish between browsing instances or instance details. In the case of browsing instance overviews, the portal displays collections of instances according to the user's selection. When viewing instance details, the user is presented with detailed information on a particular instance. Links to related instances are grouped according to the community ontology.

Instance overview. The hierarchical organization of the different concepts in the ontology is represented by a dynamic tree (see Figure 4). A user can view instances belonging to a concept from the tree (in the left pane) by expanding the tree nodes and clicking the concept of interest. The instances of this concept will then be displayed (in the right pane). By moving up and down the concept tree, a user can generalize or specialize instances. By clicking on a subtype (of the tree or in the conceptual path), the query precision should improve. This is because the instances of the supertype (i.e. the concept originally selected), including all the instances of its subtypes that do not belong to the subtype newly selected, are excluded from the result. Generalization (i.e. moving up one level in the hierarchy or clicking on the supertype displayed) on the other hand broadens the scope of the query, exploiting the concept hierarchy to expand the query to all instances of the siblings (and their subtypes) of the concept originally of interest to the user (cf. also [2]).

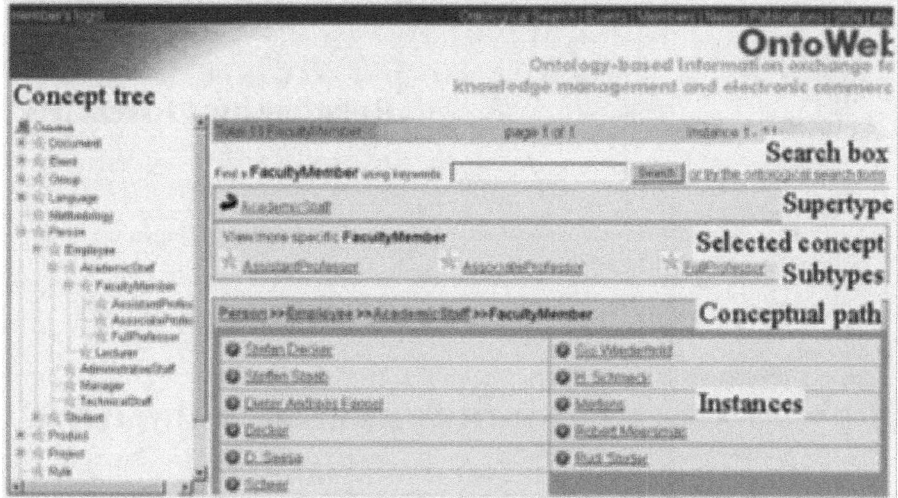

Fig. 4. Instance overview

Instance details. When viewing the detailed information for a particular instance, a distinction is made between literal and non-literal properties of concepts. While the literal properties or attributes provide a user with detailed information, the non-literal properties or relationships with other concepts (and their instances) are shown as hyperlinks, enabling a user to jump to instances of related concepts. Attributes are displayed at the top of the page. These concern e.g., in the case of a person, the name, telephone number and email. . . All the relevant conceptual relationships are displayed in the lower part of the page (with an overview in the middle). They point to instances of related concepts presented at the bottom of the page that are grouped by relationship (cf. Figure 5).

3.2 Querying

Next to the browsing of the ontology and related instances, a user may opt at any moment to enter one or more search terms. This can be considered as a conceptually driven form of interactive query refinement.

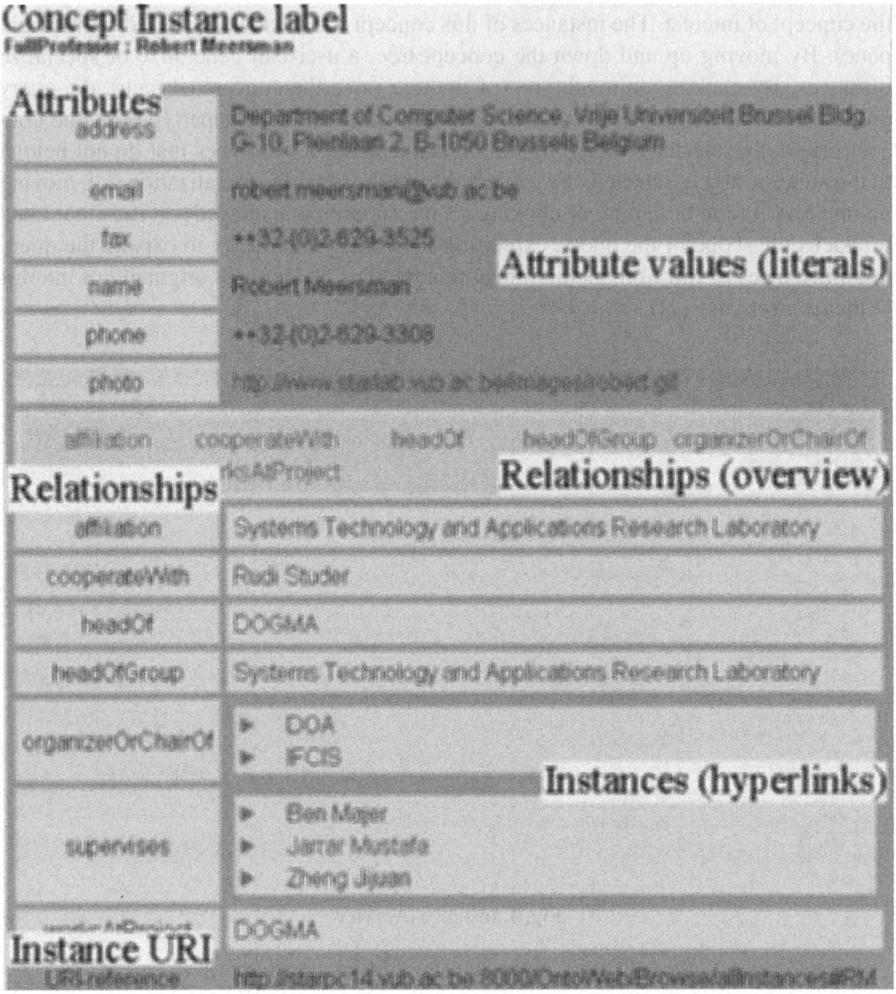

Fig. 5. Instance details

Term based. The portal offers a keyword based global search. The instances retrieved are presented to the user grouped by links pointing to the instance details page. The concept tree and conceptual path pane are dynamically adapted to the query results. When a user enters multiple keywords, the engine searches for paths between instances containing the different keywords and, if found, presents these paths to the user (cf. Figure 6). When a query is executed from an instance overview page, the results only include instances of the previously selected concept (and its subtypes).

Template based. The form-based search allows for the construction of query paths across the ontology. A user is presented with a search form containing text boxes in

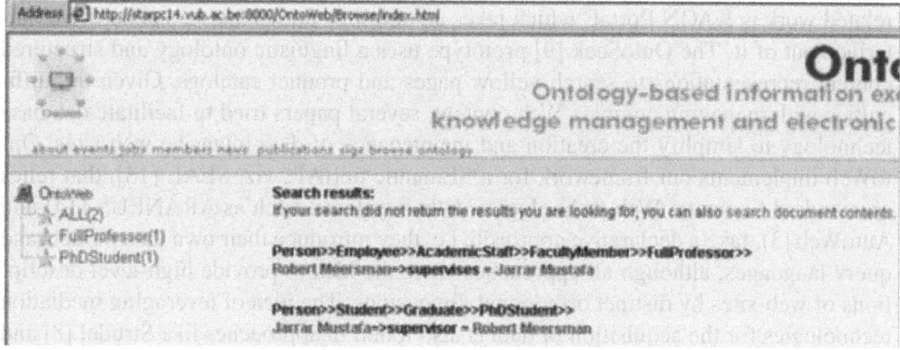

Fig. 6. Keyword based semantic search results

which attribute values can be specified. Buttons labelled with a concept give access to other forms that can be used to specify related instances. For each node in the path, a user can add restrictions on the property values. The labels for the input boxes and the buttons are dynamically adapted (cf. Figure 7). They represent the shared definition of the current concept (shown on the titlebar).

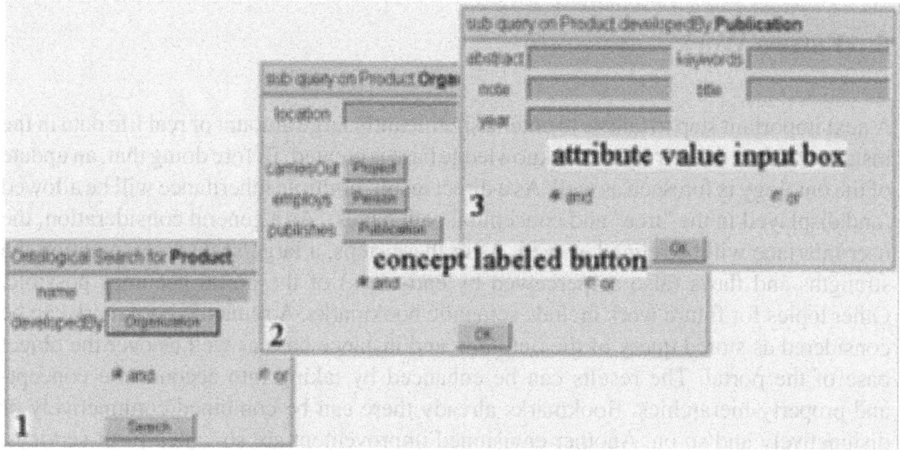

Fig. 7. Semantic query form

4 Related Work

Using an ontology to support the access of content has been discussed before. E.g., the so-called Yahoo-a-lizer [6] transforms a knowledge base into a set of XML pages that are structured like the term hierarchy of Yahoo. These XML-files are translated via an XSL-stylesheet into ordinary HTML. Within Ontobroker-based web portals [5], a Hyperbolic View Applet allows for graphical access to an ontology and its knowledge base. Another related work is KAON Portal[5] which takes an ontology and creates a standard Web interface out of it. The OntoSeek [9] prototype uses a linguistic ontology and structured content representations to search yellow pages and product catalogs. Given the difficulties with managing complex Web content, several papers tried to facilitate database technology to simplify the creation and maintenance of data-intensive web-sites. OntoWeb implements our framework for a SEmantic portAL, viz. SEAL [13], that relies on standard Semantic Web technologies. Other systems, such as ARANEUS [14] and AutoWeb [3], take a declarative approach, i.e. they introduce their own data models and query languages, although all approaches share the idea to provide high-level descriptions of web-sites by distinct orthogonal dimensions. The idea of leveraging mediation technologies for the acquisition of data is also found in approaches like Strudel [8] and Tiramisu [1], they propose a separation according to the aforementioned task profiles as well. Strudel does not concern the aspects of site maintenance and personalization. It is actually only an implementation tool, not a management system.

The importance of conceptual indexing for information retrieval has been acknowledged since quite some time in the medical information processing field [7,16,18]. However, from our point of view the OntoWeb portal is rather unique with respect to the collection of methods used and the functionality provided.

5 Future Work

A next important step to take is to enter a significantly large amount of real life data in the instance base so that a truly useful knowledge base is created. Before doing that, an update of the ontology is foreseen as well. As a direct result, multiple inheritance will be allowed (and displayed in the "tree" and conceptual path panes). As a general consideration, the user interface will be refined as well. After these steps, a large-scale assessment on the strengths and flaws (also as perceived by end-users) of the portal becomes possible. Other topics for future work include semantic bookmarks. A semantic bookmark can be considered as stored query of the ontology and instance base as well as over the object base of the portal. The results can be enhanced by taking into account the concept- and property-hierarchies. Bookmarks already there can be combined conjunctively or disjunctively and so on. Another envisioned improvement are so-called push-services. Such notify the user if a certain resource has been changed.

6 Conclusion

In this paper, a semantic portal has been presented. In particular, the components for content provision and access have been discussed in detail. It is our believe that the OntoWeb members will benefit from this portal in terms of a higher quality knowledge exchange in the semantic web community. As such, the portal serves as practical illustration and application of the scientific ideas put forward by the community members.

[5] cf. http://kaon.semanticweb.org/Portal

Acknowledgment. We like to thank Ben Majer (V.U.B. — STAR Lab) for his fruitful discussions and implementation work. Parts of the research presented here have been funded by the E.U. Thematic Network OntoWeb (IST-2000-25056), the V.U.B. and AIFB internal research grants.

References

1. C. R. Anderson, A. Y. Levy, and D. S. Weld. Declarative web site management with Tiramisu. In *ACM SIGMOD Workshop on the Web and Databases – WebDB99*, pages 19–24, 1999.
2. A. Aronson and T. Rindflesch. Query expansion using the UMLS. In R. Masys, editor, *Proceedings of the AMIA Annual Fall Symposium 97, JAMIA Suppl*, pages 485–489. AMIA, 1997.
3. S. Ceri, P. Fraternali, and A. Bongio. Web modeling language (WebML): a modeling language for designing web sites. In *WWW9 Conference, Amsterdam, May 2000*, 2000.
4. OntoWeb Consortium. Ontology-based information exchange for knowledge management and electronic commerce – IST-2000-25056. http://www.ontoweb.org, 2001.
5. S. Decker, M. Erdmann, D. Fensel, and R. Studer. Ontobroker: Ontology Based Access to Distributed and Semi-Structured Information. In R. Meersman et al., editors, *Database Semantics: Semantic Issues in Multimedia Systems*, pages 351–369. Kluwer Academic Publisher, 1999.
6. Michael Erdmann. *Ontologien zur konzeptuellen Modellierung der Semantik von XML*. Isbn: 3831126356, University of Karlsruhe, 10 2001.
7. D. Evans, D. Rothwell, I. Monarch, R. Lefferts, and R. Côté. Towards representations for medical concepts. *Medical Decision Making*, 11 (supplement):S102–S108, 1991.
8. M. F. Fernandez, D. Florescu, A. Y. Levy, and D. Suciu. Declarative specification of web sites with Strudel. *VLDB Journal*, 9(1):38–55, 2000.
9. N. Guarino, C. Masolo, and G. Vetere. Ontoseek: Content-based access to the web. *IEEE Intelligent Systems*, May-June4-5:70–80, 1999.
10. S. Handschuh and S. Staab. Authoring and annotation of web pages in CREAM. In *The Eleventh International World Wide Web Conference (WWW2002), Honolulu, Hawaii, USA 7–11 May*, 2002. To appear.
11. M. Jarrar and R. Meersman. An Architecture and Toolset for Practical Ontology Engineering and Deployment: the DOGMA Approach. In Liu Ling and K. Aberer, editors, *Proceedings of the International Conference on Ontologies, Databases and Applications of Semantics (ODBase 02)*, 2002.
12. H. Lowe, I. Antipov, W. Hersh, and C. Arnott Smith. Towards knowledge-based retrieval of medical images. the role of semantic indexing, image content representation and knowledge-based retrieval. In C. Chute, editor, *Proceedings of the 1998 AMIA Annual Fall Symposium*, pages 882–886. AMIA, Henley & Belfus, Philadelphia, 1998.
13. A. Maedche, S. Staab, R. Studer, Y. Sure, and R. Volz. Seal — tying up information integration and web site management by ontologies. *IEEE Data Engineering Bulletin*, 25(1):10–17, March 2002.
14. G. Mecca, P. Merialdo, P. Atzeni, and V. Crescenzi. The (short) Araneus guide to web-site development. In *Second Intern. Workshop on the Web and Databases (WebDB'99) in conjunction with SIGMOD'99*, May 1999.
15. R. Meersman and M. Jarrar. Scalability and reusable in ontology modeling. In *Proceedings of the International conference on Infrastructure for e-Business, e-Education, e-Science, and e-Medicine (SSGRR2002s)*, 2002. (only available on CD-ROM).

16. T. Rindflesch and A. Aronson. Semantic processing in information retrieval. In C. Safran, editor, *Seventeenth Annual Symposium on Computer Applications in Medical Care (SCAMC 93)*, pages 611–615. McGraw-Hill Inc., New York, 1993.
17. S. Weibel, J. Kunze, C. Lagoze, and M. Wolf. *Dublin Core Metadata for Resource Discovery*. Number 2413 in IETF. The Internet Society, September 1998.
18. P. Zweigenbaum, J. Bouaud, B. Bachimont, J. Charlet, B. Séroussi, and J.-F. Boisvieux. From text to knowledge: a unifying document-oriented view of analyzed medical language. *Methods of Information in Medicine*, 37(4-5):384–393, 1998.

Web Information Tracking Using Ontologies

Alexander Maedche

FZI Research Center for Information Technologies
at the University of Karlsruhe,
D-76131 Karlsruhe, Germany
`http://www.fzi.de/WIM`
`maedche@fzi.de`

Abstract. Bringing knowledge management to practice one typically has to focus on concrete problems that exist in the daily work of the knowledge worker. We consider the task of tracking relevant information on the Web as important and time-consuming, thus, as a concrete problem. In this paper we introduce an integrated approach for Web information tracking using ontologies. The overall approach has been implemented within a case study carried out at DaimlerChrysler AG.

1 Introduction

It is well-known and widely agreed that when introducing and trying to establish knowledge management one has to focus on concrete problems and provide support for knowledge-intensive tasks that appear in the daily work of the knowledge workers. We consider tracking relevant information on the Web as a typical knowledge intensive and time-consuming task, which currently lacks any knowledge management support. At the moment this is mainly done in an ad-hoc fashion via browsing the Web by looking up URL's and pursuing hyperlinks, via querying search engines, registering to mailing lists and via inspecting specialized Web portals.

In this paper we present a new approach to support Web information tracking using ontologies. The overall approach is composed of the following ingredients. First of all, we use ontologies as predefined knowledge models describing the information needs of a specific knowledge worker or a group of knowledge workers, e.g. a department within a company. Second, we identify different kinds of information available on the Web providing relevant tracking sources. Third, we provide means to connect the different forms of Web information with the ontology. Finally, interaction with the user is supported via ontology-driven Web sites.

The organization of this paper is as following. The first section introduces our notion of ontologies as a basis for knowledge modeling using a simple example. Section 3 introduces the tracking framework. Section 4 discusses our case study that has been implemented on the basis of the aforementioned framework. Before we conclude we provide a short overview on related work in section 5.

D. Karagiannis and U. Reimer (Eds.): PAKM 2002, LNAI 2569, pp. 201–212, 2002.

2 Ontologies

The application of ontologies[1] – shared conceptualizations of some domain – is increasingly seen as key to enable semantics-driven information access. There are many applications of such an approach, e.g. automated information processing, information integration or knowledge management, to name just a few.

As mentioned earlier, ontologies within our tracking approach are seen as predefined knowledge models describing the information needs of a specific knowledge worker or a group of knowledge workers, e.g. a specialized department. We use the notion of so-called OI-Models (ontology-instance models) within our approach. We refer the interested reader to [10] where a more detailed description, a mathematical model and a denotational semantics for OI-Models is provided. Figure 1 provides an example of an OI-Model.

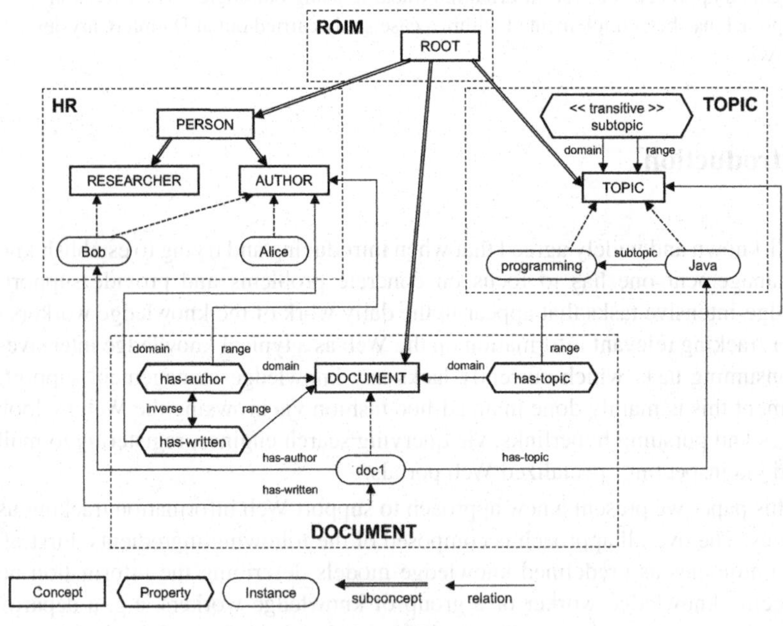

Fig. 1. Example OI-Model

An important aspect of OI-Models is that they provide flexible means of modeling concepts and instances as well as properties between them. It considers concepts and instances on the same level, providing means for modeling meta-concepts and meta-properties. Thus, we do not make any explicit distinction between concepts and instances. Additionally, means for modularization of OI-Models are provided, e.g. in our

[1] An ontology is a conceptual model shared between autonomous agents in a specific domain.

example the overall OI-Model is constructed out of a Root node, a HR model, a document model and a topic model. Furthermore, OI-Models include light-weight inferences like transitive and symmetric properties as well as inverse properties.

Furthermore, a lexical layer may be associated to each entity of an OI-Model. This is an important aspect with respect to the tracking functionality described within this paper. Figure 2 depicts a screenshot of an OI-Model within the KAON OI-Modeler[2] including the lexical layer definition of for the concept "Topic".

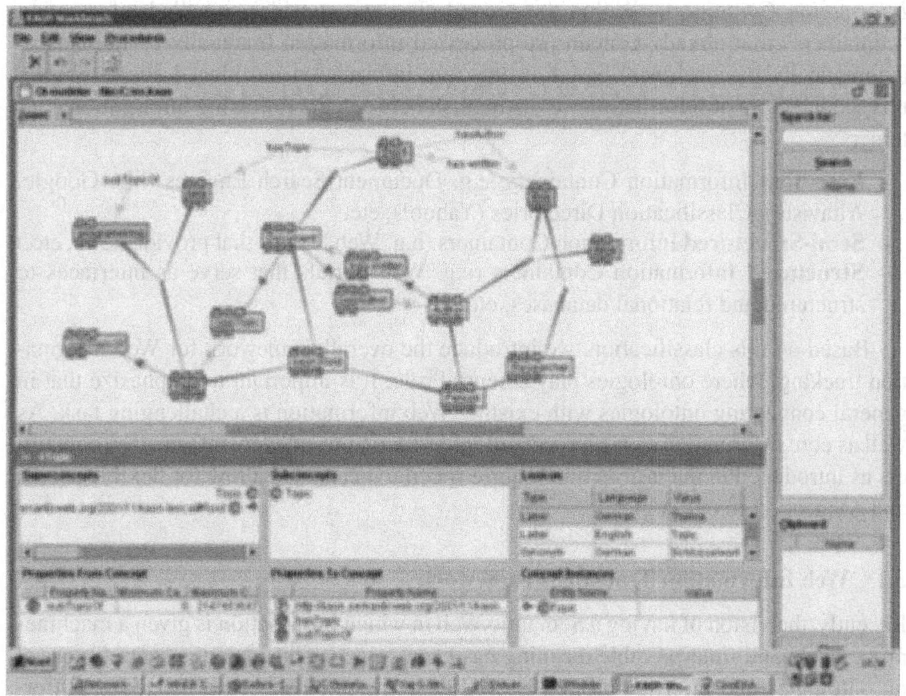

Fig. 2. Screenshot of the OI-Modeler

The reader may note that a m:n relation between the lexical layer of an ontology and its entities has to be described. We also allow to distinguish between different types of so-called lexical entries, e.g. labels, stems, etc. This aspect is quite important when using natural language processing facilities within the tracking process.

[2] http://kaon.semanticweb.org

3 A Framework for Web Information Tracking

Knowledge workers typically deal with different kind of information that is available on the Web. Within our approach we distinguish between the following two different information classes.

Core Information. The first we consider is the core information that is provided by the World Wide Web. Roughly spoken this core information is restricted to documents and hyperlinks between these documents. This information is typically accessed directly via browsing the Web.

Information Containers. Within the second class we consider so-called information "containers" that already contain pre-processed information (manually by humans or automatically by machines) based on the core information introduced above. Within this second class of information we distinguish between the following information containers:

- **Free Text** Information Containers, e.g. Document Search Engines (like Google, Altavista), Classification Directories (Yahoo!), etc.
- **Semi-Structured** Information Containers (e.g. Web Portals that provide news, etc.)
- **Structured** Information Containers (e.g. Web Portals that serve as interfaces to structured and relational databases, etc.)

Based on this classification, we introduce the overall framework for Web information tracking, where ontologies play a central role. It is important to emphasize that in general connecting ontologies with existing Web information is a challenging task. As well as core information as pre-processed information provided by information containers as introduced in the last section require specific means that allow for flexible access and connection to ontologies.

3.1 Web Information Tracking Framework

Recently, the vision of having a Semantic Web in which information is given a machine-processable and -interpretable meaning has been coined. This vision is centrally based on ontologies and information that is described via ontology-based metadata. Unfortunately, there is not much metadata available on the current Web, so that connecting ontologies with existing Web information is not so straightforward. In this paper we present a pragmatic approach to connect ontologies with available Web information. Within this approach the following points are of importance:

- Means for discovering ontology-relevant information from the Web are required. In general one has to keep in mind that one should reuse as much as possible information providers such as search engines, news providers, Web portals, etc. In this sense the ontology only provides a meta-index in top of the information containers.
- Information sources have be to indexed and integrated on the basis of the ontology. It is important to emphasize that within our approach we target to reduce human intervention as much as possible. It is obvious that there is a trade-off between obtaining a high quality connection between ontologies and Web information and the time that is invested to develop a high-quality connection.

- Based on indexed and integrated information one should provide value-adding analysis methods that allow to discover implicit relationships and patterns.
- Means for browsing and querying have to be provided to the end-user. Both, a document-driven view and a resource-centered view have to be provided to the user.

Figure 3 depicts the overall picture of our framework. In this architecture, the OI-Model builds the central backbone. It serves as input to the focused crawler, it allows to be connected to Web Services, it indexes documents, etc. Furthermore, it allows to integrate and to store materialized instances from the arbitrary information containers. Finally, it supports presentation in the form of browsing and querying.

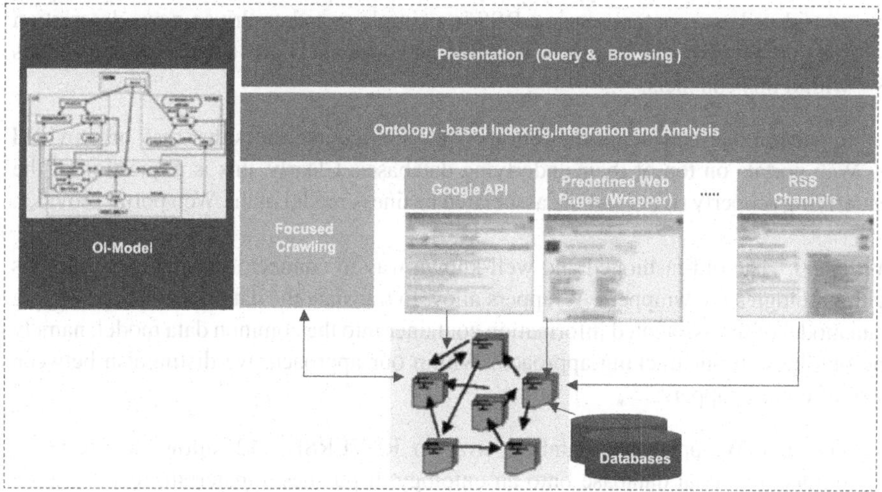

Fig. 3. Web Information Tracking Architecture

3.2 Connecting Web Information with Ontologies

In the following we give a list and description of several connectors to be used for free information on the Web as well as for free text, semi-structured and structured information containers. The overall goal is to provide a tight connection between existing information with the OI-Model. In an optimal case this means that instances and properties between instances are extracted from the existing information sources according to the predefined OI-Model.

Focused Crawler. We use a focused crawler for discovering relevant core information on the Web [9]. Actually, the crawler simulates human Web browsing behaviour by measuring the relevancy of a given Web page according to the defined ontology. If a

Web page is considered as relevant, the outgoing links are pursued. Thus, a focused search for relevant information on the Web is pursued. The ontology serves as a reference model for measuring relevancy of information.

Web Service Interfaces. For information containers containing already preprocessed information we use the different Web Service interfaces that recently have been made available:

- Google Web Service Interface: This Web Service provides a simple service allowing to query google with a set of key-words and retrieving the top ten web pages for these key words. We use the lexicon of the OI-Model to instantiate this Web Service.
- RSS (RDF Site Summary) News Syndication Format: This Web Service may be considered as a content service. RSS is a simple metadata-driven news description scheme[3]. It provides means to describe news channels and to publish news items within this channels.

In general one may adopt to arbitrary Web Service interfaces that may be provided by Web portals on top of their underlying databases. Clearly, this is a question of the underlying property rights and the associated business model of the Web portal provider.

Wrappers. The old-fashioned and well-known way to connect information containers with ontologies are wrappers. Wrappers allow to translate the data from the underlying data model of the associated information container into the common data model, namely the ontology in our tracking approach. Within our approach, we distinguish between two different wrappers:

- Database Wrapper: The database wrapper REVERSE[4] [12] allows to lift an arbitrary relational database onto an ontology. It pursues a materialized integration strategy, thus, the content of the database is copied into the ontology.
- Web page Wrapper: Recently, several Web page wrappers have been developed, e.g. the WysWyg Web Wrapper Factory W4F[5]. Typically, these tools allow to define extraction rules to extract content from Web pages.

3.3 Ontology-Based Indexing, Integration, and Analysis

The indexing and integration layer works on top of the connected information sources. This layer has to deal with different kinds of information:

- Documents (discovered by the focused crawler, or retrieved by the Google Web Service)
- News (already include some basic metadata that may be represented in the form of instances of ontologies)

---

[3] http://www.purl.org/rss/1.0/

[4] http://kaon.semanticweb.org/REVERSE

[5] http://db.cis.upenn.edu/DL/WWW8/

- Instances of the ontology (e.g. as provided from a database or Web page wrapper or obtained by calling a specialized Web Service)

Indexing of textual data (documents, news summarizations, etc.) is done on the basis of the lexical layer of our OI-Models in combination with shallow text processing techniques. Indexing in this sense can been seen as automatically adding "subjects" to the documents, where subjects are take from the concept and instance entities contained in the OI-Models. Thus, we build a materialized index associating the objects with the textual data. Furthermore, we create instances of the ontology. The instances represent materialized objects obtained by the different connectors, e.g. the database and the HTML wrapper. A detailed description of the overall integration approach is provided in [7]. In the reference implementation and case study section we will see that users may also want to define instances manually. E.g. users may add information to the OI-Model and therefore support knowledge sharing.

Additionally, the indexing and integration layer contains several value-adding analysis components that work on top of the index and the materialized instances. Three examples of analysis components that we use are the following:

- Ontology-based Document Clustering: A classical unsupervised text mining task is document clustering. In [4] it has been described how ontologies to approach the matters of *subjectivity* and *explainability* within clustering.
- Concept-based Association Rules: Association rules have been established in the area of data mining, thus, finding interesting association relationships among a large set of data items. The algorithm described in [6] learns generalized association rules between concepts.
- Instance Clustering: The instance clustering approach described in [8] takes instances and instance relations as higher level input for clustering objects. It provides means for similarity-based clustering of objects according to their semantic characteristics.

3.4 Presentation

This section is about how the end-user may interact with the discovered and ontology-enhanced Web information. Typically, one can distinguish between the following usage scenarios. First, the user may just browse for relevant information along the ontology and its relations. Results obtained by applying an analysis method as described earlier may also be inspected on the basis of browsing. Second, users may also define concrete queries ranging from keyword-based queries to SQL-like queries. Futhermore, they may be interested in executing a specific analysis method with a selected set of integrated information sources.

Browsing. Browsing gives knowledge workers to explore the information provided by the integrated information and information containers. Browsing, however, in our framework is not just clicking on hyperlinks.

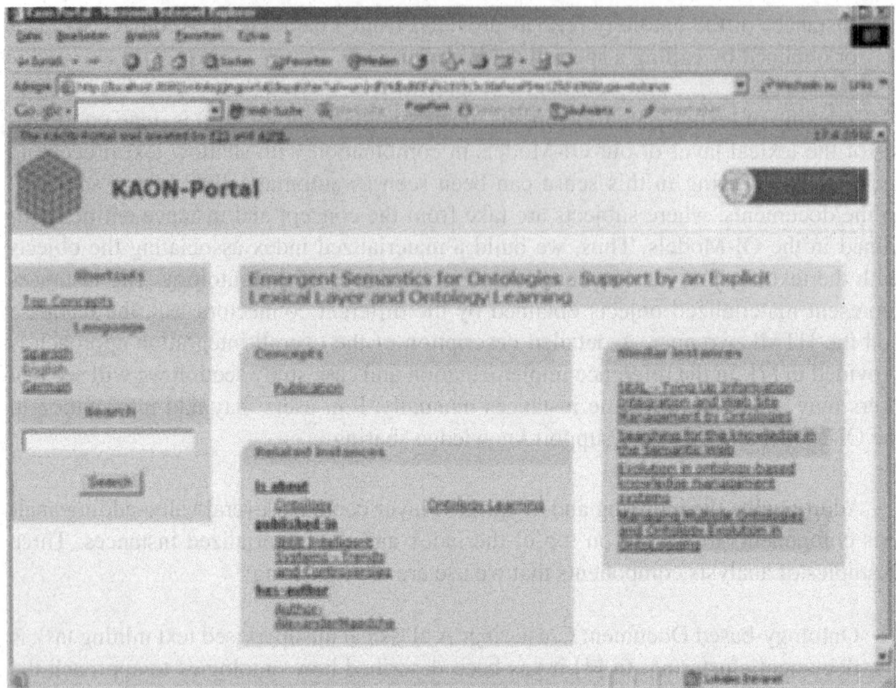

Fig. 4. KAON Portal

We consider browsing in the context of the Semantic Web vision. Thus, having a resource-centered view onto the data. Resources in this sense can be everything, e.g. documents, people, topics, projects, ideas. Users explore this resources by following the properties that exist between the different resources.

Querying & Execution. Queries may range from simple boolean keywords, queries by example and complex queries. Simple keyword-based querying is realized via mapping the key-word string onto the OI-Model as described earlier. All entities from the OI-Model are retrieved that are referred by the key-word string. By selecting one of the retrieved entities, the user switches to the browsing mode and explores associated entities by analyzing the associated properties.

The next layer of query complexity is supporting queries by example. Query by example (QBE) is a well-known technique to reduce the complexity of defining a query. QBE interfaces are directly obtained by the ontology, its entities and associated properties. A detailed explanation how this is done has been introduced in [7].

Additionally, the execution interfaces allow users to define analysis tasks. Thus, for example in [4] it has been described how the overall document clustering task may be influenced by selected a pre-defined set of concepts along clustering should be performed.

4 The HR-TopicBroker – A Case Study

The HR-TOPICBROKER is a simple tracking system that has been developed for DaimlerChrysler AG. The HR-TOPICBROKER is a system that supports the location of relevant human resource (HR) topics (strategies, trends, etc.) on the Web. Thus, the underlying idea of this system is that the HR strategy of the DaimlerChrysler group is modelled in the form of an ontology. This explicit representation of relevant tracking topics serves as input for the underlying information containers and for the presentation module.

For searching and tracking core information about the HR strategy we used the focused crawler as described earlier and initialized it with a set of predefined URLs (business schools, competitors, etc.). Additionally, we used the Google Web Service to get the top-10 pages for entity labels and entity label combinations (e.g. Google was queried for "Volkswagen and E-Learning"). Thus, in the HR-TopicBroker system we only used documents as information providers. All collected documents are indexed using the HR strategy ontology.

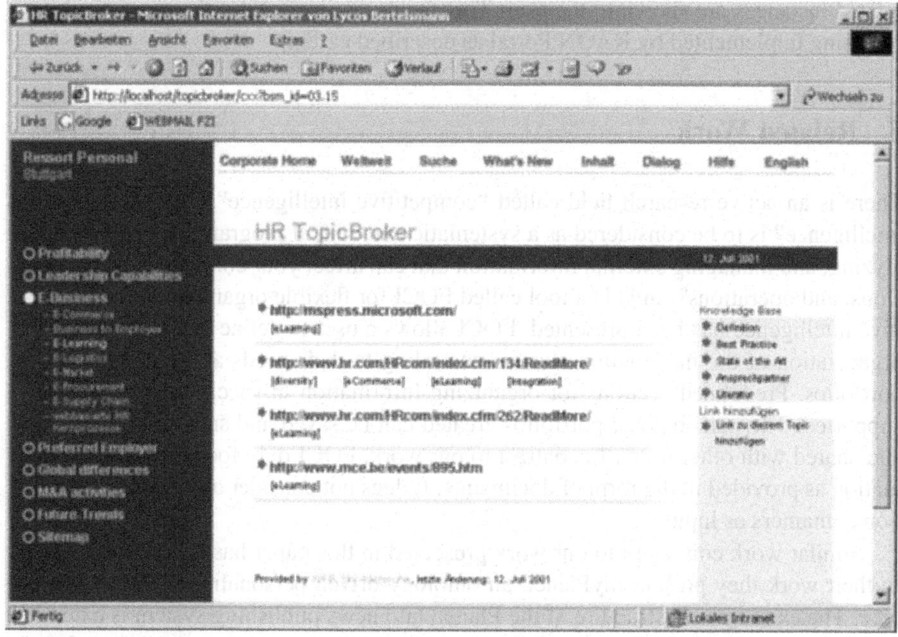

Fig. 5. HR-TopicBroker

The HR-TOPICBROKER user interface has been embedded in the DaimlerChrysler Intranet and was made accessible for human resource managers. On the presentation side we selected a Yahoo!-like, hierarchical presentation that allows for browsing, supporting a document-centric view on the ontology. Figure 5 shows a screenshot of the running application. By clicking on "E-Learning" one gets a list of relevant documents.

The system also provides means for defining additional information and for information sharing. We considered that case that people discovered a relevant Web page by browsing along the proposed Web pages. Therefore, we offered the possibility to users to define links for entities contained in the ontology. This approach has also the advantage that the focused crawler gets new starting points for its focused search for relevant information.

Additionally, we also allowed the joint definition of a "knowledge base" on top of the discovered and tracked documents. The knowledge base in the HR-TOPICBROKER application consisted of instances and instance relationships manually added to the OI-Model. For example, it is possible to define contact partners for specific topics, e.g. the definition of a relation between the entity E-Learning and a research institute in this field. We used a template-based approach within HR-TOPICBROKER system to collect these kind of instances and instance relationships. Thus, the underlying complexity of defining an instance and an instance relationship was not shown to the human resource managers. Browsing of the contents contained in the knowledge base is again done along the Yahoo!-like topic hierarchy. However, when clicking on a specific topic the related instances are shown to the user. This feature is inspired by the resource-driven browsing implemented by KAON Portal as described earlier.

5 Related Work

There is an active research field called "competitive intelligence" [13]. "Competitive intelligence" is to be considered as a systematic and ethical program for gathering, analyzing, and managing external information that can affect your company's plans, decisions, and operations[6]. In [11] a tool called FOCI for flexible organization for competitive intelligence has been presented. FOCI allows a user to define and personalize the organization of the information clusters according to their needs and preferences into portfolios. Predefined sections for organizing information in specific domains is also supported. The personalized portfolios created can be saved and subsequently tracked and shared with other users. In contrast to our work, FOCI only focuses on pure information as provided in the form of documents. It does not consider any kind of information containers as input.

Similar work compared to our work presented in this paper has been done by [14]. In their work they present myPlanet, an ontology-driven personalised Web-based service. The existing infrastructure of the PlanetOnto news publishing system is extended with ontology-based functionality focusing on the easy access to repositories of news items, a rich resource for information sharing. In contrast to our work, their approach is mainly focusing on news, whereas our approach provides a wider range of information containers as input.

With respect to using ontologies for document-indexing and information retrieval it has been shown that in clearly defined domains, ontologies are adequate means for

[6] http://www.scip.org/ci/index.asp

improving recall and precision values [1]. Recently, in the context of focused crawling much work has been done (see [2, 3]). This work distinguishes from our's in the sense that it only focuses on Web document discovery and not on connecting information containers. Furthermore, all these approaches do not provide any kind of ontology-based indexing and integration on top of the results of the focused crawler.

6 Conclusion

In this paper we presented a knowledge management module focusing on the concrete problem of tracking relevant information on the Web. Ontologies represented in the form of OI-Models have built the backbone for our tracking framework. Within this framework we distinguish between core information available on the Web and information containers that already provide a higher-level access to the information available on the Web. The distinction between these two kind of information providers has important effects on the way we connect them with ontologies. First, for the core information we provide a focused crawler that supports an ontology-driven search on the Web. Second, for the information containers we use different kind of interfaces, such as Web Services and wrappers. In the middle layer of our framework we bring the different information sources together and allow to use analysis methods for extracting implicit patterns contained in the distributed information pieces. Finally, we allow for browsing and querying the information using a document-centered and resource-centered approach in parallel.

In the future, we will further focus on research how to generate ontologies automatically, because this is one of the main drawbacks of our current approach. In this context we have introduced the concept of ontology learning [5] that allows for semi-automatic generation of ontologies from existing sources. Additionally, with respect to the costs associated for connecting existing information sources to ontologies we consider Web services as a promising direction. However, there is still much work to be done to allow for automatic connection of available services.

Acknowledgements. Research for this paper was financed by European Commission, IST, project "Ontologging" (IST-2000-28293) and by DaimlerChrysler AG, Germany. Special thanks to Lars Kuehn who implemented the HR-Topic-Broker application. Thanks to Klaus Goetz, DaimlerChrysler AG for providing stimulating comments to the HR-TopicBroker application.

References

1. S. Aitken and S. Reid. Evaluation of an Ontology-based Information Retrieval Tool. In *Proceedings of the ECAI-200 Workshop on Ontologies and PSMs, Berlin, Germany*, 2000.
2. S. Chakrabarti, M. van den Berg, and B. Dom. Focused crawling: a new approach to topic-specific web resource discovery. In *Proceedings of WWW-8*, 1999.
3. M. Diligenti, F.M. Coetzee, S. Lawrence, C. L. Giles, and M. Gori. Focused Crawling using Context Graphs. In *Proceedings of the International Conference on Very Large Databases (VLDB-00), 2000*, pages 527–534, 2000.
4. A. Hotho, A. Maedche, and S. Staab. Ontology-based text clustering. In *Proceedings of the IJCAI-2001 Workshop "Text Learning: Beyond Supervision", August, Seattle, USA*, 2001.

5. A. Maedche. *Ontology Learning for the Semantic Web.* Kluwer Academic Publishers, 2002.
6. A. Maedche and S. Staab. Discovering conceptual relations from text. In *ECAI-2000 - European Conference on Artificial Intelligence. Proceedings of the 13th European Conference on Artificial Intelligence.* IOS Press, Amsterdam, 2000.
7. A. Maedche, S. Staab, Y. Sure, R. Studer, and R. Volz. SEAL - Tying Up Information Integration and Web Site Management by Ontologies . In *IEEE Data Engineering Bulletin*, 2002.
8. A. Maedche and V. Zacharias. Clustering Ontology-based Metadata in the Semantic Web. In *Proceedings of the Joint Conferences 13th European Conference on Machine Learning (ECML'02) and 6th European Conference on Principles and Practice of Knowledge Discovery in Databases (PKDD'02), Springer, LNAI, Finland, Helsinki*, 2002.
9. Alexander Maedche, Marc Ehrig, Siegfried Handschuh, Raphael Volz, and Ljiljana Stojanovic. Ontology-focused crawling of documents and relational metadata. In *Proceedings of the Eleventh International World Wide Web Conference WWW-2002*, May 2002. (Poster).
10. B. Motik, A. Maedche, and R. Volz. A conceptual modeling approach for semantics-driven enterprise applications. In *Internal Research Report, University of Karlsruhe, 2002, online available at http://kaon.aifb.uni-karlsruhe.de/conc-model.*, 2002.
11. Hwee-Leng Ong, Ah-Hwee Tan, Jamie Ng, Hong Pan, and Qiu-Xiang Li. Foci: Flexible organizer for competitive intelligence. In *Proceedings of the 2001 ACM CIKM International Conference on Information and Knowledge Management, Atlanta, Georgia, USA, November 5-10, 2001*. ACM, 2001.
12. L. Stojanovic, N. Stojanovic, and R. Volz. Migrating data-intensive Web Sites into the Semantic Web. In *Proceedings of the ACM Symposium on Applied Computing SAC-02, Madrid, 2002*, 2002.
13. Richard G. Vedder, Michael T. Vanecek, C. Stephen Guynes, and James J. Cappel. Ceo and cio perspectives on competitive intelligence. *Communications of the ACM*, 42(8):108–116, 1999.
14. Y.Kalfoglou, J.Domingue, E.Motta, M.Vargas-Vera, and S.Buckingham Shum. yPlanet: an ontology-driven Web-based personalised news service. In *Proceedings of the IJCAI'01 Workshop on Ontologies and Information Sharing, Seattle, WA, USA, August 2001*, 2001.

A Domain-Specific Formal Ontology for Archaeological Knowledge Sharing and Reusing[1]

Chunxia Zhang, Cungen Cao, Fang Gu, and Jinxin Si

Key Laboratory of Intelligent Information Processing, Institute of Computing Technology, Chinese Academy of Sciences, Beijing 100080, China
{cxzhang, cgcao, fgu, jxsi}@ict.ac.cn

Abstract. Inherent heterogeneity and distribution of knowledge strongly prevent knowledge from sharing and reusing among different agents and across different domains; formal ontologies have been viewed as a promising means to tackle this problem. In this paper, we present a domain-specific formal ontology for archaeological knowledge sharing and reusing. The ontology consists of three major parts: archaeological categories, their relationships and axioms. The ontology not only captures the semantics of archaeological knowledge, but also provides archaeology with an explicit and formal specification of a shared conceptualization, thus making archaeological knowledge shareable and reusable across humans and machines in a structured fashion. As an application of the ontology, we have developed an ontology-driven approach to knowledge acquisition from archaeological text.

1 Introduction

With the widespread use of computers and the World Wide Web, inherent heterogeneity and distribution of domain knowledge strongly prevent it from sharing and reusing across different agents and domains. This happens to every domain, and archaeology is no exception! Archaeological knowledge is an important part of human knowledge, and is necessary in many knowledge-intensive applications, such as knowledge-based systems, information retrieval and intelligent tutoring for archaeology. However, it lacks a tool for giving itself a formal, clear and declarative description for communicating, sharing and reusing archaeological knowledge among different humans and software entities.

Formal ontologies have been viewed as a promising means to tackle this problem. However, like formal methods in software development, they are not often used directly in modeling applications because of their formalities and abstractness. We

[1] This work is supported by a grant from the Chinese Academy of Sciences (#2000-4010), a grant from the Foundation of Chinese Natural Sciences (#20010010-A), and a grant from the Ministry of Science and Technology (#2001CCA03000).

D. Karagiannis and U. Reimer (Eds.): PAKM 2002, LNAI 2569, pp. 213-225, 2002.

would argue that domain-specific ontologies are more useful and theoretically valuable.

A domain-specific ontology of archaeology in this paper captures the semantics of archaeological knowledge; gives the domain an explicit and formal specification of a shared conceptualization; and makes it shareable and reusable for agents in a structured way [2, 8, 14]. It is also a basis for an ontology-driven approach to knowledge acquisition from text [5], and serves as a guideline for defining a natural language interface for querying archaeological knowledge [9].

The rest of the paper is organized as follows. Section 2 gives a few basic definitions in our domain-specific ontology of archaeology. Section 3 discusses principles of domain ontology design, content and representation. Comparison between our ontology and the object-oriented concepts reference model of the ICOM-CIDOC (International Committee for Documentation of the International Council of Museums) is presented in section 4. Section 5 concludes the paper and raises a few problems on our research agenda.

2 Preliminaries

A domain-specific ontology of archaeology is an explicit and formal specification of a shared conceptualization of archaeology. Here, *conceptualization* refers to an abstract model of some phenomenon in the world by having identified the relevant categories of that phenomenon; *explicit* means that the type of categories and the constraints on their use are explicitly defined; *formal* refers to that the ontology should be machine-readable; and *shared* means that the ontology captures consensual knowledge (it is not private to some individual, but accepted by a group) [7, 17]. The domain ontology is composed of categories, their relationships and formal axioms that constrain the interpretation and use of these terms, as shown in the upper part of Fig.1.

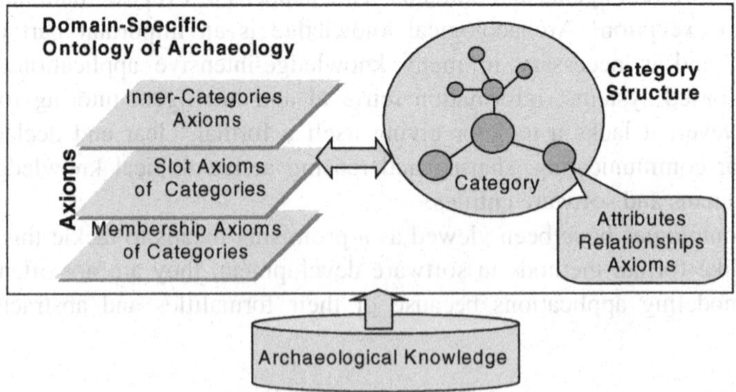

Fig. 1. Components of Our Domain-Specific Ontology of Archaeology

Definition 1. Given a category C_1 in a space of archaeological categories, the individual space of C_1 is the set of all individuals of C_1, written as $\mathrm{ind}(C_1)$.

For example, the category Person consists of all human individuals – living or dead; that is, ind(Person) is the set of all human individuals. As a point in a space of categories, a specific category is related to others in one way or another. In the following, we define a few useful relationships between categories.

Definition 2. Given two categories C_1 and C_2, if ind(C_2)$\subset$ind(C_1), we say that C_2 is a specialization of C_1, written as is-spec(C_2, C_1). In other words, C_1 is a *super-category* of C_2, and C_2 is a *sub-category* of C_1.

Definition 3. Given two categories C_1 and C_2, we define a mapping θ as

$$\theta\text{: ind }(C_1) \rightarrow \text{ind }(C_2)$$

$\forall\alpha\in$ind (C1), if $\theta(\alpha)$ is part of α; $\theta(\alpha)\in$ind (C_2); and θ is a surjection; then we say that C_2 is a *part-category* of C_1, and C_1 is a *whole-category* of C_2, written as part-of (C_2, C_1).

To articulate the part-of relationship in the domain of archaeology, we reconsider a new classification of part-of. In the classification of part-of given by [1], we find that the object/stuff relationship is not adequate of specifying the part-of relationship in archaeology. The reason is that stuff is an attribute attached to an object, and it has no independent existence. In this sense it is unreasonable to regard stuff as a category.

We summarize our classes of part-of relationships of archaeological objects as follows:

1. Integral-object /Component. For example, "The wall is part of a carcass".
2. Area/Place. For example, "A tomb is part of a graveyard".
3. Activity/Feature. For example, "The design is part of a piece of pottery".
4. Collection/Member. For example, "An artifact is part of a complete set of artifacts".
5. Mass/Portion. For example, "A block of accumulation is part of an accumulation layer".

3 A Domain-Specific Formal Ontology of Archaeology

Before building a domain-specific ontology of archaeology, we must consider some basic problems: What are principles of constructing it? How to represent it? What is the specific content of it? What are its applications? Etc.

3.1 Design Criteria

The principles of constructing ontologies have been expounded in [7, 10, 13, 14]. For the main purpose of sharing and reusing knowledge, designing a domain-specific ontology of archaeology should comply with the following criteria.

- *Sharability* and *reusability*. The domain ontology provides an explicit and formal conceptual specification and taxonomic structure of archaeological objects, so exchanging and communication between different agents will become easier and convenient. In addition, the knowledge engineers who build other domain ontologies can share and reuse our archaeology ontology.

- *Clarity* and *objectivity*. The meaning of each term is provided with objective and natural language definitions.
- *Completeness*. Definitions of categories are expressed in terms of necessary and sufficient conditions.
- *Transformation*. The domain ontology is also thought of as an object-oriented semantic model, if its axioms are ignored. Therefore it can be easily converted into other object-oriented models.
- *Readability*. Archaeological knowledge representation is natural and expressive to archaeological domain experts.
- *Appellation Standardization*. We first adopt the appellations of categories, attributes and relationships of the Standard in Archaeology [18]. If these terms do not exist in the Standard [19], they are named by consulting archaeologists.

3.2 Ontology Representation

First of all, we must emphasize that an ontology has nothing to do with any formal language. But for communicating ontologies with other people, we have to specify them in a certain formal language. Our ontology language is a combination of a frame formalism and first-order predicate calculus. It uses frame mechanism from the Generic Frame Protocol [6] and Loom [3, 20]. Fig.2 illustrates a frame-based schema for representing categories. Axioms are first-order formulae, representing a first-order theory on categories and their relationships.

The reasons that we don't adopt other representation approaches (such as description logics, full first-order logics and logic programming) are as follows. Description logic describes the hyponyms among concepts through the containing relation between different individual sets. However, it can't depict the meronyms, and doesn't represent the logical relation among concepts. In addition, knowledge about a concept or an individual, represented in full first-order logic and logic programming, is partitioned into a large number of independent pieces of propositions in the knowledge base, while the frame mechanism organizes this kind of knowledge into a frame. Furthermore, the frame representation is equivalent to the first-order logic representation, which makes it convenient knowledge inference. Our ontology language not only denotes the hyponyms and the meronyms, but also logical relation among categories.

In our language, a category specification has three parts. The *category header* begins with the keyword defcategory, followed by the name of the category to be defined.

The *category body* consists of a (unordered) list of slots. A slot is classified as an attribute or a relationship. It may have a number of facets. A slot facet provides additional information for a slot. Typically, we have

- Type: The value type of the slot. This facet is mandatory for all slots.
- Domain: The set of complete values the slot can assume
- Default: The default value of the slot
- Unit: The unit of the slot value
- Synonym: The synonyms of the slot

- Parasynonym: The parasynonyms of the slot
- Antonym: The antonyms of the slot
- Reverse: The reverse slot of the slot. For example, the reverse of the slot have-member is is-member-of.
- Property: The properties which the slot has.
- Facet: The domain-specific facets that the slot is subject to
- Related slots: The relevant slots related to the slot
- Comment: The informal comment on the slot

```
defcategory <category-name>[<related-categories>]
{
                {<definition-of-slots>}
                {<inner-category-axioms>}
}
<related-categories>::= Super-categories <sequence-of-super-category>
        [; Part-categories <sequence-of-part-category>]
        I Part-categories <sequence-of-part-category>
        [; Super-categories <sequence-of-super-category>]
<definition-of-slots>::==<type-of-slot><slot-name>
{
                :type<type-slot-value>
                [:domain<complete-value-domain>]
                [:default<default-value>]
                [:unit<units>]
                [:synonym<sequence-of-synonym>]
                [:parasynonym<sequence-of-parasynonym>]
                [:antonym<sequence-of-antonym>]
                [:reverse<reverse-slots>]
                [:property<general-properties><specific-properties>]
                [:facet<sequence-of-necessary-facet-users-define>]
                [:related-slots<other-slots-related-with-the-slot>]
                [:comment<informal-comments>
......
<general-properties>::==<Reflexive I Irreflexive I Anti-reflexive I Symmetric I Anti-symmetricI
                Asymmetric I Transitive I Anti-transitive I Non-transitive >
<specific-properties>::==<time-varyingI...... >
<inner-category-axioms>::==<Axioms-of-definition-of-category>I<Axioms-of-properties-of-
                category>I<Axioms-of-slots>I<Axioms-of-relationships-among-slots>
<Axioms-of-definition-of-category>:: ==<first-order well-formed formula>
<Axioms-of-properties-of-category>:: ==<first-order well-formed formula>
<Axioms-of-slots>:: ==<first-order well-formed formula>
<Axioms-of-relationships-among-slots>:: ==<first-order well-formed formula>
}
```

Fig. 2. Category Representation (Keywords are in bold face)

The *axioms* constrain the interpretation of the slots and the relationships between categories.

3.3 Categories and Their Backbone Structure

We identify main categories and their relationships in the domain of archaeology in appropriate terms, and combine top-down and bottom-up strategies to capture other categories. Moreover, we give precise meaningful models for the categories and their relationships at the knowledge level. So far, we have built more than 120 archaeology-specific categories. Fig.3 depicts the category Archaeological-Culture.

```
defcategory Archaeological-Culture Part-Categories: Cognition, Neo-Confucian-Orthodoxy, Archaeological-
Site, and Archaeological-Relics
{
        Attribute: Period
            :Type string
            :Domain Paleolithic-Period, and Neolithic-Period, and ......
            :Synonyms Age
            :Comment An interval of time characterized by the prevalence of a specified culture
        Attribute: Upper-Limit-Year
            :Type string
            :Facet Dating-Method, and revision
            :Comment The upper limit year of period of a specified culture
        Attribute: Lower-Limit-Year
            :Type string
            :Facet Dating-Method, and revision
            :Comment The lower limit year of period of a specified culture
        Attribute: Year
            :Type string
            :Comment The fuzzy year of period of a specified culture
        Relation: Developed-from
            :Type string
            :Comment Value domain is cultures which the specified culture developed from.
        Relation: Evolve-to
            :Type string
            :Comment Value domain is cultures which the specified culture evolved to.
            ......
        <Axioms of Properties of Category>
            Archaeological-culture (a)→(∃b)(Period(a, b)∈ Frame_a ∧b∈{sequences of period } )
        <Axioms of Slots>
            Archaeological-culture(a) ∧ Geological-Ages(a, b)→((∀c)Geological-Ages(a,c) →Equal(b,c))
        <Axioms of Relationships of Slots>
            Archaeological-Culture (a) ∧ Upper-Limit-Year (a, b_1) ∈Frame_a ∧ Lower-Limit-Year (a, b_2)
            ∈Frame_a →Earlier-Than (b_1, b_2)
......
}
```

Fig. 3. The Category Archaeological-Culture

There are a variety of relationships among categories. We mainly investigate two kinds of the most fundamental relationships in the ontology: is-spec and the part-of relationships. With these two relationships, we define the backbone structure of the formalized archaeological categories, as depicted in Fig.4. In the figure, because of the limitation of space, some branches are folded and those who are interested in the backbone structure may contact with the first author to get a full copy thereof.

3.4 Archaeological Knowledge Representation

We use Frame_a to denote the frame for object a. Frame_a consists of a set of slot-value pairs with optional facet-value pairs, i.e. Frame_a= {(slot, slot-value [,facet-1, facet-1-value, … , facet-n, facet-n-value])}.

For representing axioms, we define predicates of the form Slot(a, slot-value, facet-1, facet-1-value, ..., facet-n, facet-n-value) to denote the tuple of the Frame_a. And predicate ¬Slot(a) denotes that the object a doesn't have the slot, Predicate ¬Slot(a, b) represents that the slot value of the object a is not b. For example, Upper-Limit-Year(Yangshao-culture, about B.C. 5000 Year, Dating-Method, Radiocarbon-Dating, Revision, Yes)$\in \text{Frame}_{\text{Yangshao-culture}}$.

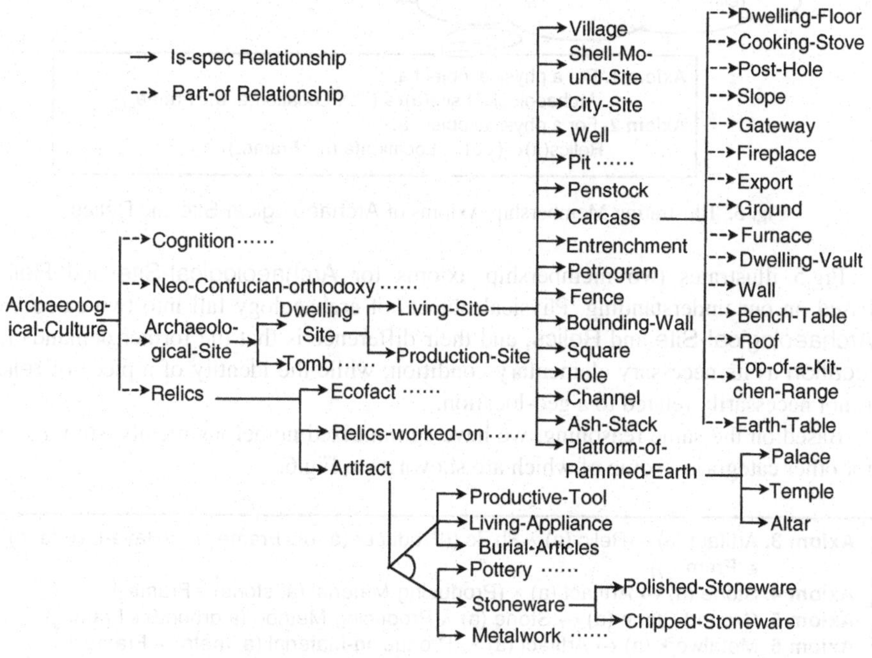

Fig. 4. The Backbone Structure of Archaeological Categories

3.5 Semantic Axioms

Axioms are a crucial part of our domain ontology, and they constrain the interpretation of ontological categories and their relationships and contents. In our ontology, axioms are classified into three types according to the objects which they describe.

3.5.1 Membership Axioms of Categories

For each category, there are some axioms for determining whether an instance or individual belongs to it. Formulating membership axioms for a category is difficult since it requires a comprehensive understanding of archaeology and its domain knowledge.

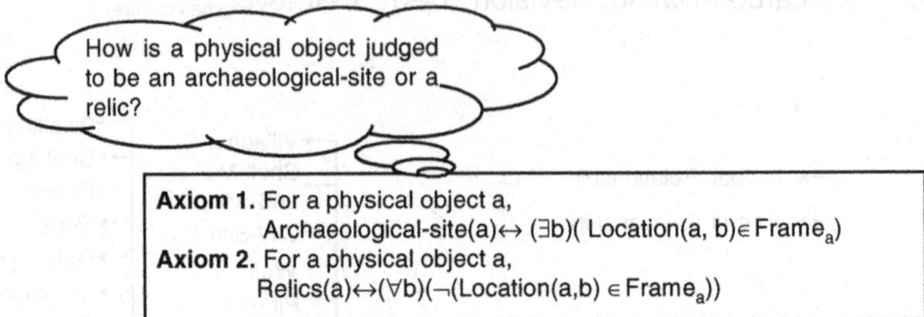

Fig. 5. Illustrating Membership Axioms of Archaeological-Site and Relics

Fig.5 illustrates two membership axioms for Archaeological-Site and Relics based on our understanding. Physical objects of archaeology fall into two categories Archaeological-Site and Relics, and their difference is that the former demands the location as its necessary elementary condition, while the identity of a piece of relics is not necessarily related to a geo-location.

Based on the same reasoning, we have summarized numerous membership axioms for other categories, some of which are shown as in Fig.6.

Axiom 3. Artifact (a) ↔Relic (a) ∧ ∃b ∃c ((Producer (a, b)∈ Frame$_a$) ∧ (Have-Use (a, c) ∈ Frame$_a$))
Axiom 4. Stone (a) ↔ Artifact (a) ∧ (Producing-Material (a, stone) ∈ Frame$_a$)
Axiom 5. Ground-Stone (a) ↔ Stone (a) ∧(Producing-Method (a,ground) ∈ Frame$_a$)
Axiom 6. Metalwork (a) ↔ Artifact (a) ∧ (Producing-Material (a, metal) ∈ Frame$_a$)
Axiom 7. Ironware (a) ↔Metalwork (a) ∧ (Producing-Material (a, iron) ∈ Frame$_a$)

Fig. 6. Membership Axioms of Artifact and Some of its Subcategories

Axiom 3 means that given an object a, a is a piece of Artifact if and only if there exists a producer b of a, and a has a specific use (denoted as c). Other axioms have a similar interpretation. From the axioms above, we can derive a lot of interesting theorems or propositions, and some are presented below.

Proposition 1. Given a physical object a, Ironware (a)→ Artifact (a).

Proof. Given a physical object a, if Ironware (a) holds, then we have Metalwork (a) by axiom 7. Further, we derive Artifact (a) according to axiom 6.

Proposition 2. Given a physical object a, Ground-Stone (a) → Artifact (a)

Proposition 3. Artifact (a) → Relics (a)

Proposition 4. Artifact (a)→∃b (Producer (a, b)∈ Frame$_a$)

Proposition 5. Artifact (a) →∃c (Have-Use (a, c) ∈ Frame$_a$)

3.5.2 Slot Axioms of Categories

In our ontology, slots are divided into two classes: attributes and relationships. As illustration, we present a few axioms in the category Archaeological-Culture in Fig. 7. Axioms 8-10 are constraints on the two attributes period and founder and the relationship located-in, respectively. Axioms 11-14 are about some slots on time in Archaeological-Culture. Axiom 8 means that if an object a is an instance of Archaeological-Culture, then the value of the attribute period of a belongs to the set-of-sequences-of-periods such as Neolithic Age, Western Zhou and Qing.

From the axioms 8-14, we can derive the following propositions.

Proposition 6. Given an abstract object a, Archaeological-Culture(a)∧Found-Time(a, b)∧Upper-Limit-year(a, c_1)∧Lower-Limit-Year(a, c_2)→Earlier-Than(c_1,b)

Proposition 7. Given an abstract object a, Archaeological-Culture(a)∧Upper-Limit-Year(a, c_1) ∧Found-Time(a, b)∧ Excavation-Time(a, d) → Earlier-Than(c_1, d).

Proposition 8. Given an abstract object a, Archaeological-Culture(a)∧Lower-Limit-Year(a, c_2)∧Found-Time(a, b)∧ Excavation-Time(a, d) → Earlier-Than(c_2, d).

3.5.3 Inter-categories Axioms

Currently in our ontology, we identify two types of inter-category relationships: category-level and slot-level relationships. By a category-level relationship we mean that the relationship does not refer to slots of the related categories. By a slot-level relationship, we mean that the relationship between categories is reflected by the relationship(s) of the slots in the relevant categories.

Axiom 8. Archaeological-Culture (a) →(∃b) ((Period (a, b) ∈ $Frame_a$)∧b∈{sequences of period })
Axiom 9. Archaeological-Culture (a) →(∃b) ((Founder (a, b) ∈ $Frame_a$)∧Human-being(b))
Axiom 10. Archaeological-Culture (a) →(∃b) ((Located-in(a, b)∈ $Frame_a$)∧Region(b))
Axiom 11. Archaeological-Culture (a) ∧ (Typical-Site (a, b1, b2,…,bn) ∈ $Frame_a$)→(Site (a, b1) ∈ $Frame_a$)∧ (Site (a, b2) ∈ $Frame_a$)∧…∧ (Site (a, bn) ∈ $Frame_a$)
Axiom 12. Archaeological-Culture (a) ∧ (Upper-Limit-Year (a, c1) ∈ $Frame_a$)∧ (Lower-Limit-Year (a, c2) ∈ $Frame_a$)→Earlier-Than (c1, c2)
Axiom 13. Archaeological-Culture (a) ∧(Period (a, b) ∈ $Frame_a$)∧(Upper-Limit-Year (a, c1) ∈ $Frame_a$)∧ (Lower-Limit-Year (a, c2) ∈ $Frame_a$)→In (c1, b) ∧ In (c2, b)
Axiom 14. Archaeological-Culture (a) ∧ (Found-Time (a, b) ∈ $Frame_a$)∧(Lower-Limit-Year (a, c2) ∈ $Frame_a$)→Earlier-Than (c2, b)

Fig. 7. Slot Axioms of the Category Archaeological-Culture

Axiom 15. Relics (a) ↔(Artifact (a) ∧¬Ecofact (a) ∧¬Worked-on-Object (a))∨(¬Artifact (a) ∧Ecofact(a) ∧¬Worked-on-Object (a)) ∨ (¬Artifact (a) ∧¬Ecofact (a) ∧Worked-on-Object (a))
Axiom 16. Archaeological-Culture (a)→ ∃b (Archaeological-Site (b) ∧ Part-of (b, a))
Axiom 17. Archaeological-Culture (a) → ∃b (Artifact (b) ∧ Part-of (b, a))

Fig. 8. Axioms of Category-Level Relationships between Categories

Axioms 15-17 represent category-level relationships between categories. For instance, axiom 15 declares that an object is a piece of Relics if and only if it is an Artifact, an Ecofact, or a Worked-on-object, where an Artifact is man-made, an Ecofact is unworked or natural, and a worked-on-object is worked-on by human.

Axiom 18. Archaeological-Site (a) ∧ ∃b ((Found-Place (b, a) ∈ $Frame_a$) ∧ Fossil (b)) → Period (a, Paleolithic-Age)
Axiom 19. Archaeological-Site (a) ∧ ∃b (Found-Place (b, a) ∈ $Frame_a$)∧ Stone-Tool (b)∧ (Producing-Method (b, ground) ∈ $Frame_a$) →¬Period (a, Paleolithic-Age)

Fig. 9. Axioms of Slot-Level Relationships between Categories

In Fig.9, axioms 18-19 are constraints on category-level relationships between categories. For example, axiom 18 is a formulation of the fact that there is no enough time to form Fossil after the Paleolithic-Age according to archaeological stratigraphy and formation process of Fossil.

3.6 Knowledge Acquisition and Inference Based on the Domain-Specific Ontology

Many endeavors have been intended to acquire knowledge from text. We can acquire about 90 to 95 percent of the domain knowledge in knowledge-based systems directly from domain texts [4, 8, 11, 12]. The ontology-driven archaeological knowledge acquisition process has as following steps [16]. First, identify categories and individuals in texts of archaeological knowledge; second, find relations among categories and individuals according to definitions of categories, their backbone structure and axioms; third, extract the attribute values and the relation values of every categories and individuals.

The domain-specific ontology of archaeology is also used for knowledge analysis, and knowledge inference, and knowledge discovery. In particular, a question answering system with a natural language interface for inquiring about archaeological information has been developed [9]. Based on the axioms of the domain ontology, we can find inconsistent knowledge, such as inaccurate attribute values and relation values of categories and individuals, and false is-spec and part-of relations. In addition, given a proposition or problem, we can deduce proposition's correctness or answer the problem through knowledge searching and inference. The procedure is divided into 3 steps. First, extract entities, attributes, relations, and interrogative. Second, search for these terms in frame-based archaeological knowledge base. Thirdly, if they are found, then give the answers, otherwise, resort to axioms to problem solving. If the problem involves only one category, then utilize slot axioms of the category, or else, use inter-category axioms.

4 A Comparison with CRM

To our knowledge, however, there exists few domain-specific ontology of archaeology so far. The project team of post-excavation on complex sites at the University of York is developing an archaeological ontology to key aspects of the archaeological process. The object-oriented conceptual reference model (i.e., CRM) of the ICOM-CIDOC could more or less be viewed as a domain ontology, and it is intended to cover all concepts relevant to museum documentation. The model was developed by the CIDOC Documentation Standards Group from 1994 to 1999 [17]. The relationship is-spec is considered in both our domain ontology and CRM.

The differences between our ontology of archaeology and CRM are:

- Our ontology of archaeology orients all objects in the generic domain of archaeology, while CRM is a description of the information categories used for developing records about the objects pertinent to museum documentation.
- CRM deals with three kinds of part-of relationships: integral-object /component, area/place, and activity/feature. Our domain ontology introduces collection/member and mass/portion part-of relationships in addition.
- The key difference is that formal axioms are an indispensable component in our domain ontology (Axioms are used for constraining the interpretation of ontological categories and their relationships and contents), while CRM doesn't provide formal meanings of the entities and properties.
- Sites and holes are classified as objects in our ontology, while they are considered as physical features in CRM. We think it is unreasonable, for if post-holes are not physical objects, then they can't occupy space and posts couldn't occupy the same space, though post-holes are attached to posts.

5 Conclusion

Sharing and reusing knowledge has become a significant research topic in information community with the widespread of Internet. In this paper, we discuss our current work of constructing an archaeological knowledge base with ontological theory and engineering. Categories, their relationships, and constraint axioms are three factors of a domain-specific ontology of archaeology. Since domain knowledge is described in a formal, explicit and structured way to provide a commonly agreed understanding of archaeology, it can be shared and reused across different agents and knowledge bases. We adopt a combination of a frame formalism and first-order predicate calculus as the ontology representation language. The language can describe the hyponyms, the meronyms, logical relations about categories and individuals. Production rules has the disadvantages: inefficient and inflexible, though its advantages include naturalness of expression, modularity and restricted syntax. A major problem with semantic network is that although the name of this language is semantic nets, there is not clear semantics of the various network representations. And it doesn't convey some kinds of facts.

Based on the domain ontology, we have developed an ontology-driven approach to archaeological knowledge acquisition, and a question answering system with a natural language interface for inquiring about archaeological information.

There are a few problems to be solved in our project: How to utilize axioms to discover unknown knowledge? How to find potential applications of ontology? How to formalize our ontology development method so that more fundamental issues can be tackled vigorously (e.g. consistency, redundancy, and completeness of ontological axioms)?

References

1. A.Artale, E.Franconi, Nicola Guarion, and Luca Pazzi.: Part-whole Relations in Object-centered Systems: an Overview. Data & Knowledge Engineering, Vol.20 (1996) 347-383
2. W.N.Borst.: Construction of Engineering Ontologies. PhD thesis, University of Twente, Enschede (1997)
3. David Brill.: Loom Reference Manual Version 2.0. http://www.cbl.leeds.ac.uk/nikos/tex2html/examples/shell/shell.html (1993)
4. Cungen Cao.: Medical Knowledge Acquisition from Encyclopedic Texts. Lectures in Computer Science, Vol.2101 (2001) 268-271
5. Cungen Cao, Qiangze Feng, et.al.: Progress in the Development of National Knowledge Knowledge Infrastructure. Journal of Computer Science and Technology, Vol.17 (2002)523-534
6. V.Chaudhri, A. Farquhar, R. Fikes, P. Karp, & J. Rice.: The Generic Frame Protocol 2.0,KSL-97-05 (1997) http://www.ksl.stanford.edu/KSL_Abstracts/ KSL-97- 05.html
7. Ying Ding, Dieter Fensel.: Ontology Library Systems: The Key to Successful Ontology Re-use. http://www.semanticweb.org/SWWS/program/full/paper58.pdf. (2001)
8. D.Fensel. Ontologies: a Silver Bullet for Knowledge Management and Electronic Commerce. Springer-Verlag, Berlin (2001)
9. Qiangze Feng, Cungen Cao, et al..: A Uniform Human Knowledge Interface to the Multi-Domain Knowledge Bases in the National Knowledge Infrastructure. To appear in The Twenty-second SGAI International Conference on Knowledge Based Systems and Applied Artificial Intelligence (2002)
10. Asuncín Gmez Péz, V.Richard Benjamins. Overview of Knowledge Sharing and Reuse Components: Ontologies and Problem-Solving Methods. Proceedings of the JICAI-99 workshop on Ontologies and Problem-Solving Methods (KRR5) Stockholm, Sweden, August 2 (1999)
11. Ruqian Lu, Cungen Cao.: Towards Knowledge Acquisition from Domain Books. In: Wielinga, B., Gaines, B., Schreiber, G., Vansomeren, M. (eds.): Current Trends in Knowledge Acquisition. Amsterdam: IOS Press (1990) 289-301
12. Ruqian.Lu, Cungen. Cao, Y.Chen, et al.: A PNLU Approach to ICAI System Generation. Science in China (Series A), vol.38 (1996) 1-10
13. Asuncín Gmez-Péz.: Evaluation of Ta xonomic Knowledge in Ontologies and knowledge Bases. Proceedings of the Knowledge Acquisition Workshop, KAW99 (1999)
14. Thomas R. Gruber. Toward Principles for the Design of Ontologies used for Knowledge Sharing. Knowledge Acquisition, vol.5, no.2, (1993) 199-220
15. R.Studer, V.R. Benjamins, and D. Fensel.: Knowledge Engineering, Principles and Methods. Data and Knowledge Engineering, 25(1-2) (1998) 161-197

16. Jinxin Si, Cungen Cao, Haitao Wang, Fang Gu, Qiangze Feng, Chunxia Zhang, et al.: An Environment for Multi-Domain Ontology Development and Knowledge Acquisition. Proceedings of Engineering and Development of Cooperative Information System. (2002)104-116
17. The ICCOM/CIDOC Documentation Standards Group. Definition of the CIDOC Object-oriented Conceptual Reference Model. http://cidoc.ics.forth.gr/docs/cidoc_crm_version 3.3.2.doc (2002)
18. The Core Data Standard for Archaeological Sites and Monuments. http://www.cidoc .icom.org/archo.htm (1995)
19. Standards in Archaeology. http://ads.ahds.ac.uk/project/userinfo/standards.html (2002)
20. Loom 4.0 Release Notes. http://www.isi.edu/isd/LOOM/how-to-get.html (2000)

Metasearch. Properties of Common Documents Distributions

Nikolai Buzikashvili

Institute of System Analysis, Russian Academy of Sciences,
9 prospect 60 Let Oktyabrya, 117312 Moscow, Russia
buzik@cs.isa.ac.ru

Abstract. The effectiveness of metasearch data fusion procedures depends crucially on the properties of common documents distributions. Because we usually know neither how different search engines assign relevance scores nor the similarity of these assignments, common documents of the individual ranked lists are the only base of combining search results. So it is very important to study the properties of common documents distributions. One of these properties is the Overlap Property (OP) of documents retrieved by different search engines. According to OP, the overlap between the relevant documents is usually greater than the overlap between non-relevant ones. Although OP was repeatedly observed and discussed, no theoretical explanation of this empirical property was elaborated. This paper considers formal research of properties of the common documents distributions. In particular, sufficient and necessary condition of OP is elaborated and it is proved that OP should take place practically under arbitrary circumstances.

1 Introduction

Different data fusion techniques, above all those which aggregate search experts opinions' and do not re-analyze retrieved documents are based on OP [1], [5]. The cause is not that OP implies better results but that common documents of the individual search results are indeed the only base of combining these results. At the same time if OP does not hold, combining search results may aggravate precision. For this reason it is important to study properties of common documents distributions, in particular OP. OP has been studied in detail as an empirical property [2]–[4]. However an explanatory base of OP as well other properties of common documents distributions is poor and these properties have not been investigated from the theoretical point of view. We construct some characteristics of these distributions.

Let's consider a Search Engine (SE) as a pair $<X_t,R_t>$, where X_t is a database of indexed documents and R_t is a relevance ranking function. SE$_t$ ranks X_t and retrieves a list of documents $s_t(X_t, R_t, R_t^{min})$ ordered by decreasing of the relevance. Thus, retrieved list is the top of ranked X_t. The retrieved ranking does not contain documents which

D. Karagiannis and U. Reimer (Eds.): PAKM 2002, LNAI 2569, pp. 226-231, 2002.

relevance is less than R_t^{min}. So if any document x is absent in s_t, it can mean either $R_t(x) < R_t^{min}$ or $x \notin X_t$.

There are two ways to interpret relevance scores. First, a score is considered as an estimation of relevance, so a number of score gradations equals to a (usually small) number of relevance gradations. The other way is that a score is a measure of confidence. In this case a relevance takes only 2 values ('relevant'/ ' non-relevant') while a number of score gradations is infinite. Suppose a relevance takes R values $r = 1,\ldots, R$, which we call relevance ranks. A document the relevance rank of which equals r is referred to as r-document. The greater the rank the smaller the relevance. If $R = 2$, then $r = 1$ is interpreted as 'relevant' and $r = 2$ as 'non-relevant'. In this case retrieved lists contain only those documents the ranks of which were detected as 1.

2 The Overlap between Samples

Let Y_0 be an 'universal' set containing N_0 objects and $\{Y_t\}$ $(t = 1,\ldots,T)$ be independent random subsets of Y_0. A size of Y_t is N_t. The probability that two subsets Y_v and Y_w include m common objects is

$$p_{com}^{(v,w)}(m) = \binom{N_v}{m}\binom{N_0 - N_v}{N_w - m} \Big/ \binom{N_0}{N_w} \tag{1}$$

and the expectation of common objects of two samples

$$E(m) = N_v \binom{N_0 - 1}{N_w - 1} \Big/ \binom{N_0}{N_w} = N_v N_w / N_0 \tag{2}$$

(Expected number of common objects of n samples is and the expectation of common objects of two samples is $\prod_i^n N_i / N_0^{n-1}$.

3 Identical Bases

Let's suppose that all bases are identical. (As we shall see below, the case of overlapping bases causes no changes and is considered in Section 6.) Let a probabilistic matrix $P_{R\times R}^{(t)} = \| p_{ij}^{(t)} \|$ correspond to each SE$_t$, and $p_{ij}^{(t)}$ is a probability that SE$_t$ identifies i-document as j-document. Each base consists of $\overline{n} = (n_1, n_2, \ldots, n_R)$ documents, where n_r is a number of r-documents. Then SE$_t$ identifies $\overline{n}$ documents as $\overline{n}^{(t)} = \overline{n}P^{(t)}$.

Let's consider two lists retrieved by SE$_v$ and SE$_w$. From (1) it can be shown for each rank r that a distribution of common documents over $[0, n_r]$ is

$$p_{com}^{(v,w)}(m) = \binom{n_r}{m} \left(p_{ij}^{(v)} p_{ij}^{(w)}\right)^m \left(1 - p_{ij}^{(v)} p_{ij}^{(w)}\right)^{n_r - m}$$

Thus, the average of common *i*–documents identified as *j*–documents

$$E(com_{ij}^{(v,w)}) = n_i p_{ij}^{(v)} p_{ij}^{(w)}$$

In particular, the average of correctly identified common *j*–documents

$$E(com+_j^{(v,w)}) = E(com_{jj}^{(v,w)}) = n_j p_{jj}^{(v)} p_{jj}^{(w)} \tag{3}$$

The average of all correctly identified common *j*–documents

$$E(com_j^{(v,w)}) = \sum_{i=1}^{R} E(com_{ij}^{(v,w)}) = \sum_{i=1}^{R} n_i p_{ij}^{(v)} p_{ij}^{(w)} \tag{4}$$

On the other hand, the average of documents identified by SE_v as *j*–documents

$$E(all_j^{(v)}) = \sum_{i=1}^{R} n_i p_{ij}^{(v)} \tag{5}$$

including

$$E(all+_j^{(v)}) = n_j p_{jj}^{(v)} \tag{6}$$

correctly identified *j*–documents.

4 Characteristics of Common Documents Distributions

Let's introduce the following characteristics of common documents distributions. The expected fraction of common documents identified by both SE_v and SE_w as *j*–documents, among all documents identified by SE_v as *j*-documents

$$\alpha_j^{(v,w)} = E\left(\frac{com_j^{(v,w)}}{all_j^{(v)}}\right) = \frac{E(com_j^{(v,w)})}{E(all_j^{(v)})} = \frac{\sum_{i=1}^{R} n_i p_{ij}^{(v)} p_{ij}^{(w)}}{\sum_{i=1}^{R} n_i p_{ij}^{(v)}} \tag{7}$$

The expected fraction of correctly identified documents among all common *j*-documents

$$\beta_j^{(v,w)} = E\left(\frac{com+_j^{(v,w)}}{com_j^{(v,w)}}\right) = \frac{n_j p_{jj}^{(v)} p_{jj}^{(w)}}{\sum_{i=1}^{R} n_i p_{ij}^{(v)} p_{ij}^{(w)}} \tag{8}$$

The expected fraction of correctly identified documents among all documents identified as *j*-documents

$$\mu_j^{(v)} = E\left(\frac{all+_j^{(v)}}{all_j^{(v)}}\right) = \frac{n_j p_{jj}^{(v)}}{\sum_{i=1}^{R} n_i p_{ij}^{(v)}} \tag{9}$$

5 The Overlap Property Condition

In terms of above characteristics, OP is $\beta_j^{(v,w)} > \mu_j^{(t)}$ for each relevance rank j observable in lists elaborated by SE_v and SE_w ($t = v, w$). Let $t = v$. As it follows from (8) and (9), we have a system of R inequalities with $R(R-1)$ independent variables p_{ij}

$$\sum_{i \neq j} n_i p_{ij}^{(v)} (p_{jj}^{(\;)} - p_{ij}^{(\;)}) > 0 ,$$

It holds if $p_{jj}^{(w)} = \max_i (p_{ij}^{(w)})$ and $p_{ij}^{(w)} < p_{jj}^{(w)}$ is carried out at least for one i. We call this sufficient (and necessary if R=2) condition the Overlap Property Condition (OPC).

Thus, OP is carried out, when diagonal elements of matrixes $P^{(t)}$ are maximal in columns, that is probability to be identified as the *r*–document most of all at the document really being the *r*–document. If only first R^* of R relevance ranks are observable, then OPC takes place over first R^* columns of $P^{(t)}$ matrixes. The alternative formulation of OPC is considered in the Appendix.

This requirement is weak enough. In particular, a quality of recognition of relevant documents may be quite poor. For example, $P = \begin{bmatrix} \varepsilon & 1-\varepsilon \\ \varepsilon/2 & 1-\varepsilon/2 \end{bmatrix}$, where probability of the correct identification of the relevant document is arbitrarily small ε, satisfies OPC.

If OPC takes place, then $\sum_j p_{jj} > 1$. Indeed, according OPC $\sum_i^R p_{ij} < Rp_{jj}$. Then $\sum_j \sum_i p_{ij} < R\sum_j p_{jj}$. But $\sum_j \sum_i p_{ij} = R$. Then $R < R\sum_j p_{jj}$, that is $\sum_j p_{jj} > 1$.

6 Overlapping Bases

Above we have considered the case of identical bases. Now, let the bases be randomly overlapping and fractions of common documents of X_v and X_w be

$$c^{(v,w)} = \frac{|X_v \cap X_w|}{|X_v|} \text{ and } c^{(w,v)} = \frac{|X_v \cap X_w|}{|X_w|},$$

Let $n_r^{(v)}$ be a number of r–documents in X_v and $n_r^{(v,w)}$ be a number of common r–documents of $SE_v \bullet SE_w$. Then, at average $n_r^{(v,w)} = c^{(v,w)} n_r^{(v)} \equiv c^{(w,v)} n_r^{(w)}$.

Thus, the average of the documents simultaneously identified as j–documents by SE_v and SE_w

$$E(com_j^{(v,w)}) = \sum_{i=1}^{R} n_i^{(v,w)} p_{ij}^{(v)} p_{ij}^{(w)} = c^{(v,w)} \sum_{i=1}^{R} n_i^{(v)} p_{ij}^{(v)} p_{ij}^{(w)} \equiv c^{(w,v)} \sum_{i=1}^{R} n_i^{(w)} p_{ij}^{(w)} p_{ij}^{(v)}$$

The average of correctly identified common j–documents is

$$E(com+_j^{(v,w)}) = c^{(v,w)} n_j^{(v)} p_{jj}^{(v)} p_{jj}^{(w)} \equiv c^{(w,v)} n_j^{(w)} p_{jj}^{(w)} p_{jj}^{(v)}$$

The formulae (5) and (6) which don't include '*com*'–components have no changes. It is clear if an original formula contains '*com*'–component only in the numerator (denominator), then the factor $c^{(v,w)}$ will appear in this part. If *com*–components enter into both parts, there will be no changes. Thus, $c^{(v,w)}$ will appear in (7), but not in (8) and (9).

Thus, the OPC will not undergo any changes in the case of overlapping bases.

7 Conclusion

It is very unlikely that OPC does not hold. However, OPC may hold exclusively due to the high probability of identification of non-relevant documents rather than an identification quality of relevant documents. In particular, it may be connected with the rejection of really relevant documents.

References

1. Dwork, C., Kumar, R., Naor, M., Sivakumar, D.: Rank Aggregation Methods for the Web. WWW10 (2001) 613–622
2. Katzer, J., McGill, M., Tessier, J., Frakes, W., DasGupta, P.: A study of the overlap among document representations. Information Technology: Research and Development. Vol.2, (1982) 261–274
3. Lee, J. H.: Analyses of Multiple Evidence Combination. Proceedings of the 20th Annual International ACM–SIGIR Conference (1997) 267–276
4. Saracevic, T., Kantor, P.: A study of information seeking and retrieving. III. Searchers, searches, overlap. Journal of the American Society for Information Science. Vol. 39, No. 3 (1988) 197–216
5. Zhang, J. et al.: Improving the Effectiveness of Information Rtrieval with Clustering and Fusion. Computational Linguistics and Chinese Language Processing. Vol. 6, No. 1 (2001) 109–125

Appendix

Let's consider as ćommon' all documents which ranks are not greater than r, i.e. instead of r-documents consider '≤r- documents'. To do this change ranks assignment, namely, reassign rank 1 to all documents with the ranks $i \le r$ and ranks $i > r$ substitute with $i - r + 1$. Next, instead of $P^{(t)}_{R\times R}$ consider matrix $Q^{(t)}_{(R-r+1)\times(R-r+1)}$, where

$$q_{ij} = \begin{cases} p_{i+r-1,\, j+r-1} & \text{if } i, j > 1 \\ \sum\limits_{l\le r}\left(p_l \sum\limits_{k\le r} p_{lk}\right) & \text{if } i = j = 1 \\ \sum\limits_{l\le r} p_l p_{l,\, j+r-1} & \text{if } i = 1, j > 1 \\ \sum\limits_{l\le r} p_{i+r-1,\, k} & \text{if } j = 1, i > 1 \end{cases}$$

where p_l is a conditional probability $p_l = p(i = l \mid 1 \le i \le r) = n_l / \sum_{i\le r} n_i$.

Q is a probabilistic matrix. Formulae (7) – (9) are applied to Q, if we replace 'p' by 'q'. Thus, OPC for Q matrix is $q_{jj} = \max_i (q_{ij})$. How OPC for Q depends on OPC for P? It is clear, if $j > 1$, then OPC for P implies OPC for Q since $q_{jj} = p_{j+r-1,\, j+r-1}$, $q_{ij} = p_{i+r-1,\, j+r-1}$ for $i > 1$, and q_{1j} is a weighted mean $p_{l,\, j+r-1}$ $(1 \le l \le r)$, i.e. not greater than $\max_l (p_{l,\, j+r-1}) \le p_{j+r-1,\, j+r-1}$. Since $q_{11} = \sum_{l\le r}\left(n_l \sum_{k\le r} p_{lk}\right) / \sum_{j\le r} n_j$ and $q_{i1} = \sum\limits_{k\le r} p_{i+r-1,\, k}$,

$$q_{11} - q_{i1} = \left(\sum_l n_l \left(\sum_{k\le r} p_{lk} - \sum_{k\le r} p_{i+r-1,\, k}\right)\right) / \sum_{j\le r} n_j \,.$$

That is if $j = 1$, then sufficient condition of OP is that $\sum_{k\le r} p_{lk} > \sum_{k\le r} p_{mk}$ for any $l \le r$ and $m > r$. More generally sufficient condition looks as follows. Let ranks r_1–th to r_2–th are united. Let ranks from the r_1–th up to the r_2–th are united. Let's select a submatrix $P' \subset P$, consisting of columns from r_1 to r_2. The overlap property appears, if in P' the sum on anyone line l $(r_1 \le l \le r_2)$ crossing the main diagonal of P is greater then the sum on any line of P' not containing diagonal elements of P.

End-User Access to Multiple Sources – Incorporating Knowledge Discovery into Knowledge Management

Katharina Morik, Christian Hüppe, and Klaus Unterstein

University of Dortmund, Computer Science Department, LS VIII
morik@ls8.informatik.uni-dortmund.de
http://www-ai.cs.uni-dortmund.de

Abstract. The End-User Access to Multiple Sources, the EAMS system integrates document collections in the internet (intranet) and relational databases by an ontology. The ontology relates the document with the database world and generates the items in the user interface. In both worlds, machine learning is applied. In the document world, a learning search engine adapts to user behavior by analysing the click-through-data. In the database world, knowledge discovery in databases (KDD) bridges the gap between the fine granularity of relational databases and the coarse granularity of the ontology. KDD extracts knowledge from data and therefore allows the knowledge management system to make good use of already existing company data.
The EAMS system has been applied to customer relationship management in the insurance domain. Questions to be answered by the system concern customer acquisition (e.g., direct marketing), customer up and cross selling (e.g., which products sell well together), and customer retention (here: which customers are likely to leave the insurance company or ask for a return of a capital life insurance). Documents about other insurance companies and demographic data published in the internet contribute to the answers as do the results of data analysis of the company's contracts.

1 Introduction

Knowledge management is the acquisition, offering, distribution, and maintenance of knowledge. Diverse users are to exploit knowledge from diverse sources for their working procedures. In the EAMS system system, we personalize the results of document retrieval to diverse user types. Since the need for personalization is not questioned, we do not introduce into this part of our work here. The second contribution to knowledge management, however, the integration of relational databases into the content of knowledge management systems is a new challenge which requires some justification. Hence, we introduce into this new aspect of knowledge acquisition, offering, and maintenance.

Knowledge management establishes new collections of information, e.g., experience reports [1] or skill profiles, most often in the form of documents that are accessed via the intranet [2], [3], [4]. Business processes are modeled and used for

D. Karagiannis and U. Reimer (Eds.): PAKM 2002, LNAI 2569, pp. 232–243, 2002.

the distribution of knowledge as well as for the integration of knowledge sources [5], [6]. Even laws and company regulations are formalised in order to justify and modify certain steps in a business process [7]. However, the preparation of new information is time consuming and could possibly lead to yet another isolated information source in the broad range of a company's systems. Therefore, the integration of given data sources is considered the major challenge of knowledge management systems. Technically, the integration is enabled by the use of ontologies ([8], originally called knowledge interchange formats [9], [10], or reference schemas [11]) together with wrappers for the knowledge source [12] or explicit annotations [13]. Some systems implement agents that gather, classify, and enter information into a memory that is organised according to an ontology [14], [15], [16]. These approaches are almost always accessing document collections, although XML document collections are sometimes called databases [17]. The main data sources that actually exist in all organisations are, however, databases or data warehouses. As far as we are aware, only the TSIMMIS project aims at accessing relational databases for knowledge management [18]. Why is the most comprehensive information source of organisations that neglected?

One reason which excludes given databases from knowledge management is the different granularity of the ontology and the database. The ontology concept of a customer, for instance, does not match any attribute or relation directly, but is spread over several tables and their attributes. The translation from an ontology concept to a database query is already quite some SQL programming. The second reason is the different answer set of database and knowledge management systems. The excerpt even of aggregated data is not yet the required knowledge. We might, for instance, create a view which lists customers together with their contracts. This table corresponds to a concept and its features in the ontology. Most likely, however, the user does not want to look at that table but would like to see answers to questions like:
Which are the frequently sold products?
What are the attributes of my most frequent customers?
On-line analytical processing is capable of answering those questions using statistical procedures and the data cube. To go even further, we want to extract knowledge from the database that answers questions like the following:
Which contracts are frequently sold together?
Which customers are most likely to sell their contract back to the company before it ends?
KDD can indeed answer such questions on the basis of the given database. Each such question corresponds to a KDD case. The collection of KDD cases forms a knowledge source of the knowledge management system. In this way, we bridge the gap between data and knowledge and indirectly integrate databases as a source of knowledge into a knowledge management system.

The paper is structured as follows. Section 2 gives an overview of the system. Section 3 presents the learning search engine which adapts to differse users. Section 4 explains how we store and retrieve KDD cases and how they are adapted to updated databases (i.e., knowledge maintenance). Section 5 shows the KDD results used in our insurance knowledge management.

2 System Architecture

The EAMS system integrates the document and the database world using an ontology. The ontology concepts are linked with search strings which are sent to the search engine and with the conceptual model of the database in the form of the meta-data model M4 (cf. section 4). Figure 2 shows the system architecture. In order to apply the system to a new application, the meta-data of the database, the conceptual meta-data (ontology), the meta-data about a KDD case (the conceptual case model), and the search strings which correspond to concepts in the ontology need be entered. Currently, we have not yet implemented an editor for meta-data which eases this task. However, within the MiningMart project, a meta-data editor for relations, concepts, and cases is under development. The integration of this is prepared. The EAMS system offers in its Graphical User

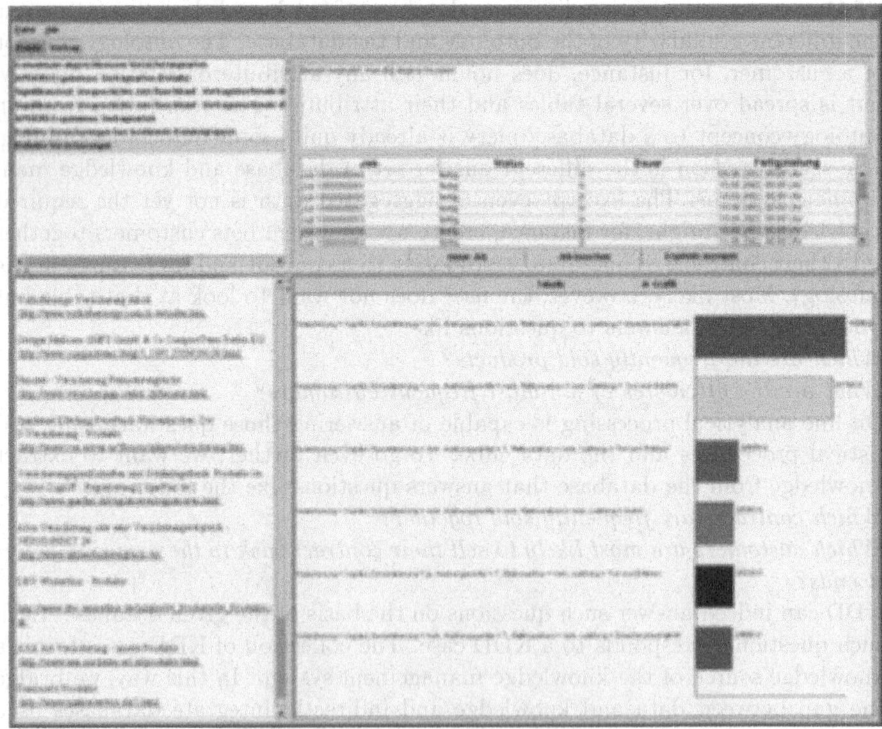

Fig. 1. Graphical user interface

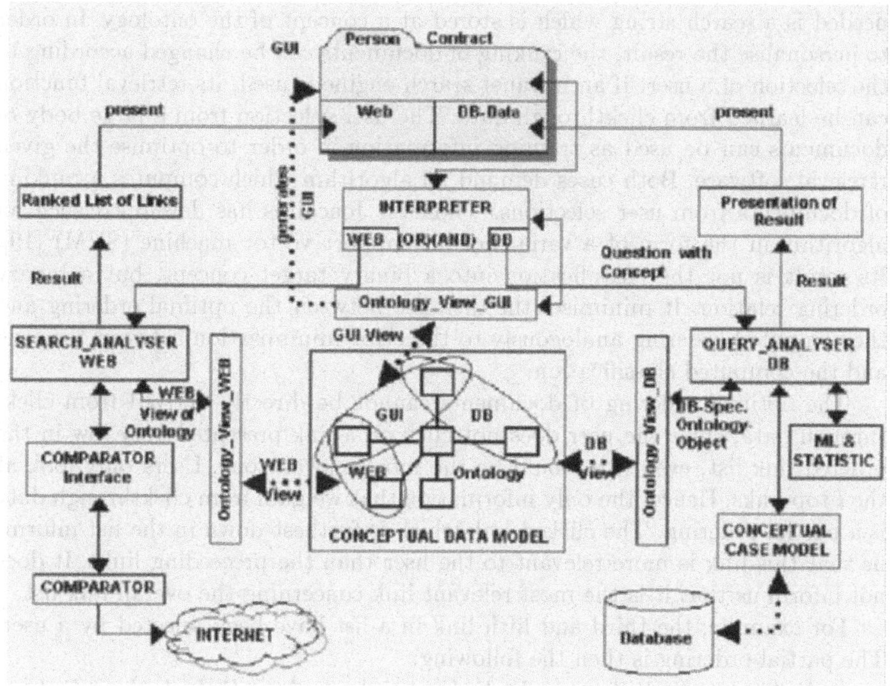

Fig. 2. System architecture

Interface (GUI) the concepts of the ontology. Each concept is presented as a folder label. The lower part of the screen is divided into one part for results from the document world and one part for results from the database world. In the middle, there is space for entering queries by selecting a query type (i.e., frequencies, segmentation, correlation, and classification). If there exist already executed KDD results for a query type and a concept, the GUI presents the KDD cases together with their date. The user may select one. If the desired combination of query and concept has not yet been executed and does not require complex preprocessing, the user may start a new KDD execution. Of course, starting a prepared KDD case anew is always possible. This is sensible, if the last execution is too long ago for the results being up to date. The results of the selected KDD case are presented in the lower database part, either as a table, or as a diagram. See figure 1 for a screenshot of the GUI.

3 Learning Search Engine

Users of the EAMS system are provided with access to a document collection. If the document collection has already been indexed by a search engine – as is the world wide web – then such a search engine can be applied. All that is needed is a search string which is stored at a concept of the ontology. In order to personalise the result, the ranking of documents can be changed according to the selection of a user. If an intranet search engine is used, its retrieval function can be learned from clickthrough data. The user selection from a large body of documents can be used as training information in order to optimise the given retrieval software. Both cases demand an algorithm which computes a ranking of documents from user selections. Thorsten Joachims has developed such an algorithm in the form of a variant of his support vector machine (SVM) [19]. Its result is not the classification into a binary target concept, but a binary ordering relation. It minimises the distance between the optimal ordering and the computed ordering analogously to the error minimisation between the true and the computed classification.

The optimal ordering of documents cannot be directly derived from clickthrough data, since the user does not click on a link presented very low in the ordered link list, even if it would be the most relevant one. Users only look at the l top links. Hence, the only information that we gain from clickthrough data is a partial ordering. The clicked link which is furthest down in the list informs us that this link is more relevant to the user than the preceeding links. It does not inform us that it is the most relevant link concerning the overall link list.

For example, the third and fifth link in a list have been selected by a user. The partial ordering is then the following:

$r : link_3 < link_2, link_3 < link_1, link_5 < link_4, link_5 < link_2, link_5 < link_1$

Joachims transforms partial orderings into the input of the SVM. For each query q_i to the document collection, such a partial ordering r_i is computed from the clicked links. The input of the SVM becomes a set $(q_1, r_1), (q_2, r_2), ..., (q_n, r_n)$. The retrieval function to be learned delivers a ranking $r_{f(q)}$.

The learning result is used in order to display the relevant documents as a list which is ordered according to the learned ranking. Since the retrieval function is learned for particular users from their data, the presentation of links is adapted to their relevance assessments. This is the personalisation which we have incorporated in the EAMS system.

4 Knowledge Discovery in Databases

KDD extracts knowledge from databases. It answers high-level questions on the basis of low-level data. The question types correspond to *KDD tasks*. Some of them are:

- Frequencies of attribute values given some other attributes' values, e.g., the number of blue cars given a car series and a year of sales;
- Segmentation (clustering or subgroup detection), e.g., characteristics of subgroups of customers;
- Correlation (or association) of attributes, e.g., products that are frequently sold together (basket analysis);
- Classification (or prediction) of a target attribute.

Each task is solved by several methods. Given that the data are already well prepared, the data mining step of KDD applies an algorithm that performs the task. Currently, the EAMS system uses the following *data mining tools*:

- statistical functions of Oracle and statistical stored procedures for simple frequencies,
- data cube [20], [21] for frequencies,
- APRIORI [22] for correlations,
- C4.5 [23] for classification in the weka-implementation J48, and
- mySVM [24] for classification.

A KDD case is a sequence of steps which lead from the original database tables to an evaluated result. Where machine learning focuses on the data mining step, KDD carefully designs the preprocessing steps which prepare the data. Usually, these consume up to 80 percent of the effort. The design of the appropriate sequence for a given analysis task and database is difficult. For each step the appropriate procedure must be selected. A procedure may be an SQL procedure, a simple statistical method, or a learning method. The best parameters of the method have to be determined. Each step requires several trials.

In the context of knowledge management, we cannot expect users to interactively apply KDD techniques in order to receive answers from the database. KDD cases must be prepared by the database department of a company and be stored within the knowledge management system. A user then selects a case which answers his or her question. The management of KDD cases is part of the knowledge management: a KDD case must be related to the ontology, be stored and retrieved accordingly. For the integration as introduced in section 1, it is not sufficient to store experience about KDD cases in the internet as done in [1]. The results of a KDD case change as soon as the content of the database is changed. Therefore, a stored question together with a KDD result will soon be outdated. Hence, the KDD case should be stored as a sequence of steps which is executable on the database.

The MiningMart project [25], [26] develops a system which stores executable KDD cases. The kernel of the project is an ontology of cases,i.e., the model of meta-data which describe a case. The model of meta-data, M4, is structured into a part describing the database and a part describing the sequence of steps. The meta-data of the database are structured into the conceptual level and the relational level. The conceptual level could be considered an ontology of the domain. The relational level describes the database with its relations and attributes. Most of the relational level comes along with standard database systems. The links between conceptual and relational meta-data are part of an application's meta-data. The sequence of steps is characterised with respect to the conceptual level of the meta-data. It is compiled into executable SQL code for the relational data and into calls to external data mining tools. The same conceptual meta-data can apply to several different relational meta-data. This eases the adaptation of a case to a new relational database, which fits the conceptual model. An engineer must only connect the conceptual meta-data to the own relational meta-data.

For our EAMS system, the storage of KDD cases is the important notion of MiningMart. The KDD cases which we have developed for the insurance application (see section 5) are linked with the ontology. A KDD case can be selected together with its already computed results or run on the database anew, if its content has changed. All the trials and errors of case design have been made by others[1], the user just selects a question from the menu and receives the results[2]. Minor modifications of a case can easily be done by the users. They select an ontology concept and a given KDD task and modify the parameters or the particular concept's features about which KDD should learn.

5 Application

The application we have developed is the support of employees of an insurance company. The main *application objectives* are:

- Customer acquisition,
- customer up and cross selling, and
- customer retention.

Different users are working towards these objectives. They are supported by the knowledge management system which provides them with up to date information about the company's customers (database world) as well as the competetors offers, demographic overviews, and related journal papers (internet world). We collaborated with the SwissLife insurance company, from where we received an anonymized database of 12 tables with at most 31 attributes and at most 1,469,978 rows. We were also given general information about the working procedures within the company.

Questions and Answers about Customers

Companies need information about their customers for offering new products to existing customers. It could be interesting to have a detailed analysis of the customers which allows the end user to look at the entire data set from a bird's eye perspective. **Frequencies** of attribute values like sex, family status, age class or profession group are shown. More complex frequencies can be displayed using multidimensional data cubes according to [27]. An advantage of the EAMS system is, that it is now possible to find out whether the customer distribution corresponds to that of the total population or not. The user might apply the integrated search engine for finding demographical information about population distribution.

[1] Here, we were the case designers, see sections 5 and 5. In general, a knowledge management team in cooperation with the database department would provide users with the required cases.

[2] In the screenshot 1 the question list is displayed in the upper half left, the list of jobs shows executed cases.

In order to acquire new content for the knowledge management system we have developed a KDD case for customer **segmentation**. In order to prevent attrition or churn it might be proper to provide special offerings to the different customer groups. We first choose different properties which allow a segmentation of the data. Some properties like profession or age have a large number of variations, so that we summarize their values into groups. Moreover, it was necessary to create a new table, in which every row contains all properties that belong to a customer. Then, we applied the Apriori algorithm to detect properties that frequently appear together. The results are frequent item-sets like

{age class: 40 to 65, male, married, insurance owner, mode of payment: pays, profession class: 1}.

If we compare the item sets found on the basis of the data about all customers with those found on the basis of only the customers who re-bought their insurcance, we encountered a significant difference for the most common group of customers (i.e., owner, payer and insured person are the same): this group makes up for 79% regarding all customers, but 94% regarding re-buy cases. In the data set reduced to surrender cases, Apriori found 91 frequent item sets. Using the criterion of certainty factors [28], the number of item-sets was reduced to 19.

{male, married, insurance owner, insured person} $\longrightarrow$ insurance surrender

For insurances it is very interesting to know if people will churn a contract, switch to other companies or keep their contract unchanged for years. The detection of high risk customers opens the possibility to offer special contracts to such people. The **prediction** of high risk customers is supplied by using two classification algorithms. On the one hand a decision tree analysis algorithm[3] and on the other hand a support vector machine[4]. However, the prediction of re-buy could not be effectively learned on the basis of customer properties, but required contract data (see below).

Questions and Answers about Contracts

In addition to the information gathered by analyzing the customers, the content needed in the knowledge management system is the structure of contracts. A contract is not a monolithical entity but is composed of different contract components, in which the contract conditions are determined. Each contract component stores the exact amount of premium, payment, for what parts does that specific component apply to, the type (pension, once-only payments, etc.) and the general framework (possibility of contract extensions, dynamic sampling, etc.). The contract itself is only an envelope around the contract components which specify the contract. **Frequencies:** The EAMS system produces a ranking

[3] J48 from the Weka project, http://www.cs.waikato.ac.nz/ml/weka

[4] mySVM according to Stefan Rüpping, http://www-ai.cs.uni-dortmund.de/SOFTWARE/MYSVM

by using statistical methods on the frequencies of each contract component ordered by their frequency[5] of occurence for a quick overview on different contract components. We contructed 214 contract types, each being characterized by a combination of the 11 most relevant attributes.[6] These types were applied to classify all contract components with a new attribute.

Correlation: Customer relationship management includes cross selling. Cross selling is the process of offering new products and services to existing customers. One form of cross selling, sometimes called up selling, takes place, when the new offer is related to existing purchases by the customers. Using data mining for cross selling helps to predict the probability or value of a current customer buying these additional products. A data mining analysis for cross selling moves beyond repeating the analysis required for customer acquisition several times, i.e. for each additional product. Here, the key is to optimize the offerings across all customers and products. The goal is to create a win–win situation, in which both the customer and the company benefit. Analyzing previous offer sequences with data mining methods can help to determine what and when to make the next offer. This allows to carefully manage offers to avoid over-soliciting and possibly alienating customers and to keep the costs low. Therefore the EAMS system aids in finding these correlations between contracts (and components) by inspecting the contract component combinations. This is achieved by using Apriori. Again we start with the previously segmented contract components, whose types are used as items for Apriori. A transaction in Apriori terminology accords to one client (the contract is assigned to the insurance holder to get a unique assignment) and his effected insurances. The resulting frequent item sets refer to combined acquired contract types, which are displayed with their support. Most frequently a capital contract with a contract on death or life were effected together.

Prediction: Churn predicition was not possible on the basis of customer data. When learning on contract data, we again applied mySVM and adopted the TFIDF-measure from information retrieval. Each property A_i of a contract component represents a **term**. The **termfrequency** TF is the number of changes of A_i in a contract component C_j defined as:

$$TF_{C_j A_i} = |\{x \in \text{year } | A_i \text{ of } C_j \text{ was changed in year } x\}| \tag{1}$$

Therefore the **document** $\text{TFIDF}_{C_j A_i}$ describes the history of changes of a contract component C_j which is calculated by

$$\text{TFIDF}_{C_j A_i} = TF_{C_j A_i} \cdot \log\left(\frac{|C_{\text{all}}|}{|\{t \in C_{\text{all}} | A_i \text{ changed in t}\}|}\right) \tag{2}$$

Based on this representation the vector for SVM training looks like:

$$C_j : \text{TFIDF}_{C_j A_1}, \ldots, \text{TFIDF}_{C_j A_{23}}, y$$

[5] Both relative and absolute frequency is displayed. The relative frequency is calculated by comparing the absolute frequency with the total number of contract-components.

[6] Note, that most of the combinations of attributes do not occur.

y is the target attribute (insurance surrender occured: yes/no). mySVM[7] delivered excellent results using a linear kernel (recall = 0, 4452; accuracy = 0, 8646; absolute error = 0, 3375). These results are sufficient for predicting an insurance surrender.

Web support: Informations from different competing insurance companies about products are rare. They aren't stored in a textual form to get processed by search engines so the results are insufficient. Therefore the aid from the EAMS system for the product designer on informations about contracts coming from the World Wide Web is rather small. Hence, the use of the learning search engine could not ne tested in this application.

6 Conclusion

In this paper, we have presented a principled approach of how to make available both, document collections and databases to users of a knowledge management system. Both types of information are glued together by the ontology which also generates the user interface. We have argued that the link to databases directly is not appropriate for the users' needs[8]. Instead, KDD bridges the gap between low-level data and high-level information needs of users. A case base of KDD cases is necessary for providing users with knowledge on the basis of their company's databases. Such a case base can be built incrementally, preparing a new case, when necessary. The acquisition of knowledge is eased since the data already given are used as its source. The maintenance of knowledge is guaranteed, since the cases of KDD are operational and run anew on the changed database whenever wanted.

For the personalisation of the ranked lists of documents, we have applied the system of Thorsten Joachims. This is particularly interesting, because it eases the search also in intranets. Personalisation of KDD results seemed not necessary. The presentation form can be selected from a menu, and so are the parameters of the data mining tools.

We have illustrated our approach with an application at the insurance company SwissLife. Since the colleagues with whom we were cooperating have left the insurance company, we could not validate our EAMS system in a practical test by real end-users. We regret this, but we hope that the ideas that were implemented in the EAMS system are nevertheless convincing.

Acknowledgment The EAMS system has been developed in a one year students project (PG402) at the university of Dortmund by Fabian Bauschulte, Ingrid Beckmann, Christian Hüppe, Zoulfa El Jerroudi, Hanna Köpcke, Phillip Look,

[7] kernel: dot, radial; mode: pattern; sample: random-sample (biased); evaluation on population.

[8] In our example, the aggregation and transformation of data into an informative and interesting form uses about 3000 lines PL/SQL for each case. No end-user could afford this affort of programming!

Boris Shulimovich, Klaus Unterstein, and Daniel Wiese under the supervision of Katharina Morik and Stefan Haustein. We want to thank Thorsten Joachims for placing at our disposal his excellent tool for the optimisation of retrieval functions in search engines. We also thank Regina Zücker, Jörg-Uwe Kietz, and Peter Brockhausen for their information about the insurance practice and the anonymised database.

References

1. Bartlmae, K., Riemenschneider, M.: Case Based Reasoning for Knowledge Management in kdd projects. In Reimer, U., ed.: Proc. of the Third Int. Conf. of Practical Aspects of Knowledge Management. (2000)
2. R., R.J.: Skills Management at Swiss Life. In: LLWA 01 - Tagungsband der GI-Workshopwoche Lernen - Lehre - Wissen Adaptivität. (2001) 227–236
3. Sure, Y., Maedche, A., Staab, S.: Leveraging Corpoate Skill Knowledge - From ProPer to OntoProPer. In Reimer, U., ed.: Proc. of the Third Int. Conf. of Practical Aspects of Knowledge Management. (2000)
4. Becerra-Fernandez, I.: Facilitating the Online Search of Experts at NASA using Expert Seeker People-Finder. In Reimer, U., ed.: Proc. of the Third Int. Conf. of Practical Aspects of Knowledge Management. (2000)
5. Karagiannis, D., Telesko, R.: The EU-Project PROMOTE: A Process-Oriented Approach for Knowledge Management. In Reimer, U., ed.: Proc. of the Third Int. Conf. of Practical Aspects of Knowledge Management. (2000)
6. Rainer, T., Dimitris, K.: Realising process-oriented knowledge management: Experiences gained in the PROMOTE-project. In: LLWA 01 - Tagungsband der GI-Workshopwoche Lernen - Lehre - Wissen Adaptivität. (2001) 206–212
7. Margelisch, A., Reimer, U., Staudt, M., Vetterli, T.: Cooperative Support for Office Work in the Insurance Business. Technical report, Swiss Life, Information Systems Research (1999)
8. Benjamins, V.R., Fensel, D., Gómez Péres, A.: Knowledge Management through Ontologies. In Reimer, U., ed.: Proceedings of the Second International Conference on Practical Aspects of Knowledge Management. (1998)
9. Gruber, T.R.: Towards Principles for the Design of Ontologies Used for Knowledge Sharing. In Guarino, N., Poli, R., eds.: Formal Ontology in Conceptual Analysis and Knowledge Representation, Deventer, The Netherlands, Kluwer Academic Publishers (1993)
10. Genesereth, M., Singh, N.: A knowledge sharing approach to software interoperation (1993)
11. Genesereth, M.R., Keller, A.M., Duschka, O.M.: Infomaster: an information integration system. In: SIGMOD 1997, Proceedings ACM SIGMOD International Conference on Management of Data, May 13-15, 1997, Tucson, Arizona, USA. (1997) 539–542
12. Vdovjak, R., Houben, G.J.: RDF-based architecture for semantic integration of heterogeneous information sources. In: Workshop on Information Integration on the Web. (2001) 51–57
13. York, S.: On-To-Knowledge. In: LLWA 01 - Tagungsband der GI-Workshopwoche Lernen - Lehre - Wissen Adaptivität. (2001) 213–216

14. Cranefield, S., Haustein, S., Purvis, M.: Uml-based ontology modelling for software agents. In: Proceedings of the Autonomous Agents 2001 Workshop on Ontologies in Agent Systems. (2001) http://cis.otago.ac.nz/OASWorkshop/Papers/oas01-27-cranefield.pdf.
15. Haustein, S., Lüdecke, S.: Towards Information Agent Interoperability. In Klusch, M., Kerschberg, L., eds.: Cooperative Information Agents IV – The Future of Information Agents in Cyberspace. Volume 1860 of LNCS., Boston, USA, Springer (2000) 208 – 219
16. Gandon, F., Dieng, R., Corby, O., Giborin, A.: A Multi-Agent System to Support Exploiting an XML-based Corporate Memory. In Reimer, U., ed.: Proc. of the Third Int. Conf. of Practical Aspects of Knowledge Management. (2000)
17. Christophides, V., et al.: Community webs (c-webs): Technological assessment and system architecture. Technical report, FORTH Institute of Computer Science (2000)
18. Chawathe, S., Garcia-Molina, H., Hammer, J., Ireland, K., Papakonstantinou, Y., Ullman, J.D., Widom, J.: The TSIMMIS project: Integration of heterogeneous information sources. In: 16th Meeting of the Information Processing Society of Japan, Tokyo, Japan (1994) 7–18
19. Joachims, T.: Optimizing search engines using clickthrough data. In: Proceedings of Knowledge Discovery in Databases. (2002)
20. Gray, J., Chaudhuri, S., Bosworth, A., Layman, A., Reichart, D., rali Venkatrao, M., Pellow, F., Pirahesh, H.: Data cube: A relational aggregation operator generalizing group-by, cross-tab, and sub-to tals. J. Data Mining and Knowledge Discovery **1** (1997) 29–53
21. Harinarayan, V., Rajaraman, A., Ullman, J.D.: Implementing data cubes efficiently. In: Proceedings of the 1996 ACM SIGMOD International Conference on Management of Data, Montreal, Quebec, Canada, June 4-6, 1996. (1996) 205–216
22. Agrawal, R., Srikant, R.: Fast algorithms for mining association rules in large data bases. In: Proceedings of the 20th International Conference on Very Large Data Bases (VLDB '94), Santiago, Chile (1994) 478–499
23. Quinlan, J.: Improved use of continuous attributes in C4.5. Journal of Artificial Intelligence Research **4** (1996) 77–90
24. Rüping, S.: mySVM-Manual. Universität Dortmund, Lehrstuhl Informatik VIII. (2000) http://www-ai.cs.uni-dortmund.de/SOFTWARE/MYSVM/.
25. Kietz, J.U., Zücker, R., Vaduva, A.: Mining Mart: Combining Case-Based-Reasoning and Multi-Strategy Learning into a Framework to reuse KDD-Application. In Michalki, R., Brazdil, P., eds.: Proceedings of the fifth International Workshop on Multistrategy Learning (MSL2000), Guimares, Portugal (2000)
26. Morik, K.: The representation race - preprocessing for handling time phenomena. In de Mántaras, R.L., Plaza, E., eds.: Proceedings of the European Conference on Machine Learning 2000 (ECML 2000). Volume 1810 of Lecture Notes in Artificial Intelligence., Berlin, Heidelberg, New York, Springer Verlag Berlin (2000)
27. Gray, J., Chaudhuri, S., Bosworth, A., Layman, A., Reichart, D., Venkatrao, M.: Data cube: A relational aggregation operator generalizing group-by, cross-tab, and sub-totals. Data Mining and Knowledge Discovery **1** (1997) 29 – 54
28. Fernando, B., Ignacio, B., Daniel, S., Maria-Amparo, V.: A New Framework to Assess Association Rules. In et al., H.F., ed.: Advances in Intelligent Data Analysis. Volume 2189 of LNCS. Springer Verlag Berlin (2001) 95–104

Data Integration for Multimedia E-learning Environments with XML and MPEG-7

Marc Spaniol, Ralf Klamma, and Matthias Jarke

RWTH Aachen, Informatik V, Ahornstr. 55, D-52056 Aachen, Germany
{mspaniol|klamma|jarke}@cs.rwth-aachen.de
http://www-i5.informatik.rwth-aachen.de/lehrstuhl/i5/index.html

Abstract. Integration of heterogeneous data is one of the greatest challenges for versatile e-learning environments, since support for different multimedia data formats is often restricted or adaptions are necessary to fit strict requirements. Therefore, we examine the opportunities given by new metadata standards like MPEG-7 and XML for knowledge management in terms of automated processing, evaluation and presentation of e-content. In Germany's first interdisciplinary and collaborative research center on "Media and Cultural Communications", we are studying the influence of transcription, localization and (re-) addressing on e-learning environments. Exemplarily, we want to introduce our Virtual Entrepreneurship Lab (VEL) as an approach to comply with these tasks in a multimedia e-learning environment.

1 Introduction

Both, knowledge management (KM) and collaboration among learners should be supported in e-learning environments [CC00]. Multimedia database systems [Ko02] can be used to organize integrated management of heterogeneous multimedia e-learning content while collaboration support in these database systems is still an open issue. The XML-based MPEG-7 standard [Ma02], introduced by the moving pictures expert group (MPEG) permits the integration of versatile multimedia data [BM02]. On the one hand, information can be categorized by an ontology and being classified that way, but on the other hand there is an increasing user interest in retrieval techniques on loose or even non-structured data. We therefore focus on opportunities given by the combination of both techniques based on multimedia database systems.

The integration of heterogeneous data as content for e-learning applications is crucial, since the amount and versatility of processable information is the key to a successful system. In this aspect we want to present the opportunities given by the metadata description standard MPEG-7 when (loosely) categorizing new information of different sources and types. Besides, it is possible to store data efficiently in XML databases and make it accessible for conventional KM techniques. Additionally XML data allows the handling of more than only meta information by making the data itself accessible for multimedia retrieval techniques. Hence, we have started several cooperations within our collaborative research center on

D. Karagiannis and U. Reimer (Eds.): PAKM 2002, LNAI 2569, pp. 244–255, 2002.

"Media and Cultural Communication" to analyze and evaluate the impact of new media on learning structures in cultural sciences [JK02].

In this paper we'd like to present and discuss KM and data integration in e-learning environments. The rest of the paper is organized as follows: In the next section we present related work concerning development of e-learning applications. In the following, the terminology of our joint collaborative research center will be introduced as basis for a discussion on current approaches. Afterwards we present our prototype for a multimedia e-learning environment, the Virtual Entrepreneurship Lab (VEL). The paper closes with a summary and an outlook on further research.

2 Current Approaches to Multimedia E-learning

Due to the interest in reducing costs of education on one hand and stimulating people to never stop learning on the other hand, prototypes of KM systems for e-learning applications have recently been developed in educational, industrial and research institutions. Latterly those applications that allow semantical enrichment of data and a loose categorization of the presented content have become very popular, since they suggest an unaffected presentation of the e-content. The KM of those data is somewhat more difficult, compared to e.g. ontology-based systems [FD98], due to the lack of underlying structures.

There exist several approaches to increase the acceptance and usage of existing platforms in education, but most of them are restricted in flexibility concerning the content and adaptation to the user's skills. In these approaches, learning and teaching is recognized as a KM task on digital archives stored in database systems. The following subsections give a brief overview on KM in distant learning community systems. Currently our analysis concentrates on infrastructure and media versatility in knowledge creation processes.

2.1 BSCW

The BSCW (Basic Support for Cooperative Work) system was developed at Fraunhofer FIT institute and acts as a common workspace to share and distribute information within a community [Kl00a]. Accessible via a web browser, the user navigates through the shared workspace consisting of folders, documents and links, organized in some kind of hierarchical file system. Besides it offers additional facilities for supporting cooperative work, like user administration, permission management or email directory services. So, a BSCW workspace can be thought of as a "web folder", which means a central repository, accessible via World Wide Web and accustomed browser software.

In our collaborative research center we introduced the system to our colleagues from the cultural sciences and started a common workspace to improve the knowledge transfer between cultural scientists and computer scientists. Because of the diverse working structure, the system was mainly used by the computer scientists. Another range of application is KM of projects and teaching at our department. Within the common workspace, students and researchers can share documents, which enhances the flow of information. The highlighting of new data by a special sign and logging of activities within the workspace makes it possible to analyze the knowledge distribution process in detail.

2.2 Notebook University

The "Notebook University" is a new aspect of multimedia e-learning environments and is currently being developed in concept and implementation. Nevertheless, some ideas have become apparent in new research projects [Ur02], [ZF02]. Most important for the notebook university is the ubiquitous access to information within the campus. Efforts in creation and management of knowledge are up to now reduced on simply making information accessible. The aim is to support knowledge sharing among all participants. Hence, a common workspace would be suitable to integrate, but isn't established yet. In future, a detailed analysis is necessary to see if and how far making information accessible at any time and anywhere will enforce conversation structures and knowledge creation.

Researchers actually developing notebook universities think, that due to the increment in mobile connectivity, the number and quality of interactions will increase. Consequently, this will add value in a speedier knowledge creation process. Courses and lectures also have to be further investigated, since new media and connectivity allow the integration of new learning tools and online discussions. So, notebook university will be a very interesting approach for the near future. Nevertheless it is doubtful, whether the approach will be successful as a stand-alone system. Probably new learning theories have to be developed and current e-learning environments have to be adapted and integrated.

2.3 Courseware Watchdog

Courseware Watchdog represents an ontology-based information system that has been jointly developed by the Learning Lab Lower Saxony and the University of Karlsruhe [SS02a]. It is designed to find and visualize relevant educational material on the WWW according to the user's needs. Automatic crawling on related websites guarantees, that documents will be categorized according to the terms of the ontology. By matching and evaluating the user's preferences with the affiliated categorizes of a document, all user relevant data will be personally addressed. Similar approaches can also be found at Fraunhofer FIT institute [JK01], e.g. in the ELFI system. Current research projects at FIT, e.g., aim at the creation of an e-learning environment.

KM in such ontology-based systems is done by classification of heterogeneous data within a predefined schema and a redistribution of the information afterwards [SS02b]. To increase the flexibility of the system, current studies cover the ontology evolution. Hence it becomes necessary to introduce new concepts when they newly appear on the web, and to integrate them at the right position of the used ontology. This will make it possible to analyze the changes in ontologies by versioning or recognizing shifts in the usage of concepts.

Fig. 1. Entrepreneurship e-learning platform for virtual communities

2.4 The Virtual Entrepreneurship Lab (VEL)

The Virtual Entrepreneurship Lab (VEL) is a joint development of Lehrstuhl Informatik V and Fraunhofer FIT institute [KH02]. It is based on theories that are taught at the MIT (Massachusetts Institute of Technology) in entrepreneurship education. Starting from a constructivist point of view, it represents an interactive learning environment combining the advantages of new metadata standards as MPEG-7 and meta information languages as XML.

The VEL represents a hyper dimensional multimedia e-learning platform (cf. figure 1). To the right there is a three-dimensional categorization schema, which allows loose filtering of the presented content. The three dimensions are predefined and fixed by specific aspects of a founding of a company. The content selection concerning entrepreneurship education segregates three parameters:

- time: the different phases of the founding process
- person: selection of a specific person, who acts as a founder
- skills: browsing aspects of relevant founders' skills

The thumbnails in the circular overview vary related to the chosen category. By dragging it from its position and dropping it in the middle, the user selects a media file. A red frame surrounding it, indicates its selection. Now the user can work with the selected media and all annotations concerning the media file are accessible. The additional metadata can now be used for better understanding of the situational background. By highlighting the appropriate buttons depending on the context of the selected media, the user shall be encouraged to investigate other entrepreneurial aspects associated with the media file.

		BSCW	Notebook University	Courseware Watchdog	Virtual Entrepreneurship Lab
Transcription	Content Adaptability	++	++	o	-
	Media Versatility	++	++	o	++
Localization	Community Suitability	+	-	o	+
	Interactivity	-	+	o	+
(Re-) Addressing	Personalization	o	--	++	o
	Interface Adaptability	--	--	--	--

Legend: ++ strongly supported, + good integration, o average support, - weak integration, -- not supported

Fig. 2. Transcription, localization, and addressing in e-learning environments

At the bottom is a screen element to maintain collections. Media files can be selected, arranged and annotated with additional information. This user-specific customization shall guarantee a continuous and gradual improvement of annotations. Collections can be seen as an approach to focus on a certain aspect: combining and customizing media files by compounding this view on single media components with additional, issue-related information with the aim to pursue creative collaboration on certain issues on which the collection is focused on.

3 Media Versatility in E-learning Environments

When we started our participation in the collaborative research center, we had to learn the terminology used by various disciplines within the cultural sciences. This disturbance - the lack to understand the terminology of another scientific domain - made it necessary to "map" the domain-specific terminology onto terms more appropriate to the computer science community. So the first step that we undertook was to transfer their terminology into terms that are widely used in the field of computer science [Ja02]. In our opinion the usage of these terms is advantageous for the computer science community. Hence, we are now trying to give an overview on how the well-defined terms of transcription, localization, and (re-) addressing can be transferred into common terms of the computer science:

- *Transcription* is a media dependent operation to make media settings more readable, like e.g. semantical enrichment of data.
- *Localization* means an operation to transfer global media into local practices.
- *(Re-) Addressing* describes an operation that stabilizes and optimizes the accessibility of global communication, as it is done by personalization.

We are now dicussing in how far existing e-learning approaches fulfill these aspects. In figure 2 we give a brief overview on our results by trying to combine the terminology of both communities, with respect to the following analysis:

- *BSCW* offers a wide range of media types to be supported as well as easy content adaptability and community suitability. Data management can simply be done as it is handled in common operating systems and the great success of this tool is a proof of excellent community suitability. Besides personalization is limited to a user specific content view that restricts the overall amount of files to those, that affect the user. Interactivity and interface adaptability are very restricted, because the system behaves as an asynchronous accessible file system.
- The *Notebook University* projects provide good opportunities in transcription, because wireless LAN allows distributing huge amounts of versatile media. On the other hand localization and personalization seem to be restricted, since current approaches do not show any more than creating a common platform for knowledge distribution.
- *Courseware Watchdog* offers average localization and transcription features. This is based on the fact that integration and reaction on new media files is possible in general, but compatibility to common standards as, e.g. MPEG-7, is missing. Semantic Web approaches might back media integration in the future. The system strongly supports personalization, as it is an ontology-based information brokering system, but lacks up to now an adaptive user interface. Same arguments also hold for FIT Fraunhofer's *ELFI* system.
- The *Virtual Entrepreneurship Lab* is based on the MPEG-7 metadata description standard. Therefore it has excellent capabilities in terms of media versatility. Besides interactivity and community suitability are well supported, as there are techniques integrated like drag&drop and the possibility to share collections among members. It also offers personalization features as personal selections and annotations. Up to now its lacks the availability of automated content integration and adaptability of the user interface.

It becomes obvious (cf. figure 2) that those system backing transcription strongly, fail more or less in addressing and vice versa. On the other hand we can see, that up to now, the community aspect in terms of localization should be improved, since the cooperation within the community will be crucial for the success of KM. In addition, the user interface adaptability needs enhancements in all systems.

4 Knowledge Management with MPEG-7 and XML

Ontology-based information systems have been developed to structure content and to support information retrieval in KM. They reach from simple catalogs to information system ontologies using full first order, higher order or modal logic [SW01]. Applications of ontologies can be found in various information brokering systems, which have been very effective for knowledge creating processes in the last few years. Especially the modeling of context for information captured in an organizational memory (OM) has been a very promising approach to support knowledge creation [Kl00b]. Furthermore, research has been undertaken to combine the resource description framework (RDF) with an information brokering system [LC02]. The problem is that an ontology has to fit into all user interpretations, which become obvious, when an ontology creation is shared [DC98].

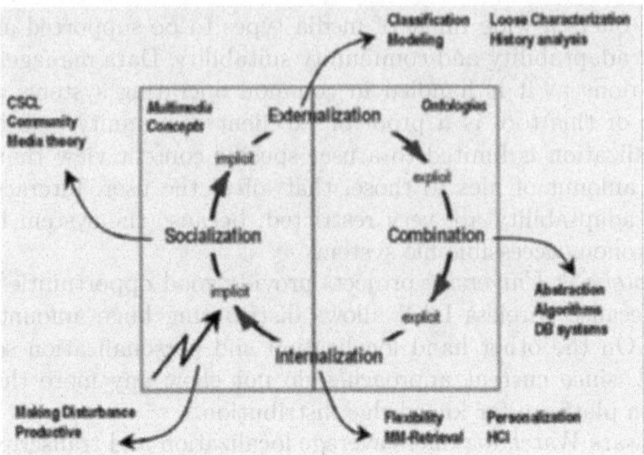

Fig. 3. Making disturbance productive: Coupling multimedia concepts with ontologies

Therefore the ontology development is usually guided by domain experts in an iterative, incremental and evaluative process [RB02].

In our collaborative research center we are currently investigating the impact of disturbances as origin of a knowledge creation process. We therefore examine a disturbance as the starting point of a learning process and try to make it productive for both individuals and the community. Due to the interests of cultural scientists in semantical enrichment of data and by transcribing already existing documents, we are trying to combine those practices with methods of computer sciences, by jointly developing new information systems based on MPEG-7 and XML. This means that we have to reduce (or even close) the gap between metadata description in multimedia concepts and strict categorization of ontologies.

4.1 Combining Multimedia Concepts with Ontologies

Nonaka and Takeuchi's approach [NT95] of classifying knowledge either as implicit or as explicit that undergoes a continuous process of knowledge creation has been of great importance for studies in the field of KM. Similar to the assumptions by [PL02], the knowledge building process can be seen as a combination of Nonaka and Takeuchi's thesis with the aspects of disturbance triggered knowledge creation (Engeström) and knowledge building communities (Bereiter). Therefore we want to point out, where disturbances commonly take place and what strategies can be applied, to make them productive.

Figure 3 shows a modification of Nonaka and Takeuchi's cycle of knowledge creation. We have divided up the process into two sections. On the left hand side we concentrate on those aspects of *multimedia concepts* that are used for socialization, as analyzing communities, which depend on social interaction among learners. On the right hand side we recognize combination as, e.g., database systems that are necessary for efficient data management, like in *ontology-based*

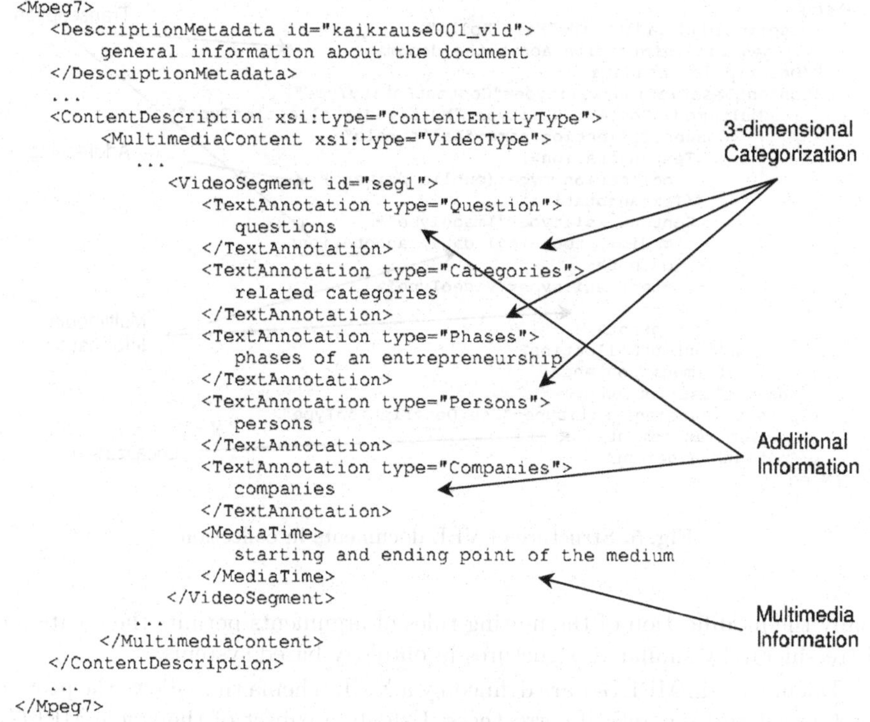

Fig. 4. Basic structure of VEL MPEG-7 documents

systems. In between are the cutting edges in terms of externalization and internalization. There, *multimedia concepts* and *ontologies* meet each other, since it becomes necessary to make implicit knowledge explicit and vice versa. Common techniques therefore are, e.g., modeling or classification on one hand and multimedia retrieval or human-computer interaction (HCI) on the other hand.

In our point of view, the transfer of explicit knowledge into implicit knowledge is most likely to be affected by disturbances, since the user often has problems to get suitable information. Consequently, we have to analyze how to overcome this problem. Therefore we are trying to optimize the personalized addressing in knowledge creation processes. In the case of the VEL we have discovered a disturbance in knowledge transfer from entrepreneurs to students.

4.2 Transcription, Localization, and Addressing in the VEL

Descriptors and description schemes (DS) are basic concepts of the XML-based MPEG-7 standard. Descriptors define the syntax and semantics of each feature or metadata element, whereas DS specify the structure and semantics of the relationships between components. In addition, the description definition language (DDL) allows the creation of MPEG-7 descriptors and DS. It provides a syntax to combine, express, extend and refine descriptors as well as DS [Hu01]. Espe-

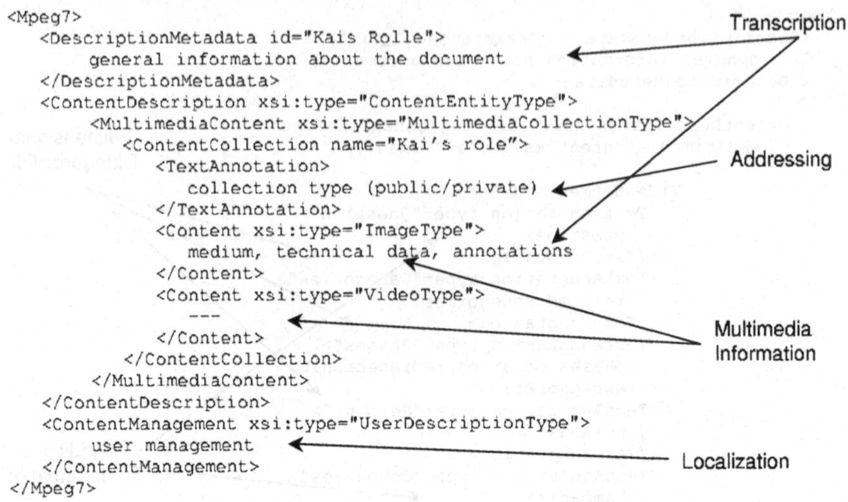

Fig. 5. Structure of VEL documents in collections

cially the modification of the nesting rules of arguments permits the creation of a tree-hierarchy similar to structures in ontology-based systems.

Documents in MPEG-7 are defined by a XML schema that allows the prove of syntactical and semantical correctness. Usually a subset of the whole MPEG-7 standard is selected and defined in a document type definition (DTD), since the whole standard is too extensive. When creating new e-content for the VEL, MPEG-7 documents will be validated against the MPEG-7 schema and the predefined DTD. Verification of the DTD ensures that all necessary information for the VEL system exist. By validation against the schema compatibility of, e.g., datatypes, which cannot be defined in a DTD, is being assured. Besides MPEG-7 metadata allows qualitative access to the content of multimedia data by searching, filtering and applying information retrieval techniques as in [GD00], [SS01]. The system features guided linking and arranging of the data, too. Furthermore, data transfer between applications compatible with MPEG-7 is made easy.

A brief overview on the structure of VEL MPEG-7 documents is given in figure 4. It allows the combination of loose categorization, annotations and multimedia information. The VEL allows the transcription of data by simply annotating documents with additional information. Even more, the integration of heterogeneous data is being made possible by the MPEG-7 description scheme.

Figure 5 indicates the substructures of a MPEG-7 VEL document concerning information about annotations and collections. Concordances with the basic structure of VEL MPEG-7 documents (cf. figure 4) are visible. The aspects of transcription, localization and addressing as well additional information on the multimedia content are specially figured out. We give the opportunity to textual annotate documents for the moment being. The user management does localization in the VEL. It administrates the users within the community and permits access to the system. Addressing on a coarse level in the VEL is done by the previously described localization tools, which manage user access to the community. On a more granular level, users can modify access rights of collections. They enable them to make collections accessible to the whole community or to keep it private. To improve the efficiency of addressing further improvements can be implemented, e.g. by analyzing the usage history [BY02].

5 Discussion

Generally, the MPEG-7 standard allows a comprehensive content description and a semantic coding of multimedia data. This is necessary, since efficient retrieval techniques for a tool like the VEL, which integrates heterogeneous data, are needed. Therefore, MPEG-7 serves as an expedient framework. However, annotation and handling of non-linear materials has still to be done manually to achieve a high quality of the e-content. In this aspect, the domain knowledge about entrepreneurship education has strongly influenced the content editing.

The cooperation with Kurt Fendt from the MIT was very effective for the design of a constructivist e-learning environment. For instance the loose categorization represents a design aspect that makes the structure of the data more transparent. It allows applying concepts of ontologies to be bound with nearly unlimited metadata information of MPEG-7. Furthermore, confining to three dimensions reduces the risk for the user to get lost while navigating through the data. Hence, the number of media thumbnails and categorization buttons is limited to retain the overview. This ensures that, the user will be guided when studying the content and is being motivated to explore associated materials.

For best exploitation of metadata information in our software applications we are currently researching on accessorily options MPEG-7 offers. The next step will be to develop adaptive user interfaces to make the content presentation dependent on the predefined settings. Hence, an integration of the extensible stylesheet language transformation (XSLT) in the VEL is currently being studied. By applying XSLT, a personalized content presentation will be possible without any other manipulation in a transcribed MPEG-7 file. The structure of valid XML documents can also be used to create a somewhat simplified ontology. Subsections of the XML and their nested arguments could be interpreted in that way. Automatic processing of the MPEG-7 files is backed by their hierarchical structure. Therefore, queries can be used to directly access selected elements of a document via XPath/XQuery [CD99].

6 Conclusions and Outlook

In this paper we presented and discussed current approaches on KM in e-learning environments. Thereby, the appearance of disturbance in knowledge transfer causes a transcription and (re-) addressing process, which becomes necessary, when information cannot be understood by all participants correctly. By example of the VEL we showed that the usage of MPEG-7 makes the transcription process transparent and flexible. Also the coupling of ontology-based information systems with metadata-enriched multimedia files can be achieved.

Multimedia retrieval techniques are also to be developed in the future to exploit the opportunities MPEG-7 gives to its extents. Further studies will be necessary to develop efficient retrieval techniques for both ontology-based data structures and metadata enriched multimedia concepts. Hence, we have started cooperations in our collaborative research center to stabilize addressing and improve personalization. Together with cinematic scientists, we are currently creating a specialized movie archive, and in conjunction with scientists of philology we are planning to develop an e-learning laboratory for sign language education.

The availability of multimedia standards enables us to develop e-learning environments that render up to date disciplinary research and didactics. By relying on metadata standards we keep flexibility for further developments. They allow us to integrate new learning modules and to seek for additional scope of duties. We hope to detect a model core common to learning processes, which can be extended to fulfill specific requirements in versatile area of applications.

Acknowledgements. This work was supported by German National Science Foundation (DFG) within the collaborative research centers SFB/FK 427 "Media and Cultural Communication" and SFB 476 "IMPROVE". We like to thank our colleagues for the inspiring discussions. Special thanks to Oliver Fritzen for reviewing this article.

References

[BM02] Benitez, A. B., Martinez, J. M., Rising, H., Salembier, P.: Description of a Single Multimedia Document. *Manjunath, B. S., Salembier, P., Sikora, T. (eds.): Introduction to MPEG-7 – Multimedia Content Description Interface, John Wiley & Sons Ltd.* (2002), pp. 111–138.

[BY02] van Beek, P., Yoon, K., Ferman, A. M.: User Interaction. *Manjunath, B. S., Salembier, P., Sikora, T. (eds.): Introduction to MPEG-7 – Multimedia Content Description Interface, John Wiley & Sons Ltd.* (2002), pp. 163–175.

[CC00] Clarke, P., Cooper, M.: Knowledge Management and Collaboration. *Reimer, U. (ed): Proceedings of PAKM2000 – Practical Aspects of Knowledge Management, PAKM 2000, Basel, Switzerland, October 30–31* (2000).

[CD99] Clark, J., DeRose, S.: XML Path Language (XPath) Version 1.0. *World Wide Web Consortium, chapter.1http://www.w3.org/TR/xpath,* (1999).

[DC98] Dieng, R., Corby, O., Giboin, A., Ribière, M.: Methods and Tools for Corporate Knowledge Management. *Proceedings of the 11th Banff Workshop on Knowledge Acquisition, Modelling and Management, KAW'98, Banff, Alberta, Canada* (1998).

[FD98] Fensel D., Decker, S., Erdmann, M., Studer R.: Ontobroker: The Very High Idea. *Proceedings of the 11th International Flairs Conference (FLAIRS-98), Sanibal Island, Florida* (May 1998).

[GD00] Gandon, F., Dieng, R., Corby, O., Giboin, A: A Multi-Agent System to Support Exploiting XML-based Corporate Memory. *Reimer, U. (ed): Proceedings of PAKM2000 – Practical Aspects of Knowledge Management, PAKM 2000, Basel, Switzerland, October 30–31* (2000).

[Hu01] Jane Hunter: An Overview of the MPEG-7 Description Definition Language (DDL). *IEEE Transactions on Circuits and Systems for Video Technology, 11(6)* (2001), pp. 765–772.

[Ja02] Jarke, M.: Wissenskontexte. *Künstliche Intelligenz, Heft 1/02* (2002), pp. 12–18.

[JK01] Jarke, M., Klemke, R., Nick, A.: Broker's Lounge – an Environment for Multi-Dimensional User-Adaptive Knowledge Management. *Proceedings of the 34th Annual Hawaii International Conference on System Sciences, Hawaii, USA* (2001).

[JK02] Jarke, M., Klamma R.: Metadata and Cooperative Knowledge Management. *Proceedings of the 14th International Conference on Advanced Information Systems Engineering, CAiSE 2002 Toronto, Canada, May 27–31; Springer* (2002), pp. 4–21.

[KH02] Klamma, R., Hollender, E., Jarke, M., Moog, P., Wulf, V.: Vigils in a Wilderness of Knowledge: Metadata in Learning Environments. *Proceedings of the IEEE International Conference on Advanced Learning Technologies, ICALT 2002, Kazan, Russia, September 9–12* (2002), pp. 519–524.

[Kl00a] Klöckner, K.: BSCW - Educational Servers and Services on the WWW. *Proc. of the International C4-ICDE Conf. on Distance Education and Open Learning "Competition, Collaboration, Continuity, Change", Adelaide, Sep 9–14,* (2000).

[Kl00b] Klemke, R.: Context Framework – an Open Approach to Enhance Organisational Memory Systems with Context Modelling Techniques. *Reimer, U. (ed): Proceedings of PAKM2000 – Practical Aspects of Knowledge Management, PAKM 2000, Basel, Switzerland, October 30–31* (2000).

[Ko02] Kosch, H.: MPEG-7 and Multimedia Database Systems. *SIGMOD Records, ACM Press, Vol. 31* (June 2000), pp. 34–39.

[LC02] Liu, P., Curson, J., Dew, P.: Exploring RDF for Expertise Matching within an Organizational Memory. *Proceedings of the 14th International Conference on Advanced Information Systems Engineering, CAiSE 2002 Toronto, Canada, May 27–31; Springer* (2002), pp. 100–116.

[Ma02] Martinez, J. M.: MPEG-7 Overview. *International Organization for Standardization, http://mpeg.telecomitalialab.com/standards/mpeg-7/mpeg-7.htm* (2002).

[NT95] Nonaka, I., Takeuchi, H.: The Knowledge-creating Company. *Oxford University Press, Oxford* (1995).

[PL02] Paavola, S., Lipponen, L., Hakkarainen, K.: Epistemological Foundations for CSCL: A Comparison of Three Models of Innovative Knowledge Communities. *G. Stahl (ed): Computer Support for Collaborative Learning: Foundations for a CSCL community. Proceedings of the Computer-supported Collaborative Learning 2002 Conference, Hillsdale, N.J.; Erlbaum* (2002), pp. 24–32.

[RB02] Reich, R., Brockhausen, P., Lau, T., Reimer, U.: Ontology-Based Skills Management: Goals, Opportunities and Challenges. *Journal of Universal Computer Science, Vol. 8, No. 5* (2002), pp. 506–515.

[SS01] Salembier, P., Smith, J. R.: MPEG-7 Multimedia Description Schemes. *IEEE Transactions on Circuits and Systems for Video Technology, Vol. 11, No. 6* (June 2001), pp. 748–759.

[SS02a] Schmitz, C., Staab, S., Studer, R., Stumme, G., Tane, J.: Accessing Distributed Learning Repositories through a Courseware Watchdog. *Proceedings of the E-Learn 2002 – World Conference on E-Learning in Corporate, Government, Healthcare & Higher Education* (2002).

[SS02b] Studer, R., Sure, Y., Volz, R.: Managing user focused access to distributed knowledge. *http://www.aifb.uni-karlsruhe.de/WBS/rvo/papers/iknow02.pdf* (2002).

[SW01] Smith, B., Welty, C.: Ontology: Towards a new synthesis. *Welty, C., Smith, B. (eds.): Formal Ontology in Information System, Ongunquit, Maine; ACM Press* (2001), pp. iii–x.

[Ur02] Urmel: Ubiquitous RWTH for Mobile E-Learning. *http://www.urmel.rwth-aachen.de/* (2002).

[ZF02] Zitterbart, M., Fruchter, R., Pehrson, B.: I am here! Mobile Learners in dSpace. *www.learninglab.kth.se/projekt/mobile_learner.pdf* (2002).

Managing Business Models for Business Application Development

Koichi Terai[1], Masahiko Sawai[1], Naoki Sugiura[1], Noriaki Izumi[2] and Takahira Yamaguchi[1]

[1] Dept. Computer Science, Shizuoka University,
{terai, sawai, sugiura}@ks.cs.inf.shizuoka.ac.jp,
yamaguti@cs.inf.shizuoka.ac.jp
[2] Cyber Assist Research Center, AIST Tokyo Waterfront,
niz@ni.aist.go.jp

Abstract. Due to the recent trend of the management science and *e*-business, it is significant to respond customers' requirements rapidly than ever before. In order to achieve the rapid response, we have to manage enterprise models and to reflect the requirements on the models. This paper proposes a management framework of layered enterprise models. Proposed framework consists of a business model repository and a software repository that support enterprise modeling, workflow modeling, and application development. This framework helps us to develop web applications in incremental deployment of analysis, design, and implementation. We have implemented a prototype environment by JAVA. Each repository's contents are described by XML so that the repositories are interoperable.

1 Introduction

Due to the recent trend of the management science[6], it has been becoming significant for managers to reflect their strategy on their enterprise structure and activity. By combining such sort of management theory with the latest topic of e-business, the target of knowledge management is about to shift from the organizational memories to enterprise activities. Especially, in order to respond the customer's requirement rapidly, dynamics of the enterprise architecture has been focused, which is called the adaptive enterprise[2]. The concept of the adaptive enterprise, however, still remains as the abstract theory. In fact, it is not easy to restructure the organizational structure of the large companies rapidly. Although the SME (small and middle enterprises) may have some possibility of agile adaptation, there is no clear guide how and what to change for the realizing of the adaptive enterprise.

From the above significance of realizing the adaptive enterprise, this paper proposes the management framework of layered enterprise models. We do not regard the innovation of new enterprise models as the emerging the whole idea, but as the combination of a small idea and the existing heterogeneous ideas of business models. In order to accelerate the spiral process of continuing innovation

D. Karagiannis and U. Reimer (Eds.): PAKM 2002, LNAI 2569, pp. 256–267, 2002.

and deployment of business idea, we focus on the e-business and concentrate on restructuring virtual enterprise architecture.

In our framework, in order to establish the strategy-driven reconstruction of enterprise, the main activities of the innovation phase are involving the related business models and merging the obtained heterogeneous models. On the phase of the deployment, a relevant application of the business model such as an on-line-store on the Web is developed.

In order to reuse and to classify business models, a number of repositories have been provided. In the field of MS (Management Science), the most famous one is the *e*-Business Process Handbook[10], called Process Handbook for short, carried out by MIT. Process Handbook is a substantial contribution as a business repository, which contains approximately 4,600 definitions of business activities from abstract processes to the specialized one to the business over the Internet. Its formality, however, is not strict since the most part of the definitions are described by natural language. This means unavailability of definitions of business activities for machine processing.

From the viewpoint of the formality on the process specification, there is the Enterprise Ontology[8] of Edinburgh University in the field of artificial intelligence. Its formality is very strong and it contributes the reuse of business models nevertheless it covers only so general and abstract concepts that it is very hard to construct concrete business models with operability.

On the other hand, a lot of software libraries for building EC applications have been proposed. Most of them are originally developed as repositories for the agent applications and extended to ones for the business applications. Furthermore, the special platform for the development of enterprise applications is provided such as J2EE[9]. Those libraries and platforms offer the strong framework for the construction of real applications. There are, however, no clear relationships between software components and business models.

From the above viewpoints, in order to develop the management of the enterprise design, we devise a business model repository based on the existing repositories to support business model development, and also devise a software repository to support application implementation from the model that is archived by the business model repository. Proposed framework support us to reconstruct the enterprise activity and to reflect the established strategy to organizational architecture of the enterprise. At the same time, our repository helps us to investigate the availability of knowledge management not only for the business process management but also management strategy.

2 Constructing Business Model Repository

Business model repository contains reusable business models on different abstraction levels. Actually, we provide two abstraction levels for business model. Higher abstracted one is called Enterprise Model that clarify the tasks an organization holds. Another is called Workflow Model that clarify how each task's goal is archived.

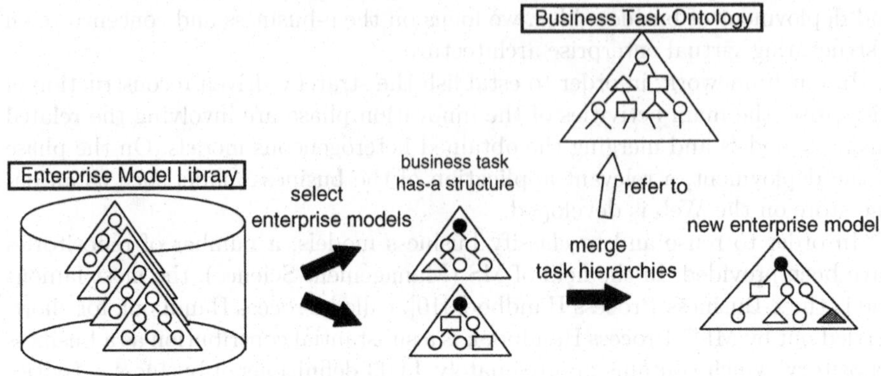

Fig. 1. Developing New Enterprise Model

Table 1. Business Process Methods

Abstract	Assign	Classify	Compare
Cover	Critique	Evaluate	Generate
Group	Match	Modify	Operationalize
Propose	Predict	Select	Sort
Specify	Verify		
Obtain	Receive	Provide	Present

An Enterprise Model contains tasks' definitions and task hierarchies to specify what to do in the business and to define relationships between tasks. New Enterprise Model is constructed by merging task hierarchies of existing Enterprise Models in the context of the task relations. In the construction of the new model, we require a library of existing models from which merged models are selected, and a overall task hierarchy which are refered to by the merging process. We construct an enterprise model library and a business task ontology for each. Figure 1 shows development processes of Enterprise Model.

A Workflow Model consists of Business Process Patterns. Business Process Pattern is substructure of Workflow Model. The pattern is constructed by sequencing its primitives that are defined by business process methods and their input and output objects. The business process methods are provided as PSMs (Problem Solving Method) based on CommonKADS's[1][7] inference primitives. Table 1 shows the list of the business process methods. Input and output objects are employed from the ones that appeared in the task definitions of Process Handbook. Figure 3 shows a example of Business Process Pattern that is for the task "Deliver product or service".

A new workflow model is constructed by exploiting Business Process Patterns from each task contained in Enterprise Model, and merging its input and output

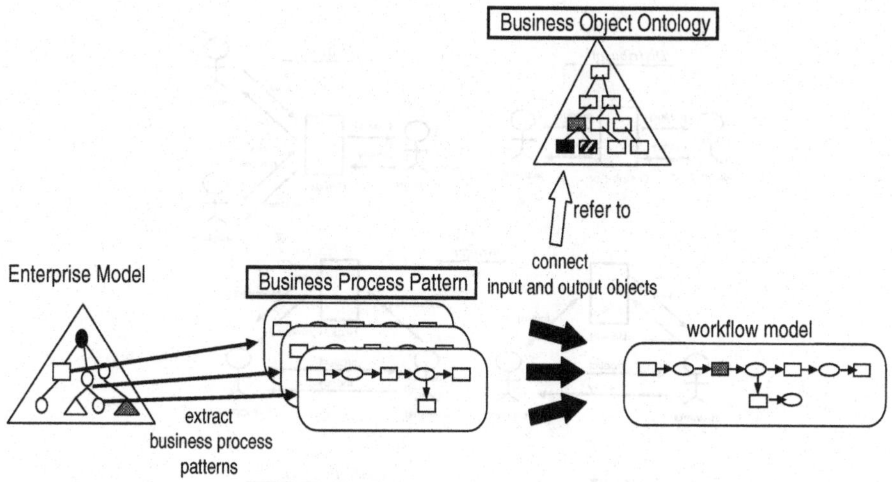

Fig. 2. Developing Workflow Model

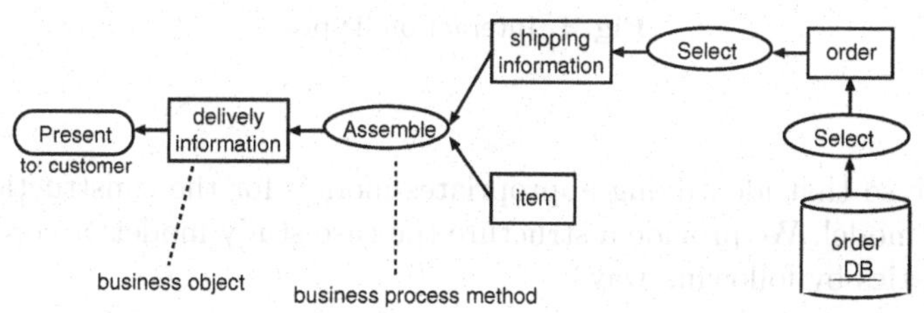

Fig. 3. A Example of Business Process Pattern

objects by unifying as a common generic object. In order to identify a common generic object among two objects, a concept abstraction hierarchy is required[5]. We construct the hierarchy as a business object ontology based on IS-A relation among objects. Figure 2 shows development processes of Workflow Model.

2.1 Constructing Enterprise Model Library

We develop an enterprise model library by restructuring the case study enterprise models in Process Handbook. Each case study model contains has-a relations between business tasks that make up the business. For example, famous online bookstore Amazon.com has the task structure that top level tasks are made up with "Buy", "Sell", "Manage", and these business tasks have followed-level tasks such as "Receive order", "Attract audience to web site", "Manage resources by type of resource", and so on. The case study models itself, however, don't have

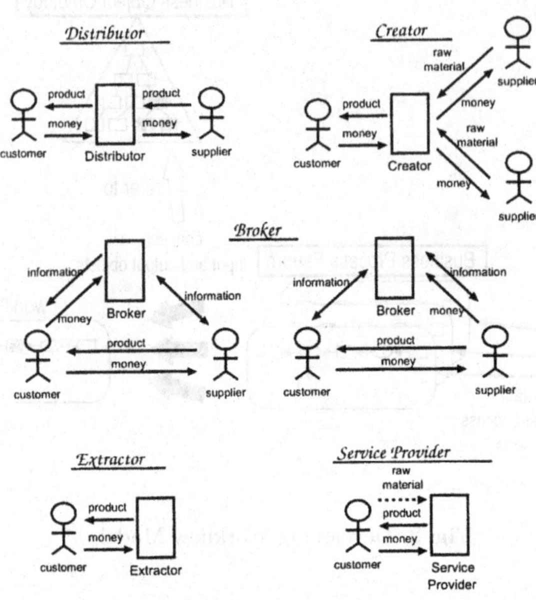

Fig. 4. Interaction Types

a structure so that identifying appropriates models for the construction of new enterprise model. We provide a structure the case study models according to its characteristics by following way.

1. Identify actors (such as customer, supplier) appearing in the case study enterprise model and interactions among those actors.
2. Categorize classes according to the type of the interaction. In this case, five classes (Distributor, Creator, Broker, Extractor, and Service Provider) are categorized (show Figure 4).
3. Provide a hierarchy for each class according to the characteristic of each case study model. Each case study has a specific characteristic such as "via Internet", "via electronic store", and those are structured according to its frequency of appearance. A characteristic that frequently appears is considered as a general one, and it is placed at top level of hierarchy. (show Figure 5)
4. Put each case study model into the hierarchy considering its characteristic. This hierarchy of the case study models is defined as enterprise model library.

2.2 Constructing Business Task Ontology

Process Handbook has a structure of business tasks. It is, however, difficult for machine processing to use the Process Handbook as it is because of its semantic

Fig. 5. Feature Hierarchy

ambiguous with informal concepts such as "what", "how", and so on. Due to this semantic problem that formal definitions like "is-a" or "has-a" relationship are not given, we rebuild the Process Handbook into the business task ontology, which contains formal inheritance structure of task properties, as follows.

1. Consider the frequency of each business task contained in each case studies of Process Handbook.
2. A task that frequently appears is regarded as a generic one, and it is placed as an upper concept of is-a relation's hierarchy.
3. Other tasks are added the hierarchy by referring to Process Handbook's task structure.

Constructed business task ontology is shown in Figure6. In this ontology approximately 500 tasks are defined.

2.3 Constructing Business Object Ontology

We employ the WordNet [3] as a general ontology that contains over 17,000 concepts, in order to reuse general concepts in the construction of the business object ontology. Main objects of the business object ontology are employed from Process Handbook by extracting terminologies from its business tasks' definitions. We construct the business object ontology as follows.

1. extract terminologies from tasks' definitions in Process Handbook.
2. Identify the structure of business objects based on WordNet, respect to the degree of frequency and the abstraction of the terminologies.
3. A structure that is archived by above way is defined as a business object ontology. Figure 7 shows a part of constructed business object ontology.

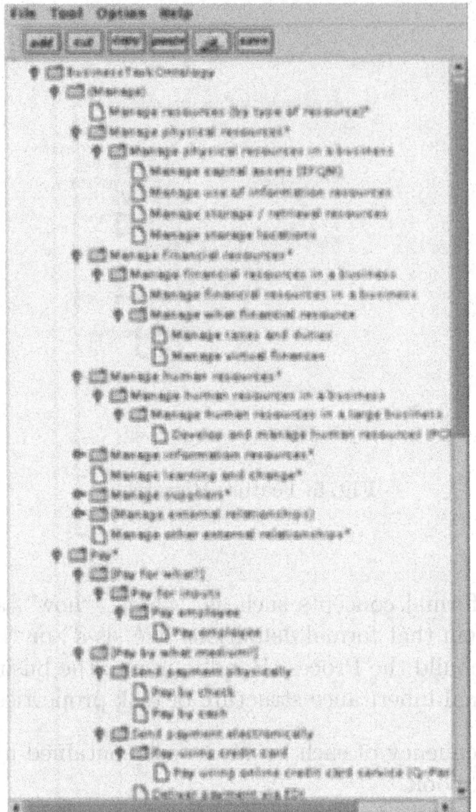

Fig. 6. Business Task Ontology (a part)

3 Constructing Software Repository

To obtain an executable application from the model that is archived by the use of the business model repository, we provide a repository of software library as a software repository. In this study, we have selected Web-store as a case study business, so software repository is specialized for Web-store application. In order to help us to write a program code of a system, the software repository contains business components, relevance information of components, and information of their use.

A business component[4] is a software package, which is used in various business applications. There is an issue in what granularity and sorts of the business component should be implemented. From a standpoint of a target application of Web-store management, we have defied seven business components by analyzing commercial business component package: Order, Shopping Cart, Inventory, Customer, Delivery, Catalog, and Payment. Each business component has API information described with XML. As a semantic unit of application model, Com-

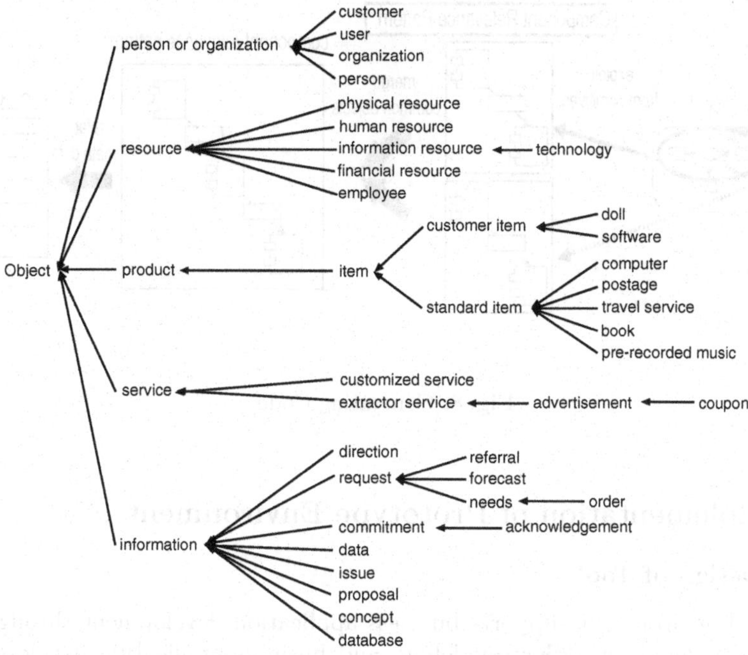

Fig. 7. Business Object Ontology (a part)

ponent Relevance Pattern is defined. Component Relevance Pattern specifies the message passings among the components in specific situations. For example, when a customer order a item, shipping information and billing information associated to the customer are passed from the Customer component to the Order component. We have collected those patterns by analyzing existing web stores and commercial applications.

In order to generate Web-store application code from a workflow model, we exploit Component Relevance Patterns from each business process method in Workflow Model. Then, we merge common objects among the patterns. Finally, we generate code by referring to the meta data contained in the pattern. Figure 8 shows the code generation process.

There are several types of participants in developing Web application such as an application architects, page designers, and Java programmers. Our environment does not support page design but can generate simple input field (HTML input form). Application architecture is fixed by underlying web application framework (Struts of The Jakarta Project[11] in this case study), but it can be changed by implementing adaptation code for each framework. Java code is generated from component relevance pattern.

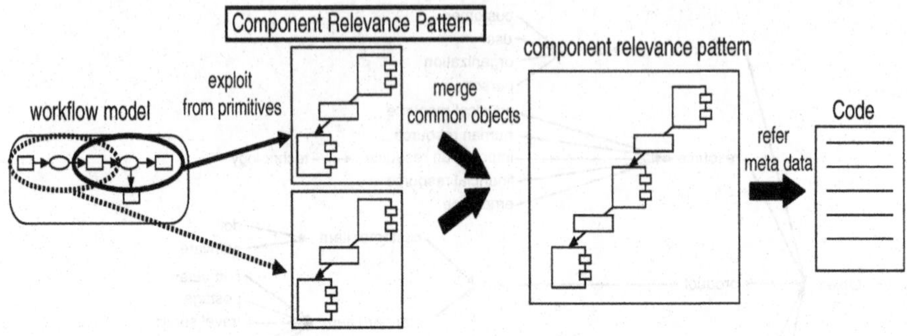

Fig. 8. Generating Code

4 Implementation of Prototype Environment

4.1 Design of Tool

Proposed environment supports business application development through enterprise modeling, workflow modeling, and business application development. Each model dealt with by each modeling step is basically composed of objects and their relations. The object corresponds to such as business object, business process method, software component, and so on. The relations are defined based on the objects defined. Because these models can be shown graphically (show in Figure 9) as the related objects, we are able to implement our environment as GUI application in order to deal with models easily. We can edit the model by intuitive way such as clicking, dragging, and so on.

In order to make it easy to implement repository management tools, we have designed common APIs for all repositories. Each repository contains various models and libraries, but its basic construction elements are concepts (business task, business object, and so on), and their relations and structure (is-a, has-a relation, and tree structure). We have designed common APIs for the concept, the relation, and the structure as follows.

- Operations against a concept
  - Edit label
  - Add and remove a attribute
  - Edit attribute value
- Operations against a relation and a structure
  - Add a concept to a structure
  - Move a concept to other place in a tree structure
  - Add and remove a relation
  - Replace a concept related to a relation

All repository management tools are based on these common APIs, and tool specific APIs are implemented by adding new APIs or overwriting these APIs.

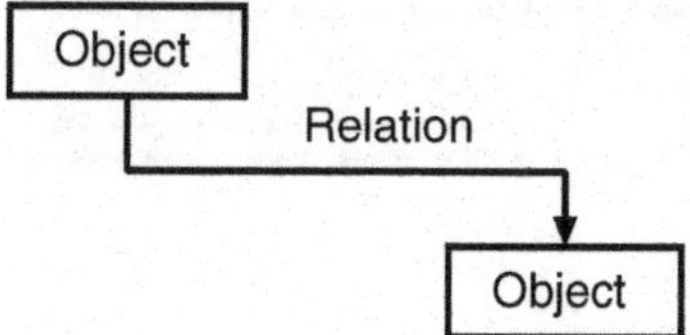

Fig. 9. Model Primitive

4.2 Implementation of the Environment

In this study, three tools have been implemented by Java language: enterprise model editor, business process editor, and component relevance pattern editor that support enterprise modeling, workflow modeling, and application development respectively. All tools input and output XML description of models so that tools can be connected seamlessly. Each tool is shown Figure 10, Figure 11, and Figure 12. Total data size of the tools and the repository contents (XML data) are 6.3MB and 1.3MB for each.

We have applied these tools to case studies , and the result of the application confirms us that we are able to manage the various information corresponding to the three repositories.

5 Discussion

Proposed environment supports the whole development processes of business application from abstract business model level to application implementation level. Many CASE tools have been developed to support business application development. These tools, however, focus on software engineering processes. Because of models unavailability among interprocess work, business modeling is supported as an isolated process by usual CASE tools. This is because there is a gap between abstract business model and business application such as information quantity and concept abstraction level. In order to bridge the gap, the environment provides business model repository. Workflow Model plays a main role in this study to bridge the gap by providing Business Process Patterns. Business Process Pattern has flexible abstraction levels due to its generic primitives that are method and object. By providing a common model as a middle model between enterprise model and software model, the participants in a organizations from manager to programmer can discussion with the model. The software repository supports business application development. The software repository contains static software components in this study. In order to develop application more flexibly and efficiently, this repository would be required to cooperate existing CASE tools and other software engineering studies. From the above discussions, we have confirmed the validity of our methodology.

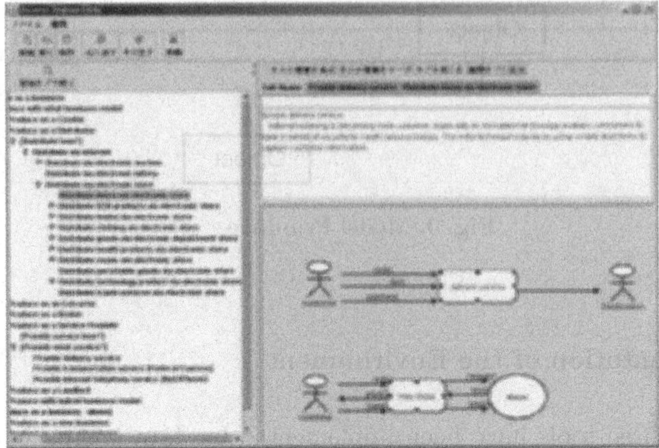

Fig. 10. Enterprise Model Editor

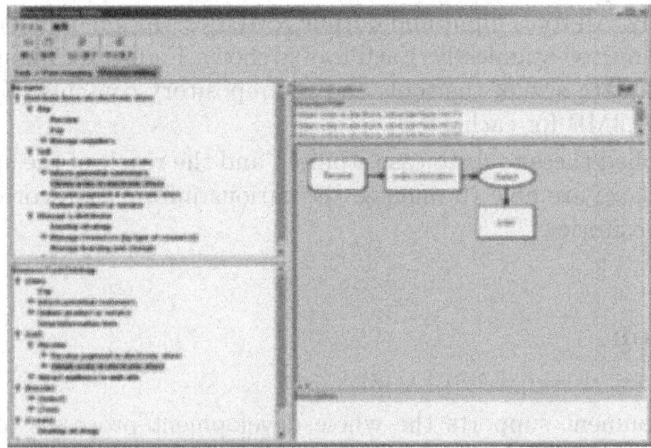

Fig. 11. Business Process Editor

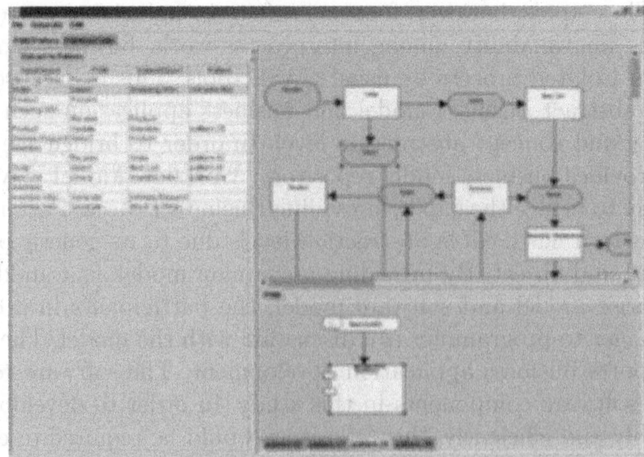

Fig. 12. Component Relevance Pattern Editor

6 Conclusion

In this paper, we have proposed an environment to develop business application. In order to manage several granularity concepts, we have devised a business model repository and a software repository, and developed libraries and ontologies such as business task ontology and business object ontology. Ontology provides us the context for integrating existing models'. Using these repositories we can develop business application by incremental development from enterprise model to application model.

We have implemented a prototype environment with Java language as GUI applications: enterprise model editor, business process editor, and component relevance pattern editor. Each editor deals with each aspect of business application development and manages repositories. By coding repository contents with XML, each editor exchanges the input information or output product seamlessly each other.

References

1. Breuker, J., W. Van de Velde.: COMMONKADS LIBRARY FOR EXPERTISE MODELING. IOS Press, and Ohmsha (1994)
2. Despres, C., Chauvel, D.: KNOLEDGE HORIZONS, Butterworth-Heinemann (2000)
3. Fellbaum, C. (ed.): WordNet. The MIT Press (1998). see also URL: http://www.cogsci.princeton.edu/~wn/
4. Herzum, P., Sims, O.: Business Component Factory. John Wiley & Sons (1999)
5. Izumi, N, Yamaguchi, T.: Supporting Development of Business Applications Based on Ontologies, 3rd International Conference on Enterprise Information Systems (2001)
6. Kaplan, R.S.:, Norton, D.P.: THE STRATEGY-FOCUSED ORGANIZATION, HBS PRESS (2000)
7. Schreiber, Guus, et al.: KNOLEDGE ENGINEERING AND MANAGEMENT. The MIT Press (1999)
8. Ushold, M., et al.: The Enterprise Ontology, Knowledge Engineering Review, Vol.13, Special Issue on Putting Ontologies to Use (1998)
9. J2EE: http://java.sun.com/j2ee
10. The MIT Process Handbook Project: http://ccs.mit.edu/ph
11. Struts: http://jakarta.apache.org/struts/index.html

A Process for Acquiring Knowledge while Sharing Knowledge

Harald Kjellin and Terese Stenfors

Department of Computer and Systems Sciences
Stockholm University and Royal Institute of Technology
16440 Kista, Sweden

hk@dsv.su.se, terese@dsv.su.se

Abstract. This study produces and evaluates a process that aims to bring out the tacit competence within professionals so that others can use it. The main conclusion in this study is that using a seminar based on interviews for bringing out tacit competence works and can be recommended. The seminar has been developed gradually through prototyping. Two larger evaluation studies have been performed as well as smaller informal studies. The results from the two test seminars as well as results from interviews and questionnaires have been analysed and compared with established criteria to measure the success of the proposed process. The competence brought out during the test seminars has been found easy to understand and predicted to be useful.

1 Introduction

For a company to cope with the present competitive market, organisations need to use their staffs' competence and knowledge in a more efficient way. The knowledge residing within the staff of a company is today considered one of the company's greatest assets. Unfortunately the potential knowledge is much greater than the used knowledge. Tacit knowledge is in many cases knowledge that people do not even know they have. It is most important that companies recognise the value of the tacit knowledge and find ways of using it. Knowledge is only a benefit to a company if it is available.

This paper has a practical approach to knowledge management theories and aims to suggest a solution to the common problem of how to induce professionals to mediate their tacit knowledge in a simple and concrete way, so that the right person can get access to it and use it.

The aim of this study is to produce and evaluate a seminar that brings out the tacit competence within professionals. The seminar will result in explicit rules of thumb describing the participants' professional competence. The rules of thumb will be presented in such a manner that they can be read and used by others within the company via an Intranet, where the results can be stored.

D. Karagiannis and U. Reimer (Eds.): PAKM 2002, LNAI 2569, pp. 268-280, 2002.

2 Method

As part of the preliminary research for this study, questionnaires were distributed to students participating in two selected courses at the University of Stockholm. The courses were selected since they both use teaching methods based on students teaching each other and learning from each other. The courses also used iterative interviews as a part of the pedagogic strategy. The reactions of the students participating in these courses have been used to evaluate the usefulness of these teaching methods. The results from the questionnaires were used only to provide initial guidance to the advantages and disadvantages in knowledge sharing seminars.

Altogether 124 questionnaires were collected and analysed. In short the students had a very positive attitude towards the teaching methods used. A large majority of the participants wanted the methods to be used in other courses at the University as well. Most of the participants also believed a seminar where the students taught and interviewed each other was a positive experience and that the interviews facilitated their learning and structuring of knowledge.

Since the process being tested in this study is new and unique the seminar was produced using an iterative process, which can also be referred to as a prototyping approach. The method for developing the seminar was chosen because of the complex character of the topic and the lack of paradigms within the area. Prototypes for parts of the concept for the seminar were tested on individuals and small groups. These first empirical studies were informal. The seminar was gradually refined based on the feedback received from the subjects of the study. Because of the large number of variables involved (competence, motivation, readability etc.) a gradual empirical evaluation was assumed to be more practical. To develop the seminar further two more formal empirical evaluation studies were made.

2.1 Evaluation Studies

Two evaluation studies were performed at the University of Stockholm. The first study had five participants and the second six. The participants were all students at the university. Questionnaires, structured interviews and observations during the two test seminars were used to collect data. The same informants were used for all three evaluation methods. The target audience for this study is professionals, not students and therefore these tests, described in the section below, only verifies whether the process is rewarding or not for students.

After the first seminar, changes to further improve the methods were made based on the feedback received from the subjects of the study and initiated co-workers and researchers at the University of Stockholm. The test seminars focused on studying working methods that are used by professionals as well as students. It was therefore assumed that students could be used instead of professionals in the evaluations studies.

During the first of the two seminars an observer participated actively in the interviews, while at the second seminar the observation was non-participating. Both observations were open, direct, passive and structured and aimed to answer the following questions: 1) Do the participants understand what they are supposed to do? 2) Are the participants able to do what they are supposed to do?

Questionnaires were distributed to all participants of the two test seminars directly after the seminars had finished. A few days after the seminars interviews were made with the participants. In connection with the interview the interviewees were asked to study the results of two anonymous participants from the seminar the interviewees themselves attended. The interviews evaluated not only the seminar itself, but also the competence brought out, and the possible use of it for others.

3 An Introductory Description of the Evaluated Seminars

The evaluated seminars started with a short introduction to knowledge and competence. The advantages with sharing knowledge were discussed and the methods that were going to be used were explained. The introduction lasted until all the participants seemed to have grasped the advantages of the process and understood the procedures that were to follow.

The participants were then divided into pairs and a few questions were shown on an overhead. The questions concerned what the participants believed to be the most important for them in their role as students, how they tried to achieve this, the methods they used for studying and how they solved specific problems that they came across. The participants asked each other the questions and the interviewer wrote down the replies on a piece of paper. The interviewer gave feedback to the interviewee's replies and they were discussed before the roles reversed and the interviewer became the interviewee. After a while the participants were asked to change partners and summarise their own answers to their new partner. New questions were shown and the procedure repeated. The participants changed partners once more and new questions were displayed. In total the participants answered approximately ten questions.

The participants were then asked to transfer their answers to a pre-designed template. The templates were collected and the results could be published on an Intranet, where people could search for a specific skill or method to solve a particular task. The recommended seminar will be described in full later in this paper.

4 Theoretical Framework

To some people a certain piece of knowledge might be mere information, because he or she does not understand it and its context, but to somebody else that information is knowledge. Allee [1] calls this the "great paradox of knowledge". Braf [2] claims that tacit knowledge is developed in parallel with competence within a new area, and that one need not be particularly skilful to at least have some tacit knowledge in a certain area. Therefore it is assumed that the seminar will be applicable for recently employed personnel as well as very experienced ones.

To transform tacit to explicit knowledge Baumard [3] believes that most of the knowledge we posses has been gained through socialisation. The seminar evaluated in this study uses socialisation to communicate and assimilate people's experiences so that we do not all need to make the same mistakes as our colleagues did when getting the experience. Maier, Prange and Von Rosenstiel [4] suggest that one way of making tacit knowledge explanatory is with interviews and this is the method that will be used in the seminar.

Nonaka and Takeuchi [5] believe that redundancy is an important condition for knowledge creation and that concepts and information need to be shared even with people who might not immediately need it. Sharing information promotes sharing tacit knowledge and therefore redundancy speeds up the knowledge creation process. When information is shared people can offer each other advice and new perspectives. Nonaka and Takeuchi refer to the phenomena as "learning by intrusion" [6].

Traditionally, knowledge has been a key to power and success, and therefore people throughout history have been keen to keep it to themselves. Allee [7] claims that this is no longer the case, since knowledge today gets outdated so quickly. Allee believes that knowledge still equals power but not until you share it with others. Knowledge is today being used as a joint source of power for a particular group of people instead of a source of individual power [2].

4.1 Competence

This study focuses on what Anttila [8] refers to as functional competence. Functional competence is developed gradually and is what is sometimes referred to as learning by doing. By focusing on a person's ability to solve a task instead of his or her qualifications this type of competence can be detected.

Haglund and Ögård [9] believe that companies have to make the methods for competence development more effective and that ways have to be found that support competence development running alongside ordinary production. They believe companies should focus on improving what they refer to as learning competence, to cope with future demands. Learning competence is the ability to teach and learn. When people have reached a certain competence level within teaching and learning, they automatically raise their levels within professional competence and relational competence. Learning competence creates a lever action and leads the company into a positive spiral.

4.2 Core Competence

"Core competencies are those unique characteristics that enable a company to generate innovative products continually and to extend market capability." [10] It is "a unique bundle of skills and technologies that enables a company to provide particular benefits to customers" [10]. Allee further believes that core competence is fundamental to a company's success. It is assumed that the seminar this study will produce and evaluate will help the participants to identify their company's core competence. By identifying core competence with colleagues, the common ground and future visions for the employees and the company will be reinforced.

Prahalad and Hamel believe core competence is "the collective learning in the organization, especially how to coordinate diverse production skills and integrate multiple streams of technologies." [11] Core competence is also about the delivery of value, the organization of work, communication and commitment to work over organisational boundaries. People must let their functional expertise, that is their core competence, unite with other people's skills, since competence grows stronger when it is shared and applied. The seminar recommended in this study will facilitate the identification of the individual participants core competence.

4.3 Learning

According to Braf [2] there are two types of learning: learning from information and learning from experiences. Via learning from information people can learn from other people's experiences and recycle their knowledge. Argyris [12] believes that a lot of people do not know how to learn, and that they sometimes block themselves from learning. People have to reflect over the way they think about their own behaviour and their reason for learning. To critically reflect over one's work performance is very difficult for many people. In fact people usually react defensively to these kinds of activities to protect themselves and their behaviour. People will try to turn the focus of the conversation from their own behaviour and towards someone else; this is what brings learning to a halt according to Argyris. Haglund and Öd [9] have found the same resistance towards learning competence. Argyris claims that teaching people how to reason about their behaviour in new ways will break down the defences that might be blocking the learning process.

Maier et al [4] point out a fact that strongly supports the aim for the seminar, namely that individuals learn from people they experience as being similar to themselves. Therefore it is assumed that for colleagues in similar job positions, the seminar will support and encourage this process, and hence stimulate learning. Maier et al also claim that the capacity of a group to store knowledge is superior to that of individuals. This memory they believe, consists in all members of the group's knowledge of what knowledge is stored within whom and also the knowledge itself stored within the individuals. The members usually specialise in certain domains, and the other members pass on relevant knowledge to the domain specialist. The better a group is at recognising its members' expertise, the better they are at making decisions. This supports the idea of a seminar where the group members' competence are discussed.

4.4 Meta-cognition

Pramling [13] explains meta-cognition by saying that it is about how we gain knowledge about how to gain knowledge. In children this ability is not yet developed. For example children cannot tell whether they have understood something or not. Flavell [14] suggests that within some domains meta-cognitive knowledge might not be possible until one has some knowledge or expertise within that area. This suggestion emphasises the idea behind this study i.e. that the professionals themselves share their meta-cognitive knowledge about their work, since they are the only ones having this meta-cognitive knowledge about a certain task.

4.5 Group Dynamics

In the process of knowledge sharing and learning that will be evaluated in this study there is a combination of team learning and individual learning. In the seminar the aim is to stimulate new insights that would not be possible without encouraging a dialogue within a group of several members. Braf [2] claims this is the general aim of team learning. After the seminar, the results will be available for the participants to study on their own and discuss with each other if they wish to do so.

Since every group is unique, different groups will come up with different results for the same task. This is one of the reasons why it is believed to be a good idea to let the same people participate in the seminar on a regular basis (perhaps every six months) in a slightly different group constellation.

4.6 Interviews

People need other people to see what they cannot see themselves. People are blind for their own implicit assumptions [15]. This is an argument supporting the proposed type of seminar. The interviewer will be able to help the other person find the rules of thumb for his or her competence, and the most important working methods. Dixon believes that a lot of people do not want to admit that they need help to identify these, and therefore the interviews are designed to gradually help people to identify their competence without demanding any definitions. By reversing the roles during the interviews everybody will both help and be helped, which will further facilitate the identification of the rules of thumb.

The Von Restorff effect shows that the hardest things to remember for people are the things they do and the methods they use on a daily basis [9]. In the seminar people will be helped to make these things explicit by discussing them with the other participants. A solution or method must be tried or analysed by someone with similar experience before one can tell whether it is useful or not [16] and by articulating the tacit knowledge together with someone, as it will be done in this seminar, this feedback will be given directly.

4.7 Templates

The results from the knowledge sharing and creating process (i.e. the rules of thumb for the participants' competence) will be stored in a specific template. The template used in the proposed seminar consists of eight headlines and adequate space for the participants to fill in their own results. The different headlines will be domain independent and valid within several different areas of use. Having all the participants' results stored according to the same template will make it easier for others to use the results [17]. It will also make updating the information easier if the seminar is repeated. A company's Intranet creates possibilities to spread and mobilise the knowledge, and by implementing an online search engine people can search for the information they are looking for.

5 Success Criteria, Results, and Validation

The success criteria for measuring the usefulness of the evaluated seminar spring from research within related areas, literature studies, and discussions with knowledgeable persons within knowledge management and other relevant areas. The fulfilment of the criteria is measured from the analysis of results from the observation of the two seminars, the questionnaires, the interviews and literature study.

5.1 Participation

The participants must experience that they get substantial support for reflecting about their situation. Argyris [12] believes that if people are made to reason about their behaviour in a new way, the defences that block learning can be broken down. 90% of the participants in the two test seminars felt supported to discuss their own working methods according to the questionnaires.

The participants must feel motivated to think critically. To critically analyse one's behaviour is one of the keys behind what Argyris [12] calls double-loop learning. 65% of the participants in the two test seminars claim that they felt motivated to critically analyse their working methods. One of the positive participants commented: "Because it helped my personal development".

Participating in the seminar must be a positive experience, and the participants must be motivated. If the person being interviewed is not motivated, he or she will not bring about the information wanted. Efficient transformations between data, information and knowledge are only feasible if the participants are motivated and prepared to share and learn. The questionnaires show that 100% of the participants thought participating in the seminar was fun and motivating. Two participants wrote "self realisation" and "It is fun to talk about oneself". Simplicity is another key to motivation. All of the participants found the instructions for the seminar easy to understand.

The participants must be able to communicate in an efficient way with one another. Dixon [18] claims that for people to send and receive knowledge they need to share context and background. In the test seminars all the participants were students at the same department of the University of Stockholm and thereby their context and background is to some extent shared. None of the interviewed participants experienced any communication problems during the seminars. According to the interviews all the participants found it easy to understand each other.

The participants must feel comfortable in the interview situation. Jğhult [19] believes that for people to share their views and opinions, a good atmosphere is needed. The environment should be as neutral as possible. According to the questionnaires all the participants felt relaxed and comfortable during the interviews.

The participants must feel that the critical feedback they receive to their presentations help them produce better results. According to Argyris [20] response to one's ideas is crucial to learning. 84% of the participants in the seminars felt that the feedback helped them produce better answers. One positive participant wrote "It is good to have a speaking partner, then you have to think extra hard about why something is in a certain way." Another positive participant wrote "Counter questions gave the chance to develop thoughts and think again."

5.2 The Contributed Knowledge

The results must be of use for the employees. Everybody has knowledge useful to somebody else within the company [18]. Knowing that the seminar will result in something of use for the participants is a motivator to perform one's best during the seminar. During the interviews all participants expressed that they believe the results from the seminar to be useful. Some participants thought they might be even more useful for professionals than for students. Many of the interviewees expressed how inspiring they found comparing their own results to others.

The participants will learn something from attending the seminar. Learning and achieving new knowledge is a strong motivator for many people. Especially learning about oneself and learning that will improve work performance. In a successful knowledge transfer the receiver automatically starts the process of learning. 82% of the participants believe that they learned something during the seminar, the remaining participants answered "I don't know". One person believed he or she learned "To reflect over my behaviour in different situations, why I do this and that."

The participants' prerequisite knowledge about one another must not affect the result to a great extent. According to the interviews none of the participants believed that the answers they wrote down were affected by who the interviewee was. To avoid participants trying to answer in a favourable instead of a true way to please or impress the interviewer it is important that there is no or little hierarchy between the participants in a seminar group

Information about the participants' working methods and competence should not be used for any other purposes than those agreed on. Dixon [18] believes that one of the main criteria for a rewarding discussion is that the participants know what the information will be used for. This goal can be achieved by the seminar leader stating what the results will be used for at the seminar, both initially and in the summary at the end of the seminar. It is also possible to produce an agreement over what the results can be used for that is signed by both participants and seminar leader. During the test seminars this goal was achieved through the introduction of the seminar and dialogues with the participants in connection with the interviews. During the observations in the test seminar, no worries concerning what the results were to be used for among the participants were detected and they did not hesitate when asked to sign the templates with full names and hand them in.

All irrelevant information must be eliminated. Dixon [18] claims that when there is too much information to read, people give up and loose interest. The conclusion after analysing the results is that they do not contain any or very little irrelevant information. None of the interviewed participants experienced any difficulties in selecting what to write down from what the interviewee said.

Employees must be able to understand the result of other participants. Davenport and Prusak [21] emphasise the importance of knowledge being coded in the way most suitable for that type of knowledge. How to organise content is critical since well-structured and accurate information supports learning [22]. Information must make sense to the user for learning to occur [22]. During the interviews the interviewee was asked to study the results of two participants from one of the test seminars. None of the participants said that they experienced any problems in understanding the results.

5.3 Areas of Use

The information should be of use in appraisals when employees meet their employer. Most interviewed participants think this is an excellent idea since the templates will reveal working methods, and also what the person wants to achieve with his or her job. The seminar, if repeated, could function as a base for such revisions. The results can also be used to discuss progress and future competence development needs.

The information should be of use when putting together a project group to find the various types of competence needed. All but one interviewee believed that the results could be used to find people working according to certain working methods. One person supported the idea since he or she believed the seminar brought out things the participants themselves were unaware of. Some people suggested that the results should be complemented with a CV or a list with other skills and achievements.

The information should be of use in recruitment situations. Most interviewees thought the results would facilitate finding an applicant working according to a certain sought after method. The templates can also be used in a recruitment situation, especially internal recruitment. If everybody involved is familiar with the seminar and the results, an employee can compare his or her results with results from people working in other departments to see where his or her competence is most needed.

The information should be of use when introducing newly employed people. This would make it possible for new employees to get an overview of how their predecessors worked, what they found important, their unique competence and the most important working methods used by the company. Most interviewees gave a positive response to this question, with one person believing it to be an ideal solution since "nothing is as useful as seeing how people work".

5.4 Summary of the Results

The results from the three sections above:

- **Participation:** All criteria concerning participation were fulfilled.
- **Contributed Knowledge:** All criteria concerning contributed knowledge were fulfilled.
- **Areas of Use:** All criteria concerning areas of use were fulfilled.

6 Description of the Recommended Seminar

Earlier in this paper a short introductory description of the seminar has been presented. Here we give a more extensive description of the recommended seminar in its final version.

6.1 Preparations and Introduction to the Seminar

The number of participants should be 15-20 and everyone taking part should be sent some information about the topic in advance. The seminar takes no more than four hours. The introduction aims to inspire and motivate the participants. The need for the seminar should be presented in a way that shows every individual how he or she is affected and an inspiring vision of the results must be created. The goals of the seminar should be clearly stated.

6.2 Introduction to the Interviews

To introduce the next part of the seminar (the interviews) the seminar leader asks the participants some questions from the templates that will be used in the interviews. The participants answer the questions as a department and not as individuals. The first question might be for example "What is most important within this department?" and another question is "Why does this department perform a certain task better than other departments in other companies doing the same thing?". The seminar leader asks the participants' attendant questions until he or she receives the type of answers he or she is looking for, and that he or she considers being useful. The interview continues until the group has grasped the concept of core competence.

6.3 Interview Part One

The participants are divided into two groups: interviewers and interviewees. Blank sheets are handed out for the interviewer to fill in. It is assumed that using a pre-designed template would restrict the participants. They might feel that they are not allowed to bring up more issues than would fit in the template. The interview builds on the funnel question technique. The interview starts with general questions and gradually they get more and more specific.

In the test seminars some rules for the interviews were presented and it is believed that they facilitated the interviews. Therefore the use of the following rules is recommended: 1) The interviewee does not have to give straight answers but is allowed to think aloud about the question asked. 2) The interviewer is allowed and recommended to use follow-up questions such as 'why' and 'how'. 3) The interviewer shall give the interviewee continuous feedback on his or her answers.

The interviewers asks the following questions:

- What is your job title? Give a short description of your job.
- What skills and attitudes are needed for doing your job?
- What is most important in your job?
- What is the most important task in your job?

The questions above should be asked by one participant to another only and then the roles will be reversed; the interviewee will perform the same interview on the other participant.

6.4 Discussion

A group discussion is assumed to be a good way of keeping motivation among the participants high. The seminar leader leads the discussion covering the following subjects: 1) The difficulty in knowing what we know. 2) Our defence system against discussing our working methods and ourselves. 3) The difficulties and advantages in interviewing each other.

6.5 Interview Part Two

This part of the interview is divided into two. The participants are first asked to find a new interview partner and start with a quick review of the answers from before the break.

- Describe your own working methods to perform the most important task in your job and the different steps in them.

A considerable amount of time should be spent on the question above since many participants in the two test seminars believed it to be the most interesting, important and useful part of the seminar. After being asked and asking another participant the question, the participants are asked to find a new partner. Again the interview starts with a short revision of the earlier answers.

- Resources needed to perform the task.
- Problems that might occur when performing the task.
- The expected outcome of the working method.

6.6 Summary and Presentation of Results

Most participants in the test seminars were keen to discuss the seminar after it had finished and this is seen as an indication that a summary is a good idea. The following issues can be discussed:

1. The bonus effects a seminar like this creates. (Getting to know colleagues better will for example probably lead to more knowledge exchange in the future.)
2. How the feedback we have received and the reflections we have made will affect our working methods in the future.
3. How addressing these issues will make us more perceptive for learning new ways of solving problems.
4. How competence develops and changes over time.

The participants can be asked to type their own template into their computer and publish it on the company Intranet. The working methods can then be read and used by everyone in the company. Rosenberg [22] believes that there might not be a better way to create a learning culture than by creating an obligation for everyone to teach each other. This is exactly what this seminar will do. By explaining their working methods the participants will teach the listener and him/herself that this job can possibly be done in a more efficient way.

7 Conclusions

Using a seminar where participants interview each other is a method that works for bringing out tacit competence. The method was highly appreciated by the participants in the two test seminars. All the criteria produced to measure the success of the study were fulfilled.

According to the participants' replies in the interviews, the results were presented in a way that allowed them to be read and used by others. None of the interviewed participants experienced any problems in understanding other participants' results or filling in the template with their own results. The interviewed participants also found the results useful and they accepted the working method used to produce the results. A large majority of the interviewed participants believe that all the suggested areas of use for the results of the seminar are feasible.

The overall conclusion is that the method used and produced in this study to bring out tacit competence can be recommended.

7.1 Future Research

The evaluation studies performed for this study could serve as a base for further research. We believe the seminar needs to be tested on a larger scale with full three to four hour seminars with large groups of professionals within different professions. The use of the results of the seminar in different contexts should also be empirically tested before it is possible to scientifically verify them.

References

1. Allee V: The Knowledge Evolution. Expanding Organizational Intelligence Newton MA: Butterworth-Heinemann (1997) 180
2. Braf E: Organisationers kunskapsverksamheter en kritisk studie av "knowledge management" (Filosofiska fakulteten, avhandling 37), Linköping: Linköpings universitet (2000)
3. Baumard P: Tacit Knowledge in Organizations London: Sage Publications (1999)
4. Maier G W, Prange C, Von Rosenstiel L: Psychological Perspectives of Organizational Learning. In Dierkes M, Bethoin Antal A, Child J, Nonaka I: Handbook of Organizational Learning and Knowledge. New York: Oxford University Press (2001)
5. Nonaka I, Takeuchi H: The Knowledge Creating Company How Japanese Companies Create the Dynamics of Innovation, New York: Oxford University Press (1995)
6. Nonaka I, Takeuchi H: The Knowledge Creating Company How Japanese Companies Create the Dynamics of Innovation, New York: Oxford University Press (1995) 180
7. Allee V: The Knowledge Evolution. Expanding Organizational Intelligence, Newton MA: Butterworth-Heinemann (1997)
8. Anttila M: Kompetensförsörjning Stockholm: Ekerlids (1997)
9. Haglund T, Öhd L: Livslågt läande. En arbetsmodell för kompetensutveckling och för att skapa en läande organisation, Uppsala: Konsult förlaget (1995)
10. Allee V: The Knowledge Evolution. Expanding Organizational Intelligence, Newton MA: Butterworth-Heinemann (1997) 20
11. Prahalad C K, Hamel G: The Core Competence of the Corporation. Harvard Business Review 68(3) 79-91 (1990) 82

12. Argyris C: Teaching Smart People How to Learn. Harvard Business Review 69(3) 99-109. (1991)
13. Pramling I: Vad ä metakognition Göteborg: Göteborgs universitet (1987)
14. Flavell J H: Metacognition and Cognitive Monitoring: A New Era of Cognitive Developmental Enquiry. American Psychologist 34. 906-911 (1979)
15. Dixon N M: Dialog pårbetet Stockholm: fakta info direkt (1996)
16. Hoberg C: Precision och improvisation Stockholm: Dialoger (1998)
17. Kjellin H, Nälund A-K, Hjerpe S : Are knowledge networks suitable, for supporting learning at university courses? Proceedings of ISECON 2002, International conference on The Future of IT Education, San Antonio, Texas (2002)
18. Dixon N M: Common Knowledge. How Companies Thrive by Sharing What They Know Boston: Harvard Business School Press (2000)
19. Jähult B: Planeringssamtalet. Malmö: Liber (1988)
20. Argyris C: Overcoming Organizational Defenses Facilitating Organizational Learning Boston: Allyn and Bacon (1990)
21. Davenport T H Prusak L: Working Knowledge Boston: Harvard Business School Press (1998)
22. Rosenberg M J: E-learning Strategies for Delivering Knowledge in the Digital Age, New York: McGraw-Hill (2001)

Knowledge in an Electronic World ?

Johann Ortner

Abstract. Understanding the way human interaction and knowledge transfer work is a fundamental issue in KM. IT supported/assisted KM strategies face the question of the extent to which knowledge can be codified, programmed into software systems, stored, extracted, distributed, organized and managed electronically. This paper examines the possibility of translating theorems rooted in socio-linguistics, epistemology, psychology, philosophy and other human sciences into a concept that fits the paradigms used in information theory.
Information is defined as a >selection process< steered by four different types of commands: Selection requests, instructions, representation and interpretation modificators. >Selections< are assumed to be (true) knowledge under four conditions: Situational relatedness (situationedness of knowledge), supposition of reality-substantiality (sense making, belief, claim), conformity with patterns of social behaviour (culture, civilization, artificial world), integratability into the image of the relation between >self< and >world< (self-identity, Weltbild). Extraction, reconstruction of >knowledge< from protocols of thoughts and mental images is performed through the execution of internalized, learned selection/action patterns applied to individual life experience, and sense making understanding of a given situation.
The translation of the logical structure of >situational understanding<, >sense making< and >selection process< into a conventional representation of functional relations between elements of an organizational situation (information processing in/of organizations by means of IT) makes >sense< if the choice between options (transparency) of selections (the content of negotiation and calibration) leads to desirable flexibility of individuals and organizations in a globalized world.

1 Language – Introductory Issues

Much thought and discussion has been given to the relationship between IT and knowledge, raising the vital question: Can a PC contain knowledge? There are two simple yet conflicting answers to this question: Yes and No. If a PC were dismantled and its inner design and technology studied in detail, it would be quite valid to claim that it contained a great deal of **embedded, incorporated knowledge**. Its developers and manufacturers were obviously very knowledgeable and others would be able to acquire this knowledge given the appropriate skills and time to investigate.

Yet this knowledge is by no means universally accessible. A century ago, this kind of technology would have been inconceivable and noone would have been able to extract the knowledge in the individual component parts. On the other hand, 15 years

D. Karagiannis and U. Reimer (Eds.): PAKM 2002, LNAI 2569, pp. 281-300, 2002.

ago the KGB in Moscow would no doubt have paid a very high price for the technology and employed large numbers of experts to extract this knowledge.

Although it is quite possible to describe the data on the hard disk as embedded knowledge, it is a different form of incorporated knowledge. If the computer works properly, a set of symbols, figures and images will appear on the screen and represent either the user's or someone else's **codified knowledge.** *But is this really the case?*

There has already been enough discussion on these basic issues and definitions and this paper is not intended as yet another theoretical discussion on the definitions of knowledge. Instead, it focuses on practical aspects of KM and the need for practical solutions to practical problems. Indeed, one of the most practical problems faced by KM is the issue of knowledge transfer. How can I effectively transfer the knowledge supposedly stored in my own brain to others and vice versa?

This problem is best illustrated using a practical example. A sociologist is carrying out an oral history study on the way people think, act and live. The study takes the form of personal interviews and the questions have been carefully selected to give the researcher the required insight into human social behavior. Understanding the way human interaction and knowledge transfer work is a fundamental issue in KM. This in turn raises another question: If we can gain real understanding of how these processes work, can we then use this understanding to create effective IT solutions?

Of course, this requires a precise description of the situation and the actual process. Here, a preliminary description of the situation might be: Two people are sitting in a room talking. One (the researcher) is asking questions because he wants to know he answers. The other (the >object of interest<) answers or tells short stories. It is assumed both participants see and understand the situation in the same way and are each playing their appropriate role.

			Category
1	I	And what religion was your mother? Protestant? Or was she a Catholic?	Aa
2	A	Protestant.	Ba
3	I	And she doesn't go to church any more either?	Ad
4	A	Uh, Uh.	Bd
5	I	Since when?	Aa
6	A	No idea. About the same time as my father.	Ba
7	I	Hm. So they stopped going before you?	Ad/Ab/Dc
8	A	Yes, yes.	Bd
9	I	Had they … when you were confirmed, had they already stopped going?	Ab/Ad/Db
10	A	Oh yes, they were radicals.	Bd/Bc
11	I	So they had stopped going to church by then. So who wanted you to be confirmed? Was it your idea?	Ad/Da/Aa
12	A	Pardon?	Ae/Cb
13	I	You wanted to get confirmed then?	Ad
14	A	Yes, yes.	Bd/Aa
15	I	Because your friends had been confirmed?	Ab/Ca
16	A	Because all I got was "he's not being confirmed". Drove me mad.	Bb/Cc
17	I	So that's the reason. I see.	Bd
18	A	Yea, you know what it's like. And you have to admit that it was then the parents who accepted the child's wishes. Don't you think?	Bc//Bb/Cc

In the analysis of this dialog sequence, words have been used as markers to identify the function of single expressions or statements. These words (representing explanatory sentences) are indicated using the following letters:

A **Requests**

a **Limitation request**: The partner is requested to draw a line (selection) between the subject matter covered by the question and his knowledge of this subject

b **Reasoning request**: The partner is requested to indicate the systematic context for categorizing his statements.

c **Evaluation request:** The partner is requested to indicate the type of relationship between the propositional content of his statement and his values hierarchy.

d **Confirmation request:** The partner is requested to confirm the message has been understood correctly (decoded).

B **Instructions**

a **Limitation instructions:** The subject gives the interviewer (or vice versa) instructions on how to construct limits between >true – false< in the proposed subject.

b **Categorization/association instructions**: The subject gives instructions on how to associate isolated subject matter (thematic element) with other elements or defines the organizational reasoning context.

c **Context/evaluation instructions:** The subject indicates to the interviewer how to relate statements to the person and his value hierarchy.

d **Confirmation of completion:** Indicates to the partner that the speaker has completed (i.e. listened to and understood) the partner's instructions.

C **Representation modificators**

a **Proposal:** The interviewer give a simultaneous indication with his request (limitation, reasoning, evaluation) of how he anticipates the subject will limit, reason and evaluate.

b **Hint/Sign:** The listener interprets the elements in the partner's statement as an indication that they find it difficult to follow an instruction or request.

c **Appeal:** An emotional identification appeal through which the speaker requests the partner to respect maxims (e.g. solidarity) in order to make him accept or provoke a non-systemisable limitation, evaluation or judgment instruction.

D **Internal/external interpretation modificators**

a **Hint:** The conversation partners act out differences directly or indirectly but in such a way that these are obvious both to themselves and external observers.

b **Sign:** One participant notices and interprets a subconscious hint of difference on the part of his partner and reacts in such a way that they are obvious to the observer.

c **Indication:** The observer (analyst) believes he has identified differences which have not been acted out by the conversation partners.

The availability of a written transcript of this dialog is of utmost importance as it provides the necessary distance and time to reflect on the situation. I would analyze the above situation in the following way:

An association chain based on the day-to-day understanding of categorizing behavior over time can be identified in the questions asked by the interviewer in the question-answer sequence 1 to 7. I classifies actions as normal or unusual and bases his judgment on his own image of a normal working class family with established ideological, social and economic freedoms and restrictions. A recognizes and accepts the notion of "no longer attending church" introduced by I. A has no current problems with this, although I indicates in 7 that his presuppositions (family image, timeframe) make it hard for him to categorize some statements, e.g. child is confirmed after parents stop attending church (Why? The statements don't really fit together).

The repeated reformulations in 7 to 14 indicate both partners are trying to change the subject. However, A does not react to I's attempt to do so and instead provides more background on the period concerned and the judgmental values, referring to working class ideology to explain why his parents no longer attend church.

The new subject of >parental/offspring relationship< in religious/ideological questions is one aspect of the judgmental framework for actions in the previous subject of >not attending church and confirmation<. To explain the difference between parental and child action, it becomes necessary to either differentiate the validity of the previous judgmental framework or introduce a new one that enables I to understand why the difference between parental and child action is neither contradictory nor implies incorrect behavior by A. For A, the link to the present in the new subject arises from the fact that every new judgmental premise forces him to reformulate his identity based on his life history. "In the past I thought differently, but now..." The reasoning proposed by I and adopted by A can be described as follows: adapting to the environment takes precedence over solidarity with parents. This becomes plausible if family ideological differences do not necessarily have negative practical consequences (exclusion/punishment), whereas environmental pressure to adapt is comparable to a threat of exclusion from the community. It indicates that internal emotional relationships are more important in family life than ideological, moral issues: love for children takes priority over class interests. Thus A limits the validity of both ends of the scale and puts them in a hierarchical relationship. I accepted and understood this – he knows how to categorize A's statement.

How did I proceed? Did I gain new insights from this analysis? If so, which ones? **I interpreted the actions of >asking< and >answering< as expressions of force and attempts to push another person to make a specific selection in his mind.**

Yet what should this selection be applied to? How should the persons sort out the relevant pieces in their memory, life experience or tacit knowledge base (or whatever the mind contains), fit them together to construct the appropriate puzzle, attach them to a learned code and give them a identifiable >name<. In other words, I applied my own mental models, my personal understanding of the situation and the (dynamic) relations between its elements.

One of my mental models is very similar to computer science models: We use commands to select from pools of structured/unstructured raw data and form specific patterns of contextualized datasets.

In other words: the word "mother" or the phrase "my mother was a protestant" actually contain no knowledge whatsoever; instead they are commands or triggers that prompt the selection of a specific pattern in the mind. Of course, we have to gain experience, learn and train ourselves from childhood to be able to follow these commands and (re-)select existing patterns in a particular way.

The observer (in this case me) would be unable to create and apply a re-interpretation of the dialog if he had had no real-life experience of similar situations.

2 Situatedness

This raises the next question: What is a situation? What do we do when we experience ourselves (consciously or intuitively) in a situation or a part of a situation? How do we (as observers) interpret situations like the one described above?

"In the Artificial Intelligence paradigm, human knowledge is thought of as if knowledge were separate-able from the private experience of individuals in situations. ...An understanding of human memory and human anticipation must be part of a framework for understanding the content of individual human experience of mental events. Memory is not memory of situations but the re-member-ment (or the aggregation) of the invariances that are experienced across many instances. It is a memory of the color red, or of texture. The context is gone. Meaning is gone. There is no semantic description of the elements of the memory store. The elements of human memory store have no context. ... These elements must be associated again in new contexts und this only occurs during experience of situationedness." (P.S. Prueitt: "Situationedness.", 2001)

In cognitive psychology >situation awareness< is "the perception of the elements in the environment within a volume of space and time, the comprehension of their meaning, the projection of their status into the near future, and the prediction of how various actions will affect the fulfillment of one's goals." (M. Endsley, 1995)

In social sciences, >knowing in a situation< (situatedness of knowledge) and >understanding of a situation< (reflexive interpretation) are differentiated between as "subjective, existential" and "objective, scientific" views. Social scientists maintain that an observer is able to describe and analyze what appears to be the situation of an actor in a way the person involved is not able to do. The view of the person acting and knowing in a situation and the view of an observer lead to completely different results caused by the "logical structure of understanding of an alter ego" (See A. Schütz, 1977, p. 53). Schütz argues that in his unit act theory, Talcott Parsons mixes "objective schemes for interpreting subjective phenomena with the subjective phenomena themselves" and overlooks the different >knowledge horizons< and >motive horizons< of actors and observers.

"Parsons defines "unit act" as the smallest elements into which a concrete action system can be broken down. A unit act is characterized by a given actor, a given purpose, a given situation (which includes condition and means) and a given normative value orientation as link between the other elements [...] Furthermore, it is easy to accept that from the subject's perspective the term "situation" refers to the determined purpose of action, which alone determines the elements relevant to reach the goal. If one considers the difference between the two component parts of a situation ("means" and "condition"), the question of whether these are under the control of the actor or not refers to the available knowledge and experience of said actor at the time of determination. This implies that the dividing line between both factors in the "situation", namely the means and the conditions, are ultimately set

solely by actors. Conversely, from an objective (i.e. "scientific") perspective what the actor considers as a means might well turn out to be a condition and vice versa. This is because, from an objective perspective, conditions are those elements of a situation over which the actor – according to the verifiable knowledge of others- can have no control, regardless of whether the actor is aware of his incapability or how highly he estimates the relevance of these factors." (See S. Schütz,1977, p. 57f).

I assume in the following that the (conscious or unconscious) perception/evaluation of a situation is in itself a selection (selective perception of the >self< & environment) and that intuitive actor and analytical observer do not have a >qualitatively< different type of knowledge (or approaches). Actor and observer are simply in different situations and thus have different motives, interests and knowledge horizons. The actor's >situation< is an element of the observer's own >situation< and, as a result, he >sees< differently (sees different things). Both are prisoners of their own situations.

(In the above example, this means I cannot reflect simultaneously on both my own situatedness and the situation of the people interacting in the interview. The "truth" of >scientific knowledge< will be discussed in Section 3).

Splitting a Situation into (Logical) Elements – Analyzing

Identification und definition of the (assumed) constitutive elements of a situation

- In order to (analytically) understand a situation, an observer has to identify several elements (factors) that play certain roles in this situation.
- He must then assume that these elements can be characterized by their attributes, qualities etc. and that these will impact the relations between the elements.

For the above example, I propose the selection of the following elements:

1. Individual or Person (my Self)

There are (obviously) two people present in the room.

We can assume each of them sees himself as a unique entity, a singular individual. We also can assume that they are both aware of each other's presence and consider themselves potential or real actors in their environment, not objects (e.g. tables). This of course is my (the observer's) projection of my own understanding of myself and I regard these elements as I would regard myself, i.e. I am a human being with all its attributes and characteristics.

2. Partner or Opponent (the other Self)

For each person there is/are one (or more) opponent(s) and we can assume that they treat and see each other as persons (the other Self) and not as other objects in the room. The presence of another person is an accepted fact to them both and results from a previous situation where interests, goals, time and location had been agreed upon or set. People have a shared or common memory of history (prior to a situation). This of course is my projection of my own knowledge of situatedness. I am >thinking<.

3. Purpose or Goal (the anticipated result, aim, task in hand)

We can assume that people act (more or less consciously) to achieve something. This means they are acting in anticipation of a future situation. We cannot assume that they necessarily know the actual or required outcome of their actions or that they share the same goal. This is a projection of my own experience of wanting to achieve something and having different goals to my partner. Negotiating the aims of spending time and communicating with another person means adjusting (calibrating, modifying or changing) visions and intentions.

4. Motives or Drivers (the reasons why)

We can assume that both observer and partner (the other Self) are able to understand another person's actions (behavior/reactions) if they receive or give an answer to the question of why. We cannot assume that the actors (in a situation) are consciously aware of their own motives or of those of their partners. Motives are the >cause< for people's actions and active participation in a negotiating process. This is my projection of my understanding of events with a logical structure of cause and effect.

5. Object or Material (topic or subject of negotiation/processing/action; content)

We can assume that people who work together or talk to each other selected a topic to be proposed as the subject of negotiation. We cannot assume that the actors always (consciously) know what they are actually working on or the subject matter of their negotiation. It does not matter whether people are working on an actual real object, a document, thoughts, shared history, priorities, values or social relationships etc. – they need something to deal with. This is of course my projection of my understanding of >doing< and >something<.

6. Knowledge as the Common/General Structure of Thinking (patterns of imagination / argumentation / behavior, mental models, language, logic, etc.)

We can assume that communication and interaction between >Selves< (people) have a >prior history<. It does not start from the beginning, rather is based on a (cultural) consensus of cognitive, normative and regulatory generalities (i.e. selections). Therefore, we cannot assume that people are acting freely and independently of these patterns. People must use these >codes< and >grammars< of thought, speech and interaction to think and communicate. They must learn and internalize them and cannot change them as easily as they would like. When people talk to each other they are selecting, differentiating and calibrating these patterns. This is a projection of my understanding of myself and my experience of life. I had to learn how to think, speak and behave and use a >language< I did not create myself.

7. Environmental Conditions (the location, time, structural, material and regulatory space for the communication)

We can assume that the actors use or chose a more or less suitable frame for their interaction and made some preparations to permit or facilitate their negotiations. We cannot assume that the participants chose optimal conditions nor that they are aware of any possible influence the chosen environment (the framework of the situation) might have on their communication. People are free to meet and talk to each other wherever they like. However, if the surroundings have a negative effect on the purpose of their meeting, they will consciously try to change this environment. This is a projection of my own experience of intentionally choosing and preparing my surroundings when I want to do something. But sometimes I have no choice.

8. Externals (unexpected from outside the situation/unconsidered interferences)

We can assume the actors see their situation as a more or less closed world. This means they selectively perceive themselves and the >here< and >now<. We cannot assume that they recognize all possible potential (external) factors that might influence or determine their situation (beyond their situational horizon).

It should of course be noted that the above assumptions, projections and elements are all differentiating selections made by an observer. The number and type of elements that will be needed to understand a situation depends on the observer's belief that he (now) can understand. Most of these elements could become subjects of negotiation or attention (i.e. content) as soon the participant(s) notice that their assumptions are problematic and questionable.

I consider most of these elements to be relevant for any situation which involves people. (Aspects of elements could become elements depending on the perception interest ("Erkenntnisinteresse") of an observer.)

It does not make sense (at least at this stage in the argumentation) to ask whether elements are real or constructed. (The answer to this question has to be discussed within the framework of a philosophical theory of science.)

We must now reassemble these pieces by describing how they are (inter-)related. In other words, we have to determine how we can imagine/think that the constituent elements of the given situation work together. To simply say "a person must have a motive for committing a crime" is not enough, because >to have< and >not to have< do not seem to be applicable for the relation between >motive< and >person< or >person< and >action<. How can we describe these functional relations?

Creating Connections and Relations – Contextualizing

Reconstruction and interpretation of relations between elements

- Observation enables us to identify effective relations (dependencies, conditions, context, activities) between elements (e.g. he is >talking *about* a subject<).
- The context should appear to have a kind of logical necessity (e.g. >we *cannot* see *without* light<).
- This contextualization has to be seen as the >constructions< an observer needs to be able to understand a situation.

The (linguistic) description of the relations represents conceptual images, which have been adjusted to fit each other (calibrated) through cultural history by means of conventional language. These linguistic images are used to describe the (logical) relationship between the elements: *>The person (who is present or has done something) has a motivating reason<.*

Neither the elements nor the relations between them can be touched, seen or measured. They are in fact interpretations, projections or suppositions. This means that (assumed real) relations between elements must be characterized as specific types/forms of interpretation activities (how or by what means do I as an observer establish the relationship?) and these in turn must correspond to the >action schemes< of particular conceptual images (>*presumptions/assumptions*< etc.). This includes the request or instructions for action for both the acting, thinking person and the observer. In the case of person and action this could be: *Relate actions to motives! Search for the reason why!*

Which terms or expressions could be used to characterize these relations? My suggestions (for a codification of interpretative functional relations) are:

Characterizing term for observer's (actor) action when creating a relation.	*Mental images expressed in language*
1 **search for/justify the reason :**	Something moves us to act.
(Psychology/Physics)	Actors are driven by a force.
Paradigm:	*A moving force. (Why?)*
Implicit instruction/request:	Mobilize your powers/motivate people!
2 **intentionalize/foresee/expect:**	Action has a goal.
(Action theory/Economics)	The object of desire satisfies this desire.
Paradigm:	*Means to an end. Pursue a goal. (Why?/Where to?)*
Implicit instruction/request:	Clarify what you want /where to go!
3 **reflecting/mirroring/projecting**	You see yourself in the mirror.
(Epistemology)	Thought/behavioral patterns (etc) can be rec(
Paradigm:	*Subject and object. (How can I know?)*
Implicit instruction/request:	Place something in front of you and step back.
4 **limit/accept:**	Some things cannot be changed.
(Cultural Anthropology/Systems Theory)	Differentiation, decision and selection means to both determine and exclude. Recognize your limits.
Paradigm:	*There are two sides to every coin (To what extent?)*
Implicit instruction/request:	Don't bang your head against the wall. Make the world fit.

5 **calibrate/adjust/align:** (Communication, Information Theory) (Sociology, Organization theory)	You can choose your friends, but you can't choose your family. The link in the chain/Me, us and the others.
Paradigm:	Let's make a compromise!
Implicit instruction/request:	*Similarities and differences (Who with?)* Look for the commonalities! Negotiate!
6 **relativize/look out:** (Systems theory)	Watch out! What you see/know is not everything.
Paradigm:	Who knows what the future holds. *The unknown/unconsidered*
Implicit instruction/request:	*(Under what circumstances?)* Keep you eyes open! Expect the unexpected!

The six (proposed) characteristics of *functional relations* between elements should not simply serve as instruments for analyzing situations and better understanding of their dynamics, but should also be considered as effective principles of the processes observed: They should make sense. (Kant would argue that we could also say: Our mind is structuring the world into two dimensions – time and space. With this background, the first three >relations< represent the >time-cause-effect< structuring activities of our mind, whilst the other three represent the >object-differentiating< activities of splitting the world into entities.)

(Although it would be interesting to discuss similarities and differences between "situatedness" i.e. this concept of >situation< and I. Nonaka's concept of "BA", this is beyond the scope of this paper. "Ba is the context, in which knowledge is shared. [...] Ba is where meaning is created. The power to create knowledge is seated not just in an individual but also in interactions with other individuals or with the environment as well as within the context in which such interaction takes place, that is, ba." (see :I. Nonaka, 2001, p. 831 also: Giesen,1991).

If we cannot assume these functional relations are in fact real >working principles< within a situation, statements about this situation would not make sense to us.

In consulting, training and organizational development, most methods are based on the assumption that certain organizational settings can be established through predefined rules and structures, which have an impact on the dynamics of a situation (open space/action learning/group dynamics/...). Such rules should not be questioned in sessions such our interview example, where the players accept the rules and roles. These techniques do not introduce new >working principles< but support some type of relational activity such as the optimization of *calibration* processes or *reflecting* mental models and behavioral patterns. However, no one single method or technique provides an answer to the question of how and why individuals can come to the conclusions: "It makes sense to participate and communicate." or: "It does not make sense for me to accept the rules set up by the other and work for his benefit." Is >sense< the identification with something as a result of a calibration process or could it be something else?

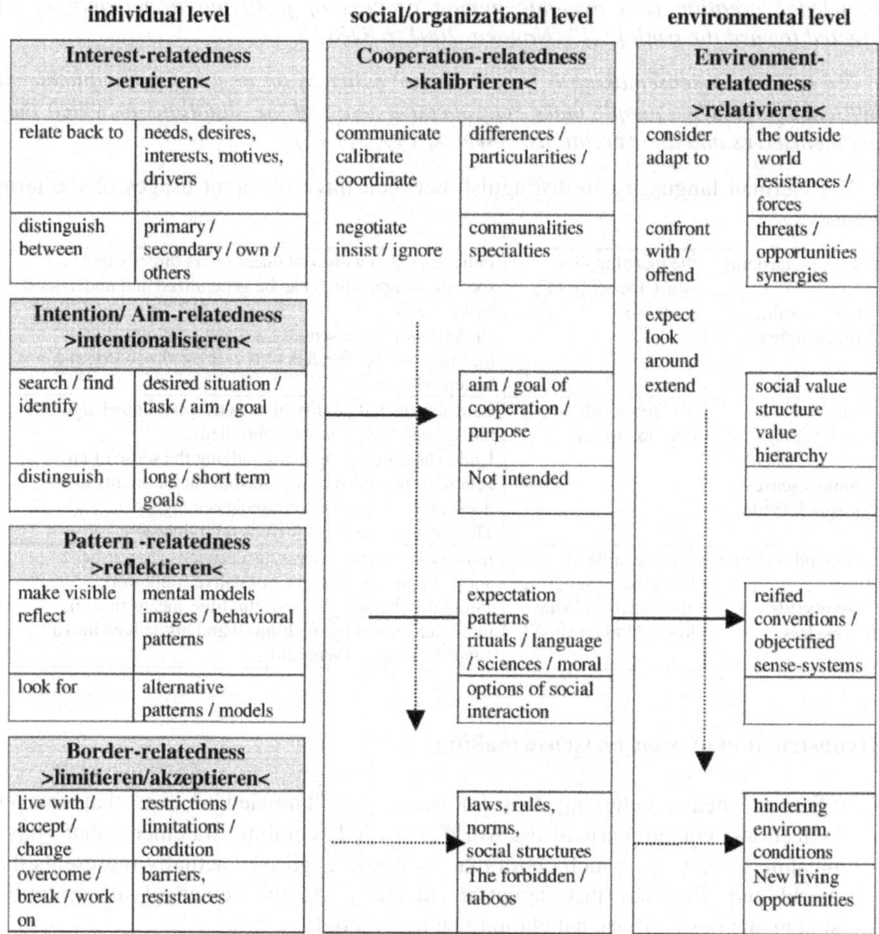

individual level
social/organizational level
environmental level
Interest-relatedness >eruieren<
relate back to
needs, desires, interests, motives, drivers
distinguish between
primary / secondary / own / others
Intention/ Aim-relatedness >intentionalisieren<
search / find identify
desired situation / task / aim / goal
distinguish
long / short term goals
Pattern -relatedness >reflektieren<
make visible reflect
mental models images / behavioral patterns
look for
alternative patterns / models
Border-relatedness >limitieren/akzeptieren<
live with / accept / change
restrictions / limitations / condition
overcome / break / work on
barriers, resistances
Cooperation-relatedness >kalibrieren<
communicate calibrate coordinate
differences / particularities /
negotiate insist / ignore
communalities specialties
aim / goal of cooperation / purpose
Not intended
expectation patterns rituals / language / sciences / moral
options of social interaction
laws, rules, norms, social structures
The forbidden / taboos
Environment-relatedness >relativieren<
consider adapt to
the outside world resistances / forces
confront with / offend
threats / opportunities synergies
expect look around extend
social value structure value hierarchy
reified conventions / objectified sense-systems
hindering environm. conditions
New living opportunities

3 Sense Making: Sense and Nonsense

"Since mankind lost its ability to see itself in any way as a partner of the afterworld, its view of the world around it darkened. Somberly, we had to find it for ourselves and then >consume< it. When things have reached this point, all that remains in a senseless world all sense in himself, resulting in the nihilistic shock caused by the realization that there is no sense. What remains is self-preservation." (Sloterdijk, 1983, p. 637)

„Knowledge is grounded in values, experience, and purposeful action. Knowledge is meaningful; it is relational and context specific for it is created in and justified in a changing environment.[…] Hence, knowledge can be defined as a meaningful set of information that constitutes a justified true belief and/or an embodied technical skill.

Knowledge creation is a dynamic human process of justifying a personal belief directed toward the truth [...]" (Nonaka, 2001. p 828)

"To talk about sensemaking is to talk about reality as an ongoing accomplishment that takes form when people make retrospective sense of the situations in which they find themselves and their creations." (Weick, 1995, p. 15)

The German language can distinguish between three different usages of the term >sense<.

sinnig – unsinnig **has meaning - meaningless**	the meaning of a word, the sense of a sentence	Indicates that a word/statement refers directly to a specific image, which can be generalized and understood by his equals. Understanding the sense of a sentence means that its meaning or what it refers to (i.e. image/knowledge) can be reproduced.
sinnhaft – widersinnig **makes sense – absurd, futile**	The sense behind a decision to act.	Indicates the judgability of an action as >knowledge based< and >expectation controlled<. Understanding/ recognizing/judging the sense of an action means it can be assumed the actor orients his decision on a specific >consequence logic<. The application of this logic is reproduceable.
sinnvoll – sinnlos **>senseful< - senseless**	The meaning of life; the sense in suffering and sacrifice; What lies behind creation?	Indicates the actor orients his decisions for one or another option to act on a normative framework (Sinnbild). Leading a >senseful life< means that an individual can integrate himself and his actions into a consistent image (Weltbild).

Reconstruction of >sense< (sense making)

1. >Sense< means believing that knowledge is "knowledge", i.e. that images (selections) contain parts of the world (knowledge claim). Statements that >have meaning< are those which claim that what was expressed actually represents the world and does not just depict it (identity). At the center of all scientific statements lies an irrational claim to be true (belief).
2. >Meaningless< statements are those which are not understood because the assumption that the identity of image and depicted, "statement" and "about" cannot be reproduced.
3. For the knower and speaker there is no >sense<, since whether or not knowledge or a statement >make sense< only becomes relevant if the sense has become lost.
4. The context of knowing (i.e. coherence between knowledge elements) is known as the Weltbild, whose consistency and relevance is supposed – it makes sense.
5. >Sense< is believing that what has been experienced can be projected forward (in the present and the future). Knowledge is the attempt to intellectually stabilize the time dimension, by denying >change<. We cannot have knowledge about >now< or the future. We are making assumptions, projections or predictions.
6. >Sense making< assumptions are suppositions that what happens can be understood, i.e. explained by an assumed coherence (consequence construction) and that experience can be turned into valid knowledge.
7. The supposed validity of projected assumptions turns into images of a time-cause structure. The essence of >being< is what it has been.

8. The sense-making context of >what has been< is secured by the dissolution of the differences in >something comes to pass – doesn't come to pass<: rational knowledge.
9. Doing something that >makes sense< means doing something because it is assumed that certain actions will lead to a particular outcome, i.e. transfer of the time/cause structure to one's self and one's relationship to the world.
10. Doing/making something that >makes sense< is the knowledge-based re-formation of the (natural) environment to make it fit to the knowledge, i.e. to ensure that what is expected happens: Artifacts/civilization.
11. >Sinnbilder< (sense systems/mythological, religious meta-narrations) bridge explanatory deficits of projected knowledge, when the expected does not happen.
12. A >sense crisis< is the threat to knowledge if the world cannot be stabilized or domesticated and if the assumptions of the knowledge fail.
13. >Senseful< is the supposition that a constructed context within knowledge is – in itself – knowledge and not just >belief<.
14. >Sinnbilder< provide the reason why threatened knowledge is not nonsense and why it is not absurd to continue to behave and act in a knowledge-oriented manner. They explain the inexplicable.
15. The assumed rationality of the relationship between the self and the world – an analogy to cause effect construction – is the context of a >motive-intention-aim-action consequence< within one's knowledge of oneself.
16. Social interaction is based on reciprocity of expectations, i.e. assumptions.
17. In order (in the social environment) for the expected to be applicable and to happen, a differentiation needs to be made between >equals< and non-equals and the behavior of equals stabilized.
18. The stabilization of behavior between equals lies in the subjugation under >reified, objectified knowledge< through
    a. Formulation of behavioral guidelines, rules, standards, laws
    b. Transformation, i.e. education of associates to >respectable< fellow men
    c. Anchoring of >good behavior< or well-being in technical artefacts and social establishments (institutions)
    d. Formulation, definition and implementation of sanctioning instruments
19. Socially binding sense systems promise more than they are able to deliver.
20. >Sense< as in a >senseful life< is therefore the bridging of the explanatory deficits of social orders and the explanation of the inexplicable human life.
21. The >evil<, the devil, the calamity etc. are necessary element of sense constructions, since they explain what cannot be in the >sense< of sense constructions. The >evil< is the reason why sense constructions (religions) exist.

(For the purpose of this paper the original >chain of arguments< had to be cut down and some links are missing. Another problem I faced was how to translate what makes sense to me in German into English. Please also compare: *(P.L. Berger, Th. Luckmann: (dt) 1980, S. 112 ff)*

You may think this is too philosophical, theoretical or abstract and not applicable to for real world problems. I disagree! It is extremely practical! Think about the following. If you had said a year ago "my Enron shares are worth $1M", this could have been assumed to be true knowledge, because you believed it and might well have been able to sell those shares at that price and believed the banknotes you received were really worth the $1M written on them. Now we assume to know better. "The evil in American business will be smoked out!" Is this >sense-making< too?

When I think or say "I am 55 years old" I do not differentiate between >statement< or >knowledge< and >about what<. I just believe that what I know and say are true facts. Only by reflecting on what I said can I raise doubts about my assumptions and consider them as >just words<.

This leads to the conclusion that there is no knowledge on a hard disk or anywhere else in IT. So what is there then? Commands, instructions and recommendations on how to select something in our minds. It is up to us to follow these commands and believe in them and turn them into >meaningful, senseful knowledge< or not. However, we function as the computers ask us to do, because these commands (recommendations) are not just any (old) commands. They represent the rules, structures, instructions and commands of the artificial, social world we made up to make us function. And this brings me to the final question.

4 The Social Structure in My PC

Let me give you a trivial example to explain what I mean. I am sitting in my office in front of my computer. An icon begins to blink and I take this as a request to look at an incoming message, i.e. to read it. I >function< as is expected of me and in the way I have learned and open the message window. This contains text, which asks me to provide more information on my special qualifications or skills (selection requests re. "matter" of calibration and option of action). Nothing out of the ordinary. Someone could also have called me or invited me to a meeting in the personnel department.

If the internal computer network is well organized, my reply would automatically be delivered to the right person in the right place, integrated into the data-structures and would be made available to appropriate decision-makers. That is the reason for sending it electronically. That's why we have integrated workflow mechanisms.

If we could *describe exactly and explain clearly* what happens in the moment I see the icon blinking, read the first line of text and then either continue reading and understanding or close it abruptly with a mouseclick, then it should be possible to use technology to create the >ultimate< software tool. This would interact with the processes that caused me to read the text, interpret my conclusions and initiate the relevant actions or not.

Because the significant text elements (selection requests) "provide information about your qualification" do not tell me the immediate benefit of following the request, I will try to find out what the consequences I would face it I ignored the message. The sender's identity and his/her function and position within the organization tells me (if I know it) that our relation is not one of >colleagues at the same level< but a hierarchical dependency relationship. A colleague of equal status could appeal to my good will or image of myself as a friendly, helpful person to consider his request amicably. The relation I might have to the sender will in any case have an impact on what, to what extent and how quickly I provide >information<.

The social organizational settings determine the type, form and >content< of the information process: identify social relation and position > select options to act > consider consequences > select "content" > etc. If we could somehow incorporate/program all the >decisions< I consciously or subconsciously perform in my mind into IT, another person would be able to play with this selectable options of selection-functions.

For example: The following symbolic codification of structural codes (i.e. IT functions, workflow, automated execution of selection requests) should illustrate how IT can interfere in sociostructural codification (i.e. positions, roles, e.g.) and change the >situation< (conditions of knowledge exchange).

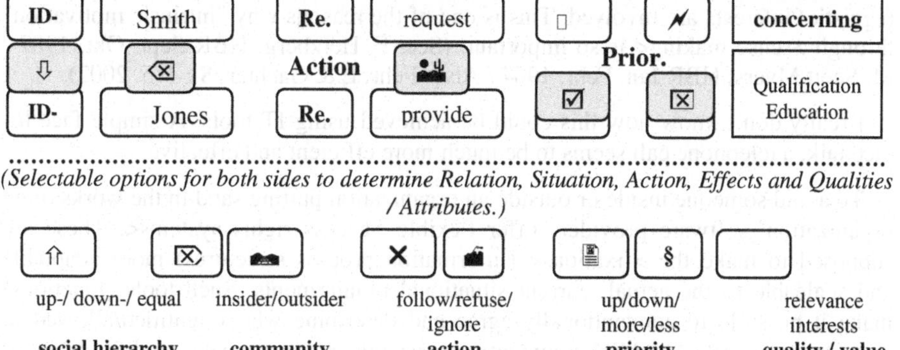

(Selectable options for both sides to determine Relation, Situation, Action, Effects and Qualities / Attributes.)

The hierarchical position of Mrs. Smith (fixed, calibrated pre-selection) is based on her >function< within the organization. This means that hierarchical up or down positioning is only possible within an organization and is legitimized by the coordination and administration functions necessary for organizing division of labor.

The priority level "very urgent", the relevance "important" and the resulting/ required form of (re-)action "provide/answer" and selection of >content< must be interpreted by Mr. Jones in relation to Mrs. Smith's position in the organization. If I (Mr. Jones) were to change the priority to "not important" because I considered other things to be more important at the moment, I would question/ignore her position.

If I were free to alter her position by a mouse click (move it up/down) or re-define her position as >not belonging to my community< and she would be able to see this on her screen simultaneously it would have an enormous impact on the information process; it would completely change the >situation< (and the organization).

It is clear that within traditional organizations (enterprises) this is and should not be possible, because icons and symbols (function keys) only represent what has been established (fixed) outside the IT structure as social, organizational structure. Nobody should be able to change the position (and rights) of a manager to that of an ordinary employee. This is why we have laws, agreements, conventions, etc. (Codification of social relations through symbolic codes are related to structural code systems. See: B. Giesen, 1991, p 10 ff)

However, it is conceivable and in principle it is not a technical problem. For example, this kind of behaviour can sometimes be observed in virtual Internet Knowledge Communities. (See: E. Reid; M.A. Smith / P. Kollock (Ed) 2000 / A. Dickinson: DU Krems 2002)

On the other hand, most attempts to incorporate and use the regulatory mechanism of social behaviour and interaction to optimize >digital knowledge exchange< did not turn out to be very effective ("digital incentives"). Appeals to fairness, warnings of punishment, promises of incentives (on TV) or threats of legal sanctions for violating intellectual property rights (in the Net) are usually >one way< requests and – as long as channels are not bi-directional - do not force the user/receiver to act accordingly. Whilst making "socially not acceptable behaviour" public can be a strong instrument, it does not really affect the actual moment of decision making when short-term (egoistic) interests are involved. This is one of the reasons why "intrinsic motivation" through >sense making< is so important. (See: F. Herzberg: HBR Sept. Okt. 1987 / M. Scott Myers: HBR Jan. Febr. 1964 / Also: Fehr, E & Gachter, S.: 415, 2002)

I really don't know how this could be achieved using IT tools. A simple face-to-face talk, a telephone call seems to be much more efficient and effective.

To avoid someone inside or outside an organization putting sand in the works of an organization, software providers offer flexible >access rights systems<. These are supposed to make the >fixations< (information process structures) more adaptable and scaleable to the actual, current situational requirements. Such tools (functions) make it possible to conventionally agree and determine who is entitled/allowed to start a process, select and link >content<, access information, create, modify, delete or distribute documents under what conditions/premises. This is because it would not make sense with respect to either business or organizational goals to leave everything open to negotiation and calibration. Usually authorized system administrators are responsible for day-to-day decision-making on who should/should not have particular access rights and decision responsibilities (concerning selection patterns/personalized content by roles and functions).

On this >meta-level< system administrators can act and decide only on the background of process definitions, organizational charts, content classifications, etc. They are and have to be educated and experienced in computer science, but usually do not have >knowledge< of organizational, management, communication or information theory. This is why >flexible access right systems< sooner or later turn into rigidly fixed (traditional) information process execution machines. (See: D. E. Smith, 2000)

5 Discussion

Combining paradigms used in socio-linguistics, cognitive psychology, gestalt psychology, systems theory, etc. to create a "unified theory of information" (R. Capurro: Information, 1978) is still a desideratum and I wonder if this could be achieved using theorems elaborated in philosophical epistemology or the biologically rooted systems theory. The need for a better theory of information and knowledge creation is best illustrated by the fact that whilst the most sophisticated computers can be used for both criminal, inhuman purposes and for creating a more peaceful world, advanced IT cannot deal with the human emotions, beliefs and social cultural behavior that determine or at least influence economic, political, technical and practical decision-making. Such a theory should give insight into how emotions, knowledge, belief systems and reified knowledge (artifacts, symbol systems, etc.) are interlinked and work together. What contribution can we expect here from IT and IT-related research?

In section 1, I argue that >social interaction< through >language games< (Wittgenstein, 1953) is steered by >commands/requests< understood as such by the actors involved based on learned (internalized) rules of behavior. (To distinguish a >statement< from a >request<, one must be able to understand and follow the sequence of a dialogue and be familiar with the guiding functions of modificators).

Most of these rules/regulators of behavior are >informal<, i.e. not known explicitly but (can be) used intentionally by the actors (mimic, gestures, intonation and other subtle signals/"form of life" - Wittgenstein). Standardization and formalization of these types of >signals< (as a precondition of speech content identification) is, in principle, possible through analytical observation of the status quo of the language game behavior of a community (see section 1: Categories of analysis of a dialogue), but it is questionable to what extent a formalization would destroy the necessary ambiguity and vagueness that maintain the interpretatory openness of a social situation: It was noted that we are dealing with conventions that must be learned and trained (and can therefore be seen as >generalities<) but function as (strategic) tools to keep a situation open for both (face-to-face) negotiation, interpretation and sense making in a given situation and reinterpretation of self-identity and repositioning in relation to others. (This is a challenge for global knowledge networks too.)

Some rules are formalized (see section 4.) and appear as explicit markers of specific social interaction patterns (structure of social systems/communities of practice). Symbol system based communication within formalized communities (organizations/non-open situations) is mainly steered by the explicit, formalized >command-modificators< which indicate the expected, desired, requested form of (re-)action, i.e. behavior (names, identities, roles, positions, relation markers, action modificators (values, priorities, etc.)). To activate these markers and release them for individual/situational choice (as subject of negotiation) means deformalizing organizational structures. KM proponents claim this is needed to stimulate knowledge production and so-called "knowledge exchange" (virtual communities/project teamwork/learning organization).

In section 2, >situatedness of knowing< is defined as the >mental activity< which projects mental activities into the outside world (reality constitution) and splits the world into relevant elements, i.e. significant differences (pattern creation) and the (assumed) relations (time, cause, effect, space, expectation horizon) between them. The assumption that elements are real objects and relations real attributes, characteristics or processes appears as >sense< in the act and moment of knowing. In the actual moment of >knowing<, there is no way to verify or falsify >knowledge claims<. New knowledge that retrospectively judges a previous knowledge claim true or false is itself a >knowledge claim<. Selection patterns are represented by so-called "explicit knowledge", which is in fact not >knowledge< per se but the conventionally stabilized ways of pattern creation in an individual's memory of life experience. They define (select) what is/must be taken as >content< (subject of attention, negotiation, calibration, work). (See: M. Polanyi: Personal Knowledge, 1958)

Following the argumentation of section 3, (incomplete for the purpose of this paper) situational >sense-making< is (per definition) the very heart of >knowing< and can in no way be performed by IT systems. However, >understanding of a situation< can be supported and encouraged using tools that support the specific mental activities which carry out situational understanding as proposed in section 6 (7).

To stabilize the orientation of behavior and action decision on medium and long term expectation horizons (enduring, non-egoistic, etc. motives), sense making in the sense of belief systems (religious, ideological, ethical, philosophical etc. value systems) is vital not only for individuals but also for communities, organizations and societies. Are some better and more rational than others, as some politicians (and religious fanatics) claim to know? What do you think?

6 Conclusion: Conservative or (R)evolutionary IT?

I ask you to accept the following concluding statements

1. Knowledge does not exist per se. It is supposed to reside in our minds when we select pieces of our (bodily) experience (tacit knowledge) and form patterns that we assume to fit to a given situation. If we believe that they fit and therefore claim that they are >true<, these patterns make sense and are taken as >knowledge<. (See: K.R. Popper, 1985)
2. Knowledge exchange through communication is not a real >exchange< of knowledge but rather requests, recommendations, instructions on what and how to select in our memory. Even it seems useful to differentiate between >knowing what< (content) and >knowing how< (structure, context), I assume there is no principal difference between knowing >what< and knowing >how<. In the act of knowing and understanding, our mind is not able to separate content and structure. Understanding and performing a selection request (through information) is itself knowledge (tacit knowledge?).
3. Symbolic communication as a request to someone to select can be seen as a calibration process using >commands< that must be learned and trained by education and are specific to communities and cultures. Thus, symbolic interaction and selection works only on the basis of reified knowledge (artefacts) and established social structures, conventions, rules and laws.
4. Information Technology represents and acts as a collection of sets of established >selection requests<. IT can either replicate social interaction patterns (traditional, conservative IT) and risk that the structures and patterns cannot be negotiated because they are technologically fixed (see: J. Ortner, 2002) or it could provide new possibilities of breaking down hindering social, administrational structures by

providing >selection options< (evolutionary IT) in a society where flexibility and mobility is supposed to be needed to survive in a globalized world: Cyberspace.

5. In addition to maintaining transparency and providing options for social interaction patterns, evolutionary IT should support situational interpretation activities (as described in Section 2):
   a. *reasoning*: cause finding, simulation tools for complex situations/case based reasoning tools
   b. *visioning*: desired situation modeling/time domain structuring for short, medium and long term expectations/decision support tools
   c. *reflecting*: visualization tools /pattern recognition/alternative modeling tools
   d. *limiting*: >element< generation through dataset clustering/situational frame definition tools/best practice proposal tools
   e. *calibrating*: negotiation supporting tools
   f. *relativizing*: environment observation tools, scenario playing

These six points (a > f) indicate the direction in which KM tools development should go and concentrate on in order to make a >sensefull< contribution to knowledge creation and exchange.

Would this make >sense making< and social interaction easier and less irrational?

"We don't understand how the mind works – not nearly as well as we understand how the body works, and certainly not well enough to design utopia or to cure unhappiness." (St. Pinker, 1998)

References

1. Berger, P.L.; Luckmann, Th.: The Social Construction of Reality, 1966; deutsch: Suhrkamp, Frankfurt 1980.
2. Dickinson, A.: Translating in Cyberspace. Virtual Knowledge Communities, DU-Krems 2002.
3. Endsley, M.: Toward a theory of situation awareness in dynamic systems. Human Factors, 1995, p 37.
4. Fehr, E & Gachter, S.: Altruistic punishment in humas. Nature, 415, 2002.
5. Giesen, B.: Die Entdinglichung des Sozialen. Eine evolutionstheoretische Perspektive auf die Postmoderne, Suhrkamp, Frankfurt 1991.
6. Herzberg, F.: One More Time: How Do You Motivate Employees? HBR Sept. Okt. 1987.
7. Kavanagh D. , Seamas K.: Sensemaking, Safety and Situated Communities in (Con)temporary Networks, Journal of Business Research, Dublin 2001.
8. Leedom, K.D.: Final Report, Sensemaking Symposium, Oct. 2001, http://www.dodccrp.org
9. Myers, M.S.: Who Are Your Motivated Workers?, HBR Jan. Febr. 1964.
10. Nonaka, I.; et al.(Ed.): Organizational Learning and Knowledge, Oxford University Press 2001.
11. Nonaka, Reinmöller, Toyama, Integrated Information Technology for Knowledge Creation, In: Handbook of Organizational Learning, Oxford University Press 2001. p 828.

12. Ortner, J.: Knowledge Barriers - Barriers to Knowledge Management; In: Anwendungsorientiertes Wissensmanagement, Bornemann, M., Sammer, M. (Ed), DUV Gabler, 2002.
13. Pinker, St.: How the Mind Works, London 1998.
14. Polanyi, M.: Personal Knowledge, 1958.
15. Popper,K.R., K. Lorenz: Die Zukunft ist offen, Piper, 1985.
16. Prueitt, P.S.: "Situationedness..", 2001; http://www.ontologystream.com
17. Reid, E.: Hierarchy and power: social control in cyberspace. In: Communities in Cyberspace; Smith/Kollock (Ed), 2000.
18. Schütz, A: Zur Theorie sozialen Handelns, 1977; Der sinnhafte Aufbau der sozialen Welt, 1932.
19. Sloterdijk, P: Kritik der zynischen Vernunft, 1983.
20. Smith, D.E.: Knowledge, Groupware and the Internet, 2000.
21. Watzlawick, P: Vom Sinn des Sinns oder Vom Sinn des Unsinns, Wiener Vorlesungen, 1995.
22. Weick, Karl E.: Sensemaking in Organizations, London, Sage, 1995.
23. Wittgenstein, L.: Philosophical Investigations, Oxford, Blackwell, 1953.

A Framework for Analysis and a Review of Knowledge Asset Marketplaces

Kostas Kafentzis[1], Dimitris Apostolou[2], Gregory Mentzas[1], and Panos Georgolios[1]

[1] Department of Electrical and Computer Engineering, National Technical University of Athens, 10682 Greece
{kkafe, gmentzas, pgeorgol}@softlab.ntua.gr
[2] Planet Ernst & Young, Apollon Tower, 64 Louise Riencourt Str., 11523 Athens, Greece
dapost@planetey.com

Abstract. An increasing number of enterprises are getting interested in exploiting knowledge, tacit or explicit, lying outside their organizational borders and augmenting the knowledge network of their organizations. A first generation of knowledge e-marketplaces has arisen to provide the platforms for knowledge exchange and trading in an inter-organizational level. This paper develops a framework to evaluate the business models, roles, processes, and revenue models of knowledge trading platforms and provides a survey of six existing knowledge marketplaces based on this framework. Finally, a set of conclusions is drawn on what issues should be addressed in a knowledge marketplace in order to eliminate the risks and gain the trust of its targeted customers.

1 Introduction

Electronic marketplaces can be said to represent a second wave in the e-commerce propagation and can be defined as interactive business communities providing a central market space where multiple buyers and suppliers can engage in e-commerce and/or other e-business activities (Bruun et. al., 2002). Their primary aim is to increase market and supply chain efficiency and create new value.

As marketplaces evolved two key elements have arisen: their ability to provide not only transaction capabilities but dynamic, relevant content to trading partners and their embracement of dynamic commerce, which involves the buying and selling of goods and services online through flexible transaction models that change over time based on multiple terms such as price, condition of goods, warranty, and shipping costs.

Nowadays we are witnessing the emergence of complex e-marketplaces that must support existing business processes and systems and facilitate the transactions of complex and context-specific products. The landscape becomes even more vague and complicated by the replacement of the so prominent value chains of entire industries by much more complex value webs embedded in an ecosystem where the growing importance of intangible assets and new technology, the existence of the right connections and alliances and the shift in focus from customer-centric to customer-driven are determinant to success.

D. Karagiannis and U. Reimer (Eds.): PAKM 2002, LNAI 2569, pp. 301-313, 2002.

As a result a new type of marketplaces has emerged to cope with an important dimension of this new ecology, which is the transaction of knowledge assets, the knowledge marketplace. Aiming to facilitate the flow of knowledge and to increase the efficiency of knowledge exchange and trading in an inter-organizational level the k-marketplace is facing a plethora of challenges.

Content is becoming even more critical for k-marketplaces. Buyers need good content description, namely content about the content, to make informed purchases and valid and appropriate knowledge assets that will satisfy their needs, while sellers need content about transactions and customer feedback as to properly market and differentiate themselves from the competition and address efficiently existing and emerging customer needs. As a result, the accessibility, usability, accuracy, and richness of content directly impacts the value that a marketplace adds on its customers.

Another development, that actually favours k-marketplaces, is the shift towards dynamic commerce, since some unique characteristics of knowledge products, such as being intangible and highly context-dependent making it difficult for the buyer to assess and value them beforehand and for the supplier to price them in a transparent marketplace of multiple buyers, do not allow static pricing.

Furthermore the increased push towards collaboration and knowledge sharing within a dynamic value web calls for powerful mechanisms that will efficiently support these functionalities and also seamlessly integrate them with corporate knowledge management systems.

A first wave of k-marketplaces has already made its appearance shifting existing knowledge markets into the Web. Examples include (Skyrme, 2001): Intellectual property trading, Recruitment agencies, Management consultancies and Research companies.

This paper develops a framework, called Knowledge Trading Framework (KTF), for analysis of knowledge asset marketplaces and provides a survey of existing k-marketplaces based on this framework. The objective of the survey is to gain a deeper understanding of the business models and methods employed by the first generation of knowledge trading initiatives.

The sample for the survey includes six k-marketplaces that were selected with the objective to cover a wide range of types of knowledge assets traded at the present time. The main criteria for the selection were the success and market penetration of the marketplaces as well as the novelty of their business models.

The Knowledge Trading Framework, which provides a holistic approach for the examination of our subject, is presented in chapter 2. The results of the analysis are presented in chapter 3 where a detailed comparison of the marketplaces is illustrated including useful and consistent conclusions we have drawn. The detailed cases of the selected marketplaces as well as an extensive questionnaire, which has been created to further facilitate our analysis effort and follows the structure of the KTF, can be provided upon request by the authors.

2 The Knowledge Trading Framework

In order to evaluate the business models, roles, processes, and revenue models of existing knowledge trading platforms, we have developed a basic framework for

Knowledge Trading (KTF), which identifies the core elements to be talked about. KTF is based on the Business Media Framework (BMF) (Schmid and Lindemann, 1998; Schmid, 1999; Schmid, 1997), which is adopted and enhanced by the addition of the Strategic Orientation and Knowledge Assets elements in order to capture in a holistic manner all the important issues that are related to *knowledge* marketplaces.

The proposed framework is depicted graphically in Figure 1.

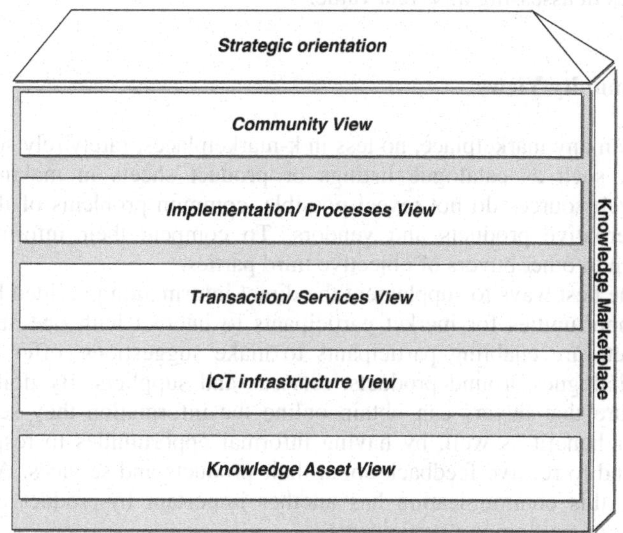

Fig. 1. The framework for knowledge trading and sharing

2.1 Strategic Orientation

The cornerstone of a knowledge marketplace positioning is the value that adds on its participants. The value proposition depends on the knowledge product or service that is offered, its uniqueness and the means of delivering it to the targeted segment of customers. A unique value proposition can provide a first mover advantage that is an important factor for success and can lead to premium pricing of the knowledge offerings. This leads to the selection of a specific niche that could be a specific customer segment, a specific knowledge domain, a capability/ expertise niche, a service niche or a focused geographic location.

Having selected a niche, the other main element of the strategic orientation is a viable business model that should carefully consider costs and resources and address issues such as *liquidity, trust and risk* and *revenue model*:

- The main struggle of a market maker is to ensure *liquidity* of participants and transactions, especially in neutral marketplaces that face the chicken-egg problem.
- Furthermore, to participate in a marketplace the potential customers need the associated *risks* to be eliminated. The more the risks are tackled efficiently the more their *trust* increases towards the marketplace. A number of risks ranging from

financial ones to risks regarding the quality of products concern participating members and need except for the proper infrastructure, clear policies and rules.
- The right balance between the created value and the imposed fees, namely the *revenue model*, should be achieved in a way that both the viability of the marketplace is ensured and the participants still consider the cost of participation fair. Major hurdles are the intangible nature of knowledge assets and the difficulties in assessing their real value.

2.2 Community View

Participants in any marketplace, no less in k-marketplaces, rarely rely solely on direct information, such as catalogue listings or product sheets in making a purchase decision. Such sources do not reveal possible, common problems of the product, or identify alternative products and vendors. To compete their information, buyers typically turn to other buyers of objective third parties.

One of the best ways to supplement the direct information provided by suppliers is to create opportunities for market participants to interact with one another. Today, many markets are enabling participants to make suggestions, offer comments, or engage in dialogues around products, services and suppliers. By doing so, market makers ensure that buyers can obtain online the information they seek from their peers. Seller benefit as well, by having informal opportunities to respond to buyer questions, and to receive feedback about their products and services. As with offline interactions, this communication has another important by-product over time: the development of trust among participants.

However, for these interactions to work successfully we need to describe and structure the *business community* of primary interest beforehand. Therefore, within the community view the *roles* of the participating market member are defined. Based on these roles the interaction of the market members is structured by the necessary *protocols*. Protocols model the admissible interactions among agents providing a set of clear rules and instructions. Apart from specifying the flow of actions they specify the way the marketplace evolves as well. Finally a common language and understanding between the market participants needs to be reached.

2.3 Implementation View

In this view the roles and protocols are realised based on the underlying services in term of specific *processes*.

There are three types of *processes* relevant to e-marketplaces. First of all, the on-line processes that allow the participants to accomplish specific tasks and activities with regard to their assigned role and the relevant protocols. These processes are either strict and pre-defined or may derive on the fly during the interaction of the members with the platform.

The second type concerns marketplace supportive processes that are associated with the support of the normal operation of the marketplace and the delivery of all the offered services in an efficient way.

Finally, the integration of on-line services with back office operations of participating companies benefits both companies and market makers, since seamless flow of knowledge increases the efficiency of interaction.

2.4 Transaction/ Service View

A market transaction can be understood by means of a phase model following the logical flow of actions. This includes the following phases:

The *Knowledge Phase* deals with providing the market participants with the necessary information about the offered products and services. Electronic product catalogues, push- and pull- services or intermediaries, can provide this information. Especially when dealing with complex products like knowledge assets are, satisfying results of this knowledge phase can only be expected, when there is a commonly agreed on logical space, for example in form of an agreed on vocabulary with a shared semantics.

In the *Intention Phase* the market agent develop concrete intentions of exchanging goods and services. The results are precise demands and offers. The primary medium to make offers public is the electronic product catalogue. The description of offers must be precise in a way that it is a sufficient basis for signing a contract.

In the *Contracting Phase* the negotiation takes place, which in case of success is finalized in a valid and secure electronic contract, possibly by integrating trusted-third parties. These contracts are based on the results intention phase.

The services needed during the *Settlement Phase* concern the settlement of the electronic contract. This includes the delivery of services, transport of goods as well as the transfer of payments, insurance and other related services.

2.5 ICT Infrastructure View

This view contains the communication-, transaction- and transport-infrastructure respectively the interfaces to the latter ones. They are used within the service view to implement the services. In general, we evaluate the infrastructure details only if they seem to have a special impact on a certain knowledge trading scenario.

2.6 Knowledge Assets

The starting point for a knowledge trading and sharing scenario is to consider what knowledge assets to commercialise. Skyrme (2001) distinguishes between two main types of exploitable knowledge assets: those that are primarily people-based and those that are object- or information-based.

Some of the most valuable knowledge-intensive services are those relying on personal knowledge. Specialist expertise associated with deep tacit knowledge, insights and experiences may be "productised" and be put on a knowledge marketplace.

Object-based knowledge assets are typically the result of synthesising many different elements of knowledge and applying a design and development process. The resulting object-based knowledge assets are most commonly packaged into two main types of media: compute-based and paper-based. The former include databases, Web pages, software (e.g. expert systems). The latter includes documents and many other types of publication – reports, books, articles, etc. The same knowledge is often packaged in different ways to meet the needs of different consumers and the different ways in which they will use it

3 Comparative Analysis

The comparative analysis presented in this section follows the same structure as the KTF. The various aspects of knowledge trading that we focused on are classified into the six components of the proposed framework and a relevant table presenting a synthesis of the results is introduced at the end of this section.

A short description of the selected knowledge e-marketplaces is presented next, while the more detailed studies of these cases can be provided upon request by the authors:

- Experts Exchange: ExpertsExchange.com has pioneered the IT Professional Collaboration Network marketplace since 1996 with the aim of bringing together professionals in the field of information technology and promoting collaboration among them, in order to provide specific solutions to specific problems.
- Knexa: Knexa.com created in 1999 the world's first person-to-person as well as business to business knowledge auction, a patent pending e-commerce application that applies dynamic pricing to digital goods such as codified knowledge, software, and multimedia content.
- Yet2.com: yet2.com founded in February 1999, aimed at being the first global marketplace for buying, selling and licensing intellectual property on the Internet with the use of an anonymous, confidential and secure process.
- HotDispatch: Hotdispatch.com, founded in 1999, provides a marketplace for IT/IS professionals, systems integrators, and channel partners to buy and sell knowledge services such as questions and answers, project outsourcing, and software exchange.
- Community of Science: CoS.com is the leading Internet site for the global R&D community. Community of Science brings together scientists and researchers at more than 1,300 universities, corporations and government agencies worldwide and provides tools and services that enable these professionals to communicate, exchange information and find the people and technologies that are important to their work.
- eWork: eWork.com operates one of the largest talent marketplaces on the Web with over 300,000 registered users. eWork is headquartered in San Francisco with additional offices throughout the United States and in Europe.

3.1 Strategic Orientation

Most knowledge e-marketplaces tend to position as neutral, playing the role of an independent intermediary who matches knowledge seekers with relevant knowledge sources without favouring any specific side. Yet, in some cases the operation of a marketplace is determined to a certain degree by participating partners intending to serve their own interests better. These partners, that may be large buyers or sellers, banks and consulting firms, often partially fund the endeavour and have a specific interest in it. For example Caterpillar, which is backing up yet2.com, wants to influence the architecture, processes and value-added services of yet2.com to suit the technology transfer needs of its industry.

One of the major advantages that knowledge marketplaces offer is the increased market reach for knowledge sellers who can have access to a broader set of potential buyers around the world and vice versa. Yet, the range of potential customers in a marketplace depends on the strategy followed by the market maker to attract participants. In parallel a strategy that focuses on building the transaction volume, which in some cases is more important than the number of members, should be formed and applied. Players who trade the most should be targeted and actively helped by the market maker to migrate their transactions on-line.

In addition to these a good brand name can be a determinant for the success of a marketplace. The name of a marketplace depends on the best part on the companies that back it up, either by investing on it or forming partnerships with it or participating as buyers or sellers. Furthermore, marketing techniques can enhance the marketplace's image.

Finally, the revenue model of a marketplace is an important strategic decision since the profits and consequently the viability of the marketplace depend on its suitability and effectiveness. It was not surprising to find out that most marketplaces prefer their revenue model to rest on a combination of fees (see Table 1) in order to become less vulnerable to competition and tie their revenue model more accurately to the value being created as perceived by the different types of customers.

Table 1. Sources of revenue selected by the k-marketplaces

Sources of Revenue	Hot-Dispatch	Knexa	yet2.com	Experts Exchange	Community of Science	eWork
Transaction fees	√	√	√			
Sales fees	√			√		√
Fees for VAS			√			√
Subscription fees				√		
Membership Fees			√		√	
Advertising fees				√	√	√

3.2 Community View

In every marketplace we examined there existed at least two clear and distinct roles:

- the knowledge seeker or buyer who has a need for knowledge, which need may vary from specific and crystallized to vague and immature,
- the knowledge provider or seller who owns a knowledge asset, which may be explicit, such as a best practices document, or tacit, like consultancy time.

Other intermediaries, like brokers or trusted third parties or service providers, were included depending on the business model. For example, Knexa houses companies, called Knowledge Agents, which carry expertise in specific business areas.

Protocols serve the model described in the community view and especially the relevant business community. Besides, the marketplaces have to adhere to general law of their country or region and to follow legal obligations given by the arising Internet law and standards, like Netiquette.

Regarding probable disputes the increased complexity to assess a knowledge asset value, which is connected to its relevancy and applicability to each specific case, may lead to several kinds of disputes. A marketplace needs clear rules and a dispute mechanism as to avoid trouble, like disappointment from the usefulness of an asset, refusal to payment etc, resulting in the loss of trust or even worse in the withdrawal of participants. Resorting to arbitration schemata within the marketplace or by independent third parties should also be stated clearly in user agreement. In most marketplaces in the survey disputes are solved on an individual basis, which is the easier way. The other mean is to call an independent arbitrator to settle the dispute under the specific country's arbitration rules, which happens in HotDispatch.

The fulfillment of an order or the support of the full transaction cycle on-line represents an important advantage for the marketplaces that provide them. Especially knowledge assets being intangible and, often, in digital format simplifies the delivery process to a certain degree. On the whole, in knowledge industry both services and products can be delivered on-line depending on the infrastructure of the marketplace. In all the marketplaces examined in the survey, apart from yet2.com and Community of Science, the business transaction cycle is completed on-line. This is because the assets traded in yet2.com (IP, technology) are very complex to transfer and hard to negotiate on-line. In the case of Community of Science, the service restricts itself to matching scientists and funding organizations and initiating a contact.

Protocols regarding the facilitation of collaboration and creation of new knowledge businesses through a virtual organization structure or a looser team formation can accelerate knowledge creation and development within a marketplace. For example, e-Work provides a secure virtual space and the appropriate collaboration and project management tools, which are the main enablers for the development of on-line synergies. The various aspects of knowledge co-creation include infrastructure, project management, legal arrangements, equity and intellectual rights etc.

Lastly, knowledge marketplaces have a two-fold role; besides enabling knowledge transactions they provide a venue for people to socialize. This venue is defined by a set of values and norms which are set by the market maker and are usually very strict regarding what is not allowed to be said or done by the participants. When relationships between members develop new groups and sub-communities can be created and evolve following the unwritten rules imposed by the specific group's mentality. A space for the social interaction of the members of the marketplace is nurtured in two cases, Experts Exchange and HotDispatch. In Knexa self-evolving, autonomous communities may grow under the wings of the Knowledge Agencies.

3.3 Transaction/ Service View

The functionality of a marketplace is based on the services that are employed to support the transaction cycle. Services should efficiently deal with all the issues regarding commerce, collaboration and content in order to enable a customer to carry out a satisfactory transaction and enjoy a pleasant on-line experience.

Therefore, the selected services should address the key inefficiencies in the specific market space and they need to be coordinated to yield synergistic effects and to create new value. Their mix should be dynamic and reflect the on-going changes in the marketplace environment. For example Experts Exchange enriched their services, both in the commercial and the content area, by providing an organized library of well-structured previously answered questions accompanied with advanced search tools. A subscription fee is charged for unlimited access to the knowledge assets of the library. By this service Experts Exchange exploits the previously untapped resource of three million answered questions.

Specifically, the commerce model is more or less specified by the selection of the trading mechanism(s) (catalogue, auction etc) and various factors have to be considered before the final selection; product complexity, available liquidity and maturity of trading participants are the most important. HotDispatch provides a reverse auction mechanism since there is the analogous liquidity to ensure the mechanism appropriate operation. An interesting case is Experts Exchange that operates a patented recognition system to induce its members to participate actively in the marketplace, whose notion is based more upon voluntary participation and reciprocity than on making profit. In the following table the pricing mechanisms employed by the marketplaces of the survey are presented.

Table 2. Pricing mechanisms employed by the k-marketplaces

Pricing Mechanisms	Hot-Dispatch	Knexa	yet2.com	Experts Exchange	Community of Science	eWork
Fixed Price	√	√		√		
Direct Negotiation [1]	√	√	√		√	√
Auction		√				
Reverse Auction	√	√				

The appropriateness of pricing mechanisms ensures that knowledge assets are priced in accordance to their market value at the specific time of the transaction. Although different kinds of mechanisms match better with different types of assets, the availability of a set of pricing mechanisms can establish trust and help to better depict the value of an asset as perceived by its potential buyer.

Credit and payment mechanisms comprise another crucial service for gaining the trust of the potential members of the marketplace. Payment mechanisms should make it easy for the customer to do business with and reduce the buyer's risk. Of course clear terms of trading go hand in hand with trust. Regarding security the technologies that are broadly used are SSL and digital certificates. Another arising issue especially for marketplaces that handle low cost transactions is dealing with micropayments. Knexa provides a mechanism for dealing efficiently with this type of payments. The payment mechanisms that have been selected by the marketplaces are presented in the following table.

[1] In the cases of CoS and yet2.com direct negotiation takes place off-line while in eWork it can take place either on-line or by traditional communication mechanisms

Table 3. Types of Payment Mechanisms employed by the k-marketplaces

Payment Mechs	Hot-Dispatch	Knexa	yet2.com	Experts Exchange	Community of Science	eWork
Credit Card	√	√		√		√
Wire Transfer	√					
Off-line	√		√		√	√
Other [2]	√					
Micropayments		√				

Moreover, value is added and trust towards the marketplace is further established by the provision of a range of payment mechanisms so that the member can choose the one fitting his needs can. For example, HotDispatch offers four different payment mechanisms, satisfying customers' various needs and establishing a strong trust relationship at first sight.

Another element that enhances the reliability of the marketplace and reduces risks for the buyer is proof of the credibility of the participant as well as the provision of a payment guarantee that shifts the risk of the transaction from the customer to the market maker. Loyalty is further enhanced by the provision of financial and other value-added services such as invoicing. e-Work provides billing and payroll services and also guarantees the professional services provider's payment regardless her client's payment attitude.

It also seems essential for the smooth interaction of the customers with the knowledge marketplace a personal account and repository to be provided to them, which will facilitate them to easily handle their knowledge assets and personal information as well as completing administrative tasks. eWork provides its users an account with which they can audit and handle all their interactions in the marketplace.

3.4 ICT Infrastructure View

In terms of the underlying infrastructure, our notices conclude to a set of characteristics that the selected technologies have to carry. First of all the platform has to be scalable as to cope with the increased volume of transactions or the number of participants. Secondly, it has to be flexible in order to adapt to possible focus shifts and increased demand. Thirdly, it should ensure security as to establish trust. Fourth, the platform must offer the possibility of frictionless integration with back-office systems of participating members and support the migration of intimate supplier networks. For example HotDispatch facilitates the migration of existing communities in the internal of companies onto the platform with the use of corporate accounts. Fifth, the platform should enable connectivity to other marketplaces as to offer to members a one-stop experience providing them with the capability to buy all relevant products and services through one marketplace. Community of Science provides this opportunity to its members by connecting them with a broad set of databases and marketplaces relevant to their needs. Finally, an important element is ease to use that is achieved by user-friendly interfaces.

---

[2] PayPal®is an email-based service created by HotDispatch to enable individuals and organizations to add a financial reward to any email request they send

With regard to the collaboration part, trading participants and / or third parties should be easily connected with collaboration tools that satisfy their specific needs for communication and team working. QuestionReader, a patented mechanism available in HotDsipatch, deals with collaboration issues with success enabling threaded discussion between participants using a mailreader style interface.

3.5 Implementation View

A successful value proposition should rely on processes that streamline and transform the traditional processes in the knowledge supply chain. How'to conduct business can be a differentiating factor by itself obtaining competitive advantage for the marketplace, both against traditional businesses and direct competitors. For example yet2.com creates value for its participants by providing them with an anonymous, confidential and secure process for technology transfer and licensing. The proposed process reduces drastically the needed time for locating a buyer or a provider of a specific licensed technology.

Furthermore, integrating the marketplace functionalities with back office systems of the participants, e.g. knowledge management systems, content management systems or workflow management systems, increases value delivered to the user. It also increases switching costs of the customer to competitors.

3.6 Knowledge Asset View

A marketplace may be focused on a specific industry and its needs for knowledge or it may cater for a variety of industries with a similar knowledge need. In both cases, it is not only the quality of content that matters but also the quantity of knowledge assets plays an important role. A marketplace that doesn't have a plethora of items available, even if it is a niche market, cannot meet and fulfill customer broad range of needs, leading to frustration and lose of trust.

Additionally, the confidence and trust of buyers is increased when the sellers have been validated before they are accepted in the marketplace by the market maker or better by third parties, e.g. commercial chambers. Yet, customer feedback and ratings on products and sellers professional behaviour can help buyers gain confidence towards specific suppliers. Knexa uses a three-star rating system for buyers to grade the quality of a knowledge asset, while HotDispatch and Experts Exchange employ a similar system for grading experts' performance.

It seems to be a common ground for most of the examined marketplaces that structuring their knowledge assets catalogue is not an underestimated operation, diminishing this way the risk of frustrated customers unable to locate a proper category suiting their needs or offers. A logical and rich structure of the classification scheme available on a marketplace in parallel to good computer searching algorithms, that make catalogues easily searchable, and items accurately described so they can be easily compared, can provide satisfactory and quick results to customers searching for specific knowledge. The customers who approximately or not very clearly know what could be helpful for their case may initiate a dialogue with knowledge providers and conversely (for example in RFQs), so that needs and offers can be refined.

Marketplaces for experts or project outsourcing provide this type of facilities, e.g. Experts Exchange and HotDispatch. Moreover, in complex knowledge assets knowledgeable human brokers can make the most accurate matchmaking giving the marketplace a distinctive advantage. A good paradigm is yet2.com, where although the patented format for describing a technology is adequate for most of the cases, a human infomediary sometimes is needed to make the proper matches.

4 Conclusions

The objective of this survey was to gain a deeper understanding of the business models and methods employed by existing knowledge marketplaces, based upon the Knowledge Trading Framework, which captures in a holistic manner all the elements that are useful for understanding and analyzing the structure and strategy of knowledge marketplaces. It becomes clear from the analysis of the selected marketplaces the fact that an increasing number of enterprise are getting interested in exploiting knowledge, tacit or explicit, lying outside the organizational borders in parallel to harnessing the internal knowledge resources. The arising need for augmenting the knowledge network of their organizations has led to the participation in various types of the first generation of knowledge e-marketplaces.

Our analysis of six of these marketplaces has helped us draw a first set of conclusions on what are the main trends in knowledge trading and how typical e-commerce issues are addressed by the existing knowledge marketplaces.

First of all, the trend of knowledge marketplaces to position as neutral business communities playing the role of an independent intermediary, achieving the increased trust of customers towards the marketplace, became clear. On a second level, regarding content, it appears that most marketplaces tend to target a niche market when launching, providing a narrow assets portfolio that is expanded aggressively as soon as a firm market share has been established in the particular focus segment. Moreover, liquidity of quality content and participants, especially in expert-based communities, are vital for survival and development and directly associated to the marketplace's potential of revenue generating.

Secondly, the two main roles in all knowledge marketplaces are these of knowledge seeker and knowledge provider, supported during their transactions by a group of agents, like brokers, certification authorities, services providers, escrow agents etc. These roles act within a business community governed by specific protocols and rules. Yet, sub-communities or socialization venues are also provided in most cases, aiming at further increasing participants' loyalty via their emotional involvement.

Thirdly, it seems to be a necessity for the marketplace in order to be accepted to support the full transaction cycle on-line. Information and intention phases are supported by category lists, search engines, requests for quotation, recommendation services and intelligent matching mechanisms. In the contracting phase negotiation occurs either off-line, in some cases for projects, or more often on-line via pricing mechanisms such as auctions and reverse auctions or direct negotiation and on-line communication tools. Finally, in the settlement phase secure payment services are always available and in general rating services allow buyers to grade the quality of content delivered.

It is certain that some of the existing knowledge marketplaces will not prove to be viable while on the other hand a number of new and innovative ones will arise as the need for knowledge from outside the boundaries of organizations increases and the relevant business domains expand. Comprehending these needs as well as the peculiarities of knowledge trading in contrast to traditional e-commerce are the main enablers to creating viable and profitable business communities that add real value on their customers.

Acknowledgement. This paper came from research conducted within the framework of the EU funded IST project 'INKASS'. We would like to thank the participating organizations, consortia members and partners.

References

1. Bichler, M.: The Future of e-Markets. Cambridge University Press (2001)
2. Bruun, P., Jensen, M., Skovgaard. J.: e-Marketplaces: Crafting a Winning Strategy. European Management Journal, article in press (2002)
3. Kearney, A.T.: Building the B2B Foundation. White Paper, A.T. Kearney (2002)
4. Muller, R., Spiliopoulou, M., Lenz, H-J: Electronic Marketplaces of Knowledge: Characteristics and Sharing of Knowledge. Proceedings of the International Conference on Advances in Infrastructure for e-Business, e-Education and e-Medicine on the Internet, Italy (2002)
5. Petra, S.: The Pivotal Role of Community Building in Electronic Commerce. In: Proceedings of the 33th HICSS Conference, Hawaii, (2000).
6. Raisch, W. D.: The E-Marketplace Strategies for Success in B2B eCommerce. McGraw-Hill (2001)
7. Schmid, B., Lindemann, M. A.: Elements of a Reference Model for Electronic Markets. In: Proceedings of the 31st Hawaii International Conference on Systems Science, Hawaii (1998) 193-201
8. Segev, A., Gebauer, J., Fäber, F.: Internet-based Electronic Markets. International Journal on Electronic Markets, St. Gallen, Switzerland (1999)
9. Skyrme, D. J.: Knowledge Commerce: Succeeding in a Global Knowledge Marketplace. Knowledge Economy Conference, Beijing (1999)
10. Stolze, M., Ströbel, M., Ludwig, H.: Knowledge Allocation Using Negotiated Agreements in Service Markets. Proceedings of the AAAI 2000 Spring Symposium on Bringing Knowledge to Business Processes, Stanford University, California, (2000)
11. Ströbel, M.: On Auctions as the Negotiation Paradigm of Electronic Markets. Journal of Electronic Markets 10(1) (2000)
12. Zimmermann, H.-D.: Understanding the Digital Economy: Challenges for new Business Models. In: Chung, M. H. (ed.): Proceedings of the 2000 Americas Conference on Information Systems, Long Beach, CA, (2000)

KM for Public Administration: Focusing on KMS Feature Requirements

Roland Traunmüller and Maria Wimmer

Institute of Applied Computer Science, University of Linz, Austria
{traunm, mw}@ifs.uni-linz.ac.at

Abstract. The information society develops a novel and comprehensive vision of governance with knowledge as core part. For building KMS a mere transferring of concepts from the private sector to the public area will not suffice; approaches of their own are necessary. For this purpose, Public Administration in general as well as in typical applications is juxtaposed with main features of KMS. Focal question is how features of KMS technology can meet requests derived from administrative work. The outcome is a remarkable picture; it shows bright options and possibilities as well as shortfalls and indications for further development.

1 Knowledge as Prime Force in Public Administration

With the emergence of the information society, establishing an integrative approach to governance is of paramount importance. So it surpasses isolated solutions such as internet portals for citizen; moreover the proclamation is an unreserved claim for a profound rethinking of administrative work. In such a novel concept of governance the role of knowledge becomes dominant and is expressed in metaphors: defining administrative action as "knowledge work" is one statement, regarding public authorities as "knowledge networks" is another. Especially the idea of a network is demanding: it is more than claiming demand for information; moreover the idea of a network suggests a qualitative increase and intensification of relevant knowledge. So building a modern administration with novel patterns of co-operation is tantamount to changing the distribution of knowledge. Redistribution of knowledge must be designed and orchestrated carefully, and so managing knowledge becomes a major responsibility for officials. Boiling this down to leads to the concept "knowledge enhanced Government." Without a doubt, prospects for KM in Public Administration are remarkable from the point of demand: nearly all administrative tasks are informational in nature, decision making is an officials daily bread, and for any agency its particular domain knowledge is an asset of key importance. In this contribution we treat a main question of introducing KM to Public Administration: how can main features of KMS meet the typical requests of administrative work.

D. Karagiannis and U. Reimer (Eds.): PAKM 2002, LNAI 2569, pp. 314-325, 2002.

2 Introducing KM

Introducing KM to the governmental domain is high on the agenda. First strategy that comes in mind is to rely upon proven concepts and systems which have been developed in the commercial sector. Yet, past experiences have shown that a plain replication from the private sector to the public one is questionable. Often in a simple transfer considerable hindrances have become apparent. A striking example has been given with the introduction of workflow management systems. Experiences drawn are clear: conceiving agencies as some sort of production plant transforming inputs into outputs has missed decisive aspects of administrative work; administrative processes differ significantly from most processes in the industrial and commercial area [3]. Hence, a strategy relying on a mere replicating concepts from the commercial sector is questionable. There are several inherent reasons - all closely connected with specific traits of administrative work. They are discussed in detail in the literature [1] [4], so here purely some demarcations are outlined in a brief way:

- The extraordinarily complex goal structure of Public Administration distinguishes the public sector from private business.
- Legal norms are a standard vehicle of communication between central authorities and executive agencies. Generally, public administrations are highly regulated by legislation which is enacted on several levels (supranational, national, regional, local).
- Neither the procedural nor the material law can fully determine outcomes – legal interpretation, deliberation and consensus building are crucial. Thus developing consensus and enter into negotiations are important modes of action.
- Legal norms give particular meaning to administrative structures. Examples are plentiful such as protecting the rights of citizens or safeguarding legal validity.
- Public Administration works via a complex tissue of cooperation of acting entities.

For these reasons, replicating concepts and systems of the commercial domain can only be a part for a strategy that brings KM to Public Administration. Moreover, it has to be supplemented effectively by a second line of action: thoroughly regarding administrative work as knowledge work and subsequently deriving particular feature requirements. Only so, the genuine requests will be met.

3 Focal Point: The Knowledge Factor in Administrative Work

Administrative Work is knowledge work and officials are knowledge workers par excellence. After a decade that was preoccupied with processes a contrasting view has taken over. No more is reengineering towards low costs/skills the objective. Quite the opposite has become the motto: fostering and cultivating expertise. A new conviction begins to spread: work in agencies is expert work and depends on knowledge available there. Max Weber, one of the founding fathers of administrative science, addressed such knowledge in his notion of Dienstwissen"– a term which we would call service knowledge or domain knowledge at the present time. This type of knowledge is a hard-to-define blend of different kinds of knowledge [9]:

- Knowledge about the policy field to be influenced
- Knowledge about the evaluated effects of previous actions

- Knowledge about legal rules, standards, political attitudes of stakeholders and other political conditions commanding and constraining action
- Knowledge about one's own capabilities to act.

Such new directions mark considerable progress as they shift focus away from a discussion on structures and processes towards issues of content – so reaching the very heart of administrative work: taking decisions. In some aspect, this regained focus on decisions is going back to roots. It connects to cybernetic thinking which in the Sixties has been widely used for explaining control in the governmental realm [7].

4 Elaborating the KMS Framework for Public Administration

In an earlier investigation, we have treated administrative work as knowledge work as well as the sophisticated intertwining of process, legal norms and administrative domain knowledge in detail [6]. This contribution now goes one step further and confronts administrative knowledge work with the features offered by KMS. In concrete, the proposal on KMS features requirements established by [2] is used for this comparison. Hence the further discussion pursues the following division:

- Domain ontology
- Content repositories
- Knowledge dissemination
- Content integration
- Actor collaboration
- Security.

Above schema will be juxtaposed with administrative work considering both: administration requirements in common and three examples of specific applications. Administrative work in common has been discussed in depth in literature (e.g. [4] [5] [8]); here we only sketch those applications used for explanation in the later sections:

1. *Application 1: Decision Making Centred on Individual Cases:* For many officials it is the principal work activity consuming a large amount of their office time Individualised case processing takes into consideration the particular circumstances of a situation and there are manifold cases in point: child allowances, tax cases, building permits etc. In praxis borders blurry: the same case that is routine for person A, for person B may become complex on special factual or legal grounds. Additional, interaction with stakeholders is often not foreseeable in detail at the beginning. To bring it to the point: there is a basic distinction between recursive production processes and complex decision processes. For later ones at the date of the initiation of the process the later stage cannot be anticipated, neither in its actual course nor in its accumulated complexity, getting advice from further experts or involving additional agencies may become necessary.
2. *Application 2: Policy Formulation*: Preparing processes of policy formulation is important for legislative and administrative work. Examples are bills of parliament, answers responding to parliamentary inquiries or complex political decisions. Also in the higher echelons of administrations cooperative decision processes are a common way of work. Policy making and its complex processes represent a case of weakly-structured processing with quite unique constraints.

3. *Application 3: Citizen Information:* Citizen information is a core part of an integrated service access management as envisaged in online one-stop Government. As organisational mode several forms are possible: kiosks, municipal neighbourhood one-stop offices, multifunctional service offices as well as home and mobile access. Many particular functions are included such as: citizen information at various stages, choice of the favoured access channel, aid for filling in forms, matching of the citizen's demand with the administrative structure, invoking human mediators for help etc.

Having outlined the examples, attention is directed toward the KMS features starting with the prime component – domain ontology.

5 Domain Ontology

Administration Requirements in Common: For domain ontology a rich kit of methods for knowledge representation exists as listed in [2]: taxonomies, semantic nets, semantic data models, hyper links, knowledge based reasoning, time modells and process graphs. Here we will raise the basic question of advantages and obstacles.

- *Sizeable formalised ontologies are scarce:* Regarding Public Administration, most needed features are taxonomies, semantic nets and semantic data models. In a concrete project[1] we have handled the task of modelling a sizeable ontology for the complex life events and associated administrative processes." Such a highly formalised description has become necessary - as request out of an international project whose software has to run in several countries. Modelling in an accurate way has further advantages as the domain under consideration is difficult: live events and processes have multiple relationships and in addition the processes have to cross various administrative boundaries. A lesson learnt is that the effort in modelling has been rather high. This experience leads to a core concern: administrative work in general lacks such precise descriptions. Being short of formalised ontologies is a key imperfection in present systems and causes multiple consequences.
- *Lack of commitment:* An obstacle is that - in contrast to e-Commerce where efforts have brought to bear ebXML[2] - Public Administration shows less commitment. Reasons are many: fragmentation of administration, competing claims on resources with high priority, intrinsic difficulties of the domain in question.
- *Intrinsic features:* Intricacy and complexity of law itself is one reason. So troubles start on the basis with legal terms themselves that all too often are not adequately defined. This is due to several reasons: vagueness that may be on purpose, genuine inconsistencies and fuzziness, dynamics in law, planned discretionary power of street level bureaucrats etc. Further, mapping administrative semantics is full of more or less inhibiting difficulties: profound differences in legal systems, adequate meaning of terms, different connotations of terms and non-existence of counterparts.

---

[1] eGOV (an integrated platform for realizing online one-stop government), IST-2001-28471, http://www.egovproject.org/

[2] http://www.ebxml.org/

Application 1: Decision Making Centred on Individual Cases: This application depends heavily on internal and external data exchange. In reality this means using workflow and EDI as tools. Therefore domain ontologies are central:

- *Formalised legal domain ontologies:* Although this is an urgent request, scarcely work on such elaborate models can be found. Often rather coarse taxonomies and makeshift classifications are used deducted from the every day work of users.
- *Taxonomies need detailing:* Sharpening is urgent as coarse classifications – although often used and sufficing for certain applications - are inadequate as requirement for KMS. Just to give an example, for running workflow a coarse grouping may do: distinguishing information objects whether they belong to the case and to the process (one class describing all the facts pertaining to a particular case, the other guiding the administrative process). Yet turning from workflow to KMS a more detailed distinctions becomes mandatory.
- *Taxonomies for information gathering:* Taking decisions means including all available information in the decision process that makes information gathering crucial. Aspects are described subsequently at multiple occasions: aspects of policy information in section 5; usage of internal memories in section 6; ways of legal information retrieval in section 7; knowledge portals in section 8.

Application 2: Policy Formulation: Turning towards planning the need for ontologies is apparent as well:

- *Information gathering:* For policy formulation the realm for information search and investigation is rather unlimited; collecting all relevant information might include exhaustive seeking for information sources. Collecting expertise and preparing information for decisions is a tough part: gathering as well internal and external information, furthermore both factual information as well as "deontic" information. Especially the latter one is crucial and manifold: norms, prior decisions, binding expectations etc.
- *Taxonomies for documentation:* For documenting negotiations and decisions is a small example is given concerning the legal status of the documents. References of legal relevance have to be marked in an unmistakable way: authorized status of minutes, binding character of decisions, liability of the decision body etc.

Application 3: Citizen Information: Following examples may give an idea about the need for a proper ontology:

- *Automatically routing of citizen demands:* The goal is an automatically routing either to relevant knowledge repositories or to the agency with competencies in the legal sense. The concrete target may be diverse: a plain data base, a sophisticated piece of software, a staffed service centre (e.g. a call centre) or an official in a particular agency. Nowadays this is done in comparing key words, yet mapping requests by means of domain ontologies is preferential-
- *Adding comprehension:* Taxonomies must be þalatable"for citizens. There is no much use providing information on the web just in an exclusively administrative-legal wording. Web-design has to resolve conflicting demands: a) citizen's requests commonly posed in a rather urgent situation, b) the need for an in-depth explanation in an unambiguous way, c) and the limited explanatory capabilities of the system.
- *A basis for static and dynamic help:* Support can be both, static and dynamic, yet an underlying ontology is needed anyway. Instruments for dynamic help are

software agents or human mediators (discussed in section 7). A static support means thoroughly editing, commenting and illustrating the taxonomy in question.
- *Continuous improvements for interaction:* Perfection starts with small steps, so with working on better comments, drawing clearer scenarios, adding better help-functions. Considerable steps concern incorporating knowledge into software. Final developments will comprise intelligent multi-lingual and multi-cultural personal assistants being integrated in electronic public services portals.

6 Content Repositories

Administration Requirements in Common: As to content repositories quite a lot of KMS features aim at one goal - enabling the exchange of data between diverse administrative bodies. Here we consider two topics, data interchange features and the inclusion of internal repositories, and start with the former ones:
- *EDI:* Evidently, in a cosmos of increasingly fragmented public organisations data exchange between administrative agencies has become the rule. Inter-organisational linkage of content repositories has been a dominant concern since decades. There is a long history with EDI as most renowned pioneer. EDI has enabled smooth computer-to-computer exchange of standardised information items and of transactions.
- *XML and RDF:* Current interest points at other exchange features such as extensible mark up languages together with resource description facilities. With them it is possible to build standards for rather complex structured concepts.

Organisational learning needs several internal repositories. They act as internal memory and may assist in many decisions:
- *Repositories filled by internal processes*: Administrations also have to maintain their organisation and for this aim several supportive activities have to be taken. There is a pure occupation of an organisation with their own internal business and often this is a legitimate objective.
- *Repositories filled by incomplete processes:* Many observing and information-gathering activities take place without producing tangible results. Then observable facts (cf. section 5 with items a and b) go in an internal memory especially when incomplete processes are involved. So many collected pieces of information are valuable; although never used directly for action they may contribute to organisational learning within an agency. Observations gathered by pure chance are a good example and not even a rare one. Such pieces of information should be considered part of a puzzle game with one piece more added.

Application 1: Decision Making Centred on Individual Cases: Here two subjects are considered, interconnection of agencies and documenting the procedural states:
- *Connecting administrative data:* It is a key topic and is touched in several sections of this contribution. Data involved in a specific administrative decision are dispersed over many locations, under the competencies of diverse agencies and residing on several systems. As for the central importance the topic has been tackled in several projects. They all aim at diverse aspects of information exchange and include a variety of approaches. The following selection of references may

illustrate the diversity: eGIF[3], IDA[4], RDF[5], XML PersonRecord in Austria[6], OSCI initiative in Germany[7].
- *Version control:* There are other vital matters as well. As a key point we present documenting the respective states of an official file during its procedural course. This objective is achieved via strict version control where all alterations of a document can be traced – a prime request for safeguarding legal validity.

7 Knowledge Dissemination

Administration Requirements in Common: Stating requirements on the general level is difficult: knowledge dissemination in Government is rather intricate and a lot of options and conditions have to be considered. Potential appearances and forms of design are numerous; in addition they are very depended on addressees and framing conditions. Here some parameters are listed that shape a concrete design:
- Tradeoffs between push- and pull-approaches
- Choice of the access channel which suits best
- Diverse organisational forms and physical settings of demand (office, kiosk, home)
- Balance of human and software mediators/knowledge bearers
- Routing of offer/demand according to administrative competencies
- Intricacies of the subject matters (legal norms and decisions)
- Translation from administrative/legal jargon to everyday world and vice versa.

The following applications 1 and 3 illustrate the dependency on users and circumstances. In the case of decision making the users are administrators and legal retrieval is a pull only situation; for the case of citizen information quite divergent aspects of dissemination come out as relevant: routing, assistance, comprehension etc.

Application 1: Decision Making Centred on Individual Cases: Main requests derives from the influence that is exerted by legal reasons on administrative decisions. Yet this demand is not easy to fulfil. Many legal information systems exists, yet the praxis shows little usage: Consequently new ways have to be explored:
- *Requests for advanced retrieval systems:* Poor usage of common retrieval is explicable because present systems are keyword oriented and lack any further elaboration in view of the particular circumstances of the case to be decided. To be frank, at the moment there remains only yearning and hope.
- *Expecting new developments:* Actually, one can find developments in the direction for retrieval that is case-oriented and handles analogy. Regrettably such approaches still belong to the scientific realm: case based retrieval, deontic logic, probabilistic measures, neuronal nets.

Application 3: Citizen Information: As stated before in the beginning of this section many options are open. For citizen information quite distinct design will result

[3] http://www.govtalk.gov.uk/interoperability/draftschema.asp
[4] http://www.ukonline.gov.uk/
[5] http://www.w3.org/RDF
[6] http://www.cio.gv.at/
[7] http://www.osci.de/leitstelle/index.html

as treated in detail in [4]. To shorten the discussion, here we will only sketch a vision of an advanced system as to illustrate the ample capabilities:

- *A vision as guidance:* We envisage a advanced system using multimedia. A citizen may go to mediating persons at the counter of public one-stop-service shops. The mediators will use the system with its diverse repositories. In case the issue is too complex it is possible to invoke further expertise from distant experts via a multimedia link between the service outlet and back-offices: dialogue becomes trialogue. As the accessed expert himself may use knowledge repositories human and machine expertise become totally interwoven - knowledge enhancement at its best.
- *Further expansion:* Above scenario may be expanded on several sides: the citizen posing ma make contact from the home-site using multimedia; for the routing of demands using software guidance (avatars) is possible; the agency may act in proactive way seting the initial step.

8 Content Integration

Administration Requirements in Common: Regarding content integration two requests are central, coping with the heterogeneity and achieving comprehensiveness.
Heterogeneous data repositories: Content integration means handling a collection of rather heterogeneous data repositories containing data of diverse type format that are originated from different sources. Content integration involves all sorts of conventional ways of keeping data: files, databases, legacy information systems. Efforts for content integration are rather high and minor or major obstacles are common:

- Content integration needs sophisticated content management. A first step is making accessible the diverse data spread over various locations.
- Joining different content may be rather problematic. The semantics of data in a particular application often has been defined long time ago. Now with the Web, data originally used locally have to be used globally.
- Problems accrue in automatic processing (e.g. in data mining), when semantic inconsistencies in data may lead to statistical artefacts causing misinterpretations.
- Another point: With many diverse data types and formats involved rendering information visible is not easy.

Comprehensive integration – a systemic view: An important point is including data from all fields of administrative action. Being well aware of privacy restrains the question points at possibilities in general. For illustrating the wide span to be covered a systemic view on administrative work may serve. Accordingly the six basic stages in executive decision processes are regarded [4]: observation, substantiating facts, decision to act, administrative intervention, execution for enforcement, evaluation. As the schema appears rather abstract some remarks may be useful:

- Above schema is conceptual and can hide a lot of complexity: e.g. substantiating facts is a stage where in reality the effort going into legal interpretation and negotiation may become massive.
- The actual weight of stages differs with the type of application. So observation and evaluation are mostly essential for policy making - yet rarely significant in decision

making in individual cases. In contrary, for decision making in individual cases attention predominantly circles around substantiating facts and intervention.
- The means of administrative actions are a rich collection of various instruments: legal methods comprise norms, directives, permits, obligations; financial measures are impeding (duties and levies) or provide stimuli (allowances and grants).
- In some stages physical-technical actions can occur as well: observation via monitors; intervention by setting up of road-signs; execution in forcible way of tax collection.

The systemic view given here may illustrate both, the span of information sources and the variety of repositories involved. Some aspects are more detailed below.

Stages, information sources and repositories: Evidently the connections are plentiful such as to give some examples:

a) *Observation and collecting information:* Obtaining information is a key condition for governance in general such as to observe the behaviour of the society or a group of citizens. So sources are copious and countless diverse repositories are involved for capturing administrative information.

b) *Substantiating facts*: The material gained from such observations is evaluated in the light of legal and policy premises. In this way, by initiative of an agency a 'case' is constituted as concrete action. In an alternative way, numerous cases are initiated by citizens themselves: claim for an allowance, request for a building permit, applying for civil marriage. In any case, substantiating and proving facts is a crucial and tough activity. In the course of action numerous dossiers are created and many repositories are involved. Repositories may concern observations (mentioned in a), may compile the data on citizens or may pertain to the internal memory (discussed already in section 6). More on b and c is pondered in application 1 below.

c) *Decision to act:* When enough material is collected and combined with the facts, administrators have to take a decision for action. The decision is documented and become part of the accumulated dossier. Decisions will go into several repositories due to the innate importance of decisions and their multiple consequences. Such repositories and their design have to mirror and balance quite differing aspects: integrity and durability of information; sensibility for privacy protection; decisions as precedence cases; access for organisational learning; freedom of information etc.

d) *Intervention*: Intervening in the fabric of society is the final goal of administrative action. This can be made by legal binding declarations of various form: granting permissions, declaring obligations, setting financial measures etc. For most administrative acts the results of the decision-making process are simply communicated to the addressees. In rare cases the intervention will mean physical action.

e) *Execution for enforcing*: If some addressees do not comply with the orders, an execution of the order may become necessary.

f) *Evaluation*: In the last step it has to be checked whether the action taken had the intended effect concerning the influence on the society. Opinion polls, case studies and claims management are examples. The results of this evaluation are collected in particular databases used for improving both, administrative decision-making and the rules guiding it. Here reference is given to section 6 discussing repositories used as internal memory.

Application 1: Decision Making Centred on Individual Cases: This application can be seen as a particular instance for the stages b, c, d. We discuss it for the life situation of civil marriage:

- *Instantiation of the systemic view*: Regarding above schema and taking civil marriage as example one gets a rather "simple case" that will commonly comprising initiation by citizens, proof of legal grounds, proclamation.
- *Variety of transactions and repositories:* Yet, it is just the opposite from simple when the view of on-line one stop service is taken. It is essential for one stop service that data are brought together from /disseminate to diverse data sources. This means that for the life situation of civil marriage a lot of transactions and number of repositories are involved. So before the event lots of documents located in different agencies have to be checked; afterwards a lot of updates on documents have to be made (change of name, civil status, common domicile etc.)
- *Interstate e-Government:* Making the example a little more complicated one may envisage two persons with different citizenship marrying in a third country. In this case the respective transactions cross state borders and so difficulties for on-line one stop service will build up.

Scenario 2: Policy Formulation: Out from several issues we will touch three:

- *Knowledge portals:* The diversity of knowledge sources, types and containers make the user feel uneasy. Hence, meta-information, the information about information, is needed and best moulded directly into the portal. This leads to the idea of dedicated knowledge portals that guide to the respective contents.
- *Joining different types of knowledge:* Combining the different forms of knowledge is not easy as hard and soft data have to be joined. For the former ones figures from controlling pose as example, for the later ones opinion polls and estimations.
- *Unique browser:* Even as it looks to be a mere technical problem it has to be mentioned. One has to ensure that a single browser copes with the multitude of heterogeneous data repositories and different data formats that are involved.

9 Actor Collaboration

Administration Requirements in Common: Actor collaboration features are essential in nearly every administrative scenario. Two basic requests are treated here:

- *Blending different modes of cooperation:* There is need for a wide spectrum of possibilities, depending whether strictly structured cooperation (workflow) is involved or more informal collaborative modes (message exchange, discussion fora, meeting rooms). A smooth transition between both modes and the inclusion of auxiliary functions such as filtering and calendaring is mandatory.
- *Usability:* This is a key word and includes a list of particular requests. Each of them, taken for its own, appears to be rather minute; yet collectively they are important for smooth work. Examples of advanced attributes include: malleability of mechanisms as an adaptability to personal preferences; indicators reminding the basic status (such as what, where, how) when managing subtasks simultaneously; semantic conformity of notational primitives corresponding to the context of usage.

Application 1: Decision Making Centred on Individual Cases: The main request is to have phases of strictly structured cooperation (workflow) are interwoven with phases of informal collaboration:

- *Enabling informal collaboration:* A key priority for internal work due to the intention to reach consensual decisions and a tendency to have consistent decisions for similar cases. Also external negotiations with clients needs collaboration.

Application 2: Policy Formulation: Key requests emerge from two dominant characteristics:

- *Unpredictable amount of negotiations:* The amount of negotiations necessary, their length, their course, the amount of parties they involve are often not foreseeable. This is because policy formulation normally takes place through multiple processes of negotiation. The negotiated character permeates all phases of the policy process and spans diverse organisational boundaries.
- *Meeting support:* Most important to policymaking activities are meetings. In order to reach adequate support environments, one has to blend conventional decision support with collaborative functions. Support system should have a set of highly-modular components as the particular nature of a task is often not foreseeable.

10 Security

Administration Requirements in Common: Knowledge security features are obviously of high relevance for agencies. Consequently actual KMS should integrate diverse security components such as encryption, access control and electronic signatures.
Applications 2 an 3: Policy Formulation and Citizen Information: For both applications demands for safeguarding data security and privacy are stringent. These directives are not easy to fulfil as they sometimes contradict other demands such as planning needs for data integration. In the same way the need for privacy may conflict with other goals such as transparency and freedom of information for the public.

11 Conclusions

First conclusion: For administrative scenarios a broad part of common basic features exists. Furthermore the set of KMS feature suggested by [2] is fairly adequate
Second conclusion: Mostly for usage in Government and Commerce there is no need for distinction in technical matters is necessary.
Third conclusion: Generally, KMS have to be adapted to a particular application and also customising to the specific circumstance of usage might become necessary. In this way non-technical factors expressing organizational and legal demands will exert a strong influence on design and implementation.
Fourth conclusion: There exists a number of features necessary that are really special for governmental work. Some examples have been mentioned: citizen card, legal retrieval systems, knowledge infrastructures for policy formulation, certain marks in citizen information, means for safeguarding privacy etc. Several features of this list still wait for adequate realization.

References

1. Bellamy, C., Taylor, J.A.: Governing in the Information Age. Open University Press, Buckingham Philadelphia (1998)
2. ICONS. Intelligent Content Management System. EC Project IST-2001-32429, project presentation, http://www.icons.rodan.pl/docs/ICONS_D01_project_descr.pdf (April 2002)
3. Lenk, K.: Business Process Re-Engineering: Sind die Ansätze der Privatwirtschaft auf die öffentliche Verwaltung übertragbar? In Traunmüller, R. (ed.): Geschäftsprozesse in öffentlichen Verwaltungen: Neugestaltung mit Informationstechnik. R. v. Decker's Verlag, G. Schenk, Heidelberg (1995) 27 - 44
4. Lenk, K., Traunmüller, R.: Öffentliche Verwaltung und Informationstechnik - Perspektiven einer radikalen Neugestaltung der öffentlichen Verwaltung mit Informationstechnik. R. V. Decker's Verlag, Heidelberg (1999)
5. Lenk, K., Traunmüller, R.: Perspectives on Electronic Government. In Galindo, F., Quirchmayr, G. (eds.): Advances in Electronic Government. Proceedings of the IFIP WG 8.5 Conference in Zaragoza (2000) 11 - 27
6. Lenk, K., Traunmüller, R., Wimmer, M.: The Significance of Law and Knowledge for Electronic Government. In Grönlund, A. (ed.): Electronic Government - Design, Applications and Management. Ideas Group Publishing (2002) 61-77
7. Luhmann, N.: Recht und Automation in der öffentlichen Verwaltung. Berlin (1966)
8. Traunmüller, R., Lenk, K.: New Public Management and Enabling Technologies. In Proceedings of the XIV. IFIP World Computer Congress. Chapman & Hall, London (1996) 11 – 18
9. Wimmer, M., Traunmüller, R: Trends in electronic Government: Managing Distributed Knowledge. In Proceedings of the DEXA, IEEE Computer Society Press, Los Alamitos, CA (2000) 340 – 345

Towards a Framework for Mobile Knowledge Management

Matthias Grimm, Mohammad-Reza Tazari, and Dirk Balfanz

Computer Graphics Center (ZGDV e.V.),
Fraunhoferstr. 5,
64283 Darmstadt, Germany
{Matthias.Grimm, Saied.Tazari, Dirk.Balfanz}@zgdv.de

Abstract. Mobile devices, such as PDAs, evolve rapidly from digital calendars and address books to hosts of more complex functionality. Screen quality, processing power and mobile networks allow for full-blown mobile information systems. However, mobility and scaled-down technology lead to specific limitations in contrast to the usage of desktop computers. It is absolutely crucial to consider these restrictions to ensure the development of usable mobile applications. In this paper, we are going to derive basic requirements for mobile knowledge management and present a first approach to possible solutions within the area of project management work. Underlying technical and human constraints are drawn from a general discussion of mobile information access and processing. We will point out focal components and problems to address. Finally, our main concept of context-aware KM will be sketched, building on the idea of Knowledge Portals and prototyped as the "BuddyAlert" system.

1 Introduction

Mobile devices, such as PDAs, evolve rapidly from digital assistants primarily serving as calendars and address books to hosts of more complex functionality. In addition to the capabilities of these devices themselves, new mobile communication technologies, such as UMTS or WLAN, enable 'anytime' and 'anywhere' access to information infrastructures and integrate the devices as the front ends of mobile information systems.

However, despite the rapid evolution of technology, certain basic limitations will remain and impose requirements on the development of the information system architecture. These limitations can be divided into technical aspects and human aspects.

Technical Limitations. As mobile devices today are a scaled-down version and merger of concurrently developing technologies, such as notebooks, phones or cameras, the processing power of these slim devices is necessarily a year or two behind the current normal-sized, non-merged equipment. This drawback will remain constant for some time to come, although there is ongoing improvement.

D. Karagiannis and U. Reimer (Eds.): PAKM 2002, LNAI 2569, pp. 326–338, 2002.

To some extent, this observation is also valid for transmission rates and display quality, for example. Wired networks reach a much higher throughput than wireless ones and mobile display quality is – for the time being – bound to the physical device size, unless high resolution retinal displays are available. Information presentation on mobile devices needs to address these shortcomings and has to provide adapted visualization; compressed or streamed media, pre-caching and other optimizing measures should be implemented. Nevertheless, the importance of these factors decreases with technical evolution.

Human Limitations. Human limitations are far more stable than their technical counterparts, because the cognitive ability of humans does not obey Moore's law of exponential growth of performance. Especially in the area of mobile information usage, there are specific drawbacks for human cognition. "Mobility" is seen here either as really being "in motion", or as working in a non-office environment with mobile, digital equipment, e.g. in a meeting. In both cases, the attention of the user is partially occupied by other tasks, perhaps even primarily. Under these restrictions, the usage of a mobile information device should not distract from, but rather should primarily support the other tasks. The cognitive ability of the user is reduced by working on several tasks in parallel and demands information retrieval and processing that is fast, effective and easy to accomplish.

These constraints result in the requirement to provide a user of a mobile information system with the rather specific information that she needs in a given situation (which certainly depends on user's current task, location, terminal, etc.), with the type of presentation or visualization that is most appropriate for that situation. As some of the constraints are highly personal (preferences and situation) and bound either to personal or organizational (context-related) history, we regard such mobile information systems as being part of a mobile (personal) knowledge management.

2 Approach to Mobile KM

Our vision is to supply the user with the right information at the right time at the right place using an optimal method of visualization. Although this vision is very appealing, it assumes that for a given task and situation, there is this specific piece of information a user needs. But in reality, this is often not the case. There are rather a number of interrelated information objects that satisfy the user's requirements. Consider, for example, a meeting situation, where often a bundle of information objects, such as agenda, protocol of the last meeting, tasks, etc., are needed. These objects form a sub-space of the whole available information space.

Therefore, new methods are needed to determine this highly dynamic sub-space of situation-related relevant information objects, retrieve the related information, and enable its mobile visualization and navigation, respectively. Our approach to this problem is to consider the user's situation and preferences within a knowledge management system. This system is able to exploit the user's context in order to filter information, which is of special interest in the current situation.

While analyzing and exploiting the user's context in her office is very difficult, mobile knowledge management seems to be a promising research area. One of the major characteristics in mobile environments is the change of user location and thus, the change of her location-related context, since the user's location is highly correlated to her current work. Therefore, knowledge about her location enables the system to select information objects that the user would probably want to access at this location. If the user is a sales-force member and meets a customer, she will most likely want to deal with information concerning the customer. An architect who meets an engineer at a construction site will most likely access information concerning the latest problems relating to this specific construction site. Another important point is the inverse case of accessing information. If a user wants to make some notes, for example, at a meeting or at a construction site, these notes can be automatically annotated with metadata describing the situation, such as the location or people present. This metadata enables the user to easily retrieve the notes by querying the creation context instead of querying the content, which she doesn't remember [4], [8]. Today, the vision is no longer the prototypical implementation of some standalone, mobile, situation-aware applications [4], but to create a framework and concept that facilitate sophisticated integrated applications that logically unify several services in combination with the technically fast-evolving mobile devices.

We regard the modelling, capturing, and supply of context information on the one hand, and context-aware retrieval and filtering of knowledge in terms of documents on the other, as two independent research areas and want to introduce our approach to these areas in the following sections.

3 Context Management

The mobility aspect of our intended framework points out the necessity of considering context data when providing the user with the necessary information [5]. With the change of the user's location, many of the operation parameters also change, for example, the available and used resources and the network infrastructure. Other factors depending on the location of the user, which may affect the behavior of mobile adaptive and proactive software systems, are the social and physical environment of the user [13]. The presence of other people who may (or may not) be cooperating with the user in order to reach a collective goal or physical parameters like temperature and noise are examples of these factors.

Different components of a mobile KM system, however, use these contextual parameters in different ways. For a component responsible for information visualization, the operation parameters and the physical parameters of the environment are the important factors to be considered. For a proactive component providing the user with the necessary information automatically, the reason why the user is at the current place is in fact more important. Nevertheless, all of these components may operate on the basis of shared context data.

Using shared data by different components brings up the question of how this data is structured and organized and which shared mechanisms are needed for using them [12]. Hence, we propose a single component called the Context-Manager, responsible for the management of the context data and for providing the necessary shared mechanisms.

3.1 Context Data and the Concept of Situation

As a result of our investigations, we identified six major types of context data (comp. [1], [5], and [13]):

- Profiles of resources relevant in a concrete situation, e.g. available devices, services, documents, etc. Each such profile describes the identity, characteristics, and capabilities of the underlying resource and "knows" about the location and the state of the resource.
- Profiles of locations, which describe the identity and the state of the location and list the available resources and the people present at that location. The state of a location results out of the perception of the physical characteristics of the location using sensor data, e.g. temperature, brightness, etc.
- User profiles consisting of user's identity, characteristics, capabilities, universal preferences, and the state of the user. User's state includes information about her location, main activity, current terminal, etc.
- The current time.
- Application-specific user preferences.
- Other application-specific data that may play a role in the process of recognizing the current situation – especially applications from the domain of personal information management (PIM), e.g. calendar, to-do list, address book, etc.

A profile in the above sense is a coherent collection of key-value pairs describing a distinct resource, location, or user. Profiles are main storage units of the Context-Manager.

Application-specific data will obviously be managed by the corresponding application. It seems justifiable to also leave the management of application-specific preferences to the application itself, unless the application implementers would like to use some of the special services of the Context-Manager. One such special service is the possibility of defining different values for the same preference depending on the situation. For example, an agent acting as communication assistant and managing, among other things, the incoming telephone calls, must consider the current situation of the user and look up user preferences to see if the user would answer the call in such a situation. Hence, the data describing the context is a combination of profile and preference data, namely profiles of devices, networks, locations, users, services, documents, and so on, plus some application-specific user preferences and data.

Some parts of context data are essentially static (like most parts of device profiles), but they may be referenced and de-referenced dynamically. Other parts are of a dynamic nature (like the location of the user and her main activity or the temperature of a location). Obviously, the user context is changing permanently. At some event, a certain combination of some items of this data may be interpreted as a *well-defined situation*. So, a *recognizable situation* is the event of some set of context items reaching some predefined set of values (comp. [13]). Hence, situation-aware applications need to analyze context data to decide about appropriate actions. A challenging task in this area is to provide a shared mechanism for managing context data along with a *situation recognition engine*. The logic about how a situation may be recognized must be provided by applications, but the Context-Manager may monitor context data, recognize the situation based on the given logic, and notify the corresponding component at the right moment.

3.2 Distribution of Context Data

We believe that the concept of context management may only then be successfully realized and employed, when the inherent distribution of context data is considered. One aspect of this distribution is discussed in the previous section and deals with the fact that some application-specific data may play an important role in recognizing the current situation (e.g. user's appointments). We discuss the other aspects in this section.

Concerning the fact that many parts of profiles are static, it is possible to put each coherent collection of key/static-value pairs as a distinct profile somewhere on the Web (independent from the context management service) once and to reuse those profiles by concrete instances of the Context-Manager. For example, the terminal being used by the user may have some extensions when compared with the standard specimen. The profile of the standard specimen may be available on the Web site of the manufacturer; then, the local profile can contain only the differences and dynamic data, such as the current IP address (comp. [7] for default values).

On the other hand, many context items are personal information that the user may not be willing to disclose (obviously, the user profile contains the majority of such data), whereas other items are public info that may be accessed by any user (e.g. profiles of public locations).[1] To simplify privacy management, there may be personal instances of the Context-Manager versus public instances of it, which reveals the next aspect of the distribution of context data.

Table 1 summarizes the above discussion. Our approach for dealing with the distribution of context data is to provide a "virtually centralized" service (i.e. the distribution of profiles is hidden by local instances of the Context-Manager) for managing all kinds of profiles, regardless of their structure and semantics. The schema describing the structure and some semantics of each profile type can then be used for accessing the concrete profile instances.

[1] There are also other categories in-between, like organizational data, which we ignore at this stage.

Table 1. Distribution of context data from context management point of view

	personal	public
internal	e.g. user profile, profile of user's terminal	e.g. profiles of concrete public resources, location profiles
external	e.g. PIM data, project plan	e.g. profiles on the Web

3.3 Exchange of Context Data

The language of choice for the exchange of context data is the XML syntax of RDF, the Resource Description Framework of W3C [9]. This is a natural choice, because context data is mostly formed from descriptions about resources. The usage of RDF as a standardized framework for the exchange of context data makes it very simple to use the external public profiles on the Web. The XML syntax of RDF allows the realization of the Context-Manager as a Web service, because of its conformity with current schemes for Web services. It also facilitates the communication within the context management service, because arbitrary sets of context data being managed at different places by different instances of the Context-Manager may be merged to determine the definite set of relevant data in a given situation.

The notion of RDF schema and its enhancement as DAML+OIL [16] can then be used for modelling user context. These schemas describe the shared and common understanding of the context data being exchanged.

3.4 Context-Manager Functionality

At first glance, context management is a special database service enabling storage and retrieval of context data. One of the fundamental requirements on the context management is hiding the distribution of context data. There must also be some support for default values: especially the public profiles on the Web may play the role of default values [7] for some local profiles (see the example about the user terminal in section 3.2).

We have also mentioned the necessity of a situation recognition engine as part of the context management service. Besides, most of the context-sensitive applications need to be notified about changes in the context. In such cases, applications normally subscribe for some event occurring in the context. Subscriptions may be simple or rule-based. Applications submit simple subscriptions in order to be kept up-to-date about the values of some context items. Rule-based subscriptions utilize the situation recognition engine in the event of changes in the context to decide if the subscriber should be notified in the current situation.

Context management, as the profile management service, must also provide a profile editor. The editor must be able to handle all types of profiles. This problem can be solved using the schema definitions of profile types. Last but not least, some context items (especially user preferences) may have different values for different situations. Hence, the Context-Manager must utilize its rule engine to accept and evaluate conditional values. While rules used in conjunction with rule-based subscriptions must be evaluated automatically in some context events, rules used in conditional values must be evaluated when an attempt is made to read the corresponding context item.

To summarize, some important requirements on context management are:

- Providing facilities to insert, update, delete, and query context data.
- Handling default values.
- Providing a situation recognition engine.
- Providing a notification mechanism for handling simple and rule-based subscriptions.
- Handling conditional values.
- Handling the distribution of data in such a way that applications have a centralized view of context data.
- Providing a profile editor.

We have implemented a context manager that realizes most aspects of the first five items above. This service is used as an integral part in our prototypical scenario described in section 5.

4 Mobile KM

There are numerous approaches to knowledge management, each of which is aimed at solving different problems. One widely accepted model for knowledge management systems is that of the knowledge elements by Probst et al [11]. According to Probst, the core processes that make up a knowledge management system are the development, dissemination, acquisistion, maintenance, identification, and usage of the knowledge.

Obviously, some of these processes can be supported very well by the usage of information technology systems – others cannot. Especially in a mobile environment, the dissemination, the maintenance and storage, and the identification of knowledge seem to play a very important role. According to Borowski, et al [2], these sub-processes can be supported very well by the usage of a `knowledge portal`, which is an access point to the Internet or to an organizational Intranet.

4.1 Personal Knowledge Portals

Portals provide several advantages. They facilitate a well-structured, well-organized presentation of knowledge and allow an efficient and purposeful access to knowledge objects. Additionally, portals facilitate the cooperation of virtual teams, because results of their work can be integrated into the portal and thus are available for all other team members. Last but not least, portals offer the possibility to personalize the access, in order to provide different views on the knowledge for different individuals or different groups of knowledge workers.

The final reason for us to choose portals for achieving our goals is that the information a knowledge worker needs cannot be stored in her mobile device. The knowledge is stored in the company's intranet and the device has to connect to this intranet via wireless or radio network. The communication endpoints are the mobile devices and the user's portal, which is technically most likely a web server.

4.2 KM and Context-Awareness

A system, which retrieves and filters information with respect to the given user context, requires a model describing which information is important in which situation. Situations are descriptions of the spatial and temporal adjacencies of the user. These descriptions are mostly vague and fuzzy. Not even the location can be described sharply. A room, for example, can be described as a rectangular region with certain corner coordinates. The coordinates of the user can be measured using an in-house GPS device. They can be compared to the coordinates of the room, and if they are inside the rectangle, the user is in the room. Nowadays, in-house tracking systems provide an accuracy of a few meters. So, if the user stands near a wall, the system might expect her to be outside the room. If there is important information attached to that room, the system won't retrieve this information, unless it is fuzzy capable and estimates probability values rather than binary values. But situation descriptions include more than only user location and time. They also comprise information about any other people present, about the user's workflow, her next working steps, etc., that are also vague and fuzzy.

Thus, a situation- or context-aware knowledge management system is far more than a system with a query interface accepting clear-cut situation descriptions in terms of data structures and returning information objects that have certain relations to these situation descriptions. It has to be a system, which knows about fuzzy situation descriptions in terms of sets of features describing the situation, and that is able to identify correlations between these features and information objects. Methods have to be explored that make it possible to describe these correlations. Ontologies might help to model situations and information objects, as well as relations between them. Using these ontologies, fuzzy classification and inference methods might be used to recognize relations between information and situations and, therefore, to retrieve and filter information that is of special interest.

4.3 Application Domain

The application domain of our work deals with project work. The information, which is presented to the user in a context-aware way includes emails, text documents, tasks, notes and appointments (we call these the `information objects`). We created a domain ontology, which describes these information resources and possible relations. Beside these resources, work-specific resources, such as projects, sub-projects, project partners, and roles and abilities of people, are modeled in ontologies and linked to the information objects (we call them `infra-structural objects`). This leads to a network structure where information objects are directly linked to infra-structural objects.

4.4 Accessing the Information

In our concept, the context-aware retrieval (CAR) of information is performed in two subsequent steps. First, metadata must be captured and attached to the information objects. In our case, the metadata describes attributes of information objects, such as the author, title and keywords of a document, or the sender and the subject of an email, on the one hand, and relations between these information objects and the infra-structural objects, such as projects, sub-projects, topics, etc., on the other. One core problem of knowledge management is that the authors do not provide this information. However, our system has a certain knowledge about the domain. It knows the user, the projects she is involved in, and the subjects she is interested in. This knowledge might help to classify information objects and automatically generate metadata.

The second step is the retrieval of information itself. To do so, we first identify the infra-structural objects that are directly linked to the current situation (e.g. knowing the construction site, we can identify the related project). Having identified the infra-structural objects, and utilizing the existing metadata, we build a query to find related information objects (e.g. tasks of the user in the corresponding project). This approach is called user-driven CAR in [3], in contrast to author-driven CAR , where authors attach the situation descriptions explicitly to the information objects. In the latter case, when the described situation occurs, there is no need to build a query (because the information object is explicitly attached to the situation) and the information object can be presented to the user instantaneously.

5 Prototypical Implementation

As a first step towards situation-aware, proactive retrieval and in order to explore the interesting field of mobile knowledge management, we have implemented a first prototype, called BuddyAlert (see figure 1). It demonstrates some of the basic functionality mentioned above and follows the key idea of supporting the user with a kind of memory aid. The user may, for instance, define tasks linked with documents and persons ('buddies'). Meeting one of the addressed persons would make the system remind her of the tasks, in addition, offering her access to the related documents. When being visualized, the documents are adapted to the user's current situation. Besides defining tasks, the user can compose memos, address them to one or more buddies and post them to a location, quite similar to the stick-e note architecture described in [10]. Figure 1 shows the main screen of the BuddyAlert system, the 'AlertSpace'. The list includes all items that are relevant to the latest recognized situations: tasks, location-sensitive memos, and notifications concerning the location of buddies. All these information objects are examples of the author-driven CAR mentioned above.

The underlying information agent is organized in different layers (see figure 2). Each layer represents a specific semantic abstraction level. The query layer enables us to connect to different database systems without any prior knowledge

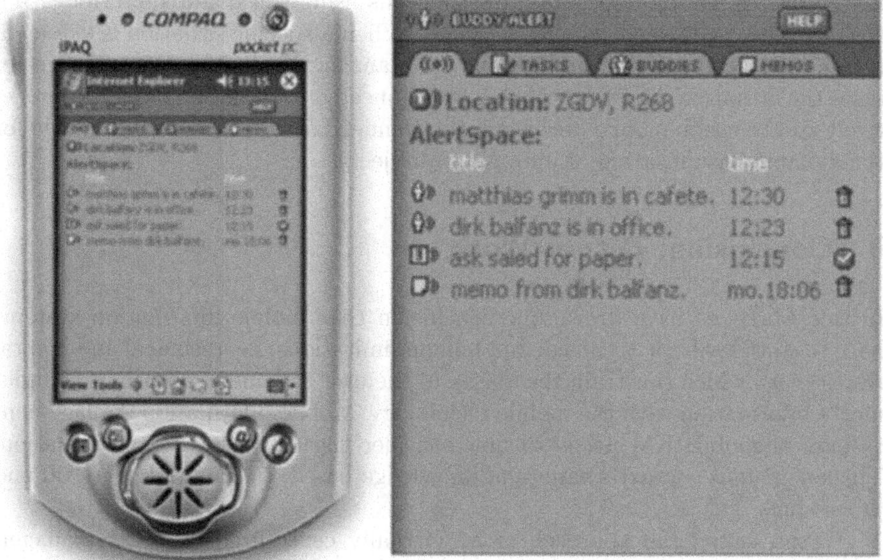

Fig. 1. The AlertSpace of Buddy Alert.

about the semantics of the underlying data. These databases can be used for storing the tasks and memos. The databases we use are MySQL, PIM applications, such as Outlook, and the World Wide Web. The Situation-Assistant is attached to the Context-Manager via a wrapper, which provides easy access to location information, user information, device capabilities, etc. The Situation-Assistant

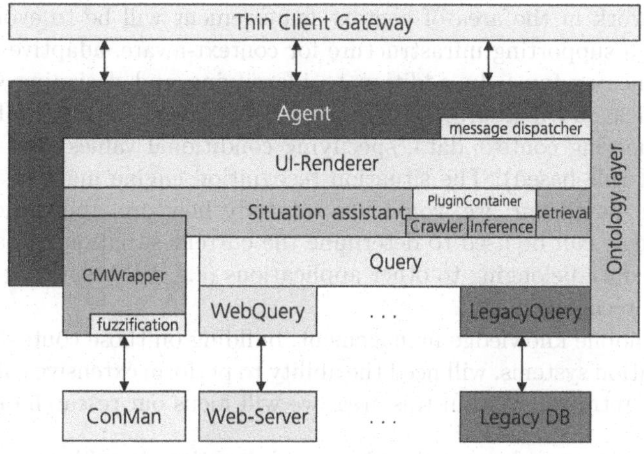

Fig. 2. Architecture of the Knowledge Agent.

is responsible for the description of situations using rules, and subscribes itself to the Context-Manager passing the rules. When a specific situation is detected, it receives a notification from the Context-Manager. Evaluating this message enables the Situation-Assistant to push the connected information object(s) proactively to the user's mobile device via the Render-Layer, which is responsible for the dynamic visualization of information objects.

6 Conclusion, Future Work

In this work, we have drawn the conclusion that mobile information systems have to consider basic technical and human limitations, i.e. technical and mental restrictions, which constrain the ability of the user to handle, absorb or communicate information with the mobile technology. Mobile information management as part of mobile KM needs to first consider the user context and situation. The key issue is context-aware (and knowledge-based) information retrieval and processing.

We presented the approach of a "virtually centralized" context manager, based on Semantic Web technologies, that is able to

- provide applications with a centralized view of context data,
- handle profiles of resources, locations, users, and application-specific user preferences,

and provide

- a situation recognition engine with
- a related notification mechanism for simple and rule-based subscriptions.

With the "BuddyAlert" system, we have depicted a prototypical usage of this approach to context management.

Future work in the area of context management will be to evolve this approach into a supporting infrastructure for context-aware, adaptive, and proactive assistance systems. In addition to identifying and designing the missing building blocks in the desired infrastructure, we plan to suggest RDF-based notions for querying context data, specifying conditional values, and subscribing (simple and rule-based). The situation recognition engine must be made more powerful. In particular, we would like to study how probabilistic calculations and fuzzy logic can be used to determine the current situation [14] and how we can include data belonging to other applications (e.g. PIM–data) in the process of situation recognition [12].

Future mobile knowledge management, building on those context-aware mobile information systems, will need the ability to perform extensive context-aware information retrieval. Within this area, we will focus our research on how to:

- provide a better abstract description of situations considering relevance to infra-structural objects,

- provide a (semi-)automatic mechanism to explore information objects and create metadata that describe information objects in terms of their relations to infra-structural objects,
- estimate the relevance of information objects with regard to dynamic queries.

Acknowledgement. This work is partially sponsored by the Information Society DG of the European Commission. It is part of the MUMMY project (IST-2001-37365, Mobile Knowledge Management – using multimedia-rich portals for context-aware information processing with pocket-sized computers in Facility Management and at Construction Site) funded by the Information Society Technologies (IST) Programme. More information: http://mummy.intranet.gr

References

1. Amberg, M., Wehrmann, J.: A Framework for the Classification of Situation-Dependent Services. Universitiy of Erlangen-Nuremberg. (2002)
2. Borowski, R., Scheer, A.-W.: Wissensmanagement mit Portalen. In: Information Management, Consulting 16 (2001) 1, 62–67
3. Brown, P.J., Jones, G.J.F.: Context-aware retrieval: exploring a new environment for information retrieval and information filtering. In: Personal and Ubiquitous Computing, 5(4) (2001) 253–263
4. Brown, P., Burleson, W., Lamming, M., Rahlff, O.W., Romano, G., Scholtz, J., Snowdon, D.: Context-Awareness: Some Compelling Applications. University of Exeter, MIT Media Lab, Xerox Research Center Europe, Motorola Labs, DARPA. (2000)
5. Chen, G., Kotz, D.: A Survey of Context-Aware Mobile Computing Research. Dartmouth College, Department of Computer Science. (2000)
6. Hong, J.I., Landay, J.A.: An Infrastructure Approach to Context-Aware Computing. University of California at Berkeley. (2001)
7. Klyne, G., Reynolds, F., Woodrow, C., Ohto, H.: Composite Capability / Preference Profiles (CC/PP): Structure and Vocabularies. http://www.w3.org/TR/CCPPstruct-vocab/, W3C Working Draft. (2001)
8. Lamming, M., Flynn, M.: "Forget-me-not" - Intimate Computing in Support of Human Memory. In: Proceedings of FRIEND21, International Symposium on Next Generation Human Interface, Meguro Gajoen, Japan (1994)
9. Lassila, O., Swick, R.R.: Resource description framework (RDF) Model and syntax specification. Recommendation, W3C, February. http://www.w3.org/TR/1999/RECrdf -syntax-19990222. (1999)
10. Pascoe, J.: The stick-e note architecture: Extending the interface beyond the user. In: Proceedings of the International Conference on Intelligent User Interfaces (1997) 261–264
11. Probst, G., Raub, G., Romhardt, K.: Wissen managen: Wie Unternehmen ihre wertvollste Ressource optimal nutzen. Gabler, Wiesbaden (1999)
12. Satyanarayanan, M.: Pervasive Computing: Vision and Challenges. In: IEEE Personal Communications. Carnegie Mellon University. (2001)
13. Schirmer, J., Bach, H.: Context-Management within an Agent-based Approach for Service Assistance in the Domain of Consumer Electronics. In: Proceedings of Intelligent Interactive Assistance, Mobile Multimedia Computing, Rostock. (2000)

14. Schmidt, A., Gellersen, H.W.: Modell, Architektur und Plattform für Informationssystemme mit Kontextbezug. In: Informatik Forschung und Entwicklung 16, Springer Verlag (2001) 213–224
15. Staab, S., Schnurr, H.-P., Studer, R., Sure Y.: Knowledge processes and ontologies. In: IEEE Intelligent Systems, 16 (2001) 1
16. DAML+OIL Specification. www.daml.org/2001/03/daml+oil-index.html. (2001)

A Situation-Oriented and Personalized Framework for Role Modeling

Irene Süßmilch-Walther

Department of Information Systems I / FORSIP
University of Erlangen-Nuremberg, Germany
suessmilch-walther@forsip.de

Abstract. *In an occupational environment every employee has to accept a role which she or he is obliged to execute depending on primarily objective criteria like the affiliation of an enterprise to a certain type, sector and life cycle. There is only little scope left for subjective preferences and resentments.* The *pragmatic research objective is to design frameworks to identify the information requirements of different roles.*

1 Introduction

Long information searching times cause inefficiency, especially for new employees. Portals offering tasks, decisions and information assigned to a specific role might reduce periods of vocational adjustment and relieve efficiency from the first working day on.

The main purpose of this study is to design role-based initial settings to distribute adequate information that supports the employee's decision-making process without overloading cognitive capabilities.

2 Theoretical Background

2.1 User Modeling

The theoretical background of user modeling has been investigated up to a certain depth for several years in many fields of research like information retrieval, web mining or semantic webs.

Some times ago an output-oriented approach was pursued in the range of information systems and it was assumed that the quality of decisions increases with the amount of available mainly internal information [1]. Today there are also approaches focusing on

D. Karagiannis and U. Reimer (Eds.): PAKM 2002, LNAI 2569, pp. 339-346, 2002.

the increasing demand for external information, for example in the field of controlling [2] or on demands of marketing managers [3].
The stereotype approach of Rich [4] assumes that facts about people are not statistically independent and therefore can be clustered into groups that frequently co-occur. Hence, the way to build a complete profile is to assign a whole set of characteristics to a user as soon as certain triggers fire.

2.2 Role Concepts

Sociology. In sociology a role is considered as a set of expectations, e.g. attitudes, beliefs and assumptions which are associated with a certain position [5]. Roles are defined independently from the actual role keeper and prescribe in particular the accepted behavior and acting.

Organization Theory. In traditional organization theory the situation of members within an organization is specified by roles. Roles are thereby groups of people at the same hierarchical level or in the same organizational unit [6].
Every company with its social entities can be regarded as a complex structure of functionally and hierarchically referred roles. In this context roles are used to represent hierarchical structures, to define rules of substitution, to allocate tasks and to determine the social position of an employee.

Functional Orientation. From a functional perspective every role is described by a set of tasks to be performed [7][8]. A role can be held by different persons, as well as a person can live different roles at the same time. Roles are thereby used to standardize ranges of operations and to ensure controlled completion of work.

Skill Management. Within the scope of competence-specific classification each role is defined by a set of skills, abilities and know-how, e.g. industry skill standards or language abilities which are necessary to execute tasks [9]. On basis of these qualification requirements every task is assigned to adequate roles.

Information Security. With regard to security matters users with equal rights are subsumed to groups, called roles [10]. Rights and permissions are assigned to roles rather than to individual users (role-based access control). Each role consists of a set of allowed transactions, e.g. documents, data or applications.

3 Role Modeling

3.1 Holistic Approach

The term role is used in different meanings depending on the range of application [11]. Therefore an integrated approach is needed which combines the various aspects of

roles and includes consolidated findings of business and organization sciences such as cognitive sciences or computer science.
Within the paper we try to combine the different theoretical views to a holistic approach and describe roles primarily by activities and responsibilities. A role is an objective set of rights, responsibilities and requirements which are associated with a role-bearer because of his or her position. Furthermore we examine the essential knowledge, skills, abilities, competencies and charges related to a certain task to enable the best possible match to the different tasks.

3.2 Expectations towards Role Bearers

Every role consists of a quasi-objective core which is defined by three kinds of role expectations (see Fig. 1): "must" or "mandatory" expectations, "shall" or "preferential" expectations and "can" or "permissive" expectations [12].

Expectations	Sources	Examples	Sanctions
Mandatory expectations	Laws, guidelines, regulations, contracts, judgments, commentaries, convictions	Obligatory supervision, duty to give information, due diligence, tax duties	Absolute obligation, legal sanctions by non-performance
Preferential expectations	Conventions, standards, usances	Job instructions, official instructions, responsibilities of office	High obligation, negative social or economic sanctions by non-performance
Permissive expectations	Practices, customs	Engagement, advanced training	Voluntariness, positive social or economic sanctions by performance

Fig. 1. Role Expectations in Companies

Mandatory expectations are endorsed by legal or quasi-legal sanctions and must be observed to avoid prosecution. Preferential expectations apply to the fundamental minimum requirements of professional role execution. These are requirements that an employee has to meet to avoid being fired or being named by others as lazy or unfit. The sanctions attached to preferential expectations are primarily economic and social. Permissive expectations bear on the way of executing occupational roles and attain social acceptance to the individual.
An analysis of the different levels of expectations gives a realistic overview of professional practice because what employees generally do is predominantly determined by what they must do.

3.3 Decisions of Role Bearers

Every employee is expected to perform certain tasks which are associated with his or her role. A product manager e.g. has to observe brand extensions or the design of new products (see Fig. 2).

Employee	Decision	Objects	Information
Product manager	Brand extension	Company / trademark	Image, range, requirements, brand equity, marketing-mix
		Environment	Mood, lifestyle, occasion, behavior of trade rivals, competition, quality distinc-tions
		Transfer object	Fit, product type, date of extension

Fig. 2. Exemplary information objects for a product manager

To fulfill these related tasks it is necessary to make different decisions. By extending a brand e.g. the product manager has to make the decision if the extension should take place in a horizontal or a vertical way, directly or indirectly [13].

In order to come up with a decision it is required to have qualitative as well as quantitative data on. In the previous example the product manager needs information about the image of the trademark or the behavior of competitors.

Employees require the same information for different functions and decisions, however in unequal combinations (see Fig. 3). The information is used for different decisions, anyhow the released information overlap.

Role	Functions	Information requirements
Executive producer	Master production schedule, material requirements planning	Waste, cycle time, stock, market growth, finishing quote, working to capacity, lot size, range, purchase time, term of delivery, target stocks
Material manager	Order management, demand forecast, redisposition	Numbers of suppliers, stock, market growth, completion quote, lot size, range, scrapping, delay quote, time of delivery
Sales staff	Customer retention, shift of market, sales promotion	Supply price, contribution margin, market growth, completion quote, marketing costs, distribution costs, time of delivery, sales area

Fig. 3. Information Demands of Employees

The information „stock"and „market growth"are used by product managers, material managers and by sales staff. The product manager needs the information to decide which quantity has to be produced in the following period. The material manager has to decide on how much material should be ordered and at which date it has to be delivered. The sales staff uses the information in order to state customer delivery dates.

3.4 Theoretical Procedure of Modeling

Role expectations are often intercorrelated. Furthermore, uncertain and inaccurate sets with fuzzy boundaries make a definition of relevant tasks rather difficult.

Due to our assumption that there is an interrelation between employees having the same functions or decisions to make, we merge individual cases to groups which we define as roles.

The resulting role concepts are hold in a knowledge base and serve as framework to model roles and companies in industrial companies. This fundament can therefore be used for the development of standard software.

3.5 Role Modeling in Practice

In an occupational environment everyone has a role which he has to execute depending on largely objective criteria. There is little scope left for subjective preferences and resentments. Basing upon monitoring in practice, e.g. job offers, job descriptions or best-practice reports, we identified tasks, related decisions and information requirements of employees. Additionally we examined information about sectors, types or lifecycles.

To get an overview of expectations assigned to special positions we inductively started with a text analysis of job advertisements with regard to job-related tasks and decisions. In a first step, we analyzed 250 ads of different German e-recruitment providers searching for an "account manager" and had to struggle with several problems:

1. There are many words which have more or less the same meaning than other words, e.g. "sales representative" and "sales manager." These synonyms must be identified, subsumed and assigned consistently to the different categories. A special case in Germany is the tendency to use English words for characterizing jobs and tasks, e.g. the English term "account manager" is for the most part congruent to the German term "Kundenmanager."
2. The job descriptions are often on a very low level and are thereby hardly significant and ambiguous.
3. Depending on enterprise size and sector, the same job title covers different fields of functions and activities.

We built up a dictionary which includes a detailed description of the role "account manager" and the assigned tasks and decisions to guarantee inter-coder reliability. The procedure has the pretension to be inter-subjectively comprehensible and to obtain complete and one-dimensional results without overlapping.

Per frequency of occurrence we identified the most relevant tasks which were e.g. the acquisition of new accounts (9%) and the hands-on of existing customers (8%). This approach submits a more enclosing view (130 tasks) than other methods like brainstorming or analysis of secondary literature (59 tasks).

After that we subsumed the different tasks to get terms of reference. The scope of duty of an account manager involves the acquisition of customers and projects, the establishment of business connections and the generation of new projects. Altogether the 7 most significant assignments cover 75 % of all single tasks.

Subsequently we subsume different tasks to develop roles. These aspects can be included in different jobs as well as a job can consist of different roles.

4 Influencing Factors

The expectations to a role represent an inter-subjective revisable and objective behavioral framework. Depending on the degree of freedom the role bearer has free hand to a certain extent in completing a particular role. The way people behave in a certain situation, is up to personal and situation-oriented factors [14].

4.1 Personalization

The precise individual role performing is provided by the subjective perception of the role bearer and his or her wishes, values and settings [15]. Referring to the core shell model, there are two categories of tasks. On the one hand there are tasks which concern every role keeper independent from sector or enterprise type. On the other hand there are tasks where the precise definitions are influenced by objective characteristics like the affiliation of an enterprise to a type, sector and life cycle or by subjective characteristics like individual preferences and aversions (see Fig. 4). Expert knowledge influences e.g. the behavior of information reception.

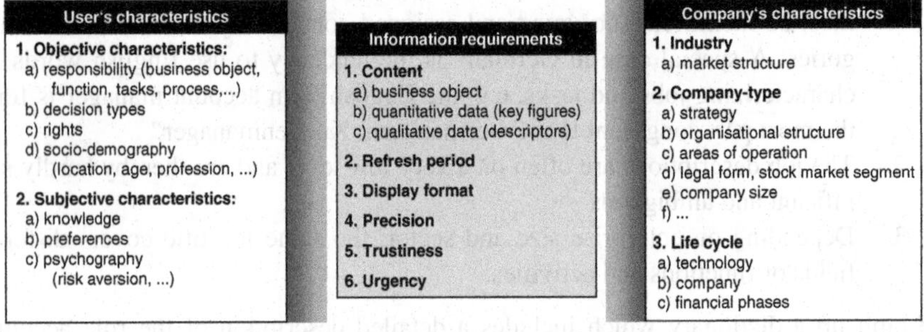

Fig. 4. Determinants of information requirements (in extension to [16])

4.2 Situation Orientation

In addition to personalization the context in which the user is situated must be regarded. On the one hand it must be analyzed in which way the presentation of knowledge depends on the output device [17], e.g. in reference to quantity or representation form of data. On the other hand the requirements of an employee are down to characteristics like sector, type or lifecycle of the enterprise (foundation, crisis, reorganization) [16] and can be classified e.g. by job specifications or legal regulations.

5 Benefits

The benefits of role-based solutions for employees consist of higher productivity and lower costs. According to the goal-setting theory [18], an employee has higher moti-

vation and improved performance if the assigned tasks and the expectations associated with them are understood. Furthermore co-workers and supervisors need not to pitch in during the transition time and can concentrate on their own job.
Additionally, the time for information search can be minimized if required information is made available automatically. Recently recruited employees know generally neither which information is necessary nor where they can find it. The demands of superordinates and workmates decrease and redundancies of work are avoided.
At last, the risk of wrong decision due to insufficient information drops off.
As a result the intellectual capital of highly educated, skilled and experienced employees can be utilized in the best possible way and the competition position can be maintained or even improved.

6 Conclusion

The research conducted by the „Bavarian Research Cooperation for Situated, Individualized and Personalized Human-Machine-Interaction”(FORSIP) aims at closing the gap between human and computer. Future software generations should be able to adapt brightly to personal preferences, situations and roles.
The objective of our partial project „Situated and Personalized Modeling of Roles and Business Structures “(SIPRUM) is to design frameworks to identify the information needs of different jobs, so the employees get exactly the information they need in order to do their job.
As a result also untrained users can apply to the systems without a long period of practice because the systems adjust to the human - not the other way round [19].

References

[1] Ackoff, Russell; Emery, Fred: On Purposeful Systems. Aldine-Atherton, Chicago 1972.

[2] Meier, Marco: Integration externer Daten in Planungs- und Kontrollsysteme - Ein Redaktions-Leitstand für Informationen aus dem Internet. Gabler, Wiesbaden 2000.

[3] Cas, Klemens: Rechnergestützte Integration von Rechnungswesen-Informationen und Marktforschungsdaten. Nürnberg 1999.

[4] Rich, Elaine: User Modeling via Stereotypes. In: Cognitive Science 3 (1979) 3, p. 329-354.

[5] Rühli, Edwin: Un ternehmungsführung und Unternehm ungspolitik 3. Paul Haupt, Bern 1993.

[6] Rosemann, Michael; zur Mühlen, Michael: Der Lösungsbeitrag von Metadatenmodellen beim Vergleich von Workflowmanagementsystemen (1996). Arbeitsbericht Nr. 48. http://www.wi.uni-muenster.de/inst/arbber/ab48.pdf, 2002-04-23.

[7] Kosiol, Erich: Grundlagen und Methoden der Organisationsforschung. Duncker & Humblot, Berlin 1968.

[8] Blohm, Hans: Organisation, Information und Überwachung. Gabler, Wiesbaden 1977.

[9] Scheer, August-Wilhelm: Wirtschaftsinformatik: Referenzmodelle für industrielle Geschäftsprozesse. Springer, Berlin 1997.

[10] Sandhu, Ravi; Coyne, Edward; Feinstein, Hal; Youman, Charles: Role-Based Access Control Models. In: IEEE Computer 29 (1996) 2, p. 38-47.

[11] Kirn, Stefan: Organisational Intelligence and Distributed AI. In: Jennings, Nick; O'Hare, Gary (ed.): Theoretical Foundations of Distributed Artificial Intelligence. John Wiley & Sons, New York 1996.

[12] Dahrendorf, Ralph: Out of Utopia: Toward a Reorientation of Sociological Analysis. In: American Journal of Sociology 2 (1958) 64, p. 115-127.

[13] Sattler, Henrik: Markenstrategien für neue Produkte. In: Esch, Franz-Rudolf (ed.): Moderne Markenführung. Grundlagen, Innovative Moderne Markenführung. Grundlagen, Innovative Ansätze, Praktische Umsetzung. Gabler, Wiesbaden 2000, p. 346-347.

[14] Lewin, Kurt: Vorsatz, Wille und Bedürfnis. In: Psychologische Forschung 7 (1926) o. A., p. 294-329.

[15] Giddens, Anthony: The Constitution of Society. Outline of the Theory of Structuration. Polity Press, Cambridge 1984.

[16] Meier, Marco; Stößlein, Martin; Mertens, Peter: Personalisierung von Management- und Stakeholder-Informations-Systemen. In: Buhl, Hans Ulrich; Huther, Andreas; Reitwiesner, Bernd (eds.): Information Age Economy - 5. Internationale Tagung Wirtschaftsinformatik. Heidelberg 2001.

[17] Bressan, Stéphane; Goh, Cheng Hian; Levina, Natalia; Madnick, Stuart E.; Shah, Ahmed; Siegel, Michael: Context Knowledge Representation and Reasoning in the Context Interchange System. In: Applied Intelligence 13 (2000) 2, p. 165-180.

[18] Locke, Edwin A.; Latham, Gary P.: A theory of goal setting and task performance. Prentice-Hal, Englewood Cliffs 1990.

[19] Mertens, Peter; Höhl, Michael; Zeller, Thomas: Wie lernt der Computer den Menschen kennen? Bestandsaufnahme und Experimente zur Benutzermodellierung in der Wirtschaftsinformatik. In: Scheffler, Wolfram; Voigt, Kai-Ingo (eds.): Entwicklungsperspektiven im Electronic Business, Grundlagen - Strategien - Anwendungsfelder. Wiesbaden 2000, p. 21-52.

Instruments to Visualize Design Engineering Working Methods in Automotive Supplier Companies

Regine W. Vroom, Imre Horváth, and Wilfred F. van der Vegte

Delft University of Technology, Faculty of Industrial Design Engineering, Landbergstraat 15, NL-2628 CE Delft, The Netherlands
r.w.vroom@io.tudelft.nl
http://www.io.tudelft.nl/research/ica

Abstract. Before implementing a PDM-system within a company, the internal processes of product and process development and the information handled herein should be organized well. To enable this organization, one should be able to see the bottlenecks. Therefore the working methods and the documents involved should be made transparent. That is why the development processes of three automotive suppliers are analyzed and documented in three representations, formatted according to a generic scheme, to gain transparency of the processes. Based on these representations a so-called induced model of product and process development is created. In this paper, the format of the representations will be shortly explained, the application method for the realization of the representations will be described and some of the results will be illustrated. Also the research problems that came up during the research will be described.

1 Introduction

In literature very little is found on details about the information handled within product and process development together with the activities in which this information is created and/or used in industrial companies. To gain insight into this area, a research project was started.

In this project, a method and instruments are developed to consistently capture the representation of the product and process development together with the relevant information in a database and in clearly structured diagrams. These instruments are a generic representation scheme defining the format of company-specific representations, a software tool to facilitate the application of the representation scheme, a method for the application of the generic representation scheme with consistent results and an induced model of product and process development.

Using the method for the application of the generic representation scheme, the development processes of three automotive suppliers were analyzed and laid down in three company-specific representations. In these representations, the organization, the relationships between documents and the activities of product and process development are represented together. The three descriptions were then compared mutually as well as with current theories. In these cases, sufficient similarities in the product and

D. Karagiannis and U. Reimer (Eds.): PAKM 2002, LNAI 2569, pp. 347-358, 2002.

process development were found to enable the creation of a more generic so-called induced model. Thus, based on these findings an induced model of product and process development, describing both activities and information, is created. This way, the knowledge and experiences of the three companies are brought together into one induced model. The induced model can be used as an initial expectation when recording an as-is situation of a company. And the induced model is useful as a resource of ideas when creating a to-be situation for a company's product and process development.

The research is carried out with the help of an industrial sounding board in which industrial companies were represented as well as consultancy and research institutes.

The instruments that are developed in this research (generic representation scheme, software tool, induced model and method altogether) act as a still camera producing a snapshot of the product and process development of a company. By doing this, it makes several aspects visible. The snapshot reveals possible bottlenecks and, at the same time, it checks the consistency. Thus, it provides the companies with a means to make the information regarding their product and process development, as well as the development process belonging to it, transparent.

2 The Research Approach

In order to determine and chart product and process development together with the information, case studies are carried out. In the beginning of the research project, it was unknown to what extent companies look alike in their development processes and information involved. That is why companies are selected with comparable clients, comparable products and comparable magnitudes etc. That way we had the greatest chance of finding similarities.

The research project is an explorative research and it can be qualified as being qualitative [2]. The research data are collected by interviewing company people and by analyzing existing documents of the companies. These documents include procedures of the working method, quality handbooks (e.g. ISO9000 and QS9000 documents), copies of engineering information documents, such as the drawings, bills of materials and all kinds of forms. The research strategy is derived from the inductive-hypothetical strategy [9], [7], [11]. The derived research strategy includes the following steps (see figure 1):

1. Selection of three companies and the development of a generic representation scheme. In this step also a first description of the companies is made (descriptive empirical models).
2. Description of three companies according to the generic representation scheme, resulting in three company-specific representations of product and process development (descriptive conceptual models). In parallel, a tool is developed to facilitate and accelerate the application of the generic representation scheme.
3. Comparison of the three company specific representations and the creation of the induced model (the prescriptive empirical model). In this step also the method used for describing the companies is laid down.

4. The prescriptive empirical model is not implemented during the research. That is why the three companies and the industrial sounding board were important to contribute to the evaluation of the prescriptive empirical model. In this step, results are evaluated, conclusions are drawn and recommendations are formulated.

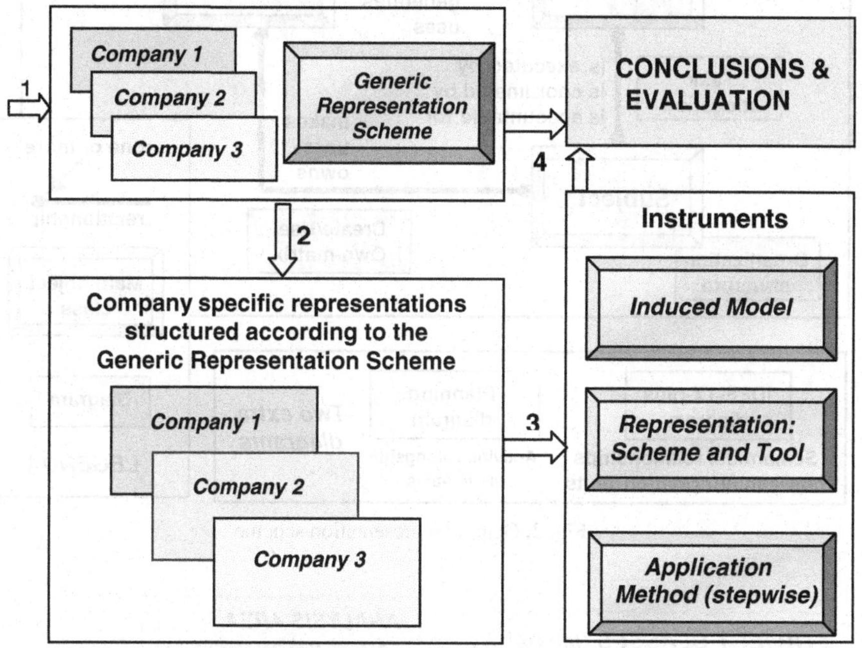

Fig. 1. Research strategy

3 Generic Representation Scheme

The generic representation scheme defines the format for the company-specific chartings. In this representation scheme, the development of a product and a production process is considered being a project having a clear starting and ending point. A project is represented by three aggregates of object classes (called main object classes, abbreviated as MOC), which are:

- Subject (to register the organization)
- Activity (for the processes)
- Information

These three main object classes represent who (subject) does (activity) what and with which information. In figure 2 the main object classes and the relationships between these main object classes of the representation scheme are represented. The three coherent main object classes together make up a three-dimensional model in which the three main object classes are the three dimensions. This three-dimensional model represents the coherence, but does not give a good overview. That is why two-dimensional pictures of the model are required and eight diagrams are defined (fig. 2).

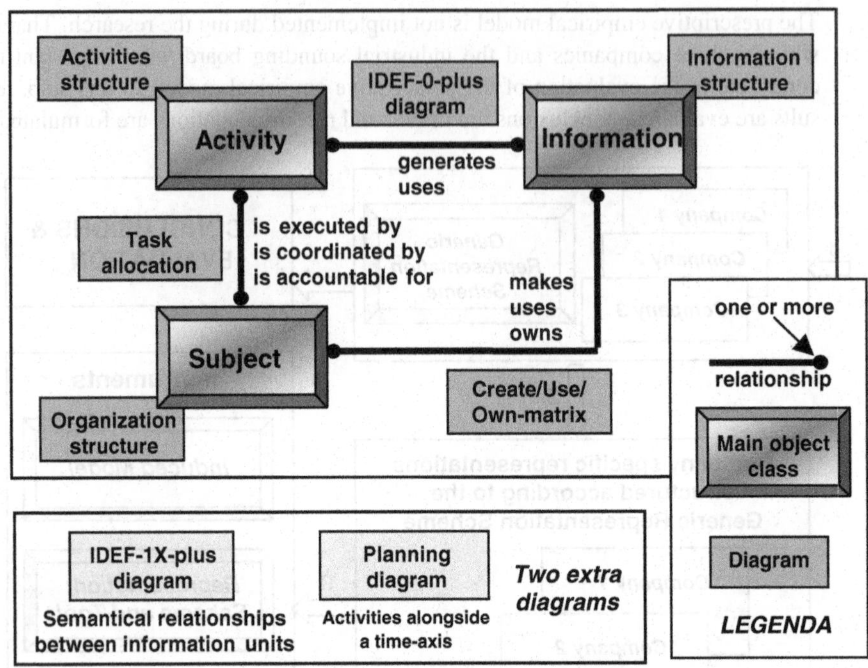

Fig. 2. Generic representation scheme

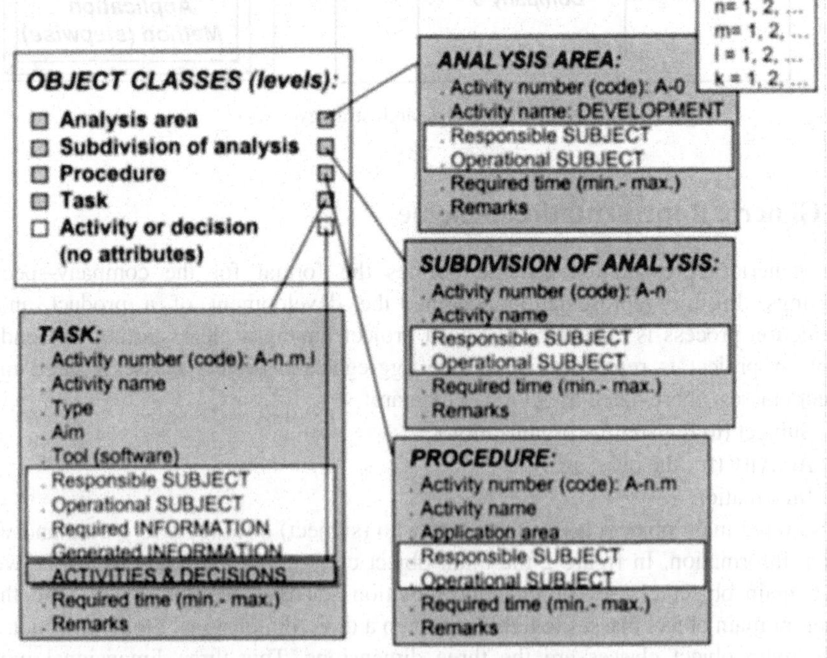

Fig. 3. Internal structure of main object class ACTIVITY

Three of which represent the relationships <u>within</u> the main object classes (the Activities structure for MOC Activity; the Organization structure for MOC Subject; the Information structure for MOC Information). Three other diagrams represent the relationships <u>between</u> the main object classes (these are the IDEF-0-plus diagram, the Task allocation matrix and the Create-Use-Own matrix). Furthermore there is one diagram representing the semantic relationships within the main object class Information and one diagram representing the activities in the proper order and frequency alongside a time-axis.

Instances of the main object classes are stored in a database. Each MOC consists of several levels. Each level got its own attributes. The attributes describe the instances and also the relationships between the instance and instances of the other main object classes. For example, the MOC Activity consists of five levels of object classes, see figure 3. At the object class (level) called Tasks, the relationships between the Tasks and the MOC Information are stored by the attributes "Required Information" and "Generated Information." In the same way the relationships between Tasks and Subjects are stored by the attributes "Responsible Subject" and "Operational Subject." By means of the Activity-number attributes at each level (as shown in figure 3: from A-0 up to A-n.m.l), the internal relationships between the levels of the MOC Activity are stored. Comparably, the main object classes called Subject and Information are leveled and attributed.

The instances of the object classes contain all information required to automatically generate six of the eight diagrams that represent the development process. That is why a software tool is developed that facilitates and accelerates the application of the generic representation scheme. In fact the tool generates pictures from the contents of the database, see figure 4.

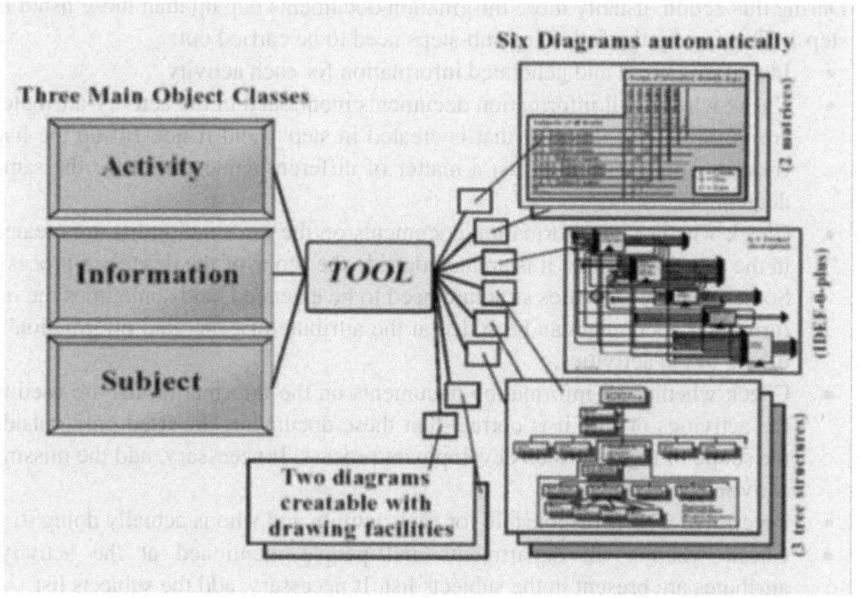

Fig. 4. Tool to facilitate the application of the generic representation scheme

4 Application Method for the Representation Scheme

The method to apply the generic representation scheme is a stepwise method. With this application method the representations of the product and process development of companies will be consistent. The application method consists of the following steps:

Step 1: Identifying the instances of the main object classes (Activity, Information and Subject). This will result in three one-dimensional lists. In this step, the induced model (illustrated in section 5 and in [13], [14], [15]) can help with a starting point.

a) Identifying the activities. A company-representative has to describe the product and process development. An initial activities structure can be set up.
b) Identifying the information documents, such as reports, drawings, pictures, documents, forms, computer files, models, parts, tools, products and available knowledge. At this point it is sufficient to make a list of all the information documents that are used and/or generated in product and process development. Information codes will be added later. Start collecting copies of the documents.
c) Identifying the subjects (departments etc.). This step mainly consists of a study of the organization graphs of a company.

Step 2: Collecting copies of information documents. During the first interviews (step 1), the collection of these copies is already started. In this step one has to identify and collect the missing copies and the copies that need to be completed.

Step 3: Describing the activities, the information documents and the subject and the relationships between all these instances.

a) Activities. Following the activities structure that is created in the first step, the attributes as described in the generic representation scheme should be filled in, for each activity. This information is gathered from interviews with company people. During this action, usually more information documents pop up than those listed in step 1. That is why the following sub-steps need to be carried out:
   - Identify required and generated information for each activity
   - Check whether all information documents mentioned in the activity-attributes are in the information list that is created in step 1 and if not, fill up the list. Beware; sometimes it is just a matter of different names, used for the same document.
   - Check whether all information documents on the information list are created in the activities or that it is created outside the scope of the described process. Sometimes the activities structure need to be extended, and sometimes the information document can be added at the attribute of "generated information" of one of the activities.
   - Check whether all information documents on the information list are used at the activities or that it is correct that these documents are used only outside the scope of the described development process. If necessary, add the missing activities.
   - Determine who is responsible for each activity and who is actually doing it.
   - Check whether all departments and people mentioned at the activity-attributes are present in the subjects list. If necessary, add the subjects list.

b) Information. In the former sub-step, the information list is extended. Copies of the new items have to be collected. Next, the information documents are given an Information number (database item code). The information names are checked with a company representative. Also the collected copies of the documents are analyzed in order to describe each instance of the information list. Then, together with the company representative, all the other attributes are filled in. Then it is checked whether all departments and people that are mentioned at the information attributes are also present in the subjects list. If not, the subjects list is filled up.
c) Subjects. The description of subjects is done in this step.

Step 4. Insert the information in the software tool. Of course, during the former three steps, most of the information collected is already inserted in the tool. In this step all the gathered information should be inserted.

Step 5. Generate diagrams. The tool generates the diagrams. These diagrams make the product and process development visible.

Step 6. Analyze the diagrams. In the resulting diagrams one could find some loose ends. For example: a document is used by a subject and in an activity, but the subject is not mentioned in that activity. This could mean that there is another activity where the document is used and another subject that uses the document. This way the model is checked as a whole. The next two-dimensional relationships are checked:

- Check whether the subjects that are mentioned as users of an information document, are mentioned together with that document within an activity. If this is not the case, that could be correct. Otherwise, the relationships are added.
- Check whether the subjects that are mentioned at the activities are also mentioned in the relationships of the information document that is involved. This could be correct, but otherwise the model needs to be filled up.

All these loose ends are discussed with company people in order to solve them. Then the model needs to analyzed again. Sometimes, solving one loose end causes another loose end. When all the loose ends are tied, a consistent model is created.

Step 7. Discuss the diagrams and the descriptions with company-people. Now that a visible and consistent model of product and process development is created, the company people can find the bottlenecks.

5 Induced Model of Product & Process Development

Using the instruments described in the former sections, three automotive supplier companies are analyzed, which resulted in three representations [13]. To improve the accessibility of the data within these three company-specific representations for third parties, the knowledge and experience at the field of product and process development of the three companies is bundled into one induced model of product and process development. This induced model is based on the similarities found in the three company-specific descriptions and is structured according to the same representation scheme. In this section, the induced model is illustrated, both for the MOC Activity and the MOC Information. In figure 5 an overview is given of the induced model at the second level of the MOC Activity (which is the level of the Subdivisions of the analysis area).

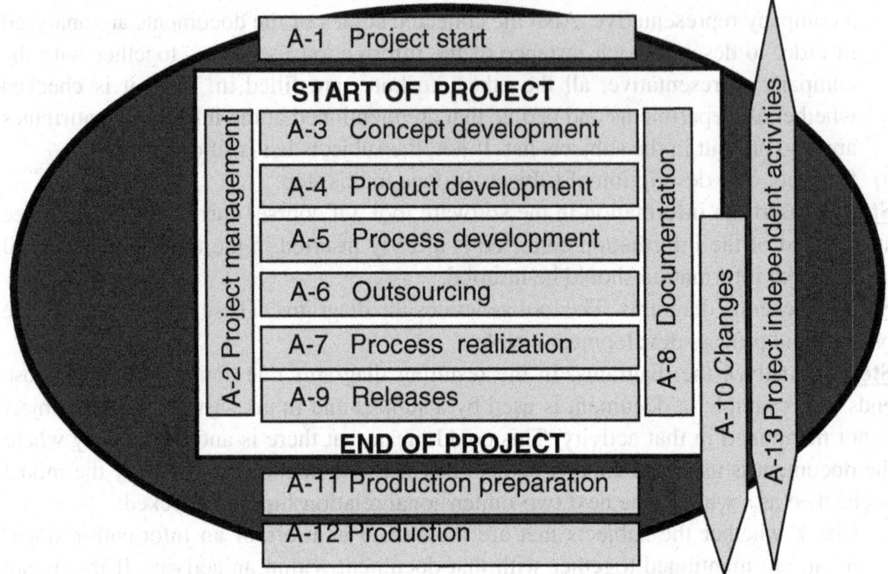

Fig. 5. Overview of the subdivision areas (activities) of the analysis area

In the activities structure of the induced model, the Subdivisions A-1 to A-13 (see figure 5) are further elaborated down to the level of Tasks. To give an impression, the results of this elaboration for A3 and A4 are presented below. The other elaborations of the activities structure of the induced model can be found in [15] and [13].

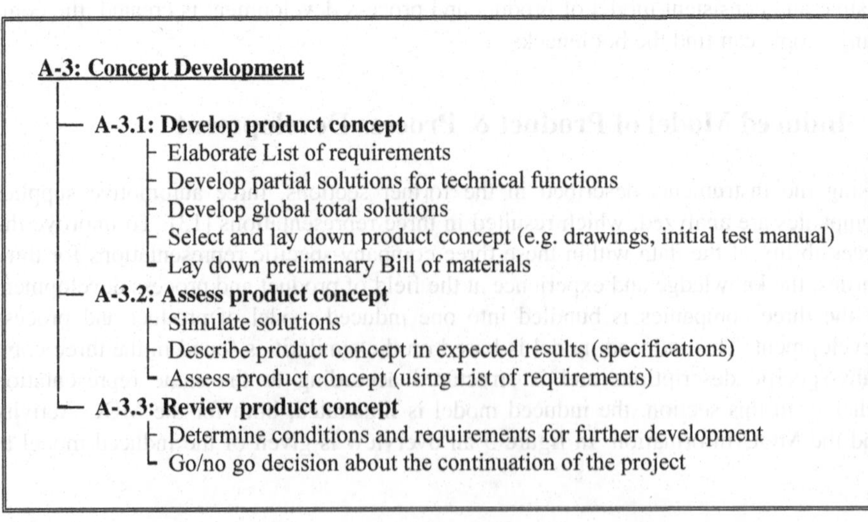

A-3: Concept Development

- **A-3.1: Develop product concept**
  - Elaborate List of requirements
  - Develop partial solutions for technical functions
  - Develop global total solutions
  - Select and lay down product concept (e.g. drawings, initial test manual)
  - Lay down preliminary Bill of materials
- **A-3.2: Assess product concept**
  - Simulate solutions
  - Describe product concept in expected results (specifications)
  - Assess product concept (using List of requirements)
- **A-3.3: Review product concept**
  - Determine conditions and requirements for further development
  - Go/no go decision about the continuation of the project

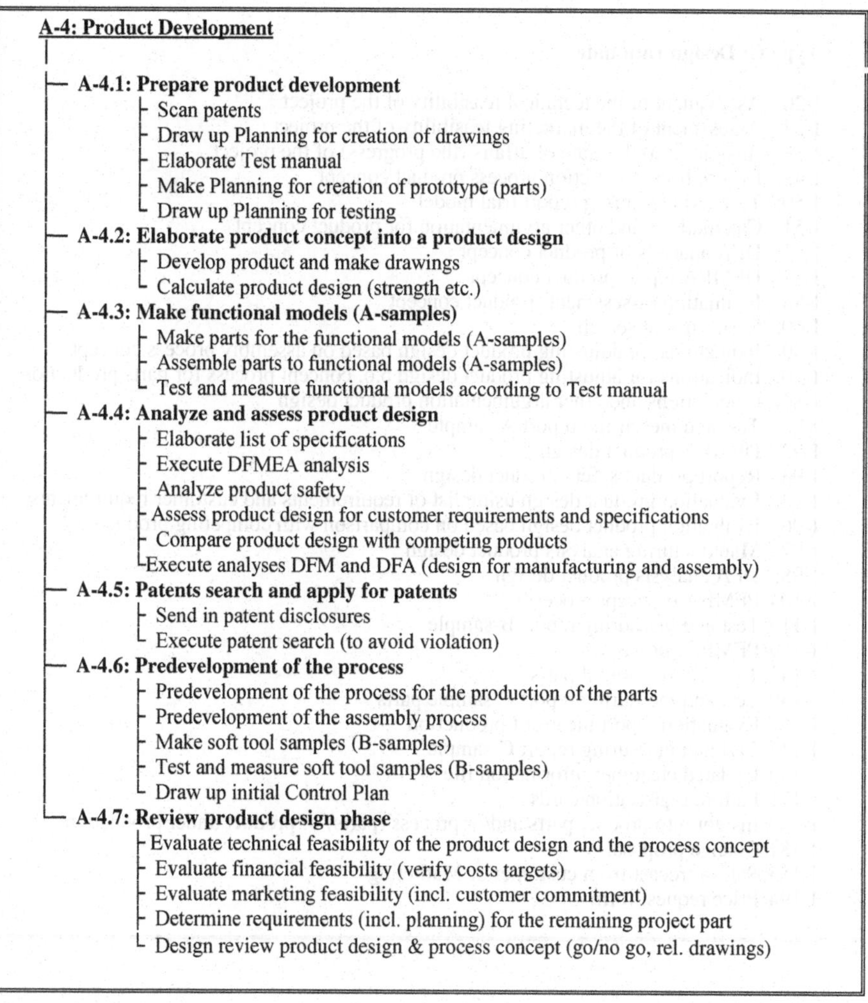
A-4: Product Development

- **A-4.1: Prepare product development**
  - Scan patents
  - Draw up Planning for creation of drawings
  - Elaborate Test manual
  - Make Planning for creation of prototype (parts)
  - Draw up Planning for testing
- **A-4.2: Elaborate product concept into a product design**
  - Develop product and make drawings
  - Calculate product design (strength etc.)
- **A-4.3: Make functional models (A-samples)**
  - Make parts for the functional models (A-samples)
  - Assemble parts to functional models (A-samples)
  - Test and measure functional models according to Test manual
- **A-4.4: Analyze and assess product design**
  - Elaborate list of specifications
  - Execute DFMEA analysis
  - Analyze product safety
  - Assess product design for customer requirements and specifications
  - Compare product design with competing products
  - Execute analyses DFM and DFA (design for manufacturing and assembly)
- **A-4.5: Patents search and apply for patents**
  - Send in patent disclosures
  - Execute patent search (to avoid violation)
- **A-4.6: Predevelopment of the process**
  - Predevelopment of the process for the production of the parts
  - Predevelopment of the assembly process
  - Make soft tool samples (B-samples)
  - Test and measure soft tool samples (B-samples)
  - Draw up initial Control Plan
- **A-4.7: Review product design phase**
  - Evaluate technical feasibility of the product design and the process concept
  - Evaluate financial feasibility (verify costs targets)
  - Evaluate marketing feasibility (incl. customer commitment)
  - Determine requirements (incl. planning) for the remaining project part
  - Design review product design & process concept (go/no go, rel. drawings)

The induced model also incorporates an information list. In this information list, the information documents are categorized into four types of information, which are:

A. Available knowledge and documentation (library information)
B. Product and process design descriptions (product dossier)
C. Design rationale (calculations etc.)
D. Project management information

To illustrate this part of the induced model, a part of type C is listed in a border below. The complete information list can be found in [14].

Type C: Design rationale

I-20: Assessment of the technical feasibility of the project
I-24: Assessment of the marketing feasibility of the project
I-33: (Insight into) the state of affairs (the progress) of the project
I-42: Description of selection process product concept
I-50: Test and measuring report trial model
I-51: Calculations and other argumentation for product concept
I-52: DFA analysis of product concept
I-53: DFMEA report product concept
I-55: Evaluation (assessment) product concept
I-60: Result patent search
I-69: Indications for adjusting product design based on assembly process concept
I-70: Indications for adjusting product design b.o. concept process for parts production
I-86: Calculations and other argumentation product design
I-90: Test and measuring report A-sample
I-92: DFMEA product design
I-93: Report product safety product design
I-94: Evaluation product design using list of requirements and customer requirements
I-96: Evaluation product design based on comparison with competing products
I-97: Manufacturing analysis product design
I-98: DFA analysis product design
I-104: PFMEA (concept process)
I-113: Test and measuring report B-sample
I-129: PFMEA (process)
I-143: Test report external parts
I-150: Test and measuring report C-sample parts
I-151: Evaluation report means of production
I-155: Test and measuring report C-sample
I-159: Updated customer information file
I-171: Failure registration cards
I-180: Insight into product parts and/or process (parts) of product under production
I-181: Change proposal
I-185: Sales forecast from customer or Marketing
I-194: Price request form

6 Research Findings of This Practice Based Research

During the research some problems came up. This section will go further into these problems and it will discuss the way the issues were handled in this research project.

The time needed to create a description of the situation in a company (i.e. to create the as-is representation according to the general representation scheme) varied between 6 and 12 months. This time frame was in fact the exposure time of the imaginary photo camera. This exposure time turned out to be too long to create a stable snapshot of the situation in a company. The working methods and processes that had to be described were changing continuously. That is why the description was frozen when it was almost complete. It was frozen in the sense that no changes would be inserted anymore, and only those corrections and additions would be taken into account, that were needed for a complete and consistent description.

A second problem was that companies usually do not have an unambiguous working method. Not nearly everything has been recorded in documents and for that reason, the researcher has to depend partly on stories told from the memory of people. Then it appears to be that different people of the same company describe the processes differently. Furthermore the processes described by people are not completely compliant with the working methods recorded in the documents. Finally, the spokesmen of the companies usually already had some ideas to improve the working method and they had also introduced those changes to some extent. Illustrative for these problems is that within a company usually more projects are running in parallel, based on different working methods. We chose to describe the "almost introduced"working method rather than the "almost obsolete"working method. The goal for the current research was to describe a working method, in which the knowledge and experience of an industrial company are captured.

A third problem is the uncertain influence of the researcher on the changes and the ideas about changes in the working method. This problem is especially important when the changes caused by the instruments developed, have to be described precisely. In that case the research method used is not accurate. In the current research, however, we chose to disregard the twilight zone of changes because for us the change was an unwanted side effect that had to be coped with, rather than the main subject of interest.

7 Conclusions

According to the company people, the used order in charting a case is required to gain insight: first analyze the parts (which means: fill in the main object classes separately) than creating the relationships and finally draw up the relationship-diagrams. The company people stated that some of the diagrams are hard or even impossible to draw up without the usage of the scheme and the application method.

Working methods in companies are not unambiguous. Not even people of one company describe the same working method the same way. They do not describe working methods in compliance with the procedures on paper either. And, when trying to reconstruct the working methods used within specific projects running in one company, it turned out that different projects have different working methods as well. These differences are caused by the many changes introduced in working methods, as well as the long duration of the development projects. In this research project, we described the method of working that was the best according to the company people.

Comparisons of the product and process development of the three cases delivered sufficient similarities for the creation of a more generic induced model for the activities and the information.

During the research, the representations of the companies that were already finished played a role as initial expectation for the charting of a next case. This helped to lay down a product and process development trajectory in detail. The intention of the induced model is that it can be used as such an initial expectation for facilitating the charting of an existing situation (the as-is situation). Because the knowledge and experience of three cases is bundled in the induced model it could also be used as a resource of ideas when creating a new product and process development trajectory (the to-be situation). This counts for companies who are not too different from the selected companies (chapter 2).

References

1. Andreasen, M.M. (2001) "The contribution of design research to industry - reflections on 20 years of ICED conferences" in S. Culley e.a. (Eds.) Proceedings of ICED01, Professional Engineering Publishing, Bury St Edmonds and London, UK, pp 3-10.
2. Baarda, D.B. and M.P.M. de Goede (1995) "Methoden en technieken" Stenfert Kroese, Houten.
3. Bots P.W.G. & Sol, H.G. (1988) "Shaping Organizational Information Systems through Coordination Support" in R.M. Lee, e.a. (eds.), Organizational Decision Support Systems, Elsevier Science Publishers, Amsterdam, pp 139 -54.
4. Cantamessa, M. (2001) "Design research in perspective - a meta-research on ICED 97 and ICED 99" in S. Culley e.a. (Eds.) Proceedings of ICED 01 - Design Research - Theories, Methodologies, and Product Modelling, Professional Engineering Publishing, Bury St Edmonds and London, UK, pp 29-36.
5. Harmsen, Hanne. (1994) Improving product development practice: An action-research based approach", Conference Proc. Meeting the Challenges of Product Development, ed. Margaret Bruce, e.a. Manchester School of Management.
6. Horváth, I. (2001) "A contemporary survey of scientific research into engineering design" in S. Culley, A. Duffy, C. McMahon, K.Wallace (Eds.) Proceedings of ICED 01, Professional Engineering Publishing, Bury St Edmonds and London, UK, pp 13-20.
7. Meel, J.W. van. (1994) The Dynamics of Business Engineering, Doctoral Dissertation, Delft University of Technology, Delft, The Netherlands.
8. Samuel, A. and W. Lewis (2001) "Curiosity-oriented research in engineering design" in S. Culley e.a. (Eds.) Proceedings of ICED 01, Professional Engineering Publishing, Bury St Edmonds and London, UK, pp 37-44.
9. Sol, H.G. (1982) "Simulation in Information Systems" Doctoral Dissertation University Groningen (RUG), Groningen, The Netherlands.
10. Verschuren, P and H. Doorewaard (1995) "Het ontwerpen van een onderzoek", Lemma BV, Utrecht, The Netherlands.
11. Vreede, G.J. (1995) Facilitating Organizational Change" Doctoral Dissertation, Delft University of Technology, The Netherlands.
12. Vroom, R.W. (1996) A general induced model for automotive suppliers of the development process and its related information, Computers in Industry, Elsevier Science, Amsterdam, The Netherlands.
13. Vroom, R.W. (2001) Zicht op product- en procesontwikkelingsinformatie - in het bijzonder bij toeleveranciers aan de automobielindustrie, DUP Science, Delft, NL.
14. Vroom, R.W., J.C.Verlinden (2002) Transparency in Documents and Activities in Product and Process Development at Automotive Suppliers, Proc.Design 2002, Croatia.
15. Vroom, R.W. Research into the Practice of Design Engineering Working methods within Automotive Companies, to be published at EdiProd2002.

Applications of a Lightweight, Web-Based Retrieval, Clustering, and Visualisation Framework

V. Sabol[1], W. Kienreich[1], M. Granitzer[1], J. Becker[1], K. Tochtermann[1], and K. Andrews[2]

[1] Know Center,Competence Center for Knowledge-Based Applications and Systems, Inffeldgasse 16c, A-8010 Graz
{vsabol|wkien|mgrani|jbecker|ktochter}@know-center.at
http://www.know-center.at

[2] IICM, Graz University of Technology, Inffeldgasse 16c, A-8010 Graz
kandrews@iicm.edu

Abstract. Today's web search engines return very large result sets for query formulations consisting of few specific keywords. Results are presented as ranked lists containing textual description of found items. Such representations do not allow identification of topical clusters, and consequentially make it difficult for users to refine queries efficiently.

In this paper, we present WebRat, a framework for web-based retrieval, clustering and visualisation which enables parallel querying of multiple search engines, merging of retrieved result sets, automatic identification of topical clusters and interactive visualisation of the result sets and clusters for query refinement. This framework is lightweight in the sense that it consists of a small, platform-independent component which can be easily integrated into exisiting Internet or Intranet search forms without requiring specific system environments, server resources or precalculation efforts.

The WebRat system extends existing approaches to web search result visualisation in many aspects: Found results are added incrementally as they arrive, labelling is performed in 2-dimensional space on clusters the user can see and rendering is optimised to provide sufficient performance on standard office machines.

The WebRat framework has been used to implement a variety of applications: We have provided enhanced web search capabilities for users doing scientific research. Overview and refinement capabilities have been implemented for the environmental domain. Finally, abstracts generated on the fly by a knowledge management system have been used to provide topical navigation capabilities to developers searching for technical information in mailing list archives.

D. Karagiannis and U. Reimer (Eds.): PAKM 2002, LNAI 2569, pp. 359–368, 2002.

1 Introduction

Todays web search engines return relevance-ranked result lists containing thousands of items for a typical query consisting of one to two keywords. Users have to do a large amount of query refinement to find the information they are looking for, especially if the query term is of general nature and the intent behind the query is obtaining an overview on a topic. Two observations describe the problem and point towards a feasible solution:

- *Some query keywords are better than others:*
  Such query keywords lead to a much better narrowing of the result set than others. Providing users with a selection of such "power keywords" - which do not necessarily form a classification pattern or hierarchy - would greatly aid query refinement.

- *Relevance cannot be measured in one dimension:*
  Ranked lists hide topical relations between found items from users, making it hard for the user to identify promising query refinement strategies. Providing users with a view of the topical clusters formed by a query result space would support query refinement.

Adressing these problems, we have designed the WebRat framework which enables querying of web sources, topical clustering of query results, extraction of keywords describing found clusters and interactive visualisation of results including topical clusters. Applications of the framework have been implemented for a number of real-world problems, and some preliminary evaluation has been done.

This paper briefly describes work related to Webrat, the standard interface through which users interact with the application and the architecture of the system behind the interface. Then, three concrete applications of WebRat are described, and the results of preliminary evaluation are discussed. Finally, we provide an outlook on future work to improve and extend the capabilites of WebRat.

2 Related Work

Our framework employs the concept of thematic landscapes to interactively visualise query results, building on existing and related work in the area. Query results can be obtained from a large number of sources, ranging from web search engines to email data or intranet information. Results are merged and then processed further, as in traditional meta-search engines.

2.1 Thematic Landscapes

A thematic landscape is a visual representation in which the spatial proximity between visualised entities in a 2D or 2.1D view is a measure for thematical similarity of the underlying documents. Similar objects are placed close to each other and the resulting 2D layout is used to generate a 2D or 3D-style overlay map. By identifying areas where groups of similar documents are located, and by computing labels which describe the underlying documents, an intuitive topical landscape is created.

The Bead system [4] is an interactive, multi-participant, information-terrain document visualisation system. It computes inter-document high-dimensional distances and applies a force-directed placement method to create the the 2.1D landscape. As opposed to WebRat the Bead system does not offer dynamically generated labels which describe the currently explored part of the landscape, nor does its visualisation metaphor faithfully reproduce a landscape.

The SPIRE project [11] provides a galaxies visualisation where documents are displayed as stars in a galaxy. ThemeView, formerly known as Themescape [13] is a further development of the galaxies visualisation. The system can produce a 2.1D map for very large document corpora.

In Kohonen's Self Organising Maps [5] every document's term vector is used to train a neural network which produces a topically organised map. SOMs can be used for creating maps containing very large amounts of documents, but they require a significant amount of time for training the network, making them too slow for creating a landscape on-the-fly.

Finally, Visualisation Islands [9],[1] can be seen as a direct predecessor of our framework. The system uses aggregation and sampling techniques to improve the separation and speed of a force-directed placement algorithm, which generates a map where related topics are presented as islands. However, Visualisation Islands failed to scale to larger document sets.

In contrast to WebRat, all aforementioned systems use static maps rendered once based on a given data set. Incremental mapping, which is defined as the process of incorporating a stream of newly added results when they arrive, and on-the-fly generation, which denotes realtime creation and modification of the visualisation according to user needs, are important features in modern retrieval and visualisation application.[2] While most existing systems succeed at one of these tasks, WebRat has been specifically designed to fulfill both.

Most existing systems employ static means of navigation and interaction, focussing on the generation of a visual representation of the data set and less on the interactions between user and visualisation. For example, labels are calculated during rendering of the map and then remain unchanged in many of the aforementioned systems. We believe that techniques like dynamic labeling, continuous hierarchical zoom or query refinement suggestions can significantly improve usability of visualisation applications and consequentially have incorporated such techniques into WebRat.

2.2 Meta-search Engines

Lighthouse [6] is system for clustering and visualisation of search results. The search query is sent to a number of popular search engines (Google, Alta Vista, Excite, etc.) and the specified number of results is analysed and thematically organised on-the-fly. A 2D or a 3D layout is computed by a force-directed placement, and the documents are visualised as spheres floating in space, with the estimated relevance being encoded through color. However, the system offers very limited means of navigation and exploration, mostly due to an inappropriate choice of visualisation metaphor. Another drawback is that the number of search results which can be processed and visualised is quite small.

Vivisimo (www.vivisimo.com) is a meta search engine with the ability to organise search results into thematically similar groups which are named after the topics covered by the corresponding documents. However, the system offers no visualisation. The produced hierarchy is displayed as a tree, so that relations between single clusters and relations between single documents can not be visualised.

Insyder [8] is another meta search system focusing on buisness intelligence and employing user relevance feedback for query refinement. While its process modell is similar to WebRat, visualisation and navigation strongly differs from our approach.

3 The WebRat Interface

Webrat allows users to enter a number of query keywords. These keywords are sent to all sources (i.e. search engines) selected by the user. Returned results are processed by the system and displayed in the visualisation. The visualisation is updated in regular intervals as more and more results arrive. Results form islands on a virtual "satellite map" which are labelled with the according keywords. Users can zoom in and out on the map, revealing more details or displaying an overview in the process. Labels are calculated on the fly, to always describe the most obvious concentrations of documents (the largest islands). Figure 1 shows the WebRat interface: the global view (left), zooming in (top right), context menu (bottom right).

For each labelled island, users can call up a context menu using the right mouse button, which allows to research any of the used sources by refining the original query with the label keywords of the selected island. This way, users can refine query terms quick and efficent. In addition, the context menu contains basic navigational functionallity like zoom in, zoom out and "home", which resets the point of view to display the whole map. A number of further features, including navigational markers which a user can set at any point of the map and to which he can return later, a navigation history of points visited on the map which can be traversed, and color-coding for meta-information values (e.g. relevance), have been implemented, too.

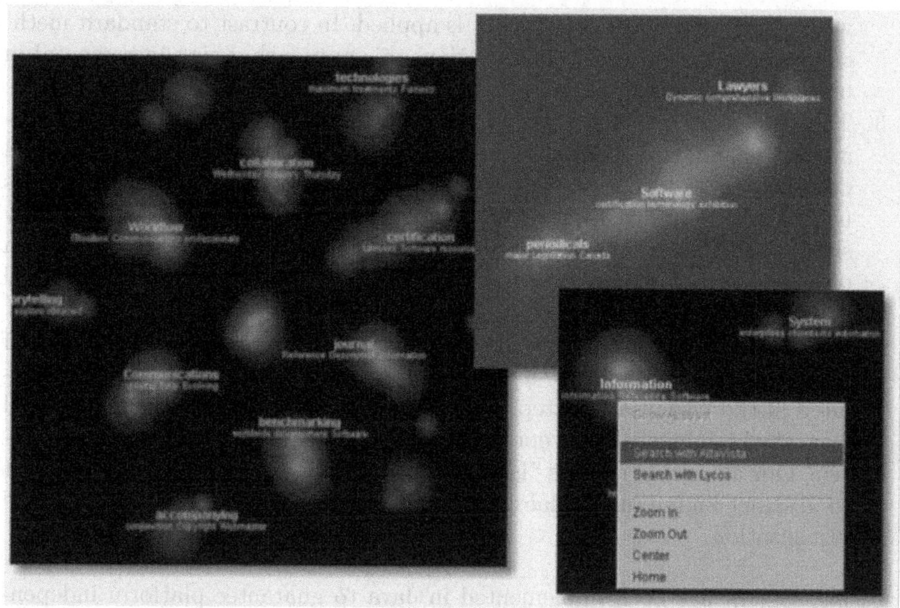

Fig. 1. The WebRat Interface:the global view (left), zooming in (top right), context menu (bottom right).

4 WebRat Architecture

The focus of this paper is on applications of the system to real-world problems. However, some specifics of the underlying techniques strongly influence possible applications. Consequently, this section briefly describes our work from an algorithmical and technical point of view.

Our framework is constituted by four stages which communicate through an object pool and event-driven control logic. All stages are exchangable through strict interface-based, object oriented design, allowing for adaption of the whole system to new tasks with minimum effort.

1. The *query and retrieval stage* sends requests to sources and parses the returned results into a generalized, internal representation using n-gram decomposition [3]. To allow merging of result sets retrieved from various sources, the URL of returned results is used as a global unique identifier. Retrieved objects are assigned a high-dimensional term vector describing object content, which is calculated using a modified TFIDF (Term Frequency Inverse Document Frequency) weightening scheme [10].
2. The *mapping and placement stage* computes a low-dimensional representation from the high-dimensional one using a method related to multidimensional scaling: A sampling-accelerated force-directed placement algorithm

with a cosine similarity coefficient is applied. In contrast to standard methods based on eigenvector computation, this approach, being incremental in nature, allows incorporation of new objects as they arrive.

3. The *visualisation stage* takes the lowdimensional representation and creates an island visualisation from it. A height map is generated from local document density distribution by combining precalculated influence cones using Porter-Duff blending rules [7]. The map is then color-coded and finally shaded using an asymetric two-dimensional filter kernel to create the illusion of a lighted, colored island topography with a minimum of computational effort.
4. The *labelling stage* identifies clusters in low-dimensional space by means of image processing applied to a downsampled version of the height map calculated in the visualisation step. Labels for found clusters are then computed from the highdimensional representation. This is a unique feature of our system: Our algorithm returns "labels for the clusters the user sees", in contrast to abstract high-dimensional clusters not necessarily related to those in the visualisation.

The system has been implemented in Java to guarantee platform independence. A typical distribution consisting of all components mentioned above packed into a JAR-file has a size of about 150kB and can be run on any browser able to run applets. The system works in real time, the user being able to watch the evolution of the result set and to interact with the visualisation as processing continues.

5 Applications

The WebRat framework has been adapted to a number of real-world problems for proof-of-concept and evaluation purposes. Framework adaptions included incorporation of specific sources as well as changes to the visualisation metaphore and interactivity. While detailed tests including precision studies under controlled conditions are still underway, preliminary results are available from user polls and interviews.

5.1 Supporting Search for Related Work in a Scientific Context

The first application of the framework provides a web meta-search form to members of the KnowCenter. The form allows querying for a number of keywords much like standard web search engines do. Two general search engines (AltaVista and Lycos) and a specialised scientific paper search engine (CiteSeer) were defined as sources, with results being merged by the system. The document snippet data returned by the search engines, which is very poor on information, was used to identify and process topics and clusters. As a visualisation, the standard interface of WebRat was used. Figure 2 shows the results on queries for "Knowledge Management Software" (right) and "Artificial Intelligence" (left).

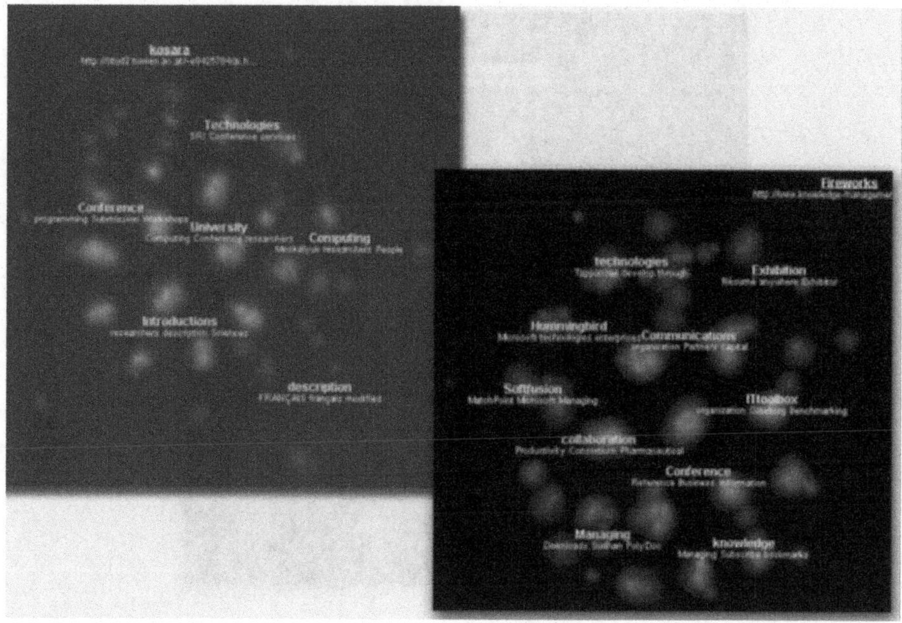

Fig. 2. WebRat results for "Knowledge Management"(right) and "Artificial Intelligence" (left). displayed.

Users were encouraged to use the system in addition to their usual means or research in the process of finding related work for scientific publications. After an evaluation period of two weeks, opinions and experiences were gathered with a questionnaire which all users filled in and by additional interviews with selected users.

Results indicate that the system was perceived as superior to conventional methods of research when users wanted to orient themselves within a new area of interest. "Getting an overview on a topic" was the most-often cited advantage of the system. Users perceived the map representation and the ability to narrow a search on one of a number of presented topics to be very helpful. However, when users knew exactly what they were looking for, and had the appropriate keywords in mind, the beneftis of the system were less obvious.

5.2 Providing Orientation Capabilities in an Environmental Context

The characteristics of environmental information make it a challenging field for search engines and query refinement tools: Environmental information is typically made up of a variety of different data types, and it is enriched with meta-information. The environmental context is saturated with abbreviations and multiple meanings of words, rendering snippet information as used in standard web queries mostly useless.

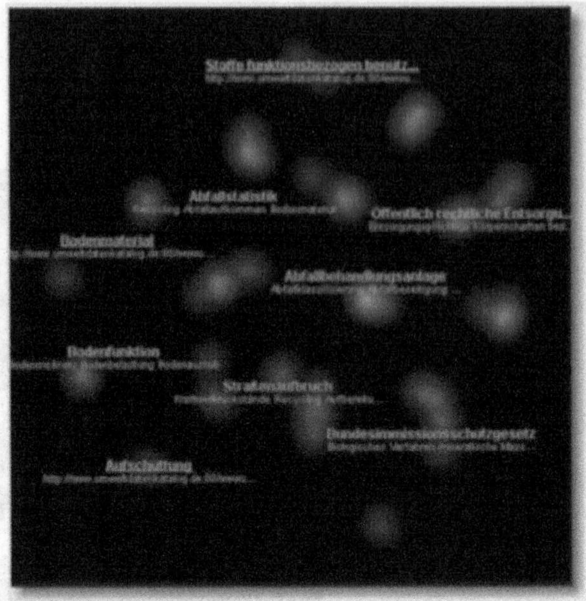

Fig. 3. WebRat displaying results for a query for "Abfallverwertung" in UDK.

In this field, WebRat was applied as a retrieval tool querying the UDK (www.umwelt-datenkatalog.de) and the GEIN search engine (www.gein.de). Meta-information returned by these systems was incorporated, and given priority compared to snippet information also queried and used. The default WebRat interactivity and metaphor was used in the application. Figure 3 shows the results for a query about "Abfallverwertung".

Results indicate that WebRat excels in comparison to strongly meta-information based systems like intelligent maps whenever users wanted to get an overview on a topic, and in situations where little meta-information was available [12]. In such cases, the additional information provided by the snippets lead to acceptable results in WebRat, whilst solely meta-information dependent query environments returned no hits at all. However, locating clearly defined information entities in an environment rich in meta-information is more quickly done in dedicated meta-information based systems than in WebRat.

5.3 Topical Navigation of Contents Stored in a Knowledge Management Systems

Email traffic as generated by discussion groups is easily stored and managed in a knowledge management system like the Hyperwave Information Server (www.hyperwave.com). However, retrieval of information in such a context is very hard, as emails contain misspelled words, abbreviations, slang and other features hindering standard search operations.

In this context, we have applied WebRat as a retrieval tool against a database of several thousand technical mailing list postings. We have exploited the capability of the Hyperwave Information Server to create high-quality abstracts of documents on the fly: Such abstracts were returned as "search result snippets" and processed in WebRat, resulting in very high quality topical clusters being generated.

No formal evaluation of the approach has been done to date. However, we have identified an interesting application from user input to this application: WebRat can be used as a trend watcher, with clusters denoting discussion hot spots and changes of clusters over time denoting changes in the general interest within a community of practice.

6 Future Work

As WebRat is an open, adaptable system, much future work will be done in the direction of applying it to new sources and application domains. As a result of the aforementioned discussion group experiment, we will implement an animated visualisation displaying the change of a query result structure over time. A hierarchical clustering algorithm will enable WebRat to process up to 100,000 information entities and at the same time generate a hierarchical topic structure which can be used for automatic directory generation. Finally, we will explore new visualisation metaphors and means of interaction.

7 Conclusions

In this paper, we presented a framework for web-based retrieval, clustering and visualisation, and a prototype called WebRat, which employed the framework in a number of applications. In the area of related-work literature survey in a scientific context, users evaluated the prototype to be most useful for obtaining an overview on a topic, while conventional search methods were perceived superior in locating individual, well-described information entities.

With the ever-increasing amount of information available to search engines in intranets and on the web, users clearly need support in navigation and refinement of large query result sets. WebRat provides this support to selected domains. It enables users to find information faster and, consequently, to complete their daily work more efficiently and satisfyingly.

Acknowledgements. The Know-Center is a Competence Center funded within the Austrian Competence Centers Programme K plus under the auspices of the Austrian Ministry of Transport, Innovation and Technology (www.kplus.at).

References

1. Andrews K., Gütl C., Moser J., Sabol V., Lackner W.: Search Result Visualisation with xFIND
In Proceedings of UIDIS 2001, Zurich, Switzerland, May 2001. pp. 50-58

2. Boerner K., Chen C., Boyack K.W. (2003): Visualizing Knowledge Domains Annual Review of Information Science and Technology 37.
3. Cavnar, W.B., Trenkle, J. M. (1994): n-Gram based text categorization. In Symposion on Document Analysis and Information Retrieval, p161-176, University of Nevada, Las Vegas.
4. Chalmers M. (1993): Using a landscape methaphor to represent a corpus of documents. In Proceedings European Conference on Spatial Information Theory, COSIT 93, pages 337-390, Elba, September 1993.
5. Kohonen, T., Kaski, S., Lagus, K., Salojärvi, J., Honkela, J., Paatero, V., Saarela, A. (1999): Self organization of a massive text document collection. In Oja, E. and Kaski, S., editors, Kohonen Maps pages 171-182, Elsevier, Amsterdam, 1999
6. Leuski, A., Allan, J. (2000): Lighthouse: Showing the Way to Relevant Information. In the Proceedings of IEEE Symposium on Information Visualization 2000 (InfoVis2000), Salt Lake City, Utah, October 2000. pp. 125-130.
7. Porter T., Duff T. (1984): Compositing Digital Images in SIGGRAPH 84, p253-259.
8. Reiter H., Mußler G., Mann T., Handschuh S.: Insyder - An Information Assistant for Business Intelligence In Proceedings of the 23rd Annual International ACM SIGIR Conference on Research and Developement in Information Retrieval, July 14-18, 2000 Athens, Greece
9. Sabol V. (2001): Visualisation Islands: Interactive Visualisation and Clustering of Search Result Sets. Master's Thesis at IICM, Graz University of Technology
10. Salton B., Buckley G. Term Weighting Approaches in Automatic Text Retrieval. Information Processing and Management, 24(5), pp. 513-523, 1988
11. Thomas, J., et al. (2001): Visual Text analysis - SPIRE Technical flier from the Pacific Northwest National Laboratory. http://www.pnl.gov/infoviz/spire.pdf
12. Tochtermann, K., Sabol, V., Kienreich, W., Granitzer, M. and Becker, J. (2002): Intelligent Maps and Information Landscapes: Two new Approaches to support Search and Retrieval of Environmental Information Objects. In Proceedings of 16th International Conference on Informatics for Environmental Protection, Vienna University of Technology , September 2002
13. Wise, J., Thomas, J., Pennock, K., Lantrip, D., Pottier, M., Schur, A. (1995): Visualizing the non-visual: Spatial analysis and interaction with information from text documents. In Proceedings of the Information Visualization Symposium 95, p51-58. IEEE Computer Society Press

Facilitating Comprehension of Normative Documents by Graphical Representations

Marite Kirikova

Division of Systems Theory, Riga Technical University, 1 Kalku, Riga, LV-1658, Latvia
marite@cs.rtu.lv

Abstract. Normative documents are used to record knowledge about "what" and "how" regarding goals or purposes the organisation must achieve, and products or services the organisation must produce or provide. In cases, when normative documents are complex and must be understood by individuals that have not been involved in their development, graphical representations of the document contents, and of the relationships between the documents may serve as facilitators of better comprehension of the documents.

1 Introduction

A considerable part of organisational knowledge is included in different types of organisational documents. Documents are used to record contracts and agreements, policies, standards and procedures, to represent a view of reality at a point of time, to act as a mechanism for communication and interaction among people, and for many other reasons [1]. In this paper the discussion concerns normative documents - those documents that are used to record knowledge about "what" and "how" regarding goals or purposes the organisation must achieve, and products or services the organisation must produce or provide. In other words, the focus is on the documents that represent particular norms that are to be followed by the organisation. Different types of regulations, agreements and standards are the most characteristic examples of that category of documents.

Most of normative documents carry textual declarative knowledge about a particular subject [2]. This knowledge may be regarded as explicit conceptual knowledge with respect to the phases of knowledge creation [3]. To be useful, the explicit knowledge represented by normative documents should be internalised by employees of the organisation. However, the internalisation of knowledge reflected in the normative documents depends on the individual comprehension of the textual declarative knowledge. Therefore different, even contradictory, interpretations of the conceptual knowledge may be internalised and cause serious misunderstandings among the employees concerning the messages carried by the normative documents [4]. We propose here to support textual documents by graphical interpretation of their contents to facilitate accuracy, easiness and speed of comprehension of normative documents by individuals [2].

D. Karagiannis and U. Reimer (Eds.): PAKM 2002, LNAI 2569, pp. 369-376, 2002.

Business process models are suggested as central tool for graphical representation of normative documents. It is essential that several normative documents may refer to one and the same business process and vice versa. On the other hand, there are certain relationships among the normative documents that are to be taken into consideration in business processes. Therefore, for achieving maximum of transparency, the normative documents are to be viewed as a system of documents.

The nature of normative documents is analysed in Section 2. Section 3 describes a correspondence between normative documents and business models. Section 4 introduces the notion of an integrated part of organisational memory consisting of the subsystem of documents and corresponding sub-system of graphical representation of a business system. Brief conclusions are given in Section 5.

2 Nature of Normative Documents

Normative documents are part of organisational memory [1], [5]. Knowledge contained in them, among other things, pictures the boundaries of workspace [4] by referring to goals and restrictions of organisational processes [6]. Normative documents are an externalised part of a deep tacit knowledge that belongs to their developers, they have a particular life cycle, and usually are organised as a set of more or less tightly related elements.

2.1 Knowledge Contained in and behind the Normative Documents

A normative document usually is a result of multistage groupwork. Tacit knowledge of individuals involved in the development of the document is harmonised during several official or non-official sessions. Part of this tacit knowledge is externalised and explicitly written down in the form of a text that in most cases is well structured.

It is essential that the normative document represents only a small part of knowledge involved in its development. Therefore easiness of its comprehension and understanding depends on the similarity between knowledge of developers and users of the document. In case developers and users of the document are the same individuals, there should not be any serious problems in the use of normative documents. However, in many cases normative documents must be understood by individuals that have not been involved in their development. In those cases understanding of the documents becomes a task of a high cognitive complexity.

Natural mechanisms of complexity reduction, such as forgetting, plausible retrieval, etc., [2] lead to the particular simplifications of the documents. Those simplifications are complemented by individual interpretations due to the differences in tacit knowledge of users of the documents. This results in different (ranging from non-essential to fundamental) misunderstandings that negatively influence organisational processes. For example, at Riga Technical University four normative documents that regulate the process of examinations were perceived as contradictory by secretaries and students [4]. After deep analysis of the documents (including interviews with their developers) it appeared that there are no any contradictions in the documents. The problem then was resolved by supplementing the documents by a graphical business process model that represented a part of explicit knowledge contained in four documents. Further details concerning relationship between normative documents and business models are given in Section 3.

2.2 Structure of Normative Documents and Their Relationships

In most cases normative documents are represented by the text organised in numbered paragraphs. Each paragraph is a portion or piece of knowledge that is related to other such portions of knowledge (paragraphs) in the same document or in other documents. For example, Regulation (EEC) Nr. 2419/2001 has more than 100 references to approximately 20 paragraphs in other EEC regulations, and more than 60 internal references [7]. As relationships between different portions of knowledge contained in the documents are represented by direct textual references or have to be derived cognitively, they are not explicitly shown at different levels of abstraction. For example, it is not possible to obtain a birds-view of the documents, that explicitly represents all links between the related documents. Therefore, it is hard to check whether all necessary relationships are taken into consideration during internalization of knowledge contained in the documents.

Electronic document representation gives an opportunity to make relationships visible in each moment of interest and at different levels of abstraction. To achieve this, each paragraph must be supported by plugs for attaching links from or to other documents. There are following types of plugs:

- document level plugs referring to the whole document
- paragraph level plugs referring to the numbered item (paragraph)
- concept level plugs (not discussed in this paper) referring to a particular concept or explanation of the concept.

The paragraph may be supported by document or paragraph level plugs. Each type of plugs should have a different appearance, e.g., a particular color may be used for a particular type of plugs. Thus each document is viewed as a sub-system of a system of documents [8] where paragraphs form its internal structure. Use of document and paragraph level plugs is demonstrated in Fig. 1. The plugs show that in Riga Seaport's normative document Regulations of ships incoming and exit'there is a reference to paragraph 5 in paragraph 4; and that paragraph 6 of this document refers to normative document Classifier of International Maritime Organisation."

Plugs and the possibility to view graphically represented links between documents at several levels of abstraction give additional information relevant in comprehension of the documents.

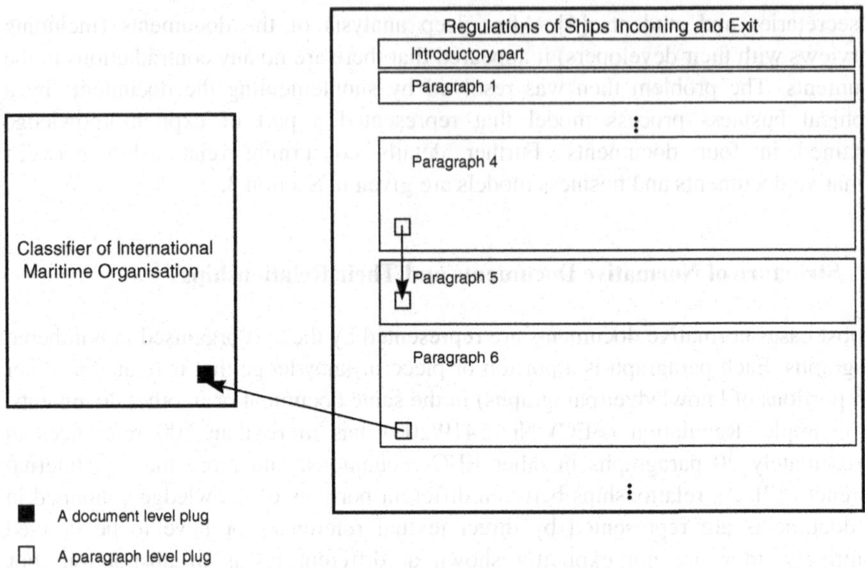

Fig. 1. Use of plugs for revealing relationships between normative documents and their subparts

2.3 Life Cycle of Normative Documents

A normative document becomes valid at a point of time t1, it may be changed at points of time t2, …, tN, and it can become non-valid at a point of time t(N+1). Changes in normative documents are usually made by other normative documents that are issued at particular points of time before or during the period of validity of the document.

Reader's first acquaintance with the document may occur at any point of time of the document's life cycle. An individual, who first time reads the document that has been changed for several times, must consider the initial version of the document and all other documents that had introduced changes in the initial document. The individual's time and effort would be saved if a current valid knowledge conveyed by the documents were at his/her disposal. Actually, this knowledge is available but is not shown explicitly. If the documents were handled electronically as systems of paragraphs, and relationships between documents made explicit, then the current valid version of the document could be generated on the basis of the initial document and all those documents that had introduced changes in the initial version. This approach, however, can be applied only if in documents' development process some rules concerning their structure are taken into consideration.

3 Correspondence between Normative Documents and Business Models

Normative documents relevant for particular organisation form a local organisational legislation system that overlaps with governmental legislation and other local organisational legislation systems. In many cases representation of information in legislation systems does not promote effectiveness of its processing. Therefore attempts to use information technology have been made with the purpose of improving the utilisation of legal information. The most common approach is an establishment of legal databases that are equipped with different search mechanisms such as search by key-words, search by subject, associative search [9] and/or are analysed by intelligent agents [10]. Legal databases facilitate information processing concerning normative documents, but they do not represent the relationship between documents and business activities. However, this relationship can be represented because many normative acts define business rules at different levels of generality, and business rules, in turn, can be translated into business process models.

Business models can be graphically represented using particular business modelling environments [4]. The models consist of a set of interrelated sub-models such as a business process sub-model, organisational structure, data sub-model, etc. according to the languages of corresponding business modelling methodologies. The business process sub-model is the kernel of the majority of business modelling methodologies [11]. The business process sub-model basically consists of the following elements [4]: external entities, tasks, information, material and control flows, data stores, performers of the tasks (actors), timers, and triggering conditions.

Normative documents contain information that corresponds to particular elements of business process sub-model and elements of other related sub-models. Therefore it is possible to translate the normative document in a particular business modelling language and represent it graphically. The best aid for comprehension of normative documents is the kernel of the business model, the business process sub-model, because it explicitly shows the sequence of activities prescribed or assumed by the normative document.

In Fig. 2 the sequence of activities prescribed by paragraphs 4 and 5 of the normative document Regulations of ships incoming and exit'is shown. The message in the normative document and the business process model is the same. However, graphical representation gives a possibility to see clearly the actions prescribed by the document and relationships between these actions in terms of sequence of activities, information flows, and material flows. Graphical representation of the document provides also a transparent pattern of responsibilities that correspond to the activities (or sub-processes) to be accomplished in an organisation.

In some cases almost all elements of the business process sub-model can be obtained from a single normative document. In other cases several normative documents are used to construct the sub-model; or autonomous elements of the business process sub-model may be defined by the normative documents.

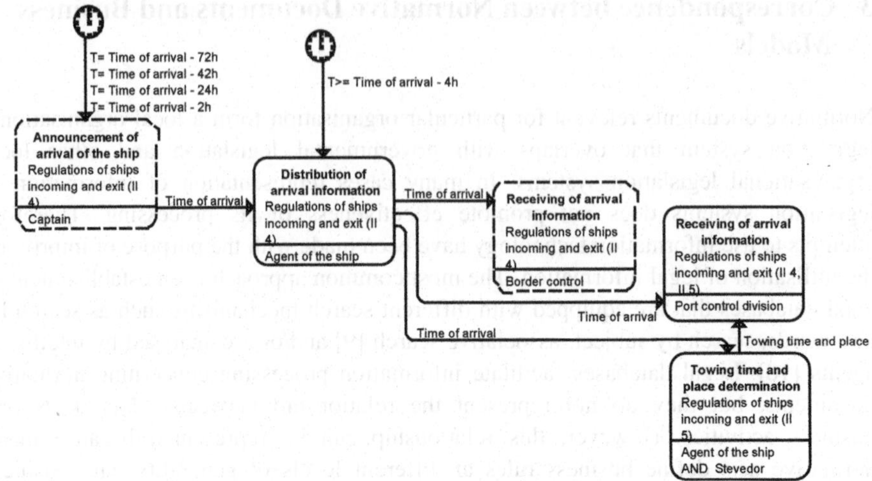

Fig. 2. Sequence of activities prescribed by paragraphs 4 and 5 of Riga Seaport's normative document Regulations of ships incoming and exit'(part II)

Graphical representations of normative documents as business models enforce additional cognitive mechanisms of individuals and thus help to minimize misinterpretations of the text and facilitate better comprehension of the documents.

4 Supporting Organisational Memory by Integrated Document and Business Model Representation System

Representation of documents electronically as systems of paragraphs, and translation of normative documents into particular business modelling languages give an opportunity to establish the integrated graphical document and business model representation system that explicitly shows the following relationships:

- relationships between documents and parts of the documents (see Section 2.2) that are established by using plugs and/or showing the relationships graphically. In Fig. 1 paragraph level plugs are represented by small blank squares and a document level plug is shown by the filled small square.
- relationships that show history of the documents (see Section 2.3). These relationships also may be represented graphically. On the other hand, even when not shown graphically they can be used for generating a full text of the current version of the document.
- relationships between particular pieces of documents and corresponding parts of the business model (see Section 3).

Relationships between documents and parts of the documents, and relationships between particular pieces of documents and corresponding parts of the business model are shown in Fig. 3 in an integrated way.

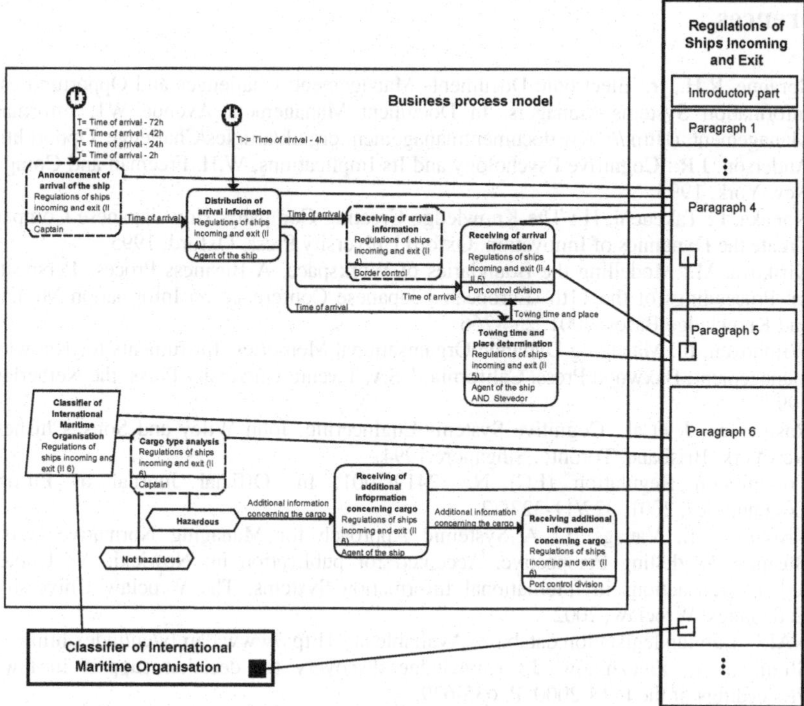

Fig. 3. Relationships between normative documents, and normative documents and a business process sub-model

Integrated document and business model representation system can be used as part of organisational memory. However, for establishing this system, particular document preparation rules, document history generation algorithms, and software tools for integrated representation of business models and documents are to be designed and developed. Currently available business modelling environments can not directly be used for the integrated document and business model representation system. Nevertheless, some elements of the system may be realised by commercial business modelling environments [4].

5 Conclusions

Graphical representation of (1) relationships between normative documents, and (2) contents of the textual normative documents as business models may be used as complementary cognitive aids for comprehension of normative documents. Textual and graphical representations of knowledge are perceived differently, and may be regarded as two sources of one and the same basic knowledge that emphasize different aspects of that knowledge. The use of graphical representations not only enriches the background of comprehension but is also a means for evaluation of complexity of the cognitive task and completeness of knowledge acquired.

References

1. Sprague, R.H., jr.: Electronic Documents Management: Challenges and Opportunities for Information Systems Managers. In Document Management Avenue W1: Information Management. (Http://www.documentmanagement.org.uk/articles/Challenge_Opport.htm)
2. Anderson, J.R.: Cognitive Psychology and Its Implications, W.H. Freeman and Company, New York, 1995
3. Nonaka, I., Takeuchi, H.: The Knowledge Creating Company: How Japanese Companies Create the Dynamics of Innovation, Oxford University Press, Oxford, 1995
4. Kirikova, M.: Modelling the Boundaries of Workspace: A Business Process Perspective. In: Proceedings of the 11th European - Japanese Conference on Information Modelling and Knowledge Bases, 2001, 254-266
5. Wijnhoven, F.: Managing Dynamic Organisational Memories: Instruments for Knowledge management, Baxwood Press, California, USA, Twente University Press, the Netherlands, 1999
6. Rasmussen, J. et al.: Cognitive Systems Engineering, John Wiley and Sons, Chishester, NewYork, Brisbane, Toronto, Singapore,1994
7. Commission Regulation (EC) Nr. 2419/2001. In: Official Journal of European Communities, 2001, 327/11-327/32
8. Kirikova, M., Vanags, J.: A Systemic Approach for Managing Normative Acts: A Business Modelling Perspective. Accepted for publication in: Nowicki, A., Unold, J. (eds.): Transactions in International Information Systems, The Wroclaw University of Economics, Wroclaw, 2002
9. NAIS - Latvian legislation database. Available at - Http://www.dati.lv/en/index.html
10. Stranieri, A., Zeleznikow, J.: Knowledge discovery for decision support in law. In Proceedings of the ICIS'2000, P. 635-639.
11. Nilsson, A.G., Tolis, Ch., Nellborn, Ch., (eds.): Perspectives on Business Modelling: Understanding and Changing Organisations. Springer, Berlin, Heidelberg, 1999
12. Vanags, J., Kirikova, M.: The role of Normative Acts Based Business Modelling in Port's Mnagement Information System. In: Scientific Proceedings of Riga Technical University, Series-Computer Science, Riga Technical University, Riga, 2001, 92-99

A Fuzzy-Graph-Based Approach to the Determination of Interestingness of Association Rules

B. Shekar[1] and Rajesh Natarajan

Quantitative Methods and Information Systems Area
Indian Institute of Management Bangalore
Bangalore 560076, INDIA
(shek[1], rn)@iimb.ernet.in

Abstract. 'Interestingness' measures are used to rank rules according to the 'interest' a particular rule is expected to evoke in a user. In this paper, we introduce an aspect of interestingness called 'item-relatedness' to determine interestingness of item-pairs occurring in association rules. We elucidate and quantify three different types of item-relatedness. Relationships corresponding to item-relatedness proposed by us are shown to be captured by paths in a 'fuzzy taxonomy' (an extension of the concept hierarchy tree). We then combine these measures of item-relatedness to arrive at a total-relatedness measure. We finally demonstrate the efficacy of this total measure on a sample taxonomy.

1 Introduction

Knowledge-based resources of a firm are difficult to imitate by competition and are socially complex. The collective knowledge of a firm, not only consists of explicit knowledge in the form of documents, rules, work procedures etc. but also tacit knowledge. Tacit knowledge, more often than not, resides in the minds of employees. Many firms, in recent times, have introduced knowledge management systems (KMS), in order to identify and leverage such knowledge for competition. KMS are a class of IT-based systems, developed to support the primary processes of knowledge creation, storage/retrieval, transfer and application of knowledge [1]. Knowledge Discovery in Databases (KDD) or Data Mining is a discipline that aims at extracting novel, relevant, valid and significant knowledge, expressed in the form of patterns from large and very large databases. They not only help in bringing out subtle and less known facts about the operations of a firm, but also help in formalizing and giving credibility to the tacit knowledge of the firm's employees.

Association rules are patterns that bring out co-occurrence of items in a database of transactions [9,11]. In the retail market-basket context, association rules tell us which items are likely to be purchased by a customer given that he/she has already purchased other items from the store. Thus, association rules, bring out the affinity between items displayed for sale in a retail store – affinity that is a result of customer purchasing behaviour. Association rule mining is a highly automated activity. User interaction is limited to his/her supplying two parameters viz. support and confidence [9,11]. As a consequence of the automated nature of the search process, a large number of association rules are extracted – numbers that exceed

D. Karagiannis and U. Reimer (Eds.): PAKM 2002, LNAI 2569, pp. 377-388, 2002.

human ability for easy comprehension. Further, many of these rules may not add any value to the user (typically, a manager of a retail store) as he/she, being a domain expert, may already be aware of them by virtue of experience. Given that a user has a limited time at his/her disposal it would be helpful to a user, if only the most interesting and significant rules are displayed by the system. Actions such as selection of items for display, arrangement of display shelves, design of discount coupons and the like can then be based on these displayed rules.

One approach adopted by researchers in this field to tackle this problem of comprehensibility involves the use of 'interestingness' measures to rank association patterns. Interestingness measures rank rules based on the 'interest' that a rule is supposed to evoke in a user examining it. Then, rules that have very low 'interestingness' values need not be examined, as they are likely to contain well-known aspects about the domain which might be common place. Hence they can either be discarded or presented later. Interestingness measures may be 'objective' or 'subjective' [8]. Objective measures classify interestingness of a pattern in terms of its structure and the underlying data used in the discovery process [11], while subjective measures, in addition to the above, also try to incorporate the views of the person inspecting the pattern [8]. Silberschatz and Tuzhilin [8] identify two aspects of subjective interestingness, namely unexpectedness and actionability. A pattern (rule) is interesting to a user if it is unexpected i.e. surprising to him/her. Further, a pattern (rule) will also be interesting if the user can act on the knowledge conferred by the rule to his/her advantage.

Here, we consider association rules discovered from market-basket transactions in a large retail store. We try to capture one aspect of subjective interestingness called 'item relatedness' using a fuzzy taxonomy (concept hierarchy) of items. Concept hierarchies have been used extensively in data mining studies to find associations between items at different levels of the concept hierarchy [6] and from multiple taxonomies [4], to find negative associations [10] and in attribute-oriented induction [6]. In our study, we deal with association rules whose items occur as leaves in the taxonomy tree. We include domain knowledge about items, their classifications and relationships in the structure of the taxonomy. This might also include the tacit knowledge that a manager has about customer purchasing behaviour. We then use structural aspects of the taxonomy to derive an intuitive measure of 'relatedness'. Graff et al. [3,4] have used taxonomies to find interesting association rules. They consider cases wherein multiple taxonomies are available for attributes [4] and attributes are fuzzy [3]. They consider an item-set (or rule) interesting if the behaviour of the item set is different from that of its parents. They estimate/compute the support of the item set from the support of its parents. If the 'actual' support of the item set (obtained from the database of transactions) is different from this estimated support, then the item set is deemed 'interesting.' Our notion of interestingness is very different from this as it is based on the structural aspects of the taxonomy. In addition, we also fuzzify the relationships between items and their parents rather than the items/attributes themselves. Chen et al. [2] have used fuzzy taxonomies to mine three kinds of association rules viz. rules with taxonomic nodes, linguistic terms and hedges. However, they do not deal with the relationships between items as done here, but are more concerned with mining generalized fuzzy association rules across higher level taxonomic nodes. More importantly, we use the fuzzy taxonomy to quantify the interestingness of crisp association rules that are inherently non-fuzzy. The study that comes closest to our current study is due to Hamilton et al. [6] who used concept hierarchies to rank generalized relations on basis of their interestingness. In their study, concept hierarchies were constructed for individual attributes, but they did not consider relationships that exist between the attributes themselves. The intuition used there was that nodes that lie between the extremes of the leaf nodes and the root node are most likely to provide new, non-trivial and previously implicit information. Here, we do not deal with attribute values explicitly, but rather consider them implicitly while constructing the 'fuzzy taxonomy'.

'Fuzzy taxonomy' is described in the next section along with three notions of item-relatedness. Subsequently we present a mechanism for calculating 'item-relatedness' existing between two items and discuss its appropriateness. We then discuss the implications of the new item relatedness measure and motivate it intuitively with the help of an example. Finally, we conclude with a summary of results.

2 Fuzzy Taxonomy

Items in a retail super-market are generally arranged by their generic category. Whenever customers purchase with a goal in mind they consider items both within a generic category and across categories. A taxonomy (concept hierarchy) of items is useful in depicting categorization of items based on the relationships between them. In a traditional concept hierarchy [6,9] each concept/category node can be the child of at the most one parent node. This restriction does not allow us to express certain relationships that might exist between items and their higher-level concepts. It becomes very difficult to categorize an item that might belong to two or more higher-level concepts at the same level [9]. Further, one also has cases wherein an item can be used in many ways, and might substitute other items to various extents. For example, a spoon can take the role of a knife to a limited extent for cutting soft items like butter and some kinds of fruits. The tip of a knife, made blunt, might serve as a screwdriver to a limited extent. Such cases of an item taking on multiple functions arise because of the presence of secondary functionalities in addition to the 'primary' functionality and the overlap of attributes required for the functions. Such relationships cannot be sufficiently expressed in a traditional concept hierarchy. In order to express the relationships arising out of secondary functionalities, we use the notion of 'fuzzy taxonomy' [2]. We use standard graph-theoretic terms [5] and standard terms from fuzzy literature [7] throughout. Other specific terms are defined as and when they are introduced.

A 'Fuzzy Taxonomy', an extension of the traditional concept hierarchy, is a tree with items represented as leaf nodes and concepts represented as non-leaf nodes [2]. A 'Parent' and 'Child' pair represent an 'is-a' relationship. A 'child' node need not be a full member of the category/concept represented by the 'parent' node. In other words, some attributes of a 'child' node may not be relevant as compared to those of its 'parent'. Another important point to note is that there are no direct connections between siblings. Siblings are connected only through their parents. We define a membership function that takes on a value between 0 and 1, and which represents the extent to which a 'child' node belongs to its 'parent' category. This value is then carried over to other ancestors (emanating from its parent) of the 'child' node. When an 'ancestor' node has two or more membership grades from the various parents of a leaf-level item, then we choose the highest membership value. This is done so as to preserve the membership value of the leaf-level item in its closest ancestor. Formally, the membership function of a child node 'c' in its parent node 'p' is given by: $\mu_{(c,p)} = x : 0 \leq x \leq 1$. For an ancestor 'a', the membership grade is given by $\mu_{(c,a)} = \max\{ \mu_{(c,a)}(k)\}$ where k = 1, 2, ….N. $\mu_{(c,a)}(k)$ is the membership grade of the child node 'c' in its ancestor 'a' by the virtue of the path 'k'.

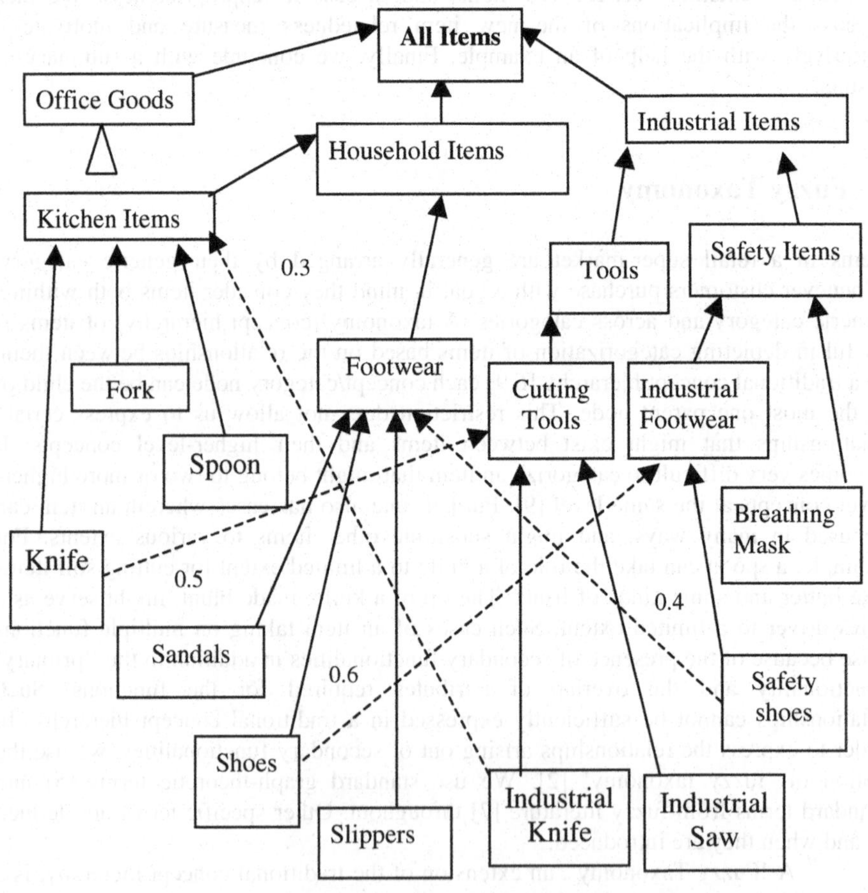

Fig. 1. A Fuzzy taxonomy

Figure 1 shows a fuzzy taxonomy. Although it is somewhat compact to aid illustration, the discussions that follow can be extended to fuzzy taxonomies of any degree of complexity. Any item can have one or more parents. For example, node *knife* is a member of both the nodes *kitchen items* and *cutting tools*, although the membership of *knife* in *cutting tools* is just 0.5, i.e. $\mu_{(knife,\ cutting\ tools)}(k) = 0.5$ while $\mu_{(knife,\ kitchen\ items)}(k) = 1.0$. We represent fuzzy membership grades (that is any membership less than 1.0) by broken lines with membership values written on them. Crisp memberships (μ=1.0) are represented by solid lines. We note that the membership of *knife* in the node *industrial items* is 0.5 because of the membership being transferred to nodes *tools* and *cutting tools*. Thus, $\mu_{(knife,\ Industrial\ items)} = 0.5$. On the other hand, the membership value of *knife* in the *All Items* node is 1, because of the direct crisp path through the node 'household items'. $\mu_{(knife,\ All\ Items)} = \max\{\mu_{(knife,\ Household\ items)}, \mu_{(knife,\ Industrial\ items)}\} = \max[1.0, 0.5] = 1.0$ In a very broad sense the transfer gives the extent to which properties of the child overlap with those of the parent node. Further, the non-leaf items themselves might have fuzzy memberships in other higher-level nodes. For example, the node *Industrial Footwear* can have a membership of say 0.6 in the node *Footwear.* However, to keep the discussions relatively simple we have not considered them here, although our discussions could be extended to such cases. We first need to find all simple paths [9] connecting the two items. A path here is a set of nodes connecting any two items.

The *highest-level node of path(A, B)*, $H_{A,B}(p)$, is defined as the node that occurs at the highest level (i.e. nearest to the root node) in the path p connecting items A and B. We have a highest- level node for each of the paths connecting A and B. The highest-level node can also be defined in an alternative way. Consider the path from the item A to the root node say, path(A, Root), and the path from item B to the root node say, path(B, Root). The two paths will have at least one common node i.e. the 'root' node, but might have more common nodes. Then, the common node from the two paths viz. path(A, Root) and path(B, Root) which is closest to A and B is the highest level node of path(A,B). For example, in the crisp path between *knife* and *shoes*, the node *household items* is the highest-level node. By the virtue of its position, the highest-level node of a path plays a significant role in determining the 'relatedness' between the two items under consideration. It is the closest common context that relates the two items. Further, the distance of the highest-level node from the root node also gives an indication of the relatedness between the two items.

3 Item Relatedness

Relationships between items are a result of the generic category to which the items belong (primary functional purpose), domains of application and secondary functionalities. Any two items say A, B can be connected by many such relationships each of which increases the extent to which the two items are related to each other. It is also important to note that mere presence of a large number of relationships may not increase the relatedness between the two items since the strength of each of them also plays an important role in determining 'relatedness'. All association rules have support (statistical significance) and confidence (predictive ability) [10,11] greater than the user set minimum values. An item-pair in an association rule is 'interesting' to a user if the items in it are weakly related to each other. The fact that these item-pairs, despite being weakly related, have a high frequency of occurrence in the database make them interesting. Thus, 'relatedness' and 'interestingness' are opposing notions.

Highest-level node membership of items A and B in path 'p', [$HM_{A,B}$ (p)] is given by the minimum of the membership values of the two items in the Highest-level Node of path 'p'.

$$\mathbf{HM_{A,B}(p) = min\,[\,\mu_{A,H(A,B)}(p),\ \mu_{B,H(A,B)}(p)]}$$

Consider the fuzzy path connecting items *knife* and *shoes*. The node *Industrial items* is the highest-level node of this path. Thus, $HM_{(knife,\,shoes)}$ (p) = min [0.5, 0.6]= 0.5. We consider 'minimum' as the operator that relates the memberships of the two items in the highest-level node. The membership value of *knife* in *Industrial Items* is 0.5 while that of *shoes* is 0.6. Therefore, both items have their presence in *Industrial Items* as members to the extent of at least 0.5. The rationale is that *knife* and *shoes* cannot be considered to be proper *Industrial items*, but they can be used together as 'industrial items' to a maximum extent of 0.5.

Relatedness between two items is determined by the path that connects them, with the highest-level node of the path playing a pivotal role. The distance from the root node to the highest-level node of path 'p' gives another component of relatedness. Nodes close to root node deal with attributes that cause the separation of the entire domain of items into various sub-domains. These attributes tend to be fundamental (or basic) as far as characterization of the domain is concerned, with their values having the ability to segregate and categorize items into various categories/sub-categories. Closer the highest-level node (of path 'p') to the root node, greater is the degree of separation between the items and consequently lower the relatedness. On the other hand, if the highest-level node of path 'p' is at a much lower level, the attribute characterizing the node will be fine-grained and probably specific to the sub-category. The path from the root node to the highest-level node of this path will be longer, with larger number of attribute values identical for the two items under consideration. Thus, the relatedness between the two items increases. We capture this notion by a measure called 'Highest-level relatedness'. The *highest-level relatedness,* $HR_{A,B}(p)$, for two items connected by path 'p' is defined as the level of the highest-level node [$H_{A,B}(p)$] in path 'p'.

$$\mathbf{HR_{A,B}(p) = level\,[H_{A,B}(p)]}$$

It is to be noted that the root node is at level 0 and subsequent levels from the root node are labeled by consecutive integers in increasing order starting with 1. Due to this nomenclature of labeling, the relatedness between two items A, B is directly proportional to $HR_{A,B}(p)$. Thus, for the crisp path connecting *knife* and ***shoes***, the highest-level relatedness $HR_{knife,\,shoes}(p) = 1$.

The length of the path (in terms of nodes) connecting items A and B in a fuzzy taxonomy gives an indication of the conceptual distance between them. Many paths, each of which represents a particular relationship between the two items, can connect two items. Each category node in the path has one of the two items (A, B) either as a 'child' or a 'descendant' node. Only the highest-level node has both items (A and B) as children/descendants nodes. Category nodes other than the highest-level node might consider attributes that are instantiated and specific to one of the two items under consideration. A large number of such distinct attributes specific to each item (resulting in a longer path) reduces relatedness between items. We define a measure of item-relatedness called *node-separation relatedness*, $NSR_{a,b}(p)$, which is the length of the simple path 'p' connecting the two items.

$NSR_{A,B}(p)$ = Length of the simple path 'p' connecting nodes A and B.

In Figure 1, node separation relatedness due to the crisp path connecting *knife* and *shoes* is 3 while that due to the fuzzy path connecting them is 5.

4 A Fuzzy Item-Relatedness Measure

In the previous section we had identified three measures that characterize the relatedness between two items A and B represented in a fuzzy taxonomy. These measures viz. highest-level node membership (HM), highest-level relatedness (HR) and node-separation relatedness (NSR) were defined for individual paths connecting two items A and B. Consider the two items *knife* and *shoes* in Figure 1. *Knife* is a crisp member of *household items* while it can also be considered as an *Industrial item* to the extent of 0.5. This arises due to the membership value of *knife* in *cutting tools* being 0.5. Similarly, *shoes* is a crisp member of *household items* while its membership in *industrial items* is 0.6. Thus, from the fuzzy taxonomy, four relationships arise between *knife* and *shoes*. One relationship arises when *knife* and *shoes* both behave or are used as *household items*, the second when both are used in an industrial context. The third and fourth relationships arise when *knife* behaves like a *household item* while *shoes* behave as an *industrial item* and vice versa respectively. Each of the four relationships, represented by a path in the fuzzy taxonomy contributes to a component of relatedness. The total relatedness between the two items is therefore a sum of these four components.

We note that relatedness between items A and B increases if either highest-level node membership (HM) or highest-level relatedness (HR) or both increase. On the other hand, relatedness between two items decreases as the node-separation relatedness measure (NSR) increases in value. Therefore, the overall relatedness contributed by the path 'p' can be stated as:

$$\mathbf{OR_{A,B}(p)} = \frac{\mathbf{(1+HR_{A,B}(p))(HM_{A,B}(p))}}{\mathbf{NSR_{A,B}(p)}}$$

Integer '1' is added to the highest-level relatedness in order to account for the case when root node appears in the path as highest-level node. Consequently, Total relatedness (summation over all paths) can be given by:

$$\mathbf{TR(A,B)} = \sum_{\mathbf{p}} \mathbf{OR_{A,B}(p)} = \sum_{\mathbf{p}} \frac{\mathbf{(1+HR_{A,B}(p))(HM_{A,B}(p))}}{\mathbf{NSR_{A,B}(p)}} \qquad \mathbf{(1)}$$

Consider a fuzzy taxonomy having a maximum depth 'k' with the root node being at level 0 (Fig. 2). Let us calculate the maximum relatedness that can be contributed by any path in this taxonomy. In order for the relatedness to be maximum here, the node separation relatedness (NSR) should take on the minimum possible value, while the highest-level relatedness measure (HR) should take on the maximum possible value and a 'crisp' path should connect the two items A and B. This condition will be fulfilled only if the path is as shown in Figure 2 (Viz, A →M →B). Here, $NSR_{A, B}(p) = 1$, $HR_{A,B}(p) = k\text{-}1$ and $HM_{A, B}(p) = 1$. This gives us $OR_{A, B}(p) = ((k - 1 + 1)/1) \times 1 = k$. This is the upper bound for the relatedness contributed by a single path for a fuzzy taxonomy of depth 'k'.

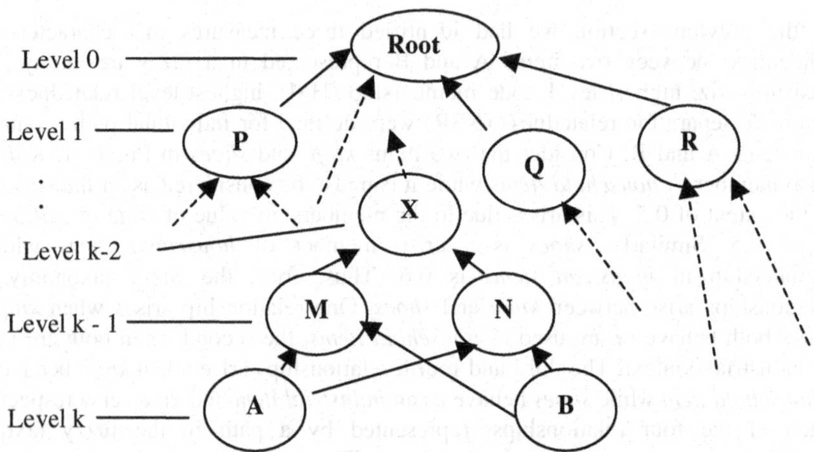

Fig. 2. A Fuzzy Taxonomy of level k

We note that in a fuzzy taxonomy of depth k, if an item A has crisp memberships in two immediate higher-level nodes, then two paths exist to the root node. Similarly, if item B also has crisp memberships in the same two immediate higher-level nodes, then a total of $2 \times 2 = 4$ crisp paths exist between the two items. The strength of total relatedness will be highest only if the length of the path is minimum i.e. the two non-leaf items are siblings, with respect to both their parent nodes (Fig. 2). There exist two paths of length 1 (we consider the number of nodes in the path and not the edges) each passing through the two parent nodes say M and N. Further, there exist two more paths having both the nodes M and N in them and some higher level nodes. The strength of the relationships will be the highest if these two paths are also as short as possible i.e. there is just one node say X that connects nodes M and N. Thus, we have four paths viz. A →M →B, A →N →B, A →M →X →N →B and A →N →X →M →B. The maximum relatedness for two items A and B that have these four crisp paths can be calculated using equation 1. This gives, Total Relatedness (A, B) = $2\times k + 2(k - 2 + 1)/3 = (2k) + 2(k\text{-}1) / 3 = (8k - 2)/3$. Based on this discussion we find that for the fuzzy taxonomy in Figure 1, the maximum theoretical relatedness for any two items A and B, having two paths each to the root node, is 10.

Let us calculate the 'Total relatedness' between *knife* and *shoes* as shown in Figure 1. Four paths exist between them and these are given below. The highest-level nodes in the path are italicized.

Path I: Crisp Path (Knife →kitchen items →*household items* → Footwear →shoes.)
Path II: Fuzzy path (Knife →cutting tools →tools →*industrial items* →safety items → industrial footwear → shoes)
Path III: Fuzzy – Crisp Path (Knife →cutting tools →tools →Industrial items →*All Items* →Household items →Footwear → Shoes)
Path IV: Crisp – Fuzzy Path(Knife →Kitchen Items →Household Items →*All Items* →Industrial Items →Safety Items →Industrial Footwear →Shoes)

Table 1. Determination of Total Relatedness between *Knife* and *Shoes*

Paths	A=Knife	B=Shoes	$NSR_{A,B}$	$HR_{A,B}$	$HM_{A,B}$	$OR_{A,B}$
I	Crisp (1.0)	Crisp (1.0)	3	1	1.0	0.667
II	Fuzzy (0.5)	Fuzzy (0.6)	5	1	0.5	0.2
III	Fuzzy (0.5)	Crisp (1.0)	6	0	0.5	0.0833
IV	Crisp (1.0)	Fuzzy (0.6)	6	0	0.6	0.1

Details regarding the measures of relatedness are shown in Table 1. Figures in the parentheses represent the membership value of the particular item in the path nodes. The total relatedness existing between *knife* and *shoes* as calculated by the proposed relatedness measure is 1.0503. We derived the maximum possible relatedness between any two items connected by four paths in the fuzzy taxonomy of Figure 2 to be 10. If we compare the two, we see that the relatedness is quite low. This is natural as *knife* and *shoes* are quite different items – varied in their application, purpose and usage. The only point connecting them is that both are *household items* and can be used together as industrial items to a maximum extent of 0.5 and not more.

5 Discussions

Here we consider a few item-pairs from the fuzzy taxonomy of Figure 1 and discuss the computed results. Table 2 shows the 'relatedness' components for five pairs of items from Figure 1. Let us consider the item pair (*shoes - safety shoes*). The 'crisp' path i.e. path I considers *shoes* as a *household item* and *safety shoes* as an *industrial item* while the fuzzy path (path II) considers the reverse. The relatedness components contributed by these two paths are quite low. This is to be expected as these paths consider the relationships when the two items behave (or are used) as items in different domains viz. household and industrial domains respectively. The fuzzy path contribution is lower than the crisp path contribution as the items cannot be considered as 'complete' members in their respective domains. Another interesting observation is with respect to the contribution made by paths III and IV. Path IV considers both *shoes* and *safety shoes* as *footwear* items under *household items*. Although the membership of *safety shoes* in *footwear* is fuzzy (0.4), the fact that the two items are siblings and thus can substitute one another in the same parent domain (household) to a maximum extent of 0.4 strengthens the relatedness between *shoes* and *safety shoes*. This aspect is reflected by a high contribution of 1.2 to the total relatedness measure. Similarly, *safety shoes* and *shoes* when used in industrial domain have a relatedness of 2.4. This is because in the industrial domain, the parent category node is one level lower than the parent of the two items (*footwear*) in the household domain and the membership value of *shoes* in *Industrial footwear* is higher (0.6).

Intuitively, we know that *Shoes* and *Safety Shoes* are footwear whose primary purpose is to protect the feet of the wearer. Naturally, we would expect a high relatedness between them, except for the fact that they are normally used in quite different settings. The primary functional purpose, which is the same, though in different settings is considered by the paths III and IV. Thus, these paths consider the extent to which the two items can substitute each other. Paths I and II however emphasize the fact that they belong to different domains. In this case the two items are likely to be used separately. The rationale for considering all paths that exist between the two items is that each path represents a particular way in which relationships can arise between items, either from the domain of application or from their functional purpose. Failure to consider any path will result in an understatement of the total relatedness.

Table 2. A comparison of Item Relatedness for sample item-pairs.

Sr. No.	Item A	Item B	Path I (Crisp–Crisp)	Path II (Fuzzy–Fuzzy)	Path III (Fuzzy–Crisp)	Path IV (Crisp–Fuzzy)	TR (A, B)
1	Knife	Shoes	0.667	0.2	0.0833	0.1	1.0503
2	Shoes	Safety Shoes	0.1667	0.0667	2.4	1.2	3.8334
3	Spoon	Shoes	0.667	----	----	0.1	0.767
4	Spoon	Safety Shoes	0.1667	----	----	0.2667	0.4334
5	Knife	Industrial Knife	0.1667	0.05	2.0	0.9	3.1167

Consider item pairs 3 and 4 from Table 2. *Spoon* and *Shoes* belong to the same domain viz. *Household Items*. Therefore, the contribution of crisp path I is greater than the contribution of the crisp path for *spoon* and *safety shoes* – items that belong to two different sibling domains. We note that *spoon* and *safety shoes* are related to a greater extent through path IV as compared to path I. This is because both are considered as items belonging to the *household* domain, even though the membership value of *safety shoes* in the *household* domain is fuzzy (i.e. 0.4). Item pair {*spoon, shoes*} is analogous to pair {*knife, shoes*} since *spoon* and *knife* are siblings. However, *spoon* does not have utility as *industrial item* unlike *knife*. This results in only two paths and lower relatedness between *spoon* and *shoes*. Item pair 5 is similar to pair 2 in the sense that the two items in each pair have their primary purpose as the same. However they are members of different domains. We note that *knife* and *industrial knife* are weakly related to each other as compared to *shoes* and *safety shoes*. This is due to lower fuzzy memberships in the case of items *knife* and *industrial knife*.

Relatedness measures can help in activities such as coupon design, shelf-space arrangement and the like by using the most appropriate relationships between items. For example, consider the item pair {*shoes, safety shoes*}. Path III gives the relationship that has the highest overall relatedness value (2.4) for these two items. Here, *shoes* and *safety shoes* are both considered as items in the industrial domain. A store manager can increase sales by giving discount coupons for the purchase of *shoes* to customers who have purchased *safety shoes*. More often than not, it would induce the customer to purchase *shoes*. On the other hand, giving discount coupons for the purchase of *safety shoes* to customers who have bought *shoes* may not be as effective in increasing sales, since all customers might not need *safety shoes*. This is brought out by a lower overall relatedness value (1.2) contributed by path IV (that considers the two items as household domain items) towards the total relatedness. Item-pairs that are deemed interesting by the relatedness measure, but that still have a frequent presence in the database of customer transactions, reflect knowledge that is at a conflict with the beliefs of the manager. Knowledge of items that sell together has direct relevance to the manager as it represents opportunities for furthering the sales of the retail store by means of actions such as cross-selling, coupon design, sales display design etc. For example, the relatedness between *spoon* and *shoes* is quite low (0.767). Therefore on frequent occurrence the pattern will be deemed interesting and brought to the attention of the manger. The manager may investigate the reasons and can consider various sales promotion schemes.

A Knowledge Management System has to support the creation of knowledge. Knowledge creation here consists of association rule mining and identification of relevant and interesting association rules that do not represent obvious knowledge. An important consequence of our taxonomy-based approach towards identification of interesting and relevant association rules is the codification of the tacit knowledge of managers in the structure of the fuzzy taxonomy tree. The fuzzy taxonomy tree represents relationships between items. These relationships are a direct reflection of the customer behaviour (purchasing and usage) as perceived by the managers. Such knowledge used to be previously resident mostly in the minds of the managers and thus unavailable in an explicit form. Now it can be made available in a more direct form viz. the taxonomy tree. Further, the action of comparing actual purchasing behaviour represented by the mined association rules and the beliefs of the managers helps the managers to update their knowledge as regards what is taking place in the field. This can lead to a revision of the manager's beliefs and can result further refinement of the taxonomy tree. Thus, the knowledge discovery and refinement process is not a static but an iterative dynamic process with the taxonomy tree getting revised as the manager learns more about the domain.

6 Summary

Knowledge Discovery in databases is an important knowledge creation activity of Knowledge Management. Here, we have introduced the notion of 'item-relatedness' to measure 'interestingness' of item-pairs occurring in association rules. The fact that these discovered item pairs despite being weakly related have a high frequency of occurrence in the database makes them interesting. We have introduced three notions of relatedness, which are then combined to give the strength of an individual relationship. We then combine the strengths of all relationships existing between items of an item-pair to get a total relatedness measure. We have also demonstrated its appropriateness and intuitiveness. Factors affecting 'relatedness' between items in an item pair include their primary and secondary functions, and domain of application contributing to different relationships. Each relationship is represented by a simple path. Strength of the 'relatedness' contributed by a path depends on length of the path, distance of the path from the root node and membership values of items in the path. Relatedness between two items increases if many such paths connect the two items. Identification of related patterns can help the manager concentrate on the few relevant patterns, draw appropriate conclusions and convert them into concrete actions.

References

[1] Alavi, M., Leidner, D.E.: Review: Knowledge Management and Knowledge Management Systems: Conceptual Foundations and Research Issues. MIS Quarterly Vol. 25(1), March, (2001) 107 – 136

[2] Chen, G., Wets, G., Vanhoof, K.: Representation and Discovery of Fuzzy Association Rules (FARs), Institute of applied Economic Research (ITEO), Limburg University Centre (LUC), Belgium, Research Paper Series, ITEO No: 00/01, March, (2000)

[3] de Graaf, J.M., Kosters, W.A., Witteman, J.J.W.: Interesting Fuzzy Association Rules in Quantitative Databases. In Proceedings of PKDD 2001 (The 5th European Conference on Principles of Data Mining and Knowledge Discovery), De Raedt, L., Siebes, A. Lecture Notes in Artificial Intelligence, Vol. 2168 , Freiburg, Germany, (2001) 140-151

[4] de Graaf, J.M., Kosters, W.A., Witteman, J.J.W.: Interesting Association Rules in Multiple Taxonomies, presented at BNAIC'00, Kaatsheuvel, November 1/2, In: A. van den Bosch and H. Weigand (ed.), (2000) 93-100

[5] Deo, N.: Graph Theory with Applications to Engineering and Computer Science, Prentice Hall of India Private Limited (1989)

[6] Hamilton, H.J., Fudger, D.R.: Estimating DBLEARN's Potential for Knowledge Discovery in Databases. Computational Intelligence, Vol. 11, No. 2, (1995) 280-296

[7] Klir, G.J., Yuan, B.: Fuzzy Sets and Fuzzy Logic: Theory and Applications, Prentice Hall of India Private Limited, New Delhi (1997)

[8] Silberschatz, A., Tuzhilin, A.: What makes Patterns Interesting in Knowledge Discovery Systems, IEEE Transactions on Knowledge and Data Engineering, Vol. 8, No. 6, (1996) 970-974

[9] Srikant, R., Agrawal, R.: Mining Generalized Association Rules, In Proceedings of the 21st VLDB conference, Zurich, Switzerland, September (1995) 407-419

[10] Subramanian, D.K., Ananthanarayana, V.S., Narasimha Murty, M.: Knowledge-Based Association Rule Mining using And-Or Taxonomies, to appear in Knowledge Based Systems (2002)

[11] Tan, P., Kumar, V., Srivastava, J.: Selecting the Right Interestingness Measure for Association Patterns, accepted for the Eighth ACM SIGKDD Int'l Conf. on Knowledge Discovery and Data Mining (KDD-2002), July 23-26, (2002)

Collaborative Knowledge Flow – Improving Process-Awareness and Traceability of Work Activities

Schahram Dustdar

Information Systems Institute, Distributed Systems Group,
Vienna University of Technology,
Argentinierstrasse 8/184-1, 1040 Wien
dustdar@infosys.tuwien.ac.at

Abstract. Next-generation business solutions in the domain of collaborative knowledge work require the integration of process modeling, groupware, and workflow technologies. This paper aims at discussing the fundamentals required for improving process-awareness for group collaboration. Prospective process-aware collaborative tools are required to record, map and manage processes involved in knowledge work: from creating ideas to their development into profit contributors. Development activities involve distributed teams working across organizations, time, and locations. We present a case study and an implementation of a collaborative knowledge flow solution, enabling the traceability of collaborative work activities for team members. This leads to increased efficiency of New Product Development teams as well as to faster time-to-market of product and services.

1 Introduction

Innovation and the development of products and services are the heart of every organization. Companies operating in highly competitive markets have an intensive need for continuous innovation and faster time-to-market for their products and services. Those products and services are the result of complex and expensive business processes. Involved processes and outcomes are highly knowledge intensive and therefore require sophisticated tools for capturing and managing knowledge capital within the enterprise, with partnering organizations, and with customers. Prospective process-aware cooperative tools are required to record, map and manage processes involved in knowledge work: from creating ideas to their development into profit contributors. Development activities involve distributed teams working across organizations, time, and locations. Every day the need for creating and replicating collaborative and innovative processes of the organization rises.

Solutions required for highly efficient and effective knowledge logistics (i.e. who does what, when, how, why, using which resources) [4] require new technological concepts, which go well beyond current software systems such as groupware, workflow [3, 5, 6, 7, 8, 12], project - and knowledge management. The reason is that processes as in product and service development require highly integrated and flexible

D. Karagiannis and U. Reimer (Eds.): PAKM 2002, LNAI 2569, pp. 389-397, 2002.

systems supporting multiple organizational structures interlinked with business processes and resources [e.g., 11]. A flexible state-of-the-art software architecture for distributed, cross-organizational and multi-disciplinary teams using multiple devices [2], is of paramount importance. To solve this problem future solutions must go further than current systems, which are solely based on documents, shared folders, workspace structures, modeling projects and processes without integration and feedback to their real execution. Some fundamental requirements are to

- provide a chain of linked information, which represents the results (what), who created them, how, when and why they were created (context).
- automatically build "knowledge trails" of activities and their relationships to knowledge processes as well as "Best practice" libraries.
- provide views on contextual information of work activities, how they relate to the work of others and their relationships to business processes. All relationships, activities, and actors described above may be distributed on the Internet.

Capturing the process by which knowledge is collaboratively developed is as important as documenting the output of group collaboration. In other words, "results" must provide more than data and information - they must also serve as resources for documenting "how we arrived at the outcome". We propose to streamline the connections between people and processes. People are the greatest factor in an organization's ability to compete based on knowledge. Successful results depend on knowledge transfer among various business processes. In every kind of business, core knowledge processes are intertwined and interdependent.

The remainder of this paper is structured as follows: Section 1.1 presents related work in this research area as well as states the main contribution of this paper. Section 2 analyses the requirements for collaborative knowledge flow systems based on a New Product Development (NPD) case study, including aspects on organizational modeling, processes and activities, data management and business objects, and the management of knowledge flow itself. Section 3 discusses design- and implementation issues related to the software presented in this paper. Finally, section 4 concludes the paper.

1.1 Contribution and Related Work

Collaborative systems can be categorized using multiple criteria and dimensions. Ellis [9], for example, presents a functionally oriented taxonomy of collaborative systems, providing the required understanding for integration of workflow and groupware systems –the fundamental information systems for support of collaborative knowledge flow within and between organizations. Ellis distinguishes between (i) Keepers, (ii) Communicators, (iii) Coordinators, and (iv) Team-agents. Keepers follow a shared workspace metaphor (e.g. a database) and provide access control on artifacts, versioning, and concurrency control. Communicators are messaging oriented and support explicit communications between participants. Coordinators are based on an organizational model and provide support for the ordering and coordination of activities.

Team-agents (e.g. applications or user-interface agents) provide domain-specific functionalities, such as meeting scheduling.

The contribution of this paper is the design and implementation of an innovative collaborative knowledge flow system - Caramba [4, 10] - motivated by a case study in the area of New Product Development. The proposed system integrates three of the categories discussed above: Keepers, Communicators, and Coordinators.

2 Collaborative Knowledge Flow

Advances in the area of Workflow (WfMS) and Groupware are often seen as substantial for supporting distributed knowledge work. Collaborative knowledge work in teams is increasing and as a consequence the use of collaborative knowledge flow solutions are becoming increasingly pervasive. WfMS have been defined as "technology based systems that define, manage, and execute workflow processes through the execution of software whose order of execution is driven by a computer representation of the workflow process logic" [13].

Groupware systems usually provide very low knowledge context information but enable users to retrieve, share, organize their work in workspaces, and to distribute artifacts. Document Management systems are increasingly integrated with WfMS as recent mergers demonstrate (e.g. Lotus Notes/OneStone). Project management (PM) software is still mostly viewed as software for individuals (i.e. project managers) and rarely offers collaborative or business process-aware solutions. Moreover, in most cases PM software is not integrated with corporate information systems and in fact is only utilized as a graphical modeling tool for outlining tasks. Most Knowledge Management (KM) systems on the market today are workspace-oriented and provide very simple support for modeling organizational structures (e.g. using roles only, but not skills). It is interesting to note that nearly no KM system provides interfaces to business process modeling and enactment systems (the domain of WfMS). Most KM-systems enable users to retrieve knowledge artifacts from repositories, but rarely allow distribution and process-awareness of collaborative work activities.

Knowledge can be viewed as information enriched with context. With context we mean information about the “who, when, how, and why”. As an example, consider an “Explorer”-like view on a file system. This view allows the person to see documents (artifacts) stored inside folders. The name of such folders might reflect project names themselves. The mentioned view on these documents does not contain further contextual information on what a person (yourself, or others) actually have to do (did) with it (e.g. create another document, send an e-mail to customer, call partner organization, etc.). For example if the person in the above example needs to see who actually received a document stored in any given (project) folder, he is required to manually retrieve his e-mail box in order to find this information. This simple example shows that links between artifacts, such as documents or database information, and activities performed by persons are usually not stored in information systems such as Groupware, KM or WfMS. However this linkage is of paramount importance for knowledge-intense business processes in order to provide contextual information on knowledge artifacts for processes such as New Product Development, which cannot be modeled using a WfMS. The reason for this is that NPD processes are semi-structured by nature and many exceptions occur during enactment of the processes. This makes it impractical to remodel the process model every time an exception occurs in order to continue the process flow.

2.1 Case Study

Consider a New Product Development (NPD) process such as in software development. In our case the team consists of 9 *persons* and has the goal to jointly develop a new product and some product extensions. All team members have a set of *skills* (e.g. Java, Oracle, etc.), which are fundamental for the success of the overall development process. The overall NPD process consists of a set of *subprocesses* (e.g. architectural design, database design etc.). Since team members have different skill-sets, they also have different *roles* (e.g. Product manager) in the NPD team. Based on the roles, team members have different *tasks* (e.g. estimate project costs) to fulfill. The NPD team requires a collaborative knowledge flow system in order to model and to enact their NPD process. Furthermore, it is required to model the organizational structure of the team (persons, roles, skills, tasks etc.). Finally the system should allow integrating NPD artifacts (e.g. source code, management reports etc.) to the appropriate activities the team members are supposed to work on.

2.2 Organizational Modeling

In order to manage structural information of the work team, we [4] have implemented a component (Caramba Object Center) managing three categories of objects: Organizational, Dynamic, and Business Objects. The *Organizational Objects* category contains the following objects: Persons, Roles, Groups, Skills, Units, Organization, Tasks, and Document-Templates. The *Dynamic Object* category consists of Processes (i.e. templates consisting of linked activities modeled as directed graphs) and Workcases (enacted Processes). The *Business Objects* are a means of integrating corporate databases into our collaborative knowledge flow system. The underlying metamodel enables modification and customization of the attributes of the objects and their relationships (e.g. a Person may have many Roles).

Figure 1 depicts a graphical view on the Object Center objects with all Skills to be found in the NPD team. Figure 2 depicts a matrix view on the Persons and the Skills to be found in the team and their relationships. Additional links (relationships) can be modeled by double-clicking the appropriate cell. Figure 3 provides an example of our case study, where the object *Person* (in this case Everitt Lynn) is associated with *Tasks* from a modeled process, (Fig. 3, left window) and Links (artifacts associated with the Person, e.g. database objects (bug reports) and other documents (e.g. a Word document).

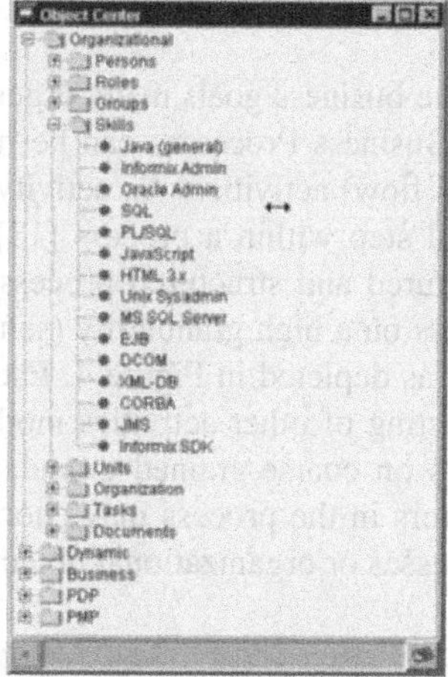

Fig. 1. Object Center: Skills

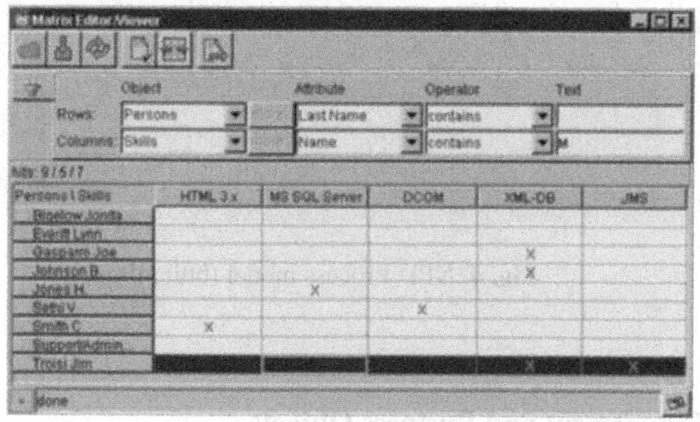

Fig. 2. Matrix Editor: Association of Person and Skills

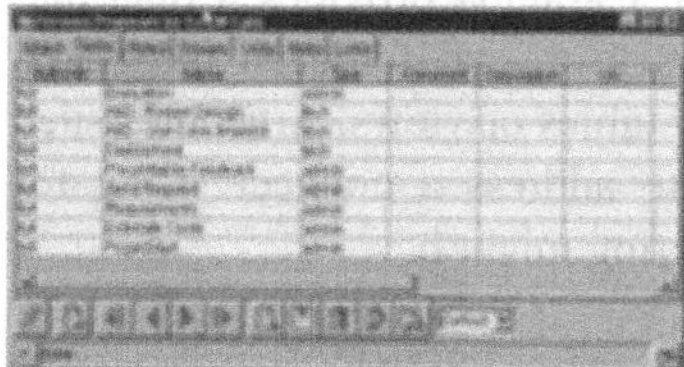

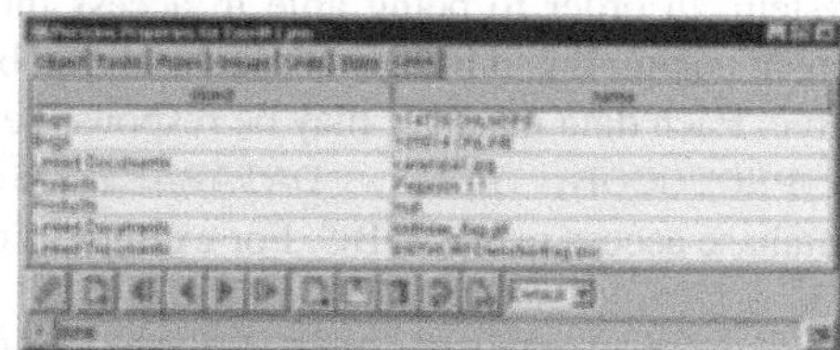

Fig. 3. Person associations: Tasks and associated artifacts

2.3 Processes and Activities

In order to efficiently achieve business goals many organizations model their business processes and enact them. Business Processes can be represented as directed graphs consisting of linked (control flow) activities. An activity constitutes a logical piece of work, which forms a logical step within a process [13]. The literature differentiates between ad-hoc, semi-structured and structured processes [e.g. 8]. In our case study we modeled the NPD process on a high granularity (semi-structured) by modeling six main phases (subprocesses) as depicted in Figure 4. Each activity box in Figure 4 represents a subprocess consisting of other activities modeled as a directed graph. The NPD process shown here is on coarse-grained granularity level and will serve as a template to be enacted. Actors in the process may choose to "coordinate" work item (activities) to other subprocesses or organizational objects (e.g. exceptions).

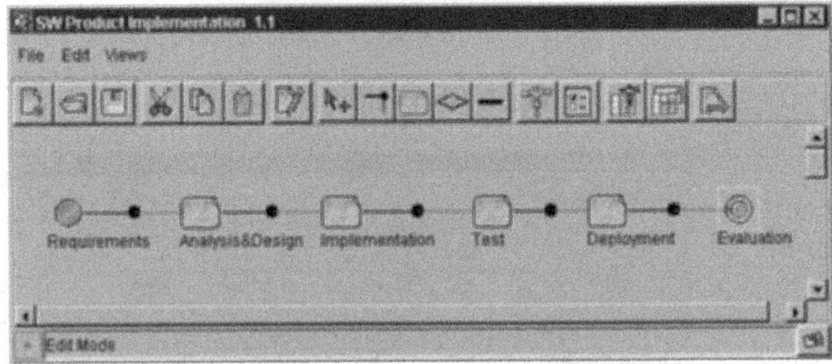

Fig. 4. NPD Process model (build time)

2.4 Data Management and Business Objects

Caramba utilizes data managers, which enable organizations to integrate corporate database tables (e.g. bug report tables) into the Caramba collaborative work management system. In order to being able to access those tables, Caramba provides a data manager containing information such as database name, user, etc. for each integrated table. Each data manager may be responsible for many tables or views. Attributes such as `PROTOCOL`, `PORT`, `DATABASE` are utilized to address a connect string for database access using JDBC. For example a connect string might be:

```
jdbc:oracle:thin:@dbserver:1844:Caramba,PROTOCOL=jdbc.ora
cle.thin,SERVER=dbserver, PORT=1844, DATABASE=Caramba
```

Integrated database tables are called Caramba Business Objects (CBOs). Utilizing the Caramba metamodel the administrator may configure attributes of the table to be displayed inside Caramba. CBO-records may be "attached" during the coordination activities of team members, similar to file-attachments. In our case study CBOs are used for tables such as source code, bug reports, management reports, review reports etc.

When a Caramba object is accessed the appropriate Caramba data manager is loaded and access to the database table is provided. Figure 5 shows the database model of Caramba data manager and its relation to the Caramba tables.

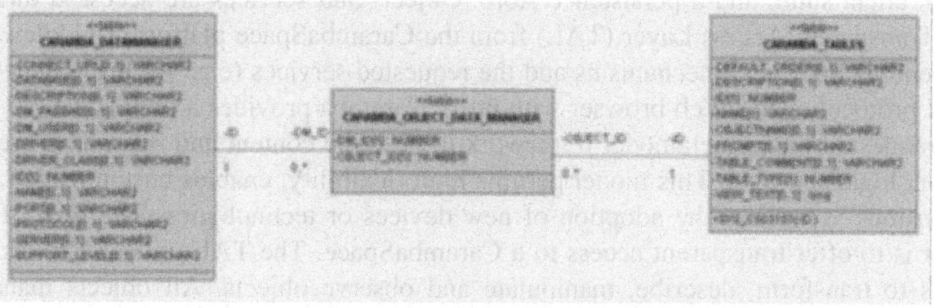

Fig. 5. Caramba Data Manager

2.5 Knowledge Flow Management

The main end user component (Caramba Activity Center) provides the management hub for managing personal worklists consisting of *work items*, personal *actions* performed on work items, and personal *scheduling* information on work items. The Activity Center is based on a messaging metaphor and aims at integrating the first three collaborative systems paradigms discussed by Ellis [9]. The Object Center provides the features required by *Keepers*. The Activity Center implements the *Communicator* features, and the *Coordinator* is realized by the Caramba Process Editor.

Caramba users (in our case study software engineers working on joint projects) may access work items being routed to them (coordination) and retrieve a knowledge trail of all "coordinations" based on any work item they are associated with. This allows each team member to monitor the progress of the overall project and increases the process-awareness of personal activites. Figure 6 depicts the Caramba Activity Center with windows for personal actions, time/cost related information, personal scheduling information, and a view on the overall progress for a selected work item.

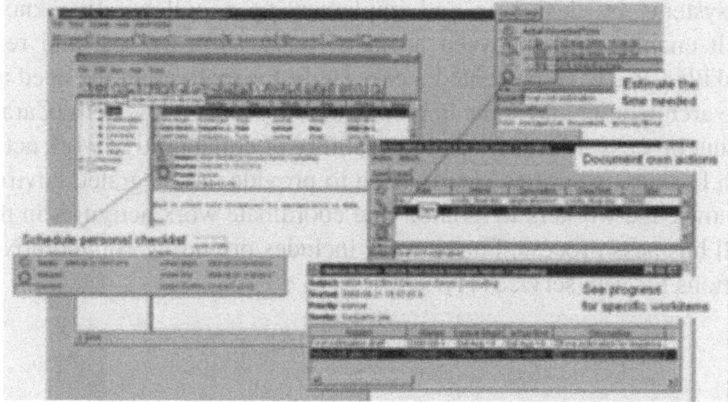

Fig. 6. Caramba Activity Center

3 Design and Implementation

The Caramba software architecture [4, 10] is composed of multiple layers: middleware, client suite, and a persistence store. Objects and services are accessed through the Transparent Access Layer (TAL) from the CarambaSpace platform (middleware). Depending on access mechanisms and the requested services (e.g. via Java client with RMI protocol or via Web browser with http), Caramba provides a unique way to handle requests using a metamodel framework to describe content and separating presentation, logic and data. This model permits high flexibility, enables customization, and extensions as well as the adoption of new devices or technologies. The goal of this layer is to offer transparent access to a CarambaSpace. The TAL utilizes various services to transform, describe, manipulate and observe objects. All objects managed through a CarambaSpace are well described using a metamodel description framework. Objects can be customized in their structure (e.g. adding columns to tables, adding relations to objects) and their presentation by adopting their metamodel description. Any changes are dynamically reflected by client components. Based on the metamodel description framework Caramba enables various options to customize data and content and to integrate data from different resources (e.g. corporate databases). This layer also provides facilities for fine-grained object notification services and the implementation of customized services based on object observers. The middleware does not manage states and persistence of objects. Objects are stored, manipulated, and retrieved via the Persistence Layer (PEL). Caramba middleware and client are written in Java and leverage standard Java based technologies (e.g. JDBC, JNDI, HTTP, etc.) and Internet standards (e.g. SMTP) to access and integrate corporate information systems.

4 Conclusion

This paper contributes to the goal of building process-aware collaborative work management systems by designing and implementing a collaborative knowledge flow solution. It enables *links* between artifacts, business processes, and resources (e.g. persons, skills). We have presented a case study for motivating the need and have discussed the architecture and some implementation issues of a system (Caramba) aiming at improving process-awareness and traceability of collaborative work activities. Next-generation business solutions clearly have to provide an integrated environment, supporting knowledge workers to monitor and coordinate work activities in the context of the overall business process. Future work includes providing collaborative knowledge flow solutions for web services [1].

References

1. Baina, K., Dustdar, S. (2002). Web-Services Coordination Model. International Workshop on Cooperative Internet Computing (CIC 2002), in conjunction with VLDB conference, August, Hong Kong, Kluwer Academic Press.
2. Bolcer, G.A. "Magi: An Architecture for mobile and disconnected Workflow", *IEEE Internet Computing*, May and June 2000, pp. 46 -54.
3. Bussler, C. "Enterprise-wide Workflow Management", *IEEE Concurrency*, 7(3), pp. 32-43.
4. Caramba Labs Software AG (2002) http://www.CarambaLabs.com
5. Casati, F. et al., "Developing e-Services for composing e-services", *Proceedings CaiSE 2001*, Computer Science Lecture Notes, Springer Verlag, 2001, pp. 171-186.
6. Chen, Q. et al., "Peer-to-Peer Collaborative Internet Business Servers", HP-Labs Technical Working Paper HPL-2001-14.
7. Craven, N. and Mahling, D.E. "Goals and Processes: A Task Basis for Projects and Workflows", *Proceedings COOCS International Conference*, Milpitas, CA, USA, 1995.
8. Dayal, U. et al., "Business Process Coordination: State of the Art, Trends, and Open Issues", *Proceedings of the 27th VLDB Confererence, Roma, Italy*, 2001.
9. Ellis, C. (Skip), A Framework and Mathematical Model for Collaboration Technology, in. Coordination Technology for Collaborative Applications –Organizations, Processes, and Agents (Conen and Neumann, Eds.), Springer Verlag, 1998, pp.121-144.
10. Hausleitner, A. and Dustdar, S. "*Caramba - Ein Java basiertes Multimedia Koordinationssystem*", In Erfahrungen mit Java. Projekte aus Industrie und Hochschule. Silvano Maffeis, et al. (Eds.), dPunkt-Verlag, Heidelberg 1999.
11. J. Puustjävi, and H. Laine, "Supporting cooperative inter-organizational business transactions", *Proceedings DEXA 2001*, Computer Science Lecture Notes, Springer Verlag, 2001, pp. 836-845.
12. Schal, T., *Workflow Management Systems for Process Organizations*. New York: Springer 1996.
13. Workflow Management Coalition (WfMC), *Workflow Management Specification Glossary*, http://www.wfmc.org

Process–Oriented Knowledge Management Systems Based on KM-Services: The PROMOTE® Approach

Robert Woitsch[1] and Dimitris Karagiannis[2]

[1] BOC-ITC, Baeckerstraß 5, A-1010 Vienna
robert.woitsch@boc-eu.com
[2] University of Vienna, Department of Knowledge Engineering, Bruennerstraß 72, A-1210 Vienna
dk@dke.univie.ac.at

Abstract. This article describes the PROMOTE approach, to define and implement a service-based Knowledge Management System (KMS) that has been developed during an EC-funded project. The aim is to define a modelling language that is used to analyse, document and implement a KMS on the basis of so-called Knowledge Management Processes (KMPs). KMPs define the knowledge interaction between knowledge workers in a process-oriented manner and consists of activities that are supported by knowledge management key actions (KA) like searching, categorising or storing information. These knowledge management key actions are supported by IT-based knowledge management services (KM-Service). The prototype of PROMOTE® is briefly mentioned to discuss the KMP-models and the service based KMS.

1 Introduction

Since 95 [1] the number of knowledge management (KM) publications are growing constantly, the KM tool market is rising and KM becomes a serious management discipline in today's economy [2]. Within the EC-project PROMOTE® [3] an overall framework of KM has been defined based on three layers of KM [4][5]:

- **Knowledge layer**: The knowledge layer is seen as the application layer of the KMS. It defines the application scenario of KM. The selection of the right scenario, the risk analysis and the focus of the KMS are critical success factors. The selection of the application scenario is a strategic decision and often seen as KM strategy.
- **Organisational memory layer**: This layer describes the organisational memory that is defined by (Hedberg81) as "The Organisational Memory defines the cognitive structure of information proceeding processes of the whole organisation, the **Theory of Action**" (translated from German) [6]. For an efficient management of the organisational memory these cognitive structures and information proceeding processes have to be defined, analysed and documented in an explicit way. To describe the cognitive structure there are modelling languages such as Ontologies [7], Topic Maps (TM) [8] or Mind Maps [9], that describe the static view of the organisational memory. There are different approaches to describe the information proceeding processes based on

D. Karagiannis and U. Reimer (Eds.): PAKM 2002, LNAI 2569, pp. 398-412, 2002.

process chains [6][10][11]. PROMOTE® defines a modelling language, that include both the static view of TM and the dynamic view of KMPs. The aim was to embed the new KM models into already existing working environment, business processes and resource models.

- **Technological-Layer:** This layer describes the Solution of the KMS, that are mainly IT-based. The PROMOTE® approach defines categories of KAs to associate functionalities supporting these activities to enable a service based framework. This leads to a service based architecture of the KMS. The idea of this concept is to enable a model based integration of KM-Services, that can be provided from several tools, whereas the PROMOTE® models are used for co-ordinating and integrating these services. PROMOTE® can be seen as a knowledge based application integration platform, that is managed by models.

Using the above terminology, this article focuses on the organisational memory layer and describes the interfaces to the technological layer. In the following some key issues of the implementation of service-based KMS are depicted, the organisational memory layer is described in more detail and an overview of the implementation scenario at the technological layer will be given.

2 Key Issues of Service Based KMS

There are some fundamental questions when implementing a service-based KMS. The following list gives an overview of the challenges and depicts the focus of this text.

Why implement knowledge management?

There are theoretical thoughts about knowledge enhancing by sharing and having a positive production factor [12]. This led to the wrong assumption that KM in general improves business. There are many KM projects that clearly missed their goals [13]. KM has to be carefully planed in certain business areas under well defined and well analysed situations. Considering this leads to success stories in KM like the Siemens ShareNet [14]. The selection of the "certain business areas" and the analysis is part of the strategic decision of an organisation. The result of this selection is the exact definition of an application scenario including a risk-analysis. This leads to the next question that is the focus of this text.

How to implement a KMS, considering the business objectives?

KM is an interdisciplinary approach including human-, technical- or organisational-oriented approaches. The focus of this text are organisational aspects using a process based method [15]. There are three challenges that are expressed in quotations of existing KM definitions [16]:

KM should "enhance customer value" (Beckman), "aim to achieve the company's objectives" (van der Spek) or "produce biggest payoff" (Hibbard). These quotations define the first challenge which can be expressed as follows: "How can a method guarantee, that a KM approach creates additional value to an organisation?".

"KM is the systematic, explicit, and deliberate building, renewal and application of knowledge" (Wiig) as well as "the explicit control and management of knowledge" (van der Spek). The second challenge can therefore be expressed as: "How can a

method support the explicit control of knowledge, in a transparent, well structured and platform independent way?".
In this context knowledge is seen as "humanised information" (Karagiannis) where information can reside in "databases, on papers, or in people's heads" (Hibbard). This leads to the third challenge: "How can a method describe the context and the content of the organisational knowledge?".

The following text depicts the PROMOTE® approach that addresses theses three challenges first by starting with the analysis of business processes to identify "knowledge intensive tasks" and to select activities where "an explicit control of knowledge" leads to a better performance of the business process. The second step is to introduce a model language that defines the knowledge interaction between knowledge worker in a process oriented manner and to combine the dynamic aspects with static aspects by a so-called "Knowledge Structure Model" that categorises knowledge resources and defines access rights to address the third challenge. Section 3 addresses this challenge by introducing the PROMOTE® model language and the PROMOTE® method.

How to finally realise the KMS?
The realisation of a KMS is the implementation of an integration platform that combines IT-Based and non IT-Based KM-Service. IT-Based Solutions are tools like Search Engines, Data Warehouses, Document Management Systems or Groupware tools, whereas non IT-Based Solutions are Coffee Corners, Space Management, Job-Rotation or the organisational culture. The challenge is therefore the heterogeneity of the tools that have to be integrated. PROMOTE® uses a model based approach for integration. The tools are seen as collections of KM-functionalities, that are interpreted as KM-services. The integration platform provides KM-Services to the user that are structured by KMPs.

The Components of PROMOTE® are seen as proxy-containers of KM-Services that are KM-functionalities of external KM-tools. Section 4 addresses this topic by introducing the KM-Service concept and depicts an example of the application scenario tested within the project.

How to evaluate the benefit?
The evaluation of KM is a critical issue and an interesting research field. PROMOTE® addresses this topic by enabling an interface to a Balanced Score Card (BSC) tool ADOScore® [17] to adapt the BSC concept to the needs of KM. This topic is only briefly mentioned in section 5.

3 Organisational Memory Layer – PROMOTE® Models and Method

This section depicts the PROMOTE® models that describe the Organisation Memory Layer and gives an overview about the method that is used to analyse the Organisational Memory (OM).

3.1 Organisational Memory Models

After a requirement analysis from the PROMOTE® application scenarios, a model language has been defined that is sufficient to describe KM approaches in a method and tool independent way [18][19].

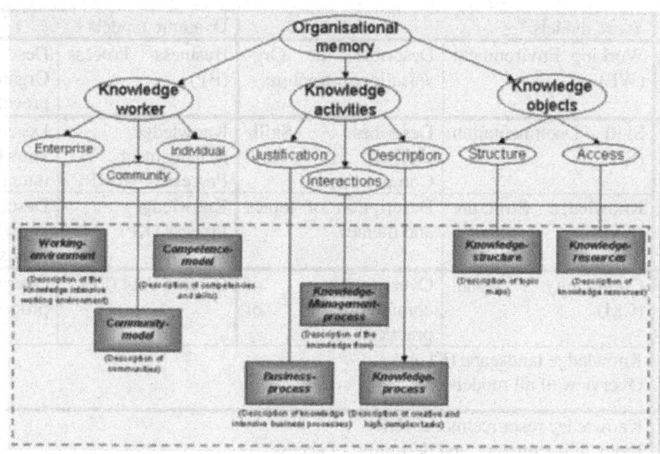

Fig. 1. Depicts the PROMOTE® model language that is used to describe the OM and the knowledge interactions between knowledge workers

This model language is based on the grammar of the natural language using "subject", "predicate" and "object" whereas the subjects are the knowledge workers, the predicates are the knowledge activities and the objects are the knowledge objects.

The "knowledge workers" are described on an individual level using skill profiles (skill model), on a community level to describe communities of practice (community model) and on an enterprise level to describe the competence profile of departments (working environment).

The already mentioned "knowledge activities" are justified by business processes, the interaction with the OM is defined using the previously mentioned "Knowledge Management Processes" and knowledge intensive tasks (that have been defined as critical due the analysis of the business process) are described in detail using a special type of process a so-called "Knowledge Process".

The "knowledge objects" are categorised using "Knowledge Structure Models" and accessed using a modelled index, the "Knowledge Resource Model".

3.2 Organisational Memory Formal Model

The knowledge modelling graph (KMG) is a formal concept for describing knowledge process modelling in PROMOTE®. A KMG is composed by the tupel KMG:=<BG,KG>. BG is a business graph with BG = $\{BP^*, KE, \rho_{ij}\}$ where BP is the business process, KE is the knowledge environment and ρ_{ij} denotes the relations between BP and a specific KE [20]. The second part of the tupel is the Knowledge management graph KG defining specific knowledge actions related to business activities. KG is a knowledge management graph with KG={KnMPr*}. The Business Graph and the Knowledge Graph can be transformed to Business Execution Graph and Knowledge Execution Graph ($BG \rightarrow BG_e$ and $KG \rightarrow KG_e$).

Table 1. PROMOTE® model language. The different model types are listed below

	Static models		Dynamic models	
Business models	Working Environment (WE)	Describes the Organisational structure.	Business Process (BP)	Describes the Organisational processes.
Knowledge models	Skill Documentation (SD)	Describes Skill-profiles and Competences.	Knowledge Management Processes (KMP)	Describes knowledge interaction.
	Knowledge Structure (KS)	Description of topics and themes.	Knowledge Process (KP)	Describes knowledge intensive tasks.
Overview model	Community Model (CM)	Overview of communities of practice.	Process Pool (PP)	Overview of processes.
	Knowledge landscape (KL) Overview of all models			
Index	Knowledge resource model (KR) Index of documents, and definition of access			

The following section depicts the formal model that defines the PROMOTE® model language.

In the following examples for handling structured knowledge are given. Basically knowledge actions KA (query, E-Mail etc.) are used as operators drawing a conclusion for a specific query. Basically we have

$$Q\,(KA_1, KA_2, KA_3,\ldots, KA_P)$$

This means that the execution of the logical sequence of KA_p provides an answer for a given query Q. Here the logical sequence of the executed knowledge activities is very important. The answer may also be negative, e.g. the knowledge item requested was not found.

This model will be more complex by taking into account the respective business processes and the knowledge environment. For example, if we want to know how many employees E have a specific skill (SK) o, we have the query

$$Q(\#E, SK_o, \{KA_1, KA_2, KA_3,\ldots, KA_P\})$$

which can be resolved by finding the KA_p: $\forall\, E_k$ count sk_o.

An entry into the OM is for example realised by

$$E(E_k, OU_l, b_{kl}, \{KA_1, KA_2, KA_3,\ldots, KA_P\}).$$

This means that a new employee E_k belongs (b_{kl}) from now on to the organisational unit OU_l. This realised via the "programs" $\{KA_1, KA_2, KA_3,\ldots, KA_P\}$. In practice only one "program" KA_p will be necessary (e.g. entry in database).

3.3 Use Case of Organisational Memory Model

This section describes the Use Case "Enhanced Quality Management in Software Development" of the project PROMOTE and depicts the method how the OM has been modelled in this Use Case. Starting point of this Use Case was a "Software Development" process, that defines the critical activities within an application implementation process. Three "knowledge intensive tasks" have been analysed in more detail, "Functional Specification", "System Design" and "Program Design". These three activities have been insufficiently supported by Lotus Notes, an intranet search engine and a HTML portal. The challenge was to support these three activities in a process-oriented manner using PROMOTE and to integrate the models in the existing environment.

Business Process and Working Environment as Starting point
The first step was to collect all existing processes as the BP "Software Development" was already modelled in an event-process-chain format, whereas the description of the working environment only existed in a Lotus Notes Database.

The existing BP "Software Development Process" has been imported into PROMOTE® and stored as a "Knowledge Based Business Process" to distinguish between the BP that is managed by the organisational department and the new Knowledge Based Business Process that is managed by a new KM group. The working environment model has been imported from Lotus Notes using an Adapter.

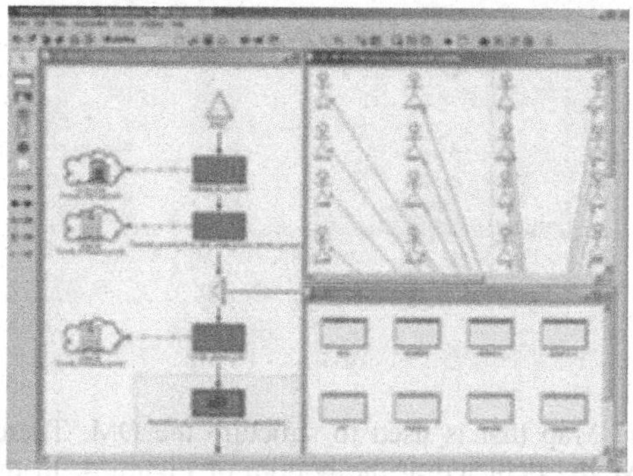

Fig. 2. Depicts the BP "Software Development Process" where three critical activities have been marked as "Knowledge Intensive Tasks" (KIT) and important Knowledge Resources have been linked to activities. The Working Environment model including employees and organisational units have been imported by a Lotus Notes Adapter listing the employees and the organisational units

Knowledge Management Processes and Skill Profiles
Based on the models depicted in Figure 2 the BP has been analysed for knowledge interaction in a process oriented manner at KITs. The Working environment model has been analysed in more detail introducing Skill-Profiles.

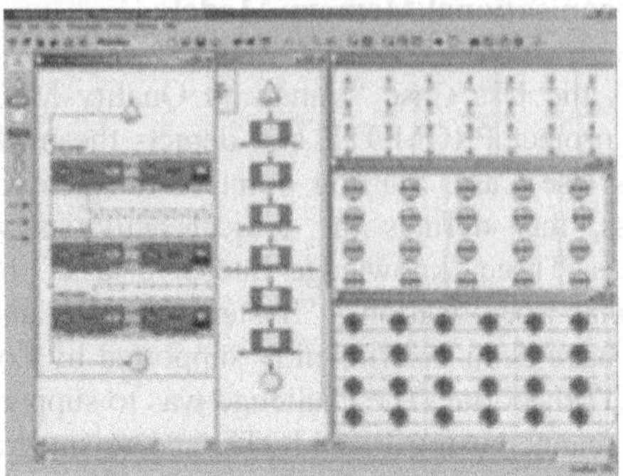

Fig. 3. Depicts a screen shot of KMPs and Skill models, that have been derived out of workshops. The KMPs define the knowledge interaction between knowledge worker in a process oriented manner, whereas the skill-documentation defines the structure of the skill profiles. In this scenario four different types of Skill-Profiles (Ability-self, Ability-manager, Interests, Products) have been defined

Knowledge Structure and Knowledge Resources

The third step, was to define the Knowledge Structure via Topic Maps and the different types of knowledge resources in workshops.

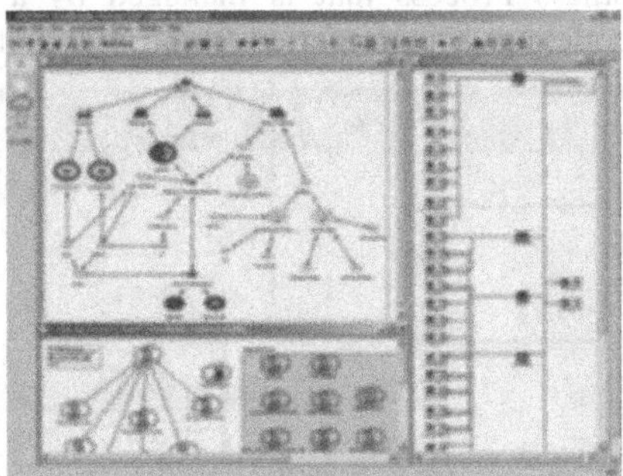

Fig. 4. Depicts a Topic Map that is used to structure the OM. There are references to the Knowledge Resource Model depicted at the bottom of Figure 4. In this application scenario HTML, Multi Media files, Lotus Notes and Office Documents have been selected as types of Knowledge Resources

In overall there are 44 models that have been defined, 15 out of them have been generated automatically from Lotus Notes (3 out of the 15 automated models had to be maintained manually). Four of the remaining 29 models are Topic Maps that have been imported from an existing tool using the ISO13250. One BP was imported from a different format. 12 models are reference models that are application scenario independent and have been copied into the model repository. The remaining 12 models have been modelled manually specially for this application scenario.

These models describe the OM of that application scenario and define an organisational memory index. To make this index operational is discussed in the next section.

4 Technological Layer - Making KMPs Operational

This sections depicts the realisation of a KMS based on models. There is a static aspect describing an index of the organisational memory and a dynamic aspect describing the integration of different KM Services. In the following KM-Services are depicted in more detail and the integration using a platform like PROMOTE® is discussed.

4.1 KMP an Evolutionary Approach

Process-oriented KM using KMPs is seen as the third step of an evolutionary approach for integrating KM-Services.

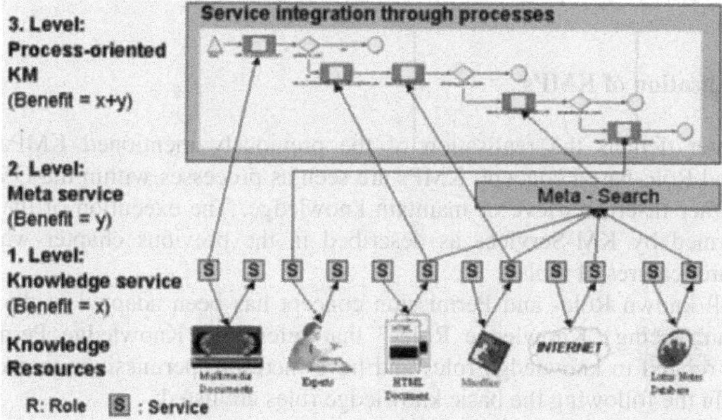

Fig. 5. Depicts the tree levels of Service integration where knowledge resources (REm) are defined as knowledge carrier. These knowledge resources are accessed via KM-Services to provide a certain benefit

This means that the knowledge activity KA1 is executed by the KM-Service KMS_1 as $KMS_1(KA_1)$. KMS_1 could be a Query (Q) or an Entry (E) to achieve a benefit B=x, where $x=f(r_1)$ is a function of the result. Benefit B is seen as a factor between 0 and 1 that influences a criterion of the business process like time, cost or quality, whereas r is a tupel from quality and quantity of information $r:=<i_{qn},i_{qu}>$.

The next evolutionary step is to combine several KM-Services to a Meta-Service like a query consisting of several sub-queries $Q(\{Q(KA_1),Q(KA_2),\ldots,Q(KA_p)\},KA_m)$ to achieve a benefit B=y, where $y=f(r_1+r_2+\ldots+r_p)$. KA_m is the knowledge activity performing the meta-query that is most likely a trivial service like the addition of results and rarely a sophisticated service like a pattern comparison.

The benefit f(r) must not be linear as there exists a paradigm within KM like "Information is useful, but too much information is useless due to information-overflow". This leads to the assumption that if $r_x < r_y$ it is likely that the benefit $f(r_x) < f(r_y)$ as one single service hardly creates an information overflow. Based on this theory, meta-services like Meta-Search Engines are common approaches within a KMS.

The third evolutionary step is to combine several KM-Services in a process-oriented manner using KMPs for $Q(KA_1,KA_2,\ldots KA_3)$ as described in section 3.2. The benefit now depends on the process model that has different elements. A sequence has the benefit $B=f(r_1)+f(r_2)$, a parallelism has $B=f(r_1+r_2+\ldots+r_p)$ whereas decisions in a process influence the benefit with $B=\max(f(r_1),f(r_2))$. With these elements it is possible to define a process like in Figure 5 where sequences, parallelism in form of meta-services and decisions are used to optimise the benefit.

This concept is useful to optimise the benefit of KMPs linked to the BPs. As there are many KMPs supporting different criteria of the BP, it is likely that the KMPs interfere each other. These effects have to be analysed by using e.g. a Balanced Score Card concept to define knowledge goals and knowledge sub-goals and check the performance.

The next chapter describes how the KM-Service concept has been put into praxis during the PROMOTE® project.

4.2 Realisation of KMPs

This chapter depicts the realisation of the previously mentioned KMPs using a Service and Role-based concept. KMPs are seen as processes within the OM that are used to either insert, retrieve or maintain knowledge. The execution of these KMPs are performed by KM-Services as described in the previous chapter where KM-Services are features of tools.

The well known Role- and Permission concept has been adapted to the needs of KMPs, introducing "Knowledge Roles" that refers to "Knowledge Permissions". Users are related to knowledge roles and have therefore permissions to access KM-Services. In the following the basic knowledge roles are listed:

- **Knowledge User (KU): "*Read*"**

The KU takes advantage from the system to use knowledge. This role has no responsibilities within the OM.

- **Knowledge Worker (KW): "*Content*"**

The KW enters, evaluates and maintains the knowledge within the system

- **Knowledge Process Designer (KPD): "*Structure*"**

The KPD is the formalist, who describes the OM in a specific format that is used by the KMS as an index.

- **Knowledge Manager (KM): "*Organisational Responsibility*"**

The KM is responsible for the selection of the trial case, the risk analysis and strategic knowledge goals. The responsibility is to achieve the strategic goals and knowledge strategies with KM approaches.

- **Knowledge Interface Engineer (KIE): "*Customizing, Adaptation, Configuration*"**

The KIE is responsible for the transfer between different formats of organisational memory indices.

The Components of PROMOTE® (Model Editor, Yellow Pages, Search Engines, Document Co-ordinator, Micro Articles, Model Viewer, Knowledge Cockpit and My-Workbench) define a logical relationship of KM-Services. Each component consists of several KM-Services that define the functionality.

The KMPs of PROMOTE® define a sequential relationship of KM-Services for the six categories Knowledge Model Building Processes, Knowledge Identification Processes, Knowledge Accessing Processes, Knowledge Storage Processes, Knowledge Distribution Processes and Knowledge Evaluation Processes.

These processes are defined using the model language described in chapter 3.1, and executed by Instances of KM-Services.

4.3 KM-Services

The concept of Web-Service is a common concept when implementing Web-Applications, this chapter depicts the adaptation of the Service-based concept to the needs of KM.

4.3.1 Web-Services vs. KM-Services

The technical definition of a Web-Service can be formulated as "basically a messaging framework, with the only requirements to be capable of sending and receiving messages to the application code" [21]. These web-services are kept within a service container, the web application server, whereas the application code is a piece of software that actually performs the task. The Web-Service can be seen as a translator between the Web-User Interface and the application without any specification of the application size. This means, that the application code of a service can be a piece of software that only makes an entry in a log-file, or it can be a high sophisticated Search-Engine that automatically searches through the Internet, categorises Web-Pages and updates the pattern on a regular basis.

This architecture enables the access of platform independent Web-Services whereas the service application code is performed on a specific platform. It does not matter whether the application service are written in Java and the browser written in C++, or the application services deployed on a Unix box while the browser is deployed on Windows [21].

The Web-Based architecture is obviously a common design when realising a KMS. Within PROMOTE® this architecture has been mapped to the concept of KM-Services. A KM-Application code is seen as a piece of Software that is an enabler of a Knowledge activity (KA), that can be accessed by a KM-Service. The KM-Service are managed by the KM integration platform of PROMOTE®.

The Component "Yellow Pages" for example collects KM-Services for expert search. The KM-Service "Categorised Person Search" is a Search Engine, that searches for experts based on Topic Maps. The PROMOTE® integration platform manage these KM-Services as described in chapter 4.2 whereas the KM-Services are translations objects, that transform the User request into a tool specific command. The actual task is executed by a program that is either implemented as a module of PROMOTE® or as an external tool independent of platform and interface.

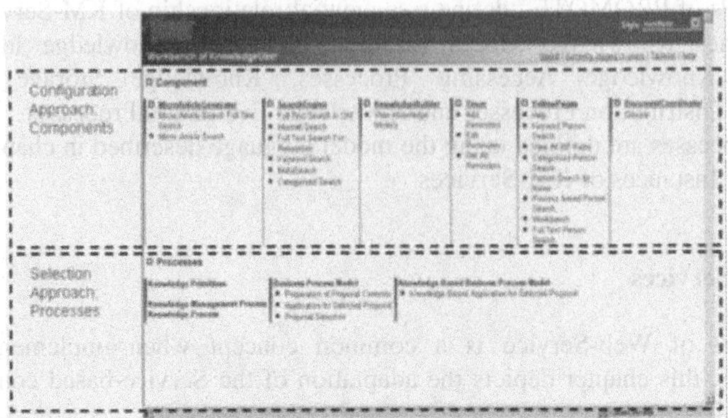

Fig. 6. Depicts a screenshot of the Knowledge Users Workbench, where services are configured for each Component and processes are selected out of the OM-repository

4.3.2 Execution of a KM-Service Based KMP

This section depicts an application scenario from PROMOTE®, to explain the different Knowledge roles, the KM-Service concept and the KMPs as an integration platform.

The scenario is, to import skill-profiles from a Lotus Notes Database by the Knowledge Interface Engineer (KIE), to adapt the model using a graphical model editor by the Knowledge Process Designer (KPD), to maintain the model by the Knowledge Worker (KW) and finally to use the model for a "person search" by the Knowledge User (KU). This scenario is implemented based the service- concept, so the actual application code supporting this scenario are different external tools.

The situation is that the users responsibilities for products are stored in a Lotus Notes Database. The task is to import these skill data into PROMOTE® using the "Skill documentation" model.

First the KIE has to generate a view in Lotus Notes that selects the documents representing the product skills. In this example the view is stored as "PROMOTE-Productrelation" in the database "products.nsf". The second step is to generate a mapping file, that translates the structure within the Lotus Notes Database into the structure of the PROMOTE® model language. In this example a model named "Productrelation" of the modeltype "Skill-documentation" has to be generated, that consists of Skill-Profiles for each user and stores the product-responsibility.

The following mapping file depicts the transformation from a Lotus Notes Database to the PROMOTE® skill-model. First the database and the selected view is defined, followed by some necessary model informations like modelname and modeltype. For each user, that is stored in the Lotus Notes Database in the Field "FAG" a Skill-Profile is generated. The relations to the products are stored in a separate view called "PROMOTE-Productrelation\Skill" that is included into the Skill-Profiles in line 19.

```
[0]<view name="PROMOTE-Productrelation" include="yes">
[1]<database server="" name="c:\promote\products.nsf">
[2]    <applib name="PROMOTE-WE-library_v_3.2" />
[3]    <modeldata>
```

```
    <name>
        <const value="Productrelation" />
     </name>
     <modeltype>
        <const value="Skill documentation" />
     </modeltype>
  </modeldata>
  <instancedata>
      <class>
        <const value="Skill-Profile" />
      </class>
      <name>
        <field name="FAG" />
      </name>
      <components>
        <record name="Profile" view="PROMOTE-Productrelation\Skills"/>
      </components>
  </instancedata>
</view>
```

The KIE uses this mapping file to generate a XML stream, based on the PROMOTE® model language described in chapter 3.1, using the KM-Service "Import View-Based Lotus Notes" implemented in Visual Basic. The KPD has now the possibility to change the model by using the KM-Service "Change Knowledge Model" of the component "Knowledge Model Builder" that opens a graphical online model editor implemented as a Java-Applet.

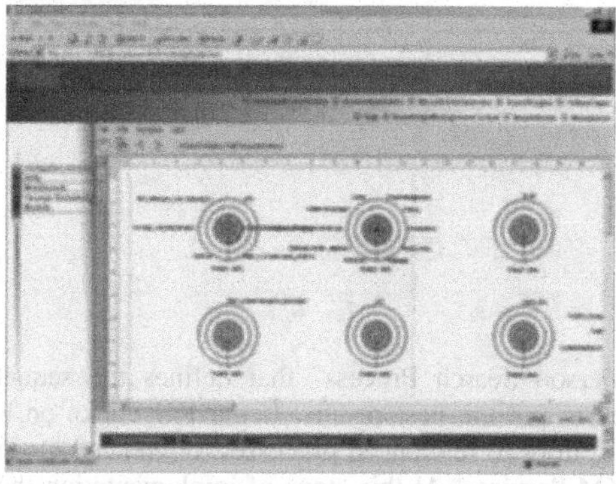

Fig. 7. Depicts the imported skill profiles that are linked with the product model

After the final changes the model is stored and used by the KW, who changes the relation of this model using the KM-Service "Skill-Profile Categoriser".

This service is implemented as a Java Application and the Web-Interface is implemented using Java Server Pages.

Finally the Knowledge User can take advantage from the model by using the KM-Service "Categorised Person Search". If the search is not successful the KU can select other KM-Services like "Full Text Person Search", "Keyword Based Person Search" or "Full Text Search in the models".

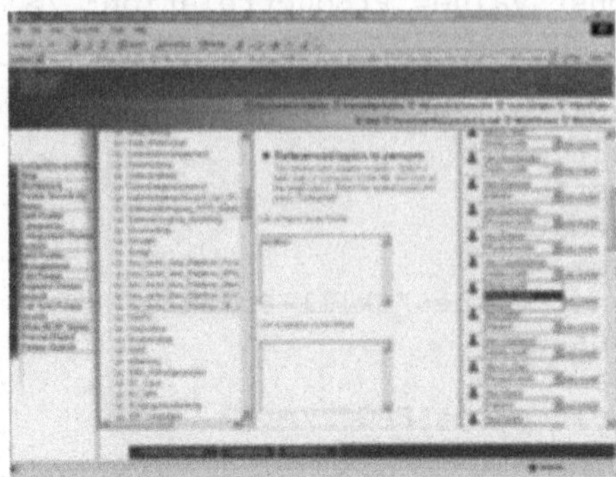

Fig. 8. Depicts a screen shot of the KM-Service "Categorising skill profiles", where the left frame shows a list of all products, the middle frame shows the selection, and from the right frame the skill-profile to be linked can be selected

The most promising sequence of the above KM-Services is modelled as the KMP "Person search KMP". The Knowledge User can start the Person - Search KMP to run all the above mentioned KM-Services.

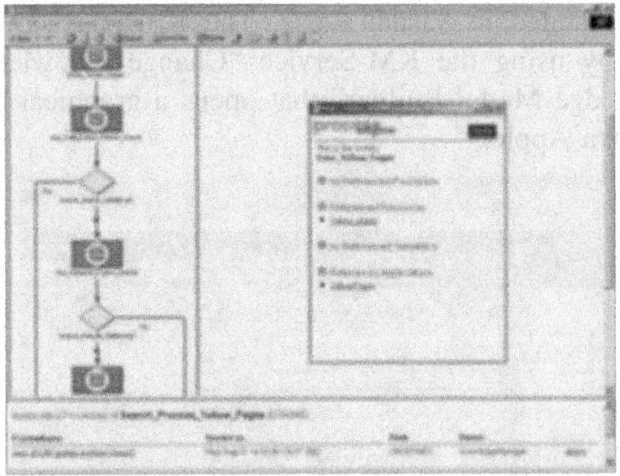

Fig. 9. Depicts the "Person Search Process" that defines the sequence of the previously mentioned KM-Services to get the best results. If the KU clicks on an activity an assistant window opens providing links to referenced processes, referenced resources, referenced Topic Maps and referenced KM-Services. At this stage of implementation the KM-Services have to called manually by clicking on the activity. The next step of implementation is, to automate these process adapting the Workflow concept to the needs of KMPs.

This scenario depicts the KMP as an integration platform, to manage different KM-Services in a process-oriented manner. Best practice processes are defined on a model base to enable the management of the OM. KM-Services have to be implemented as Web-Service accessing either PROMOTE® modules or external software application. KM-tools that provide Web-Services are easily integrated in this process oriented platform, KM-tools that do not support the Web-Service concept, have to accessed by implementing a Web-Service Adapter.

The next section gives an overview of the evaluation approach of such a KMS.

5 Evaluation of the KMS

The evaluation strategy of the KMS-PROMOTE® is twofold, first the evaluation of the prototype and the applicability to the application scenario has been tested, second an evaluation framework to monitor the performance of the KMS has been developed. A Test Scenario has been introduced, a prototype was installed on a Linux server to test the scenario with selected users. The focus was the usability, the user-interface as well as the coverage of the functional requirements.

The second and probably more interesting aspect was to provide an evaluation framework to evaluate the performance of the KMS. This evaluation scenario is based on the Balanced Score Card that has been modelled with the tool ADOScore® to define goals like "Improve Skill Management", "Additional Quality Management" and "Increase Multimedia Based Learning". These strategic goals have been broken down to specific criteria like "Within 1 year guarantee access to yellow pages at 95% of sites/branches for employees of the software development department (SDD)". These goals and criteria have been modelled and exported into the KM Cockpit to provide the Knowledge Manager with an evaluation tool.

The Cockpit enables the management of strategic goals, operative goals and criteria. At the moment there are two Test Users that implement the prototype of PROMOTE® and test the evaluation concept.

6 Outlook and Further Investigation

PROMOTE® is a prototype that has been evaluated by the European Commission, and is tested at two Test User Sites on Linux and Windows. The market launch of PROMOTE® is planned by the beginning of 2003, where performance and the reliability of the system will be improved.

The KM-Service concept will be analysed in more detail to completely embed the concept in the PROMOTE® method. The functionality of PROMOTE® will be enhanced including Workflow concepts and better groupware functionality.

The vision is, that PROMOTE® becomes a model editor to combine all KM-Services implemented from tool-vendors on the KM-market.

References

1. Despres C., Chauvel D., How to map knowledge management, Financial Times Mastering Information Management, March 4-6, 1999, www.esc-marseille.fr/publication/article.htm, access: 08.08.02
2. Wickli A.;Jonischkeit R., Kunkler B., Geben Sie Ihren Leuten Kanus und Kompasse, in Chemie und Fortschritt, Clariant 2/2000 in Muttenz, p28-31.
3. PROMOTE, www.boc-eu.com/promote, access 08.08.02
4. Telesko R., Karagiannis D., Woitsch R. Knowledge Management Concepts and Tools: The PROMOTE Project, in Gronau N. Wissensmanagement Systeme-Anwendungen-Technologien, Shaker Verlag, Aachen 2001, p95-112

5. Dilz S., Gronau N., Haak L.,Laskowski F., Martens S., Forschung im betrieblichen Wissensmanagement –Bedarf und erste Ergebnisse, in Gronau N. Wissensmanagement Systeme-Anwendungen-Technologien, Schaker Verlag, Aachen 2002, p1-24
6. Lehner F., Organisational Memory –Konzepte und Systeme fü das organisatorische Lernen und das Wissensmanagement, Hanser Verlag, Müchen 2000, p93
7. Ontology, www.ontology.org, access 08.08.02
8. Topic Maps, www.topicmap.com, access 08.08.02
9. Mind Maps, www.mind-maps.com, access 08.08.02
10. Abecker A., Mentzas G., Legal M., Ntioudis S., Papavassiliou G., Buisness-Process Oriented Delivery of Knowledge through Domain Ontologies, Proceedings of the second Workshop on Theory and Applications of Knowledge Management (TAKMA), Munich, 3-7 September 2001
11. Dengel A., Abecker A., Bernardi A., van Elst L., Maus H., Schwarz S., Sintek M., Konzepte zur Gestaltung von Unternehmensgedähnissen, in Küstliche Intelligenz 1/02, Gesellschaft fü Informatik, arendtap, Bremen 2002, pp5-11
12. Wilke H., Systemisches Wissensmanagement, Lucius & Lucius Stuttgart 1998
13. Schneider U., Die sieben Todsüden im Wissensmanagement, Frankfurter Allgemeine Buch 2001
14. ArsDigita, www.clasohm.com/cv/siemens090700.html, access 08.08.02
15. Abecker Andreas, Hinkelmann Knut, Maus Heiko, Müler Heinz Jügen, Geschäts-prozess-orientiertes Wissensmangement, Springer Verlag, 2002, Berlin
16. Karagiannis, D., Telesko, R., Wissensmanagement. Konzepte der Küstlichen Intelligenz und des Softcomputing. Oldenbourg, 2001, Müchen
17. ADOScore®, www.boc-eu.com, access 08.08.02
18. Karagiannis D., Woitsch R., Modelling Knowledge Management Processes to describe organisational knowledge systems, proceedings of 15th European conference on Artificial Intelligence, WS Knowledge Management and Organizational Memories, Lyon, 21-26 July 2002
19. Woitsch R., Karagiannis D., Renner T., Model-Based Process Oriented Knowledge Management, the PROMOTE Approach, Proceedings of the I-Know, Graz, 18-19. July 2002
20. Karagiannis D., Junginger S., Strobl R., Introduction to Business Process Management System Concepts, in: B. Scholz-Reiter, E. Stickel (Eds.): Business Process Modelling, Lecture Notes in Computer Science, 1996, Springer, pp. 81-106.
21. Snell J., Tidwell D., Kulchenko P., Programming Web Services with SOAP, O'Reilly, Sebastopol 2002

Knowledge Management for Industrial Research Processes of an Industrial Research Center

Christian Frank[1,2] and Mickael Gardoni[2]

[1] EADS Corporate Research Center, 12, rue Pasteur
92152 Suresnes, France
christian.frank@eads.net
[2] GILCO Laboratory, INPF-ENSGI, 46, av. Félix Viallet,
38000 Grenoble, France
gardoni@gilco.inpg.fr

Abstract. Knowledge management can support industrial research processes. Indeed, these industrial research processes are situated between a system of operational units, requiring and using research results, and a system of technological providers and academic laboratories. The knowledge flow between these systems is exposed to certain industrial constraints. The research center needs to optimize internal and external knowledge flows. In this purpose we identified a knowledge typology of industrial researchers. Based on a research process model, the knowledge typology and a theoretical knowledge management model we propose a portal solution. This portal solution allows manipulating information and knowledge more flexible in order to assure a certain dynamic for the knowledge management system. In future work we will integrate a knowledge evaluation process to focus on this dynamical aspect. This article discusses the introduction of a knowledge management system for industrial research processes at the EADS Corporate Research Center.

1 Introduction

For companies the managing of knowledge constitutes a strategic perspective [2]. If knowledge and know-how are not under control, they represent an element of weakness. On the other hand, if they are under control, they become a resource and a strategic factor for continues improvement of product and process quality and for the development of new knowledge [4].

An industrial research center stands between an *external information provider system* (e.g. technology suppliers, academic laboratories, etc), and an *industrial operational system,* (operational units like the design office, the assembly factories, etc). The industrial operational system represents the most important final user of the industrial research results and thus can be considered as the industrial research customer. An information exchange process takes place between the operational system and the external information provider system with the industrial research center in the middle of this process (Fig. 1).

D. Karagiannis and U. Reimer (Eds.): PAKM 2002, LNAI 2569, pp. 413-424, 2002.

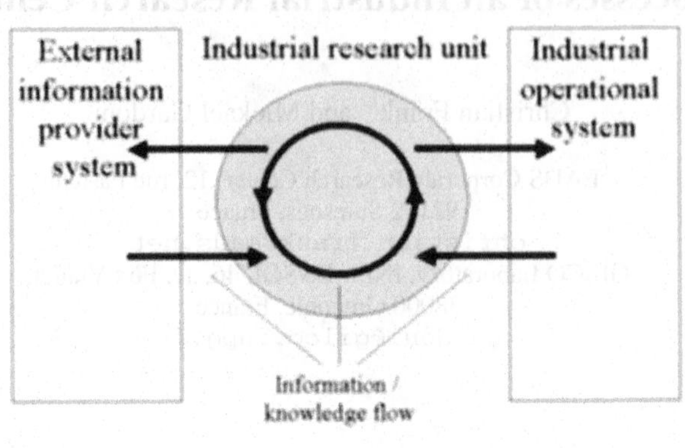

Fig. 1. Industrial research processes -a macroscopic description

The role of industrial research is to experiment, illustrate and validate models with new technological and methodological solutions, to combine them in order to propose new possible solutions for the requirements coming from the operational system. The role consists of creating new technological and methodological competencies and knowledge and to transfer them into the industrial operational system [1].

The position of industrial research implies information and knowledge flows. These flows have to respect certain constraints. In the next chapters we will expose knowledge relevant problems for industrial research and show how we count to face these problems with a knowledge management solution.

2 Problem Description and Objectives

The fact that industrial research activities are directly linked to the customer environment and the information supplier environment causes external influences and constraints on the internal research processes [6]. Products and processes of the customers are under constraints like costs, quality, risks and delay. These constraints have a direct influence on industrial research processes: the results of the industrial research processes are dedicated to improve products and processes of the customers and thus need to respect the customers constraints. The industrial research customer constraints become the industrial research constraints. These constraints on research processes affect the information flow between the different systems and the management of knowledge: the control of knowledge in industrial research processes under constraints gets a crucial factor.

Knowledge management relevant problems can concern (some examples coming from interviews with industrial researchers and research managers):

- The knowledge acquisition: find external knowledge to integrate in research projects, get access to new internal knowledge, be always informed about the needs of the operational units, etc.
- Knowledge distribution: reach and contact the right people, exchange new ideas with experts, inform operational units about new research results, etc.
- Knowledge preservation: preserve knowledge when people are leaving, update rapidly new arrivals and assure knowledge continuity, formalize and keep feedback concerning the application of research results, etc.
- Knowledge evaluation: use the right and useful knowledge to produce new knowledge, know the maturity of internal knowledge compared to external knowledge, etc.

These problems need to be addressed in order to improve the efficiency of industrial research processes of a research center and to counter the existing constraints.

In order to be able to control and manage the knowledge in industrial research processes we propose to introduce knowledge management. The objective is to propose a knowledge management system (or parts of a system) which demonstrates the feasibility of knowledge management functions useful for industrial research processes. Even if the introduction of such a system might imply reflections on knowledge management methods (communities of practices, communities of competences, etc.), our focus lies on system characteristics specific for industrial research processes.

In the following chapters, we will basically present the achieved results concerning a requirement analysis, a process and knowledge structure analysis. The knowledge management solution proposition is not yet fully developed and thus needs further reflections.

3 Requirement Analysis – A Functional Analysis

To reach our objective, we first conducted a requirement analysis with a group of researchers and research managers. In several meetings we tried to identify potential and desired KM functions, which should be provided by a KM system. These desired functions represent an important part of the knowledge management requirements and complete the expressed problems of the chapter above.

The first part of the analysis is to determine the environment interfaces of a potential system. The environment interfaces should represent the environment of an industrial researcher: he is in interaction with external information suppliers, internal information suppliers, information resources concerning the customer requirements (operational units), and teams of researchers (Fig. 2).

The potential functions of such a system, identified during the work sessions, combine and link the different interfaces (Fig. 2). The functions are described below:

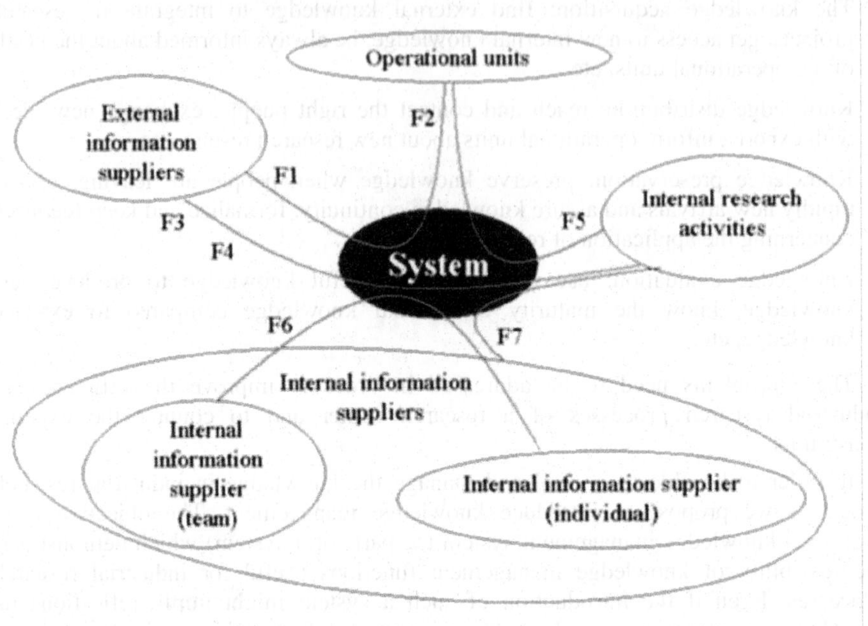

Fig. 2. The environment interfaces of a potential knowledge management system for industrial research processes and its potential functions

- *F1*: The system should help to identify external industrial problems comparable with the problems of the research customers. The objective is to identify external industrial problems, industrial requirements among industrial partners, competitors, etc. similar to the problems and requirements of internal research customers. Certain external problems could be equivalent to the implicit customer needs not yet identified.
- *F2*: The system should help to identify external solution proposals (methods and technologies) for the research customer requirements. The objective here is to support the identification of technologies and external methods which could support the solution development for customer problems.
- *F3*: The system displays the gap between the research activities conducted by external research organizations and the internal research activities. This function allows the visualization of an evaluation of external research activities compared to internal research activities concerning a research subject. It could show in which way external research problems are treated. After such a comparison, it would be possible to decide whether to integrate external research activities and results and to orientate the internal research activities. The knowledge management system can thus contribute to an evaluation on for knowledge and supports to select between obsolete, basic and new knowledge [8].
- *F4*: The system helps to identify external elements (concepts, methods, technologies, tools, and competencies) in order to carry out internal research activities.

- *F5*: The system should show in which way the research activities cover the customer requirements. The objective here is to visualize the difference between the customer research requirements and the requirements treated and covered with internal research activities. This difference indicates the need for future research activities and the need to deepen already existing research activities and initiates actions to create new knowledge.
- *F6*: The system should support a sense of sharing among internal researchers working in the same research area. In order to create this sense of sharing between researchers, it will be necessary to develop competencies references, to rely similar professions, similar project environments, and perhaps transverse organizations [8].
- *F7*: The system should help to identify internal elements (concepts, methods, technologies, tools, and competencies) that help to carry out internal research activities.

These potential functions transform the requirements in wishes for a knowledge management system. They are the starting point for process analysis and solution development.

4 Industrial Research Processes – Process Analysis and Knowledge Flow Description

In order to introduce a KM system, it is important to understand the functioning of processes and information flows. In this purpose we analyzed in more detail the organizational structure, the research processes, the information and knowledge flow and the knowledge structure of industrial researcher.

4.1 The Organizational Structure of the Research Environment

The research activities are embedded in our case in an organizational structure. The most important parts of this organizational structure concern a quality certification, a stable intranet structure with its document organization, a regularly reporting about the project advancements and regular project meetings and reviews.

The quality certification implied to introduce procedures describing and defining certain work processes and defining the production of certain documents. Documents have to be produced at the beginning of a research project (research programs) after every meeting concerning this project (minutes of meetings), at milestones and at the end of the projects (reports). This guarantees a minimum of information distribution and preservation. The quality framework is supported by an intranet which helps to manage the different documents required by the quality procedures. The documents are structured according to the research project structure. This concerns also external relevant documents important for certain research projects. Regularly project reporting and review meetings are another mean to assure the distribution of the information concerning new research project results.

Of course, this structure is very specific to our work environment. The fact of having quality certification for research processes might not be easy to accept for every researcher [3]. The introduction of quality certification implies to respect certain organizational rules and predefined processes. This might be seen as a handicap for research activities. Nevertheless, the trend nowadays is to introduce quality certifications for more and more academic and industrial research organizations [3].

This basic framework will play an important role for our further analysis and solution development. It is possible to better analyze already existing knowledge and information flows. On the other hand this framework with its existing and defined information flow and document creation is an opportunity to build knowledge management solution on existing practices and structures and to take them into account for new solution development.

4.2 The Activity View of Industrial Research Processes and the Knowledge Flows

Industrial research processes are characterized by the anticipation of industrial operational unit requirements. This obliges the industrial research units to know and understand the customers' problem environment. Providers of new external technologies and information constitute knowledge resources.

A research process is initiated by a need to improve processes and/or products of the operational system. A research process can also be initiated by the discovery of the importance of new innovative concepts. According to the maturity degree of the researcher's knowledge, the research process can be decomposed into three phases: *investigate, focus, transfer*:

- The activities concerning the investigation characterize the identification of new research domains, the observation of new technological possibilities and activities and aims to constitute state-of-the-arts about new technologies and new methods. Therefore, the industrial researcher transfers and transforms external information or external knowledge into internal knowledge: a knowledge flow from the external environment to the internal environment. The monitoring activity is very important for this phase of the research process. Before transferring external knowledge into internal knowledge, the researcher evaluates the utility of the external knowledge for his future research activities.
- The objective of the next phase is to focus on new technologies and methods and to acquire new knowledge and competencies. Experimenting and illustrating prototypes by using new technologies and methods help to acquire new knowledge and competencies. The activity allows combining internal and external knowledge with given problems. This combination is characterized by learning processes for researchers, by knowledge exchanges among researchers and initiatives of innovations.
- Transfer driven research is directly related to the operational units requirements. The objective is to experiment illustrators, prototypes and methods with concrete data coming from the operational units. By proposing improvements for the identified problems, the research units transfer their knowledge into the operational units. As in the "focalization" phase, researchers combine internal and external

knowledge to come up with suitable solutions. However, the role of internal knowledge dominates the role of external knowledge. Internal knowledge, coming from exploratory research activities and the experimental phase has to be adapted to research customer problems. This transfer of knowledge is also accompanied by learning processes for researchers: the feedback of the operational units about implemented research solutions (Fig. 3).

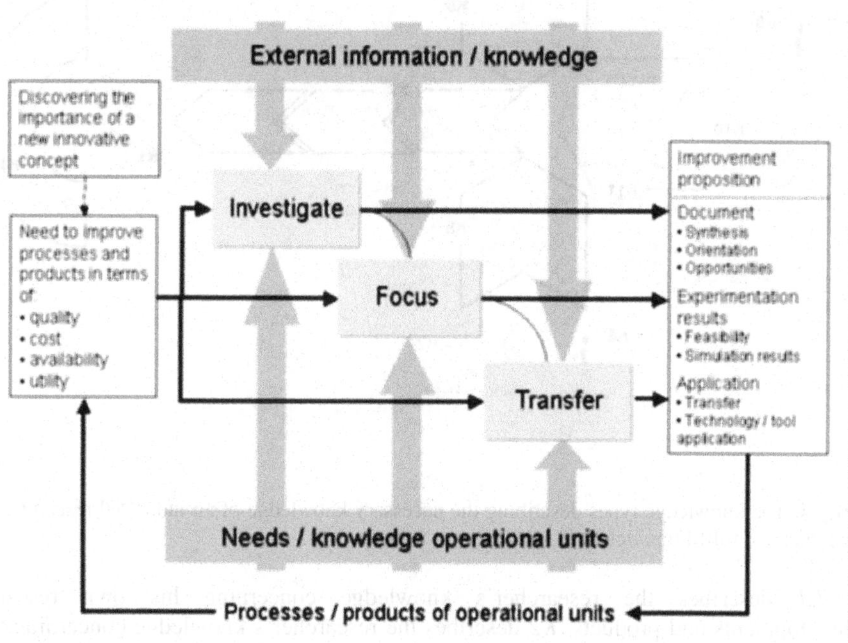

Fig. 3. Industrial research process – an activity view

4.3 The Twelve Knowledge Types of Industrial Researchers

Managing knowledge in industrial research processes requires knowing which knowledge is manageable. Besides, it is also important to know which knowledge will be necessary to conduct research activities and to come up with research results. These two aspects encouraged us to find a *knowledge typology* of industrial researchers necessary to develop research results. In order to identify the different knowledge types, we analysed documents and held interviews with researchers. This analysis was based on a systemic analyse: which are the people concerned in a project, which decisions are made, what are the different activities, where are information shared.

The typology tries to describe and categorize 12 knowledge types as objects (Fig. 4).

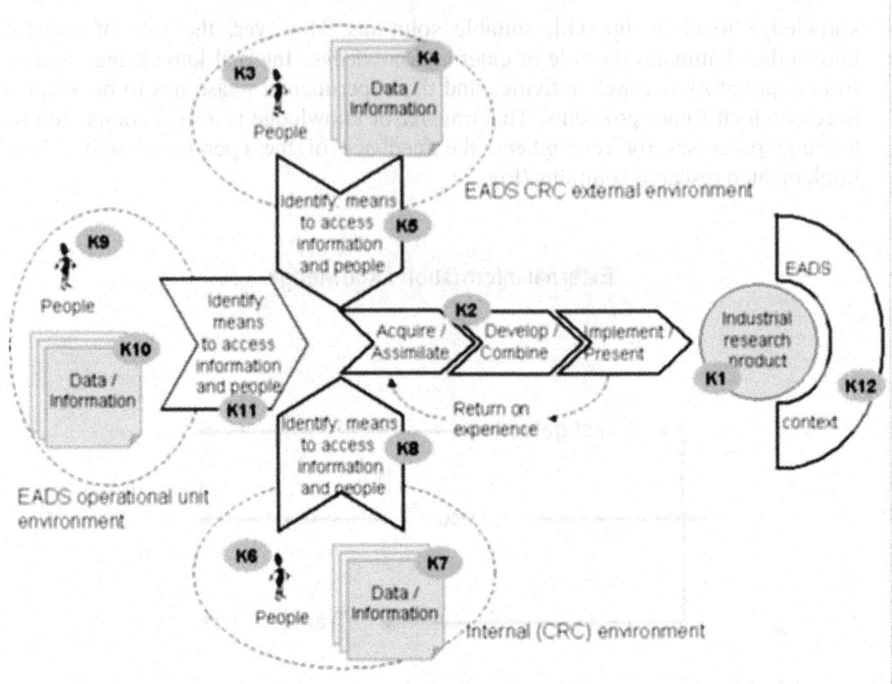

Fig. 4. The knowledge types describing the necessary knowledge of an industrial researcher to conduct and fulfill research activities

K1 describes the researcher's knowledge concerning his own research developments and products. *K2* describes the researcher's knowledge concerning the process and daily activities to reach research results and products. *K3* describes the researcher's knowledge he has about existing external knowledge resources. These resources are a part of the external information provider system (e.g. technology suppliers academic and industrial laboratories, etc.) and provide the researcher with new information and knowledge, characterized with *K4.* K4 is the concrete information a researcher has to know and to take into account for new research results. We distinguished three main categories in K4: the researcher has knowledge about academic / industrial laboratories, technology suppliers, and external user (competitors / partners). For each main category we found sub-categories describing knowledge objects. As an example, the knowledge objects for technology suppliers are *orientations, innovative concepts, methods, tools, means, and experimentations.* This allows us to precise the knowledge of researchers and to identify, where knowledge does exists and where is a lack of knowledge. For the other knowledge types we defined similar categories. *K5* describes the researcher's knowledge he needs to access to external information and resources. He knows how and where to get external information for his research activities and objectives. He owns knowledge about conferences, articles, presentations, etc. K3, K4 and K5 describe the entire knowledge of an industrial researcher concerning his knowledge about the external information provider system.

K6 describes the researcher's knowledge concerning the internal research unit resources. These internal resources (people, projects and units) provide him with knowledge or information (*K7*) which he includes in his research activities and results. *K8* describes the researcher's knowledge which enables him to access the internal information and resources. K6, K7 and K8 are the counterpart of K3, K4 and K5 and describe the entire knowledge of an industrial researcher concerning his knowledge about the internal industrial research system. *K9* describes the researcher's knowledge about operational unit resources. These problems and needs are characterized with *K10*. With his knowledge *K11* the industrial research knows how and where to access to the operational unit information and research needs. *K12* describes the researcher's knowledge concerning the global group context of his research results.

5 The Knowledge Management Architecture

The knowledge management architecture we propose is based on three models: the industrial research process model (chapter 4.2), the knowledge typology model (chapter 4.3) and on an external theoretical knowledge management model form Romhardt [9]. As a basic model we will use the industrial research model which helps to categorize the different research activities in three phases : investigate, focus, transfer. These activities can be supported by knowledge management activities as described in the knowledge management model of Romhardt (Fig. 5).

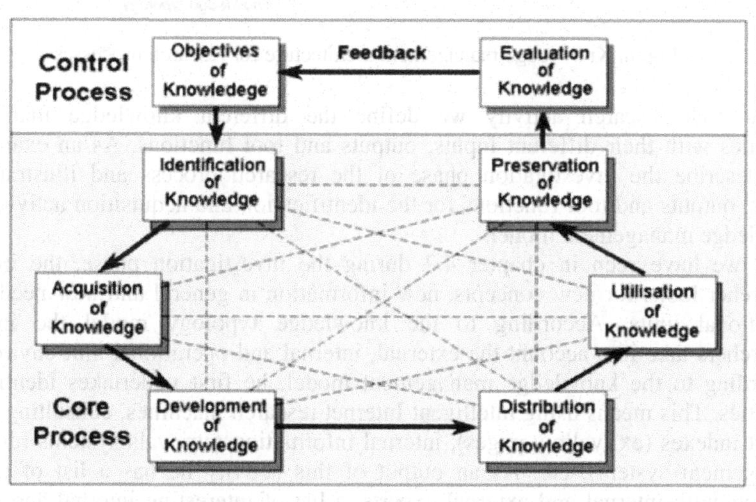

Fig. 5. Knowledge management model according to Romhardt [9]

In order to support the different knowledge management activities in the different research phases we propose a toolbox for each activities of the knowledge management model. This toolbox enables the execution of the different activities from the knowledge management model. Each toolbox contains an information input field, a specific toolbox area according to the activity of the knowledge management model and an information output field. The information input and output field are structured according to the knowledge typology model. As the typology model represents the necessary knowledge for research activities this structure assures the availability of critical knowledge. This three level architecture allows to coordinate the different knowledge management activities and to integrate a process view, an activity view and a knowledge management view (Fig. 6).

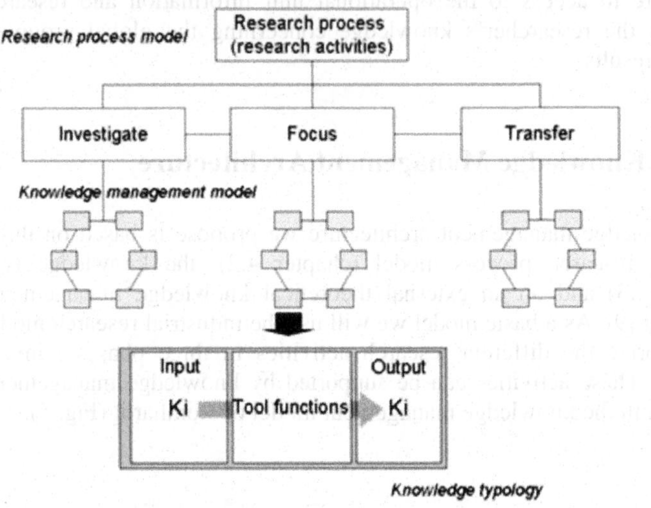

Fig. 6. Knowledge management architecture for research processes

For each research activity we define the different knowledge management activities with their different inputs, outputs and tool functions. As an example we will describe the investigation phase of the research process and illustrate some inputs, outputs and tool functions for the identification and acquisition activity of the knowledge management model.

As we have seen in chapter 4.2 during the investigation phase, the industrial researcher looks for new concepts, new information in general and new needs in the operational units. According to the knowledge typology model the industrial researchers take into account the external, internal and operational unit environment. According to the knowledge management model, he first undertakes identification activities. This means using intelligent Internet research machines, consulting internal expert indexes (ex. yellow pages), internal information retrievals systems (document management system), etc. As an output of this activity he has a list of potential contacts with internal and external experts, a list of interesting internal and external documents, a list of potential interesting conferences to visit, etc. After the identification of these information sources the industrial researcher needs to transform the information into internal knowledge. This happens during the acquisition activity of the knowledge management model. The output of the identification activity is the input of the acquisition activity. The tools for this activity are a mixture between organizational tools and technical tools: in order to make use of the potential contacts the industrial researcher has to meet people, hold presentations to get feedback, assist to conference and read the collected information. As one of the technical tools for this activity we provide an electronic form to review the exchanged information in meetings (minutes of meetings) and to summarize the different internal and external documents. This electronic form is structured according to the knowledge typology. As an example we give the electronic form describing the information concerning a technology supplier (see also detailed description in chapter 4.3) (Fig. 7).

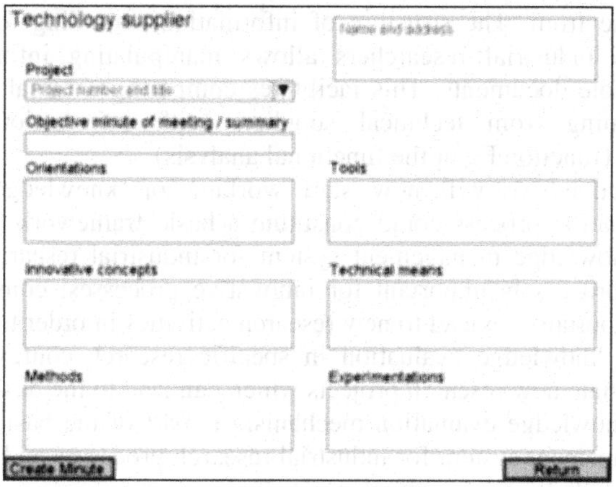

Fig. 7. Electronic form structuring the information concerning a technology supplier according to the knowledge typology

As output the industrial research creates structured information according to the knowledge typology. This information can be considered as important information describing the knowledge of the industrial researcher concerning a technology supplier. Technically it is also possible to create an official minute of meeting according to the quality certification requirements.

After the acquisition activities follow the other activities according to the knowledge management model. The different tool functions are integrated in a portal solution. The above demonstrated forms play an important role among the tools. We propose similar forms to formulate other documents or reports. Important is that via the portal it is possible to manipulate the different "information objects" created by the forms in order to link different information, to oppose and combine different information. This is a mean to create new knowledge in a more effective way.

6 Conclusion and Perspectives

In order to realize a knowledge management solution for industrial research processes we first described the different research activities in a research process model and illustrated the knowledge of industrial researchers in a knowledge typology model. With a functional analysis we tried to describe, in a "systematic way", the demanded functions of a potential knowledge management system. Based on these models and the existing organization environment (ex. quality certification) and with an external theoretical knowledge management model we constructed a knowledge management solution for industrial research processes. For the different research activities we proposed different knowledge management solutions. All these solutions are integrated in a portal.

The knowledge management architecture takes into account most of the requirements. There is a better structure of information and there exists a better overview of the different external and internal environments where the different information come from. The structure of information according to the knowledge typology of the industrial researchers allows manipulating information without manipulating whole documents. This facilitates comparing external information like information coming from technical suppliers with information coming from operational units (function F2 of the functional analysis).

As a perspective, we will now start working on knowledge evaluation. A knowledge evaluation process could constitute a basic framework for the functions included in a knowledge management system for industrial research processes [7]. The evaluation process is important for innovative processes: considering external knowledge as important can lead to new research activities in order to obtain the same knowledge. The knowledge evaluation in specific research context and for given problems can initiate new research projects which can lead to the development of new knowledge. A knowledge evaluation mechanism is part of the basic functions for a knowledge management system for industrial research processes and gives a dynamic framework to knowledge management.

References

1. Carneiro, A.: How does Knowledge Management influence innovation and competivness in: Journal of Knowledge Management, No. 2 (2000)
2. Dieng, R. et al : Méthodes et outils pour la gestion des connaissances, DUNOD, N°2 10 004574 1, (2000)
3. Gardoni, M., Frank, C. : Finding and Implementing Best Practices For Design Research Activities, International Conferemce on Engineering Design, ICED 01 Glasgow, August (2001)
4. Liebowitz, J.: Knowledge Management Handbook. CRC Press, Boca Raton (1999)
5. Nonaka, I., Takeuchi, H.: The Knowledge Creating Company. How Japanese Companies Create the Dynamics of Innovation, Oxford University Press (1995)
6. Schulz, A.,: Applied KM in innovation processes. In Professionelles Wissensmanagement – Erfahrungen und Visionen. Shaker Verlag (2001)
7. Sveiby, K.-E.: Methods for Measuring Intangible Assets, http://www.sveiby.com.au/ (2001)
8. Tiger, H., Weil, B.: La capitalisation des savoirs pour l'innovation dans les projet, Communication au Colloque : Mobiliser les talents de l'entreprise par la gestion des connaissances, Paris (2001)
9. Romhardt, K.: Die Organisation aus der Wissensperspektive –Möglichkeiten und Grenzen der Intervention. Gabler, Wiesbaden (1998)

Knowledge Processes Embedded in Task Structures: Implications for the Design of a Technical and Organisational Solution

Anthony Papargyris, Angeliki Poulymenakou, and Kostas Samiotis

Athens University of Economics and Business, Department of Information Systems,
76 Patission Str., 10434 Athens, Greece
{apaparg, akp , samiotis }@aueb.gr

Abstract. In this paper, we elaborate on the idea that the processes of managing individual and organizational knowledge are situated in the context of work and emerge from the workplace practices. We address the relationship between Business Process-orientation and work practices as they represent the formal and the situated perspectives on work respectively. We examine the mediating role of information and communication technologies in the creation of collective knowledge within communities of practice from a Business Process-oriented viewpoint. The paper proposes a series of design implications and presents a prototype solution for a knowledge management system.

1 Introduction

Knowledge is singled out as a key driver of organisations' longevity. However, there still is no wide accepted practice (or even definition) regarding the management of corporate knowledge; still, practitioners start to realise that there is a tremendous potential for economic growth behind the "capturing" of this intangible asset.

The research presented in this paper, argues an approach to organisational Knowledge Management, which combines formal understanding of an organisation's strategic and operational behaviour on the notion of business process, with situated conceptions on organisational work anchored on the notions of work practice and Communities of Practice. We argue that Knowledge Management constitutes an organisational and technological intervention that should be related to both these perspectives. Through our research, we identify a number of design implications for researchers and practitioners involved in such intervention.

We present MODEL,[1] a technical and organisational solution, and we claim that along with a methodology, it is possible to provide and support a social network, such an organisation, with a capability to "manage" both: a) *collective knowledge*, and b)

[1] M.O.D.E.L (Multimedia for Open and Dynamic Executives Learning) is funded by European Commission's INFORMATION SOCIETIES TECHNOLOGY (IST) programme. Partners: Lambrakis Research Foundation, University of Cologne, Research Center of Athens University of Economics and Business, Oracle Italia srl University of Brighton, Scienter (societa consortile a responsabilita limitata), Intrasoft International, University of Erlangen-Nurnberg-FIM

D. Karagiannis and U. Reimer (Eds.): PAKM 2002, LNAI 2569, pp. 425-436, 2002.

process knowledge. To explain this claim, we have grounded our analysis on the ideas of Business Process knowledge and the collectiveness of practice as reflected through the notion of Communities of Practice.

In the first section, we draw on important organisational and technological issues, while we propose the design implications for IT implementation and mediation in Processes Knowledge. In the last section we present the MODEL, and address its ability to support our design implications.

2 The Process-Oriented Approach

In general, a process describes the order of action and decisions taken while constructing a product [1] or service, and consists of tasks and a set of requirements and resources required by an actor to accomplish each task. The structural element of business operation, the Business Process (BP), reflects and embodies an organisation's unique characteristics and its ability for market differentiation. While the centre of strategy formulation concerned building with competitive advantage, BPs are the reference point for continuous investigation and efforts for increasing effectiveness and efficiency of an organisations operation. This may involve efforts to decrease the product's time-to-market and production costs and at the same time, to increase the product quality and customer satisfaction.

The notion of Business Process comprises many distinct tasks, process steps (or activities), roles and resources. A process step is a single operation needed to complete a particular task and is usually triggered by an event. Roles are independent of specific resources and hence they can be assigned to several of them [2]. The resources may be parts and raw materials, workers as well as equipment or services. Each task requires a hierarchical description of the steps need to be followed and completed, before we move to the next task. Consequently, a Business Process represents the formal definition of work, that is, the structural way things were actually planned to be executed, in a manner that creates and adds value to organisational outputs.

A single Business Process may have common tasks with other processes, it may cross many different departments and sections, or it may even extend outside the organisation itself and crosses different organisations in a market alliance. Each employee involved in a BP has his/her own work practices, based on his/her mental models, different epistemological assumptions and worldview, resulting the creation of an alternative evolving reality. Knowledge is hidden in the cultural heritage of each employee, in the way they comprehend reality, and this can be best expressed by communicating or doing-executing a task. Consequently, this multi-view of nested individual contexts synthesises a canvas of ideas, lessons learned, insights and visions. In this sense a BP becomes a whole new concept, and while "process" remains a misunderstood term, it presents a massive challenge to the organisation, due to a knowledge layer associated with it that can be identified and managed as a whole.

We argue that this knowledge layer is the real (and only) way an organisation is actually behaving and acting, both internally (intra-organisationally) and environmentally (extra- organisationally). The true owners of this intangible asset are the BP stakeholders, no matter if they take part in the execution or in the management of a BP. These actors are combining their coordinated efforts, acting and reacting towards a common objective, formally outlined as the BP. Their abilities and experiences are manifest in their routines and work practices, while at the same time they constantly try to learn, evaluate and adjust them to meet personal satisfaction and work efficiency. In the vein of such an argument, we can conclude that work practices are the manifestations of both tacit and explicit knowledge each actor possess regarding an activity of a skill operation he is taking part of. In other words, they are the situated action that reflects individuals knowing of doing by their ability of contextualising and expressing their knowledge. This rich knowledge is the "reason" of acting and thus the catalyst of practice changing (innovating).

In order to gain new experiences and generate knowledge, actors need to meet their "knowledge neighbourhood", that is to communicate with their colleagues, to share their practices and mutually evaluate them. This requires by the stakeholders of a BP to have a mutual understanding of the process's context and a common abstract or formal communication language. The former means that actors should be aware of the BP event horizon and should gain an objective and subjective view of each task, and more necessarily, to be familiar with the knowledge processes embedded in its task structures. The latest means that a mutually accepted cultural compatible communication language (vocabulary) should be established and used in order to establish the optimum medium for sharing ideas and knowledge without misunderstandings and loss of meaning. For example, one informal way to share experience and tacit knowledge is storytelling and is quite popular in social communities because it's rich contextual encoded details and it's ability to be memorable [3] By using a vocabulary, actors and especially the newcomers will be able to understand current situation, adapt in the (new) procedures and apply their working practices. In MODEL, we are using the description of a BP to apply a common vocabulary among actors. When employees want to communicate with stored information or with their colleagues regarding an abstract situation such as their work practices, they use the concrete- formalised description of BP to be "fine-tuned" and establish a similar communication context. Summarising, we come to our first implication.

Design Implication 1: Exploit the formal communication vocabulary created by Business Processes, to achieve common grounded context and enable shared understanding.

3 Communities of Practice

Within the knowledge rich environments surrounding a Business Processes, people cope with complex tasks, communicate and exchange tacit knowledge with their environment and seek new innovative ways of practising. Tacit knowledge cannot be specified, and hence be put in information blocks and communicated. It must be sensed and felt rather than defined or written down, otherwise knowledge providers will be trapped in the nuances of meaning of each word they are trying to use. Usually, people working in the same processes, start to behave more socially and gradually they are creating Communities of Practice (CoP) [4]. Wenger [5] points out that CoPs emerge naturally around things that matter to people. These *social networks* become what Nonaka and Nishiguchi [6] call "Ba", a place where people develop relationships and share knowledge. The CoP formation is a very common phenomenon inside organisations and lately their study is in the centre of strategic and managerial research.

Design Implication 2: It is not enough to create formal designs of work, i.e. BPs, you also need to encourage the creation of CoPs around them.

The employees inside an organisation, as social units interact and communicate with each other and build relationships that strengthen workforce integrity. Individuals with the same interests and common recognised targets may form a community where they will share experiences and knowledge while they will work towards the benefit of the collective. Especially, employees participating in a same BP may form a community that will place high interest in experience share and in the common effort to find practicable solutions, by learning the "culture of practice" [7]. Within these communities, the knowledge creation and sharing among the members, is an ongoing continuous process, while everything is a subject of questioning and revising.

A common characteristic of CoPs is that their members share the same practices and that's why they share knowledge collectively [8]. Its members may be located on the same place and/or time, or they may be geographically dispread, while they may come with different intellectual backgrounds and interests, ethics and cultures. In a knowledge fruitful environment like a CoP, people learn to construct shared understanding amidst confusing and conflicting data [9], [10]. Personal relationships between the members are created and hence mutual respect and trust is established. These two elements are essential in enabling communication and share of tacit knowledge and are catalysts in community's knowledge enrichment. Perhaps the most attractive characteristic of CoP is its increased capacity to assimilate unexpected environmental stimulus and in return to produce strong feedback loops and situated action. Each CoP encompasses a collective knowledge repository that is actually the organisation's intellectual capital or collective expertise of the workforce [11]. This is considered to be the most valuable resource for the parent organisation. Yet, the intellectual capital is an extremely soft intangible resource and difficult to be managed.

In fact, each individual has certain skills and capabilities. But before these competencies are externalised and applied, they are melded with the individual's personal cultural (social) and epistemological (cognitive) “filters”. Although an organisation promotes its own policies and practices and tries to achieve a cultural equilibrium, there will be always the individual's norms and beliefs that will mediate in employee's actions. However, inside a CoP, such equilibrium can be achieved. Within a CoP there is a natural effort for common understanding, towards a collective perception of reality, which in results result the creation of a “communi” among its members. Instead of applying a-priori knowledge, its members are sharing their situated contexts, promoting dialogue and osmosis of their ideas and experiences. They learn from each other's actions and they adopt the most appropriate one, not by imitation but by evaluation and by “...appreciating the subtleties of behaviour of other team members” [12].

A set of practical guidelines has been introduced along with the MODEL application, with a critical mission to stimulate the formation of CoPs around organisation's BPs. On the one hand, each actor is directly associated with a BP's structure, so that everyone can associate his/her position in respect with each other's job position. In this case, BP serves as the common reference point. Additionally, there is a competence and skill map, regarding the association between the skills and competencies each activity need in order to be executed, and the skills and competencies each actors posses. On the other hand, and based on these two perspectives of work place around a BP, we guide managers to encourage their employees to communicate, exchange their opinions and progressively to meet each other personality. These actions will strength their work relationships, and will seed the seeds for CoPs.

3.1 Collective Knowledge

Within a CoP's trustful environment, members learn to share and comprehend others tacit knowledge. Story-telling, informal meetings and dialogues using a common language are the basic elements of sharing experiences, thoughts and ideas. The knowledge of an individual tends to be shared with everyone in the community and eventually, to achieve equilibrium where the knowledge is common for the whole collective and unlike community's productivity, knowledge is more than the sum of its parts [13].

Continuous cogitation, brainstorming and interaction among the members will lead to new knowledge creation and eventually to new improvisational or innovative ways of doing things. Leonard and Sensiper [14] describe the process of innovation is a rhythm of search and selection, exploration and synthesis, cycles of divergent thinking followed by convergence. Indeed, innovation is the indeterminate change that can happen "at a glance" in a work practice in order to change selected procedures, find alternative resources and reengineer routines. Eventually, innovation may be adopted in the BP and each individual involved will learn the new knowledge hidden behind the change and will adapt in the new working parameters.

In a recent paper, El Sawy concludes in the implication that "the creation of useful collective knowledge around business processes is facilitated by organisational environments that enable informal group meetings in which shared views can be developed" [15]. Knowledge creation involves high levels of tacit and explicit knowledge and one way to convert and share the tacit to explicit knowledge is through the socialisation and externalisation, in the Spiral of Organisational Knowledge Creation [16], [17]. Indeed, knowledge sharing is a social phenomenon and conceptualisation of tacit knowledge is highly context depended. Nevertheless, context is an individual construct [18] and is based on personal experiences. Argyris [19] notes that the same information does not have the same meaning for different recipients. Yet, each member in a CoP will learn and make the practice knowledge actionable and operational [20] independently from the content of the new knowledge and his context. This work-based learning process is a collective property [10] and involves the sharing and exploration of real-time emerging experiences, linked with Business Processes.

Design Implication 3: We need designs where work-based learning process is explicitly supported.

Based on this implication, in MODEL we used the notion of "case study" to create a work-based educational environment. The case study ensures that the narrative BP structure is common to everyone, while individual story-telling can be accommodated through annotations. Annotations are used to enrich the initial content with true stories originated in the commonly understood work environment, and gradually, this input will "grow" the initial description. The case study will evolve and become more and more realistic, tending to describe actual situated actions, while actors will be familiarised with each other's work practices.

3.2 Process Knowledge

As we noted previously, in each BP, there are specific procedures and practices to be followed in order to achieve the BP's primary target, the production of a product. We also mentioned the existence of dynamics and characteristics of the CoPs forming to support the activities around a BP. One of them, is the *process of knowledge enrichment*, and can help us to better understand the way knowledge flows and should be supported form special practical managerial actions and guidelines. Knowledge enrichment is a continuous process in which each member of the community contributes by adding valuable personal meaning in knowledge about a practice. Respectively, the *process knowledge* is knowledge *about*, *in* and derived *from* a process and it can be communicated as context depended information [2] and this process may support the flow of knowledge between Business Processes and business units [21]

Eppler [2] identifies three types of process knowledge, the knowledge about, within and derived from a process. The first type refers to the experience-relating know-how regarding the management of business and is usually codified and formally described in process execution documents. Respectively, it may be also in "unwritten" format (i.e. knowledge that accompanies the use of a resource). This type of process knowledge is asymmetrically available to any actor involved in the process and to the process owner. The second type, the knowledge within process includes knowledge that is constantly generated in the process's social-technical environment, such progress and evaluation meetings. Finally, the third type of process knowledge regards new experience and "lessons leaned for continuous improvement" (p. 227). The knowledge derived from a process, is the result of feedback loops between the actors and the process itself.

Quinn [22] proposes an intellectual scale, that is a hierarchy pyramid where he categorises the process knowledge: the *know-what* (cognitive knowledge), the *know-how* (advanced skills), the *know-why* (systems understanding) and the *care-why* (self-motivated creativity). According to Quinn, as an organisation operates and moves from the know-what to care-why, its professional intellect will increase. Organisational knowledge is embodied not only in the individuals' cognition, but also in the collectives' practices and cultures [23], that is the relationships between actors and the effects of interaction between actors and organisational artefacts.

Design Implication 4: We need to support know-what, know-how and know-why

Knowledge generation could be achieved through employee's encouragement for experimentation, while the sharing of knowledge is possible through employee's motivation to do so. But most of the times, motivation is not enough, and certain barriers that block knowledge sharing should be hurdled. In MODEL, with the right technological and organisational support in place, users-actors need special treatment in order to understand the value of knowledge sharing and learning. Moreover, guided tutoring using on-line material and seminars, is needed to help them understand and appreciate the different dimensions of process knowledge and the importance of information packaging when they try to express themselves.

4 ICT Mediation in Processes Knowledge

While knowledge creation is a social process [17], many attempts to isolate the common factors that affect the knowledge creation have been made. Information and Communication Technology (ICT) may be used in order to support the business process and its embedded knowledge. There is an array of categorised IT services available such as e-mail, decision support systems, workflow systems, CAD/CAM tools, document management systems and the so-called Knowledge Management Systems (KMS), claiming the ability of an IT application to support the capture, store and knowledge dissemination within a community of users. Knowledge Management aims at the support and augment of knowledge process inside an organisation. Its role is to build strategic knowledge assets and core competencies with respect to strategic business fields [22]. We are convinced that modern technological tools can support the human activities within a CoP, by enhancing and extending the community's memory and communication ability.

Our current understanding in organisational knowledge is context-specific, relational, dynamic and human-centred related to human action [26]. Explicit (or codified) knowledge is the knowledge that is objective and rational and can be expressed in formal and systematic language [17], [6]. Tacit is highly personal and hard to formalise, making it difficult to communicate or share with others. Tacit knowledge has a personal quality, it is deeply rooted in action and understanding, involves both cognitive and technical elements, and is non-transferable without personal contact [17], [6]. Within an organisational work-based context, we need an *enabling technology* to enhance communication between different organisational areas and levels. In such cases, modern ICT applications may play an important role. Communication is at the hub of knowledge sharing and effective communication requires the members of an organisation to agree on the labels, categories and distinctions used to represent the things important to the organisation [24].

Hansen [25] addresses the use of a digital repository of codified and explicit knowledge and the use of ICT means to facilitate communication networks within organisations. In other words, IT can be used to codify and create virtual networks that diffuse knowledge. However, the current conception of IT-enabled knowledge management doesn't address the processing of tacit knowledge, which is deeply rooted in an individual's action and experience, ideals, values, or emotions [26]. Alavi and Leidner [27] define KMS as a class of IT that focus on creating, gathering, organising and dissemination an organisation's knowledge. In fact, a KMS, in our context of Business Process Knowledge, must be seen as a situated combination of an information artefact management and a communication support system, enriched with appropriate guidelines that will promote knowledge dissemination through collaboration and learning, throughout a social network.

With minimum ICT support, it is possible to keep track of employees with particular expertise [28] and to enhance the collaboration and communication in an organisation. Collaboration is the degree to which people can combine together their mental efforts so as to achieve common or congruent goals [29] and an KMS should support the dissemination of these mental efforts, while providing a trustful communication highway to enhance collaboration and knowledge sharing. These tools however should be designed and treated in such a way that will be easily accepted and used by the community in the knowledge processes. Technological orchestration within a social environment such an organisation should fulfil the user needs while it should be synchronised with the organisation's culture. Moreover, special attention should be given in the system's User Interface (UI), which is perhaps the most critical element of a KMS because this is the final frontier and the bridge between the codified knowledge and the provider-receiver. Eventually, human-centred UI design will reinforce the cognitive transfer and thus the objectification of the transferred knowledge by the receiver.

Design Implication 5: A KMS should be able to enhance communication, enable collaboration and the dissemination of situated mental efforts, while at the same time it should provide a user-friendly user interface to support learning.

Perhaps this is the most critical design implication concerning the design and use of a technological intervention for KM. As we learned from MODEL implementation, in order to succeed a work-based knowledge-sharing environment, where actors are continually encouraged to communicate and collaborate, the supporting technologies used should be able to provide the means and mediums towards that direction. This has been achieved using synchronous and asynchronous communication techniques such as bulletin board, chat and e-mail. Additionally, because this technology serves as a communication hub, it should considers and adopts UI designing techniques that will be familiar to users, and will not block the knowledge transfer. For example, annotation was designed using the user-familiar sap green colour, like the sticker notes we are using to note something.

5 A Technological & Organisational Proposal for Knowledge Enablement of Work Anchored on BPs

Based on the theoretical assumptions and design implications analysed previous in this paper, a new tool-set is presented below that comes to fill the gap between the individualised BP practices and the knowledge sharing in a work context intensive environment. The MODEL solution comprises a portal, and a set of practical guidelines, and although currently exist as a prototype, it has be tested and improved based on user feedback reports.

Business Process is the "ground zero" of knowledge creation, and comprises the anchoring point for the knowledge and learning services supported by the system. MODEL has incorporated the narrative of BP, the concept of Case Studies, as the codified knowledge and learning medium for packaging the business process knowledge and the corresponding learning services applied on that knowledge. The tool-set operationalises learning and knowledge management, and aims at supporting the users in their daily activities in terms of problem solving and guidance but on the same time could comprise an organisational repository of information and knowledge sources. At the core of the system lies its ability to manage information and thus, by providing context to it, knowledge, both tacit and explicit. As shown in next figure (figure 1) MODEL employees a number of mechanisms to capture the tacit knowledge through the interaction of the users with the MODEL Case Studies.

The methodological intervention using practical guidelines for the parameterisation, deployment, familiarisation and effective use of MODEL application, has a central role The methodological intervention using practical guidelines for the parameterisation, deployment, familiarisation and effective use of

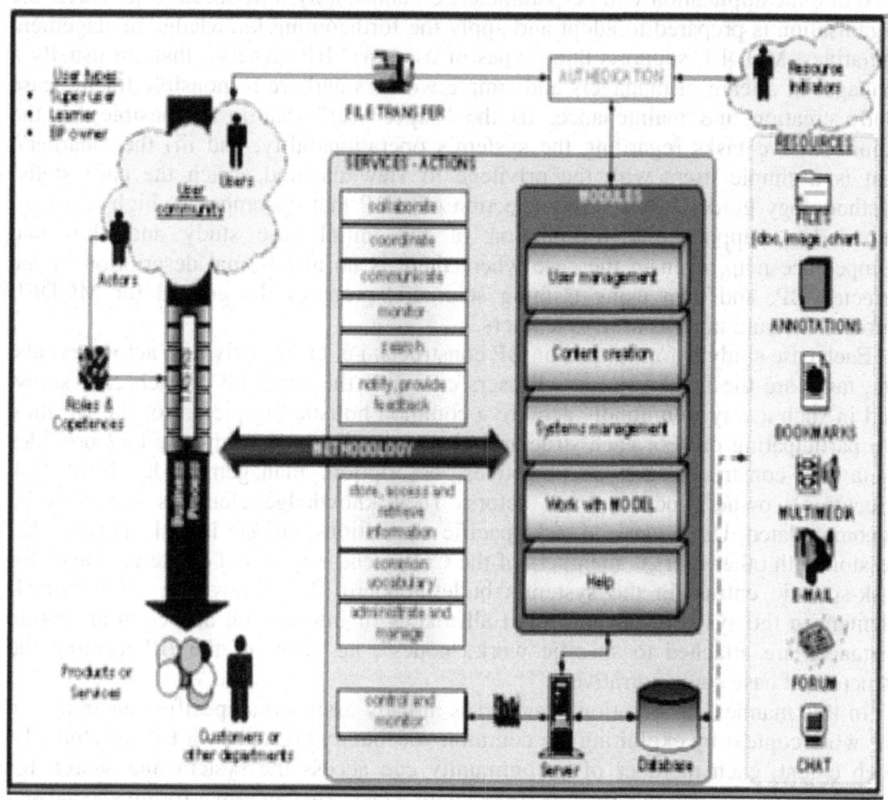

Fig. 1. The MODEL system concept

MODEL application, has a central role in system's support. The scope of MODEL methodology is to comprise a "holistic" approach that addresses two issues. First, the capture and diffusion of knowledge anchored on organizational work practices, manifested through Business Processes, taking into account organizational realities affecting the motivation of knowledge providers, knowledge flows, tool-set usability, etc. Second, the professional development, the learning aspect of the methodology, that is a systematic activity that focuses specifically on the personal development of the practitioners that are involved in the Business Process.

The importance of these issues is reflected in the methodological tools and techniques to assist managers to deploy a knowledge philosophy (organizational culture and individual behavior). In general, it consists of five phases: i) Generic MODEL Application Scenarios, ii) Organizational Needs Assessment, iii) Supporting System Set-up and Case Study Development, iv) Supporting Work-practice & Users and v) Embedding MODEL in strategies on professional and organizational development. The most crucial part is to help users to assimilate the new systems into their work procedures, while they learning how to use it and take the most of its content.

While the application will be parameterised and finally introduced to its users, the organisation is prepared to adopt and apply the forthcoming knowledge management initiatives. MODEL supports three types of users: i) "BP owners", that are usually a manager of a team of managers and simple workers and are responsible for the case study creation and maintenance. ii) the "super user" that is responsible for the administrative tasks regarding the system's operationability, and iii) the "learner", that is a simple users with the privilege to view the and enrich the case study. Methodology guides towards the selection of a BP that encompasses high levels of knowledge, supports the formulation of the initial case study and skill and competence map, even in the case where there is no any formal description of the selected BP, and then using training seminars, prepares the ground for MODEL introduction and initialisation to learners.

Each case study is formulated on BP constructs, i.e. tasks, activities, actors, events, etc; tasks are the focal objects. All users can view the structure of each case study, and in such a way to mutually acquire a common holistic big picture of the BP they are participating on. For each structural element of the case study, the tool provides meta-data constructs such as objectives, description, management level (of task execution), owner, location, and actors. Tacit knowledge elements can then be accommodated. Users can add task-specific annotations, engage in task-specific chat session with other users (- members of the CoP), send e-mail and create messages for task-specific entries in the system's bulletin board. The innovative (and critical) element in the systems design is that all tokens of information and communication instances are attached to specific work "nodes", i.e. tasks of the BP forming the structure of case study narrative.

In this manner, information provided is already assigned a specific "meaning" in the work context by exploiting the common vocabulary created by a BP structure. To such extent, each member of a community can access the system and search for relevant resources and other actors linked with a task. He can join a forum specialised in a task-specific thematic area and to communicate with other colleagues by sharing experiences and problem-solving ideas. Alternatively, he/she may send e-mail or start a chat session, and invite other colleagues to contribute collectively towards, for example, the solution of a problematic situation. These activities resulting the initial case study population with emerging experiences and descriptions of work practices.

The continually guided user-to-user interaction will result the objective initial seed capital (case study) to be transformed into a multi-subjective enriched content that will reflect the organisation's intellectual capital. At this point, the enriched case study will still be the "aurora borealis", a compass to provide users with the same focus of though, a common grounded context of discussion. In the long turn, knowledge providers and knowledge seekers will be motivated to engage in Communities of Practices and to share their understandings with the rest of the community.

6 Conclusions

Knowledge Management is a social process that can be supported from a variety of ICT. Technology can be used to promote the experimentation of new ideas, work practices simulation, and knowledge sharing through experiences and lessons learned.

To this extent, technology has a supporting role, but due to the soft aspects of Knowledge Management, specific design issues need to be addressed and considered by system developers, consultants and managers.

The new challenges emerging in the knowledge-based market require by organisations to cultivate, explore and reinforce their organisational knowledge. Organisations may need to reinvent the way of working, by providing to their workers a direct access to the knowledge layer that coexists in each Business Process. We propose some critical design implications and a techno-organisational intervention plus a set of guidelines that are dealing with issues that cannot be addressed by the application, due to the existence of the human factor and the cognitive constraints observed in its behaviour. This solution is based on the notion of collective knowledge and uses the concept of Case Studies to provide a narrative description of a Business Process at its stakeholders. Members of such community, are enabled to share task-specific knowledge and enrich their work practices.

Knowledge has a timeless value and we should pay more attention on the critical factors that provokes people to share their insights, and to enrich their experience to deal with new knowledge. We should also take into account the cognitive (individual) and behavioural (social) issues that may have considerable impact in resistance of an individual or a community to behave collectively and learn. And all these, with bearing in mind that modern organisation is continually transforming in all levels, by adopting new technologies, by refining their processes, and changing the way they doing business.

References

1. Rolland C., et al: Enterprise knowledge development: the process view, Information & Management, 36, (1999) 165-184
2. Eppler M., et al.: Improving knowledge intensive process through an enterprise knowledge medium, Proceedings of the ACM SIGCPR conference on Computer personnel research (1999)
3. Swap, W et al.: Using Mentoring and Storytelling to transfer Knowledge in the Workplace, Journal of Management Information Systems, Vol. 18, No. 1, (2001) 95-114
4. Lave, J.: Cognition in practice, Cambridge University Press, (1988)
5. Wenger, E.: Communities of Practice - Learning, Meaning and Identity, Cambridge University Press, (1998)
6. Nonaka, I., Nishiguchi, T.: Knowledge Emergence: Social technical and evolutionary dimensions of knowledge creation, Oxford University Press (2001)
7. Lave, J., Wenger, E., : Situated learning. Legitimate peripheral participation, Cambridge University Press (1991)
8. Hutchins, E.: Organizing work by adaption", Organization Science, Vol. 2, No. 1, (1991) 14-38
9. Brown, J., Duguid, P.: Organizational learning and communities-of-practice: toward a unified view of working, learning, and innovation, Organization Science, Vol. 2, No. 1, (1991) 40-57
10. Raelin, A. J.: A model of wok-based learning, Organization Science, Vol. 8, No. 6, (1997) 569-578
11. Banks, E.: Creating a knowledge culture, Work Study, Vol. 48, No. 1, (1999) 18-20
12. Ciborra, C.U.: Teams, Markets and systems, Cambridge University Press, (1993)
13. Brown, J., Duguid P.: Knowledge and Organization: A Social-Practice Perspective, Organization Science, Vol. 12, No. 2, (2001) 198-213

14. Leonard, D., and Sensiper, S.: The role of tacit knowledge in group innovation, California Management Review, Vol. 40 no 3, (1998) 112-132
15. El Sawy, O.A., Eriksson, I., Raven, A. and Carlsson, S: Understanding shared creation spaces around business processes: precursors to process innovation implementation, Int. J. Technology Management, Vol. 22, Nos. 1/2/3, (2001) 149-173
16. Nonaka, I.: The Knowledge-Creating Company, Harvard Business Review, Nov-Dec, (1991) 71-80
17. Nonaka, I.: A Dynamic theory of Organizational Knowledge Creation, Organization Science, Vol. 5, No. 1, (1994) 14-37
18. Polanyi, M.: Personal Knowledge: Towards a Post-Critical Philosophy, Chicago University Press, (1962)
19. Argyris, C.: Good communication that blocks learning, Harvard Business Review, Vol. 72, No. 4, (1994)
20. Brown, J., Duguid P.,: Organizing Knowledge, California Management Review, Vol. 40, No. 3, (1998) 90-111.
21. Maier, R., and Remus, U.,: Towards a Framework for Knowledge Managements Strategies: Process Orientation as strategic Starting Point, Proceedings of the 34th Hawaii International Conference on System Sciences, (2001)
22. Quinn, B. J., et al.: Managing Professional Intellect: Making the Most of the Best, Harvard Business Review, March-April, (1996) 71-80
23. Pentland, B.T.: Information Systems and Organizational Learning: The Social Epistemology of Organizational Knowledge Systems," Accounting, Management and Information Technology (5:1), (1995) 1-21.
24. Von Krogh, G., and Roos, J.: Organizational Epistemology, New York: St. Martin's Press, (1995)
25. Hansen, T.M., et al: What's Your Strategy for Managing Knowledge?, Harvard Business Review, March-April, (1999)
26. Nonaka, I. and Takeuchi, H.: The Knowledge Creating Company, Oxford University Press, (1995)
27. Alavi, M., Leidner, D. E.: Knowledge management systems: issues, challenges, and benefits, Communications of the AIS, (1999)
28. Bloodgood, J., Salisbury D. W.: Understanding the influence of organizational change strategies on information technology and knowledge management strategies, Decision Support Systems, 31, (2001) 55-69
29. Nunumaker, J., et al.: Enhancing Organization's Intellectual Bandwidth: The Quest for Fast and Effective value Creation", Journal of Management Information Systems, Vol. 17, No. 3, (2001) 3-8

Web Based Knowledge Management Community for Machine and Plant Construction Industries Technical After-Sales Service

Florian Kupsch[1], Silvia Mati[2], and Richard Schieferdecker[2]

[1] Institute for Information Systems at the German research Center for Artificial Intelligence, Saarbrüken
kupsch@iwi.uni-sb.de

[2] Research Institute for Operations Management at Aachen University of Technology
{mtl, sd}@fir.rwth-aachen.de

Abstract. The research project ServiceWorld[1] aims at developing a virtual community to support knowledge management in the field of after-sales service for machine and plant construction industries. Based on an existing service management reference model, a service community reference model and a service knowledge model were developed. Relevant services were identified and implemented in a community software prototype. First experiences of the pilot implementation at a heavy weight machine manufacturer will be available by the end of the year 2002.

1 Introduction

The economic pressure on companies of the German machine and plant construction industry is steadily increasing because of the actual cost structure in comparison with the international competitors.[2] In respect of big enterprises with strong market positions, small and medium-sized enterprises (SMEs) need to focus their efforts on increasing customer loyalty and acquiring customers. Customer loyalty is therefore a crucial factor for SMEs. One possibility of strengthening customer loyalty can be found in the improved worldwide technical after-sales service. In addition to the differentiation from competitors through price or an enhanced service offer, even aspects like reliability, quality of service, reaction speed on new customers' requests and knowledge on customers' desires are getting more and more important. Considering all these aspects, it is possible both to strengthen the competitive position and to increase the company's profit.

Through supply of service it is even possible to raise knowledge about customers and identify their specific requests. This is particularly important for SMEs, because customer-specific and product-specific knowledge is very difficult to imitate by competitors[3]. Therefore, service becomes a decisive competitive factor as well as price, technology and quality. Through knowledge, e.g. on customer-specific operative conditions of a machine, the service assistant is able to identify and remove defects more rapidly.

D. Karagiannis and U. Reimer (Eds.): PAKM 2002, LNAI 2569, pp. 437-446, 2002.

Today this (service-) knowledge is systematically identified, gained, developed, distributed, used, and preserved following the cycle of knowledge management only in few sectors. It concerns implicit knowledge: experience, professional skills and personal values of the individual service assistant. It is difficult to be formalized and express oneself only through concrete actions. Implicit knowledge covers the informal knowledge of service assistants, which is difficult to document and is known as *know-how*. However, as far as service is concerned, this implicit knowledge is of great importance.

Against the background of specific service requests and SMEs belonging to machine and plant construction industry (i.e. small number of service assistants, service assistants as know-how-carriers, world-wide customers, small number of service subsidiaries,...) the accomplishment of knowledge management in the field of after-sales service is only possible by using modern information and communication technology. While, the use of the Internet becomes steadily more usual e.g. for the sale of products, the technical after-sales services do not exploit the full potential of the Internet. The potential of the Internet for service means, e.g. time and cost-savings, a reduction in expensive data-transfers as well as in a waste of time. The availability of (service-) knowledge independent of time and place is a decisive aspect for the successful supply of service as well as the fact that the available knowledge is up-to-date. In spite of the above-mentioned advantages, which are associated with the use of the Internet, only isolated examples of a successful and purposeful use of the Internet for knowledge management in service exist at present.[3]

2 Research Objectives

In the course of the research project, an Internet based virtual community (ServiceWorld) was designed for the service and after-sales area. On this platform, the manufacturer, his sales and service partners as well as his customers can melt to a product- or manufacturer-oriented community. ServiceWorld offers different service utilities to all members of the community and supports an individual, topic-oriented information and knowledge exchange (see Fig. 1). The service platform enables enterprises (particularly manufacturers) to establish a personal contact with customers through knowledge-intense service utilities, and, in this manner, helps generate customer loyalty. Additionally, knowledge exchange and knowledge generation are promoted by the communication between the community members.

3 Service Community Concept

Based on an existing service management reference model[4], the service community concept consists of a service community reference model as well as a service oriented knowledge model, a concept for the organization of this knowledge under SMEs' boundary conditions and distributed structures, and a description of the identified services.

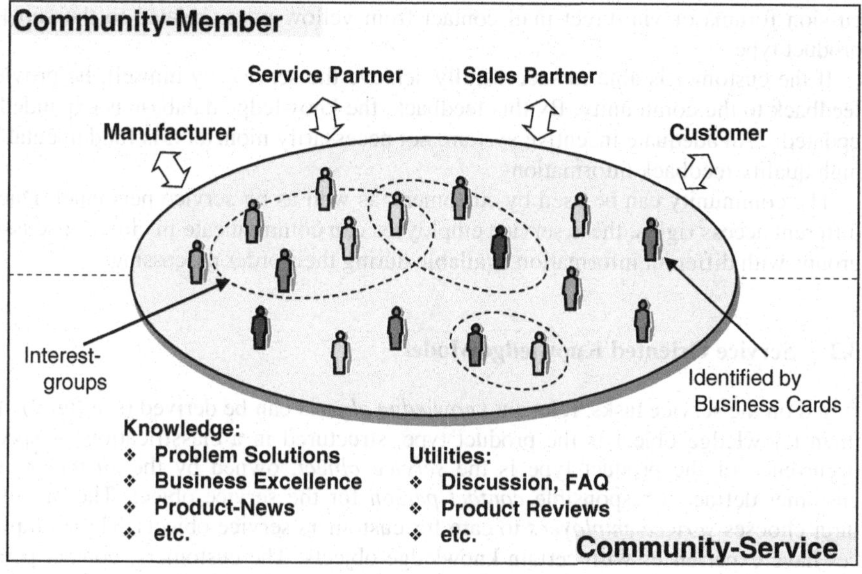

Fig. 1. ServiceWorld user and community services

3.1 Service Community Reference Model

Relevant knowledge shared by community users depends on after-sales service relevant tasks. Following the task model of the used service management model[4], relevant tasks were identified as *record request, identify problem/service, process order* and *confirm order*. Relevant data were identified as *customer, service objects (machines)* and *service employees.*

The use of the community starts with a customer request. The user is identified by registration. Accordingly any information related to the customer is available, e.g.

- service objects (machines) owned by the customer,
- related information and documents,
- service employees serving the customers' service objects as well as
- service requests or service activities already discussed in the community.

The customer describes problem causes related to his service object. Based on the service knowledge model (see chapter 3.2), information and documents related to the service object, the superior product type, cause and effect relations and resulting possible activities are displayed. If there is no useful information available, the community is involved, e.g. by posting a request in the product type specific discussion forum.

In order to specify the necessary service, i.e. the measures required to solve the customer's problem, the existing information in the community is used. If no appropriate service information is available, the user tries to retrieve information from discussion forums or via direct mail contact from yellow pages related to the superior product type.

If the customer is able to successfully achieve the service by himself, he provides feedback to the community. By this feedback, the knowledge database is expanded or updated. . An adequate incentive system, not necessarily monetary, is fundamental for high quality feedback information.

The community can be used by customers, as well as by service personnel. Due to different access rights, these service employees can communicate in closed discussion groups with different information available during their order processing.

3.2 Service Oriented Knowledge Model

Based on the service tasks, relevant *knowledge objects* can be derived (see fig. 2). The main knowledge object is the product type, structured in a classification. A special occurrence of the product type is the *service object*, owned by the *customer*. The customer defines a responsible *contact person* for the service object. The manufacturer chooses *service employees* to care for customers service objects. These employees have experiences with certain knowledge objects. The customers' contact person as well as the service personnel can be identified in a virtual community by business cards.

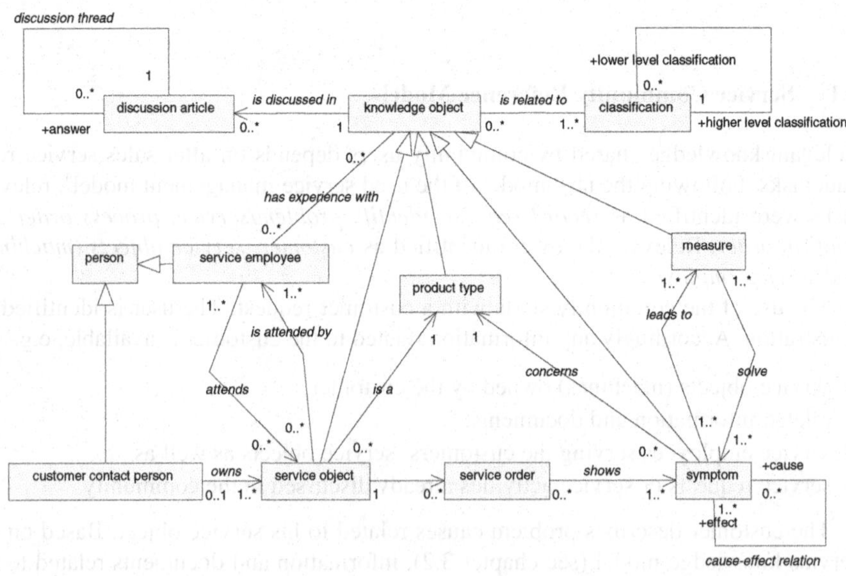

Fig. 2. ServiceWorld knowledge model

Problems dealing with service objects lead to *service orders*. Service objects show *symptoms,* which are part of a cause-effect relation network. The symptoms or the underlying causes result in specific *measures* solving the problems. Symptoms and measures can be considered as relevant knowledge objects too.

A basic service of a virtual community is a *discussion forum* where relevant knowledge objects are discussed.

The described knowledge objects and their relations are ServiceWorld's basic knowledge model. It can be extended by additional information, e.g. product information or business excellence cases.

4 Service Community Implementation

Within the scope of the implementation of the service community, different service utilities were designed and developed to support exchange, generation and search for information, under which it is possible to specify the yellow pages, the discussion forums, the error database and its FAQ section.

Every utility is accessible to every user through a comprehensive research engine even if not every user can access every piece of information. This is done in order to avoid on the one hand the spreading of enterprise internal information and on the other hand to facilitate the search for knowledge objects through an aimed reduction of the number of accessible documents per user. Service objects provide for access differentiation: the customer is only able to search for knowledge objects regarding his own service objects. Employees can execute an unrestricted search.

4.1 Discussion Forums

This utility offers the possibility to all partners of an enterprise to pursue an exchange of experience and knowledge about items concerning the products of the enterprise. In the discussion forums it is possible to get in touch with other community-users by starting a new thread about a specific problem solution or reading an inquiry and, if necessary, replying to it. Therefore, the forums represent the virtual places where knowledge is generated, distributed and applied through knowledge exchange among the community-users. Thus, the employment of the forums speeds up the creation of a knowledge database and accelerates the process of externalization of internal knowledge.[5]

Every community-user has the possibility to access every forum concerning his service objects and to virtually meet other users dealing with the same topics. By taking part to the forums, service employees can make sure that an answer to the inquired problem solution is provided and in this way avoid disappointment.

This utility also offers additional rights to employees: with the publication of a new article, employees have the possibility to determine the readership of the article by releasing it for all the community-users or only for employees. This characteristic enables internal topics to be discussed without the necessity of a separate forum. The advantage here is the centralization of all information concerning a specific problem and the simplification of a possible editorial revision, necessary e.g. to create a new document for the error database.

In order to increase attendance at forums and to ease the determination of knowledge objects' relevance, an incentive system has to be implemented: in this way every customer has the possibility to assess those articles whose content he tried out and to make his assessment in form of school grades, depending on how much a specific article turned out to be useful for the solution of a problem. Such an incentive system enhances the motivation of the community-users to take part in the forums and to write only useful articles, since a positive evaluation lets the article's author receive service-scores, which lead to an increase in his score account. With a negative evaluation, service-scores are subtracted from the score account. If the score account exceeds a certain threshold, the user can be classified as an *expert* automatically. This is the case for employees. On the other hand, classification is not automatic for customers as they can choose to set their status on *expert* by activating the proper option in their personal profile. For both user-groups the classification as an *expert* is cancelled automatically if the score account falls below the threshold.

4.2 Yellow Pages

The yellow pages support the search for carriers of service knowledge within the community, i.e. of users who demonstrated to have made experiences or have acquired knowledge about a certain service object (*experts*). This utility consists mainly of two different search functions: a free-text search for internal purposes and a tree search which provides user-specific data and allows users to establish direct contact with each other.

After a successful search request, this utility offers the functionality *call me back* in case the knowledge carrier is a service employee and a phone call is whished, and the function *direct mailing* to take direct writing contact with the knowledge carrier by electronic mail. In this case, one can also choose whether the mail should appear in a discussion forum or not. In the affirmative, the help inquiry is posted automatically to the correct forum.

4.3 Error Database and FAQ's Utility

In the error database, all documents, which have been filed and classified, describe the instances necessary to a troubleshooting. Problem symptoms, groups and types of engines and assemblies make the classification of the documents.

If a document of the database is accessed frequently by users, it grants the status of *frequently asked questions* and, for a certain amount of time, it can be found in the section FAQ. After a certain amount of days of permanence, the document is checked and, if necessary, removed from the FAQ section.

Like in the utility *discussion forum*, customers have the possibility to make an assessment of the documents' usefulness and, if they please, they can leave a commentary to complete or correct its content. In case of this additional feedback, an editorial revision takes place: the technical editor estimates whether a reworking, a rewriting, or a deletion of the document in question is necessary and, if so, he performs it. Also these procedures are assessed trough positive or negative service-scores.

Other similar aspects of the two utilities can be found in the user-specific access to documents defined through service objects and in the thematic cross-linking of every utility section among different utilities.

5 ServiceWorld Prototype

To figure out whether the kind of knowledge representation and management described in the chapters above is supporting a suggestive distribution of service-relevant knowledge, a prototypic implementation of a web-based application was accomplished. Its objective was to install and introduce that prototype within an enterprise belonging to the plant engineering and construction branch.

In this context, a suitable data model for the mapping of data structures was developed as well as the process chains implied in standard ServiceWorld operations. Therefore, common modeling techniques such as the Entity Relationship Model (ERM) for data structures and the Event driven Process Chain (EPC) for process models were used.[6]

Moreover, a high value was set on the use of Open Source software because of its free availability and the option of being customized to the user's needs. After an evaluation of the most common software components, the following products have been selected:

- Operating System: *Debian Linux*
- Web server: *Apache HTTP Server*
- Database: *mySQL*
- Programming languages: *PHP 4, Java Script* and *HTML*

Fig. 3 provides an overview of the ServiceWorld architecture. The Apache web server generates HTML code that can be interpreted by every web browser.

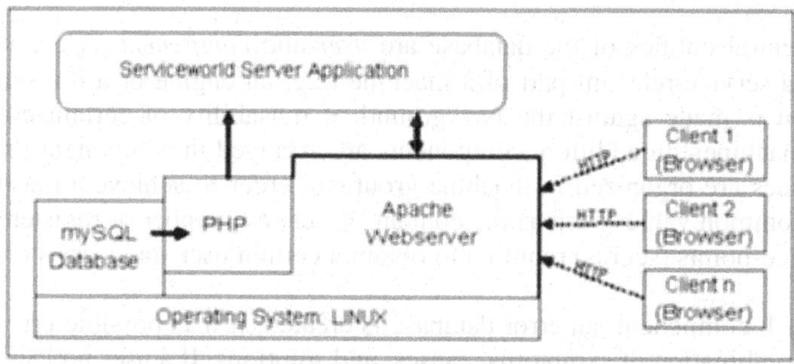

Fig. 3. ServiceWorld software architecture

To perform a unified layout, Cascading Stylesheets (CSS) are used. Dynamic elements are created by PHP scripts that are embedded into the HTML source code which describes the content of a website as well as its presentation. The particular data sets required by the scripts are obtained via the mySQL Database. It allows simultaneous access by several users and it is structured with an underlying data model illustrated in a simplified form in Fig. 4. Confidential information such as user data and password is stored with an encryption to save privacy and security.

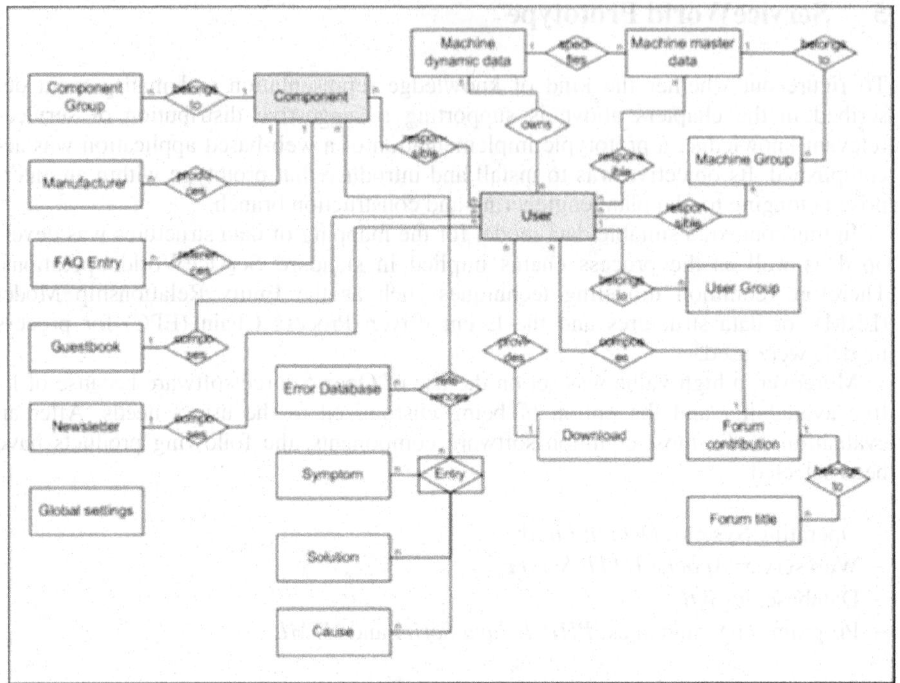

Fig. 4. Simplified ServiceWorld data model

The central entities of the database are *user* and *component*. A component is defined as a service-relevant part of a machine (e.g. an engine or a transmission). This separation is made against the background of reusability of certain components in several machines. In addition, components are arranged in component groups as well as machines are organized in machine groups in order to achieve a reasonable structuring. Common values such as the content of tickers, number of registered users, and the service-points (scores) required to obtain a certain user status are stored in a separate table.

For each component, an error database is created. It lists possible errors on the basis of a combination of symptoms, causes, and solutions. If a user notices an error in a machine, he only needs to select the faulty machine. ServiceWorld performs a decomposition of the machine in its particular components and offers all relevant services in a personalized manner. These services are presented in a networked way in order to be able to offer all kind of interesting data and information of different structure in an integrated platform. Besides common information about the machine, specific forum messages, associated downloads, qualified contact persons and common FAQ are also displayed. Fig. 5 shows a screenshot of the first prototype to give an impression of how networked knowledge is presented.

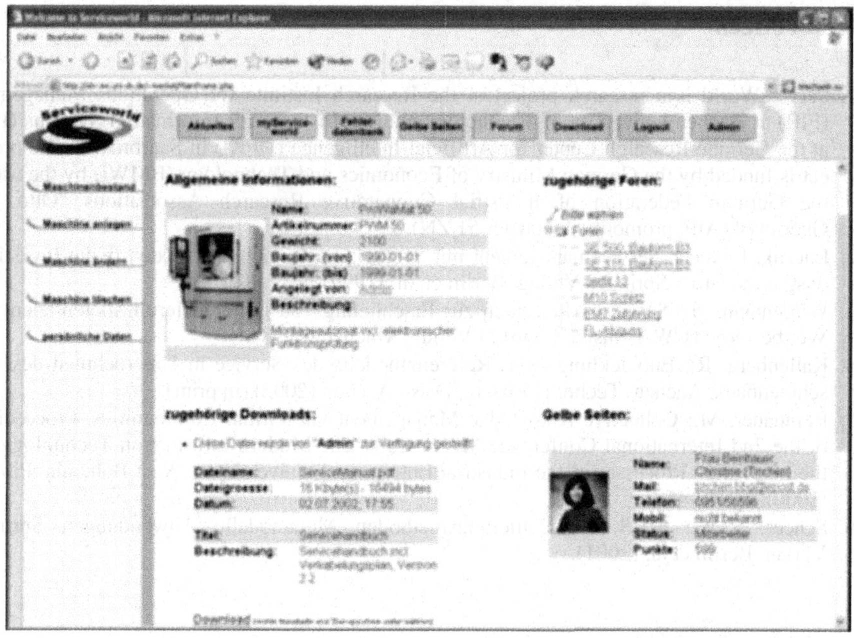

Fig. 5. Screenshot of the ServiceWorld prototype

In order to measure success and acceptance of ServiceWorld, the prototype implementation will be accompanied by several surveys to find out whether virtual communities are an adequate communication instrument in the field of service management. In order to take suggestions for the improvement of navigation and design into consideration, a performance index will be created. This will consider criteria such as number of successful contacts, number of page impressions, inquiries and so on.

6 Conclusion

The developed concept and software prototype will be tested in a heavy weight machine manufacturing company. With 60 employees, they generate an annual turnover of 10 million Euros with a ratio of 70% after-sales service.

ServiceWorld will be integrated in the service organization to support the international after-sales service efforts. For this purpose, relevant service processes as well as the described product and service knowledge must be identified and implemented in ServiceWorld.

First experiences of the pilot implementation will be available by the end of the year 2002.

References

1. ServiceWorld is a research project at the Research Institute for Operations Management (FIR) at Aachen University of Technology and the Institute for Information Systems (IWi) at the German Research Center for Artificial Intelligence (DFKI) in Saarbrüken. The project is funded by the German Ministry of Economics and Technology (BMWi) by the use of the German Federation of Industrial Cooperative Research Associations "Otto von Guericke" (AiF, promoting identifier 51 ZN).
2. Luczak, H. (ed.): Servicemanagement mit System: erfolgreiche Methoden fü die Investitionsgüterindustrie. Springer-Verlag, Berlin et. al. (1999).
3. Wildemann, H.: Service – Leitfaden zur Erschließng von Differenzierungspotentialen im Wettbewerb. TCW Transfer-Centrum Verlag, Müchen (1998).
4. Kallenberg, R.: Entwicklung eines Referenzmodells des Service in Unternehmen des Maschinenbaus. Aachen, Techn. Hochsch., Diss., Aachen (2002) (in print).
5. Beinhauer, M.: Collective Knowledge Management via Virtual Communities. Proceedings of the 2nd International Conference MITIP 2000 „The Modern Information Technology in the Innovation Processes of the Industrial Enterprices," University of West Bohemia, Pilzen (2000), pp. 40-46.
6. Scheer, A.-W.: ARIS – Modellierungsmethoden, Metamodelle, Anwendungen. Springer Verlag, Berlin et al. (2001).

Dynamic Generation of User Communities with Participative Knowledge Production and Content-Driven Delivery

Sinuhé Arroyo [1] and Juan Manuel Dodero[2]

[1] Intelligent Software Components (iSOCO) S.A.,
Francisca Delgado 11, 28108 Alcobendas, Madrid, Spain
sinuheag@isoco.com

[2] Laboratorio DEI, Universidad Carlos III de Madrid,
Avda. de la Universidad 30, 28911 Leganés, Madrid, Spain
dodero@inf.uc3m.es

Abstract. In a distributed knowledge management system, knowledge is firstly produced and then delivered to a person or community of users that is interested in it. Knowledge creation or production is a set of cooperative tasks that need to be coordinated. A multiagent architecture is introduced for this aim, where knowledge-producing agents are arranged into knowledge domains or marts, and a distributed interaction protocol is used to consolidate knowledge that is generated. The knowledge that is produced in this way is used as the source data to dynamically build user communities that can drive the delivery of knowledge amongst users.

1 Introduction

Knowledge Management (KM) is the group of processes that transform intellectual capital of an organization or group of persons into a value [18]. Amongst those processes, KM authors quote creation, acquisition, distribution, application, sharing and reposition of knowledge [17]. Knowledge emerges from the social interaction between actors, and frequently it is not formally structured to be appropriately used and exploited. In this sense, knowledge management acts as a systematic programme to profit from what the organization knows. KM processes can be summarized in production, acquisition and delivery of knowledge. In one hand, acquisition and delivery tasks allow to share and reuse the group-wide available knowledge. On the other hand, production is a creative process to formulate new knowledge in the group, that has to be validated.

When a group of people is participatively creating (or producing) a complex object, it is advisable to establish a set of rules to coordinate its development. This is the situation, for instance, when several people are building a software object. We will follow a concrete example for a better explanation of the problem. Let's suppose two developers who are designing respective modules, which will be part of the same software object. During the design, the necessity to develop two sub-elements for the

D. Karagiannis and U. Reimer (Eds.): PAKM 2002, LNAI 2569, pp. 447-456, 2002.

same purpose can be detected by both developers. Each one usually has his/her own pace of work in developing the common element. As well, they can be differently skilled in that work. If the development process is not appropriately coordinated, the following problems can arise:

- A developer could get her work crushed, depending on the required speed and quality of the design, in comparison to her partner's competency.
- When speed is more important than quality, a more elaborated and reusable product can be readily thrown away.
- In the best case, effort will be duplicated in several phases of the project.

Therefore, the coordination of knowledge production should meet the following objectives:

- Bring together participants' different pace of creation.
- Take advantage of participants' different skills in the problem domain and the tools that are managed.
- Reduce the number of conflicts provoked by interdependencies between in-production knowledge components.
- In a more general sense, avoid duplication of effort.

Knowledge needs to be constantly updated and delivered to the right places at the right time. Such delivery is a continuous process of transferring knowledge that is interesting to a person or community of users. These and other questions are raised in order to distribute knowledge among interested users:

- Which communities are users member of?
- How are the communities initially spawned, after setting up a group of users who are generating knowledge?
- What would it happen if a user changes the kind of knowledge that it produces, and this is better classified in another community?
- As time progresses, may knowledge that is produced in a community be biased towards a different category?

2 Agent-Mediated Knowledge Production

Several authors on Knowledge Management cite production or generation of knowledge referring to the creation of new knowledge [3, 15, 17]. When Davenport and Prusak tell about *knowledge generation*, they are referring both to externally acquired knowledge and to that developed within the bosom of an organization, without making any difference between acquisition and generation. In our study, we consider *generation* as distinct from *acquisition*. From our point of view, knowledge generation or production is the creation of new knowledge as the result of the social interaction between actors in a workgroup or organization, according to their interests and the regulations that apply. On the other side, knowledge can also be acquired, that is, when it comes from outside of the organization or workgroup —i.e., it is generated externally and thereafter adopted by the organization.

Coordination is a key pattern of interaction needed to obtain a good quality knowledge that has been validated by means of contrast and/or consensus in the group. Although distributed KM research in knowledge acquisition and sharing efforts are worth to be considered, knowledge production still lacks interaction models and methods to coordinate a group of autonomous users in the cooperative generation of knowledge.

Multiagent systems have been successful in the distributed implementation of KM processes. Knowledge acquisition agents have been one of the most successful applications of software agents, specifically in the Internet [7], were knowledge-collector agents operate within available information resources, and validate them in accordance with the users' interests. On the other hand, knowledge delivery lies in an end-to-end routing of knowledge that is generated by some actor. This is a task that has been typically realized by software agents [9, 10]. Therefore, it is reasonable to approach the multiagent paradigm for knowledge production. Knowledge-producing agents need to do formulations that keep with a validation scheme supporting the knowledge construction. Sice agents have been proven as a helpful tool for the coordination of human people who are performing a given task [13], multiagent systems can support the coordinated interaction needed to achieve an agreement on the knowledge that is eventually generated, and even on the validation scheme.

Agent interaction protocols govern the exchange of a series of messages among agents, i.e. a conversation. There are some popular interaction protocols and architectures, used heavily by multi-agent systems, like blackboards [14], contract protocols [16] and computational economies [19]. Nevertheless, these approaches tackle rather general aspects of agent interactions, usually characterized as competitive, cooperative or negotiative. During knowledge production, agents try to convince each other in a group to accept a given knowledge in some domain, so building the corpus of shared knowledge. The aim is to allow agents to *consolidate* knowledge that is continuously produced. Consolidation in a group of producers is to establish a given knowledge as accepted by the group as a whole, with every member knowing about that circumstance. Agents can reach a consensus on the knowledge that is consolidated by the exchange of messages, using the consolidation protocol described below.

The architecture and protocol presented below is a multi-agent approach to the production of knowledge. The working hypothesis is that a group of agents can help in the participative production of knowledge, by coordinating their creation activities. Therefore, different agents can act as representatives of knowledge-producing actors, according to the following principles:

- Agents can be structured into separable knowledge domains of interaction. This structuring reflects the knowledge differences between producers.
- A dynamic re-thinking of the structure of interactions in different domains can help to reduce the inter-dependencies during the process.

2.1 A Multi-agent Architecture for Knowledge Production

In our architecture, knowledge-producing agents can operate within the boundaries of a specific domain or knowledge mart, as shown in fig. 1. Nevertheless, interaction among different domains is also supported through a number of proxy agents. In order to facilitate interaction between domains, marts can be structured in a hierarchical way. In this architecture, domains can be modelled as knowledge marts, and marts are arranged into knowledge warehouses. A *knowledge mart* is a distributed group of agents that is trying to produce a piece of knowledge in a given domain. A *knowledge warehouse* is the place where knowledge produced in foreign marts is merged in a structured fashion.

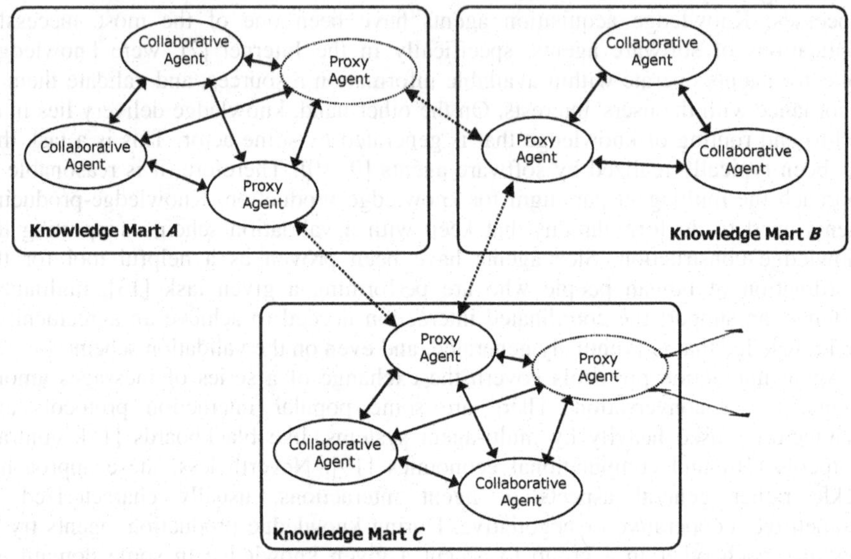

Fig. 1. Participative knowledge marts

Two or more marts can interact using representatives in a common warehouse. When knowledge produced in a mart can affect performance in some other domain, a special proxy agent can act as representative in the foreign mart, according to the proxy design pattern [8], so that interaction between marts is not tightly coupled.

2.2 Knowledge Consolidation Protocol

The function of the protocol executed by agents is to consolidate knowledge that is created in our agent-coordinated interaction environment. By *consolidation* we mean the establishment of knowledge as accepted by every agent in the mart, in such a way that every member agent eventually know about it. The consolidation protocol, described in [5], is a two-phase process:

- The *distribution* phase begins when an agent submits a proposal, i.e. when the agent starts the protocol. A given timeout t_0 is defined to set the end of this phase.
- The *consolidation* phase begins if there is a proposal waiting to be consolidated. This event can occur whether the distribution timeout t_0 expired or a t_0-waiting agent received a proposal that was evaluated as preferred. A distinct timeout t_1 is used for the consolidation phase.

An agent can participate in several interaction processes. Each interaction process is handled separately, by initiating a new execution thread of the protocol. Two different timeouts are used over the course of the protocol. Timeout t_0 is used for the distribution phase, that occurs after an agent submits a *proposal(k,n)* message, where n represents an interaction process and k is a piece of knowledge that wants to be consolidated in the mart. During t_0, messages can arrive from any other agent, consisting in new proposals, referring to same interaction process. The message used to consolidate a proposal has the form *consolidate(k,n)*, and its aim is to establish a previously submitted proposal k as consolidated in an interaction process n.

At any moment, the reception of a message from another agent may provoke a momentary retraction from a previously submitted proposal, until a counter-proposal is elaborated. An agent that has not reached this state will be waiting for t_0 timeout. Then, if the agent receives a proposal that is evaluated as preferred, a new timeout t_1 is set to give it a chance. But if the preferred proposal is not eventually ratified, then the agent goes on about its aims and will try again to consolidate its own proposal.

Agents' rationality needs to be modelled in terms of preference relations or relevance functions, in order to allow them to evaluate and compare proposals. The relevance of a proposal is defined as the set of proposal attributes considered when interacting, while the preference relationship denotes which of two proposals is preferred.

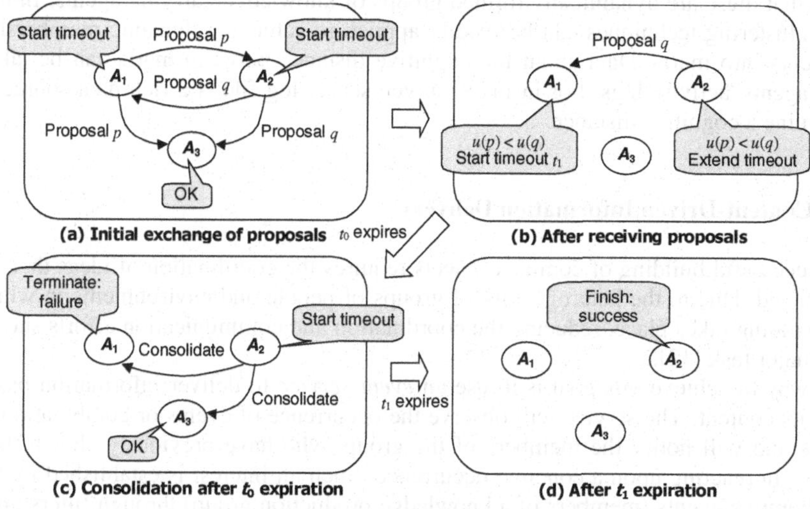

Fig. 2. Execution example of the protocol

The sequence of events spawned by the execution of the protocol by two agents trying to consolidate their proposals at the same time is depicted in the fig. 2. The interaction begins when agents A_1 and A_2 submit proposals p and q respectively.

(a) Both A_1 and A_2 receive each other's proposal and begin the distribution phase, so starting timeout t_0. Proposals p and q also arrive to A_3, which is not participating in the process and silently receives them.
(b) A_1 compares q to p, resulting p worse evaluated than q. Then, A_1 starts timeout t_1, giving q a chance to be consolidated. On the other hand, A_2 compares both

proposals as well and reminds A_1 about the results by sending it q again. Then, timeout t_0 is extended in order to give a chance for other agents' proposals to come.

(c) When timeout t_0 expires, A_2 sends a consolidation message for q to every agent in the mart. When received, A_1 finishes the protocol because it is expecting the consolidation for q. A_3 simply accepts the notification.

(d) Finally, when t_1 expires, A_2 is confirmed about the end of the consolidation phase for q and its execution thread of the protocol ends up successfully. Therefore, every agent in the mart will eventually know about the consolidation of the proposal.

3 Content-Driven Knowledge Delivery

Bringing forward the answers to knowledge delivery issues, it seems reasonable to dynamically establish the membership of agents into marts. As well, division and/or fusion of marts can be needed to better reflect the knowledge-driven structure. To represent the differences between knowledge marts, we define a *cognitive distance* between two agents as a measure of the similarity between the knowledge produced by both agents. The cognitive distance can be also defined between two marts, in the sense that these are dynamically formed groups of knowledge-carrying agents. In that case, clustering techniques can be readily applied to achieve a dynamic membership of agents into marts. Data about the cognitive distance between marts can be taken from agents' activity logs. For instance, a web server log file is a rich data source to determine a cognitive distance.

3.1 Content-Driven Information Delivery

The successful building of complex objects requires the coordination of ideas that are exchanged. Due to the heterogeneity of groups of people and environments in which this building takes place, reducing the coordination and communication efforts should be a major task [12].

A way to achieve this goal is to use an *event service* to deliver information based upon its content. The service will observe the occurrence of events or combination of events and will notify the members of the group, who have previously shown their interest in reacting upon a concrete occurrence. Such an interest is established by the collaborative agents (members of a knowledge production group) through filters upon the contents produced in the knowledge mart. The main advantage of this approach resides in the expressiveness that may be obtained in the communications, since the filters apply to the whole content of the notification, allowing a greater degree of freedom in the way the information is codified [1]. Filters are used to deliver contents of interest to the appropriate recipient.

Addressing is concern of the underlying transport protocol that guarantees a reliable delivery, and it can be done using some multicasting facility in the underlying transport. The main disadvantage of multicasting is the loss of expressiveness, due to the necessity of mapping expressions to IP groups in an scalable way [1]. Since multicasting never relates two groups of different IP addresses, a notification that matches two or more filters, corresponding to agents located in different groups of IP addresses, should be routed in parallel with the rest, so reducing the protocol effectiveness and increasing the communication efforts.

A workaround to overcome that issue is to use a set of connected brokers, which can also work as entry points for collaborative agents. Such brokers will be responsible for the routing of notifications or, in the last case, to deliver them to other agents. In order to do the addressing, each broker holds a table with filters, to send notifications matching a concrete filter to the appropriate addresses. Eventually, when notifications arrive to a broker who acts as an entry point for some agents, they will be forwarded to those whose filters are matched [2].

3.2 OKAPi as a Content-Driven Knowledge Broker

OKAPi (Ontology-based Knowledge Application Interface) is an implementation of a multiprotocol adapter for a content based-router. The main purpose of the system is to facilitate the request delivery of information in networked environments, independently of the communication protocol (HTTP, SMS, SMTP, etc). There is no limitation to the interoperability of different protocols, and so, an agent may establish a filter using HTTP, and receive notifications by SMTP or SMS, whilst the publisher used a third protocol to explicit the contents.

The filters to select the contents of interest are established by an ontology as vocabulary and reference model, in order to provide every agent with a shared way of communication within the domain of a concrete complex object.

Agents play one of two very well-defined roles in OKAPi, according to the necessity or availability of information showed by the agent:

- Subscribers: Agents who want to gather some information referred to a particular complex object. They are responsible for the establishment of filters using the appropriate ontology corresponding to a particular object.
- Publishers: Agents that make some information explicit to the rest of the community by sending it to the broker that acts as its access point to the delivery service.

Both roles are not mutually exclusive, and in some cases an agent can act as a subscriber for some complex object, and as a publisher for another.

A filter is said to be covered when for each of its attributes, there is a publication which holds values that accomplishes all the properties of the filter, according to a logical operator (=, ≤, ≥, etc.) defined for each. Once a filter has been set, it is propagated to every broker in the knowledge mart that holds an interested agent, in a least-information transferring basis. This means that if a broker situated upstream holds a more general filter that contains the current one, it won't be forwarded any further that way, since all the publication that fit the former will fit the current subscription. This mechanism guaranties that an agent is part of all the knowledge marts it is interested in, and so, that the contents produced within the interested domains will be forwarded from one router to another, following the reverse return path established by the filter, until it reaches the appropriate access point. This is true for every agent interested in that particular knowledge. From the access point, the contents of the notification are formatted according to the agent's desires and sent using the addressee' protocol (SMTP, SMS, HTTP, etc.)

4 Dynamic Generation of Agent Communities

In order to obtain a more effective communication mechanism, the interest of agents that make up the service (subscriptions and publications) are analysed using clustering techniques. As a result, agents that share similar interest (sharing the same mart) are relocated into communities located in the same access point, or close to those that at that moment have shared interests, reducing in this way the amount of information that brokers must share to complete the service.

As mentioned earlier, an agent may take two different roles, either subscriber or publisher. In both cases it holds some degree of interaction with a concrete mart, whether it is producing or is interested in receiving some content. The affiliation of an agent to a mart has to take into account both circumstances.

OKAPi provides a mechanism to overcome the agent relocation based on the amount of knowledge produced within a mart. The bigger the amount of knowledge produced among two agents (number of related publications or subscriptions sent or received), the bigger the probability that they are relocated closer to each other with respect to the marts they are interacting with. That probability is measured as the number of messages they interchange as reflected in the servers' logs (so shrinking their cognitive distance). According to this, if eventually the relocation of an agent to a new access point takes place, the chance that it sends or receives messages to/from the mart or marts they were member of will be smaller than the chance of receiving or sending within the current one.

A more specific case of agent relocation could occur when not only some agents of the community are relocated, but the hold community is resettled. Such relocation could be originated by three different circumstances:

- Significant reduction of the cognitive distance among marts. The contents produce by some marts are very much alike, which suggests that they could be merged into a single one.
- A change in produced contents: The knowledge produced can change, and it seems clear that the previous thread of contents is left aside due to obsolescence, or just lost interest.
- There are more than one thread of contents: Knowledge can be produced according to well-defined but divergent paths within the mart. In that case, the mart should be divided and their agents relocated to different access points.

These issues can be addressed by means of clustering techniques, but in some cases there are collateral considerations for the appropriate functioning of the knowledge mart, as which should be the optimal size of marts, or which could be the cost rate of agent relocation relative to the reduction in brokers' communication efforts.

An agent's cognitive distance to each existing mart is represented by the matrix of fig. 3. By analysing these distances, an optimal agent's placement could be deduced. An accurate algorithm to obtain the dissimilarity matrix, and therefore, agents' and mart's best access points location is COBWEB, which applies a hierarchical incremental method using an heuristic evaluation measure called *category utility* to determine the correct agent placement [11].

$$\begin{bmatrix} 0 & & & & \\ d(2,1) & 0 & & & \\ d(3,1) & d(3,2) & 0 & & \\ \dots & \dots & \dots & \dots & \\ d(n,1) & d(n,2) & \dots & \dots & 0 \end{bmatrix}$$

Fig. 3. Dissimilarity matrix.

Fig. 4 represents an example of agent relocation due to the birth of a new thread of knowledge within the mart. In the first stage (left side) there are two marts composed by four agents each one of them.

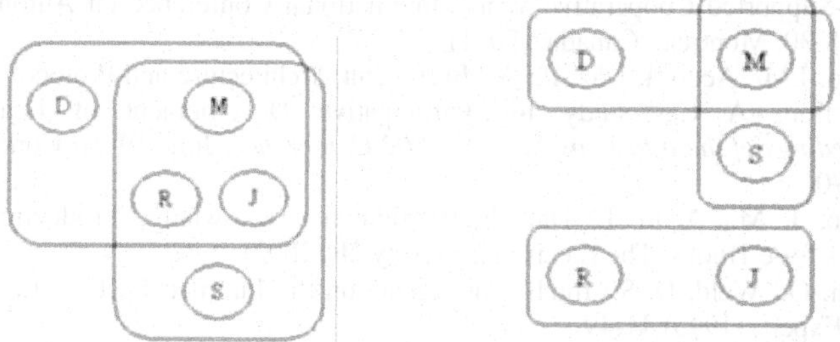

Fig. 4. Distribution of agents into communities

Due to a change of interest, a new mart is developed by the knowledge production of two agents (see fig. 4, right side). The cognitive distance among agents R and J have been reduced with respect to each other, but it did increase with respect to the mart, originating the creation of a new mart in a different access point. M and S are still part of the same community and the same happens to M and D. M is member of two marts, which means that it must be positioned in an access point not much far from those communities.

5 Conclusions

The participative approach presented in this work is applicable to several CSCW (Computer-supported cooperative work) tasks. It has been successfully applied to the instructional design of learning objects [4, 5] and electronic books composition [6]. In these scenarios, reduced-sized groups of helper agents have been found to facilitate the coordination of creational activities. Nevertheless, further validation is needed to assess the scalability of the solution in both qualitative and quantitative scenarios. We are conducting tests on the impact of the number of agents in the overall effectiveness of the model.

References

1. Carzaniga, A.: Architecture for an Event Notification Service Scalable to Wide-Area Networks. PhD Thesis. Politecnico di Milano (1998)
2. Carzaniga A., Wolf, A: Content-Based Networking: A New Comunication Infraestructure. NSF Workshop on an Infrastructure for Mobile and Wireless Systems. In conjunction with the International Conference on Computer Communications and Networks ICCCN. Scottsdale, AZ. (2001)
3. Davenport, T. H., Prusak, L.: Working Knowledge: How Organizations Manage What They Know. Harvard Business School Press. (1998)
4. Dodero, J. M., Sicilia, M. A., Garcá, E.: A Knowledge Production Protocol for Cooperative Development of Learning Objects, Proceedings of the 2nd Workshop on Agent-Supported Cooperative Work, International Conference on Autonomous Agents, May 28-30, Montreal, Canada, (2001)
5. Dodero, J.M., Aedo, I, Dáz, P.: A Multi-agent Architecture and Protocol for Knowledge Production. A Case-study for Participative Development of Learning Objects. *Proceedings of the Informing Science 2002 Conference*, June 19-21, Cork, Ireland (2002) 357-370
6. Dodero, J. M., Aedo, I., Dáz, P.: Participative Knowledge Production of Learning Objects for e-Books, The Electronic Library **20** (2002)
7. Etzioni, O., Weld, D. S.: Intelligent Agents on the Internet: Fact, Fiction, and Forecast. IEEE Expert. (1995) 44-49
8. Gamma, E., Helm, R., Johnson, R., Vlissides, J.: Design Patterns. Reading, Massachusetts: Addison-Wesley Publishing Company (1994)
9. Genesereth, M., J. Tenenbaum, J.: An agent-based approach to software. Stanford University Logic Group. (1991)
10. Gruber, T. R.: Toward a Knowledge Medium for Collaborative Product. Proceedings of the 2nd International Conference on Artificial Intelligence in Design. Kluwer Academic Publishers. Pittsburgh (1992) 413-432
11. Han, J., Kamber, M.: Data Mining: Concepts and Techniques Morgan. Kaufmann Publishers (2001)
12. Liebowitz, J. (ed.): Knowledge Management Handbook. CRC Press LLC (1999)
13. Maes, P.: Agents that reduce work and information overload. Communications of the ACM **37**(7) (1994) 31-40
14. Newell, A.: Some problems of the basic organization in problem-solving programs. Proceeding of the Second Conference on Self-Organizing Systems. Spartan Books. (1962) 393-423
15. Nonaka, I., Takeuchi, H.: The Knowledge-Creating Company. Oxford University Press. New York. (1995)
16. Smith, R. G.: The Contract Net Protocol: High-Level Communication and Control in a Distributed Problem Solver. IEEE Transactions on Computers **29** (12) (1980) 1104--1113
17. Swanstrom, E.: Knowledge Management: Modeling and Managing the Knowledge Process. John Wiley & Sons (1999)
18. Stewart, T.A.: Intellectual Capital: The New Wealth of Organizations, Doubleday, New York, 1997.
19. Wellman, M. P.: A Computational Market Model for Distributed Configuration Design. Readings in Agents. Morgan Kaufmann. San Francisco, California. (1997) 371-379

Knowledge Sharing in Cyberspace: Virtual Knowledge Communities

Angela M. Dickinson, MAS (KM)

Abstract. The past years have seen an explosion in the number of virtual knowledge communities and community membership is assuming an increasingly important role in the working lives of their members. Many communities have a number of common, key constituent elements.
This paper examines the characteristics of real and virtual communities, identifies key elements and proposes a model for analysing and evaluating them over time. Focusing on the interaction and knowledge exchange activities in a virtual community of freelance translators, an empirical study of life in a thriving knowledge community is presented and recommendations made for continued success.

1 Introduction

Over the past two decades, virtual communities and communities of practice (CoPs) have emerged across many fields of commercial and private interest to assume an increasingly important role in the working and social lives of their members. My own interest in virtual communities began when I was invited by a translator colleague to join ProZ.com[1], a virtual community for freelance translators. I became intrigued by the obvious identification of members with this community and sought to understand their motivation for membership and for sharing knowledge so freely with each other.

Much of the literature and research material on virtual communities focuses primarily on virtual social communities, transaction communities or CoPs within organisations and corporations. It often overlooks the relevance of virtual knowledge communities that have emerged without a common corporate goal and thrive without the motivation of fulfilling corporate targets or financial rewards for members. There is little scientific material available on the emergence, motivation and management of professional (extra-organisational) virtual communities, and the publications available from commercial community solution providers are generally superficial and without theoretical or empirical backing.[2]

"The notion of community has been at the heart of the Internet since its inception. For many years, scientists have used the Internet to share data, collaborate on research, and exchange messages. In essence, scientists formed research communities that existed not on a physical campus but on the Internet.[3] Indeed, it was out of a need for reliable academic collaboration that the Internet arose.

[1] www.proz.com

[2] See Schobert & Schrott (2001), p. 519

[3] See Armstrong & Hagel, 1996, p. 86

D. Karagiannis and U. Reimer (Eds.): PAKM 2002, LNAI 2569, pp. 457-471, 2002.

This paper provides a theoretical and practical look at virtual communities, identifies core elements and proposes a model for studying these communities over time. Particular emphasis is placed on motivation for membership and active participation in virtual communities, their structure and dynamics and the role they play in the lives of their members. The emergence and importance of virtual communities for knowledge exchange is also considered.

2 Communities

The concept of community is diverse and includes social, organisational, business and knowledge communities. These can be either real-life or virtual interactions in cyberspace. There is no longer any doubt that people make real connections on the Internet and thousands of groups of people already meet there regularly to share information, discuss mutual interests, play games and carry out business.[4]

In general, communities are made up of three components: people, places and things. "They are composed of *people* who interact on a *regular* basis around a *common set of issues, interests or needs*."[5]

Communities often center on geographical locations, but in recent years, sociologists have noted the role of place is becoming less important and that community networks can be maintained even over long distances. The foundations of these communities are *social networks*. "This conceptual revolution moved from defining community in terms of space – neighborhoods – to defining it in terms of social networks."[6]

2.1 Organisational Communities

Formal and informal communities and networks have long played a role in business communication, but it is only recently that both the business and the KM worlds have started to pay them serious attention. Wenger sees organisational communities as "… the new frontier for organizations, the promise of great opportunities for pioneers of the knowledge age"[7] and differentiates between communities of practice, formal workgroups, project teams and informal networks.

Communities of Practice, formal and informal networks play increasing roles in business life and are a fundamental part of learning and knowledge exchange. Whilst the social aspects of learning and knowledge sharing play a key role in such networks, the need to network and share knowledge through a chain of interdependent organisations (globalisation) means members are often not located at the same site or even in the same country. This has led to the emergence of virtual communities to keep members of these networks in touch even without face-to-face meetings.

---

[4] See Smith & Kollock (1999), p. 16.

[5] Lesser et al (2000), p. vii

[6] Wellman & Gulia (1999), p. 169

[7] Wenger (2000), p. 5

2.2 Knowledge Communities

"Since the beginning of history, human beings have formed communities that accumulate collective learning into social practices. [...] Such communities do not take knowledge in their specialty to be an object; it is a living part of their practice even when they document it. Knowing is an act of participation."[8]

Virtual knowledge communities are organised groups of experts and other interested parties, who exchange knowledge on their field of expertise or knowledge domain in cyberspace within and across corporate and geographical borders. Virtual knowledge communities focus on their knowledge domain and over time expand their expertise through collaboration. They interact around relevant issues and build a common knowledge base.

Botkin describes knowledge communities in business as "groups of people with a common passion to create, share and use new knowledge for tangible business purposes". He goes on to recognise a close relationship to CoPs with the difference that knowledge communities are purposely formed to shape future circumstances and they are highly visible to every business person in the organization and suggests that communities are the answer to unlocking knowledge.[9]

However, knowledge communities do not necessarily have to arise in a corporate environment. Many freelance workers also look to (virtual) knowledge communities to fill the need in their working lives for collaboration, exchanging information and knowledge, learning from each other and sharing work.

Since membership in extra-organisational virtual communities is usually voluntary, members join because of their interest (be it social or business) in the subject matter discussed. This makes them ideal "places" for constructive knowledge exchange.

Knowledge sharing in virtual communities takes many forms, from parenting lists on how to deal with a sick child, Yellow Pages, recommendation systems for buyers and sellers, mailing lists, to the term translation seen in ProZ.com. According to Wenger, community builders must first establish the knowledge they want to share, the kinds of activities that will facilitate sharing and the core competencies of the target group.[10]

2.3 Virtual Communities

"Millions of people on every continent also participate in the computer-mediated social groups known as virtual communities, and this population is growing fast."[11]

Virtual communities are social or business relationships in cyberspace based around a specific boundary or place (e.g. website or mailing list) where members "meet" to discuss their particular shared purpose. Whilst members go to a particular address when visiting an online community, it is not the actual physical location they

[8] Wenger (1999), p. 4
[9] See Botkin (1999), p. 15, 30
[10] See Wenger (1999), pp. 5-13
[11] Rheingold (1993), Chapter 0 - Introduction

are looking for but the subject matter it represents. However, there appears as yet to be no unified agreement among experts as to what they refer to when they talk about a virtual community. The term is used to refer to both virtual communities in the form of social groups and also business-oriented communities in cyberspace.

The term "virtual community" was coined in 1968 by the Internet pioneers J.C.R. Licklider and R.W. Taylor who, when wondering what the future online interactive communities would be like, predicted that they would be communities of *common interest*, not of common location made up of *geographically separated* members. Their impact will be great – both on the individual and on society.[12]

At first glance, "virtual community" appears to be a contradiction in terms. Community is traditionally associated with people who live near one another, have something in common and communicate on a face-to-face basis. Virtuality, on the other hand, is more abstract and is often associated with computers and cyberspace. Members of virtual communities can live on opposite sides of the world, yet still form a community around a common interest. Their communication is generally text-based, with computer networks allowing "people to create a range of new social spaces in which to meet and interact with one another."[13] In the future, advances in virtual reality may considerably enhance the means of communication beyond simple text.

Yet, both traditional and virtual forms are essentially about people and interaction and all communities share certain characteristics. "People in virtual communities use words on screens to [...] engage in intellectual discourse, conduct commerce, exchange knowledge [...] People in virtual communities do just about everything people do in real life, but we leave our bodies behind … a lot can happen within those boundaries."[14] In other words, Internet communities bring the Web to life.

Whilst technology plays an important a role in virtual communities, its importance should not be overestimated. A virtual community is not the actual site were people meet, but the *people* who meet there. Virtual communities are not about using the best or most powerful technologies and although the future of virtual communities almost definitely lies in the Internet, community builders should initially select a technology that will best help foster their community.[15]

This leads to the assumption that there is much more to a virtual community than just the technology behind it and to consider communities primarily as human associations in which the members (i.e. the human aspect) form the centre of the community. As Allee notes: "Knowledge seeks community. Knowledge wants to happen, just as life wants to happen. Both want to happen as community. Nothing illustrates this principle more than the Internet. Communities of knowledge are so powerful that they now involve people in conversation with each other all over the globe."[16]

[12] Licklider (1968)
[13] Smith and Kollock (1999), p. 3
[14] Rheingold (1993), Introduction
[15] See Armstrong and Hagel (1997), p. 171
[16] Allee (1997)

3 Core Elements of (Virtual) Communities

Based on a study of available literature and an observation of translation communities, I have tried to identify the essential core elements of (virtual) communities, thereby developing a model for analysing and understanding the performance (both actual and expected) of virtual communities.

A community centres around a common interest linking all members (*shared purpose*). It needs a critical mass of distinctive members who meet membership requirements (*identity and boundaries*), form personal relationships (*trust and reputation*) and see the need to communicate over an extended period of time (*motivation and loyalty*) in an manner (*standards and values*) established by the community over the period of its existence (*history*). A suitable structure and communication medium focuses on member-generated content (*structure and content*), especially in knowledge sharing communities. Communities need a leading figure or host (*leadership*) and place to meet (*platform*). To thrive and grow, links must be established to other possible members and communities (*network effects*).

3.1 Shared Purpose

The shared purpose or common interest forms the centre of a community and serves as the connecting element between members. Without this purpose, a community will find it difficult to establish itself and survive. This shared purpose must be strong enough to encourage the community members to come together to achieve something collectively that they could not do alone. The importance of shared purpose should not be underestimated as it goes beyond merely sharing a common interest, which alone is unlikely to be enough to sustain a successful community.

3.2 Identity and Boundaries

Communities need the right kind of members (e.g. those who demonstrate some kind of expertise in and/or can contribute to the community domain). Membership in communities is generally voluntary and most members join because they realise they share the purpose and will benefit from the communication. Since members do not "know" each other personally, they need persistent, stable identities in the community to make them recognisable to other members. Identities represent both the reason for communicating with their "owners" and the history of interaction. An "identity" is not necessarily a real name; an alias is also a persistent identity, as it serves to uniquely identify a member to the community.

A community must also define boundaries, i.e. determine who can/cannot join. If it does not do so, anyone could join, regardless of qualification or interest in the community purpose. Boundaries are more relevant in communities with free membership, as subscriptions often deter "lurkers" or non-interested parties. Furthermore, without boundaries, it becomes difficult to ensure those who join might actually (be in a position to) actively participate and contribute to the shared purpose.

3.3 Reputation and Trust

However, an identity only imparts to the community what the person behind it has chosen to reveal and says little about their reputation. Reputation has to be earned and is based on a member's actions and behaviour in the community and predominantly the impression this leaves on other members (history of interaction). Reputation provides members with a context to judge each other and the value of individual contributions and forms the basis for a member's status, standing and peer recognition in the community. Some virtual communities make awarded status visible to other members (e.g. by recording it in member profiles), thus making it something worth attaining and encouraging members to remain in the community.

With reputation comes trust, a prerequisite for commitment to a community and its longevity. Trust forms the basis for reliable, mutually beneficial member interaction.

A virtual community is rather like a virtual singles club. It is a place where people meet and exchange ideas and slowly relationships, loyalty and trust evolve. Before interaction can take place, members must be confident that others will behave the way they expect. Members must be able to judge the motives of others without fear of being (ab)used. However, trust is manifold and includes both the trust relationships between community members and the members' trust in the community leadership.

3.4 Motivation and Loyalty

Members must find a community interesting enough to motivate them to return and maintain their membership. This should encourage them to contribute to the community, thereby generating new content, which in turn is of interest to other members. If a community does not invest enough in reliability and ways of retaining its members, it will disappear before loyalty has a chance.

If visiting a community is a motivating and satisfying experience, members are more likely to remain loyal and not look for other solutions. Thus, community organisers must work to offer an appropriate balance of content and interest. In knowledge sharing communities, this is a real focus on the shared purpose. Members will quickly turn away from a community if content and discussion drift off topic.

Identification with (and loyalty to) a community encourages repeated interaction and creates the feeling of belonging and core group of loyal members a community ultimately needs and wants. Generating loyalty is essential to long-term survival as it plays a key role in the community being able to reach a critical mass of members.

3.5 Standards and Values

Virtual communities are often long-term (or permanent) establishments. As they grow and members interact over an extended period of time, common standards and values need to be established to set the community's rules of etiquette. Most members take membership seriously and behave in an appropriate manner, automatically establishing the standards that form the basis of the rules or codes of conduct for community interaction. These guidelines will differ from community to community and must be clearly transmitted to new members. Rules and charters also help to build trust among members, because they lay down the boundaries of personal and group interaction (e.g. privacy rules or the types of discussion permitted).

In open communities, these shared values and standards are of particular importance since they help to establish the image the community presents to the outside world.

3.6 Leadership and Structure

Whilst a high degree of self-rule and democracy is common in and vital to virtual communities, they do not manage themselves. If no one takes charge, they run the risk of dissolving into an unstructured mess or fading away due to lack of postings and interest. Leaders (or hosts) play a fundamental role in the structure and continuity of a community. Not least, they bring a human touch to an otherwise impersonal medium. They often define the initial rules/guidelines and ultimately take important decisions (e.g. to delete inappropriate postings, moderate discussions or ban errant members).

Community leaders promote a community, provide direction and guarantee continuity both in the community and its concept. It is more important for a community leader to have strong social and organizational skills than subject expertise, although this is an added bonus. Leaders also play a key role in conflict management in the community, as they make the ultimate decision on what to do in the conflict situations (or flames) common in virtual communities.

As communities grow, it can become increasingly difficult for one person to manage all activities and these responsibilities then have to be shared with other members. Often, groups of core members evolve or are elected to assist the leader and act as motivators for new members or moderators of individual sub-communities.

3.7 History and Dynamics

As loyalty and a sense of community grows and the community boundaries, standards and values become established, history and tradition start to play an increasingly important role. A shared history and tradition reinforces the feeling of belonging and sense of community and facilitates repeated interaction. History and tradition are the cornerstones on which members base their behaviour in a community.

In most communities, the majority of members respect established standards and values and behave accordingly. However, occasionally one (or more) individuals attempt to dominate a community and attract attention by proliferating their views and ideas wherever they can. This can make a community very unbalanced and threatens the standards and values established through the history. Such actions should be discouraged and a social balance maintained or restored. Often the best thing to do is to ignore the protagonists thus depriving them of the attention they seek.[17]

[17] See Figallo (1998)

With history also comes the need to forget. It is essential to define what the community needs to remember in order to develop a shared community history. For example, members should be allowed to delete things they think are no longer relevant and redeem mistakes they might have made in the past. A successful community must be able to learn and profit from its mistakes.

3.8 Interaction Platform and Content

The primary collaboration tools in virtual communities are digital and physical meetings are the exception, not the rule. They need a common interaction medium and environment that is both easy-to-use and suits the community's purpose and needs. Not all communities need all the functionality available for online communication. A professional knowledge community may not need the chat functionality more common in social communities, but will need a well-designed discussion forum or information exchange area.

Content is one of the most important things in making a community attractive, as it is one of the reasons people return. This is particularly the case in knowledge sharing communities where easy and well-structured access to the shared knowledge will make the community all the more beneficial to its members. Although it is difficult to manage content, a community will both distinguish itself by and benefit from a high proportion of useful, member-generated content. "A community full of half empty rooms offers visitors a very unsatisfactory experience."[18]

3.9 Network Effects

One of the biggest strengths of a virtual community is having access to a target group. Network effects are the economic term for the increase of value that accrues to a network when more people join it, thereby encouraging ever-increasing numbers of members. The network effect is often the result of word-of-mouth testimonial and a community is often itself a "great word-of-mouth marketing engine for attracting more users with similar values."[19]

Network effects are important for a community to attract and retain the critical mass (and quality) of members it needs to survive. Community standards and boundaries determine the upper limits. If a community does not have a sufficient number of members, there is unlikely to be enough content to make the community attractive to new members.[20] Furthermore, more content will encourage members to stay longer in the community and then contribute new content, which, in turn, attracts new members or other members to also create new content.

---

[18] Armstrong and Hagel (1996), p. 89

[19] Figallo (1998)

[20] Morris & Ogan (1996)

4 Model for the Core Elements of Community

Figure 1 demonstrates a model for the core elements of communities described above, which serves as the basis for analysing and understanding communities.

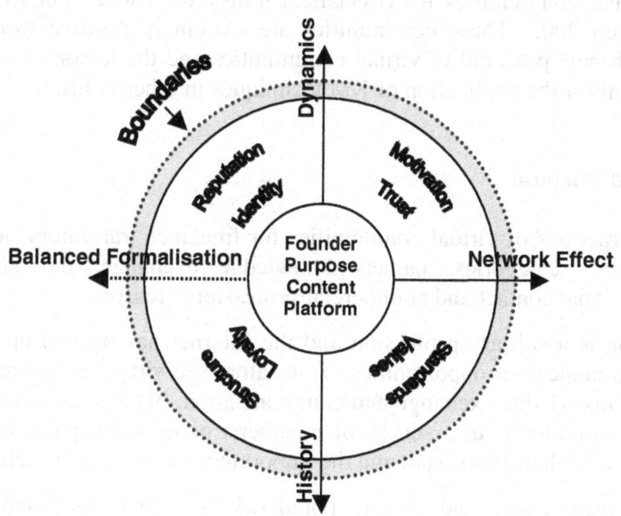

Fig. 1. Model: Core Elements of Community

Figure 2 shows this model projected over time and illustrates the importance of a community's history in its analysis.

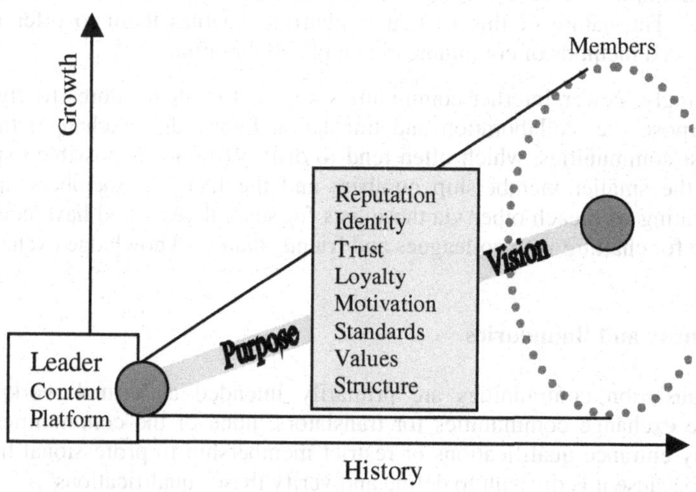

Fig. 2. Model of Core Elements of Community over Time

5 Knowledge Sharing in Virtual Translation Communities

Virtual communities provide an ideal environment for communication, collaboration and knowledge sharing and many freelance workers are now making increased use of virtual communities for these reasons. The observations that follow are based on a study of virtual communities for (freelance) translators carried out from December 2001 to March 2002. These communities are extremely positive examples of the knowledge sharing potential of virtual communities and the lessons learned could be very beneficial for the application of KM techniques in other fields.

5.1 Shared Purpose

The main attractions of virtual communities for freelance translators can be grouped into four main categories, namely knowledge exchange, individual learning, social/professional contact and commercial/professional reasons.

Translation is a solitary profession and the Internet has opened up a whole new range of communication opportunities. Translators see virtual communities not only as places for knowledge exchange and communication, but also as meeting places for like-minded individuals. In a survey of members, many participants commented on the solitariness of their profession and the importance of "no longer feeling alone".

The high membership and obvious popularity of virtual translation communities indicates that there is more than just a great deal of interest among translators. Practice shows that there is a real need for them and that these communities are developing from what might have started as virtual, fun meeting places into extensive communities of knowledge exchange.

Whilst the early communities observed function as mailing lists or newsletters, the newer communities were established from the outset as Internet communities or workplaces. The nature of this particular platform enables them to offer members more advanced methods of communication and collaboration.

Interestingly, newer Internet communities appear to adhere more strictly to their shared purpose (i.e. collaboration and translation knowledge exchange) than older mailing list communities, which often tend to drift off topic. A possible explanation might be the smaller membership numbers and the fact that members have been communicating with each other via these lists for several years and have come to use them more for chatting with colleagues and friends than for knowledge exchange.

5.2 Identity and Boundaries

Whilst translation communities are primarily intended as virtual workplaces or knowledge exchange communities for translators, none of the communities studied require any entrance qualifications or restrict membership to professional translators (not least because it is difficult to define and verify these "qualifications").

This illustrates the conflict between the principles of free access (open membership) and the need to protect the professional image of a community against an influx of unqualified members. Currently, anyone can join the communities studied and there are often links from affiliate sites on the Web. Initial solutions are in place to resolve this conflict, however these will remain cosmetic restrictions as long as membership boundaries remain completely open. This issue is discussed at great length in community forums and also reflected in the survey results.

5.3 Reputation and Trust

Since a translator is ultimately responsible for the quality of a delivered text, they need to be sure that information received from other sources is reliable. One benefit of peer support in a traditional "real" community is that members know each other's individual skills and weaknesses. Their history of collaboration has resulted in a trusting relationship. It is a quite different matter to receive assistance from someone who is an "unknown entity" and translation communities must find ways of overcoming this problem (e.g. through access to member histories) to enable members to build reliable reputations in the community. As Gaudiani notes: "Trust, like reputation, must be earned by members of a community ... through their actions."[21]

As they spend time together in a virtual community, members get to know each other and develop their own opinions of each other, both with respect to reputation and to translation and social skills.

A system of peer rating responses[22] helps build trust, as it provides access to answers provided in the past and thereby an indication of member's expertise. Discussion forums also help to build up reputation and trust, as the type and tone of postings can help members to form opinions of each other. Such systems also act as a form of benchmark for the overall quality and accuracy important for the community's reputation to the outside world. In the study, many participants commented on having built up invaluable working relationships and "virtual friendships" through community membership.

Translation communities often request members to store information on language pairs, areas of expertise, specialist fields, experience, rates, etc. in an online profile. This information is included in the member database and made accessible both to other members and to any potential clients searching the site. When a client posts a translation job, the requirements are checked against stored profiles and details of the job forwarded to all members whose profiles fit the requirements (usually by e-mail).

5.4 Dynamics and History

"Successful communities share a common story and a common set of beliefs as much as they share a common set of goals or activities. Their members share a way of

---

21 Gaudiani (1998), p. 66

22 E.g. the KudoZ term translation points system used in www.proz.com.

thinking, a value system that enables them to predict and usually respect each one another's actions."[23]

Translation communities are no different and also develop a shared history. The growth in members over time and the history generated by their interaction can lead to a need to redefine roles and adjust the community structure and standards accordingly. Although the role of the founder remains extremely important, it may be necessary to extend this role to other key figures, e.g. sub-community moderators.

The natural structure for a translation community is to divide itself into sub-communities based on language pairs. In some sub-communities, moderators play a key role in helping to develop the community spirit, whilst in others they are watched very closely and criticised for almost everything they do. This would appear to be linked to the predominant national culture behind the particular communities.

As new members join and community interaction grows, roles and structures change and the interaction between members forms recognisable patterns in the way they communicate with each other and the importance and relevance certain individual members will place on particular issues.

5.5 Knowledge Sharing and Barriers

Translators are knowledge professionals who need a wide range of skills and knowledge for their chosen profession. These include language and linguistic skills, country and cultural knowledge, specialist subject matter knowledge and IT skills. As is usually the case in knowledge sharing activities, some knowledge is easier to share than other.

Knowledge exchange in translation communities centres on language and linguistic knowledge, expertise and experience. Translators appear unaffected by the barriers to knowledge sharing seen elsewhere, e.g. in scientific communities, where initiatives face a discouraging culture based on the "fear of losing ownership of the intellectual property"[24], or in corporate environments, where knowledge is seen as power.

On the contrary, there is no indication of any fears or risks to their personal situation as a result of sharing knowledge or contributing to projects such as global glossaries. This indicates a clear recognition of the underlying reciprocity of knowledge sharing.

5.6 Drawbacks

Whilst active participation in virtual communities can be beneficial, it is also time-consuming and may even be (temporarily) addictive. Members of online communities may also find themselves confronted with a kind of "virtual office politics" (usually battled out in community forums). Indeed, these "virtual office politics" are by no means specific to translation communities and can be observed in many communities.

[23] Gaudiani (1998), p. 63
[24] See Hyams (2001)

The main areas of contention in translation communities are job bidding issues (low rates), negative forum contributions (and dominant members) and non-professional members (e.g. lack of qualification or translating outside language pairs). Although flames are a direct breach of accepted behaviour, if they do take place in translation communities they can be particularly linguistically vindictive due to the text communication dexterity of translators.

6 Conclusion

Communities can be geographical, social or business oriented, and can exist both in the real world and in cyberspace. However, regardless of their physical "location", at the heart of all communities lie the people who make up their members and determine the purpose they share. There are both differences and similarities between real-life and virtual communities, but these are not as significant as expected.[25]

Since membership in virtual communities is generally voluntary, most members participate because they want to and thus behave in an appropriate manner. This means that many virtual communities are largely self-regulating (and surprisingly well organised). However, as communities evolve and grow, they often experience an increasing need to complement self-regulation with guidelines, structures and rules, particularly if they have a large membership and/or high volumes of traffic. Members increasingly assume clear individual roles in the community and structures develop. These are then expressed in behavioural rituals, norms, standards and values that can be best understood if the community is looked at both from a synchronous and diachronic view to determine how it has developed and how these developments have affected both the members and the community as a whole.

Since one of the most important aspects of communities is social interaction, the people in and behind a community and their individual histories play a key role in any interaction. The need for and success of virtual translation communities is rooted in the specific characteristics of the translation profession and the way translators work.

When emotions run deep, it is inevitable conflicts will arise in almost any community and virtual translation communities are no exception. Virtual communities must develop ways of resolving these problems to maintain stability and the status quo. In most cases, it will be enough to ignore troublemakers, depriving them of the attention they seek. However, if this does not work, ultimately the community leader will have to step in to resolve the problem (e.g. by banning a member from the community.)

Whilst community interaction centres on common goals, the process that occurs in an interaction between members is more elaborate and rooted in their shared and individual histories. It is often expressed using informal channels (e.g. insinuations, smilies, personal comments) to indicate emotion, personal sympathies or animosities.

Relevant content is essential to knowledge communities and professional benefits are reduced if discussion regularly drifts off topic. The particular communities studied

[25] See Dickinson, A. (2002)

deal primarily with language. Language is by definition the medium through which knowledge and social interaction come together. This means "language" is not only the basis for community interaction, but also the subject and purpose of work for members of these communities.

Web-base communities play an increasing role in virtual knowledge sharing and may over time replace mailing lists (not least as a result of the increased knowledge sharing possibilities offered). The only limits to the number of members in a Web community are ultimately the hardware supporting it and the potential number of interested users it can attract. However, the community will set internal limits as members form relationships and interact with each other.

The core elements identified appear to be essential for the success and longevity for all communities, both virtual and face-to-face. However, if a community is only analysed at one particular time, this will only provide a snapshot of the community in a given situation and at a specific stage in its life. Analysis gains real relevance when reapplied at different stages over the development of the community, thereby considering the essential aspect of community history and so providing a basis for understanding and analysing the reasons for prosperity and giving an indication of future growth or decline. Studying a community with a view to its history reveals that not the community site is important; rather the sense of belonging and essence of being that develops in a community over time. Therefore, the core elements are designed to help a community master the issues it will face as it grows and develops.

Statistics show that in the United States alone, there are currently over 35 million freelance workers and this trend is on the increase, with many knowledge workers moving from a corporate environment to the benefits of freelance work[26]. Consequently, the possibilities offered by virtual knowledge sharing communities merit increased consideration and more detailed studies will have to be carried out.

References

Allee, V. (1997): 12 Principles of Knowledge Management. In: Training and Development, Nov. 1997. http://www.vernaallee.com (Accessed 25.10.02)

Armstrong, A. & Hagel, J. (1996): The Real Value of Online Communities. In: Lesser et al, 2000

Armstrong, A. & Hagel, J. (1997): Net Gain: Expanding Markets Through Virtual Communities. Boston: Harvard Business School Press, 1997

Botkin, J. (1999): Smart Business: How Knowledge Communities can Revolutionize your Company. New York: Free Press, 1999

Dickinson, A. (2002): "Translating in Cyberspace. Virtual Knowledge Communities for Freelance Translators, 2002, Master Thesis to MAS (KM) Donau-Universität Krems

Figallo, C. (1998): Interview with Amazon.com. http://www.amazon.com/exec/obidos/ts/feature/6731/104-1868321-1274338 (25.10.02)

Gaudiani, C. L. (1998): Wisdom as Capital in Prosperous Communities. In: Hesselbein et al, 1998

Hesselbein, F., Goldsmith, M., Beckhard, R. & Schubert, R. (Ed.) (1998): The Community of the Future. The Drucker Foundation. San Francisco: Josey-Bass Publishers, 1998

[26] See Pink (2001), pp. 47-50

Hyams, E. (2001): Real Services will Survive the dotcom downturn. The 4th Intl. Conference on Virtual Communities. In: The Library Association Record 103(10) October 2001, p. 602

Lesser, E., Fontaine, M. & Slusher, J. (Ed.) (2000): Knowledge and Communities. Boston: Butterworth-Heinemann, 2000

Licklider, J.C.R. (1968): The Computer as a Communication Device. In: Science and Technology: For the Technical Man in Management, 1968

Morris, M. & Ogan, C. (1996): The Internet as Mass Medium. In: Journal of Computer-Mediated Communication 46(1), 1996. http://jcmc.huji.ac.il/vol1/issue4/morris.html (25.10.02)

Pink, D. (2001): Free Agent Nation: How America's Independent Workers are Transforming the Way We Live. New York: Warner Books, 2001 (e-Book version)

Rheingold, H. (1993): Virtual Communities: Homesteading on the Electronic Frontier. Online Version, 1998 (http://www.rheingold.com/vc/book/) (25.10.02)

Schoberth, T. & Schrott, G. (2001): Virtual Communities: In: WIRTSCHAFTSINFORMATIK 43 (2001) 5, pp. 517-519

Smith, M. & Kollock, P. (Ed.) (1999): Communities in Cyberspace. London: Routledge, 1999

Wellman, B. & Gulia, M.(1999): Virtual communities as communities. Net surfers don't ride alone. In: Smith & Kollock (Ed.), 1999

Wenger, E. (1999): Communities of Practice: The Key to Knowledge Strategy. In: Lesser et al, 2000

Are the Knowledge Management Professionals Up to the Job?

Ivana Adamson[1] and Donna Handford[2]

[1] University of Edinburgh, College of Science and Engineering, Sanderson Building, Kings Buildings, Mayfield Road, Edinburgh, EH9 3JL, Scotland
ivana.adamson@ed.ac.uk

[2] Scottish Institute for Enterprise, Sanderson Building, Kings Buildings, Mayfield Road, Edinburgh, EH9 3JL, Scotland
donna.handford@ed.ac.uk

Abstract. The objective of this paper was to explore the role of a Knowledge Management professional in today's blue chip companies, to examine if and how the KM professionals differ from each other, and if Knowledge Management professionals on the whole match the earlier proposed models of an 'ideal' KM professional. The findings suggested that employing organisations did not have a clear idea of the KM role. This ambiguity was picked up the newly appointed KM professionals, who as a result felt uncertain and insecure in their KM role. Further, the findings supported earlier studies, in what the participants perceived the KM role to be (2/3 change agent, 1/3 information systems technology) although they perceived themselves primarily as management consultants/entrepreneurs rather than technicians/managers.

1 Introduction

The objective of this paper was to explore the role of Knowledge Management (KM) professionals in the UK organisations, and to examine to what extent the practising KM professionals posses the personal attributes and competencies described by the current management literature as desirable to help companies to survive and succeed in today's rapid pace of the online business environment.

The quantity and speed of information proliferating today's organisations has unquestionably influenced the way business is done today. The cost of managing information is still high, although the cost of not managing it adequately is estimated to be even higher (Di Miao 2001, Stewart 1997, Evans 1999, Von Krogh *et all* 1996). In the industrial economy the masculine industrial processes were built on forecasting, and networking and innovation were the key strategic movers. Organisations in today's knowledge economy leverage their knowledge to 'sense' and 'respond' to changes in the global business environment (Prichard 1999, Curley 1998). This shift of business priorities from resources to intellectual assets has motivated organisations to systematically audit their knowledge pool and to monitor how it is used (Hansen *et al* 1999).

D. Karagiannis and U. Reimer (Eds.): PAKM 2002, LNAI 2569, pp. 472-489, 2002.

Wenger (1998) suggested that within the global business environment creating and leveraging knowledge is not yet fully understood, and therefore, to manage knowledge effectively organisations must learn to rationalise the process. However, there is an added problem of defining what constitutes organisational knowledge.

1.1 Defining Knowledge and Knowledge Management

Plato defined knowledge as a belief supported with an account or an explanation. Today's definitions suggest that knowledge comes from our increased ability to make use of and sense of available information within our social and workplace contexts (Bentley 1999, Broadbent 1998). Knowledge is a dynamic process of justifying personal beliefs as the 'truth', although beliefs can and do fall short of becoming always knowledge (Morton 1997, Havens and Knapp 1999). Knowledge thus is a *'cognitive contact with reality arising out of acts of intellectual virtue'* (Zagrebski 1999: 109).

A survey of the current management literature suggests that there does not seem to be one and only accepted KM definition (Earl and Scott 1999, DiMattia and Oder 1997, Bicknell 1999, Boisot 1998, cited in Prichard 1999). Existing KM definitions tend to focus around an organisation's abilities to generate wealth from within its knowledge-based assets with the aim of capturing, integrating and using existing in-house expertise, employee 'know-how' and 'lessons learned' (Havens and Knapp 1999). The current management literature further shows divided opinions regarding the necessity of creating a role of a Knowledge Manager in order to launch a KM initiative, further complicating the issue of KM definition (Earl and Scott 1999, Bicknell 1999, Stewart 2000, Davenport and Prusak 1998). An empirical study of the US and UK KM professionals carried out by Earl and Scott (1999) illustrated the present confusion about the role of KM professionals in their organisations. They concluded that while the observed organisations provided a job specification for most professional positions; this was not always the case for the KM officer's. Most of the sample were employed in the KM position for less than two years, and not all their job titles contained the word 'knowledge'. Undeniably, the role of a Knowledge Manager is a relatively recent creation in organisations and accurate job specifications are still rare, despite the fact that in the above study the KM appointments were made by the CEOs themselves.

Back in 1999 KPMG consultants carried out a survey of senior managers of mid- to large-size companies from a variety of industries (De Ven, 1999). The objective of the survey was to explore to what extent companies regarded KM as important, and subsequently, to what extent and how they initiated initiatives to implement and master their 'knowledge pool'. The findings further showed that eighty per cent of respondents believed that globalisation, rapid technology development and shorter product life cycles (PLCs) were regarded as the major cause of organisational change today (eighty four per cent), and only four per cent regarded their company's current level of managing knowledge as appropriate. The findings further showed that in most of the surveyed companies knowledge creation was an unstructured process where employees' competencies were mapped in an ad hoc manner. Employees often received an overflow of information, and given little time to share their thoughts with

colleagues. This resulted in often re-inventing the wheel, and the newly created knowledge pool was seldom used.
A more recent survey of 200 senior executives carried out by the KPMG Management Consulting showed that virtually no one now thinks that KM is another management fad that will soon be forgotten. That compares with as many as a third in the 1997 poll. Some forty per cent of senior executives questioned claimed to have KM projects under way.

Some argue that KM is not a new concept, and that it has been practised for years without being succinctly defined (Hansen *et al* 1999, DiMattia and Oder 1997, Krammer 1998), and therefore cannot and should not be apportioned to any one profession as its domain. The new KM is a corporate proposition based on organisations attempting to control their intellectual capital or intangible assets, which are the intellectual capacities and experiences of employees (Donkin 2002).

1.2 Management and Knowledge Management

The process of management stretches back to ancient times, although turning it into science did not happen until the ninetieth century. The formal study of management began as an offshoot of engineering, and since then three major management theories emerged with their distinct ideas about how management should behave to ensure the success of an organisation: the 'technical-rational', the 'behavioural', and the 'cognitive'. The 'technical-rational' paradigm focuses on technical competence, the 'behavioural' paradigm emphasizes the importance of the internal and external environment, and the 'cognitive' paradigm focuses on turning information into knowledge as a path to success. Each still today provides a rationale for building management information systems. Laudon and Laudon (2000: 99) concluded that '*after 100 years of writing about management, it comes down to the fact that organizational success has something to do with technical competence, organizational adaptability to environments, and finally with the know-how and intimate knowledge of the product and production processes*'.

Back in the 1990s the process of reengineering of companies, followed a period of downsizing, and was considered as a precursor of today's knowledge management. The two are often considered as identical approaches to managing knowledge in order to bring about change. However, reengineering is a 'top-down' approach to a structured co-ordination of people and information, and is based on a conviction that corporate knowledge could be contained in technological systems. It is a process of passing on 'know-how' in a stable and competition free environment. The re-engineering process treats employees' knowledge as something to which the company has an inalienable right, and this subsequently resulted in a critical loss of knowledge and expertise in organisations (Stewart 2002). The Knowledge Management, on the other hand, assumes an unpredictable competitive environment, and is a 'bottom-up' approach. The focus is on effectiveness rather than efficiency, where knowledge professionals foster knowledge by responding to the inventive, improvisational ways people think and do things (Brown and Duguid 2000).

Most organisations' understanding of KM oscillates somewhere along a bipolar continuum from the 'recognition' end, where organisational knowledge is an indispensable source of competitive advantage in value creation, to the 'realisation' end, where managing knowledge involves a process of learning.

The process of KM was described by some as consisting of two thirds change management and one third understanding of human learning (Coleman, 1998, Nonaka and Takeuchi 1995, Bentley 1999 and Ryan 1998), and on the whole, definitions of KM tend to be placed within the 'emerging' (Broadbent 1997), the 'evolving' (Earl and Scott 1999), and the 'forming' (Gourlay 1999) learning paradigms. What KM is not is stockpiling information on facts and figures, or tackling all knowledge opportunities as they arise (Lank 1998 and Bentley 1999, Snowden 1998).

Polayi (sighted in Gelwick 1977) theorised that knowledge is neither subjective or objective but a transcendence of both, and should be thought of as an interwoven fabric (Bottomley 1998). Nonaka and Takeuch (1995) used the ontological dimension approach to explain the development of individual's knowledge and its transfer to the group or organisational levels. They segmented tacit (subjective) and explicit (objective) knowledge into three categories. Explicit knowledge represents: (i) a body of knowledge gained through experience, (ii) simultaneous knowledge or 'here and now', and (iii) knowledge gained through practice. Tacit knowledge, on the other hand, represents: (i) rational or knowledge of the 'mind', (ii) sequential or 'there and then' knowing, and (iii) theory or 'digital' knowledge. The key to group knowledge creation thus lies in the mobilising and conversion of individual's tacit knowledge.

Bentley (1999) disagreed that individuals' knowledge could be pooled and stored for organisational use. He reasoned that organisations consist of separate individuals units, it is not an organic whole. Therefore, pooling of information becomes a complex process, since: i) it is the individuals who are the gate keepers of knowledge and not the group or the organisation, ii) information will not be freely exchanged just because a new system (treating information as commodity) has been implemented. The reasons for his reasoning are based on fear of: i) sharing ('giving away') knowledge without sharing ('being given') power, and ii) 'technical' approaches could supplant the 'social' interactive values (Wilmott 1998, Pritchard 1999).

Leveraging corporate knowledge as a corporate strategy to gain competitive advantage must be built on a foundation of challenging what is true and nurturing the organisation's culture, and not just of knowledge creation and innovation (Williams 1999). Therefore, KM professionals must seek to facilitate this interactive process and suffuse it through the organisation, although caution should be taken not to regard blindly all knowledge as true, and not to repeat some of the TQM mistakes of impracticability and exaggeration of achievement (DiMattia and Oder 1997, Bentley 1999, Havens and Knapp 1999).

1.3 Why Knowledge Management?

The reason for companies going multinational in the past was their knowledge of the international marketplace (Von Krogh *et all* 1996). The European Knowledge Survey (Bailey and Clarke 1999) has found that KM expenditure in European companies was predicted to rise between 1999 and 2002 by seventy per cent. The figures in the survey were supported by statements from interviewed chief executives, who stated that that KM was seen as critical to the success of their companies (Havens and

Knapp 1999) and was second their 'must do' list after globalisation (Bicknell 1999, Verespej 1999). However, eighty per cent of those organisations that undertook a KM project failed to meet their objectives and fifty per cent of those found that the costs outweighed the value (Bray 1999); therefore questions must be asked why would an organisation wish to pursue this kind of management method? Gourley (1999) outlined five possible reasons, why organisations embark on KM programmes:

1. Lost knowledge after downsizing:
   Organisations have slowly awoken to the fact that knowledge is a human asset (Bentley 1999) and that it is knowledge, not information, that is the primary business asset (Stewart 1997, Broadbent 1998)
2. The 'customer interface' employees possess information about customers:
   For example, sales persons or delivery drivers visit customers on a regular basis, and therefore are in a strong position to build good relationships and gather useful information about customers.
3. Pressure to innovate to gain competitive edge:
   In the aftermath of a corporate merger, for example, when the value of 'acquired' assets has been exhausted, a pressure for organic growth may become the new strategy for competitiveness and innovation. The ability to innovate is then directly linked to a successful KM.
4. Information and communications technologies advances:
   Phenomenal advances in systems and software provide endless opportunities to utilise available data managed within KM settings.
5. Focus on core competencies
   Identification of core competencies has shifted from products or services to focus more on managing knowledge.

Effective information management, organisational learning and new technology are accepted as facilitators of change (Broadbent 1998, Offsey 1998, Nonaka and Takeuchi 1995), although it is the depth of understanding of what, how and who should lead the implementation, that organisations have to learn. Projects and objectives are diverse in different organisations, and successful KM projects must be multidisciplinary in terms of bringing together technology, culture, economics and politics in a combination that enables flexibility in dealing with whatever project and objective (Coleman 1998, Aadne *et al* 1996).

1.4 Who Are the KM Professionals and What Do They Do

There are two schools of thought of what constitutes KM: One is based in the IT domain and then there are the Others (Offsey 1998). Davenport *et al* (1998) studied thirty-one KM projects and within those were as many different objectives as there were knowledge demands.

The challenge of KM is to gain the trust of employees that sharing knowledge is power in itself by facilitating changes in organisational behaviour.
The challenges for a KM professional therefore are:

- How to deal with knowledge as a commodity
- How to deal with information politics
- How to create change environment through IT and people

Prusak (2000) suggested that managing knowledge requires 'hiring smart people and let them talk to each other'. In today's fast moving business environment an adequate although time constrained definition of 'smart' behaviour would not be probably very difficult to formulate. Then to operationalise the definition by developing a concept of a 'smart knowledge manager', and transfer it into a reliable and valid measurement tool (for the purposes of selection and assessment of potential applicants for the job), is another matter. Earl and Scott (1999) empirically examined the role of a Chief Knowledge Officer (CKO) and suggested that he or she should understand the company's business model, know what knowledge is relevant for the strategy building purposes, and be capable of adding value to the company. In other words, ideal CKOs should exhibit leadership characteristics, be excellent communicators, competent negotiators, understand process management, be IT designers, and be good at managing relationships.

On the more realistic level, knowledge in organisations is managed in two steps. Firstly, the in-house already available knowledge is identified, and secondly, if the knowledge is of some value, it is then disseminated throughout the organisation. Managers generally find the balancing act between the way things are formally organised (process) and the way things are actually done (practice) difficult to handle. This appears to be a no-win situation, since relaxing the formal structure for capturing knowledge may make it difficult to harness new ideas, and a knowledge work structures with too little freedom may restrict the flow of ideas. The role of the knowledge professional is to bridge the gap between free flowing ideas and technology platforms by helping to articulate new ideas and creating appropriate knowledge work systems.

Identifying organisational knowledge and best practices is not easy either. Brown and Duguid (2000) suggested that there is a difference between a job description and how jobs are carried out in reality, i.e.: what people think they do and what they really do. To complicate the matter further, most business processes are 'top-down' creations, where managers fill them with what they think is useful, and then appoint IT professionals to turn them into formal management information systems. The majority of KM studies tend to focus on the nature of knowledge within structures and the processes that aid or hinder organisational learning, such as ERP, multi-project management, external databases, and others. However, less attention is paid to the individual and personal nature of knowledge, which is the basic step of a firm's knowledge creation process. Individual knowledge is related to subsequent action and the context within which it takes place, therefore, the Knowledge Manager's personal qualities, preferences and expertise are likely to significantly influence the process of formulating the intellectual capital creation and its execution.

Table 1 summarises the KM professional's desired competencies as identified by Nonaka and Takeuchi (1995), Davenport and Prusak (1998), Stewart (1998), and Earl and Scott (1998). From the Table 1 we can see a strong synergy and emphasis on IT between Davenport and Prusak (1998) and Stewart (1998) and Earl and Scott (1998), although a more strategic and less technological approach by Nonaka and Takeuchi (1995). However, since 1995 the new developments in IT capabilities have been phenomenal, therefore a stronger emphasis on the role of IT could be anticipated. Sharing knowledge is important, and it is the most natural thing in the world, except in corporations (Stewart 2000). Knowledge Management systems were developed to elicit and hold information, so that it stays there when the source of knowledge leaves the company. A pragmatic summary of the KM professional's skills competencies and personal attributes in the Table 1 are the following three points three points:

1. The KM professional builds a knowledge culture
2. The KM professional creates a knowledge work system (KWS) infrastructure
3. The KM professional works within the organisation's strategic vision

The Earl and Scott's (1998) model of an ideal KM professional comprises a technologist, an environmentalist, an entrepreneur and a management consultant.

Table 1. The KM Professionals' Competencies

Nonaka & Takeuchi (1995)	**Davenport & Prusak** (1998)	**Stewart** (1998)	**Earl and Scott** (1998)
Articulates knowledge vision Sets challenging goals	Leads knowledge strategy development		Leads
Communicates knowledge vision	Advocates/ 'evangelises' knowledge	Creates conditions for freedom of speech	Communicates
Justifies quality of created knowledge	Measures value of knowledge	Balances competing claims of getting best value from knowledge	Negotiates &Persuades
Selects the right project leader		Understands information politics	Manages
	Designs and implements knowledge & codification approaches	Sets company wide standards of format, access and technology	Designs
	Designs, implements & oversees knowledge infrastructure	Responsible for technical infrastructure	IT literate
Team 'hands on' approach	Manages external information	Audits knowledge assets, creates expert communities	Manages relationships
Facilitates knowledge creation	Provides critical input into & facilitates knowledge creation	Packaging & presentation of knowledge	Process Manager

An ideal Knowledge Manager is said to come from a professional services company, where knowledge is a primary resource, and is likely to competencies in functional management areas such as Finance, Law, Marketing, HR or IT (Stewart 1998, and Davenport and Prusak 1998).

The objective of this paper was to explore the role of a KM professional in today's organisations, if and how the role differs from organisation to organisation, and most importantly, if their personal attributes and skills competencies match the current models of an 'ideal' KM professional. The models in Table 1 are easily to run with, without pausing and asking a simple question about the reality of the above models. After all, within the human community as a whole, there can be found some individuals whose interpersonal skills can be defined as exceptional, others developed high technical competence, and still others were born with or developed desirable leadership skills. A debate, about finding a critical mass of individuals who possess these three exceptional gifts, and who are available (or be even recognised as such by the interviewing panels) to populate the KM roles in today's organisations would be appropriate at this stage, although the discussion would be likely to take us far beyond the boundaries of this study. Therefore, study's prediction was that:

- the role of a KM professional would significantly vary between companies, and so would the strengths and weaknesses of individual Knowledge Managers, and
- no single individual in the present study would possess all three well developed skills competencies and personality attributes (i.e.: high interpersonal communication skills, desirable leadership skills, and a high technical competence) as outlined by the current KM literature models.

Finally, based on the data from the surveyed current management literature and the findings of this study, a 2002 profile of a KM professional was developed.

2 Methodology

2.1 Study Design and Rationale

The current literature review suggests that the organisation's intellectual capital plays a decisive role in the strategic decision making processes. Therefore, it is important to understand how best to capture value from employees' knowledge and competencies. It is the role of the KM professional to manage the organisation's knowledge creation and utility. However, the role of the KM professional is still an evolving one. An objective of this study was to answer the question who are the KM professional, what personal qualities and competencies do they bring into their job, and are they up to the job?

There a number well developed and tried competency based models developed by Boyatzis (1982) and others, who use the trait approach to measuring competence. These competence models were designed to measure individual's analytical reasoning, tendencies to action (Mumford 1990), and aiding the HRM selection and development programmes. The techniques used to elicit understanding use repertory grids, skill profiles, behavioural event interviews, structured questionnaires, and others. Any of these methodologies would have been adequate for this study, however, this study uses an in-depth structured interview supported by observation of individual participants in their workplace to explore the KM role and the role holders, and to attempt to validate earlier empirical research findings of Earl and Scott (1998). Therefore, the major objective was not to measure the level of any particular trait. The advantage of the qualitative research method is in providing an in-depth understanding of the study's participants, although the disadvantage of this method is that the research findings are not generalisable to the whole population of KM professionals, but stay with the sample.

2.2 The Sample

Fifty blue chip companies in the U.K. were approached with a request to interview their KM officers. From these twenty self-identified Knowledge Managers affirmatively responded, and an appointment with each individual participant was arranged on the telephone. Twelve participants were men and eight women, aged between late twenties to late forties. The sample titles ranged from a Project Manager through to a Chief Knowledge Officer (CKO). Not all had the word 'knowledge' in their title, making the KM role identification rather difficult. Job titles may not always be representative of their function but are specific to the needs and style of their organisation (Stewart 1998). 60% were the first to hold a KM role in their organisation. The majority (80%) were appointed to the job the company's CEO or other key senior executives, while the rest (20%) were appointed by line managers. 33% had a formal IT qualifications or training and in the past carried out IT projects of varied complexity.

2.3 Data Collection

The sample were visited in their companies at least once (four were visited twice and one three times to further clarify issues) for an approximately three hours session consisting of i) an in-depth one-to-one interview and ii) accompany the participant on 'walk about'. The questionnaire consisted of open ended questions, which were recorded by hand using paper and pencil. No notes were made during the 'walk about', although a summary of observations were recorded on leaving the company.

2.4 The Questionnaire

Questionnaire consisted of forty-five open ended questions and statements regarding the KM role in the organisation. Using the questions to facilitate answers, the participants were then left to freely talk about their job, their personal qualities to do the job, the reasons for applying for the job in the first place, and where do they plan to take the KM function in creating the organisational intellectual capital. The were grouped into the following categories with which to build a profile of today's KM professionals in large blue chip companies: 'The KM's Personality Attributes Profile', 'The Ideal Knowledge Manager', 'The KM's Role in Organisations', 'Testing the KM Model', and 'Are KM Professionals Entrepreneurs or Managers?'.

3 Results and Analyses

3.1 The KM's Skills and Personality Attributes Profile

The sample's job titles varied from Knowledge Manager to Learning Director, Head of Information Services, Director of knowledge and Sustainability and Project Manager. Only 20% of the sample's job titles included the word 'knowledge'.

The sample's career background and skills were surprisingly varied stretching from sales, social services, R&D, academic, IT, and HRM, to financial services. Large U.S. companies employed those who were not the first incumbents. All except one (5 years) were in the job for less than two years (from 2 months - $\leq$ 2 years).

The Figure 1 below summarizes the study's Knowledge Managers' skills background profile; the KM's previous employment, the skills they developed in their previous employment, and the rank order of collectively pooled competencies. The summary suggests that the most prominent pooled skill competencies the sample offered to their new KM role were: formalised approaches to problem solving and to collecting/disseminating information. The Personality Attributes included the following: analytical, rational, negotiator, and influencer behaviours.

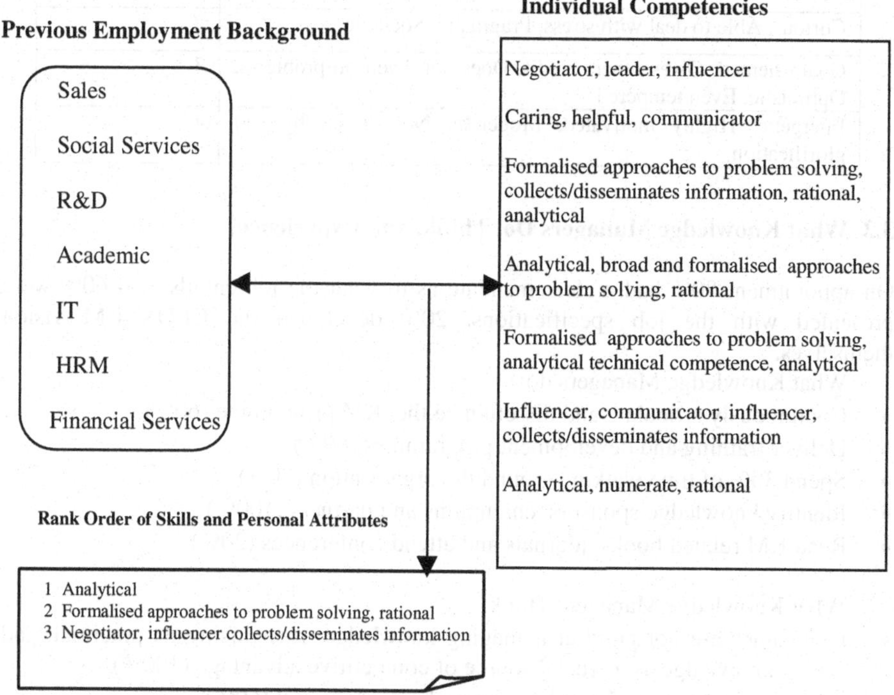

Fig. 1. The Study's Knowledge Managers' Skills Background Profile

3.2 The Perceived Ideal Knowledge Manager

The sample stated that Knowledge Management consists of two dimensions: 65% organisational culture change, and 35% IT competence. Managing relationships effectively was considered a significant part of the job. 80% saw the KM professional's role as a leader consisting of entrepreneur/consultant (70%) and management (30%) activities. 20% agreed strongly and 60% somewhat agreed that a knowledge manager must have a broad career experience background, and posses multiple competencies (80%). From a list of given personality attributes the sample ranked enthusiasm, interest in change, and tolerance as the most important. The ranking of the whole list of attributes is in Table 2.

Finally, the sample stated that Knowledge Managers must have a full-hearted support and sponsorship of their company's CEO, without which they would become vulnerable and unable to perform their job (100%).

Table 2. Ranking of Knowledge Manager's Personality Attributes

KM Personality Attributes	Ranks
Enthusiastic, Tolerant, Interested in Change	1
Curious, Able to deal with stress, Pragmatic, Sociable	2
Goal oriented, Gives others credit, Does not dwell on problems, Optimistic, Even tempered	3
Energetic, Highly motivated, Moderate, Not driven by self glorification	4

3.3 What Knowledge Managers Do, Think, and Experience?

On appointment 80% had a clear mandate as to what the job entails, and 60% were presented with the job specifications. 20% developed the CEO's KM vision themselves.

What Knowledge Managers do:

- Continuously articulate and disseminate the KM programme (60%)
- Deliver training and development programmes (60%)
- Spend 30% of time walking around the organisation (70%)
- Identify knowledge sponsors, champions and partners (100%)
- Read KM related books, journals and attend conferences (20%)

What Knowledge Managers Think:

- Companies are not good at managing knowledge, recognising its potential, and seeing knowledge as a crucial source of competitive advantage (100%)
- KM must understand the organisation's business model (60%)
- KM needs to have a clear idea what kind of knowledge is relevant and will create value (50%).

The Knowledge Managers' up-to-date experiences:

- They found managing relationships as a part of the job difficult (100%)
- Their first initiatives were IT based (100%)
- They feared that their position in the organisation was risky; i.e. when business gets tough, the KM role would be first to go (90%).

The findings in this section were interesting and somewhat disturbing. Firstly, the sample defined the KM role as consisting of organisational change (65%), and new technology dimension (35%). This means that one of the most crucial KM competency skills must be the ability to manage human relationships, and to be particularly skilful at managing stress. The findings, however, were not surprising, since being 'effective at managing interpersonal relationships' did not prominently feature on the sample's essential criteria list. The reported key personal skills and attributes were analytical thinking (Figure 1), and enthusiasm, tolerance, and interested in change (Table 2). Further, the findings of this study suggest that only 33% of the sample were technologically literate. This finding is interesting, since the whole sample started their new career of a Knowledge Manager by facilitating technology based.

In summary, the whole sample's first initiatives in their organisations were championing new office automating systems designed to increase productivity; i.e.: management processes (explicit organisational – capabilities), directories and tools (explicit technological – exploration). The least attended and least favourable areas of attention was given to groupware (explicit organisational – exploration), meeting spaces tacit organisational – contactivity) and setting up facilities such as teleconferencing (tacit technological – connectivity). Snowden (1998) suggested that it is easier to manage explicit knowledge, since it symbolizes safety and security and therefore it is easier to use as a starting point for KM initiatives. This study's finings supported Snowden's assertion, since a significant part of the knowledge manager's time was spent on exploration and facilitating organizational explicit capabilities rather than dealing with tacit knowledge.

Testing Earl and Scott's (1998) Model Knowledge Manager

In this study, KM was defined as 35% technology and 65% culture change, which differs from Earl and Scott, who defined the role of KM as 20% technology and 80% culture change. The explanation could be that IT advances and a lesser need to change culture today may contributed to this shift of balance. However, Earl and Scott (1998) identified the Technologist and Environmentalist dimensions as the preferred Knowledge Manager's capabilities, followed by entrepreneur and management consultant. Earl and Scott's model proposes that Knowledge Managers must be capable of both effectively leading and managing KM programmes, and that Knowledge Managers need to posses multiple competencies and personality attributes to carry out the role effectively. This means that their KM professionals were expected to be exceptionally competent in managing the organisational environments using technological solutions. These are to be supplemented by an entrepreneurial attitude in looking for opportunities and filling organisational know-how or expertise gaps.

The sample in this study identified an ideal Knowledge Management professional as Management Consultant (47%) and Entrepreneur (23%), and to a lesser degree Technologist (15%), and Environmentalist (15%). Their definition of the KM role in organisations is a natural progression from data processing to Management Information Systems (MIS), where KM enables an active capture and sharing of relevant organisational knowledge to add value, improve knowledge and sustained business performance. There is clearly a serious discrepancy between the Earl and Scott's findings and findings of this study. The findings of this study did not support the Earl and Scott's Model as far as the sample did not possess the necessary technological expertise themselves to appropriately evaluate the different technical solutions on offer. This alone would detract to some extent from their expected leadership ability to manage the organisational landscape.

Finally, earlier studies reported that knowledge managers identified themselves as tolerant, enthusiastic and interested in change. The Table 2 shows that this study sample ranked the above personality attributes equally as the most important for a Knowledge Manager to possess.
In conclusion, the sample of KM professionals did not fundamentally differ from Earl and Scott's model in what they did, although their perceptions of themselves as entrepreneurs and management consultants differed with Earl and Scott's technologists and environmentalists.

4 Discussion

This study sought to explore the Knowledge Management role in organisations regarding the of KM professional individuals' skill competencies and personality attributes. In doing so, an attempt was made to cross-validate Earl and Scott's empirical research with an in-depth qualitative study. Both the above literature review and the findings of this study broadly agreed about the KM role and the KM professional's personal competencies to perform the function. The KM function in organisations is that of a facilitator of organisational change towards 'sharing knowledge' culture and building intellectual capital resources by aligning information technology with the company's strategic aims to enable an organisation to achieve its competitive edge.

On the individual's level, the role of KM is a complex one where the individual job boundaries start with the job title and mandate. This study showed that some Knowledge Managers did not have the word 'knowledge' in their titles, possibly due to some companies being unclear about the KM functional responsibilities, and therefore the subsequent hesitation about placing the KM role at the centre of their decision making hub. Whatever the explanation, the reality is that most of the companies in this study showed what could be described as communicative incompetence, which left the newly appointed individuals unsure about their job, about their position in the company and about their future in the company.

The Earl and Scott's (1998) model defined a KM professional as someone possessing competencies as technologist, environmentalist entrepreneur, and management consultant. It is easy to understand that such a multidisciplinary individual would be desirable to most organisations, although, such a combination of the four very different personality types is riddled with conceptual problems.
Let consider:

1. *A technologist*'s priority is maintain and bring up to date the technological platform. This is done under often-difficult resources and political conditions. He or she tends to have little interest, or understanding of the business model, and invariably does not possess the right skills and mind-set to carry out alignments between the technology and an organisation's strategic vision (Sauer and Willcock 2002).
2. *Creating the best environment* involves building co-operative relationships and a culture of 'trust'. Ninaka and Takeuchi's (1995) solution is a hypertext organisational structure, combining the benefits of a bureaucratic structure and a task force to build a knowledge base. However, Eckert (1989) reminds us that

information travels differently within different socio-economic levels and groups even in organisations, and tacit knowledge is unlikely to be given freely for too long without any offers of sharing power in return.

3. *An entrepreneur* is an independently minded individual, who sees and takes an opportunity when it arises, often taking personal risks. This, by definition, means making and following one's own rules. Organisations, unless they are hi-tech and small, manage to exist only because of having set rules and procedures how to go about business. On the whole, organisations do not tolerate 'non-conformist' behaviours.
4. *A consultant* is entrepreneurial by nature, by bringing external expertise (or filling in 'know-how' gaps) to organisations in a form of short-term contracts. As a rule, consultants are valued, because they are not a part of the organisation's culture and therefore keep out of the politics. A Knowledge Manager, on the other hand, is at best an internal consultant without the advantage of being independent.

Knowledge managers spent between fifteen to fifty per cent of their working time walking around the organisation and identifying business concerns ('consultant' and 'entrepreneur' competency activities). Identification of knowledge sponsors, champions and partners was reported an important activity, although not identifying sceptics and having difficulties managing relationships was unique to this study relative to the earlier ones. Identifying sceptics and effective management of professional relationships is as important to objectivity as finding one's sympathisers, particularly, if the KM role is newly created and is not clearly defined in terms of responsibilities and power.

The initiatives the sample undertook since being appointed as KM professionals were based on 'technologist' or 'explicit' knowledge competencies, which conflicts with what the sample identified as their strengths (i.e. 'entrepreneurial' and 'management consultant'). Their technology based projects were relatively simple, although 'visible', and noticeable activities. By doing so the relatively newly appointed KM professionals did not take risks by starting their career with bridging technology and the more complex and difficult to quantify 'tacit' knowledge projects.

The conclusion to this study suggests that the KM role is still evolving, it consists of managing the organisational complex communications, and deploying new technology to innovate and speed up management information systems. The findings of this study seem short of the ethos of KM as a moving, knowledge creating concept, and the observed participants did not measure up to the current KM literature's 'ideal'. It too may have something to do with the problem of definition and this state of affairs is likely to stay so until the management and employees own up to and accept team responsibility for the collective knowledge creation. One way of 'resolving' this problem in the short term is to contract KM professionals on a project basis along the lines of the management consultancy industry. External expertise has both advantages (i.e. an intensive pace of work, staying out of internal politics, bringing objectivity from outside) and disadvantages (unknown quality, lack of loyalty, no extras fired by enthusiasm/motivation, relationships clearly defined by a contract) of those offered routinely by management consultants. This approach assures a close fit between his or her competencies with a presented project objectives. However, even in this case there is clearly a need for the KM professional to be facilitated into a constructively supportive team culture with open communication channels throughout the organisation, which given the 'top-down' structure of organisations could is difficult to achieve.

Managing relationships effectively and with relative ease is a necessary prerequisite for a successful KM professional. A successful Knowledge Manager becomes a facilitator in helping to determine what conditions made excellence possible and how this could encourage those conditions within the organisational culture (Cooperrider and Srivastva 1987, Bushe 1995, Cooperrider 1996, Hall and Hammond 2002).

As KM becomes embedded in the daily activities and organisational culture, this should lead to a less specific analysis of individual knowledge dimensions. This should explain why 'tacit' and 'explicit' knowledge was thought to be of equal value by this study's sample, while at the same time they spent most time on explicit conversion initiatives.

Sauer and Willcock (2002) introduced a role of 'organisational architect' as someone able to bridge the divide between the strategists and technologists. Organisational architect is someone who is neither all strategist ('tacit' knowledge) nor technologist ('explicit' knowledge), but someone who guides the translation of a strategic vision into a flexible integrated platform. The process is a form of a dialogue between the organisational visionaries and technologists as they define and design the right combination of structures, processes, capabilities and technologies, which are better, aligned and are capable of responding to the organisational goals. True synergy becomes possible by building a technological platform shaped by vision and in turn the vision is reshaped by the characteristics of the technology that enable vision. The organisational architect must possess the necessary competencies and personality attributes to understand the enablers and constraints.

Conceptually, Sauer and Willcock attempted to narrow down the Knowledge Management role into the domain of organisational change through the process of understanding how the two parties can learn from each other and to align their skills with organisational vision. Organisational architect does not undertake technology based projects, and as a consequence steps outside his or her area of expertise, but through effective communication and deep understanding of differences in individuals' skills, brings the two together to implement/initiate/facilitate a project.

It is important not only to understand the KM concept and role but also to keep pace with developments and changes, as the 'lessons are learned' (Havens and Knapp 1999, Stewart 1997), both organisations and individuals should benefit from maturation. The Knowledge Manager's job specifications and representation on the organisational charts are becoming the norm, indicating a more established role that has performance measures in place. There seems to be a more confident approach to the design of a clear mission and a mandate as senior executives play their part in closing the 'knowledge gap'. The Knowledge Managers' brief profile based on this study suggests a female or a male in their 40s and 50s, coming from not one particular or dominant professional background, although of broad mindset and career experience, tolerant, enthusiastic and interested in change.

The significance lies in the realisation that:

- The Knowledge Manager needs multiple competencies in order to effectively adjust the organisation's competency focus (Leader/Entrepreneur)

- The role of Knowledge Manager becomes temporary or contracted as specific skills are brought in to match the organisational development (Leader/Consultant)
- The role becomes 'custodial' as the team members take over according to competency possession versus competency requirements (Manager/Technologist/Environmentalist)

An earlier developed approach based on the Appreciative Inquiry theory is well positioned to be re-evaluated in becoming a tool of facilitating organisational understanding by replacing the traditional negative approaches such as 'gaps' and 'needs' analyses. The Appreciative Inquiry is a product of the socio-rationalist paradigm (Gergen 1982, 1990, Bushe 1995), treating the social and psychological reality as a product of the moment, open to continuous reconstruction. The rationale behind the Appreciative Inquiry is that search for knowledge and a theory of intentional collective action are designed to evolve the normative vision and will of a group or an organisation. In other words, it is an understanding that whatever is wanted more of, already exists in organisations. The assumptions of Appreciative Inquiry therefore are:

- in every society, organisation or group, something works
- what we focus on tends to become our reality, and it is determined by the language used
- there are multiple realities
- individuals have more confidence in approaching the future with the best from the past
- differences between individuals and groups are to be valued.

While logical positivism assumes that social phenomena are enduring, stable and replicable to allow for generalisations, socio-realism contents that social order is fundamentally unstable (Gergen 1990, Ormerod 2001). 'Social phenomena are guided by cognitive heuristics, limited only by the human imagination through the linkage of ideas and action (Cooperrider and Srivastva 1987). To build an appreciative inquiry intervention then rests on three parts: (i) discovering the best of …, (2) understanding what creates the best of …, and (3) amplifying the people and processes who best exemplify the best of … The enhanced imaginative capacity that flows from this relational process builds engaged, alert, self-aware, conscious organisational members in this Century of softer skills, effective team participation and an intimate informed understanding own one's own strengths and weaknesses.

The measurement of outcomes, the quality and impact of relationships, and sharing that with others so that they too can learn from the experience is not easy. Development for an individual and an organisation is hardly ever a linear process, although the organisations inherited from the industrial revolution continue to perpetuate assembly line mental models (Hall and Hammond 2002). Given the dynamic acceleration of change present in the global marketplace today, and if the KM professionals are to be successful in this demanding environment, a dramatic overhaul of our organisational information sharing and power relationships is required.

In conclusion, KM is not anyone's permanent expertise domain, since by nature the concept shifts its focus as it develops. A Knowledge Manager must articulate and launch the key KM objectives into an organisational culture after which the role should become owned both by the individual and the organisation where the individual and collective competencies fit the current business strategy.

References

1. Aadne, J.H., G. Von Krogh and J. Roos: *Managing Knowledge: Perspectives on co-operation and competition,* Sage: London (1996)
2. Bailey,C. and M. Clarke: 'Going for Gold', in *Human Resources,* March (1999), pp.69-72
3. Barney, J.:'Looking inside for competitive advantage', *Academy of Management Executive,* (1995) Vol. 17(1): 99-120
4. Bentley, T.:'Knowledge Management? Humbug!', *Management Accounting,* April (1999)
5. Bicknell, D.: 'Knowledge Managers Don't Work', *Computer Weekly,* (1999) May 27, pp.26
6. Bottomley, A.: 'Complexity and KM', in S. Rock (Ed.), *Knowledge Management: A Real Business Guide,* Caspian Publ.: London (1998)
7. Bray, P.: 'Do you know what you want?', *Sunday Times, Knowledge Management Supplement,* (1999) April 25, p15
8. Broadbent, M.:'The phenomenon of knowledge management: what does it mean to the information profession?', *Information Outlook,* (1998) 2(5): 23-39
9. Brown, J.S and Duguid, P.: 'Balancing Act: How to Capture Knowledge Without Killing It', *Harvard Business Review,* (2000) 78(3): 73-79
10. Bushe, G.R.: 'Advances in Appreciative Inquiry as an Organisation Development Intervention', *The Organisation Development Journal,* (1995) 13(3): 14-22.
11. Cooperrider, D.L.: 'Resources for Getting Appreciative Inquiry Started: An Example OD proposal', *OD Practitioner,* (1996) 23(1): 23-32
12. Cooperrider, D.L. and S Srivastva: 'Appreciative Inquiry in Organisational Life', in R. Woodman and W. Pasmore (eds), in *Research in Organisational Change and Development:* (1987) *Vol. I,* 129-169
13. Curley, K.: 'The Role of Technology', in S. Rock (Ed.), *Knowledge Management: A Real Business Guide,* Caspian Publ.: London (1998)
14. Coleman, D.: 'The Challenges of Electronic Collaboration in Knowledge Sharing', in S. Rock (Ed.), *Knowledge Management: A Real Business Guide,* Caspian Publ.: London (1998)
15. Davenport, T.H. and L. Prusak *Working Knowledge,* Harvard Business School Press: Boston (1998)
16. De Ven, F.: *Knowledge Management Survey,* KPMG Consulting Publ.:London (1999)
17. Di Mattia, S. and I.A. Scott 'KM: Hope, hype or harbinger?', *Library Journal,* (1999) Sept 15, 122(15): 33
18. Di Miao, P.: 'The key to successful searches: Taxonomies and Classification Structures' *The Financial Times,* (2001) Nov 7, 2001 p3
19. Donkin, R.: 'Getting to know a developing discipline: Attaching monetary value to the knowledge in a companies an important contribution to understanding an old field', *The Financial Times,* Feb.14, 2002 p12
20. Earl, E.J. and Scott, I.A.: 'What is a chief knowledge officer?', *Sloan Management Review,* (1999) 40(2): 29
21. Eckert, P.: (1999) *Jocks and Burnout,* Teachers Press: New York (1999)
22. Gelwick, R.: *The Way of Discovery: an introduction of the thought of Michael Polyani,* Oxford Univ. Press: USA (1977)

23. Gourlay, S.: 'Knowledge Management and HRM', *Croners Employee Relations (Review),* (1999) *March, Issue 8, pp.21-27*
24. Hansen, M., N. Nohria and T. Tierney: 'What's your strategy for managing knowledge?', *Harvard Business Review,* (1999) 77(2): 106
25. Havens, C. and E. Knapp: 'Easing into Knowledge Management', *Strategy and Leadership,* (1999) 27(2): 4
26. Lewis, M.: 'Six steps to orchestrating the best value from your corporate knowledge', *Computer Weekly,* (2000) January 27, p 41
27. Morton, A.: *A guide through the Theory of Knowledge,* Blackwell Publ.: Oxford (1997)
28. Nonaka, I. and H. Takeuchi: *The Knowledge Creating Company,* Oxford Univ. Press: Oxford (1995)
29. Offsey, S.: 'KM: Capitalising on your intellect', *Boston Business Journal,* (1998) May 1(7)
30. Ormerod, P.: *Butterfly Economics,* Faber and Faber: Great Britain (2001)
31. Prichard, C.: *Embodied Knowing, KM and the Reconstruction of Post-Compulsory Education: A case of of find a knowledge market, suck it, satisfy it and move on?,* Paper for Critical Management Studies Conference, Manchester School of Management, UMIST, July (1999)
32. Prusak, L.: 'Exploding the Myth: strategies for harnessing organisational knowledge', IT Directors' Forum, Cranfield School of Management, (2000) January
33. Ryan, F.: 'Librarians and Knowledge Management', in S. Rock (Ed.), *Knowledge Management: A Real Business Guide,* Caspian Publ.: London (1998)
34. Sauer, C. and L.P Willocks: 'The Evolution of the organisational Architect', MITSloan Management Review, (2002) 43(3): 41-49.
35. Snowden, D.: 'Knowledge and Differentiation', in S. Rock (Ed.), *Knowledge Management: A Real Business Guide,* Caspian Publ.: London (1998)
36. Stewart, T.A. *Intellectual Capital,* Doubleday Publ.: New York (1997)
37. Stewart, T.A.: 'The House That Knowledge Built', *Fortune,* (2000) 142(7): 278-282
38. Stewart, T.A.: *The Wealth of Knowledge, Intellectual Capital and the Twenty-first Century Organisation',* Nicholas Brealey: Great Britain (2002)
39. Verespej, M. 'Knowledge Management: System or culture?', *Industry Week,* (1999) August 16, 248(15): 20
40. Von Krogh, G. Ross and G. Yip: 'A note on the epistemology of globalizing firms', in G. Von Krogh and J. Ross (Eds.), *Managing Knowledge: Perspectives on co-operation and competition,* Sage: London (1996)
41. Wenger, E.: 'Communities of practice: learning as a social system', *Systems Thinker,* (1998) June, (www.co-I-l.com/coil/knowledge-garden/cop/lss.shtml)
42. Williams, M.: 'Skepticism', in J. Greco and E. Sosa (Ed.), *The Blackwell Guide to Epistemology,* Blackwell Publ.: Oxford (1999)
43. Zagrebski, L.: 'What is knowledge?', in J. Greco and E. Sosa (Eds.), *The Blackwell Guide to Epistemology,* Blackwells Publ.: Oxford (1999)

KEx: A Peer-to-Peer Solution for Distributed Knowledge Management

M. Bonifacio[1,2], P. Bouquet[1,2], G. Mameli[2], and M. Nori[2]

[1] Dept. of Information and Communication Tech. – University of Trento (Italy)
[2] Istituto per la Ricerca Scientifica e Tecnologica, Trento (Italy)

Abstract. Distributed Knowledge Management is an approach to Knowledge Management based on the principle that the multiplicity (and heterogeneity) of perspectives within complex organizations should not be viewed as an obstacle to knowledge exploitation, but rather as an opportunity that can foster innovation and creativity. Despite a wide agreement on this principle, most current KM systems are based on the idea that all perspectival aspects of knowledge should be eliminated in favor of an objective and general representation of knowledge. In this paper we propose a peer-to-peer architecture (called KEx), which embodies the principle above in a quite straightforward way: (i) each peer (called a K-peer) provides all the services needed to create and organize "local" knowledge from an individual's or a group's perspective, and (ii) social structures and protocols of meaning negotiation are defined to achieve semantic coordination among autonomous peers (e.g., when searching documents from other K-peers).

1 Introduction

Distributed Knowledge Management (DKM), as described in [6], is an approach to KM based on the principle that the multiplicity (and heterogeneity) of perspectives within complex organizations should not be viewed as an obstacle to knowledge exploitation, but rather as an opportunity that can foster innovation and creativity.

The fact that different individuals and communities may have very different perspectives, and that these perspectives affect their representation of the world (and therefore of their work) is widely discussed – and generally accepted – in theoretical research on the nature of knowledge. Knowledge representation in artificial intelligence and cognitive science have produced many theoretical and experimental evidences of the fact that what people know is not a mere collection of facts; indeed, knowledge always presupposes some (typically implicit) interpretation schema, which provide an essential component in sense-making (see, for example, the notions of context [18,7,13], mental space [12], partitioned representation [10]); studies on the social nature of knowledge stress the social nature of interpretation schemas, viewed as the outcome of a special kind of "agreement" within a community of knowing (see, for example, the notions of scientific paradigm [16], frame [15]), thought world [11], perspective [3]).

Despite this large convergence, it can be observed that the high level architecture of most current KM systems in fact does not reflect this vision of knowledge (see [5,6,4] for a detailed discussion of this claim). The fact is that most KM systems embody the assumption that, to share and exploit knowledge, it is necessary to implement a process

D. Karagiannis and U. Reimer (Eds.): PAKM 2002, LNAI 2569, pp. 490–500, 2002.

of knowledge-extraction-and-refinement, whose aim is to eliminate all subjective and contextual aspects of knowledge, and create an objective and general representation that can then be reused by other people in a variety of situations. Very often, this process is finalized to build a central knowledge base, where knowledge can be accessed via a knowledge portal. This centralized approach – and its underlying objectivist epistemology – is one of the reasons why so many KM systems are deserted by users, who perceive such systems either as irrelevant or oppressive [9].

In this paper we propose a peer-to-peer (P2P) architecture, called KEx, which is coherent with the vision of DKM. Indeed, P2P systems seem particularly suitable to implement the two core principles of DKM, namely the principle of autonomy (communities of knowing should be granted the highest possible degree of semantic autonomy to manage their local knowledge), and the principle of coordination (the collaboration between autonomous communities must be achieved through a process of semantic coordination, rather than through a process of semantic homogenization) [6]. In KEx, each community of knowing (or Knowledge Nodes (KN), as they are called in [4]) is represented by a peer, and the two principles above are implemented in a quite straightforward way: (i) each peer provides all the services needed by a knowledge node to create and organize its own local knowledge (autonomy), and (ii) by defining social structures and protocols of meaning negotiation in order to achieve semantic coordination (e.g., when searching documents from other peers).

The paper goes as follows. In section 2, we describe the main features of KEx, and argue why they provide a useful support to DKM; in 3, we describe its implementation in a peer-to-peer platform called JXTA; finally, we draw some conclusions and future work.

2 KEx: A P2P Architecture for DKM

KEx is a P2P system which allows a collection of KNs to search and provide documents on a semantic basis without presupposing a beforehand agreement on how documents should be categorized, or on a common language for representing semantic information within the system. In the following sections, we describe the high-level architecture of KEx, and explain what role each element plays in a DKM vision.

2.1 K-Peers

KEx is defined as a collection of peers, called knowledge peers (K-Peers), each of which represents a KN, namely an individual's or a group's perspective on a given body of knowledge. Each K-peer can play two main roles: *provider* and *seeker*. A K-peer acts as a provider when it "publishes" in the system a body of knowledge, together with an explicit perspective on it (called a *context*, e.g. a topic hierarchy used to categorized local documents [8]); a K-peer acts as a seeker when it searches for information by making explicit part of its own perspective, and negotiates it with other K-peers.

Each K-peer has the structure shown in Figure 1. Below we illustrate the main modules and functionalities.

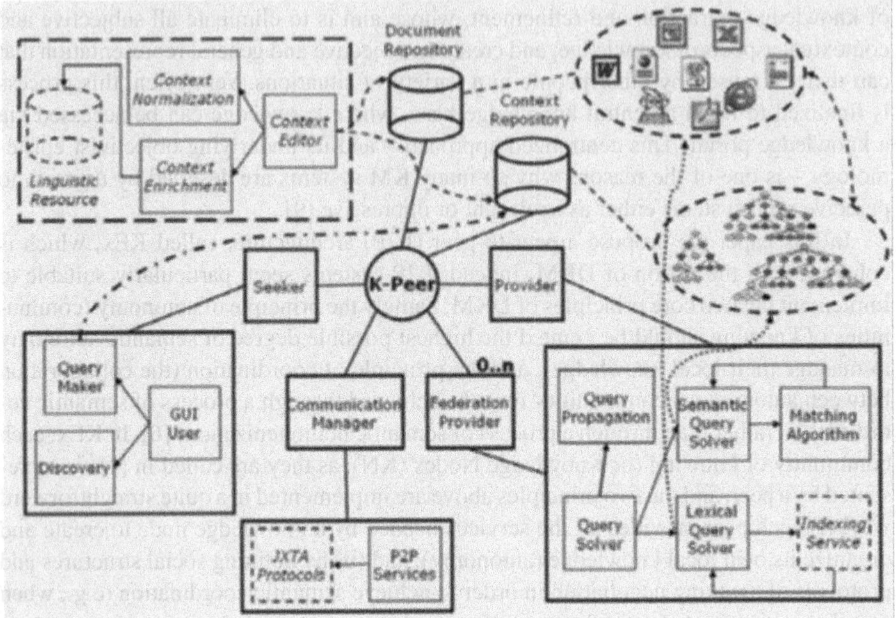

Fig. 1. The KEx's main components

Document Repository. A *Document Repository* is where each KN stores its own local knowledge. We can imagine a private space in which the KN maintains its document and data, possibly using a local semantic schema (e.g., a file-system structure, or a database schema), or a document management system in order to organize and access them.

Context Repository. Following [2], we define a context as a partial and approximate representation of the world from an individual's or a group's perspective. The reason why we adopt this notion of context is that it provides a robust formal framework (called Local Models Semantics [13]) for modeling both contexts and their relationships.

In order to use contexts in KEx, we adopted a web-oriented syntax for contexts, called CTXML. It provides an XML-Schema specification of context for document organization and classification[1].

In KEx, each context plays the role of a category system for organizing and classifying documents, or any other kind of digital information identifiable by a URI, stored in a document repository. Each peer can use more than one context to classify local knowledge; a K-peer's contexts are stored in a *context repository*.

From the standpoint of DKM, contexts are relevant in two distinct senses:

[1] Currently, contexts are trees, whose nodes are labelled with words defined in some name space. Arcs are Is-A, Part-Of or generic relations between nodes. Details can be found in [8].

- on the one hand, they have an important role within each KN, as they provide a dynamic and incremental explicitation of its semantic perspective. Once contexts are reified, they become cognitive artifacts that contribute to the process of perspective making [3], namely the consolidation of a shared view in a KN, continuously subject to revision and internal negotiation among its members;
- on the other hand, contexts offer a simple and direct way for a KN to make public its perspective on the information that that KN can provide. Therefore, as we will see, contexts are an essential tool for semantic coordination among different KN.

It is important to observe that contexts provide only a common syntax for classification structures. Indeed, we could see them as a language for wrapping any classification structure (e.g., like directory systems, databases schemas, web directories). This means that in principle people can continue to work with their preferred document management system, provided it can be wrapped using CTXML.

Context management module. The context management module allows users to create, manipulate, and use contexts in KEx. The module has two main components:

- **Context editor**: provides users with a simple interface to create and edit contexts, and to classify information with respect to a context. This happens by allowing users to create links from a resource (identified by a URI) to a node in a context. Examples of resources are: documents in local directories, the address of a database access services, addresses of other K-peers that provide information that a KN wants to explicitly classify in its own context.
- **Context browser**: is part of Seeker component (GUI User in Figure 1) and allows users to navigate contexts in the context repository. The main reasons for navigating a context in KEx are two. The first is obviously to find document in the local knowledge repository by navigating the semantic structure. The second, and more important reason, is to build queries. The intuitive idea is that users can make context dependent queries (namely, from their perspective) by selecting a category in one of the available contexts. Once a category is selected, the context browser builds a *focus*[2] – namely a contextual interpretation of the user's query – by automatically extracting the relevant portion of the context to which the category belongs. The focus is then used as a basis for meaning coordination and negotiation with other K-peers during the search.

2.2 Roles of K-Peers in KEx

Each K-peer can play two main roles: seeker and provider. Their interactions are represented in Figure 2, and described in detail in the following two sections.

Seeker. As a seeker, a K-peer allows users to search for documents (and other information) from other K-peers and federations (see Section 2.3). The seeker supports the

[2] See [17] for a formal definition of focus.

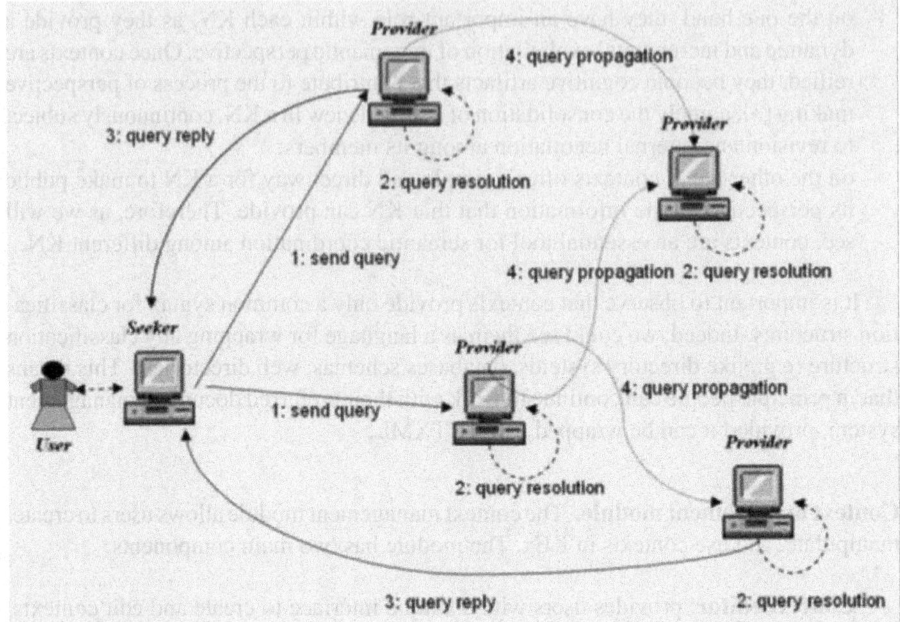

Fig. 2. The KEx system: interaction between Seeker and Provider roles

user in the definition of context-dependent queries through the context browser. A query is composed by a query expression and a focus. A query expression is a list (possibly empty) of one or more keywords provided by a user; a focus is a portion of a context determined by the category that the user has selected. Moreover, the seeker provides the discovery mechanism, used to find resources to which the query is to be sent. The user decides to send the query to some of the available K-peers and federations. When the user submits the query, the seeker activates a session associated to that query (there can be only one active session for each seeker). In a session, a seeker can receive several asynchronous replies from the providers which resolved the query (through the meaning negotiation protocol, see below) and called back the seeker. The results returned to the user are composed by the aggregation of all the results received from the providers; each result is made up of a list of document descriptors (i.e., name of the document, short description, and so on). Each result is presented together with the part of context that the provider has matched against the current query. This relationship between contexts can be used as an opportunity for learning relationships across contexts of different KNs that the seeker can store and reuse for future queries (see section 2.3). Finally, if one or more interesting documents are found, the seeker can contact the K-peers that have the documents and, if possible, download them.

Provider. The provider is the second main role in the KEx system. It contains the functionalities required to take and resolve a query, and to identify the results that must to be returned to the seeker. When a K-peer receives a context-dependent query (keywords + focus), it instantiates a provider (which is configured to use a set of contexts and to provide documents in a given portion of the knowledge repository), and tries to resolve the query in two ways:

- **Semantic resolution**: using a context matching algorithm [17], the provider searches for relations between the locally available contexts and the query's focus. More specifically, the matching algorithm searches categories whose associated contextual information in the provider's contexts matches (in a sense defined in [17]) with the query's focus. If a match is found, the URIs of the resources associated to the provider's context are returned to the seeker, together with a short information on the reason why a semantic match was found. If the matched category contains also links to resources in other K-peers, the provider propagates the query to those K-peers.
- **Lexical resolution**: using a keyword-based indexer, the provider searches for the occurrence of specific keywords into the set of documents of the local repository.

If the query contains only keywords, the provider will use only the lexical search; if it contains only a focus, the provider will use only the semantic search; if both are available, the outcome will be the result of intersecting the semantic and lexical results.

2.3 K-Services

KEx provides a collection of services which have an important role in supporting knowledge exchange (that's why they are called K-services). The main K-services are described in the following sections.

Context normalization and enrichment. This service allows to perform a linguistic normalization (e.g., deleting stop words, tokenizing, part-of-speech tagging, etc.) on user defined contexts, and to use knowledge from an external linguistic resource (e.g., WordNet) to add semantic information to the categories in a context.

Normalization uses pretty standard NLP techniques, so we do not discuss it here. As to enrichment, it is applied offline to a context defined by a user (see [17] for details). It takes a user-defined context (e.g., a context built with the context editor) as input and returns a semantically enriched context as output. In our current implementation, the result is that linguistic knowledge (e.g., senses, synonyms, hierarchical relations with other categories, and so on) is extracted from WordNet and is "attached" to each context node label.

It is important to say why enrichment is not equivalent to introduce a shared ("objective") semantics in KEx. Indeed, the intuition is that the meaning of a label in each context node has two components:

- the first is the linguistic component, which means that the words used as labels have a meaning (or, better, a set of meanings) in a "dictionary". This is used to record that many words have different meaning (e.g., "apple" as a fruit, "apple" as a tree, and "apple" as a computer brand), even if only one of them is likely to be the relevant one in a given context;

– the second is a sort of pragmatic component, which is given by its position in a context (e.g., its position in the path from the context root). This helps in understanding what the user means on a particular occasion with a word (e.g., "apple" in a path like "computer/software/apple" is different from "apple" in a path like "computer/hardware/printers/apple", even though "apple" has the same dictionary meaning').

The first component of meaning is dealt with in the normalization and enrichment phase (for example, given a context, some potential senses are deleted because of the position of a label in that context); the second is dealt with in the meaning negotiation protocol, and cannot be computed beforehand, as it expresses a user's perspective in making a query (so this is the more "perspectival" aspect of meaning).

It is extremely important to stress that different linguistic resources can be used to enrich a context. So far, we've been using only WordNet, but there's no reason why other resources (like CYC or any other domain-specific ontology) can't be used to replace WordNet. Of course, this introduces a further problem, as the enriched contexts cannot be compared as directly as in the case of a shared resource. In this case, what happens is that each provider, after receiving a query from a context which is normalized with a different linguistic resource, applies a runtime normalization-and-enrichment of the query's focus, this way interpreting the query from its perspective. Then the query can be matched against local contexts. Of course, this introduces a further degree of semantic heterogeneity, and the returned results could be unsatisfactory for the seeker even if the semantic match good from the provider's perspective.

K-federation. A *K-federation* is a group of K-Peers that agree to appear as a unique entity to K-peers that perform a search. Each K-federation can be though as a "social" aggregation of K-peers that display some synergy in terms of content (e.g., as they provide topic-related content, or decided to use the same linguistic resource to create a common "vocabulary", thus providing more homogeneous and specific answers), quality (certify content) or access policies (certify members).

Seekers can send queries directly to K-federations, and the query is managed internally at the federation. In our current implementation, the query is simply distributed to all the members of the federation (and therefore the result is the same as if the query was sent directly to each member of the federation, the only difference being that K-peers explicitly answer as members of the federation), but the idea is that in general each K-federation can implement different methods to process queries.

To become a member of a K-federation, a K-Peer must provide a K-federation Service (the Federation Provider in Figure 1). It implements the required federation protocol (reply to queries sent to the K-federation) and observes the federation membership policy.

Discovery. Discovery is a mechanism that allows the user to discover resources in the P2P network. The user needs to discover K-peers and K-federations available in the network to contact and query them. A peer advertises the existence of resources by publishing an XML document (called *Advertisement*). In the KEx system, two types of resources are advertised:

- **K-peers** that have a provider service to solve queries. The main elements of the advertisement are a description of the peer's contexts, and the peer address to contact it, to send it queries, and to retrieve documents;
- **K-federations**, namely sets of peers that have a federation service to solve queries. The federation assures that a query sent to a federation is propagated to all active peers that are member of the federation. In this case the main elements of the advertisement are the federation topic, its address and information for joining the federation.

To discover resources, a peer sends a discovery request to another known peer, or sends a multi-cast request over the network, and receives responses (a list of advertisements) that describe the available services and resources. It is possible to specify search criteria (currently only keywords or textual expression) that are matched against the contents provided by the advertisement related to each peer or federation description.

Query Propagation. This functionality allows the KEx system to distributed queries in a highly dynamic environment. When a provider receives a query, it can forward it to other providers. To decide to which peers the query is to be forwarded, a peer has two possibilities:

- *physical proximity*: the query is sent to peers known through the discovery functionality. This way, peers or providers that are non directly reachable from a seeker, or have just joined the system, can advertise their presence and contribute to the resolution of queries;
- *semantic proximity*: this functionality exploits the fact that contexts can be used not only to classify resources like documents or database records, but also other peers. Thus, if the provider computes some matching between a query and a concept in its own context, and other peers are classified under that concept, the provider forwards the query to these other peer, this way increasing the chances that other relevant peers are reached.

The propagation algorithm is based upon a cost function which allows choosing peers that are regarded as providing more relevant information (assigning a higher value to peers discovered through the semantic method than to peers reached through physical proximity one).

Obviously, several parameters and mechanisms controlling the scope of the search can be implemented to prevent a "message flood". For example, the time-to-live (TTL), the number of hops, the list of peers already reached, and so on.

Learning. When the matching algorithm finds a semantic correspondence between concepts of different contexts, the provider can store this information for future reuse. This information is represented as a semantic "mapping" between concepts (see [8]), and can be used in three ways:

- when the K-Peer receives a query from a seeker, it can reuse stored mappings to facilitate (and possibly to avoid executing) the matching algorithm;

- a provider can use the existing mapping to forward a query to other peers that have a semantic relation with the query's focus;
- the seeker can search into the available mappings to suggest the user a set of providers with which it already had previous interactions and are considered qualified with respect to the semantic meaning of the concept selected in a query.

Using this mechanism, the K-peer network defines and increases the number and quality of the semantic relations among its members, and becomes a dynamic web of knowledge links.

3 Development Framework

In this section we briefly show how the non-functional requirements of a DKM system drive the choice of a particular architectural pattern design (a *peer-to-peer* system) and an underlying technology framework (the *Jxta* Project). In particular, KEx is under development within the business setting of an Italian national bank, and of an international insurance company[3].

From an implementation point of view, we started from *JXTA*[4], a set of open, generalized peer-to-peer protocols that allow devices to communicate and collaborate through a connecting network. This P2P framework provides also a set of protocols and functionality such as: a decentralized discovery system, an asynchronous point-to-point messaging system, and a group membership protocol. A *peer* is a software component that runs some or all the JXTA protocols; every peer needs to agree upon a common set of rules to publish, share and access resources (like services, data or applications), and communicate among each others. Thus, a JXTA peer is used to support higher level processes (based, for example, on organizational considerations) that are built on top of the basic peer-to-peer network infrastructure; they may include the enhancement of basic JXTA protocols (e.g. discovery) as well as user-written applications. JXTA tackles these requirements with a number of mechanisms and protocols: for instance the publishing and discovery mechanisms, together with a message-based communication infrastructure (called "pipe") and peer monitoring services, supports decentralization and dynamism. Security is supported by a membership service (which authenticates any peer applying to a peer group) and an access protocol (for authorization control). The flexibility of this framework allows to design distributed systems that cover all the requirements of a DKM application, using the JXTA P2P capabilities, completed and enhanced through the implementation of user-defined services. As shows in the previous sections, in the KEx system we combine the P2P paradigm (characterizing a network of knowledge nodes as a network of distributed peers) and JXTA as an implementation infrastructure.

[3] This architecture is under development as part of EDAMOK (*Enabling Distributed and Autonomous Management of Knowledge*), a joint project of the Institute for Scientific and Technological Research (IRST, Trento) and of the University of Trento.

[4] JXTA is a P2P open source project started in 2001 and supported by Sun Microsystems. See `http://www.jxta.org/` for details.

4 Conclusions and Research Issues

In this paper, we argued that technological architectures, when dealing with processes in which human communication is strongly involved, must be consistent with the social architecture of the process itself. In particular, in the domain of KM, technology must embody a principle of distribution that is intrinsic to the nature of organizational cognition. Here, we suggest that P2P infrastructures are especially suitable for KM applications, as they naturally implement meaning distribution and autonomy. It is perhaps worth noting at this point that other research areas are moving toward P2P architectures. In particular, we can mention the work on P2P approaches to the semantic web [1], to databases [14], to web services [19]. We believe this is a general trend, and that in the near future P2P infrastructure will become more and more interesting for all areas where we can't assume a centralized control.

A number of research issues need to be addressed to map aspects of distributed cognition into technological requirements. Here we propose two of them:

- **social discovery and propagation**: in order to find knowledge, people need to discover who is reachable and available to answer a request. On the one hand, broadcasting messages generates communication overflow, on the other hand talking just to physically available neighbors reduces the potential of a distributed network. A third option could be for a seeker to ask his neighbors who they trust on a topic and, among them, who is currently available. Here the question is about social mechanisms through which people find – based on trust and recommendation – other people to involve in a conversation. A similar approach could be used in order to support the propagation of information requests;
- **building communities**: if we consider communities as networks of people that, to some extent, tend to share a common perspective [3], mechanisms are needed to support the bottom-up emergence of semantic similarities across interacting KNs. Through this process, which are based on meaning negotiation protocols, people can discover and form virtual communities, and within organizations, managers might monitor the evolving trajectories of informal cognitive networks. Then, such networks, can be viewed as potential neighborhoods to support social discovery and propagation.

References

1. M. Arumugam, A. Sheth, and I. Budak Arpinar. The peer-to-peer semantic web: A distributed environment for sharing semantic knowledge on the web. In *WWW2002 Workshop on Real World RDF and Semantic Web Applications. Honolulu, Hawaii (USA)*, 2002.
2. M. Benerecetti, P. Bouquet, and C. Ghidini. Contextual Reasoning Distilled. *Journal of Theoretical and Experimental Artificial Intelligence*, 12(3):279–305, July 2000.
3. J.R. Boland and R.V.Tenkasi. Perspective making and perspective taking in communities of knowing. *Organization Science*, 6(4):350–372, 1995.
4. M. Bonifacio, P. Bouquet, and R. Cuel. Knowledge Nodes: the Building Blocks of a Distributed Approach to Knowledge Management. *Journal of Universal Computer Science*, 8(6):652–661, 2002. Springer Pub. & Co.

5. M. Bonifacio, P. Bouquet, and A. Manzardo. A distributed intelligence paradigm for knowledge management. In *Working Notes of the AAAI Spring Symposium Series 2000 on Bringing Knowledge to Business Processes*. AAAI, March 18-20 2000.
6. M. Bonifacio, P. Bouquet, and P. Traverso. Enabling distributed knowledge management. managerial and technological implications. *Novatica and Informatik/Informatique*, III(1), 2002.
7. P. Bouquet. *Contesti e ragionamento contestuale. Il ruolo del contesto in una teoria della rappresentazione della conoscenza*. Pantograph, Genova (Italy), 1998.
8. P. Bouquet, A. Donà, and L. Serafini. ConTeXtualizedlocal ontology specification via ctxml. In *MeaN-02 – AAAI workshop on Meaning Negotiation*, Edmonton, Alberta, Canada, 2002.
9. G. C. Bowker and S. L. Star. *Sorting things out: classification and its consequences*. MIT Press., 1999.
10. J. Dinsmore. *Partitioned Representations*. Kluwer Academic Publishers, 1991.
11. D. Dougherty. Interpretative barriers to successful product innovation in large firms. *Organization Science*, 3(2), 1992.
12. G. Fauconnier. *Mental Spaces: aspects of meaning construction in natural language*. MIT Press, 1985.
13. C. Ghidini and F. Giunchiglia. Local Models Semantics, or Contextual Reasoning = Locality + Compatibility. *Artificial Intelligence*, 127(2):221–259, April 2001.
14. F. Giunchiglia and I. Zaihrayeu. Making peer databases interact – a vision for an architecture supporting data coordination. In *6th International Workshop on Cooperative Information Agents (CIA-2002), Universidad Rey Juan Carlos, Madrid, Spain, September 18 - 20, 2002*, 2002. Invited talk.
15. I. Goffaman. *Frame Analysis*. Harper & Row, New York, 1974.
16. T. Kuhn. *The structure of Scientific Revolutions*. University of Chicago Press, 1979.
17. B. Magnini, L. Serafini, and M. Speranza. Linguistic based matching of local ontologies. In P. Bouquet, editor, *Working Notes of the AAAI-02 workshop on Meaning Negotiation. Edmonton (Canada)*. AAAI, AAAI Press, 2002.
18. J. McCarthy. Notes on Formalizing Context. In *Proc. of the 13th International Joint Conference on Artificial Intelligence*, pages 555–560, Chambery, France, 1993.
19. M.P. Papazoglou, J. Jang, and B.J.Kraemer. Leveraging web-services and peer-to-peer networks. October 2002.

An Expertise System for Supporting the Sales and Distribution Process of a Software Vendor

Philip Hartmann, Reimer Studt, and Attila Kral

Bavarian Research Center for Knowledge-based Systems (FORWISS),
Äßrer Laufer Platz 13-15, 90403 Nuremberg, Germany
{Philip.Hartmann, Reimer.Studt}@wiso.uni-erlangen.de
http://www.wi1.uni-erlangen.de/

Abstract. Goal of the research presented in this paper is to generate an expertise document analyzing the potential of a document and workflow management system (DMS/WMS) for a specific customer. Addressee of the expertise is on the one hand the possible client who receives decision support for the investment decision in the DMS/WMS (like the expected ROI, quantitative and qualitative benefits, or potential risks), and on the other hand the software vendor himself who obtains detailed technical information about the potential project (achievable contribution margin, technical problems in similar projects, or code snippets used in comparable situations). Moreover, the paper presents the relevant part of the corresponding business process of a vendor of DMS/WMS, a description of the deficits of the current sales staff to analyze the potential of complex software systems (focus on DMS/WMS), and a concept together with a prototypical implementation of an expertise system. Since in a project-oriented distribution of a DMS/WMS many pieces of internal and external knowledge can be useful, the design of an ontology of the domain DMS/WMS which is realized in form of a Semantic Network is described. This domain knowledge serves as a means to store experiences, e.g. from past projects. Additionally, a rule base is presented in order to process business rules.

1 Introduction

The investment in complex software systems is rarely confirmed by a thorough analysis of the potential of the according system. This is also valid for the investment decision in DMS/WMS. Arguments in favor of this technology are often apparent deficits in the handling of business documents and corresponding business processes. Whether the DMS/WMS can compensate these shortcomings with an acceptable ROI and what other benefits are likely to arise from this technology is rarely being investigated in this decision making process. In this paper WEXPERT (**W**orkflow **Expert**ise System) is presented, an expertise system which analyzes the situation of the potential customer by performing a requirements analysis, and as a result generates an expertise document about the potential of the technology of DMS/WMS. WEXPERT was developed in cooperation with and is run by the COI GmbH, Herzogenaurach (Ger

D. Karagiannis and U. Reimer (Eds.): PAKM 2002, LNAI 2569, pp. 501-512, 2002.

many), the vendor of the DMS/WMS COI-BusinessFlow®. Thus, the expertise focuses on the analysis of the potential of COI-BusinessFlow® in a certain situation, taking into account on the one hand data from historic projects and on the other hand experiences from the participants in the DMS/WMS market.

1.1 Objectives

Computerized support of business processes usually means the involvement of modern document related technologies (DRT) that are also referred to as DMS/WMS. The aim of this paper is therefore to build a knowledge repository prototype that provides useful decision support information (e.g. a cost-benefit analysis, identification of special conditions and extraordinary efforts)

a) for everyone who is interested in DRT, especially for companies which are planning to launch DRT projects, i.e. to introduce, enhance, or extend a DMS/WMS.
b) for companies offering DRT solutions.

This repository will be based on knowledge extracted from the experiences of former DRT projects. Like any other IT projects, the introduction and application of DRT requires special management knowledge. Managing and representing this knowledge can be an important issue not only for software developer and IT consulting companies offering DRT solutions, but also for their (potential) customers who are more interested in the costs and benefits of implementing these technologies than in technical details. However, these details are very important for internal use by developer and consulting companies. Both from the users' and implementers' point of view, typical questions that arise before an investment in DMS/WMS technology could be the following:

1. Which business activities can be supported effectively by DRT?
2. What expectations and needs for DMS/WMS do different companies have?
3. What benefits can be achieved for a specific company using DRT?
4. What are typical, successful solutions implemented in specific business areas?
5. What circumstances could cause problems or extraordinary efforts during the implementation and therefore need special attention?
6. What product components and system configurations led to success in former projects and which ones could be the most appropriate for the current case?
7. What implementation costs and ROI can be expected?

From the implementers' special point of view, some more typical questions can be:

1. Which solution features are the most demanded and most applicable?
2. What special skills are needed, and who are the experts (or partner firms) having these skills and experiences?
3. How successful can DRT projects be for the implementers in financial terms?

1.2 Related Work

The current work builds up on different kinds of research. The concept of the experience base for the projects founds on the **Experience Factory** approach by Basili et al. [1]. The fundamental difference lies in the objects from which the knowledge is collected. For Basili et al., experiences around software development projects like algorithms, methods, or techniques are assembled [1, p. 12], whereas in the current work implementation projects of DMS/WMS are regarded, although they also comprise the development and reuse of pieces of code based on customer demands. Basili et al. provide a second loop besides the original software development process in which the collection of experiences takes place. This second loop is completely separated from the primary loop, so each could work without the other. Recently, the approach of the Experience Factory has been extended to support not only the process of software development, but rather every aspect of a business like e.g. business practices [2].
Currently, the concept of the Experience Factory is being advanced at the Fraunhofer Institute for Experimental Software Engineering (IESE). The IESE developed an approach for the reuse of experiences in the software development process [3]. Their **Corporate Information Network (CoIN)** bases on the methodology of the Experience Factory in order to build a repository to collect experiences from projects done at the IESE [4].

The storage of the case studies follows the concept of the **ICF** (Industry, Characteristics, Functions) **toolset**, a system for the requirements analysis for IT systems developed at the Department of Information Systems I at the University of Erlangen-Nuremberg [5]. ICF analyzes the correlation between the characteristics of a company and the resulting demand for IT systems [5]. The structure of the DMS/WMS case studies is similar to that of the cases from the ICF, thus enriching this tool.

The extraction of useful information from the project description of the case studies takes place with the help of XML (Extensible Markup Language). Therefore, domain specific markups have been developed in order to structure the experiences contained within the cases. Current research in this area like **DIAsDEM** (Data Integration of Legacy Data and Semi-Structured Documents Using Data Mining Techniques) focuses on the semantic tagging of domain-specific (text) documents [6]. The process of information extraction from the case studies is performed by using Microsoft Word macros; however, in current research there are approaches to automate this extraction procedure (for an example see [7]).

A platform for the knowledge-based configuration of complex technical products illustrate Wright et al. [8]. Their system **PROSE** (Product Offerings Expertise) configures selected network products and generates up-to-date, valid and consistent sales proposals.

2 Concept

This paper is part of the research done by the Bavarian Research Center for Knowledge-based Systems (FORWISS) in cooperation with the COI in order to support the sales and distribution process of complex software products by the means of knowledge-based technology. While the research project comprises the whole process and the information demands of the participants concerning former experiences, the focus in the present paper lies on the requirements analysis for the potential customer which takes place between the first contact by the sales department and the generation of an offer for the customer (see figure 1).

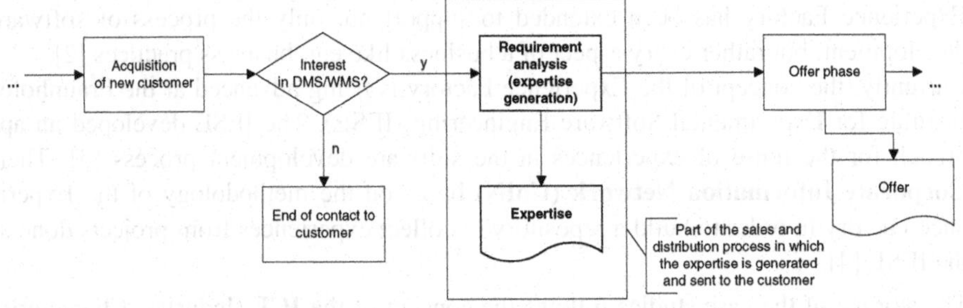

Fig. 1. Fragment of the sales and distribution process for DMS/WMS

The expertise is a means to better inform the customer of the potential of the DMS/WMS, and at the same time a tool for the vendor in order to collect information about the possible project which may result in case the customer accepts the offer. In the following paragraphs, the architecture, the input and output relations as well as the experience base will be explained.

2.1 Structural Overview

Figure 2 displays the architecture of the prototype: WEXPERT requires certain input parameters, is based on the experience repository, and finally generates two expertise documents (see chapter 3).

2.2 Input Parameters

In order to analyze the situation for a specific customer, the following information has to be obtained. This takes place in the context of the organizational analysis that usually precedes the introduction of a DMS/WMS.

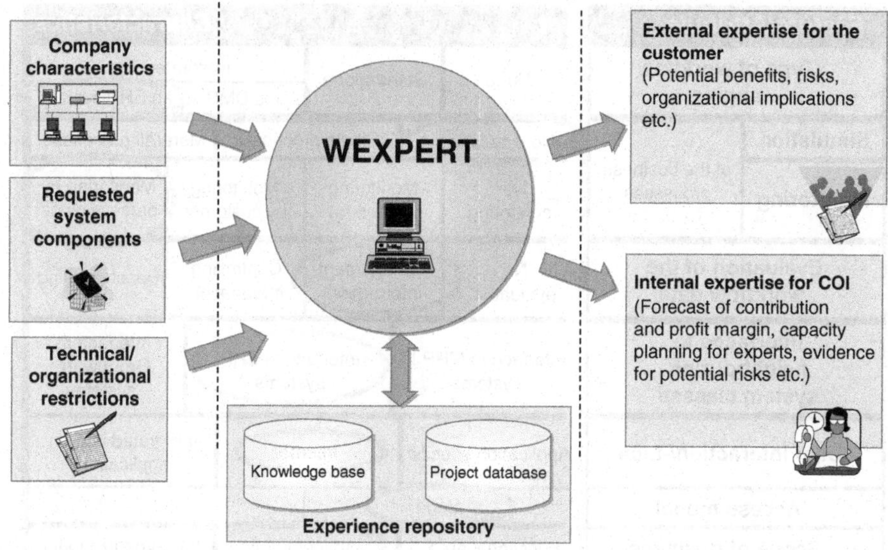

Fig. 2. Architecture of WEXPERT

1. The companies' characteristics influence the impacts of an installation of a DMS/WMS. For the ICF, about 700 characteristics have been identified, describing the entire company. However, only a small subset is relevant for WEXPERT. For example, it is irrelevant for the impacts of a DMS/WMS whether the state of an input factor is "hard", "liquid", or "gas", but there are consequences if the degree of specialization of the employees is "rather high" compared to "rather low", because workflow systems are suited for rather distributed business processes with high specialization of the processors of single activities. The most important characteristics are:
    a. The industry sector of the customer company
    b. The organizational and personnel structure (centralized or decentralized, degree of specialization etc.)
2. The automatic pre-configuration of the DMS/WMS underlies certain restrictions. An example are certain system components requested by the customer, who might prefer certain configurations or hardware vendors. Sometimes the budget of the customer doesn't allow to invest in the ideal configuration, so some components have to be left out. Figure 3 shows a possible classification of an implementation of a DMS/WMS.
3. Finally, technical and/or organizational circumstances influence the potential of a DMS/WMS, like pre-installed software or the technical infrastructure. An example is a pre-installed ERP system (see figure 3).

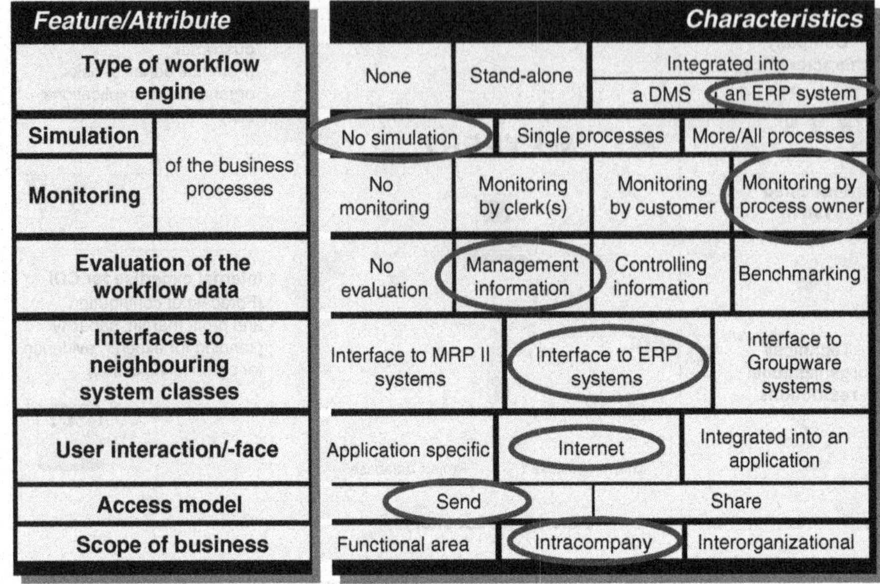

Feature/Attribute
Characteristics
Type of workflow engine
None
Stand-alone
Integrated into
a DMS
an ERP system
Simulation
of the business processes
No simulation
Single processes
More/All processes
Monitoring
No monitoring
Monitoring by clerk(s)
Monitoring by customer
Monitoring by process owner
Evaluation of the workflow data
No evaluation
Management information
Controlling information
Benchmarking
Interfaces to neighbouring system classes
Interface to MRP II systems
Interface to ERP systems
Interface to Groupware systems
User interaction/-face
Application specific
Internet
Integrated into an application
Access model
Send
Share
Scope of business
Functional area
Intracompany
Interorganizational

Fig. 3. Classification of a sample implementation of a DMS/WMS

2.3 The Experience Repository

As mentioned above, there exist two distinct sources for WEXPERT. The project database contains information about past projects, the knowledge base comprises meta-information about the technology of DMS/WMS, project management, the current market situation, research results etc.

Project Database
This data source is divided into two parts: On the one hand the detailed descriptions of completed COI-projects, on the other hand a collection of external projects (case studies), e.g. projects performed by other vendors of DMS/WMS systems or by third-party consulting companies.
The **internal COI project database** existed already at the start of the research, but contained only a minimum of project information. To a large extent, this data source had to be enhanced by project-related experiences. Furthermore, it has been built to support IT systems other than WEXPERT, like project monitoring and project income statement calculations.
Case studies from literature that represent various implementation projects of DMS/WMS are the second part of the project database. These cases stem from different DRT solution suppliers, most typically from their web pages, where they are presented as success stories or user reports. These documents serve primarily marketing purposes, therefore their processing needs special awareness (e.g. to ignore unimpor-

tant details or even exaggerations). WEXPERT currently contains 73 literature case studies. The storage of these case studies (see figure 4 for the concept of the editorial workbench) is harmonized with the ICF toolset. Relevant pieces are e.g. remarks on benefits ("decreased staffing in accounts payable areas by 65 percent, allowing the company to redeploy personnel to other areas"), shortcomings, technical requirements ("the system must be capable of generating reports on handling times"), or risks which resulted from the DMS/WMS.

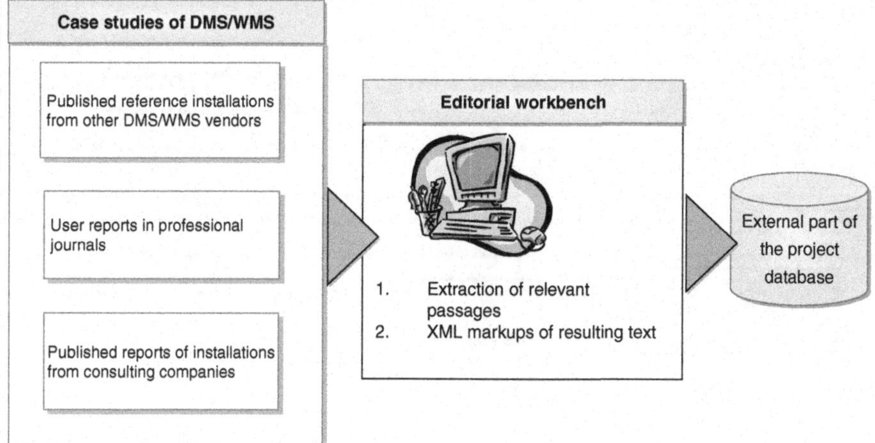

Fig. 4. Processing of case studies regarding the introduction of DMS/WMS

The data stored within the project database is primarily used to find similar projects by the means of case-based reasoning. For a marked case study see figure 5.

Knowledge Base

The repository contains formalized pieces of knowledge about the domain of DMS/WMS. If applicable, rules are derived from the knowledge that has just been acquired.

The experience repository contains non project-related material and is divided into an internal and an external area. The internal knowledge stems from experiences of the project participants at COI ("lessons learned"), the external material from results of research, market studies etc. Koennecker et al. present an example of how to integrate organizational knowledge into an experience factory [9]. A concept for a control station in which an expert collects and structures new pieces of knowledge is currently developed. At the moment, new experiences have to be added manually (see figure 6). When a new (external or internal) source comes in, it is filtered in order to remove irrelevant pieces, and then processed to extract the know-how within the data source. Sometimes, additionally a rule can be derived. This is especially the case if the document contains obligatory information like for example new legal norms. For the classification, the pre-defined XML tags like <description>, <benefit>, or <requirement> are used. Finally, the structured document is stored in a relational database.

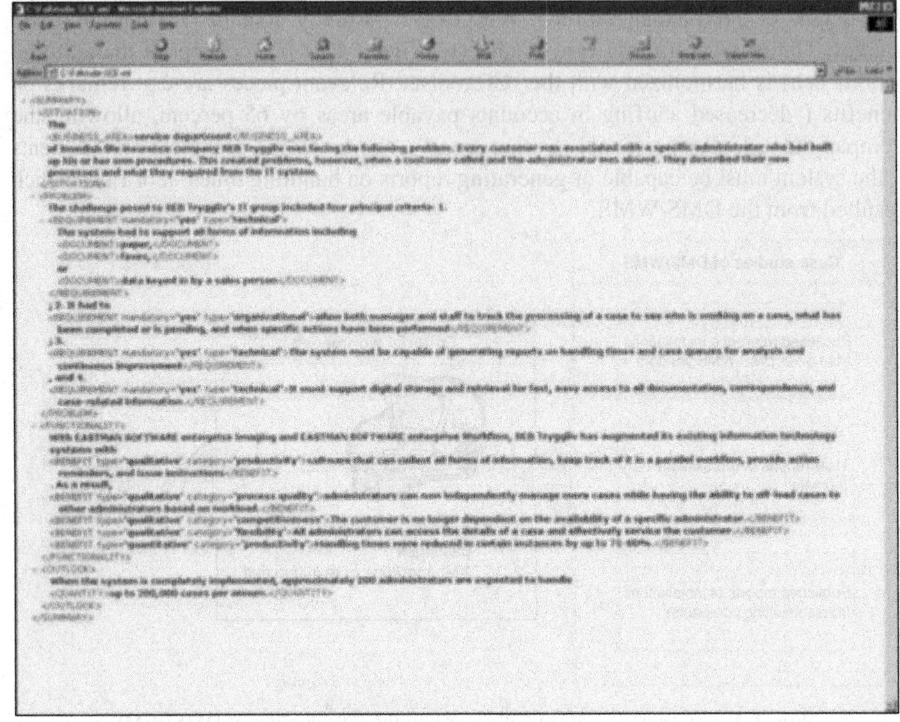

Fig. 5. Example of a marked-up case study

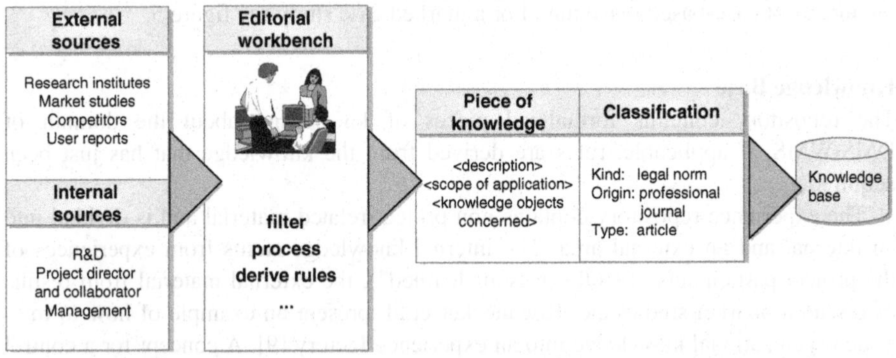

Fig. 6. Concept of an editorial workbench for new pieces of knowledge

An example of a result of research as a piece of knowledge is an investigation of business processes with regard to their potential to be automated with WMS [10]. Becker et al. provide criteria for business processes like for example "number of functions" or "frequency" that determine the potential of a workflow automation. In WEXPERT, if the values of these criteria are comparable to the current inquiry, the corresponding process will be evaluated as more or less suited for workflow automation.

3 The Expertises as the Output of WEXPERT

3.1 The External Expertise for the Customer

Since the external expertise contains information about projects done by other DRT solution suppliers, it represents a comparison of the performance of the document and workflow management industry with COI. Measurable, quantifiable output has more value for customers than simple textual information. Therefore, this data must be printed out with priority, i.e. displayed at the top level. Confidentiality of business information must be preserved. This means that in those cases where the output contains confidential elements (e.g. information about costs) it must be either made anonymous or aggregated. The expertise is presented as a dynamically generated web site with hyperlinks in order to navigate through the different sections. It consists of the following parts:

1. **Basic information** like the estimated duration of the project, the functional areas concerned, the documents that would be handled by the new system etc. in order to give the recipient an idea of the potential system and possible consequences.
2. **Cases** (= DMS/WMS projects) which are similar to the situation of the new customer.
   a. Ranking of comparable **case studies**: Based on a degree of similarity, WEXPERT presents case studies which have comparable characteristics, for example take place in the same industry and concern the same business process. The degree of similarity is calculated from a comparison of the input parameters (characteristics, components, restrictions) together with weights (a case from the database is more similar to a new case if the two companies act in the same industry sector, than if both have highly specialized employees) and is displayed as a percentage value: the higher the number, the more similar the case study is to the current new customer. Clicking on the linked case study displays the full text.
   b. Ranking of **completed internal projects of COI**: Contains key figures like number of users, amortization time, industry, number of process instances per day, number of processed documents per day etc. Because of non-disclosure agreements, some data is disguised. The complete information (including the company name) is only available for the internal project leader of COI, in case the customer should issue an assignment for the project (this requires consequently more precise information in order to learn from the project).

   By comparing both resources, the customer can get an idea of the performance of COI in a certain area. Thus, it makes the market performance of COI comparable to other providers.
3. **Cost-benefit analysis** of the projected DMS/WMS: WEXPERT generates a prediction of the quantitative and qualitative benefits as well as of the estimated efforts for the installation and customization. Key figures like the net present value are also calculated upon these estimations. Benefits of DMS/WMS divide into cost reduction, quality, productivity, flexibility, employee satisfaction, and com-

petitiveness. For each of these categories, this happens in relation to the business process concerned, e.g. benefits in the dimension quality refer to additional process quality, not product quality.

4. The **risk analysis** is a means to anticipate and learn from mistakes done in previous projects. It serves furthermore the purpose to give an impression to the customer that COI is aware of the most common problems that can arise when implementing an DMS/WMS in similar situations.
5. **Technical and/or organizational requirements** give an impression of the changes that have to take place in the customer's company. Since not the complete situation of the customer is known (see section 2.2), only selected implications are discussed.

3.2 The Internal Expertise for the Software Vendor

The internal part of the expertise addresses the project managers of COI who would be allocated to the project in case of an assignment by the customer. The document is supposed to provide them with all information that is necessary considering the new project.
The internal expertise consists of the following components:

1. **Basic information** like a description of the characteristics of the customer company or the desired configuration (on top level, no details).
2. **Automatic pre-configuration** of the DMS/WMS: based upon the input parameters (company characteristics, system requirements, technical/organizational restrictions) and the experiences from former projects, WEXPERT suggests a best practice configuration for the DMS/WMS. This constitutes an initial point for the sales assistant who prepares the offer document in the case of an assignment.
3. **Details** about the core COI-components: in which other projects have they been used, which are the known bugs, and who are the corresponding experts within COI?
4. Predictable **system behavior** (consequences for the customer): this information is useful for the project manager who shall be sensitized with respect to potential reactions of the customer. This part is comparable to an FAQ (frequently asked questions) containing the most probable questions and answers for this type of configuration. For example, several former projects of this kind may have resulted in the client company wanting to know how to perform a specific task which they formerly realized with their paper documents.
5. (Internal) **profit analysis**, estimating the potential contribution margin and the profit margin of the project for COI.
6. **Capacity planning** for the relevant experts: since for certain activities (like customizing the DMS/WMS in order to work as an SAP archive with SAP ArchiveLink®[1]) there are only few experts at COI, their workload has to be planned carefully, so that the necessary capacities for the relevant projects are available. A

[1] SAP and SAP ArchiveLink® are registered trademarks of SAP AG.

lack of planning might result in a delay of the whole project because of missing human resources.

7. (Internal) **risk analysis** ("lessons learned" from former projects, predicting the probability of risks for the current project). Most risks which have a more or less high probability of occurrence aren't suited to be presented in the external expertise. The reason for this is that unlikely risks shouldn't be mentioned there in order not to unsettle the potential customer. Thus, the internal risk analysis is more comprehensive and contains much more precise data about potential stumbling blocks in the resulting project.

4 Conclusion and Outlook

WEXPERT is right now applicable only in the limited domain of DMS/WMS projects. Other domains require an adjustment of the knowledge base, especially of the way experiences are structured. Hence, there is a need to discuss the portability of the expertise into other domains than DMS/WMS, for example other complex software system classes like ERP systems. But also in a horizontal orientation, there is a need to look beyond: the preliminary and succeeding activities within the sales process could be integrated into this knowledge base, what has already happened to some extent (e.g. in the automated pre-configuration for the offer document).

References

1. Basili, V., Caldiera, G. and Rombach, D.: The Experience Factory, in: Marciniak, J. (ed.), Encylopedia of Software Engineering, Volume 1, p. 469-476, New York 1994.
2. Basili, V., Lindvall, M., Costa, P.: Implementing the Experience Factory concepts as a set of Experience Bases, in: Proceedings of the 13th International Conference on Software Engineering & Knowledge Engineering (SEKE 2001), Buenos Aires 2001.
3. Jedlitschka, A., Althoff, K.-D., Decker, B., Hartkopf, S., Nick, M.: Corporate Information Network (CoIN): The Fraunhofer IESE Experience Factory, in: Aha, D.W., Watson, I. and Yang, Q.: Proceedings of the workshop program at the fourth International Conference on Case-Based Reasoning (ICCBR 2001), Vancouver 2001.
4. Decker, B., Althoff, K.-D., Nick, M., Jedlitschka, A., Rech, J.: Corporate Information Network (CoIN): Experience Management at IESE, in: Proceedings of the third congress Knowledge Engineering and Management (Knowtech 2001), Dresden 2001.
5. Kaufmann, T., Lohmann, M., Morschheuser, P.: Die Informationsbank ICF – eine wissensbasierte Werkzeugsammlung fü die Anforderungsanalyse, working paper of the Bavarian Information Systems Research Network (FORWIN) 2001-002, Nuremberg 2001, in German.
6. Winkler, K., Spiliopoulou, M.: Semi-Automated XML Tagging of Public Text Archives: A Case Study, in: Proceedings of EuroWeb 2001, p. 271-285, Pisa 2001.
7. Kushmerick, N.: Wrapper induction: Efficiency and expressiveness, in: International Journal of Artificial Intelligence, Volume 118, p. 15-68, Amsterdam 2000.

8. Wright, J., Weixelbaum, E., Vesonder, G.: A Knowledge-Based Configurator that Supports Sales, Engineering, and Manufacturing at AT&T Network Systems, in: Klahr, P., Byrnes, E.: Proceedings of the fifth Conference on Innovative Applications of Artificial Intelligence (IAAI-93), Washington 1993.
9. Koennecker, A., Ross, J., Low, G.: Implementing an Experience Factory Based on Existing Organizational Knowledge, in: Proceedings of the 12th Australian Software Engineering Conference (ASWEC 2000), Queensland 2000.
10. Becker, J., von Uthmann, C., zur Mhlen, M., Rosemann, M.: Identifying the Workflow Potential of Business Processes, in: Sprague, R. (ed.), Proceedings of the 32nd Hawaii Conference on System Sciences (HICSS 1999), Los Alamitos 1999.

More Efficient Searching in a Knowledge Portal – An Approach Based on the Analysis of Users' Queries

Nenad Stojanovic[1], Ljiljana Stojanovic[2], and Jorge Gonzalez[1]

[1] Institute AIFB
University of Karlsruhe
Germany
{nst,jgo}@aifb.uni-karslruhe.de

[2] FZI - Research Center for Information Technology at the University of Karlsruhe
Germany
Ljiljana.Stojanovic@fzi.de

Abstract. In this paper, we present a novel approach for the managing the clarity of queries which users post to a knowledge portal. The approach is based on the (i) measuring the ambiguity of a query and (ii) suggesting the refinement of the original query, based on various ambiguity analyses: structure of the query, knowledge repository and user' behaviours. The approach is mainly based on tracking users' interactions with the portal. Since the approach requires more semantic information about users' querying activities (for example, how many results are retrieved), which are not contained in the traditional Web server log, we have developed the new, client-based, method for tracking users' activities which is presented in the paper as well. The short evaluation study shows the benefits of applying our approach in a real-world portal.

1 Introduction

One of the vital processes in a knowledge management system is knowledge sharing. A knowledge management system usually provides a simple knowledge-access mechanism (so called knowledge portal), which enables searching for relevant knowledge resources by querying the portal using terms for which a user believes that are relevant to her problem at hand. As the response on querying, the system generates a list of resources which description of the content has been syntactically matched with the terms used in searching. However, the percentage of the problem-relevant (from the users' point of view) resources in this list is quite low, imposing serious problems for the usefulness of a knowledge management system[1]. One of the most frequently listed sources for this drawback is the ambiguity in the interpretation

1 According to the KPMG Knowledge Management Report 2000, based on the 423 CEOs, CFOs, Marketing Directors from US/Europe: "65% of organizations that have implemented a knowledge management system still complain of information overload".

D. Karagiannis and U. Reimer (Eds.): PAKM 2002, LNAI 2569, pp. 513-524, 2002.

of user' interests, when such interest is represented only by 2-3 searching terms [1], i.e. the query posted by a user does not define user's information need clearly. Although there are several approaches which cope with this problem, e.g. the interactive query expansion [2], recommendation systems [3], query-language modelling [4], all of them treat just one side of the query management problem and do not provide an integral analyses.

In this paper we present the structure of the query management component in a knowledge portal, which performs two essential functions: (i) the measurement of the ambiguity of a query and (ii) the refinement of the query, based on various ambiguity analyses: the structure of the query, the knowledge repository and user' behaviours. In order to avoid explicit feedback of users, the analyses are based on the data captured from the portal's log file. The logging system is based on the logging web-server transactions and it is independent of the concrete KM system. The traditional web-server logging approach is extended by capturing the semantic information about pages which the user has visited so far, so that various semantic analyses can be performed. The approach is novel and very promising – in the large term it ensures the continual improvement of the searching mechanism of a knowledge portal.

The paper is organised as follows: In the second section we give the requirements for the efficient searching in a knowledge portal. The third section presents the conceptual architecture of the query management component that fulfils these requirements. In the section four we present the implementation details and some initial results from our case study. In the section five, concluding remarks summarize the importance of the presented approach.

2 The Efficient Querying in a KM System – The Requirements

The problem of satisfying a user's requirement posted to the Information Portal [5] is the question of whether a relevant information resource exists in the information repository, and if the answer is positive, whether the resource can be found by a user. Therefore, the efficient searching depends on (see Fig.1):

1. the "quality" of the information repository in the portal,
   - if information resources reflect the needs of users, e.g. if the information repository contains information resources which users are interested in
2. the "quality" of the searching process, i.e. when a relevant information resource exists in the repository, how easily (if any) the resource can be found. This problem can be divided into two sub-problems:
   a) if a resource which is relevant for the user's information need can be found by the querying mechanism and
   b) if the resource which is highly relevant for the user's information need can be found easily by the user in the list of retrieved results.

The first criterion (1) is the matter of the so-called "collection management policy", which manages the deletion of old information resources and enter of new ones, corresponding to the changes in the user's interests.

The retrieval of resources which are relevant for the user's need (2a) depends on:

1) the clarity of the expression of the need in the query which is posted to the system [1], [5]

2) the quality of the annotation (indexing) information resources in the repository

The part of this problem, a so-called prediction game between providers and users of information, can be resolved by using a commonly-agreed vocabulary, i.e. an ontology [6] as the semantic backbone of the portal. We assume that such an ontology exists in the given domain, and that the system, consequently, benefits from using such a conceptual structure in searching for information.

Finding (easily) an information resource which satisfies the users' information need (2b) depends on the capability of the system to interpret the term "relevance" in the right manner. One of the possibilities is the personalisation which leads to the collaborative and/or content filtering of the retrieved results [3], but it is out of scope of this paper.

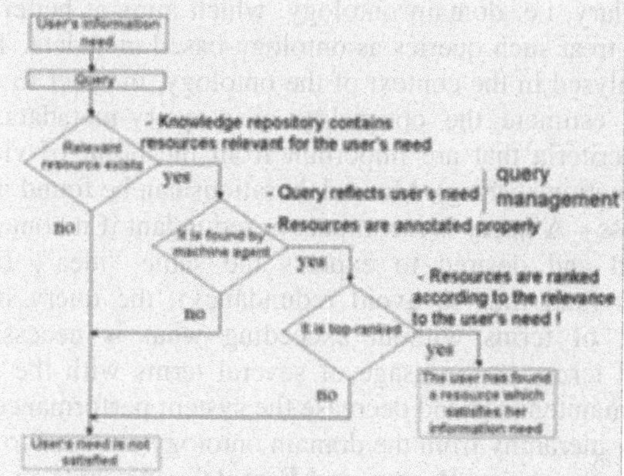

Fig. 1. The factors which the efficient searching for information depends on

In this paper we are focused on the managing the clarity of the queries posted by users, so called query management (see Fig.1).

3 The Query Management

The query management component (QMC) in a knowledge portal should supports the refinement of a query posted by a user in such a way that the new query describes the original information need of that user more clearly. In order to perform this refinement in the most efficient manner, QMC has to analyze the clarity of the query, first of all by measuring the ambiguity of the query. In the rest of this section we elaborate more on these two essential functions of a QMC.

3.1 Measuring Query Ambiguity

Recent analyses [4] have shown that the precision in searching for information depends strongly on the clarity of the query which a user posts to the system. When the query is formulated in an ambiguous manner, one can expect that a high percent of irrelevant results can be retrieved, independently of the mechanism which is used for searching. Therefore, we see the query disambiguation as the initial step in searching for information in a KM system.

The QMC observes the query ambiguity in two dimensions:

1) the structure of the query
2) the content of the knowledge repository

3.1.1 The Structure of the Query

Regarding ambiguities in the structure of the query, two other issues are defined:

a) structural ambiguity
b) clarity factor

a) Since our approach is ontology-based, the user's queries are generated from the common vocabulary, i.e. domain ontology, which aims at better understanding of a domain. We can treat such queries as ontology-based metadata. Therefore, the user's query can be analysed in the context of the ontology, in order to determine its clarity (ambiguity). To estimate the optimality of a query-metadata, we introduce the following three criteria that are important from the point of view of more precise searching (information sharing). More elaborations can be found in the [7].

1. **Compactness** – A query is incompact or redundant if it contains more terms than it is needed and desired to express the same "idea". In order to achieve compactness (and thus to avoid redundancy), the query has to comprise the minimal set of terms without exceeding what is necessary or useful. The repetition of terms or the usage of several terms with the same meaning only complicate maintenance and decrease the system performance. Concept hierarchy and property hierarchy from the domain ontology are used to check this criterion. For example, the query "**Person and Female**" represents an incompact metadata, because it is not clear whether the user is interested in all persons (including males) or only in females. Consequently, some of the results retrieved in searching will not correspond to the users' interests.
2. **Completeness** – A query is incomplete if it is possible to extend the query just by analysing the existing terms in the metadata, in order to clarify its semantic. It means that the query requires that some additional metadata have to be filled up. This criterion is computed based on the structure of the domain ontology. For example, one criterion is the existence of a dependency in the domain ontology between the domain entities which are already used in the annotation. The query "**Aspirin and Headache**" contains concepts with many relationships between them (e.g. properties "***cures***" and "***causes***" exist between concepts **Therapy** and **Disease**). The interpretation is ambiguous, e.g. when that is a query, if the user is interested in the information resources about how a disease (i) can be cured by a therapy, or (ii) caused by a therapy. In order to constrain the set of possible interpretations, the annotation has to be extended with one of these properties.
3. **Aggregation** – A query is aggregative if it contains a set of terms that can be replaced with semantically related terms in order to achieve a shorter query, but without producing any retrieval other than the original query. This structural ambiguity occurs in the situations (among others) when a query contains all sub-concepts of one concept. An example is the query "**Female and Male**". Considering the ontology-based searching, the list of retrieved resources should be the same for the query containing the combination of concepts (e.g. **Female**

and **Male**) or the query containing only the parent concept (e.g. **Person**). However, since the standard approaches for the ranking results of querying [8] exploit conceptual hierarchies, these queries will produce different lists of top-ranked results, which influences the probability that a relevant resource will be found by a user.

b) The Clarity factor represents the uncertainty to determine the user's interest in a posted query, regarding the vocabulary (ontology) used in the system. For example, when a user makes a query containing only the concept **Person**, which is refined into two subconcepts, **Female** and **Male**, in the ontology, it could be a matter of discussion whether she is interested in the concept **Person** or in its subconcepts. It is possible that she failed to express the information in a clear manner - our experience shows that users who are not familiar with the given ontology used to use a more general concept in searching for knowledge resources, instead of using more specific concepts. The Clarity factor makes the calculation of the users' interest more sensitive to the structure of the ontology by taking into account possible ambiguities in the query formulation.
The formula for the clarity factor depends on the underlying domain ontology O and the entity type:

$$Clarity(E,O) = \begin{cases} k(E,O) \cdot \dfrac{1}{numSubConcepts(E,O)+1} & E \text{ is a concept} \\ k(E,O) \cdot \dfrac{1}{numSubPropeties(E,O)+1} \cdot \dfrac{1}{numDomains(E,O)} & E \text{ is a propetry} \end{cases}$$

$$0 < Clarity(E) \leq 1,$$

whereas numSubConcepts(E) is the number of subconcepts of a concept E, numSubProperties(E) is the number of subproperties of a property E, and numDomains(E) is the number of domains defined for the property E.
The coefficient k is introduced, in order to favour the frequency of the usage. It is calculated using the following formula:

$$k(E) = \frac{1}{numLevel(E)+1} \qquad (0 < k \leq 1)$$

where numLevel(E) is the depth of the hierarchy of the entity E.
The clarity factor should be calculated only for the queries which do not contain structural ambiguities. The Librarian Agent performs the determination of the structural ambiguity of a query as the first step in processing the query.

3.1.2 The Content of the Knowledge Repository

The ambiguity of a query posted in a knowledge repository is obviously repository-dependent. For example, when a user interested in the competitors in 2002 Soccer World Cup gives the query "World Cup" against the collection of the news articles in which the articles about Chess World Cup Tournament are predominant, it is simply impossible for the system to return soccer articles consistently ranked higher than related to chess.
We introduce the Response factor for taking into account the specificities of the knowledge repository content in determining the ambiguity of a query.
The Response factor of a query Q is the measure how the terms from that query cluster the resources in the underlying knowledge repository (KR)

$$\mathrm{Response}(Q,KR) = \min_{allQ'} P(not\,\mathrm{Relevant}(Q,KR)/(\mathrm{Relevant}(Q',KR)) =$$
$$= \max_{allQ'} \frac{NumberOf\,\mathrm{Relevant}(Q',KR) - NumberOf\,\mathrm{Relevant}(Q,KR)}{NumberOf\,\mathrm{Relevant}(Q',KR)}$$

whereas

$NumberOf\,\mathrm{Relevant}(X,KR)$ denotes the set of knowledge resources stored in the KR which are annotated with the X – in other words, it is the number of results by querying for X the repository KR and

$Q' = \{x, x \subset Q, x' \neq \{\}\}$ is the set of all non-empty subsets of the Q

The special case is when the Q contains just one term

$$\mathrm{Response}(Q,KR) = P(Q) = \frac{NumberOf\,\mathrm{Relevant}(Q,KR))}{TotalNumber(KR)}$$

whereas $TotalNumber(KR)$ is the total number of resources in the repository.

The Response factor describes the probability that a knowledge resource relevant for the query Q will not be relevant for the one of the non-empty subsets of the Q –

$$P(not\,\mathrm{Relevant}(Q,KR)/(\mathrm{Relevant}(Q',KR))$$

When this probability is very low, it means that the query Q is "covered" by a Q', i.e. that query Q results in almost all results which query Q' produces. Consequently, query Q should be extended (refined), in order to return more precise results. The difference between Q' and Q is the set of terms which effect the querying process very low, and probably they should be refined (see the next section). However, this is only a recommendation how to get results which are closer to the information need of the user – it is possible that the user is satisfied with the original query (see the example below).

We treat the Response factor as a measure of how introducing new searching terms can improve the clustering process. For example, when a new searching term causes very slight difference between the old and new cluster, we treat this new query as an ambiguous one – the added searching term is too ambiguous for the meaning of the query, i.e. does not focus the query.

However, it is possible to interpret this situation in various manners, but in the scope of this research, we follow the presented analogy.

Therefore, we define the query ambiguity (QA) of the query Q regarding the ontology O and the knowledge repository KR as follows:

$$QA(Q,O,KR) = \frac{1}{Clarity(Q,O) * \mathrm{Response}(Q,KR)}$$

For each query posted to the system, the QMC checks the structural ambiguities, and if they are present, it suggests the improvements of the structure of the query. Next, the QMC calculates ambiguity (i.e. QA factor) of the query and gives the users the recommendations how to change the query in order to refine their information needs. Nevertheless, the users can initiate the query refinement on their own.

3.2 Query Refinement

One of the reasons for the ambiguity in a query is the scarce interpretation of the user's information needs in the form of a query. Most of the recommendation systems

do not make a distinction between the user's unarticulated information need and the query which results from that [9].
The QMC uses three strategies for the query refinement:

1. according to the structure of the underlying ontology
2. according to the content of the knowledge repository
3. according to the users' behaviour (usage - query refinement done by users)

1. The structure of the ontology
In case that the query contains a structural ambiguity, it has to be resolved by considering the structure of the ontology. In the previous section, by describing the structural ambiguities, we have mentioned the strategies for resolving each of them.

2. The capacity of the knowledge repository
The extension of the query terms should correspond to the characteristics of the document term space. The most popular method in the information retrieval is the so-called local context analysis [10], [11] in which the top-ranked documents are used for the query extension. The extension is usually done by using a variation of the Rocchio coefficients [12]. The query is extended by increasing the influence of the most frequently appearing terms from the top-ranked (i.e. relevant) documents, and by decreasing the influence of the terms from non-relevant documents.
In Sect. 3.1.2, we have defined the Response factor as the measure of the ambiguity regarding the knowledge repository. Obviously, it is very useful for refining the query.
In case that a query Q is ambiguous because the Response factor is too low, i.e. there is a sub-query Q' for which the list of retrieved results is almost identical to the list of Q, then such a query can be refined by refining the terms for the set containing the difference between Q and Q'.
However, since our approach is ontology-based, the extension we provide is ontology-based, as well. We are not interested in the frequently appearing terms per se, but in the semantic extensions of those terms. For example, when the query is about "ontology+researcher" and the most frequently appearing terms in the top-ranked documents (beside "ontology" and "research") are "professor", "assistant" and "student", which belong to the hierarchy of the concept "researcher", probably the relevant strategy is to expand the query with the information about the "researcher".

3. The user's behaviour
By searching the portal, a user makes a query, observes the list of retrieved results, probably refines the query in some manner, then observes the new list and "clicks" on the information resource when she notes a relevant one; when not, she refines the query again... This is the ordinary user's behaviour, and can be very useful for predicting what can be relevant for a user in a situation. By analysing such information, the system can learn how to rewrite a query in case the user is not satisfied with the retrieved results.
We define three types of query-rewriting patterns based on the users' behaviour described in the rest of the section: expansion-, reduction- and generalization/specialization- pattern.
Considering that a query represents an interest of the user, we can assume that two users who make the same query have the similar interests, regarding the query (situation). They also have the same goal in the searching – to find an information

resource about the topic of interest. This assumption allows us to make another one, about the behaviour of users during searching: users with similar interests (goals) should behave in a similar manner. Consequently, for a given query, the system can suggest a user to repeat the behaviour of the users who have already posted the same query. For example, when a lot of users **expand** the initial query "aspirin and headache" with the term "young" or "old", in order to get more precise results, we can conclude that the treatment of headache by aspirin heavily depends on the age of a patient. Every time the user makes such ambiguity in a query, the system should suggest the user to expand the query with the information about age. It is worth noting that this analysis is performed on the ontological level – "young" and "old" are only two values for the property "age" of the concept "patient". The user should be asked to expand the query not only with the terms "young" or "old", but to select any valid value for "age", e.g. "middle-aged".

The same principle can be used for **reducing** too specific queries, in case no results were retrieved for such a query. The case that users often reduce the query "aspirin, headache, female, young" to the query "aspirin, headache, young" can be interpreted as the irrelevance of the patient's gender for curing the headache by using aspirin. The system should recognise this reduction pattern and recommend such a change every time a user makes this ambiguity in a query. By generalising this pattern on the ontological level, the system can process/treat the previously unseen examples. For example, in case the discovered recommendation is that "queries about side-effects of using aspirin in the patient who suffers from rheumatoid arthritis should not contain information about age", the query "side-effect, rheumatoid arthritis, aspirin, young, male" can be reduced to "side-effect, rheumatoid arthritis, aspirin, male", although the initial query has not been seen previously.

4 Implementation / Evaluation

4.1 Embedded URL Technology

Our research presents a conceptual solution for the improvement of searching for information in an (ontology-based) information portal. The only prerequisite is to have a mechanism for tracking the users' behaviour in the portal, particularly, user's queries. One of the portal-independent realisations can be to reuse the data from the Web Server logs [13], but the quality of such data is not appropriate for our analyses because of the spider-effects, pages loaded from cache, etc. Moreover, the big problem is that the traditional Web Server log does not contain any metadata related to the content of the visited page. It means that it is not possible to get information which query is posted and which results are retrieved.

In order to get more information about the content of the visited web pages, we developed a new technology for logging the users' interactions in a portal, called Embedded URL. This technology is based on incorporating a piece of JavaScript code into a footer of each web page a potential user is interested in. This code captures useful information about the content of the visited page and stores this information with other information related to visiting a web page, i.e. URL, data/time, User_Agent, Referer_URL, etc. These data can be transformed in the Log metadata by applying some heuristics in order to cope with the missing data.

An entry in the Embedded URL log looks like:

127.0.0.1 - - [05/Jun/2002:09:19:26 +0000] “GET /ontology/asp/main.asp HTTP/1.1” 200 10240 “http:/localhost/ontology/asp/search.asp” “Mozilla/4.0 (compatible; MSIE 6.0b; Windows NT 5.0; DigExt)” “<query>Ontology+Editor+Evolution</query><NumOfResults>2</NumOfResults> <Results><1>http:// www.aifb.uni-karlsruhe.de/WBS/projects/Ontologging/ proposal.html</1><2>http://www.aifb.uni-karlsruhe.de/WBS/persons/ysu/ methodology.html</2></Results>”

Fig. 2 depicts the basic steps in recording EmbeddedURL information. In the following, we describe these steps briefly:

1. The Web Site - the user requests to view a particular page on the website.
2. The web server receives the request from the user and gathers the necessary information.
3. The web server returns the page requested containing:
   3.1 The initial HTML code.
   3.2 Metadata information specific to the page, plus a piece of code referring to a JavaScript file. This file is usually placed in the footer of the page, in order to facilitate its inclusion for the web designer.
4. Once the requested file is shown on the user’s browser, the JavaScript code will be activated. First, the code collects the metadata information of the particular page viewed along with the various other parameters. Then, a 1x1 pixel image (whose source is a URL) refers the information to a logging script on the devoted Embedded URL server.
5. In the Embedded URL server, the logging script collects the information obtained from the JavaScript file, and inserts it into the relevant columns of the Embedded URL database.

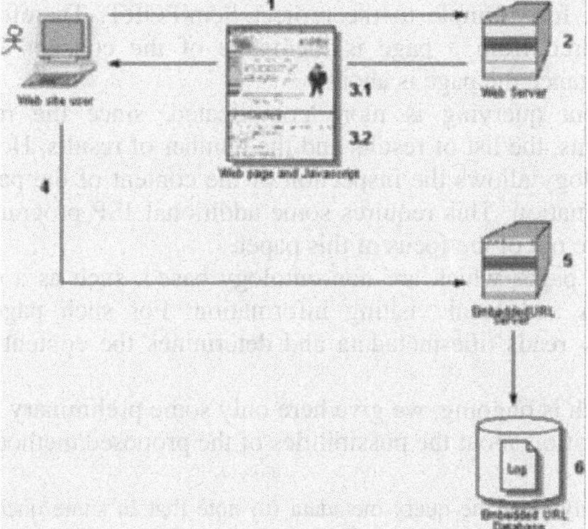

Fig. 2. Process involved in recording Embedded URL information

The Embedded URL database allows the information retrieved to be recorded in an understandable manner that can be easily accessed. The data captured in an embedded URL database may vary according to the information the web administrator wishes to record. Only one entry is recorded for every page viewed.

In order to prove the validity of our research related to rewriting the users’ queries, we applied Embedded URL technology in the web portal of our Institute. Some of the initial results are given in the next section.

4.2 Analysis of Users' Queries in the SEAL

The Semantic Portal (SEAL) [8] is an ontology-based application, which provides a "single-click" access to the almost all information related to the organisation, people, researches and projects of our Institute. It is widely used by our research and administrative staff as well as by our students. One of the most usable features is the possibility to search for people, research areas and projects on the semantic basis, i.e. using corresponding Institute Ontology. Especially is the hierarchy of research areas comprehensive – it contains more than 100 concepts. The portal provides a very user-friendly interface, which enables formation of arbitrary queries using entities from the underlying ontology. The search is performed as an inference through metadata, which is crawled from Portal pages. As the inference mechanism we use the Ontobroker [14].

AIFB Portal is implemented in the Zope technology (http://www.zope.org/). Zope is a leading open source application server, specialising in content management, portals, and custom applications. Zope enables teams to collaborate in the creation and management of dynamic web-based business applications, such as intranets and portals. Consequently, the Embedded URL technology is transferred into the Zope environment. The code related to gathering semantically based web usage information is put in the standard header file, which is reused in all pages in the Portal. Since the Portal is ontology-based, each of the pages corresponds to an instance in the ResearchInstitute Ontology, for example to the project SemiPORT. Therefore, the semantic information captured from a page is the name of the concept and the identifier of the concrete instance the page is about.

Gathering information about querying is more complicated, since the required information is searching terms, the list of results and the number of results. However, the Embedded URL technology allows the inspection of the content of the page and capturing all required information. This requires some additional JSP programming, but more technical details are out of the focus of this paper.

The Portal contains tens of pages which are non-ontology based, such as a contact page, pages about partners and local visiting information. For such pages, the Embedded URL technology reads title-metadata and determines the content of the visited page.

Since this part of the research is ongoing, we give here only some preliminary results, which can serve as an illustration about the possibilities of the proposed methods.

Table 1. The result of the analysis of the query-metadata (to note that in some queries two inconsistencies were found)

Criteria	Optimality		
	Compactness	**Completeness**	**Aggregation**
% of queries which failed regarding criteria	20	55	2

- *The rate of compactness is high* – The most frequently found ambiguity was in queries containing research areas, for example "Ontology and Modelling", "Semantic Annotation and Information Extraction". The reason can be found either in the weak understanding of the domain ontology, or in the weak modelling of some parts in the hierarchy of the research-areas.

- *Completeness is medium* – As expected, this is the most frequently found ambiguity in users' queries. The queries are too short to incorporate full understanding of users' interests (about 75% of queries contain only 2 terms). The users usually forget to provide a property between two concepts.
- *Aggregation is very high* – The non-aggregate cases we found are related to the hierarchies with only two subconcepts (the parent node has only two child nodes). For example "PhDStudent and MScStudent" (these are direct subconcepts of the concept Student in our ontology). However, most of the hierarchies contain more than two subconcept for a concept.

This part of the evaluation showed that the initial user queries contain a lot of ambiguities, which should be resolved in the query rewriting process.
Considering query rewriting we found that about 30% of users tries to refine their queries and that the most of them (about 70%) generalise/specialise the query. About 17% of query rewriting is related to the expanding the query and 5% to the reduction. The rest of rewriting contained two or more different rewriting patterns.
Naturally, the generalisation/specialisation is dominant by queries containing concepts that have many subconcepts. The most frequently appeared pattern is the specialisation of the query containing concept Ontology. Most frequently appeared changes are the substitution with subconcepts Ontology Development, Ontology Editing or Ontology Evolution.
The small number of query expansion/reduction can be explained with the relative small number of non-taxonomical relationship in the ontology. An example is the extension of the query "Person and Project" with the one of the properties between these concepts ("researchs_in" or "manager_of").

5 Conclusion

In this paper, we gave an analysis of the factors which influences the efficient searching in a knowledge portal and presented a component which support managing the clarity of queries which users post to a knowledge portal – so called query management component (QMC). This component performs two essential functions: (i) measuring the ambiguity of the query and in case of high ambiguity, (ii) suggesting the user the most effective reformulation of the query. The information about users' searching activities is gathered from the semantic log file, which supports various semantic analyses in the query reformulation process.
The benefits of the proposed approach are manifold: dynamic adaptation of the system to the changes in the business environment, dynamic analysis of the users' needs and the usefulness of particular knowledge resources and the organisation of the knowledge repository to fulfil these needs, to name but a few.
The evaluation experiments show that our approach can be applied in the real-world applications successfully. We find that it represents a very important step in the achievement of self-adaptive knowledge portals, which can discover some changes from the user's interactions with the system automatically and evolves its structure correspondingly.

Acknowledgement. The research presented in this paper would not have been possible without our colleagues and students at the Institute AIFB, University of Karlsruhe. Research for this paper was partially financed by BMBF in the project "SemiPort" (08C5939) and by EU in the IST-2000-28293 project "Ontologging"

References

1. Wen, J.-R., Nie, J.-Y. and Zhang, H.-J.: Clustering User Queries of a Search Engine. WWW10, May 1-5, Hong Kong, (2001)
2. Bruza, PD., Dennis, S.: Query Reformulation on the Internet: Empirical Data and the Hyperindex Search Engine. In: Proceedings of RIAO97, Computer-Assisted Information Searching on Internet, Montreal, (1997)
3. Balabanovic, M., Shoham, Y. : Content-Based, Collaborative Recommendation. Communications of the ACM 40 (3) (1997) 66-72
4. Cronen-Townsend, S. , Croft, W.B.: Quantifying Query Ambiguity, in the Proceedings of HLT (2002) 94-98.
5. Baeza-Yates, R., Ribeiro-Neto, B.: Modern Information Retrieval, Addison-Wesley-Longman Publishing co. (1999)
6. Guarino, N., Giaretta, P.: Ontologies and Knowledge Bases: Towards a Terminological Clarification. In N. Mars (ed.) Towards Very Large Knowledge Bases: Knowledge Building and Knowledge Sharing, IOS Press, Amsterdam (1995) 25-32.
7. Stojanovic, N., Stojanovic, L.: Usage-oriented Evolution in the Ontology-based Knowledge Management Systems. Proceedings of the First International Conference on Ontologies, Databases and Application of Semantics (ODBASE), Springer (2002)
8. Stojanovic, N., Maedche, A., Staab, S., Studer, R., Sure, Y., SEAL — A Framework for Developing SEmantic PortALs, ACM K-CAP 2001 October, Vancouver, (2001)
9. Saracevic, T.: Relevance: A Review of and a framework for the thinking on the notion in information science. Journal of the American Society for Information Science, 26, (6), (1975) 321-343
10. Salton, G., Buckley, C: Improving retrieval performance by relevance feedback. Journal of the American Society for Information Science. 41(4) (1990) 288-297
11. Cui, H., Wen, Ji-Rong, Nie, Jian-Yun, Ma, Wei-Ying: Probabilistic Query Expansion Using Query Logs, WWW2002, Honolulu, Hawaii, USA, ACM (2002)
12. Rocchio, J.: Relevance feedback in information retrieval. The Smart Retrieval system---Experiments in Automatic Document Processing. G. Salton. (ed) Prentice-Hall Englewood Cliffs. NJ. (1971) 313-323.
13. Haigh S., Megarity, J.: Measuring web site usage: Log file analysis. Network Notes #57. ISSN1201-4338. Information Technology Services National Library of Canada, (1998),
14. Ontoprise GmbH – Ontobroker http://www.ontoprise.de/download/ontobroker.pdf (2001)

A Generic Framework for Web-Based Intelligent Decision Support Systems

Vladimir Simeunović, Jelena Jovanović, Milan Sarić, and Sanja Vraneš

The Mihajlo Pupin Institute, Volgina 15, 11060 Belgrade, Yugoslavia
{vlada, jeljov, milans, sanja}@lab200.imp.bg.ac.yu

Abstract. Web-based Intelligent Systems Environment (WISE) offers generic, modular, flexible and scalable system solutions for information retrieval, extraction, fusion, knowledge discovery and intelligent decision support, using heterogeneous, distributed data and knowledge sources in information rich, open environments. WISE consists of multiple, interacting, software modules, connected if and when needed, allowing for the development of complex, multiparadigm, intelligent applications. Two illustrative examples of WISE application are described in more detail – a web-based system for water remediation technology assessment and selection, and an intelligent investment advisory system, FIDES. The former one has opted predominantly for multicriteria decision making algorithms (MCDM), particularly outranking methods, while the rule-based systems, and fuzzy rule-based systems in particular, have been added in financial and economic decision making in the latter one. WISE proved flexible enough to satisfy the needs of both, albeit completely different web-based intelligent systems.

1 Introduction

Decision support systems (DSS) very often have a specific usability domain and they are usually constructed to satisfy specific user requirements [1]. Therefore, using one DSS for different purposes is very difficult. This refers especially to knowledge organization and acquisition that is used in target DSS environment. The creation of a new system requires considering an enormous amount of time, human and financial resources, since the reusability of previously developed components is rather low.

However, Internet technologies and Java language have opened new horizons in the area of intelligent system development. An Intranet/Internet environment provides architecture for building distributed applications with distributed knowledge, and using Java platform allows creating operating system independent environment.

WISE represents a generic framework for the construction of intelligent decision support systems, based on Java environment and heterogeneous knowledge sources. It has been developed using Java 2 Platform, Enterprise Edition (J2EE) [2], and can be embedded into small system like applets, or into large applications based on J2EE architecture.

D. Karagiannis and U. Reimer (Eds.): PAKM 2002, LNAI 2569, pp. 525-536, 2002.

2 Standard DSS Architecture

The purposes of decision support systems are to:

- Improve decision-making ability of managers by allowing more or better decisions within constraints of cognitive, time and economic limits
- Increase productivity of decision makers
- Supplement one or more of a decision maker's abilities (i.e. knowledge collection, formulation, knowledge derivation and problem recognition)
- Facilitate one or more of the decision-making phases (intelligence, design, choice)
- Facilitate problem-solving flows
- Aid a decision maker in addressing unstructured or semi-structured decisions
- Enhance a decision maker's knowledge management competence, supplementing human knowledge management skills with computer-based knowledge capabilities.

It is necessary to distinguish decision support systems from other kinds of computer-based systems such as data processing and management systems. The main difference is that one DSS must have the ability of knowledge acquisition, selection ability of related knowledge and generation of new knowledge. Newly created knowledge can be used as new input data for the decision support system.

The basic architecture of a decision support system consists of [3]:

- A knowledge subsystem – this subsystem consists of different heterogeneous knowledge sources (database systems, textual organized files, Internet based Unique Resource Identifiers (URI) for uniquely identifying every knowledge source element)
- A knowledge representation system – the knowledge must be structured in related forms (i.e. organization of data in XML files, or in relational database systems)
- A presentation subsystem – the available knowledge must be presented to the end user (a decision maker), and also to the system engineer (responsible for the collection of knowledge)
- A problem solving subsystem – a decision maker activates this subsystem and starts the process of generating the best recommendation and ranked alternatives.

This standard decision support system design approach generates special cases like:

- Text oriented systems (knowledge sources represent textual data files and man machine interface is also text oriented)
- Systems where information is collected within relational databases (standard widely available database systems)
- Decision support systems that use spreadsheet-oriented application like MS Excel (knowledge is organized in the form of user-readable tabular data, and a decision maker can use that information quickly and easily
- Rule based systems (systems based on the sets of facts and rules, capturing the expert heuristics, and inference engine that derives the recommendation out of these facts and rules).

3 WISE Architecture

WISE represents a set of Java packages with specific organization and usage that could be freely and easily combined into a consistent whole, according to the specific problem at hand. The following are the three main functional packages:

- WISE.ES – the package facilitating the development of conventional, rule-based expert systems in Java language
- WISE.MCDM – the package facilitating the multicriteria decision making process, offering the two most widely used methods, PROMETHEE II and ELECTRE III [4]
- WISE.FUZZY – the package facilitating fuzzy sets, fuzzy production rules, and fuzzy linguistic functions (usually used together with WISE.ES package).

Using WISE packages it is very easy to crate the skeleton of every web based intelligent decision support system (Fig 1. shows the core WISE based DSS architecture).

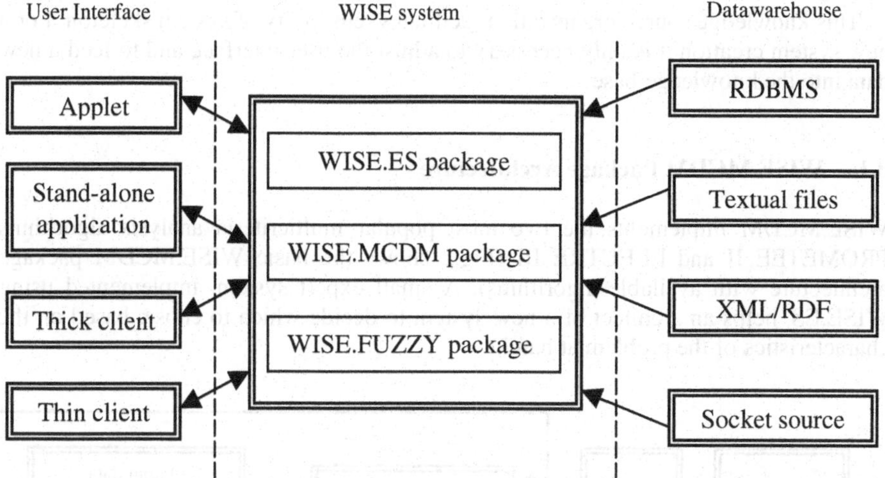

Fig. 1. WISE based decision support system architecture

A concrete web based decision support system consists of graphical user interface (GUI), central WISE layer and knowledge and data warehouse. GUI can be realized as:

- Standard Java applet - that can be embedded within a standard Internet browser (Internet Explorer, Netscape Navigator etc.)
- Stand alone Java application - when that application has a direct access to WISE packages (WISE functions must be called explicitly within the source code of target desktop application)
- Thick Java client - a client with a significant share of business logic in it, where the access to WISE packages is performed through the client side of system

- Thin Java client – a server side subsystem is using WISE packages in the complex, multiple-tier Java application
- Standard Web application – realized using standard script languages (it is possible to use Java Server Pages and also Active Server Pages technologies with JavaScript and VBScript languages).

The central part represents the core of WISE system and consists of three types of packages. It facilitates a direct access to related packages and their functionality (for a stand alone application), and support for using Java Beans technologies as an infrastructure for data interchange between clients and servers.

Knowledge data warehouse consists of heterogeneous data sources. The system also supports direct communication through TCP/IP protocol and a special high-level protocol for data transmition. Knowledge sources within WISE environment can encompass heterogeneous types of data storage. It is possible to use:

- Standard database systems, with connection through Java Database Connectivity (JDBC) interface
- Standard textual data files with a related data structure
- XML files (also in the RDF/XML format) with related schema structure.

This knowledge source organization facilitates reusability of system skeleton. For a new system creation it is only necessary to adjust the user interface and to feed a new data into the knowledge base.

3.1 WISE.MCDM Package Architecture

WISE.MCDM implements the two most popular multicriteria analysis algorithms PROMETEE II and ELECTRE III (Fig.2 shows the basic WISE.MCDM package architecture with available algorithms). A small expert system, implemented using WISE.ES, helps an architect of a new system to decide which to chose, based on the characteristics of the problem at hand.

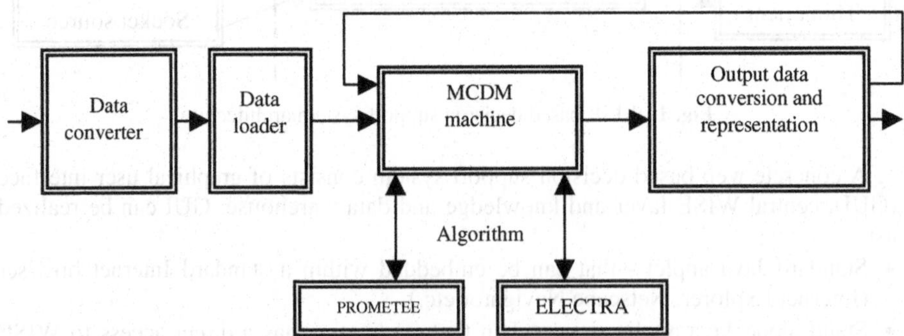

Fig. 2. WISE.MCDM package architecture

A *data converter* module converts input data from related knowledge sources into a format recognizable by WISE. For every type of knowledge sources a separate converter is used. For example, there are converters for RDBMS systems (that convert data from one type of database to a meta database that is used as a standard WISE input devices) or XML file converters if we need to translate data from a XML file to WISE expected XML schema format.

A *data loader* module feeds data into internal data structures. Organization of these structures is similar to the entity relationship diagram for data in the related database (Fig. 3 shows organization of data for WISE.MCDM package).

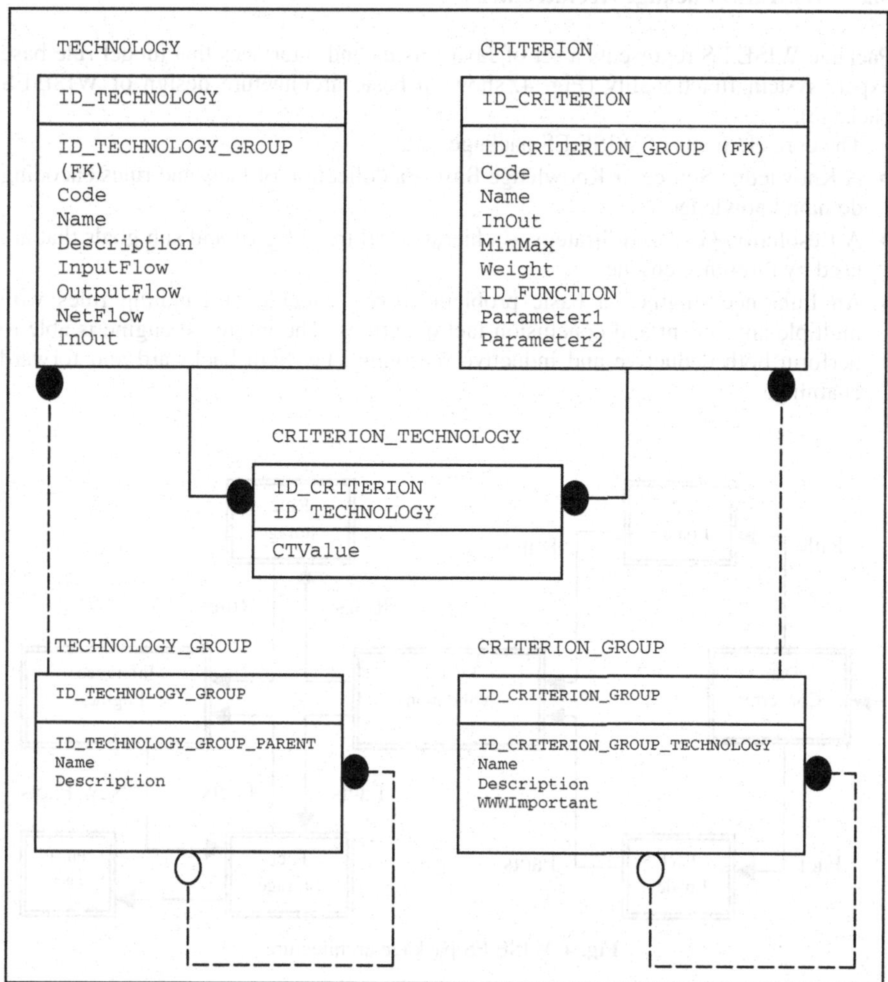

Fig. 3. Entity relationship diagram for data in WISE.MCDM package

A MCDM machine module represents a core module that is responsible for coordination of other modules, and it is used to start and stop multicriteria analysis when input data have been loaded. Before the start of analysis process, the user must decide which algorithm will be used.

Output data conversion and representation – will be activated after finishing the analysis process. The end user can change the input data and start the process again, or accept the system recommendation (or any of the feasible alternatives ranked by the system).

3.2 WISE.ES Package Architecture

Package WISE.ES represents a set of Java classes and interfaces that model rule base expert system functionality (Fig. 4. shows a basic architecture design of WISE.ES package).

The core elements of WISE.ES packages are:

- A Knowledge Source or Knowledge Base – a collection of facts and rules encoding domain knowledge
- A Resolution Goal and Strategy – a hierarchical tree of goal and sub goals that are used by inference engine
- An Inference Engine –a basic problem solver, capable of handling rules with multiple antecedent and conclusion fact quantities. The inference engine is able to perform both deductive and inductive reasoning, i.e. both backward and forward chaining.

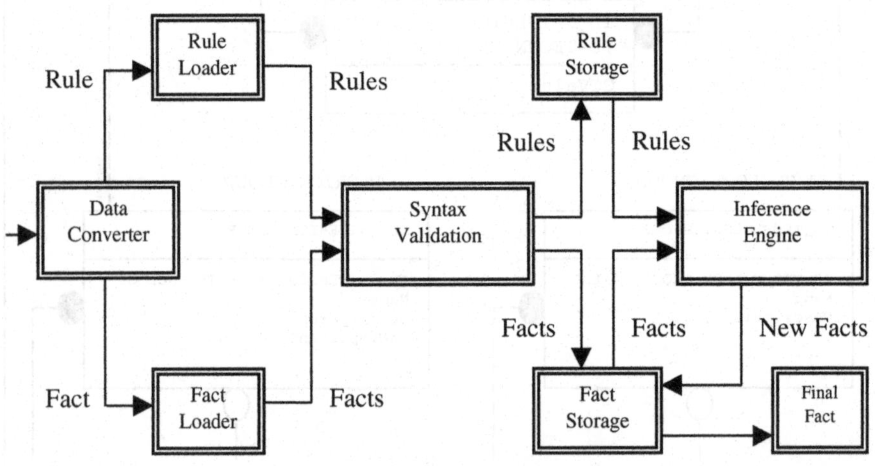

Fig. 4. WISE.ES package architecture

A data converter module is used for conversion of input data into a form recognizable by the system. Similarly to the WISE.MCDM package, there are also a few converters for translation of heterogeneous knowledge sources such as databases, textual files, XML files, etc.

Rule loader module may load rules from existing files, memory, or dynamically as they are created. When a rule is loaded, the syntax of the rule is checked. If a rule is syntactically incorrect, it is discarded and the user is alerted. If the rule is syntactically correct, the rule is placed into the related internal data structure of the inference engine rule list. Every rule has a priority associated with it. This means that when the rule is loaded, it is placed into the rule agenda, in an order based upon this priority, and "fired" accordingly.

Facts can also be loaded and asserted from an existing file, external network connection or dynamically as they are created. The same syntax parser used for loading rules is also used for facts. Assertion of facts is also performed as a consequence of rule execution by the inference engine.

The inference engine uses two types of rules - forward chaining and backward chaining rules. The current method of rule evaluation applies changes to the fact base immediately. As a rule is evaluated, all of the facts created or destroyed due to a rule firing are immediately added to, or retracted from, the list of active facts. The next rule that is evaluated will operate on the new set of facts.

4 WISE Based DSS Examples

The WISE environment has already been successfully used for the development of several rather different intelligent applications. We have chosen to present here in more detail the two of them, i.e.:

- FIDES – a financial decision support meant mostly for investment project appraisal, end
- CCR – a decision support system for water remediation technology assessment and selection.

4.1 About FIDES

FIDES (**FI**nancial **DE**cision **S**upport) performs investment project valuation in accordance with the well-known UNIDO standard [5] and makes recommendations on a preferable investment, based on multicriteria analysis of available investment options [6]. FIDES provides a framework for analyzing key financial indicators, using the discounted cash-flow technique, and also allows for non-monetary factors to enter the multicriteria assessment process, whilst retaining an explicit and relatively objective and consistent set of evaluation conventions and clear decision criteria.

Moreover, since virtually every investment and financing decision, involving allocation of resources under uncertain conditions, is associated with considerable risk, FIDES integrates the risk management module. The basic principle governing risk management is intuitive and well articulated, taking into account investor's subjective appetite for and aversion to risk, and the decision sensitivity to the uncertainty and/or imprecision of input data. Thus, with FIDES, financial analysts and decision-makers are provided with effective modeling tools in the absence of complete or precise information and the significant presence of human involvement.

The decision aid is implemented using multiple programming paradigms (Internet programming, production rules, fuzzy programming, multicriteria analysis, etc.), using a three-tier architecture as a backbone. Being Web based, the application is especially convenient for large, geographically dispersed corporations.

4.2 Fides Realization

FIDES enables the decentralized creation, analysis and appraisal of the investment projects in large enterprises, banks or governmental institutions (Fig. 1). As a basis for the investment project appraisal and the preparation of the feasibility study, the methodology of the United Nations Industrial Development Organization has been chosen. The methodology is based on modifications of integrated standard analytical tables, where financial and economic analysis is based on discounted cash-flow values.

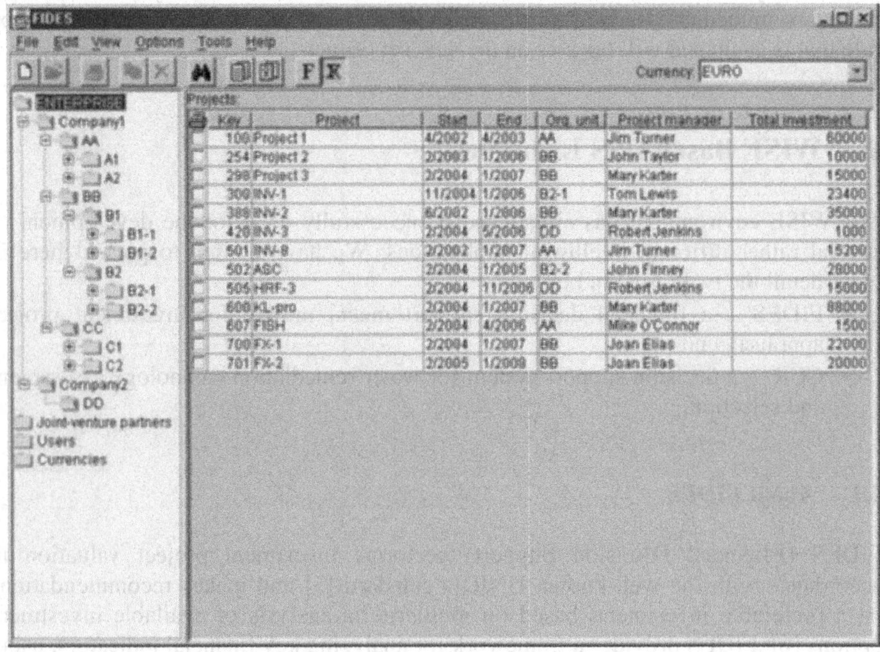

Fig. 5. FIDES application main window

The framework facilitates:

- Creation of the organizational tree that fully mirrors the enterprise topology
- Definition of the application users and their rights
- Creation of the personnel records
- Definition of joint-venture partners
- Creation of the currency list
- Investment project analysis and appraisal

The application is primarily aimed for use in large enterprises, banks, or governmental institutions, where a large number of investment projects is expected, though it can be used for the appraisal of single projects. To localize the investment projects and employees, the organizational tree has been introduced. The organizational tree is composed of the Org.-Units hierarchically organized within at most 5 levels. To each Org.-Unit a project, or an employee, can be assigned.

Recently the three-tier architecture has become a standard in the development of distributed applications. This architecture has several advantages in comparison with the classical client-server (two-tier) architecture such as the functional decomposition of the application (presentation, business, data store), which eases the development and testing to a great extent, component reusability, extensibility, portability and scalability.

In the three-tier architecture the first tier is the presentation tier, the second tier is the business tier, while the third tier is the data tier. In the Enterprise Java Beans (EJB) technology the first tier corresponds to the J2EE client (runs on the client computer), the middle tier represents the J2EE server (runs on the server computer) with the EJB container, while the third (EIS-Enterprise Information System) tier includes the database or the file system (on the database server computer).

FIDES is based on the session bean. MCDM Session Bean contains the WISE.MCDM package, while the Heuristic Classification Session Bean integrates the WISE.ES package.

Development of FIDES within the WISE environment has proven extremely convenient and efficient, using Java Beans and WISE packages for business logic and any type of Java clients for GUI. This way, the FIDES development and testing time was dramatically reduced. The estimated manpower for the FIDES development from scratch (i.e. without the help of WISE environment) was 36 man months, while with J2EE and WISE packages, the total effort was reduced to 12 man months. Almost 30 percent of source code for business logic is now in WISE packages that is separately tested and verified.

4.3 About CCR System

Remediation of contaminated water is a field of technology that has developed and grown recently. An initial approach to eliminate a hazardous waste from a particular location was to move it somewhere else, or cover it with a cap. These methods use water disposal as the solution to the problem. With an increasing number of cleanups underway, demand developed for alternatives to water disposal that provided more permanent and less costly solutions for dealing with contaminated materials. Development and use of more suitable remediation technologies has progressed and a large number of cleanup alternatives have evolved or been suggested over the past decade. Also, the technology developers and environmental service companies have sprung up in the hope of securing a place for their process in the market. As a consequence, there has been a remarkable decrease in unit cost for water treatment options. However, both site owners and environmental managers confront the challenge of making decisions to select and deploy the most suitable water remediation technologies to address a variety of problems and satisfy a number of conflicting criteria [7].

These choices are increasingly more complex because a greater variety of contamination problems are being defined and innovative technologies are becoming available every day as potential (sometimes cheaper and/or more effective) alternatives to existing technologies [8]. Innovative remediation technologies, which lack a long history of full-scale use, do not have the extensive documentation necessary to make them a standard choice in the engineering/scientific community.

However, many innovative technologies have been used successfully at contaminated sites in the United States, Canada, and Europe despite incomplete verification of their utility. Some of the technologies were developed in response to hazardous waste problems and some have been adapted from other industrial uses. Only after a technology has been used at many different types of sites and the results fully documented, is it considered an established technology. The majority of technologies in use today are still classified as innovative.

Decisionmakers are further challenged because they are compelled to integrate information about relative risk into their considerations of remedial actions and also are required to balance information about technology performance and risk with fixed or limited budgetary resources and regulatory constraints. In addition, information about the concerns of stakeholders, as well as their meaningful involvement in the larger decision process, influences the ultimate technology selection and deployment decision. Therefore, all involved parties (environmentalist, policy makers, local community representatives, site owners, other stakeholders) need better tools to help them assemble and synthesize information to respond to these challenges and conflicting interests.

Therefore we have chosen this problem to develop a CCR (Credence Clearwater Revival) system to be used for evaluation and comparison of some conventional and innovative technologies for environmental remediation. CCR provides a set of indicators for criteria for evaluating technologies to address site-specific cleanup activities and accomplishes the following:

- Enables its users to identify and systematically compare information about innovative and conventional technologies to meet remediation goals, highlighting their strengths and weaknesses
- Establishes a structure of technology evaluation and selection process, which simplifies the decision making and streamlines the variety of factors involved in the remediation process
- Defines consistent, measurable indicators for key technical, environmental, economic, and legal criteria that influence selection and deployment of technologies
- Provides documented, reproducible evaluation which can be updated as needed information becomes available
- Provides a flexible, multicriteria optimization approach allowing tradeoffs among criteria on the basis of contaminant type and site-specific needs
- Favors communications and helps focus dialogue between local community, environmental managers and stakeholders, including regulators and policy makers
- Enables explanation and justification of the choice by offering evidence on the advantages and disadvantages of the possible choices in a concise and consistent way
- Fastens development of a feasibility study of remedial options
- Provides site owners, environmental managers and other stakeholders with the opportunity to explore alternative options quickly, etc.

4.4 CCR Functionality

CCR system has been produced as a standard Java stand-alone application that uses WISE.MCDM package for multicriteria analysis. The DARTS presents its users with a variety of configuration and input parameters from which to choose. Several are mandatory (such as identifying technologies to be evaluated), but there are many that the user can choose to leave blank or use the supplied default values. This way, the user decides how to tailor the analysis to satisfy his/her specific needs.

Application configuration and data entry process encompasses several tasks: entering available technologies and their descriptions; entering criteria to be considered simultaneously; setting values of chosen criteria and selecting the type of preference function. The application's main window (Fig. 6 shows CCR main screen) consists of the current data configuration, and a few dialogs for data entry purposes.

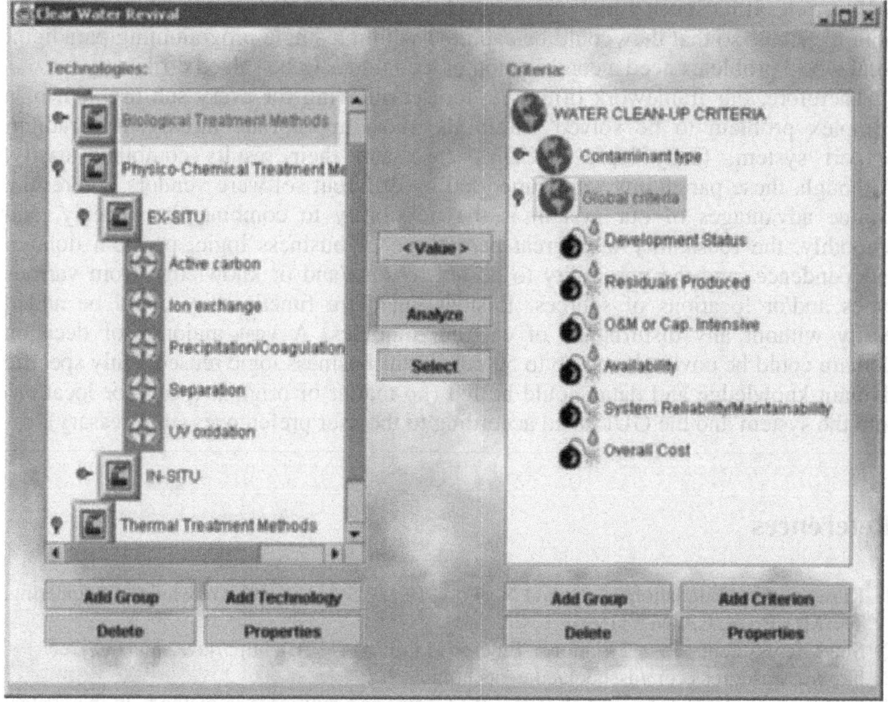

Fig. 6. CCR application main window

It is connected to the database that contains previously entered information on available technologies and selection criteria. Application uses JDBC-ODBC Bridge for accessing database. Therefore, the database should be registered by ODBC Administrator application.

First version of CCR system was stand-alone Java application with only database support for knowledge sources. The GUI and business logic have not been encapsulated in different modules (only database layer was separated). The development and testing time was almost 6 man months. Building a new application with WISE.MCDM package took only 2 man months and 50 percent of source code for business logic was in the generic packages. Besides, a new version is much more flexible, able to use different types of knowledge source and select the most appropriate algorithm for multicriteria analysis. A small wizard is currently being developed, using the MCDM.ES package that will help WISE user to select its packages and tune the configuration parameters according to his/her problem domain.

5 Conclusions

In this paper a framework for Web-based intelligent decision support systems has been described. The framework facilitates a development of multiparadigm intelligent systems that combine conventional expert systems, fuzzy logic, multicriteria decision-making, etc. It has been widely recognized that complex decision domains are rarely homogeneous, so that they could be captured within a single programming paradigm. Real world problems need a combination of techniques to be solved efficiently.

Therefore, our framework offers the toolset allowing for every sub problem of a complex problem to be solved within the most appropriate intelligent paradigm (expert system, fuzzy logic, MCDM, etc.) and their results combined easily. Although, these paradigms were supported by different software vendors before, the unique advantages of our system is the possibility to combine them freely, and smoothly, the reusability of a great percentage of business logic, problem domain independence, and the possibility to be fed by data/and or knowledge from various types and/or locations of sources. Besides, an extra functionality could be added easily without any disturbance of existing modules. A vast majority of decision domain could be covered, and up to 50 percent of business logic reused. Only specific domain knowledge and data should be fed (no matter of original format or location) into the system and the GUI tuned according to the user preferences (if necessary).

References

1. Kasabov, N.: Foundations of Neural Network, Fuzzy Systems and Knowledge Engineering. The MIT Press, CA, MA (1996)
2. Sun Microsystems: Java 2 Platform, Enterprise Edition (J2EE), http://java.sun.com/j2ee/
3. http://dssresources.com/dssbook/contents.html
4. Salminen, P., Hokkanen, J., Lahdelma, R.: Comparing multicriteria methods in the context of environmental problems, European Journal of Operational Research 104 (1998) 485 – 496
5. United Nations Industrial Development Organization (UNIDO): Manual for the Preparation of Industrial Feasibility Studies, Vienna (1991)
6. Vraneš S., Stanojević, M., Stevanović, V.: Investment decision making, in Leondes (ed.) Expert Systems, Academic Press (2002)
7. Brans, J.P., Vincke, Ph.: A Preference Ranking Organisation Method, Management Science, Vol. 31, No. 6 (1985) 647-656.
8. Economic Commission for Europe, Compendium of Water Clean-up Technologies and Water Remediation Companies, United Nations, Trieste (2002)

Mining Knowledge from Text Collections Using Automatically Generated Metadata

John M. Pierre

Interwoven, Inc.
101 2nd Street, 4th Floor
San Francisco, CA 94105
jpierre@interwoven.com

Abstract. Data mining is typically applied to large databases of highly structured information in order to discover new knowledge. In businesses and institutions, the amount of information existing in repositories of text documents usually rivals or surpasses the amount found in relational databases. Though the amount of potentially valuable knowledge contained in document collections can be great, they are often difficult to analyze. Therefore, it is important to develop methods to efficiently discover knowledge embedded in these document repositories. In this paper we describe an approach for mining knowledge from text collections by applying data mining techniques to metadata records generated via automated text categorization. By controlling the set of metadata fields as well as the set of assigned categories we can customize the knowledge discovery task to address specific questions. As an example, we apply the approach to a large collection of product reviews and evaluate the performance of the knowledge discovery.

1 Introduction

Businesses and institutions often have a great deal of information technology infrastructure devoted to maintaining various repositories of text documents. These repositories include local and networked file systems, document management systems, email, discussion groups, and portals. Much of the collective knowledge in an organization is contained within these repositories of text documents. However, text repositories typically go untapped as a source for knowledge discovery. Instead documents are often used only once, and stored away for possible future reference. Users may have the ability to search for relevant documents and retrieve them based on a query. Analyzing large numbers of documents to find trends, patterns, and rules of thumb is usually not possible without a great deal of manual effort and expert knowledge. In order to recover and utilize the valuable knowledge contained in these document collections we must develop efficient and effective methods of analyzing large amounts of unstructured text.

In this paper we describe an approach to knowledge discovery in text collections. Our methodology uses automated text categorization to create structured metadata which can then be analyzed using traditional data mining techniques.

D. Karagiannis and U. Reimer (Eds.): PAKM 2002, LNAI 2569, pp. 537–548, 2002.

The result is a set of associations or rules involving a pre-defined set of concepts. By using this approach it is possible to efficiently analyze large document repositories and discover new knowledge. This approach combines aspects of computer science and cognitive science within a framework that solves a real world business problem.

Due to recent advances in computer science in the areas of text categorization[5] and text data mining[1] it is now possible to accurately and automatically analyze unstructured text documents. The use of efficient algorithms as well as the availability of ever powerful computers mean that large collections of text documents can be processed quickly, inexpensively, and with a minimum of human intervention. While computational methods still do not come close to matching the reasoning abilities of a human knowledge worker, they do allow tedious and time consuming tasks to be performed automatically and permit human users to concentrate on higher level problems. Even though a purely manual process may result in more accurate knowledge discovery, it is usually not feasible or cost effective to have a human spend the time and effort to read, understand, analyze, and extract comprehensive insights from a text collection containing tens of thousands of documents.

A crucial part of our approach is the use of *faceted metadata*[6], which is a specialized form of knowledge representation that draws from principles of cognitive science. Individual facets represent orthogonal conceptual dimensions. In our approach the set of facets as well as the set of possible concepts in each facet must be determined by a knowledge engineer. By controlling the set of facets as well as the available set of concepts in each facet we can customize the metadata database schema for targeted mining tasks. For example we can control the level of generality or specificity in the concepts, or constrain the mining to the discover relationships between concepts within specific facets of interest. This allows us to probe different aspects of the knowledge contained in the underlying document collection. In addition, the implied semantic relationship between different facets allows knowledge workers to more easily interpret the meaning of the mined rules and associations.

This approach provides a solution that allows a business or organization to repurpose large untapped text repositories to unlock the knowledge within. The ability to customize the knowledge discovery to answer specific questions is important to ensure actionable results. In our approach the metadata schema is not rigid and does not need to be determined before the documents are created or collected. This is in contrast to traditional database systems where the schema is fixed before data is gathered and therefore data mining is more constrained. Our flexible approach allows the schema to be adjusted to suit the knowledge discovery task, and takes advantage of the rich complexity of relationships between concepts that are inherent in a large document repository. This allows the user to formulate a specific hypothesis or question and to configure the system to test the hypothesis or answer the question based on the contents of the text collection.

In section 2 we discuss in detail the approach to creating suitable metadata as an input to the knowledge discovery process. In section 3 we provide an example where we applied the approach to a large collection of product reviews. Related work is discussed in section 4. We state our conclusions and suggestions for further study in section 5.

2 Methodology

The approach presented in this paper uses automated text categorization to assign faceted metadata records to text documents. These metadata records serve as a bridge between a corpus of free text documents and a highly structured database with a rigid schema. Statistical techniques and traditional data mining can then be applied to the set of structured metadata records to discover knowledge implicit in the underlying document collection. By choosing the metadata schema and the set of concepts in each facet we can control the knowledge discovery process.

In traditional data mining (or *Knowledge Discovery in Databases*) the database schema is rigid and is usually fixed before the data is even collected. In contrast a corpus of documents is inherently more flexible, and since the metadata schema can be changed at any time, the corpus can be re-purposed to address different kinds of questions.

Our basic approach is:

1. Gather a document collection that covers the domain of interest.
2. Segment documents into an appropriate set of transactions.
3. Construct a metadata schema with facets and concepts that suit the goal of the knowledge discovery task.
4. Train text classifiers to populate the metadata fields using machine learning techniques.
5. Apply automated text categorization to create a metadata database.
6. Use data mining to discover associations between concepts or derive rules.

In the rest of this section we describe these aspects in more detail.

2.1 Document Selection

Successful knowledge discovery requires a sufficient document collection. The document collection must span the domain of interest so that the concepts and associations between them are adequately represented. In addition the collection must provide enough transactions so that statistically significant rules can be mined. Furthermore, each document should be granular enough to provide crisp associations between a focused set of concepts.

2.2 Document Segmentation

In this framework, the issue of what constitutes a document is an important one. In our approach each document defines a "transaction" that creates the associations between concepts. In analogy with a traditional data mining example, each document is like a market basket and the concepts assigned in the metadata constitute the items in the basket. Given a collection of large documents it may be useful to further segment into chapters, paragraphs, passages, *etc.* to achieve the right level of granularity.

2.3 Metadata Schema

Metadata is often defined as "data about data" and when associated with documents is usually intended as an aid to searching, organizing, and summarizing in large collections. In this work we use metadata in a generalized way to gather structured information about free text documents. Faceted metadata is a form of knowledge representation akin to templates or frames and slots. Metadata facets represent orthogonal sets of concepts (for example "People", "Locations", "Dates"). By constraining the data mining to analyze the co-occurrences of concepts in particular facets we can exercise considerable control over the knowledge discovery process.

Most approaches to text mining use natural language processing or information extraction to select the set of keywords or phrases to be analyzed. This can lead to the "vocabulary problem" where differences in word usage such as synonyms, homonyms, or spelling errors can lead to spurious results. By establishing a fixed set of concepts in each facet we can control the vocabulary used in the rule mining phase.

2.4 Text Categorization

Creating metadata can be tedious and expensive, and it can lead to inconsistent results if done completely manually. Automated text categorization has become a practical way to create metadata records for large collections of documents. The main cost is in training and tuning a classifier. Classifiers are fairly easy to adjust, which allows the metadata schema to be changed according to the needs of the knowledge discovery project.

Text categorization is the assignment of relevant categories to documents, and a number of machine learning techniques have been developed to automate the process[5]. After training with a sufficient number of example documents, associations are made between the words in documents and the concepts in the categorization scheme. Several different classifiers can be trained to assign categories from conceptually distinct taxonomies to populate each metadata facet.

The accuracy of the text categorization is an issue. With sufficient training, automated classifiers can achieve close to human levels of accuracy, but there is always some inherent error rate. Since data mining usually relies on statistically significant co-occurrences of concepts, inaccuracies in category assignments will be somewhat mitigated if they lead to spurious co-occurrences which are not statistically significant. However if classifier inaccuracies are biased (which is often the case) this will reduce the quality of the mined rules.

2.5 Data Mining

The data mining phase can be comprised of statistical techniques or algorithms to discover knowledge, rules, and relationships between concepts. Successful data mining leads to the discovery of facts which are non-trivial and previously unknown. In our approach this phase is more similar to traditional data mining in databases than to text mining because we operate on structured metadata records instead of directly on the free text itself. Since our concepts are typed by the metadata schema we can achieve greater semantic richness in our mined rules and associations than in traditional text mining [12].

In this paper we apply a common association rule induction technique to discover pair-wise relationships between concepts in different facets. However, more complicated learning algorithms could be applied to the metadata records to derive higher order rules.

3 Example

We apply our approach to a large collection of product reviews as an illustrative example. Individual text classifiers were trained to assign metadata for each facet, and data mining techniques were applied to discover associations between the concepts in different facets. The correct metadata records for each document as well as the expected set of associative relationships between concepts was known ahead of time and used as a basis for testing the quality of the text categorization and knowledge discovery phases.

3.1 Document Collection

To build a suitable document collection for experimentation, we spidered a web site containing product reviews for audio equipment[7]. The site arranged products into high-level product categories (*e.g* Speakers) and low-level subcategories (*e.g.* Main Speaker, Bookshelf Speakers, Subwoofers, *etc.*). Each product review included an overall rating as well as a free text summary expressing the reviewer's opinion of the product. We downloaded the most reviewed products in each category for a total of 47,923 individual product reviews.

We randomly split the document collection roughly in half to form a training set and test set. The first set of 24147 documents was used to train our text classifiers. Automated text categorization was performed on the second set of 23776 documents, and data mining was performed on the automatically created metadata.

3.2 Metadata Schema

The metadata was organized into four facets: Category, Subcategory, Products, and Rating. The metadata schema is shown in Table 1.

Table 1. Metadata Schema

Metadata Facet	Number of Concepts
Category	11
Subcategory	49
Products	1610
Rating	2

In our document collection there were 11 high-level product categories divided into 49 subcategories. A total of 1610 products were represented. Products were originally rated on a scale from 1 to 5 which we consolidated into two concepts, *GOOD* and *BAD*.

3.3 Classifier Training and Evaluation

We trained a separate text classifier for each of the four metadata facets. Separate Naive Bayes classifiers[8] were trained to assign product categories and subcategories. A simple Boolean classifier was constructed from the list of products derived from the pre-assigned metadata in the training set. The Boolean classifier checked if all tokens in a product name occurred in the document in order to score a match. We trained a Naive Bayes classifier to distinguish between "GOOD" and "BAD" product ratings. The text classifiers and their estimated performance are summarized in Table 2.

Table 2. Text Classifiers

Metadata Facet	Classifier	Precision	Recall
Category	Naive Bayes	0.79	0.79
Subcategory	Naive Bayes	0.54	0.54
Products	Boolean	0.31	0.18
Rating	Naive Bayes	0.91	0.91

Classifier performance was estimated using the standard micro-averaged precision and recall measures[9]. The Naive Bayes classifiers for Category, Subcategory, and Rating assigned only a single concept (and only a single concept was assumed to be correct), therefore precision and recall were equivalent.

The Boolean classifier for products was able to assign more than one product. For each review only one product was considered to be "correct" even though other (competing or complementary) products may have been mentioned in the summary or even if no products were explicitly mentioned at all. Therefore this strict interpretation of precision and recall somewhat underestimated the performance of the product classifier. A cursory inspection of the results indicated good performance of the classifier at finding products mentioned in the reviews.

3.4 Mining

To discover associations between concepts we applied the Apriori algorithm given in [10][11]. We limited our results to association rules of the form $A \rightarrow B$ with a single antecedent and consequent, each restricted to different specified facets.

Rules were selected according to thresholds on confidence and support. The support of a rule is defined by

$$Support(A) = (|A|/|T|) \times 100\%,$$

where $|A|$ is the number of transactions in which the set A occurs and $|T|$ is the total number of transactions.

The confidence of a rule is given by

$$Confidence(A \rightarrow B) = \frac{Support(A,B)}{Support(A)} \times 100\%.$$

We tested rules selected with support thresholds of 0.1% (corresponding to approximately 10 transactions), 0.05% (approx. 5 transactions), and 0.01% (approx. 1 transaction). In all cases we used a confidence threshold of 60%.

We mined four kinds of simple association rules:

$$Subcategory(A) \rightarrow Category(B)$$
$$Product(A) \rightarrow Category(B)$$
$$Product(A) \rightarrow Subcategory(B)$$
$$Product(A) \rightarrow Rating(B)$$

In the first case we found associations between instances of subcategories and high-level categories. In the second type of association rule product categories were inferred from product instances, and given products we inferred product subcategories in the third type. In the last type we found the association of individual products with a *GOOD* or *BAD* review.

3.5 Results

In Table 3 we show some selected examples for each rule type. Each rule type corresponds to the pair-wise association of concepts in two different facets. Though some of the associations are conceptually related between rules types, each was derived independently.

Table 3. Example Rules

Rule Type	Example
Subcategory(A) → Category(B):	
	A/V Receivers → Amplification
	DVD Players → Home Video
	Main Speaker → Speakers
Product(A) → Category(B):	
	Yamaha RX/V795 → Amplification
	Samsung DVD/611 → Home Video
	Paradigm Atom → Speakers
Product(A) → Subcategory(B):	
	Yamaha RX/V795 → A/V Receivers
	Samsung DVD/611 → DVD Players
	Paradigm Atom → Main Speaker
Product(A) → Rating(B):	
	Yamaha RX/V795 → GOOD
	Samsung DVD/611 → BAD
	Paradigm Atom → GOOD

3.6 Evaluation

We attempted to quantify the accuracy of mined association rules based on the ability of the system to re-derive a known set of associations between sets of concepts. To estimate the performance of our data mining tasks we have defined analogs of the standard precision and recall measures used in information retrieval and text categorization:

$$Precision = \frac{\#\, of\, correct\, rules\, mined}{\#\, of\, total\, rules\, mined}$$

$$Recall = \frac{\#\, of\, correct\, rules\, mined}{\#\, of\, rules\, known\, to\, be\, correct}$$

In order to compute these evaluation metrics we must have some prior knowledge of which rules are correct, which rules are incorrect, as well as the total number of possible rules. In more complicated mining tasks these values could be difficult or impossible to deduce, but using our constrained approach we are able to estimate them.

Since all products were known to be assigned to a specific product category and subcategory, we assumed that this defined the correct set of associations of the type *Product*(*A*) → *Category*(*B*) and *Product*(*A*) → *Subcategory*(*B*). To estimate the correct set of associations of the type *Product*(*A*) → *Rating*(*B*) we computed the average numerical score of the individual product reviews in our test collection and mapped them into the *GOOD* and *BAD* categories. Each product category was divided into several subcategories which defined the set of correct associations for $Subcategory(A) \rightarrow Category(B)$.

The concept of collecting the "right answers" for evaluation of association rules is based on some key assumptions. When the association relationship in our control set is based on instances (*e.g.* products) assigned to classes (*e.g.* categories), the associations discovered from mining can be the result of other types of relations besides class membership. For example in our data the occurrence of particular kind of audio amplifier commonly used to test high-end speakers can result in an association that would be considered incorrect according to our evaluation but not necessarily a bad rule as far as useful knowledge discovery is concerned. Likewise a highly rated product might often appear in reviews for a product with a low rating as a good alternative. Another assumption is that a complete set of right answers can even be defined. Nevertheless similar assumptions are also made when evaluating information retrieval (relevance judgments) and text categorization (category assignments) systems, and this type of evaluation has proven useful as a basis for comparison and optimization despite its limitations.

Table 4. Rule Evaluation Results

Rule Type	Support Threshold	# of mined rules	Precision	Recall
Subcategory(A) → Category(B):				
	0.1%	16	1.0	0.33
	0.05%	20	1.0	0.41
	0.01%	26	1.0	0.53
Product(A) → Category(B):				
	0.1%	168	0.88	0.10
	0.05%	341	0.84	0.18
	0.01%	475	0.74	0.29
Product(A) → Subcategory(B):				
	0.1%	86	0.74	0.05
	0.05%	210	0.60	0.08
	0.01%	443	0.39	0.11
Product(A) → Rating(B):				
	0.1%	259	0.91	0.17
	0.05%	474	0.92	0.28
	0.01%	881	0.89	0.5

In Table 4 we present evaluation results for our mined association rules. For each rule type we show the total number of mined rules, precision, and recall at the specified minimum support thresholds of 0.1%, 0.05%, and 0.01%. In general lowering the support threshold resulted in decreased precision and increased recall. Even though precision decreased the number of "correct" mined rules generally increased substantially as the support threshold was lowered.

In most cases we were able to discover rules with high precision, but low recall. Though we have shown that recall can be increased at the expense of precision by adjusting the support threshold, it is also likely that we could achieve higher recall values given a larger document collection. The relatively high levels of precision achieved show that assumptions made for generating the sets of correct answers where generally justified.

The associations of the type $Product(A) \rightarrow Subcategory(B)$ resulted in lower performance values. This is probably because of the relatively poor performance of the classifier for subcategories. The fairly subtle distinctions between some subcategories (*e.g.* Amplifiers vs. Integrated Amplifiers), were difficult for our classifier to distinguish between. In these cases the classifier tended to be biased toward the subcategories that had the most documents in the training set, and this bias was reflected in the mined rules.

4 Related Work

Text mining and applications of data mining to structured data derived from text have been the subject of much research in recent years. Most text mining has used natural language processing to extract key terms and phrases directly from the documents[2][1].

Some approaches have used external knowledge as an enhancement. In [12], a focused set of terms was generated from the document collection and arranged into a hierarchical taxonomy to refine their mining tasks. Loh *et al.*[13] use automated categorization to assign a collection of pre-defined concepts to a corpus of documents. Statistical techniques were then applied to the sets of assigned concepts to find associative rules and concept distributions. However, their concepts required a significant amount of domain knowledge to construct via manual training and were not typed into facets.

In more recent work, machine learning techniques have been used to derive complex structured data from text to which data mining techniques such as rule induction can be applied. In [3], a knowledge base was constructed around a set of predefined conceptual entities (*i.e.* companies) and various web pages were analyzed using text categorization, information extraction, and wrappers to derive specific features for each entity. Traditional data mining was then applied to the derived knowledge base to discover various rules. Their approach, while very similar to what we've presented here, is more difficult to apply to a generic collection of unstructured documents since each of their input documents must be keyed to a specific entity and some amount of effort is required to develop customized wrappers for certain types of documents. In [4], information extraction was used to construct a database of structured records from a document corpus. Data mining was applied to the database to discover prediction and association rules. The accuracy of prediction rules was evaluated by measuring the average ability to predict each slot value based on all other slot values. Basu *et al.* [14] present a method to evaluate the quality of mined rules based on their "novelty." A system for exploiting faceted metadata in a browsable user interface is described in [6].

5 Conclusions

By dynamically creating faceted metadata for a large collection of documents, we can construct a system for mining specific aspects of the knowledge implicit in the underlying corpus. Creating an appropriate set of text categorizers allows us to control the nature of the knowledge discovery and provides an automated system for deriving structured data from unstructured text. The main cost of the project is then shifted to collecting appropriate training data for the categorizers and defining facets and taxonomies. This type of system could be applied to a dynamic and growing document collection to monitor specific aspects of information that may change over time.

Our approach provides a practical solution for businesses and organizations that want to leverage and repurpose their document repositories in order to uncover useful knowledge. Since the metadata framework can be customized for specific domains, this approach could be applied to a wide variety of settings such as customer relationship management, human resources, competitive intelligence, message boards, intranets and the web. For example customer feedback email could be analyzed to determine relationships between user preferences, complaints and specific products, services or marketing campaigns. As another example, human resources documents such as resumes and performance reviews could be analyzed to find associations between people, departments and areas of expertise.

An interesting area of further study would be to explore the integration of this type of text based knowledge discovery with applications that feed on knowledge such as decision support systems, automated alert systems, agents, or expert systems. Another important area for further research is to understand how the presentation, filtering, and use of automatically discovered knowledge in the context of users' work processes leads to the most value.

References

1. M. A. Hearst. Untangling Text Data Mining. In *Proceedings of ACL'99: the 37th Annual Meeting of the Association for Computational Linguistics*, 1999.
2. H. Ahonen and O. Heinonen. Applying Data Mining Techniques in Text Analysis. *Report C-1997-23*, University of Helsinki, Department of Computer Science, March 1997.
3. R. Ghani, R. Jones, D. Mladenic, K. Nigam, and S. Slattery. Data Mining on Symbolic Knowledge Extracted from the Web. In *Proceedings of the Sixth International Conference on Knowledge Discovery and Data Mining (KDD-2000) Workshop on Text Mining*, 29-36, 2000.
4. U. Nahm and R. Mooney. Text Mining with Information Extraction. In *Proceedings of the AAAI 2002 Spring Symposium on Mining Answers from Texts and Knowledge Bases*, 2002.
5. Y. Yang and X. Liu. A re-examination of text categorization methods. In *Proceedings of the 22nd Annual ACM SIGIR Conference on Research and Development in Information Retrieval*, 42-49, 1999.

6. J. English, M. Hearst, R. Sinha, K. Swearingen, K.-P. Yee. Flexible Search and Navigation using Faceted Metadata. *Submitted for publication*, 2002.
7. AudioREVIEW.com
   http://www.audioreview.com/
8. A. McCallum and K. Nigam. A Comparison of Event Models for Naive Bayes Text Classification. In *AAAI-98 Workshop on Learning for Text Categorization*, 1998.
9. D. Lewis. Evaluating Text Categorization. In *Proceedings of the Speech and Natural Language Workshop*, 312-318, 1991.
10. R. Agrawal, H. Mannila, R. Srikant, H. Toivonen, and A. I. Verkamo. Fast discovery of association rules. In U. Fayyad *et al.*, editors, *Advances in Knowledge Discovery and Data Mining*, 307-328. AAAI Press, 1996.
11. C. Borgelt. Apriori.
    http://fuzzy.cs.uni-magdeburg.de/~borgelt/apriori/apriori.html
12. R. Feldman, M. Fresko, H. Hirsh, Y. Aumann, O. Liphstat, Y. Schler, M. Rajman. Knowledge Management: A Text Mining Approach. In *Proceedings of the 2nd International Conference on Practical Aspects of Knowledge Management (PAKM98)*, 29-30, 1998.
13. S. Loh, L. Wives, J. P. M. de Oliveira. Concept-based Knowledge Discovery in Texts Extracted from the Web. *SIGKDD Explorations*, 2(1): 29-39, 2000.
14. S. Basu, R. J. Mooney, K. V. Pasupuleti, and J. Ghosh. Evaluting the Novelty of Text-Mined Rules Using Lexical Knowledge. In *Proceedings of the Seventh ACM SIGKDD International Conference on Knowledge Discovery and Data Mining (KDD-2001)*, 233-238, 2001.
15. J. Han and Y. Fu. Discovery of Multiple-Level Association Rules from Large Databases. In *Proceedings of the 21st VLDB Conference*, 1995.

Challenges and Directions in Knowledge Asset Trading

Dimitris Apostolou[1], Gregory Mentzas[2], Andreas Abecker[3], Wolf-Christian Eickhoff[4], Wolfgang Maas[4], Panos Georgolios[2], Kostas Kafentzis[2], and Sophia Kyriakopoulou[1]

[1] Planet Ernst & Young, Apollon Tower, 64 Louise Riencourt Str., 11523 Athens, Greece
dapost@planetey.com

[2] Department of Electrical and Computer Engineering, National Technical University of Athens, 10682 Greece
{gmentzas, pgeorgol, kkafe}@softlab.ntua.gr

[3] DFKI GmbH, Erwin-Schroedinger-Strasse, D-67608 Kaiserslautern,
aabecker@dfki.uni-kl.de

[4] Institute for Media and Communications Management, University of St.Gallen, Blumenbergplatz 9, CH-9000 St.Gallen
wolf-christian.eickhoff@unisg.ch

Abstract. This paper addresses the area that is at the intersection of Knowledge Management and Electronic Commerce. This area refers to the exchange and trade of explicit and implicit knowledge at an inter-organisational level. Electronic knowledge marketplaces are currently emerging to address the opportunities and risks found in the purchase and selling of knowledge at the business-to-business (B2B) environment, the need for supporting long-lasting relationships of knowledge exchange and the requirement for facilitating virtual community contexts where knowledge seekers can find suitable knowledge providers and knowledge providers can advertise and sell their available knowledge. The paper describes the business challenges associated with the design of Internet-based knowledge marketplace. INKASS, a European IST project, has stimulated this work and has provided real-life verification on the arguments raised and on the positions adopted herein.

1 Introduction

Organisations are in the midst of two significant transformations. The first is the positioning of knowledge centre stage as a valuable resource and a driver of wealth creation. The second is the impact of the Internet, leading to the evolution of business into e-business. Until recently these developments were considered in isolation (Gartner, 2000). But there are connections, and these are becoming increasingly apparent. Knowledge is an asset that can be re-packaged into knowledge-based products and services. The Internet provides an effective vehicle for marketing and delivering knowledge. The new term knowledge trading captures the convergence of these two strands.

The first focus of many knowledge initiatives in organisations is one of identifying and sharing existing knowledge more widely: "if only we knew what we know". Better management of this knowledge is used to improve business processes, increase

D. Karagiannis and U. Reimer (Eds.): PAKM 2002, LNAI 2569, pp. 549-564, 2002.

productivity, and reduce new product development times. Beyond these initial benefits, organisations then turn to ways in which knowledge management can be used to improve their external performance. Much internally generated knowledge is applicable externally and can be converted into viable knowledge-based products and services. As in many types of business, network connectivity, and in particular extended connections offered by the Internet, offers many advantages for a knowledge business. It reduces transaction costs, extends market reach and allows round-the-clock trading.

Already the idea of knowledge trading is an exciting topic with manifold implications in both technological areas and business engineering. Early adopters of the knowledge trading idea are already working towards this goal, some of them dealing with some facets of the overall scenario, maybe unaware of the bigger picture behind, like researchers building Expert Finder Systems which are mainly thinking about significant technical solutions for the matchmaking between information needs and expert competency profiles, but paying less attention to other business-related topics around, like market mechanisms, revenue models, etc., which are required to run a business. Existing approaches:

- neither take into account the fact that knowledge is not just a book which can be described and retrieved with a simple keyword retrieval, but has manifold complex context and content features which determine its applicability and usefulness in a given situation;
- nor take into account that the real power of electronic marketplaces lies not in copying ways of working known from traditional business (like book selling with a catalogue and a simple, sequential seller-intermediary-buyer relationship), but in exploiting the strength of manifold synchronous and asynchronous communication and community-building means, which is of utmost importance when dealing which such a sensible good as knowledge;
- nor take into account that setting up a Web-portal is far from designing sustainable business which means thinking about customer relationship, advanced revenue models, appropriate pricing mechanisms for different kinds of knowledge, etc.

This paper aims to identify the core elements associated with knowledge trading. The paper is largely based on the research and early findings which have taken place at the framework of the European Community IST project [Intelligent Knowledge Asset Sharing and Trading (INKASS, 2000)] that is going to design and implement knowledge trading tools, and develop and validate business models for electronic knowledge marketplace. In the following sections we introduce the concept of a knowledge marketplace and we discuss its economics based on the overall economics of electronic marketplaces and the special characteristics that knowledge assets possess when considered as tradable products. We present how these ideas apply in the design of a knowledge marketplace for a consultancy and we conclude by providing key challenges and issues that need to be considered in similar initiatives.

2 The Emergence of Knowledge Marketplaces

A knowledge market is a place where knowledge is traded. Within organizations, the need for continuous access to knowledge has spurred the development of various knowledge initiatives. Davenport and Prusak (1998) suggest that knowledge movement within the organisations is powered by market forces similar to those that animate markets for other, more tangible goods. Like markets for goods and services, the knowledge market has buyers, sellers, and brokers, as well as market pricing and exchange mechanisms, even though money is rarely the form of payment. Outside the organization, similar knowledge exchange mechanisms exist in knowledge networks, whether these are professional societies or special interest groups in informal networks. Knowledge is also exchanged as part of everyday business conversation. The more aware individuals are of the value of the knowledge they possess, the more care they will take in giving it away freely outside of their close network or a formal trading relationship. The growing importance of knowledge indicates that the time is right for the creation of mechanisms to improve the flow of knowledge and to increase the efficiency of knowledge exchange and trading. The pervasiveness of the Internet has already started to shift existing knowledge markets into the Web. Examples include (Skyrme, 2001):

- **Intellectual property trading.** Copyright material, patents and designs are increasingly traded online, widening creator access to a broader market base. Trading sites can also serve as rights clearing houses.
- **Recruitment agencies.** Many types of recruitment, such as computer contracting, are fast shifting into online mode. The pool of job seekers and recruiters is larger. Computerized testing and profile-to-job matching helps both parties more quickly find mutually beneficial matches. Portal sites such as Carrermosaic.com give hints on writing CV's, links to recruitment fairs etc.
- **Management consultancies.** Their business is knowledge, but they are increasingly packaging it, both for internal use (on their intranets and knowledge bases) and externally, such as Arthur Andersen's Global Best Practices and Ernst & Young's Ernie.
- **Research companies.** Market and industry researchers, such as Nielsen and The Welding Institute now deliver much of their material over the Web or transfer it to clients' intranets.

Other developments are also influencing the creation of online knowledge markets. One is the growth of the Internet as a vehicle for e-commerce and knowledge exchange. Many of the commerce models of e-marketplaces, such as auctions, can be adapted to the marketing of knowledge. Business–to–business exchanges, in particular, offer significant potential for increasing the efficiency of buying and selling. The popularity of online communities demonstrates the high interest in seeking and sharing knowledge with like-minded people. Here the same factors that apply in internal knowledge markets-reciprocity, repute and altruism (Prusak and Davenport, 1998)-are also important. But many knowledgeable people who are not active in these communities may be encouraged to do so, too, if they were compensated financially for their time and expertise.

Apart from buyers and sellers, markets need a market-making mechanism to work. As a minimum an online website will need facilities to capture and process details of needs and offers. It may add intelligence that includes matchmaking capabilities and a set of business rules. These rules may filter out specific matches, based on personal preferences of buyer and seller, or they may include rules for dynamic pricing to maximize revenues. If the market is a full trading hub, order processing and account management facilities will be needed. They may even host various delivery mechanisms, including online knowledge repositories and communities. In return for providing these facilities, the market maker will seek revenues from one or more sources, such as commissions from buyers and/or sellers, advertisers, sponsors, or from affiliate fees for successful referrals to complementary websites.

3 The Economics of E-knowledge Marketplaces

3.1 The Economics of E-marketplaces

Electronic marketplaces can be said to represent a new wave in the e-commerce propagation and extending the Business and Consumer combinations (B2C, C2B and C2C) aiming primarily at the Business-to-Business (B2B) area. E-marketplaces can be defined as interactive business communities providing a central market space where multiple buyers and suppliers can engage in e-commerce and/or other e-business activities (Bruun et. al., 2002). They present structures for commercial exchange, consolidating supply bases and creating sales channels. Their primary aim is to increase market efficiency by tightening and automating the relationship between supplier and buyer. Existing e-marketplaces allow participants to access various mechanisms to buy and sell almost anything, from services to direct materials.

The products and services offered on e-marketplaces may either be industry-specific or horizontal across many applications. A number of classification schemata exist in the literature for e-marketplaces (Kaplan and Sawhney, 2000), (Dou and Chou, 2002), (BuyIT, 2002). Overall we may distinguish between three primary e-marketplace models:

- **Direct or Private B2B e-marketplaces.** These are one-to-many models that reflect a company developing their own e-marketplace to support their own customers and suppliers.
- **Coalitions or consortium e-marketplaces.** These models reflect a many-to-many model in which major industry players come together to aggregate their buy-side and supplier-side leverage to increase operational efficiencies and leverage buying power around an industry supply chain.
- **Independent e-marketplaces.** This is a many-to-many model, typically hosted by a neutral intermediary providing Net Market Maker services, such as aggregation, transaction services to participants.

These three types of e-marketplaces vary in different characteristics, such as member structure, value, business model, or financing and business impact (Table 1).

Table 1. Characteristics of e-Marketplaces (adopted from BuyIT, 2002)

	Independent	Coalitions/ Consortium	Direct
Member Structure	Many-to-many Open membership	Few-to-Many Anchored by a number of companies Open membership on the "many" side	One-to-Few/Many Anchored by sponsoring company
Value	Market efficiency Liquidity Transparency Shared benefits	Market efficiency Liquidity Transparency Shared benefits	Deep collaboration Value chain optimisation Speed and flexibility Privacy and control Retention of all benefits Customer satisfaction Service/process excellence
Business Model	Revenue based on transaction %, services, membership, advertising, etc.	Revenue based on transaction %, services, membership, advertising, etc.	Revenue based on benefit sharing, margin sharing, speed of innovation, service fees
Financing	Net Market Maker	Core members	Anchor members
Business Impact	Dis-intermediation, Re-intermediation	Dis-intermediation, Re-intermediation	Expand competitive advantage Control value chain

3.2 The Economics of Knowledge

The positioning of knowledge assets centre stage in B2B exchanges is in line with the recent trend in the strategic management that positions knowledge as the primary resource (Drucker, 1994), that is the primary assumption in the Knowledge-Based-View of the firm (Eisenhardt and Santos, 2001). The specific knowledge base, the ability to make use of the available knowledge determines the competitiveness of organisations in the emerging knowledge society (Franke, 2000).

Knowledge assets are different from other firm resources; see e.g. Glazer (1991) and Day and Wendler (1998). They are not easily divisible or appropriable. This means that the same information and knowledge can be used by different economic entities at the same time. Moreover, knowledge assets are not inherently scarce (although they are often time-sensitive). This implies that they are not depleatable.

Knowledge assets are essentially regenerative. This means that new relevant knowledge may emerge from a knowledge-intensive business process as additional output besides products and services. They may not exhibit decreasing returns to use, but will often increase in value the more they are used. This characteristic is of crucial importance for senior management; see e.g. den Hartigh and Langerak (2001). Most assets are subject to diminishing returns, but not knowledge. The bulk of the fixed cost in knowledge products usually lies in creation rather than in manufacturing or distribution. Once knowledge has been created, the initial development cost can be spread across rising volumes.

Network effects can emerge as knowledge assets are used by more and more people. These knowledge-users can simultaneously benefit from knowledge and increase its value as they add to, adapt, and enrich the knowledge base. In traditional industrial economics, assets decline in value as more people use them. By contrast, knowledge assets can grow in value, as they become a standard on which others can build.

Finding appropriate prices for knowledge assets is a challenging task (O'Hara and Shadbolt, 2001). As knowledge assets have an intangible character, there are certain specialities for the price-finding which are derived from its general characteristics:

- Because of the lack of visible capability characteristics, the price can be viewed as an indirect criterion for rating the quality of the knowledge asset.
- A direct comparison of prices is usually difficult without actual utilization of the knowledge asset.
- Due to the intangible character of the knowledge asset it is difficult to find out in advance about the customers' willingness to pay a certain price for an asset.

In the following we provide an overview of the factors that set value on knowledge, when considering knowledge assets as tradable goods.

Context of knowledge

One central problem lies in the fact that knowledge is by definition highly context-dependent, whereas all explicit representations (at the seller side) will necessarily de-contextualise it to some extent. Furthermore, in an electronic marketplace, such representations should also express aspects like knowledge quality and knowledge actuality, which can hardly be dealt with in a generally applicable manner, but must be considered separately for different types of knowledge products and knowledge requests. Knowledge has manifold complex context and content features, which determine its applicability and usefulness in a given situation.

Affiliation and branding

Affiliation is also a significant factor to be considered when setting a price on knowledge. Knowledge purchases are immensely affected by the degree of affiliation between the buyer and the seller. Because of the criticality, sensitivity and high customisation of knowledge products and services, the need for trust and established relationships increase proportionally. Branding plays also a significant role, because it associates a purchase with a certain level of quality of service, guarantee and after-sales support.

Refined and customised knowledge

The value of knowledge increases as it is refined, improved and formatted ready to be used. Users will value most knowledge that is relevant to them and provided ready to be used by them. Generalised knowledge will be priced toward the lower end of the scale, while customised knowledge on a critical purchasing decision, for example, that combines the latest data with analysis from experts will command a higher value.

Timing of knowledge

Timing is also an important ingredient of the value of a knowledge offering: knowledge is most valuable at the exact moment that is needed for critical business requirements. Knowledge is also valued by the timing that it is received in advance of the competition. As knowledge product and services are offered on the marketplace, the value of these services will be determined by the timeliness and impact of this knowledge on the person purchasing this knowledge.

Tacit knowledge

A powerful combination is that of tacit and explicit knowledge. While codified generic knowledge may have relatively low value, the addition of human judgment and experience can considerably enhance value. Capturing the information is the first step, followed by rationalizing the data so that it can be shared by appropriate people. It is the expert nevertheless that can add his/her experience and can assist in putting knowledge in context or solving a particular problem.

Aggregated knowledge

Aggregated knowledge is often worth more than the sum of the parts (Skyrme, 2001). The buyer will benefit from one-stop-shop, because it reduces the time and effort needed to collect information form multiple sources. Expertly collated and edited information can eliminate overlaps while highlighting contrasts. The richness and depth in one place aids understanding and offers new insights.

Quality of knowledge

The quality of knowledge products can be related to different criteria, like accuracy, reliability, presentation, timeliness, completeness, highlighting of main issues, relevancy and usable format (Rolph and Bartram 1994). In general there are two different perspectives to consider when talking about quality of information: on the one hand an individual or a company creates knowledge-based products and on the other hand they are distributed on a marketplace to other individuals or organisations. This leads to a constructivist and a receptive view on the quality of the product. For both views it is necessary to develop methods that ensure that only high-quality products are used in problem solving processes (Nohr and Roos, 2001).

Constructivist Quality	The constructivist quality includes all measures that are taken to ensure quality assurance during the production and distribution processes of knowledge products. Thereby attention is paid to the quality of the process, besides of the quality of the result
Receptive Quality	The receptive quality refers to measures concerning the evaluation and rating of external products. It is most commonly related to the sources of information or the creator, because the knowledge asset itself is not available for direct evaluation.

Compared to other products, knowledge products have the special characteristic that they cannot be previewed and tested before the purchase. Though the quality can generally not completely be experienced beforehand. Nevertheless, there need to be some indicators to assess it in advance. Concerning the receptive quality there are five general possibilities to improve customer's trust for the product: (1) Trust in the source of knowledge due to earlier experiences; (2) Quality assessment by trusted-third parties; (3) Quality assessment by the users or customers; (4) Trial versions; (5) Description by Meta-Information.

3.3 The Right Model for Knowledge Marketplaces

Evans and Wurster (2000) group potential benefits of e-marketplaces in three "dimensions of advantage": (i) reach, which means how many customers a business can connect with and how many products it can offer to those customers; (ii) richness, is the depth and detail of information that the business can give the customer, as well as the depth and detail of information; and (iii) affiliation with participants, especially buyers. By affiliating with customer a net market maker can make money by providing value–added services such as advice.

The traditional economics of information suggest that rich information requires proximity and dedicated channels, imposing thereby limits on the reach potential of the same information. Evans and Wurster (2000) suggest that our economy is on the verge of a new era characterised by the gradual removal of the trade-off between the *richness* and the *reach* of information. The emergence of independent e-marketplaces is a proof of the aforementioned analysis. Independent marketplaces have emerged with the objective to capitalise on the increased reach capability of the Internet, coupled with sophisticated Information Technology applications able to manage and process rich information.

Nevertheless many analysts (Bruun, et.al., 2002); (Gartner, 2001); (Davenport et. al. 2001) believe that independent e-marketplaces have had difficulty achieving both high levels of reach and richness, even in non knowledge-intensive sectors. This market reality combined with the special characteristics of knowledge assets as tradable products render the direct or private marketplace type as the prominent one, because it offers the: (a) required deep collaboration between buyer and seller; (b) speed and flexibility required for timely provision of critical, sensitive knowledge products; (c) privacy and control needed to create trusted relationships; and (d) quality of service that is a prerequisite for customer satisfaction.

4 The INKASS Project Approach

The INKASS project tries to overcome some of these challenges by spending due diligence to both technological and methodological developments, investigating issues like creation of trust and customer satisfaction.

Figure 1 gives an overview of the functional architecture to be developed. For building such a platform and validating it in realistic case studies, the INKASS approach is guided by the following principles:

- *Integrate e-commerce with knowledge management software technology*: The decision the INKASS consortium has taken is to build upon Intershop's *Enfinity*, which is a backbone E-Commerce platform, and Empolis' *Orenge*, which is an E-Commerce middleware solution for intelligent retrieval and assistance.
- At the technological side, *focus on the critical questions which distinguish knowledge trading* from other E-Commerce areas; we see crucial points (i) in a powerful, knowledge-based matchmaking mechanism comparing offers and demand; (ii) in flexible, intuitive interfaces and intelligent assistance helping users to express their demands and interactively search for appropriate offers; and (iii) in elaborated networking and community-building facilities to exploit the power of customer groups exchanging and further developing knowledge in direct communications, assessing the value of products, etc.
- At the operational side, focus on *how to cost-effectively use the platform for the novel problem of trading knowledge*. In order to do this, at least the following elements must be worked out:
  - The very *basic ontological foundations* for the utilization of E-Commerce systems for knowledge trading, plus *cost-effective methods for up-front knowledge engineering*.

– An overall system design (eg. *business engineering*) and configuration of existing mechanisms (eg. different pricing mechanisms) which take into account the particularities of knowledge trading.
– Appropriate *business models, roles, processes, and revenue models* for installing and running knowledge trading platforms.

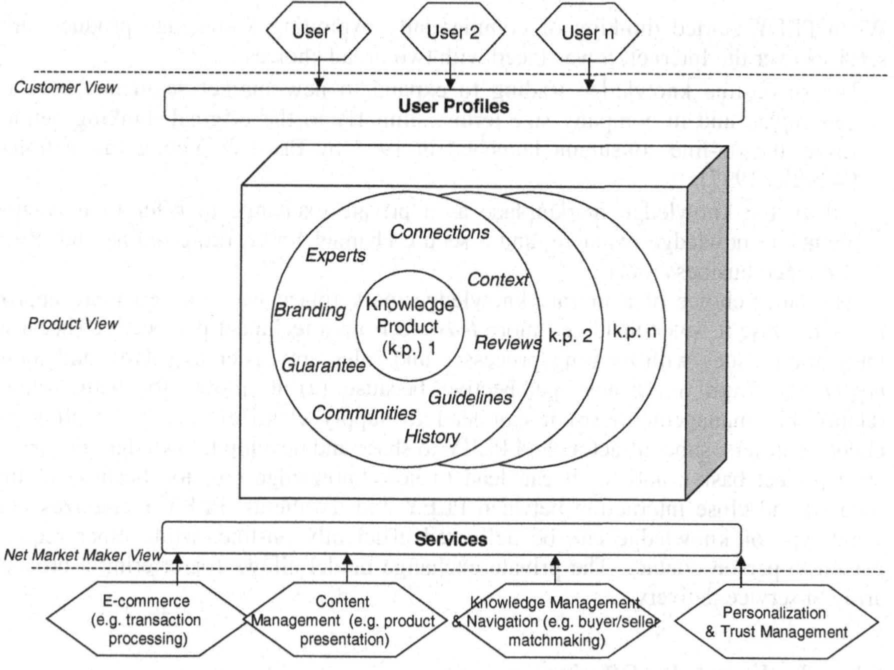

Fig. 1. The INKASS Functional Architecture for Knowledge Trading

INKASS will pilot knowledge trading in the *Business Management and Engineering areas*, with the participation of three knowledge-intensive organisations: The Welding Institute (a research and technology organisation), Planet Ernst & Young (a consultancy), and the Athens Chamber of Commerce and Industry.

5 Designing a Knowledge Marketplace for a Consultancy

Planet Ernst & Young (PLEY) is a multinational consulting firm providing management and engineering consulting services in southeast Europe[1]. PLEY provides a wide spectrum of consulting services mainly to sizable private and public sector organisations. PLEY's consulting practice has focused on developing and expanding their relationship with key large organizations in the region. There is plenty of opportunity within this customer-base and PLEY's full-service capabilities

[1] The company was formed following the merger of PLANET S. A. and the Southeast Europe Management Consulting network of Ernst & Young.

to enable them to continually meet the needs of this type of client. Despite the recent slow down in the management consulting services at the global level, PLEY has seen a growth of 20% per year over the past five years.

5.1 Strategic Orientation

When PLEY started thinking of commercially exploiting knowledge products and services over the Internet, it was faced with two broad choices:

- Utilize on-line knowledge trading to expand to new market segments, both in geographic and in company size terms, similarly to the original thinking behind Ernie, the on-line consultant launched in 1997 by Ernst & Young International (Whittle, 1997).
- Utilize the knowledge marketplace as a private exchange to offer to its major clients a knowledge resource, and a secure channel for working online and using dedicated business tools.

The latter choice of a private knowledge marketplace was deemed more appropriate because it was considered more *feasible* from a technical perspective (because integration issues with existing processes and roles are easier to solve), and more *meaningful* from a business perspective because (a) it allows for better client relationship management; (b) it can lead to supply chain efficiency by allowing clients, partners, subcontractors and PLEY to share and develop knowledge (primarily on a project basis); and (c) it can lead to new knowledge creation because of the focused and close interaction between PLEY and its clients. PLEY recognizes that some type of knowledge can be delivered efficiently on-line, while other require person-to-person contact. The private exchange model allows for offering a broader array of service delivery.

5.2 The Knowledge Offerings

The knowledge offerings that PLEY is putting on-line cover the core services (Strategy and Policy Development, Programme and Change Management, Process Improvement, Knowledge Management, Financial Management, Human Resources Management, Supply Chain Management, Marketing & Communications, Technology and IT Consulting) as these are provided to the major industries (Financial Institutions, Comm. Media & Entertainment, Commerce and Tourism, Transport, Energy and Utilities, Government and Health Care).

Each service is represented by a collection of information that include: methodologies, assessment or analysis tools, expert profiles, links to related documents and sources (internal/external), case studies and related training material. This core package is accompanied by metadata that aim to assist the user in finding and customizing content. These include: meta-information (taxonomical data, summaries, abstracts), historical data (identity, modification history), validation data (performed by internal experts), as well as marketing and pricing data.

Contextualisation of knowledge is accomplished by two mechanisms. *First*, content is filtered according to the user profile (e.g. if the user is working for a specific industry, then only relevant segments that have been classified accordingly are represented). *Second*, by offering a range of "self-service" tools (such as methodological components) that can help the user put prior knowledge in context. Nevertheless, irreplaceable human intelligence is accounted for by providing the option of providing expert advice, as part of the service offering.

5.3 The Trading Mechanisms

The traditional subscription scheme is retained mainly to serve the firm's major clients, but additional pricing mechanisms, appropriate for the one-to-many trading model, are considered. These include:

- Pay-per-document, to allow ad hoc users to buy just the items they need. The document-based knowledge product may be sold (a) at a fixed price or/and (b) by biding that includes the setting up of an initial asking price, and controlling the price fluctuation based on the number of sales and the inactive time intervals.
- Negotiation subsystem, to allow users to develop a request for the purchase of more complex products and to reach to an agreement for provision of a knowledge product (that perhaps involves buying expert consulting time). If a buyer cannot find the exact items or at the price they wish to pay, they may initiate a Request for Quote (RFQ). In composing the details of the RFQ, the buyer can elect to allow certain fields within the description of the product to be able to be modified by the seller. The RFQ can be used to negotiate a long-term contract, in which the prices, qualities and dates are to be agreed between the two parties.

5.4 Operational Considerations

In addition to the external market challenges facing PLEY there are significant internal issues that need to be addressed. There is a need to determine how to make the connection from the user to the expert. To this end the existing internal knowledge management infrastructure is exploited: Internal Knowledge Managers, who are already responsible for managing and updating knowledge at the service level, are also assigned the additional responsibility to manage the content that is available externally and to make sure that the user of the system succeeds in contacting the appropriate expert.

The quality of the knowledge offerings on the marketplace is of critical importance. The ways these offerings are used by the firm's clients can have a significant impact on the business, and care must be taken to ensure knowledge is not being misused. Quality is ensured by the experience and expertise of the Knowledge Providers. Additionally there are plans for receiving direct feedback from customers to monitor client satisfaction. The "closed group" nature of the marketplace allows for consultants to have a close relationship with the clients and to trigger feedback. Furthermore it allows for ensuring that clients are using the system properly and understand how to take advantage of its features.

6 Directions for Designing Knowledge Marketplaces

The personal nature of much knowledge means that human and social factors loom large in many areas of trading and exchanging knowledge. When professionals and managers seek advice, their first port of call is usually someone in their knowledge network, for example a work colleague or a peer in another organization. If their knowledge needs are greater or not easily obtained through their network, they tend to go first to people and suppliers they already know and trust. Established relationships count for a lot. Much existing buying of knowledge, especially that which is more people-based, takes place through established supply chains.

Traditional marketplaces on the contrary are more dynamic. They bring together buyers and sellers who do not necessarily know of each other. They allow participants to compare what's on offer and learn more about what products and services are available. They engender competition and innovation. They also foster cooperation in that suppliers get together to address common concerns. In the real world, trade exhibitions and competitive tendering for services are situations that show some of these characteristics. Conferences are other occasions where professionals can top up their knowledge for a fee. Between such events, professional workers seeking knowledge have to rely on their network or other means, which do not necessarily get them the best knowledge at the keenest price.

The concept of interoperable knowledge hubs evolved as a trade-off, a compromise between the prominent traditional model of conducting knowledge business in closed, private networks, such as the PLEY case, and the market efficiency, liquidity and transparency of broad, open, public networks. During analysis of the knowledge requirements of the INKASS pilot users and their business partners, an environment that would enable their business partners to have easy and real-time access to up to date information and custom-made solutions to their inquiries was acknowledged as a significant advantage. The business partners could be kept aware of the latest knowledge in their domain, gain a rich representation and good understanding of knowledge products on offer, query about costs and even decide to consult an expert on-line. Furthermore, the possibility to reconstruct and contextualise the knowledge offering taking into account the specific needs of the client was deemed essential.

However, most business partners confessed that, in the usual case, a certain knowledge provider, which they mainly co-operate with, does not have all the expertise required to address their needs. These needs may go beyond the specialist capabilities of any single business partner, or in fact, any private knowledge marketplace. To cater to broader knowledge requirements, marketplaces may link to each other creating networks based on the exchange and trading of knowledge. Knowledge networks can be formed in two general ways:

- through an infomediary business body that will manage the information flow across the marketplaces (resembling the centralised or star network model), or
- through a "knowledge hub", that connects one marketplace with one or more other marketplaces (resembling the distributed or hub network model).

Either model results in linking effectively and extending the knowledge offerings without giving up "control" of the buyer. The ability of marketplaces to interoperate extends the idea of liquidity and network effect by joining more buyers with more suppliers, but it does not sacrifice the ability of each knowledge marketplace to be highly specific to the supply-chain node or target buyer group it serves.

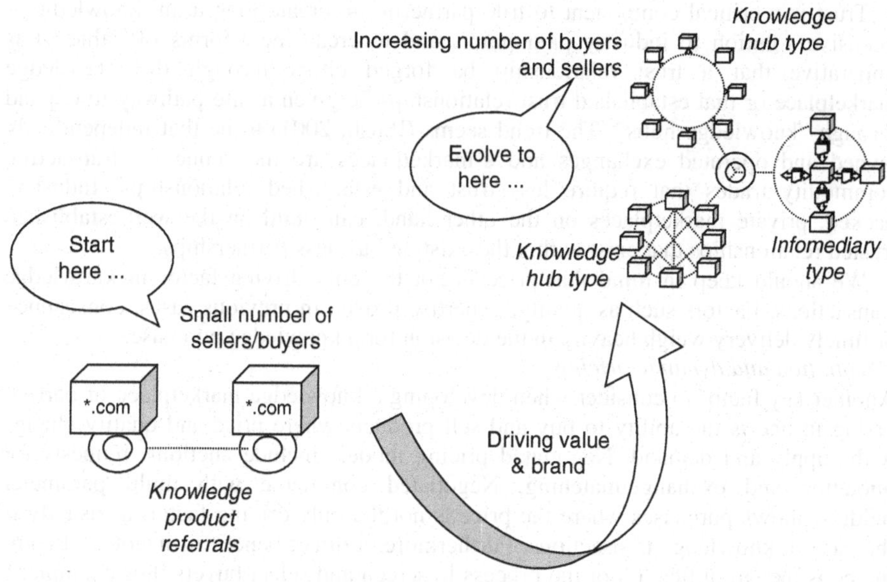

Fig. 2. Connected knowledge marketplaces

Independently of which model is followed, for effectively exploiting the network effect for conducting knowledge exchanges our analysis shows that interaction must be based on value added service, relationships must be increasingly based on trust, negotiation skills will become paramount, and there must be ample security, standards and community cohesiveness.

Value based services

The acceptance and success of knowledge marketplaces is dependent on the development and delivery of true value-added services that are offered in both digital and physical delivery systems through the evolution of trusted trading communities. The value offered by the knowledge marketplace should be greater than the traditional means of conducting the business process. We should not expect that selling knowledge assets can only be done in the digital domain, by offering only explicit knowledge. The knowledge offering should only have a tacit dimension; careful planning is needed to accommodate the selling of tacit knowledge, in terms of offering expert advice through physical (e.g. selling consulting time) or virtual (e.g. through on-line collaboration) channels.

Trusted relationships

As the critical dependency of highly customer-specific knowledge product and services increases, the need for trust and established relationships increases proportionally. For example if a company is planning to purchase some standard maintenance products, then it may be willing to try some suppliers that it has never used before. However, if a company needs expert advice on a safety-critical metal joining application that feeds the production of an aviation component, it would be most likely to rely more on trusted relationships with established knowledge providers.

Trust is a critical component to true partnering to create long-term, knowledge – intensive solution to industry pain points and to create new forms of value. It is imperative that a trust relationship be forged either through the knowledge marketplace or that established trust relationships be given a safe pathway to expand through "knowledge hubs". The trend seems (Raish, 2001) to be that independently owned and operated exchanges and e-marketplaces are the venue for transacting commodity trades that require less trust and established relationships. Industry-backed, private marketplaces on the other hand, can build on the well-established trusted relationships that exist within the existing business partnerships.

We should keep in mind that price is not the only driving factor in knowledge transactions. Factors such as quality, expertise proven in previous cases, consistency or timely delivery weigh heavily in the decision for a knowledge purchase.

Negotiation and dynamic pricing

Another key factor to consider when developing a knowledge marketplace or participating in one is the ability to buy and sell products where price and quality change with supply and demand. Negotiated pricing models include auctions, requests for quotation and exchange/matching. Negotiated commerce with multi parameter bidding allows purchases where the price is not the only driving factor, as usually is the case in knowledge transactions. Furthermore, a direct benefit of negotiated commerce is the simplification of the process to screen and select buyers. For example, a company needs a feasibility study for opening a new branch within two days. Since the company does not have the time to call each of the potential organisations that can provide this service, and does not want to award the contract to the lowest bidder automatically, a multistage, multi-parameter negotiation format may be used for the selection process. At any point, the purchaser or seller can accept, reject, or counter an offer. In the end, the negotiation process allows companies to transfer sophisticated, knowledge-intensive business transactions to the Internet.

Community cohesiveness

For knowledge marketplaces to foster a greater level of buyer loyalty and community cohesiveness they should combine the reach of the Internet with the flexibility to adapt to the changing nature of specific market needs. The real power of electronic marketplaces lies not in copying ways of working known from traditional business, but in exploiting the strength of manifold synchronous and asynchronous communication and community-building means, which is of utmost importance when dealing which such a sensible good as knowledge.

Standards

HTTP servers and XML enhanced Web content are proving effective (Ontology.org, 2002) as the foundation for small groups of co-operating commerce agents operating over the Internet. However, doubts remain whether these representations will scale to support interoperability between large, loosely coupled trading groups of buyers, sellers, brokers, aggregators and integrators, in scenarios where the full potential of the global reach of the Internet can be realised. Initiatives are already underway to agree standard XML modeling within vertical industries or markets in initiatives such as RosettaNet, CommerceNet's eCo and OASIS' ebXML.org.

7 Conclusions

Within organizations, the need for continuous access to knowledge has spurred the development of various knowledge initiatives. The pervasiveness of the Internet has already started to shift existing knowledge markets into cyberspace, with examples including Intellectual property trading, copyright material, patents and designs traded online, management consultancies packaging knowledge both for internal and external use and research companies deliver much of their material over the Web. Knowledge trading refers to the trade of explicit and implicit knowledge for specific needs at an inter-organisational level. It addresses the opportunities and risks found in the purchase and selling of knowledge at the business-to-business (B2B) environment, the need for supporting long-lasting relationships of knowledge exchange and the requirement for facilitating digital community contexts where knowledge seekers can find suitable knowledge providers and knowledge providers can advertise and sell their available knowledge.

The real challenges of knowledge marketplaces lie in best exploiting the economics of knowledge. Knowledge exchanges require timeliness, trusted relationships, ability to adopt to the customer needs, to name a few. Our findings provide evidence that the most prominent model for knowledge marketplace appears to be the private one, in which organisations exploit their business partners and clients to offer highly targeted knowledge through established relations. This would potentially form a polarization between the private marketplace "clubs" and the neutral, independent knowledge marketplaces, which would be left to serve the more fragmented industry players. However, even companies that choose to build their own private knowledge marketplace will want to be connected to other knowledge networks in order to gain access to others' pools of knowledge as well as their own. Regardless of which marketplace model will prevail, knowledge marketplaces offer new means for knowledge access, delivery and application.

References

Aberdeen Group (2000) White Paper - The e-Business Marketplace: The Future of Competition. April 2000.

Bruun, P.; M. Jensen; and J. Skovgaard (2002) e-Marketplaces: Crafting a Winning Strategy, European Management Journal, article in press.

Burke, R. (1999) Integrating Knowledge-Based and Collaborative-Filtering Recommender Systems. In: AAAI-99 Workshop on Artificial Intelligence for Electronic Commerce, Orlando Florida 1999.

BuyIT (2002) e-Business Models and how they apply to you, A BuyIT Best Practice Guideline, issued by the BuyIT Best Practice Network, January 2002.

Davenport, T. and L. Prusak (1998) Working Knowledge: How Organisations Manage What They Know, Harvard Business School Press, 1998.

Davenport, T; J. Brooks; and S. Cantrell (2001) Do independent e-markets have a future? Accenture Institute for Strategic Change.

Day, Jonathan and Jim Wendler (1998) The New Economics Of Organisation, The Mckinsey Quarterly, 1998, NUMBER 1 19.

den Hartigh, E. and F. Langerak (2001) "Managing Increasing Returns", European Management Journal Vol. 19, No. 4, pp. 370–378, 2001.

Dou, W. and D. Chou (2002) A Structural Analysis of Business-to-business Digital Markets, Industrial Marketing Management, 31 (2002), 165-176.

Drucker, P. (1994) Knowledge Work and Knowledge Society: The Social Transformations of this Century. Transcript of the Edw in L. Godkin Lecture delivered at Harvard University's John F. Kennedy School of Government

Drucker, P. (1997) The Future that has Already Happened, Harvard Business Review, September-October 1997.

Eisenhardt, K. M., Santos F. M. (2001) Knowledge-Based View: A New Theory of Strategy? in Pettigrew, A., Thomas, H., Whittington, R. (Eds.), Handbook of Strategy and Management, Sage Publications.

Evans, P., and T. S. Wurster (2000) Getting Real About Virtual Commerce, Harvard Business Review, Aug 1, 2000

Franke, U. (2000) The Knowledge-Based View (KBV) of the Virtual Web, the Virtual Corporation, and the Net Broker, in Y. Malhotra (ed.) Knowledge Management and Virtual Orgsanisations, Idea Group Publishing, 2000.

Gartner Group (2000) Strategic Planning, SPA-09-4188, Research Note, 8 October 2000.

Glazer, R. (1991) Marketing in an information-intensive environment: strategic implications of knowledge as an asset. Journal of Marketing 55(October), 1–19.

INKASS (2000) The INKASS Project Web Site, www.incass.com (1 August 2002)

Kaplan, S. and M. Sawhney (2000) E-hubs: The New B2B Marketplaces, Harvard Business Review, May-June 2000.

McGuiness, D.L. (1999) Ontologies for Electronic Commerce. In: AAAI-99 Workshop on Artificial Intelligence for Electronic Commerce, Orlando Florida 1999.

Nohr, Holger; Roos, Alexander W. (2001) Informationsqualität als Instrument des Wissensmanagements. In: Wissensmanagement 3 (2001) 2, S. 24-27

Ontology.org (2002) The need for shared ontology, white paper, www.ontology.org (1 August 2002)

O'Hara, K., Nigel R. Shadbolt (2001) Issues for an Ontology for Knowledge Valuation. In Proceedings of the IJCAI'01 Workshop on E-Business and the Intelligent Web, Seattle, WA, USA, August 2001.

Raisch, W. D. (2001) 'The E-Marketplace Strategies for Success in B2B eCommerce', McGraw-Hill.

Rolph, Paul; Bartram, Peter (1994) The Information Agenda: Harnessing Relevant Information in a Changing Business Environment. London: Management Books 2000, 1994

Skyrme, D. J. (2001) "Capitalizing on Knowledge: From e-business to k-business", Butterworth-Heinemann, London.

Whittle, R. (1997) The Evolution of Ernie – The online Business Consultant, Marshall School of Business, University of Southern California

A Methodological Basis for Bringing Knowledge Management to Real-World Environments

Mark Hefke and Ralf Trunko

FZI Research Center for Information Technologies at the
University of Karlsruhe
D-76131 Karlsruhe, Germany
{hefke, trunko}@fzi.de
http://www.fzi.de

Abstract. This paper describes our ongoing work on developing a holistic approach for the introduction and improvement of KM in an organization. The described methodology does not focus on a specific area but considers all layers of an organization, the organizational, the process and the technology layer. The overall approach will consist of two main components: a KM Measures Repository and a KM Maturity Model. The KM Measures Repository contains best practice measures for each layer. The KM Maturity Model allows an organization to describe itself. Both components will be made "machine executable" and included in a self assessment tool which uses different KM technologies.

1 Introduction

From our viewpoint companies consist of three different layers: the technological, the process and the organizational layer (see Fig. 1.). These layers interact with each other and should not be regarded isolated. The introduction and use of KM can significantly support all three layers but should also not be regarded isolated for one specific layer. If you use KM in one of these layers it has impacts on the other ones. Unfortunately, KM is often regarded as a purely technical discipline. Thus, in most of the cases organizations keep only an eye on the technology layer when introducing KM. Furthermore, the introduction of KM into a company should consider already existing structures, processes and technical infrastructures.

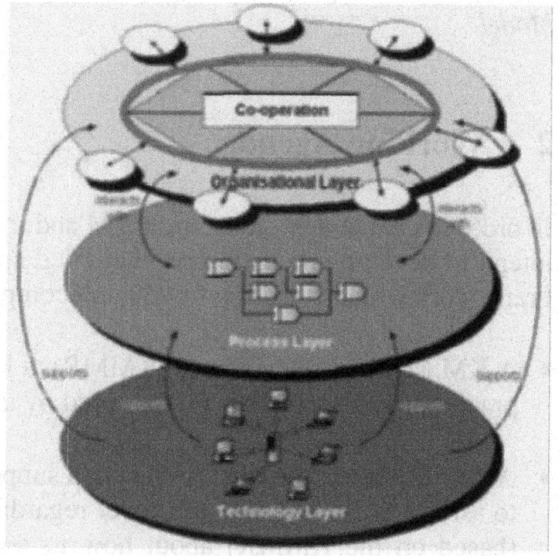

Fig. 1. Organisation Layers

D. Karagiannis and U. Reimer (Eds.): PAKM 2002, LNAI 2569, pp. 565-570, 2002.

Nowadays, most companies are aware of the importance of KM for their daily business. But to be aware of something is very different from introducing and using it. The introduction and maintenance of a KM solution is not easy and has to overcome several barriers. It is very important to have a strategy which shows you the way how to proceed. Many KM projects fail because of an insufficient know how about conceptions for KM strategies. To introduce and use KM it is necessary to know where you are and how to improve your position [1].
KM is no static concept. It should "live" with the company, i.e. it should permanently be adjusted to the company requirements and structure. Regarding already implemented KM solutions companies often do not know how to improve, advance or adjust their solutions. Our holistic and integrated approach will cover the above mentioned problem fields by supporting companies to assess their KM maturity level and giving recommendations how to reach a higher level.

In this paper we will discuss a holistic approach for the development of a methodological framework supporting organisations in improving their organisational and technological infrastructure by pointing out to them next generation KM technologies and their successful implementation, by providing necessary organisational strategies in this regard and by identifying and optimising their knowledge-intensive processes.

The content of this paper is structured as follows: The *working agenda* describes the necessary preliminary work before starting the development of the Methodological Framework. In this section we particularly focus on the Requirements and State-of-the-Art Analysis by using the three different Organisation layers in order to receive best practice cases for the KM Measures Repository. After that we illustrate the structure and components of the *KM Measures Repository* as well as the *KM Maturity Model.*

2 Working Agenda

In order to enable next-generation KM and to solve the above mentioned problems we intend to develop a holistic and integrated approach in the form of a Methodological Framework which consists of two main components:

- A KM Measures Repository (KMMR), a knowledge base, which contains KM best practices. The repository is structured by using Semantic Web technologies.

- A KM Maturity Model (K3M) which supports a company to describe itself in order to assess its current maturity level regarding KM and to receive recommendations (based on the KMMR) about how to reach a higher maturity level. The K3M-Model will be synchronized with the KMMR by "feeding" it with successful new KM best practices.

Before the development of the Methodological Framework we have to analyse successful completed as well as running KM projects regarding their used approaches and their achieved concrete results. This will be done by interviewing project catalysts, selected officials and employees in the organisations and analysing their business processes, organisational structure and used technologies concerning KM. Then we have to assess the state of the art of existing KM technologies and products as well as important KM standardization initiatives and their strengths and weaknesses. We will also collect show cases and experiences which include lessons learned and best practices of KM projects in the form of case studies, surveys, qualitative studies and statistical studies. The fourth input stream consists of the collection and description of user requirements concerning the development and practical use of KM solutions.

The collected data will be analysed considering the three different company layers and their connections among each other.

In the *organizational layer* the data will be analysed with regard to best practice business rules and strategies for the successful introduction and maintenance of KM solutions in a company, the common understanding of the role of KM for the daily business, the connections to the other layers concerning KM aspects etc.

In the *process layer* metrics for the measurement and evaluation of knowledge-intensive business processes with regard to quality, time, flexibility, reusability and costs have to be developed in order to compare existing projects/show cases [2]. Then the knowledge-intensive business processes and also the information about the processes themselves have to be analysed and benchmarked with regard to the above mentioned metrics. After that the best practice knowledge-intensive business processes will be selected. The next step will be to analyse the requirements and needs for the technical support of these knowledge-intensive processes with modern KM technologies or a combination of these technologies with existing workflow management systems.

In the *technology layer* the state-of-the-art KM technologies, products and standards will be analysed in order to identify the enabling KM technologies. The next step will be to identify possible integration capabilities between these core enabling technologies and between them and other technologies already used (e.g. integration of workflow management systems into a KM platform) as well as the capabilities of KM technologies to support the other layers.

The results of these analyses will flow into the development of the self-assessment tool consisting of the KM Measures Repository and the KM Maturity Model which will be described in the following. Fig.2 gives an overview about our plans for developing and setting-up the methodological framework, in particular the interaction of the main components of the framework as well as the input and output streams. The right side illustrates the implementation phases starting with the *requirements and state-of-the-art phase* and ending with the *validation phase*. The main components of the architecture will be described detailed in the following.

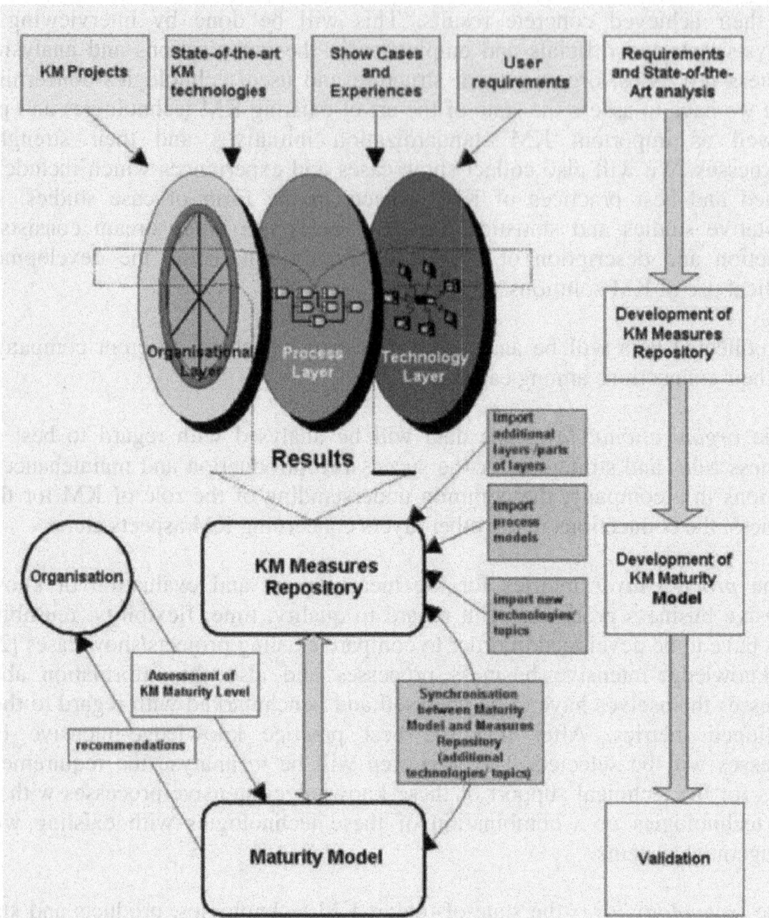

Fig. 2. Methodological Framework

3 KM Measures Repository

The analysed input streams will be combined to best practice cases in terms of a successful KM approach. The reasonable combination of enabling technologies, knowledge-intensive business processes, organisational requirements and KM relevant topics to these above-named best practice cases will be supported by using Knowledge Discovery methods.
After received the best practice cases they are once more classified into categories (e.g. implementation costs, implementation time, etc.) and finally transformed into instances of an ontology in order to receive the KM Measures Repository.

The KM repository also possesses different interfaces for importing additional aspects in order to respond to new organisational KM practices, new KM standards, technology changes or additional KM topics. The update mechanism could be supported by a Crawler which is searching new topics in the field of KM and matching these topics with the existing ones.

4 KM Maturity Model

The KM Maturity Model will consist of four components, the Auditing Component, the Measurement Component, the Recommendations Component and a Feedback Loop with integrated Learning Component.

- The **Auditing Component** provides a web-based self-assessment for interested organisations. Supported by an auditing process an organisation will have the possibility to define its current organisational and technical infrastructure as well as the core business processes, and requirements. Concerning the technical infrastructure this means for instance a precise description of all used systems, tools, databases, etc and the current integration status. On the other side the organisation describes requirements to the functionality and usability of a KM solution they would implement. With regard to the organisational infrastructure the organisation defines its size, industrial sector, structure, short term and long term objectives, organisational instruments and strategies in the field of KM. Finally, the organisation defines objectives with regard to target costs.

- The **Measurement Component** evaluates the collected data from the auditing process by the use of predefined metrics and transforms the gained results into a new instance of the KM Measures Repository. After that the new instance will be matched against already existing best practice instances of the same cost/ implementation time category. Finally the Measurement Component determines the current maturity level by directly comparing the organisation's instance with the most similar located best practice instance. For this purpose, appropriate maturity levels have to be defined.

- The **Recommendations Component** automatically provides recommendations to the organisations about how to reach the next maturity level in KM. This will be done by providing the identified best practice scenario to the requesting organisation and combining it with a respective ROI. To reach this scenario, the component supports the organisation in optimising its business rules, business strategies and knowledge-intensive processes as well as helping them in selecting appropriate KM technologies for the successful KM support of their requirements. This means that the Recommendation Component provides on the on hand approved organisational instruments and methods to implement new KM solutions, to overbear technical/ organisational barriers and on the other hand recommendations how to integrate the three organisational layers as well as time and cost saving potentials. Furthermore, the recommendation makes organisations aware of important KM topics.

- The **Feedback Loop with integrated Learning Component** adds successful completed KM implementations of organisations as a new measure to the KM Measures Repository. Furthermore, a Synchronisation Mechanism between the KM Maturity Model and the KM Measures Repository guarantees the timeless and reusability of both models with regard to additional topics by updating the Measures Repository or the Maturity Model if necessary. The Learning Component will collect lessons learned regarding inappropriate recommendations given.

5 Conclusion

In this paper we addressed the problem of an isolated approach and the lack of a suitable strategy for the introduction and realization of KM in an organization by implementing a holistic integrated methodological framework.

For the development of this framework an extensive state-of-the-art analysis in the field of KM is necessary regarding completed and running projects, technologies, show cases and experiences as well as user requirements. The data and information collected at this will be analysed with regard to organization, process, and technology layer of a company and combined to KM best practice cases. After that the best practice cases will be transformed into instances of an ontology in order to receive a KM Measures Repository. Based on these results we intend to develop a machine executable approach, i.e. a self-assessment tool which allows organizations to assess their current KM maturity level and get recommendations about how to reach a higher maturity level. For the future we intend to validate this methodological framework under real-life conditions which might be realized in the context of a concrete KM project.

References

1 META Group Deutschland GmbH: Der Markt füKM in Deutschland, 2001
2 Andreas Abecker, Knut Hinkelmann, Heiko Maus, Heinz Jügen Mller: Geschäftsprozessorientiertes Wissensmanagement, 2002
3 Prof. Dr. Wolfgang Scholl, Christine Köig, Bertolt Meyer: The Delphi Study on KM, Humboldt-Universitä Institut füPsychologie
4 KPMG Consulting: KM Research Report 2000

Openness and Cross-Functional Risk Reduction – The Key to a Successful Development Project? – "Hindsight in Advance" within and between Organizations

Geir J. Husoy, Edgar Karlsen, and Arnt Hugo Lund

The Organizational Development Alliance AS
Akersgaten 43. 0158 Oslo

Abstract. Organizational defensive routines and lack of ability to early identify and involve critical competence and knowledge, is a main cost driver in developments projects today. We argue that through systematic cross functional risk assessment (PPA- potential problem analysis), culture and competence will be strengthened towards open, involving and proactive handling of own risk factors and potentials. The project not only has to handle its technical risk, but also continuously be able to provide the best organisational preconditions for reaching own defined objectives. The focus is on barriers and effective interventions. The theory and method is put extra to the test, through a cross, -country, -linguistic, and -cultural attempt to handle common risk between a customer and supplier.

1 Introduction

"Organizational politics is such a perversion of truth and honesty that most organizations reek with its odor. Yet most of us so take it for granted that we don't even notice it... A political environment is one which "who" is more important that "what"... A non-political climate demands "openness" – both the norm of speaking openly and honestly about important issues, and the capacity continually to challenge one`s own thinking."(Senge 1990;273-274)

Senge here describes the political side of organizational dynamics, where data and information is deliberately hidden or twisted, as a result of culture and /or individual calculation. Another is the organizational inability to identify and use valid and important information. This aspect points more to organizational inability and "incompetence" to use information present, than conscious calculating and political dynamics at the individual level. A combination of these two features - a highly political organization with inability to identify and involve critical competence - will hardly promote excellence through openness, cross functional involvement and effective risk reducing working processes.

D. Karagiannis and U. Reimer (Eds.): PAKM 2002, LNAI 2569, pp. 571-584, 2002.

Openness and honesty will seldom be manifest in organizations that don't systematically and strongly promote them. The barriers to openness are many, and the negative consequences extensive. Problems will most often be explained by rational and business-appropriate, acceptable reasons, hardly ever as due to a lack of openness, power play or inability to identify and use knowledge that all along was present in the organization. What are often traditionally regarded as "soft issues", alongside the tough, everyday business aspect, can to an increasing degree be traced to and documented at the "bottom line" of projects and business operations.

In this paper, we argue that a deficient work culture concerning openness and work methods to manage risk, especially at the early stages of development projects, are of the most cost increasing and limiting factors in many organizations today. Main focus is on critical development projects where the goal is to strengthen the organization's competitive and market position. We initially examine some of the most fundamental barriers to openness and cross-professional interaction internal in organizations. The last section focuses on additional challenges presented in the relationship between customer and supplier. We follow a specific case where a customer and a supplier of different commercial, linguistic, and cultural environments accomplish a 2-day cross-professional workshop to identify and manage shared risk. Focus is on barriers and the interventions to overcome these.

Through theory and empirics, we in this paper contend that:

- Development projects in organizations characterized by openness and *actionable knowledge*[1] will have more success in achieving defined goals (quality, progression, cost, etc.) than projects in other organizations
- Development projects that are not only able to manage technical risk, but also their own organizational preconditions[2] to solve their task at hand, will have a greater likelihood of achieving defined goals than other projects. The project will also contribute to a development of culture and attitude towards increased openness and appreciation of cross-functional cooperation
- Cross-functional risk assessment between companies demands even stricter requirements for structured and facilitated preparation and execution than internally in an organization

Through a research project supported by The Norwegian Research Council through the TYIN project, ODA AS[3] (The Organizational Development Alliance AS) has, in cooperation with Norwegian companies and organizations, developed and tested methods for risk prevention in development projects.

---

1 Knowledge shared by several individuals, such that as a group deal in a conscious and planned manner
goal, resources, organization, attitude and work processes

2 Goal, resources, organization, attitude and work processes

3 ODA AS was established in 1993 and is a consulting firm in organizational development that specializes in effective project completion and cross-professional cooperation

2 Barriers to Openness and Cross-Professional Involvement Internal in Organizations

Lack of openness and insufficient use of existing knowledge are well documented defensive organizational protective mechanisms seen in different cases. The Challenger misfortune's precourse shows clearly that even though knowledge in the organization of a potential disaster was present, launching was not prevented (Argyris 1990:37). Similar mechanisms, albeit without such catastrophic results, are observed on different levels in different organizations. The following are illustrations of dynamics in organizations characterized by "passive knowledge" vs. "actionable knowledge".

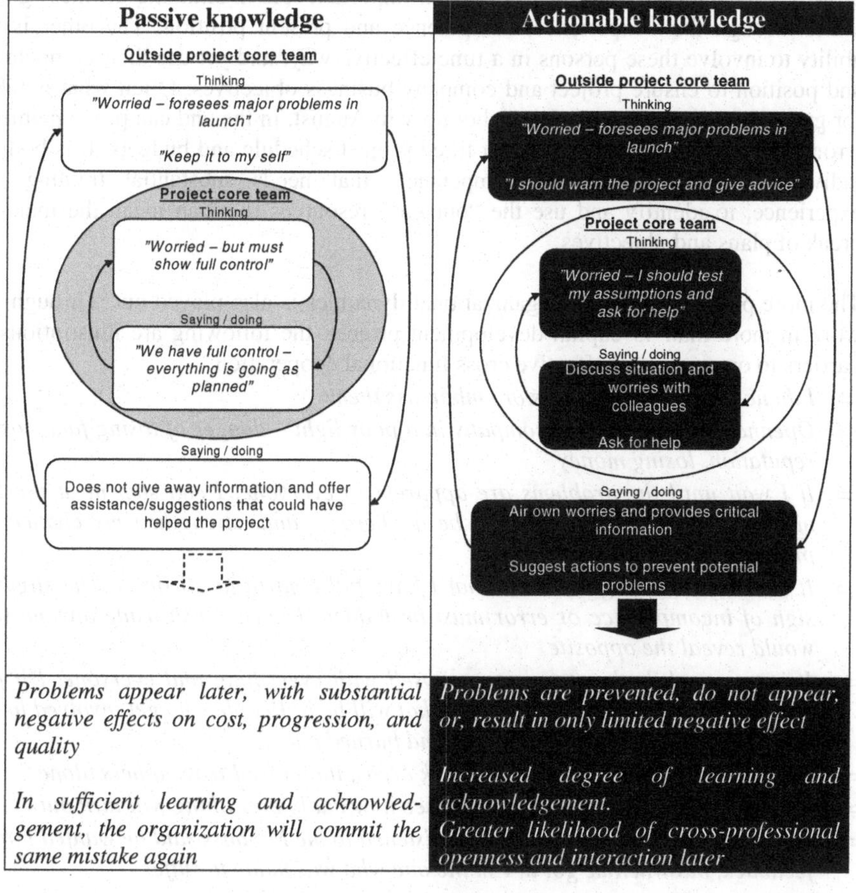

Fig. 1. Passive vs. actionable knowledge

Negative feedback causes individuals to feel hurt and insecure (Argyris 1990; 59). This is an observation and knowledge that leads us to filter out what we think from what we express. This filtration is important in order for organizations to function. At the same time, this type of "censoring" inhibits competitive strength and the ability to learn if it hinders important commercial information from emerging.

It can be assumed that openness will be a dominant feature in a relationship where associates see more long term and short term advantages to being open rather than other alternatives. Barriers to openness and interaction can manifest themselves in different ways. The following are mental models and dynamics we have observed in different organizations:

The Organizational inability to identify, involve and use existing knowledge can have different aspects. One is to recognize and identify key players in the "outskirt" of the project, which actually will or can play an important role in realizing business goals, either through their experience, competence and present position. The other is the ability to involve these persons in a time effective way, and yet use their competence and position to ensure project and company business objectives. Often what is taken for granted, ie. the capacity of the laboratory in August, in the end can prove painfully wrong and the "small problem" that tilted project schedule and budgets. It is both an individual and organizational competence, that needs substantial training and experience, to identify and use the "outskirt" resources that can mean the make or break of plans and objectives.

The more political aspect of organizational dynamics is also played out. Through our work in more than 45 capital development project, the following are illustrations of barriers to openness and effective cross functional cooperation:

⇒ *I do not want to hurt others or embarrass them*
⇒ *Openness will put me/my company in a poor light – danger of losing face, losing reputation, losing money*
⇒ *If I wait until the problems are apparent to everyone, I can step in at the last minute, take care of things and be a "hero", and, strengthen my chances of promotion*
⇒ *It is to my advantage to show that I have full control at all times. The slightest sign of incompetence or error must be hidden. I must brush aside anyone who would reveal the opposite*
⇒ *It is too much bother to concern myself with everything and everyone. I'll just stick to my own responsibilities and that will be it. People who get involved in too much wind up becoming exhausted and burned out*
⇒ *I don't want others to invade my work areas, therefore I leave others alone*
⇒ *I wasn't asked, so now they can just see how badly everything will turn out*
⇒ *I told them so last time, but nobody listened to me My boss said he wanted honest feedback, but when he got it, I'm the one who was made to suffer*

In practice, the main challenge is to demonstrate that openness is to the advantage for both the individual and the organization. An understanding must be established that openness in critical situations will result in better and less encumbered projects, and that it is worthwhile and profitable. Not only should it be permissible, but required to express concerns or worries.

This involves a fundamental alteration of mental models and culture for companies that manifest a strong element of *political climate* and *defensive routines*. Senge (1990) and Argyris (1990) contend that an overwhelming majority of companies the world over are strongly influenced by these driving forces. Argyris (1990) draws up 4 different methods to handle what he calls *"skilled incompetence, organizational defenses, fancy footwork(bypass and cover up) and malaise (hopelessness, cynicism, distancing, blaming others)"*

1. *"Appreciation Learning Experiences"* – facilitated case methodology to establish insight in the gap between an individual's espoused theory and theory in use
2. *"Appreciation and Implementation"* – as in 1 but involving only individuals from the same organization. More thorough dialogue and understanding concerning organizational dynamics
3. *"Dealing with Actual Business Problems (Away from Office)"* – seminar where relevant, critical questions concerning operations are dealt with by those who both create and manage these
4. "Dealing with Actual Business Problems at the Office" – structured exercise to establish both a mutual problem understanding and actions to handle negative elements that hinder the organization in achieving its goals

Levels 1 and 2 have traditionally been used in management groups because of the requirement for maturity and because of the substantial resources necessary to identify and to develop dynamics (time and money)[4].

Our experience shows that to begin working with this change, a well-planned and gradual implementation is necessary, along with continuous success stories. To process levels 3 and 4 we have found no better place to start than in the critical development projects. These generally have clearcut and measurable success parameters as well as strong cross-professional elements[5]. Development projects are time-limited and result-oriented with participants who are "lower" in the organization's hierarchy. Adequate effects have not been achieved working through levels 1 and 2 due to a perception of inadequate time, maturity, motivation, and money. The challenge lies in working with levels 3 and 4, with what is perceived as a useful and relevant business case, while at the same time to as great a degree as possible uncovering and revealing dynamics that hinder the project and operation to achieve its goals.

Even though the best technical conditions might be in place, this does not guarantee resolution in a satisfactory manner. Objectives can be unclear, incentives differing, organization inappropriate, trust and openness can be lacking, and the work processes cumbersome. All of these elements on their own can destroy a project, but together can be a powerful negative spiral difficult to reverse (Borgen et.al. 1998). The ODA

---

4 Generally facilitated workshops over several days involving a consultant fee of 4-5000 US$ per day

5 Dependent on the complete value chain to succeed - marketing, innovation, production, sale, storage, technical expertise, prognosis, laboratory, etc.

model has been implemented in more than 40 development projects as a tool to analyze and strengthen the requirements a project needs in order to reach its goals. The model shows that work processes and results within and between organizational units are a product of 3 organizational preconditions or ground requirements.

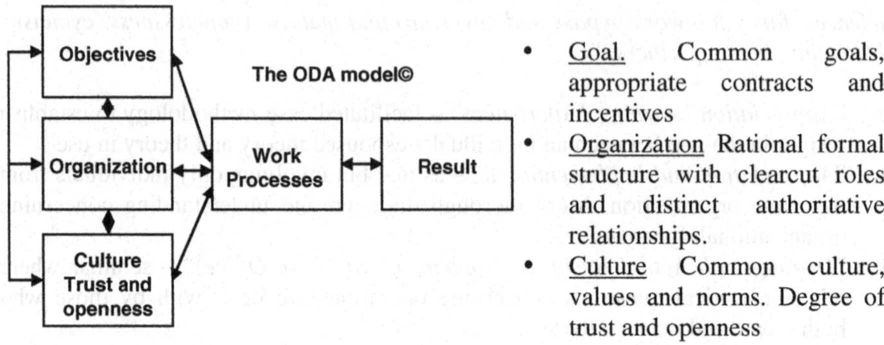

- Goal. Common goals, appropriate contracts and incentives
- Organization Rational formal structure with clearcut roles and distinct authoritative relationships.
- Culture Common culture, values and norms. Degree of trust and openness

Fig. 2. The ODA Model

To reflect over and effectively manage ones own conditions as a project is a very demanding task. Engineers and other professionals are trained to be experts in ”single loop learning” (Argyris 1990), and can easily have developed a ”blindness” to the model we have developed as well as the mental models that direct our behavior and shape our results (double loop learning). The ODA model

In this paper we will not go into detail concerning internal development work in development projects, rather, we will illustrate how these barriers have been dealt with in a case involving 2 organizations.

This means that we go one step further than Argyris' 4 levels of developing, to level 5 - ”Dealing with Actual Business Problems between Businesses.

3 “How to Deal with Actual Business Problems between Businesses in Development Projects”

A major Norwegian company implemented in winter and spring of 2001 a series of facilitated workshops in their ongoing development project to strengthen results, risk management and a culture marked by “*actionable knowledge*”. In the first few months ODA was facilitator of the meetings that were initiated by central management. After having first been implemented ”by force” by management, this method is today used highly actively on a “voluntary” basis, facilitated by the company itself.

"The PPA method has become a standard exercise in the projects that we use today and facilitate on our own initiative. It has become a part of both culture and individual accomplishments, and is used today without external assistance or press from above"

"The PPA method is highly active in organizations, and is a combination of communication- and problem-solving concepts. It provides a cross-professional involvement and participation from management on downwards"

From initiative taken by project management in one of the most critical and challenging development projects, the question was raised whether PPA could be an appropriate intervention to strengthen trust, communication and common problem solving regarding the main supplier. The supplier was contracted to engineer, construct, transport, install and commission a new prototype machine critical for launch and production of a new product. Preparation, execution and follow up of this intervention illustrates both the PPA concept, results and the additional challenges that the customer-supplier relationship creates. The fact that the customer was located in Norway, and the supplier in England, made the language and cultural challenges even greater.

3.1 Main Challenges Related to Openness in a Customer-Supplier Relationship

Strong contractual regulations, differing economic goals, and a traditionally unbalanced authority relationship, assumedly will lead to a high potential for political play and a low degree of openness in the relationship between customer and supplier. Trust will often be based on calculation – built on a fear of negative economic consequences from undesirable behavior (Lewicki and Bunker, 1996). There will often be clear suspicions on both sides that the contract will be used by the other solely to their own interest. Respect for reputation in the market and a mutual wish for long term relations will assumedly act as a counterbalance to these obstacles of trust and openness (Borgen et.al. 1998).

A lack of organizational administrative mechanisms (an established hierarchy) is an indication that contractual and trustworthy mechanisms will constitute an important foundation towards a degree of open cooperation. To strengthen this, the work method PPA (Potential Problem Analysis) has been used as a "crow bar" in work towards achieving an open and constructive common management of problems and actions.

3.2 Independent 3rd Party with No Interest Other than Best Mutual Result

It is by the involved parties emphasized that successful accomplishment with good result from both supplier and customer is especially dependent on an independent 3rd party who is trusted by both sides. This concerns both preparation and completion. Through preparations and execution, the 3rd party must be able to demonstrate independence and balance the interest and views of all parties, and through this promote an environment of trust and openness.

In order to carry out the workshop 2 facilitators are necessary. One directs the dialogue, ensures that all topics and conditional factors are thoroughly considered, and prepares problems, causes and actions. A major challenge for the facilitator is to dig deep enough into problem understanding such that the group is able to define effective initiatives and to understand eventual contraproductive dynamics that hinder the project. The groups have a tendency to be drawn into "safe technical problems", which usually have much more difficult discussable, underlying issues. The other facilitator accurately documents problems, priorities, causes and actions via PC and projector. In this way, the concluding document is mutually consistent and created right then and there in the meeting. This requires a high degree of attentiveness, ability to rapidly document via PC, and ability to clarify problems and actions.

3.3 Planning and Preparation

The most important step in preparation is to identify key players who will influence the project's success (cross-professional), and to tailor an agenda that retains the project's most important challenges and requirements. Especially important additional requirements in the case between the Norwegian customer and the British supplier were:

- Choice of a strategically important and appropriate case
- Balanced understanding of goal and PPA methodology and underlying models
- Agenda that encompassed the most important topics – and that dealt with the project's conditions to succeed

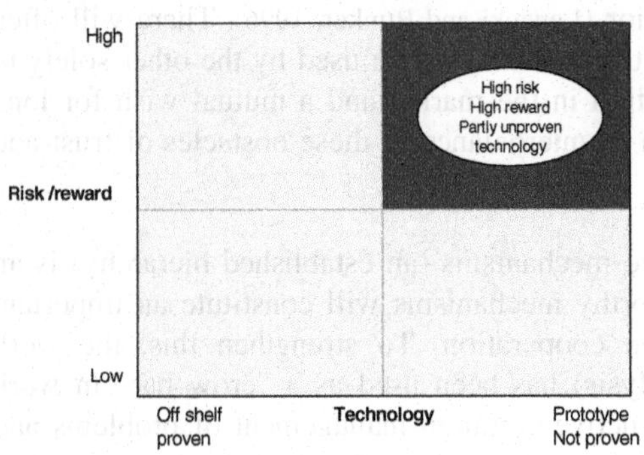

In order to defend time spent and investments, the project must have considerable upside and downside potentials, and technical insecurity related to untested technology /prototype equipment.

The project had all of these features. In addition, a very challenging plan of action including little possibility of daily communication on a face-to-face basis

Fig. 3. Technology, risk and strategic importance

It is important to prepare the workshop in a way which ensures that both sides see and understand the objectives, method and value of the work. The customer in this case was very familiar with the concept, so focus had to be turned on the supplier. Sloppy preparation will create the risk of meeting a supplier that is negative, suspicious, and not open. In such an environment the PPA is of limited value, as the true common risk factors are not identified and worked on.

The following preparations were done to create a common understanding and motivation:

- Contact by mail, phone and meetings between facilitator, supplier and customer
- 2 page paper describing objectives and method distributed to key supplier personnel
- 2 hour individual interviews with both customer and supplier personnel at "home sites"
- Development of balanced agenda through several steps, ensuring that both sides felt the critical issues of the project were dealt with in a positive manner
- Individual preparations on both sides (developing test rig, introductions etc.)

3.4 Execution of the PPA Meeting

The agenda covers 2 days, and the work methodology can be illustrated as follows:

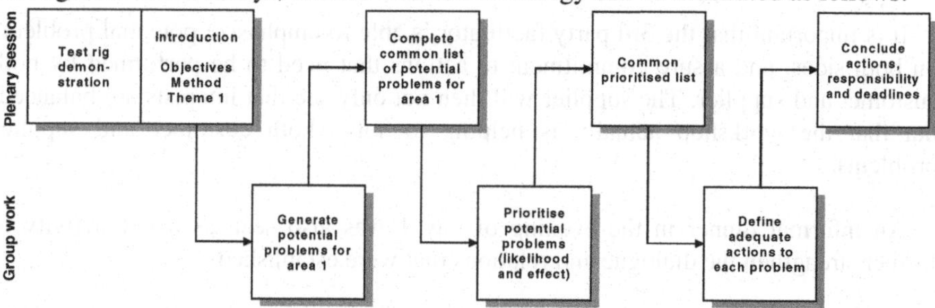

Fig. 4. Illustration of working method and agenda of PPA workshop

A total of 4 different main topics were considered in this manner. In the evening of Day 1 the participants shared an informal dinner together.

Particularly important conditions for a successful work meeting between supplier and customer were:

- Management's commitment and engagement
- Test rig demonstration
- Avoidance of addressing commercial issues in the meeting
- Active use of small groups
- Balanced responsibility

One success factor was that the supplier management wished this would be a success. Through the complete preparation process they became truly engaged, and expressed to their own members a clear expectation of maximum openness both prior to and during the work meeting. The customer's motivation was already high since the initiative had come from their side.

A visit to the supplier assembly hall including a test rig demonstration, proved very valuable. The supplier had carefully planned an especially illustrative test rig demonstration. Customer personnel got a range of their up front questions answered, and the whole group a highly specific and common framework to base further discussions. The visit probably saved time later on in the session, and increased the level of trust between the parties.

Another critical issue is to separate contractual/commercial issues from technical and organizational issues. Both in preparations and in the workshop, explicit instructions were given that commercial issues were to be dealt with later by senior project management. If commercial consideration were to become a part of the PPA workshop, a factor would be introduced that could greatly reduce openness and introduce positioning and suspiciousness. This would reduce the value of the meeting, or even prove the meeting counterproductive.

Senior project management handled contractual issues at day 3 when the rest of the organizations were not present. This greatly contributed to the openness, focus and efficiency of the workshop.

It is important that the 3rd party facilitator is able to emphasize potential problems on both sides, and assure commitment to actions that need to be performed by both customer and supplier. The supplier will then not only see that interests are balanced, but that the workshop actually is helping to solve both customer and supplier problems.

An informal dinner in the evening of day 1 was also seen as a key activity to further strengthen the dialogue and relations that were established.

Cross supplier-customer small group sessions proved to be a very valuable and productive way of working. Groups of 4-5 were used to generate potential problems, prioritize these problems, and identify adequate actions. The plenary sessions were used for introductions to group work, generating a common and complete list of potential problems, and to summarize priorities and actions. The following is an illustration of how one topic was dealt with:

All personnel involved in the work shop should receive a copy of the minutes from the meeting including an action list, and some encouraging words on their efforts to make the workshop an open and productive forum. This should be done in order to:

- Anchor and inform about decisions and actions
- Implement and follow up critical actions
- Ensure that a positive attitude will be a part of similar activities in future

3.5 Result of the PPA Workshop

After 2 well prepared for and intense days, results can be summed up in different ways and in different areas. The workshop established trust and valuable contacts across the companies, which otherwise would not have been established. This promoted also an increased climate for problem solving across the companies in the aftermath – one knew now who to contact concerning what issues. This gave increased security and confidence surrounding the project, and the customer to perceive own increased priority. Even though it was later seen that the project experienced its share of technical and commercial challenges, both sides perceived cooperative efforts as relatively open and trustworthy. The development work in

England is believed to have laid a positive foundation towards the advancement of the relationship and cooperation.
The usefulness of the work must be evaluated according to the delta created between the initiatives established because of the meeting, and the potentially negative consequences that were avoided (based on the assumption that these problem areas would not have been considered adequately enough or early enough). This is a contra factual evaluation which obviously can be neither proven nor verified. What we rely on are the evaluations given by central project collaborators. 1 year later, the following are illustrating comments from key personnel involved in the project and the workshop:

- *"This was a fantastic experiment we were a part of over there in England. It gave us a good start and better rapport and contact with the supplier than we've seen in a long time"*
- *"Personally, I'm very happy we did this a year ago, and I'm certain that everything would have been much more difficult if we hadn't "*
- *"The project was boosted considerably in the areas that were prioritized and focused on through the PPA meeting"*
- *"Even though there were a few problems, we've had a consistently good and relatively open attitude. I think we benefited in these areas by the PPA session. Afterwards, we were more accommodating from both sides and I have received clear feedback from the supplier that this is the way one should really work"*

The most concrete results are still the problem- and action areas that were identified and considered. In the course of 1,5 days more than 50 problem- and action areas were worked on. All were followed up afterwards where of 15 were mutually prioritized as the most critical. Another important aspect is that these were made known and made manageable in a relatively short period of time. Great positive surprise over the quantity and importance of potential problems that were identified were expressed both during and after the PPA meeting.

It was unexpected for both the supplier and the customer to see that so many and important action items fell to the customer. This was an area that dealt with fundamental conditions regarding the supplier's responsibilities. Experience shows that in traditional customer-supplier transactions, dialogue is much more unbalanced and contractual, where the customer dominates and is the demander. In these cases the supplier will be less aggressive and open, and rather push problems ahead to contractually "clean up" afterwards.

When a closer look is taken at the priority areas, the balance of responsibility and "single" vs. "double loop" philosophy indicates something about the quality of the dialogue process. We define "double loop" problem areas as actions directed against the project's goal, plan, resources, or the environment in which the machine will operate at the customer. "Single loop" are more traditional technical actions directed against the machine that the supplier/customer's project team develops and controls.

Table 1. Classification of top 15 prioritized problem- and action areas of the PPA customer-supplier workshop

	Supplier	Customer
Single loop	1. Improve spread out and stability of gate system 2. Ensure resources and time for valid and timely documentation 3. Ensure spare part list and sufficient spare parts in installation period	4. Glue, print, wrapping to be defined by customer ASAP 5. Clarify and prepare cabling at installation site 6. Ensure on site pneumatic requirements 7. Provide test samples (100 000 pieces) in time for FAT
Double loop	8. Ensure time and resources for corrective actions before shipping –2 week acceleration of plan 9. Establish FAT plan with clear acceptance criteria 10. Ensure actions to provide "early warning of bad news" (milestone slippage, progress, technical problems)	11. Improve molding quality of pieces to be wrapped by machine 12. Establish customer site test plan and resources in both England and Norway 13. Prevent low ownership and negative attitudes to project and machine in customer organization 14. Provide data on customer site conditions regarding vibrator control (absorbance/resonance) 15. Simulate storage of empty trays at the working station

3.6 1 Year Later

No case is ever completely a golden success story, neither here in this particular instance. The customer is profiting from the product, and is selling in relation to the defined plans. In that respect the project is fairly successful. On the negative side, the machine was delayed for startup, and a main challenge in the start up period has been to ensure desired productivity.

The value of the PPA methodology and the workshop was nonetheless, as we saw, regarded as highly worthwhile. Alternative costs of not performing the session were at the same time regarded as potentially harmful for the project. All 50 problem areas were addressed and actions defined and accomplished. It was mutually agreed that a number of problems that were addressed at this early stage would eventually have surfaced at a later point and would have been more problematic, time-consuming and costly to resolve.

Technically, a problem that arose was one that both customer and supplier had brushed aside as being rather straightforward. The argumentation was that elements were standard shelf items. The problem, though, was that shelf items were now incorporated in a new prototypical context in which they had not functioned earlier. The project tried to "shrink" the machine considerably at the same time that productivity and effect were to be much greater than before. The lesson learned was the necessity of being extra alert and wary of blindly accepting anything as being "straightforward", especially in dealing with standard components that are to be incorporated in an untested framework. The topics which caused uneasiness, and subsequently received time and focus, resulted in resolution above all expectation.

The key aspect of the methodology is not to perform a traditional risk assessment. It is to "massage" both relations, barriers and defensive organizational routines at the individual and organizational level, and at the same time handle the critical business issues in the most effective way. It is to make organizations see that well prepared and untraditional ways of cross functional involvement is not only profitable, but also fun. It is fun to succeed, and through this a culture of cross functional cooperation and appreciation can be built. It requires high management commitment and follow up. But if the result is that the entire organization starts to take responsibility for uncovering potentials and reducing risks for the common good, it should be worthwhile.

References

1. Argyris, Chris (1990) *Overcoming Organizational Defences*. Prentice Hall
2. Argyris, Chris (1992) *On Organizational Learning*. Blackwell, Cambridge.
3. Borgen et.al (1998): The ODA Model - Incentives, Authority and Trust in Integrated Offshore Organizations, ODA Oslo
4. Haugland, Sven (1996) *Samarbeid, allianser og nettverk*. Tano Aschehoug. Oslo.
5. Lewicki, Roy J and Bunker, Barbara B. (1996). Developing and Maintaining Trust in Working Relationships. In Kramer, Roderick and Tom R.Tyler (eds.) «*Trust in organizations. Frontiers of theory and research*»Sage, Thousand Oaks.
6. McArthur, Philip Woods (1994) NAVIGATING A TASK, The Dynamics of Alignment in Time-Limited Project Teams, Harvard University
7. Mishra, Aneil K. (1996). Swift trust and temporary groups. In Kramer, Roderick and Tom R.Tyler (eds.) «*Trust in organizations. Frontiers of theory and research*»Sage, Thousand Oaks.
8. Moss Kanter, Rosabeth (1997). *Rosabeth Moss Kanter on the Frontiers of Management*. Harvard Business Review Book. Boston.
9. Olsen, Bjørn Erik, Edgar Karlsen and Knut Ivar Karevold (1997). Evaluation of the 2/4X Topside Alliance. ODA, Oslo.
10. Senge, Peter M (1990). *The Fifth Discipline. The Art and Practice of The Learning Organization*: Currency and Doubleday, New York

Attachment: IT Tool for Support and Self-Facilitation of PPA

Based on experience with preparation and execution of different PPA meetings, ODA has developed a database IT tool. The IT tool is both a support and an automation of the work involved in facilitating the PPA group. Through use of the PC and overhead projector, the group is lead through the necessary steps at the same time that a common product is prepared which reflects direct verification of reports in the meeting. Important functioning areas are:

- Supervisor module. Leads the group automatically through steps and topics. Ensures, for example, reflection of "double loop" factors by automatically asking about adequate conditions surrounding the goal, organization, plan, attitude and whether work methods are in place

- Experience database Stores all previously defined potential problems and solutions. Here one is able to systematically retrieve previous problems and solutions that are sorted according to project or topic. If earlier problems/actions are relevant for the project at hand, these are automatically recorded on to the project list
- Prioritizing from a visual risk matrix. One enters 1 of 9 possible classifications of risk based on probability and effect. The program automatically calculates score and ranking
- Cause module. Leads participants to reflect deeper around the causes of each individual problem. Strengthens conditions to define effective actions
- Action module. Ensures that all problems are assigned defined actions, responsible individuals, and time limits. Individuals names are previously defined, thus just clicked off and not necessary to enter more than once
- Report module. Generates different modules based on the project's needs

Inspection Process Support System for Software Engineering Education and the Lessons from Its Application
- Towards Constructing a Knowledge Sharing Environment -

Atsuo Hazeyama

Department of Mathematics and Informatics, Tokyo Gakugei University,
4-1-1 Nukuikita-machi, Koganei-shi, Tokyo 184-8501, Japan
hazeyama@u-gakugei.ac.jp

Abstract. Software development is knowledge intensive work. Therefore in this kind of education it is necessary not only to teach theories and/or methodologies according to textbooks but also for students themselves to acquire knowledge through exercises, especially group learning because software development in practical setting is done in the form of project. Knowledge through exercises is acquired by a learner or learners' group through problem-solving, or by interactions between learners' group and the teacher side (teacher and teaching assistants). This paper deals with software inspection as one interaction between learners' group and the teacher side, describes a support system of the interaction and the results of application of the system to an actual software engineering class in a university. According to the results, the author also describes design on a knowledge sharing environment for software engineering education.

1 Introduction

With the rapid permeation of information technology like the Internet into our society, the demands for software system development and the complexity of such systems are increasing. From such social background, people who are capable of designing and developing such systems are required. Software development is knowledge intensive work [8]. Development of software systems has several phases such as planning, analysis, design, programming, and testing. Via these phases, a software system is released for use. Software systems are usually developed by organizing a project which consists of several to hundreds of members. Therefore project management techniques that allocate members to tasks, create schedules and manage the progress are also important. Software development in a practical setting is essentially collaborative work [2].

However there is little opportunity that students in university experience total software systems development in the form of project like a practical setting [11]. Based on the background, we have been offering a class called "system design" since 1997. The class aims at designing and developing a software system in the form of group learning. The goal of the class is to help students learn and acquire the skills

D. Karagiannis and U. Reimer (Eds.): PAKM 2002, LNAI 2569, pp. 585-594, 2002.

they need to design and develop software systems, especially system analysis and design, project management, and collaboration and cooperation techniques [6]. The workload of students in this class is high, so it is indispensable to support for students to learn effectively and efficiently. To overcome this problem, we have also been developing a group learning support system [5], [7].

Software inspection has been widely acknowledged as an effective technique for detecting defects in artifacts [3], [4]. Our experience showed inspection was effective for the students' exercises [6]. However because of time constraint on university education, time for sufficient face-to-face inspection meetings in the classroom was not allowed. We therefore provided a Web-based inspection process support system. This paper describes our inspection process support system and some lessons learned from its application.

2 Related Work

Some inspection process support systems have been developed thus far in the field of software engineering or CSCW (Computer-Supported Cooperative Work) (ex. [1], [4], [11]). They provided the following common features for inspection process support:
* Support various roles in inspection meeting [1], [4], [11]
* Realization of paperless inspection [1], [4], [11]
* Inspectors can perform their inspection on their workstation [1], [4], [11]
* Comments can be shared. [1], [4], [11]
* Inspection for multi-media documents [4], [11]

In addition to these features, hyperCode is a Web-based asynchronous code-inspection support environment. Perpich et al. showed a result that asynchronous inspection is more cost effective than face-to-face inspection [10].

AISA is a Web-based asynchronous inspection support environment, too. It deals with not only text-based documents but also documents with multimedia [12].

Design policy for our inspection process support environment is also Web-based, asynchronous, and the environment should deal with documents with multimedia as well as text. The reasons are as follows:

- Our class performs inspection for requirement specifications and design documents. Our experience showed one inspection for a group in the classroom (in face-to-face fashion) took around one hour. A group may have to do their inspection for several times according to modification requests from the teacher side. Therefore it is impossible for all groups to spend their inspection meetings within the classroom because of time constraint on the university class. Furthermore it is not so easy to set up a face-to-face inspection meeting outside the class because the students, teaching assistants, and teacher have their own schedules. Based on the backgrounds, we decided to provide an online asynchronous inspection environment.

- The students tackle their exercises at their home as well as in university. The system should be used by the students from any places and at anytime. We decide to construct the system by using the WWW.
- Quality of artifacts in the upstream phases affects success or failure of the project. We think that as this is the first experience for almost all students to develop a software system, it is effective to give comments for the artifacts from the teacher side. The artifacts in the analysis and design phases are created with not only texts but also figures, tables, diagrams, images, and so on. We had to deal with such multimedia information.

Our experience found that in addition to the supporting facilities mentioned above, the following two aspects should be supported for the exercises in a software engineering class. However they are not taken into consideration in the previous research projects.

* **Monitoring the progress of several groups:** In education in university, several groups do their exercises in parallel (in our case, around eight groups run in parallel each year) and each group often creates several types of artifacts. The teacher side (teacher and teaching assistants) has to be able to grasp the progress of each artifact of each group (which artifact of which group has (or has not) finished the inspection, which artifact an inspector has or (has not) given his/her comments, and the progress of other inspectors), and give advice and/or suggestions if necessary. It is a hard task as the number of artifacts increases.

* **Managing the comments associated with the artifacts (comments in an inspection meeting must be taken over in the next inspection meeting):** From our experience we found the following: based on the inspection comments from the teacher side, the group revised the artifact. When re-inspection was performed, the comments needed to be taken over for the next inspection meeting, because the inspectors check the submitted artifacts by referring to the previous inspection comments.

In the next section we describe our inspection process support system that took into consideration the above requirements.

3 Web-IPSE: Web-Based Inspection Process Support Environment

We provide the following three major facilities.

3.1 Support of the Inspection Process

The inspection process is as follows: prior to the inspection meeting, a group registers the artifacts for inspections into the system. The system analysis and design specifications are usually created with not only texts but also diagrams, figures, tables, and so on, by using word processors, presentation tools, drawing tools. The documents created by using the tools are uploaded into the system.

Once a group selects the artifacts and requests inspection, the notification message for requesting inspection is sent to the teacher side. When an inspector (teacher or teaching assistants) selects an artifact of the group, a window appears to display the artifact and describe comments. Each inspector can write comments independently, and can view the comments of other inspectors. After describing the comments the inspector decides whether re-inspection is needed or not. When all inspectors finished to inspect, the result is notified of the group automatically. An inspector who judged no need for re-inspection does not have to participate in the next inspection meeting. However he or she can give comments to the artifact. The artifacts that finished the inspection are opened to outside the group.

3.2 Monitoring the Progress

The teacher side does inspection for all groups. Each group may have several types of artifacts for inspection. It is difficult for the teacher side to grasp the progress on inspection of the artifacts. We therefore provided the progress monitoring functions. We represent the progress of each artifact by the status value and the inspection process flow by the state transition of each artifact. We have "waiting for inspection", "in progress", "finished" as the status value. "Waiting for inspection" means that the group is creating or modifying the artifact and the teacher side is waiting for the group requesting inspection. Once the group submits the artifacts and requests for inspection, the status value is changed to "in progress". After all inspectors write their comments and decide necessity of re-inspection, the status value is changed to "waiting for inspection" and the results are notified of the group. Once all inspectors approve the artifact, then the status value will be "finished". The system also shows the number of inspection. This value is counted up when the students requests for inspection.

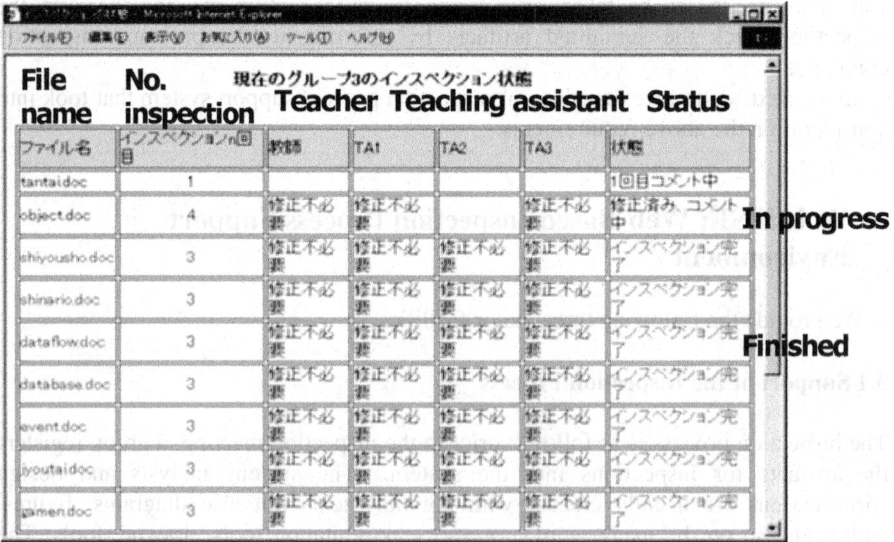

現在のグループ3のインスペクション状態

ファイル名	インスペクションn回目	教師	TA1	TA2	TA3	状態
tantai.doc	1					1回目コメント中
object.doc	4	修正不必要	修正不必要		修正不必要	修正済み、コメント中
shiyousho.doc	3	修正不必要	修正不必要	修正不必要	修正不必要	インスペクション完了
shinario.doc	3	修正不必要	修正不必要	修正不必要	修正不必要	インスペクション完了
dataflow.doc	3	修正不必要	修正不必要	修正不必要	修正不必要	インスペクション完了
database.doc	3	修正不必要	修正不必要	修正不必要	修正不必要	インスペクション完了
event.doc	3	修正不必要	修正不必要	修正不必要	修正不必要	インスペクション完了
youtai.doc	3	修正不必要	修正不必要	修正不必要	修正不必要	インスペクション完了
gamen.doc	3	修正不必要	修正不必要	修正不必要	修正不必要	インスペクション完了

Fig. 1. Progress monitoring function for artifacts of a group

Fig. 1 shows a screen shot of the progress list. An inspector selects the artifacts whose status is "in progress" and blank of his/her status column. The status of each inspector shows his/her judgment whether re-inspection is required or not. By this function, both the students and the teacher side can grasp the progress of inspection for each artifact.

3.3 Support of Version Management and Configuration Management

As development makes progress, the artifacts (documents and/or programs) may have to be revised. Version management is therefore very important. In the inspection process, this is true. As the results of inspection, new artifacts may have to be created. This means configuration management is also required. In configuration management, which version of which artifact is valid must be specified by the group.

Based on the inspection comments from the teacher and teaching assistants, the group revises the artifact. There is a case re-inspection is required. When re-inspection is performed, the comments needed to be taken over for the next inspection meeting, because the inspectors check the submitted artifacts by referring to the previous inspection comments. When registering an artifact in the system, if a user can specify its file name, comments cannot be taken over. Therefore the system manages the file name.

4 Application of the System

4.1 Profile of the Application Class

We applied our Web-IPSE to the actual 2000 and 2001 classes. We had seven groups in the 2000 class and five in the 2001 class. Each group consisted of three or four students. We inspected the following kinds of documents: additional specification descriptions for the task description by the teacher, scenario (use-case descriptions), diagrams by the OMT (Object Modeling Technique) method (i.e. object model diagram, event trace diagram, state transition diagram, dataflow diagram), user interface design specification including functional descriptions, and database specification.

4.2 Evaluation for Progress Monitoring and Comments Association with the Artifacts

We asked three teaching assistants in the 2000 class to answer a questionnaire for usefulness of the system from efficiency viewpoint of the teacher side. All teaching assistants and the teacher answered the progress list was effective.

Although we can't show the efficiency as quantitative data because of small number of people, almost all inspectors responded that the comment reference function contributed to improve efficiency when inspections were iterated several times. Without this function, an inspector has to manage his/her inspection comments for all artifacts, but it takes efforts for him/her.

The students desired quick response of inspection results. As the progress list showed who finished or did not to write inspection comments, the teacher could urge those who did not finish to write inspection comments to return them as soon as possible.

We also asked the students to comment on the progress list from the developer's viewpoint. We found the followings:

* comments association with an artifact was effective for students as well as for the teacher side. Some students described they checked the status of the documents they were responsible for at first, and then they checked the status of the other members' documents.
* some students utilized this function to grasp the progress of the teacher side for their group and the function worked to give motivation that they want to pass the inspection phase as soon as possible.

On the other hand, the following improvement requests were raised:

* some students required the time when inspection was started
* a student, who was a leader, wanted information whether the other members except for him/her checked the inspection comments from the teacher side or not when the result was notified via E-mail notification message.

Although we originally intended to provide this function for the teacher side to grasp the progress of each artifact of all groups, from the above mentioned results, we found our web-based asynchronous inspection process support environment useful for both the teacher side and students.

4.3 Analysis of Inspection Data and Consideration toward Constructing a KM

The author analyzed all the inspection comments that were stored in the system.

Table 1 and 2 show the number of inspection sessions for each artifact of each group in the 2000 and 2001 classes respectively. Note that groups with less small number of inspection sessions do not always create good artifacts because they may not have completed their artifacts through inspection. These tables show that inspection for a document is usually iterated several times (two or three times).

Table 1. The number of inspection by group in the 2000 class

	spec.	scenario	object	event	STD	DFD	DB	UI
Group1	1	1	1	1	1	1	1	1
Group2	3	2	1	2	1	1	1	1
Group3	2	2	3	2	2	2	2	2
Group4	3	3	3	2	3	2	2	2
Group5	1	2	2	2	2	2	1	2
Group6	2	3	3	2	3	3	2	3
Group7	3	3	4	3	4	3	3	3
Average	2.1	2.3	2.4	2.0	2.3	2.0	1.7	2.0

Table 2. The number of inspection by group in the 2001 class

	spec.	scenario	object	event	STD	DFD	DB	UI
Group1	2	2	3	2	4	2	2	4
Group2	2	2	2	2	2	1	2	2
Group3	2	2	2	1	2	2	2	3
Group4	4	3	3	3	3	3	3	3
Group5	3	2	3	2	2	2	2	3
Average	2.6	2.2	2.6	2.0	2.6	2.0	2.2	3.0

As eight types of documents are reviewed by a few inspectors at one inspection session, and the teacher returns the result after receiving the comments from all inspectors, it usually takes three or four days to finish one inspection session. The group examines the comments and has to modify the artifacts according to the comments. It takes around one week for an inspection cycle. Each group can make its development plan at its will. Inspection date of all groups often concentrates on almost the same period. It takes two or three weeks to finish the inspection phase from the above mentioned fact. The total calendar period for the exercises is three months (around twelve weeks), therefore the inspection should be passed as soon as possible.

On the other hand, from the viewpoint of education, students should consider by themselves and prepare artifacts at first, and then the teacher side helps over presenting past good examples if necessary. Past data should be stored and accessed.

I surveyed all inspection comments from all inspection sessions in the 2000 and 2001 classes by manual. Total number of inspection comments were 563 (342 in the 2000 class and 221 in the 2001 class). I classified them into the following thirteen categories (Table 3).

Table 3. Categorization of inspection comments

ID.	Explanation
(1)	Shortage of description
(2)	Over description
(3)	Abstract description
(4)	Difficulty in understanding of the contents of description
(5)	Terminologies needed to be defined
(6)	Inconsistency among artifacts
(7)	Error of the contents of descriptions or model diagrams
(8)	Design rationale is not understandable
(9)	Lack of consideration for requirements the teacher gave
(10)	Lack of correspondence to comments in the previous inspection
(11)	Poor presentation
(12)	Improvement proposal for a specification
(13)	Lack of description on the format of document

Fig. 2 shows the classification result of all comments that were pointed out in the classes of both years.

From this figure, we found four major items pointed out: “shortage of description”, “inconsistency among artifacts”, “error of the contents of descriptions or model diagrams”, and “lack of description on the format of document”.

Items of “shortage of description” and “error of the contents of descriptions or model diagrams” should be essentially detected in inspection. This means inspection is effective.

As examples of inconsistency among artifacts, we found some concept was represented with different terminologies or some documents should be closely related but they did not seem so. For example, classes in the object model should be reflected on the classes or tables in the DB design documents, but not. As with inconsistency of terminologies, we can provide some sort of solution by creating and sharing a dictionary, therefore we will tackle this theme.

As for document format, items such as title, author, date, version number and revision history lacked. From a viewpoint of the teacher side that checks several documents from several groups at several times, description of revision histories was expected. As this is the first experience for the students to write business documents, we found they did not know why they should describe the items. We explained the reason why it was important and the teacher should show good examples in addition to providing the template.

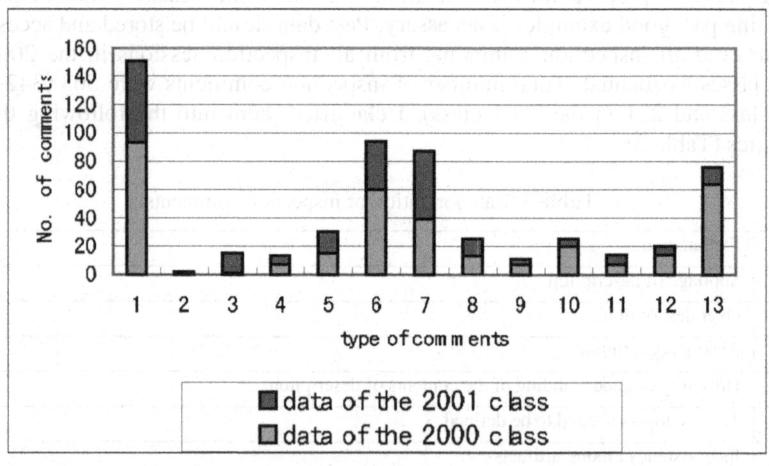

Fig. 2. Categorization result of all inspection comments

5 Design toward Constructing a Knowledge Sharing Environment

Based on the considerations from the previous section, this section describes design toward constructing a knowledge sharing environment.

Hirai et al. describes the relationship between the number of inspection and software quality in a software organization [9]. This is one knowledge gained from software inspection.

From the teacher side educational viewpoint, the result of Fig. 2 itself is very valuable. Each inspection comment is merely a datum. However we could obtain some knowledge by analyzing, collecting, and categorizing each inspection comment and displaying the result in a graphical manner. We performed this task by manual, but the system should support this process itself. Concretely speaking, the followings should be provided by the system:

- to define the items of categorization
- to associate each inspection comment with the categorization
- to display the result based on various queries

These data enable the students of succeeding years to find notices in analysis and design phases and their documentation and to reach examples for each problem to know what were problems.

Fig. 3 shows a data model for inspection data management.

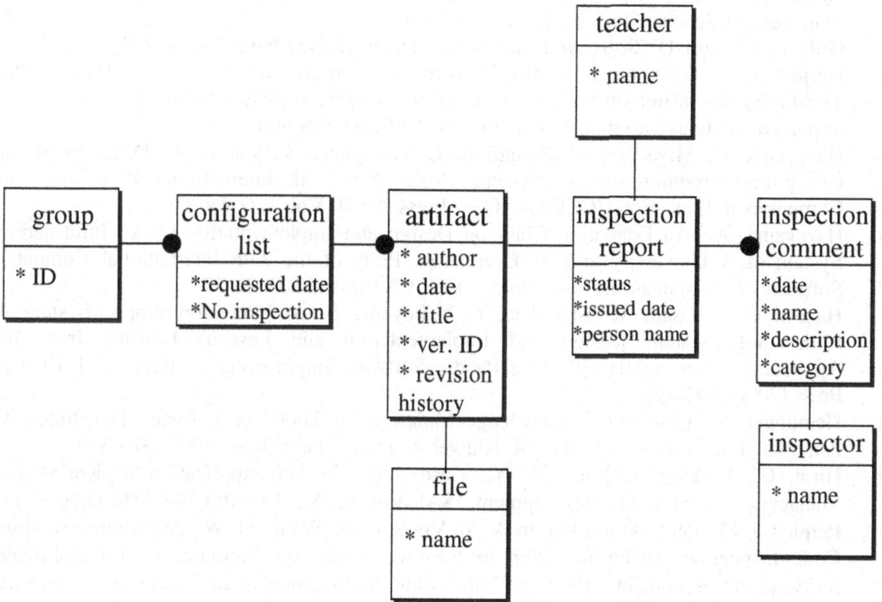

Fig. 3. Data model for inspection data management

6 Conclusion

This paper has described a Web-based inspection process support system for software engineering education. The main features of this system are progress monitoring and comments association with an artifact. Some results from its application. Though qualitative results, students and the teacher side felt useful for progress monitoring function.

We also categorized thirteen items based on all inspection comments accumulated by practice of two years and four items were detected as major pointed-out items. We proposed a data model for knowledge sharing environment for inspection process in software engineering education in universities.

Acknowledgements. This study is supported by a Grant-in Aid for the Encouragement of Young Scientists (No. A 12780120) from The Ministry of Education, Science, Sports and Culture of Japan. The author would like to thank K. Osada and A. Nakano for implementing the system.

References

1. Brothers, L., et al.: ICICLE : Groupware for Code Inspection. Proc. of the ACM Conference on Computer Supported Cooperative Work (CSCW'90), ACM Press (1990) 169 – 181
2. Faraj, S. Sproull, L.: Coordinating Expertise in Software Development Teams. Management Science, 46, 12 (2000) 1554-1568
3. Gilb, T., Graham, D.: Software Inspection. Addison Wesley Publishing (1993)
4. Harjumaa, L., Tervonen, I.: Virtual Software Inspections over the Internet. Proc. of the Third ICSE Workshop on Software Engineering over the Internet (2000) http://sern.ucalgary.ca/~maurer/icse2000ws/ICSE2000WS.html
5. Hazeyama, A., Miyadera, Y., Xiangning, L. Yokoyama, S., Souma, T.: Development of Group Programming Support System. Proc. of the 7th International Conference on Computers in Education (ICCE99), IOS Press (1999) Vol. 1, 669 – 676
6. Hazeyama, A.: An Education Class on Design and Implementation of An Information System in A University and Its Evaluation. Proc. of the 24th International Computer Software and Applications Conference, IEEE CS Press (2000) 21-27
7. Hazeyama, A., Osada, K., Miyadera, Y., Yokoyama, S.: An Education Support System of Information System Design and Implementation and Lessons Learned from Its Application. Proc. of the 7th Asia Pacific Software Engineering Conference, IEEE CS Press (2000) 392-396
8. Henninger, S.: Case-Based Knowledge Management Tools for Software Development. Automated Software Engineering 4, Kluwer Academic Publishers (1997) 319-340
9. Hirai, C., Kudoh, Y., Furuhata, Y.: Case Study 3: The Application of Knowledge Management to Software Development. JSAI, Vol. 16, No. 1 (2001) 59-63 (In Japanese)
10. Perpich, J. M., Perry, D. E., Porter, A. A., Votta, L. G., Wade, M. W.: Anywhere, Anytime Code Inspection: Using the Web to Remove Inspection Bottlenecks in Large-Scale Software Development. Proc. of the 19th International Conference on Software Engineering, IEEE CS Press (1997) 14 - 21
11. Shoenig, S.: Supporting a Software Engineering Course with Lotus Notes. Proc. of the International Conference on Software Engineering Education and Practice, IEEE CS (1998)
12. Stein, M., Riedl, J., Harner, S. J., Mashayekhi, V.: A Case Study of Distributed, Asynchronous Software Inspection, Proc. of the 19th International Conference on Software Engineering, IEEE CS Press (1997) 107 – 117

Knowledge Reuse: CE^2-Focused Training

Keren Mishra, Rajkumar Roy, Petros Souchoroukov, and Victor Taratoukhine

Department of Enterprise Integration, School of Industrial and Manufacturing Sciences, Cranfield University, Bedfordshire, MK43 0AL, UK
{k.mishra;r.roy;p.souchoroukov,v.v.taratoukhine}@cranfield.ac.uk

Abstract. This paper presents a methodology to define areas within the costing profession which require training, based on the expert categorisation of essential knowledge types for the *commercial and engineering activities within cost estimating (CE^2)*. Ten knowledge types (comprising of both commercial and engineering) were identified as being essential for CE^2. A lateral transfer of these cost-knowledge types is required across the CE^2 existing experts, and for the professions' novices. If the knowledge used within the costing domain is successfully transferred across it, the comprehension of the interacting cost experts, and the communication between them will increase: Resulting in the consistent production of faster, more accurate estimates. A training analysis (DIF) was performed per knowledge type, in order to determine which required formal training; and which would suffice with informal. The relevant knowledge was then grouped into training modules for development. The primary focus for this training development is within the aerospace and automotive industries.

1 Introduction

Industrial product costing within large organisations involves more then one knowledge type, primarily that of commercial and of engineering. These cost-disciplines both contribute to the overall activity, of costing a product: They are the means by which a product is assessed for cost, throughout its lifecycle. This includes the cost estimating requirements, from conceptual design stages, where there is very little actual product data to base costs upon: Through to the final stages of development, production, utilisation and more increasingly, disposal. During the latter stages of the lifecycle, product costing is essentially more straightforward (as there is more data; thus uncertainties and risks will have become apparent, and so forth). However during the conceptual design stages, (with low actual data, and high assumptions) the issue of cost can be obscure. It is also at these early stages, that CE^2 activities experience high pressure, to produce fast and accurate results. This is because budgets, bid proposals and cost targets, (among other requirements), for the project duration, are necessarily derived from the cost estimates. In order to produce both high speed and accurate cost results, it is essential that these costing disciplines work in an integrated manner; as they are costing the product from different angles. The *commercial* domain provides key business information for decision making in a

D. Karagiannis and U. Reimer (Eds.): PAKM 2002, LNAI 2569, pp. 595-612, 2002.

top-down fashion. This costing discipline tries to evaluate and optimise a combination of requirements -principally customer and business- with potential and selected solution(s), across a wide range of business processes, with cost as the common denominator. Therefore a broad business overview of product-cost is taken by the commercial cost expert. This view includes issues such as overheads, legislation, marketing, company strategy, annual cost breakdowns, and supplier interaction. In contrast to this wide cost angle, the *engineering* cost expert is more focused on the actual product knowledge. This includes aspects as material, labour, skill level, functionality, product and design knowledge and costs. Clearly these costing disciplines require a high level of fluid interaction when costing a product. Targeted and specially designed cost-training will improve the understanding between these interacting cost-disciplines, and consequently aid an improved communication between them.

1.1 Industrial Challenge

There is currently a gap in the communication between the commercial and engineering experts within CE^2 (Roy et al. June 2001). It has been observed that these cost experts possess a lack of understanding and appreciation of each others role within the business. Consequently this knowledge-rich profession is not utilising its costing expertise to capacity. The lack of interaction is detrimental to the outcome of product costing; it results in a decreased accuracy and speed of the cost estimate, due to a lack of access and flow of necessary information and knowledge. The lateral transfer of costing knowledge can provide the necessary understanding between the disciplines; and thus promote greater levels of communication and interaction. One of the evident causes of the lack of internal costing comprehension is due to a lack of consistent cost-terminology; and general inconsistencies within the overall language utilised within the profession.

1.2 Costing Terminology (CE^2)

The costing profession across a number of industries has a broad and varied use of terminology. This is noticeable at the highest levels of observation. For instance, when examining the professional titles of the costing expert, a number of variations can be depicted. There are many terms used to relay very similar roles within the costing domain. These include: *Cost Estimator, Cost Engineer, Proposals Manager, Bid Team leader, Pricing analysis Manager; Project Cost Engineering Manager; Head of Pricing and Estimating; Product Profitability Manager,* and so forth (ICOST, April 2001). Throughout this research, in order to avoid any confusion in relation to the expert domain under examination; a term has been derived, by the researchers and industrial experts, which refers generically to all specialists involved within product costing: $\boldsymbol{CE^2}$.

1.3 The ICOST Industrial Research Project

ICOST is the industrial parent project, from which this PhD research is derived. The focus of ICOST is to improve internal costing practices within organisations, across industry. The overlap in working practice, between the commercial and engineering aspects of CE^2 is confused and often ambiguous (refer to Figure 1). The aim of the ICOST project is to align these areas, in order to promote a lateral transfer of costing information and knowledge between the relevant cost-disciplines, within the overall scope of costing, see Figure 1. The research presented within this paper focuses on the knowledge and training aspects of ICOST: What knowledge is present within the costing profession? Which knowledge is essential for the CE^2 expert? And subsequently which knowledge needs to be transferred, to which area of expertise? Thus the overall aim of ICOST will be reached, in part, by the development of

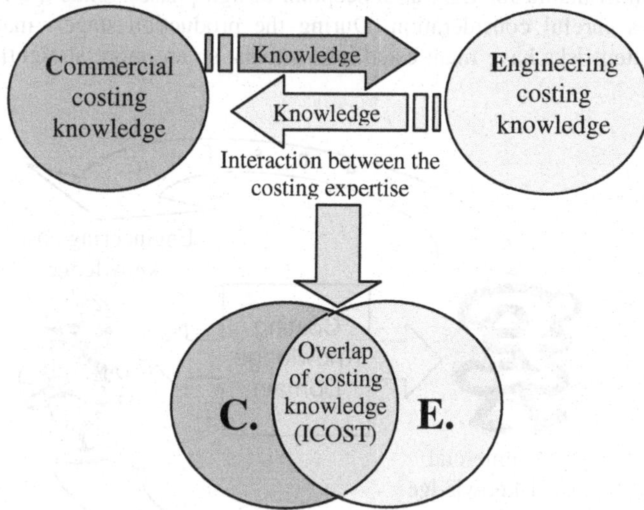

Fig. 1. Commercial and engineering costing disciplines interact, creating an overlap of unstructured, confused knowledge. ICOST will help the alignment & lateral transfer of this knowledge. (Mishra et al, July 2002)

training material. This will promote the reuse and transfer of costing knowledge and expertise within the profession of CE^2 (see Figure 2). Although the scope of the ICOST observations has spanned across a number of industries, the main focus is within the aerospace and automotive industries.

1.4 Areas in Need of Development within CE^2 Profession

As previously mentioned, one of the causes of the lack of essential costing interaction between these two interlinked costing disciplines (of commercial and engineering) is due to an inconsistent terminology between them. This issue is more complex then that which is discussed in section 1.2. The need for a common language, (as well as constant role-titles), is important as it is imperative that these experts understand each other. Thus consistent terminology, inclusive of commonly known, utilised and understood meanings being attached to frequently occurring terms will aid in improving expert interaction.

1.4.1 A Common Costing Language: However the researcher has found that within industry, there are misinterpretations not solely linked to the inconsistent usage of the same words, by different, but interacting departments. Conflicts are also created when these words are utilised to communicate during different stages of a project, but the same words have varied implications dependent of which stage of the project they are used at. For example, the consideration of the Risks involved has a higher weight placed upon it, during the conceptual design phases of a project, then in the later phases, such as production. This is due to the fact that there is very little actual data and information available for CE^2, at conceptual design phases. Thus the calculation of risk requires careful consideration. During the production stages, many of the potential predicted risks have manifested into actuals, so are more straightforward to asses.

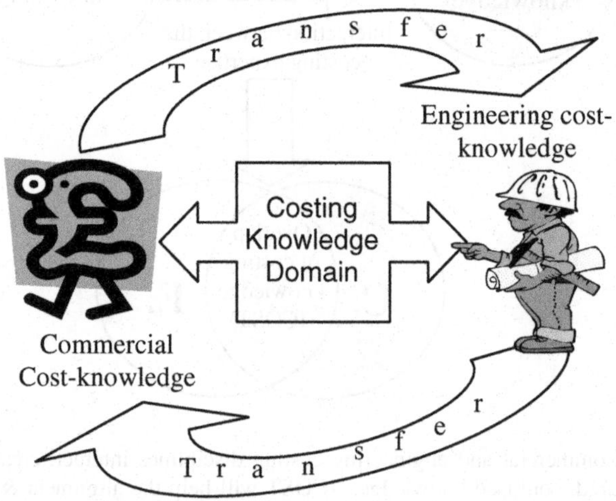

Fig. 2. Essential aspects of commercial and engineering cost -knowledge need to be laterally transferred across the costing profession. (Mishra et al, 2002)

Thus an understanding of not only the different usage of the same words, but how and why their meanings change, is an important factor in CE^2. The elimination of such ambiguity lies in developing a method in which a transparent culture of costing is created, across the disciplines. The comprehension of the experts will promote communication between them; see Figure 2.

1.4.2 Across-the-Board Comprehension of the Specific Costing Disciplines. This need for understanding and communication is also applicable to the specific requirements of the different CE^2 experts' functions: I.e. it is important that a commercial cost expert understands the role of the engineering cost expert, and vice versa, see Figure 2. For instance, a commercial expert must understand that product cost reductions are potentially undergone at the expense of product functionality (within the engineering area of expertise). This will have an impact on the competitive strength of the product: I.e. if budget reductions are deemed necessary, will the product still have all the requested customer features? Or will it be at the same standard as the direct competitor product, in relation to price? An understanding of each others role, within costing is thus essential, in order to promote high caliber CE^2, and faster, more accurate estimates, first time!

1.5 Structure of Paper

The aim of this paper is to identify areas in need of training for the costing profession, from the essential cost-knowledge types identified; and to categorised them into formalised training modules for development. The authors describe how CE^2 knowledge-reuse through training development, will aid in the required alignment between CE^2 disciplines. Having identified the knowledge categories within CE^2, and the types of knowledge that are essential to CE^2, the authors illustrate the need for a lateral transfer of costing knowledge within the costing profession, across industries. There has been no previous documented research in the development of training which is aimed specifically at the CE^2 profession, but of which is generic; i.e. not specific to any organisational costing practice. Therefore this training aims to enhance the knowledge and skills of the CE^2 expert. These skills will be transferable across organisations and ideally across industries (initially focusing on the aerospace and automotive industries). Within this paper the author outlines: Why CE^2 training is needed; What training is needed; Who the training is aimed at (Figure 2); and presents a brief structure of actual training modules identified for development (see Table 6).

2 Training Relevance

2.1 Importance of Relevant Industrial Training

"A 25-year old graduate will have to be re-educated 8 times in the course of a 40 year career" (Oriorne and Rummler, 1988); hence the need for continuous training and development. Carayannis states that an entry level employee is not only required to posses specific knowledge and skills to address the work /tasks at hand, but also needs to hold a repertoire of abstract knowledge that includes computer knowledge, leadership skills, teamwork qualities, ability to communicate, and to be mobile (Carayannis et al.1998). This highlights the fact that CE^2 is not the only profession that demands the utilisation of a multitude of skills and knowledge. As higher education does not address all of these necessities; targeted, continuously updated corporate training and development is imperative, in order to survive the ever-increasing Strategic global competitiveness'. Adequate training is essential for the continued high performance of organisations, the improvement of the workforce; and sustained, if not increased moral, and motivation. Therenou discusses the possibilities of training motivation to the resultant benefits gained from the training; and also to

participation (Therenou, 2001). Not surprisingly the results supported the idea that training development and higher participation occurred when it was supported by supervisors. Also, that the link from knowledge and skills gained from the training should be visibility associated with promotion, job security and pay.

2.2 Training Needs Analysis (TNA)

A number of TNA focus on the specific organisational strategy, when Human Resource Development (HRD) will initially identify the required skills and active management of employee-long-term learning, in relation to explicit corporate business strategies (Hall, 1984). It is recognized that both individual and organisational training development needs, require attention. Thus the course needs to be in-line with the organisational culture, to ensure the enthusiasm and learnt skills can be put into practice, once back in the work place; not met with skepticism and cynicism (Fairbarns, 1991). A more generic design of program should follow as TNA, Figure 3, when considering the introduction of training intervention. This is a systematic approach to determine the real training needs that exist in an organisation or department. Without a systematic and formalised approach to TNA training could be provided that is not required, that does not transfer to the work environment, that is too early or late to be useful, that is training for training's sake'. TNA is generally considered on three conceptually distinct levels: Organisational, Occupational, and Personal. (Goldstein et al., 2002). At organisational level, TNA will confirm that a training intervention is the most appropriate action, and allow occupational and personal analysis to be placed into the organisational context. Additionally, in organisational settings the introduction of a training program is one of many possible interventions introduced to improve performance and/or well being in the workplace. Occupational level analysis, (also known as operational level analysis), is focused on defining

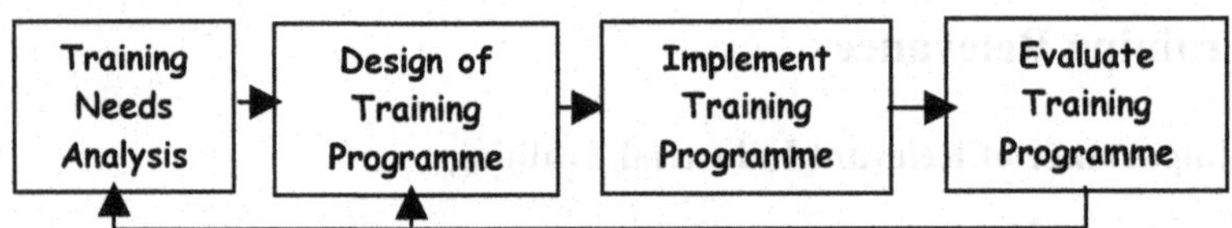

Fig. 3. A Systems approach to training

the specific training objectives in terms of actual job functions. Personal level analysis involves specifying the individuals who are to receive training; this level of analysis may not always be required. For instance an occupational analysis may be sufficient to justify team expenditure in team training. In such situations it is desirable to train the entire team, regardless of the level of competencies held by individual team members. Thus, TNA identifies the \$kills / knowledge gaps' between what level of competency is required, and the level of competency currently held by the job incumbents. To address this gap, decisions need to be made with regards to targeted formalised training intervention. Task analysis protocol has allowed managers to observe highly skilled workers, and identify the precise activities required to perform the variety of jobs performed in manufacturing, (Gael, 1988). Once a specialisation and its components had been analysed and documented, it could then be utilised to aid in the training of the domain novice. (Clark et al 1997). Prior to this job breakdown, training was undergone almost exclusively by observational, on-the-job learning, and formal apprentices. This is not only a time consuming method of learning, but without standardised procedures, inconsistencies in the training outcome would inevitably occur.

2.3 Training Methods

Carayannis et al noted that a training technique within modern organisations was to focus on strategic learning from experience, tacit learning and how- to- learn' skills within trainees. For instance trainees are encouraged to find new ways of confronting and resolving involved technical problems, (Carayannis et al.,1998). This type of philosophy is aligned with the *General principles* theory, where emphasis is placed on why' to do it, as opposed to the *Identical element*, which is what' to do (or seeing and doing, as prior mentioned). The maximum similarity is required, between the training and work environment (Patrick, 1992). The latter is useful for technical and motor skills. The former is more relevant to management, fault diagnosis and CE^2. It focuses on the principles underlying the actions. Therefore the training is designed to develop an understanding of why actions are taken, not simply what actions to take. The overview outline of the training instruction is: Direction, telling trainee what to do (lecture form): Demonstration, showing trainee what to do; and Guidance, allowing trainee to perform task under supervision.

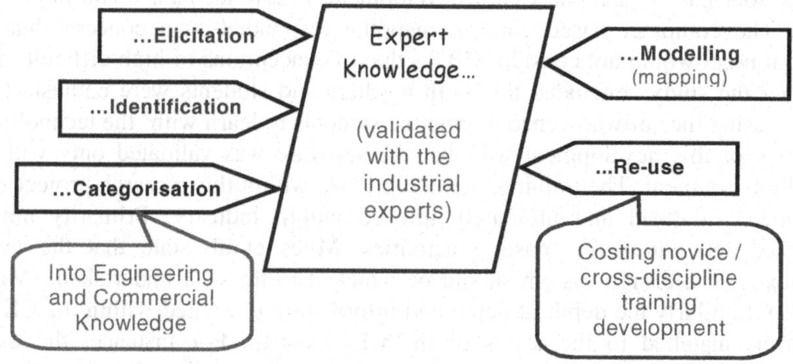

Fig. 4. A basic overview of the methodologies utilised within this research.

2.3.1 Active and Passive learning: Passive learning is a more traditional one-way method of learning, where the student is usually receiving information from an instructor / tutor. Although this is an effective method, it is generally agreed that a more interactive process ensures productive results. The following listed methods are among the processes which actively involve the recipient of the training: On the job training; Mentoring, shadowing ('Sitting with Nellie', SWN) and job rotation, off –the-job training, workshops, case studies, role playing, simulations, problem solving, interactive computer learning packages, videos and audio tapes, CBT. Drawbacks of the above include an inconsistency in the specifics of the training; and also that often the expert being shadowed or mentoring has not been trained as a trainer (Beardwell et al, 1997).

2.4 Computer Based Training (CBT) Tools

The training material developed will incorporate CBT tools: These will act as an aid to the lecture based material; to reinforce the knowledge bestowed from the lectures. CBT is useful with respect to implementing training material within industry, as it can be undergone in conjunction with on-the-job learning. The majority of published results with regards to CBT development and usage are within the area of health and educational sectors. It can be noted that much of the reported developments have been favourable. Veldenz, et al. concluded that CBT modules offered a promising training supplement towards the decision-making skill development for surgical education. It allowed interactive CBT modules that were compatible with windows, whilst being flexible enough to incorporate sophisticated multimedia; allowing the modules to act as both testing and teaching, (Veldenz et al, 1999). Further development into the area of surgical education will require more exposure, experience and investment. However care should be taken when appointing a CBT to training in decision making; all possible answers will not be supported within a CBT, thus it should act only as a support to the area of training. Thus as mentioned previously, this is the intention of the CE^2 CBT development: To reinforce the lecture based training. Knowledge representation, in forms as concept mapping and semantic networks, integrated with a training tool has been a successful development within secondary education (Rye, 2001). The computer based concept mapping responded to a concern that many potential users would not consider CBT's due to conceptions of high difficulty levels. However the study concluded that both teachers and students were enthusiastic and enjoyed using the software, encouraging the students to learn 'with' the technology. A drawback of this development was that the software was validated only within the school-environment. The training, including CBT, within this research project will be developed, validated and ultimately utilised within industry: Primarily aimed at aerospace and automotive costing activities. Miles et al. state that the level of complexity of a design system should be matched to the task undertaken. (Miles, et al.2002). Similarly the depth of detail and information presented within the CE^2 CBT should be matched to the needs of the CE^2 expert. For instance, the material knowledge module will only need to cover the aspects of material that effect cost. This does not include aspects as molecular composition of material; this would be too in-depth, and thus not relevant for the CE^2 experts. The author has observed that few publications have specified how knowledge was elicited, and then subsequently transferred into a training tool. The publications generally discussed the results and impact of the training and CBT. This often highlighted the need for further development of the tool; and the presented cases were often limited in the domain application.

3 Knowledge within CE^2

The methods used by the authors within this research to date are illustrated in Figure 4. CE^2 knowledge was identified and elicited. Seventeen organisations from a variety of industries, (primarily based within the UK and with a minority from the USA) were examined, see Table 1.

Table 1. The level and types of participating industries within this research (Mishra et al 2002)

INDUSTRY:	*NUMBER OBSERVED:
Aerospace	4
Automotive	5
Defense	4
Manufacturing	5
Software	3

*Note: In total 17 companies were examined throughout the investigations; some of which fell into more then one industrial category.

Cognitive, semi-structured interviews were conducted with between one and fifteen experts per organisation, depending on the time available within each company (which spanned between two hours and seven working days). Most of the interviews were taped, as well as physically documented. Validation was generally conducted on-sight, with the experts. The researchers designed specific cost-workshops, when group expert knowledge elicitation was available. The interviews were often accompanied by a costing questionnaire, developed in order to determine the interface between the costing disciplines, (Mishra et al, 2002). The knowledge elicited was thus modelled (mapped) in order to highlight both the classification of knowledge type, and any gaps between the CE^2 knowledge. The authors then categorised the knowledge into either commercial or engineering cost knowledge (in conjunction with expert industrial input). This revealed the ten most essential knowledge types identified as imperative for expert-use within CE^2; refer to Table 2 for the listing.

4 CE^2 Knowledge Reuse

Having identified the essential knowledge required within CE^2, the next stage of research was to determine the relevant training requirements associated with each of the knowledge categories. The method utilised for this purpose is called DIF analysis. DIF equals a measure of the **D**ifficulty, **I**mportance and **F**requency of the task in question for training.

4.1 DIF Analysis

DIF analysis is a term for techniques that attempt to rate which aspects of a task should be included in a formalised training programme; and task aspects that do not need to be trained so formally. Table 3 highlights the focus of DIF analysis. There are not any particular set rules associated in this selection method: On the contrary DIF is based primarily on expert judgment; being more art than science. Generally DIF is used within safety critical industries. It was selected for use within this research due to the straightforward manner and speed in which it could be conducted; as well as the ability to produce usable results from a number of experts. Additionally, DIF analysis has not previously been utilised within the costing profession to asses training needs. The outcome of DIF analysis decides which aspects of job or role, and which tasks should be trained formally; and which tasks can rely on informalised training. DIF analysis is performed by the subject matter expert (SME). The rating is based on either ȴow' or ȟigh' values of expert judgment. The initial stage determines whether a task is of low Ðifficulty' (D) or high.

Table 2. The ten knowledge types essential for CE^2, and the relevant categorisation of each knowledge domain (Mishra et al 2002).

KNOWLEDGE TYPE:	TRADITIONAL CATORGORISATION:
Process Knowledge	Engineering
Supplier Knowledge	Commercial
Risk Knowledge	Commercial
Material knowledge	Engineering
Costing Process Knowledge	Commercial
Product knowledge	Engineering
Knowledge of company strategy	Commercial
Design Knowledge	Engineering
Market Trend knowledge	Commercial
Contact knowledge	Engineering / Commercial

The measure of low or high values, for difficulty, in this research was generally dependent on the time taken to complete the task; i.e. time to locate information required? (-Refer to section 4.3.1). The next step is to determine the Ímportance' (I) of task, again low or high: This was generally a measure of cost, i.e. financial penalties linked to performing the task inaccurately. The concluding stage was a value of how often the task is performed or Ƒrequency' (F) of task, i.e. is the task undergone regularly, throughout the lifecycle of the product? Or only done at the conceptual stages?

Table 3. DIF analysis training selection guidelines

D	Difficulty	Difficulty in learning / performing task.
I	Importance	Level of criticality of task to job performance; or consequences of error
F	Frequency	How often task has to be performed

4.2 DIF Results

With use of the grid in Figure 5, DIF analysis was conducted on aspects of each of the ten knowledge types. Figure 5 illustrates how the final conclusions of training development per knowledge type, were assessed. The outcome of the high and low judgments made by the SME or job analyst, results in the type of training determined. If the grid illustrated in Figure 5 is followed, it can be seen that the results fall into three classifications: NO TRAIN'; TRAIN'; OVERTRAIN'.
4.2.1 Training Categories: No Training': The result of No training, did not in fact imply that a complete lack of training should be adopted for the knowledge transferal. What is determined is that no formalised training is required. The knowledge and competency can be obtained via more informal routes. An example of which is the simple observation of a competent job incumbent i.e. an informal acquisition of competency ("Sitting with Nellie", SWN). The SWN approach is more appropriate for simple tasks, where an informalised method of training will suffice. Observation is also a lower-cost training alternative. Training': Training needs, as defined by DIF indicate the need for formalised, structured training interventions. Over Training': Is where training continues after initial level of competence is obtained. This is considered to be critical for infrequent tasks which may need to be performed under sub-optimal conditions, for example where the job incumbent is under stress, or for emergency procedures. For example the need to be able to rapidly bestow first aid to injured parties, in a life threatening crisis. Subsequently these types of tasks are deemed to have high importance, and often a high difficulty.

4.3 Expert Analysis of the ten Essential CE^2 Knowledge Types

An in-depth analysis of the knowledge identified as being essential for use by the CE^2 expert, (Table 2), was undergone by five experts within three different industries (aerospace, software vendors and automotive). Each of the individual knowledge types was assessed individually by each expert. The expert relayed practical, industrial applications with relation to the knowledge types. A DIF analysis was then conducted on each activity, within each knowledge domain. In other words, one knowledge type out of the ten was taken, and then broken down into costing activities, which fell into that knowledge type. DIF analysis was then performed on each one of these activities. Each expert bestowed thus a high and low rating of the Difficulty, Frequency and Importance of day–to-day costing activities, for activities within all ten knowledge areas. Table 4 presents an example of a singular analysis of one knowledge type: The knowledge involved in the overall process of costing. A breakdown of related activities, and the subsequent rating given is highlighted. Brief reasons, explaining the reason for the experts' specific rating, have also been included. The result of this DIF analysis is to Train (see Table 4 in conjunction with Figure 5). Therefore the need for some formalised training has been established.

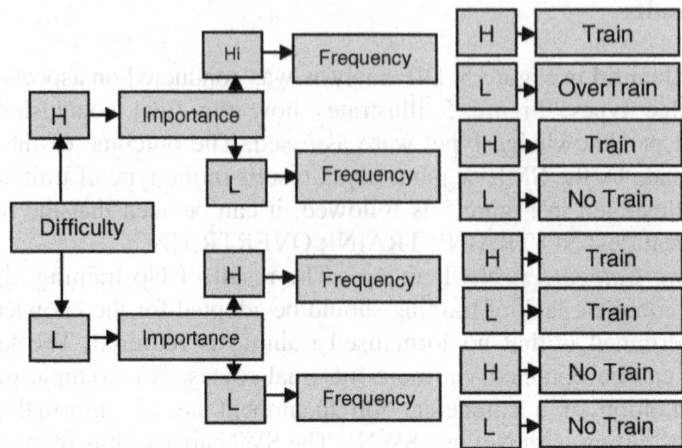

Fig. 5. The *DIF process breaks down the potential training –domains into types of training to be developed for each subject. The focus of this selection process is by means of assessing the Difficulty, Importance and the frequency of each subject area for training (Buckley and Cable 2000, p80).*

4.3.1 Measures of DIF: Difficulty can be linked to the ease at which the knowledge /information required can be accessed (i.e. difficult to obtain, or readily available?): It also refers to how time consuming and changeable the processes are. For example process knowledge was classed as high within aerospace, due to the high level of new processes, which the expert has to continuously be aware of: It was classed as low by the automotive expert, as it was assumed that the fundamentals of most processes would be known and transferred to updates/ modifications. The level of difficulty can also be related to the SMEs' background, i.e. are they á polymers expert, working with steels, specifically austenitic stainless steels? In which case, the overall domain may be materials, but the difficulty can vary, when specifics are accounted for. Where such a result has been deemed possible, (potentially low D for one expert, High D for another within the same knowledge type) it has been represented in brackets in Table 5, with the bracketed result being the less usual one. Table 4, (and analysis as in-depth as Table 4), thus determined the focus for the assessment of training development for each of the other identified knowledge types (within Table 2). The training modules designed through this method are presented in Table 6: A full DIF analysis of the ten identified CE^2 knowledge types were analysed by the stated DIF method. Table 5 shows the industrially validated results of the ten knowledge types, with both aerospace and automotive experts: It is a summary of the compilation of the sets of results obtained, from the more in-depth analysis (Table 4).

5 Training Development

The results of DIF analysis revealed a trend towards structured training development (for eight out of the ten knowledge types). Both Market Trend and Company Strategy have been assessed as requiring No Formal training' by the DIF analysis method of training requirements; thus training development is not applicable within these domains. The other CE^2 essential knowledge types, have been categorised into training development areas within Table 6. Although discrepancies in expert opinion can be observed within a number of the knowledge assessments; often this judgment differential did not affect the overall outcome of the training requirements.

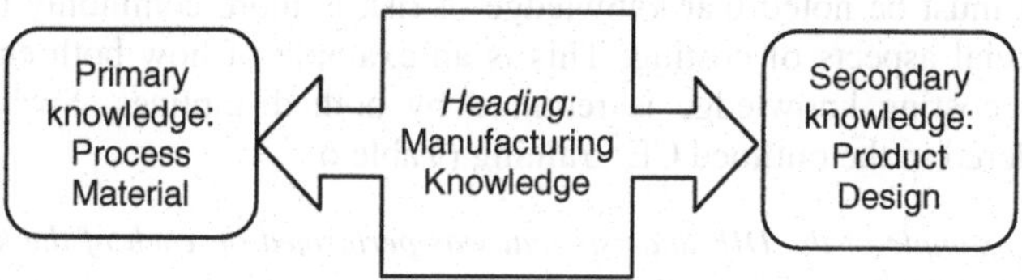

Fig. 6. *The grouping of CE^2 knowledge types that can be placed into a collective area for training development*

5.1 Industry Focus Preference (Aerospace /Automotive)

Table 5 displays a minority of inconsistencies (two) in the expert opinion with relation to importance, difficulty and frequency of use of the knowledge type. The discrepancy of Risk knowledge illustrates a specific industrial difference, in the usage and need for that particular knowledge type. Thus it can be seen that knowledge of Risks is high, high and high (respectively for each D-I-F), as judged by the aerospace specialist. This is due to the nature of the industry: An aerospace project may run for the duration, or in excess, of 20 years. The risks involved in this time span can be costly if estimated incorrectly. Alternately the automotive experts classified Risk knowledge as low, low and low for difficulty, frequency and importance. This is due to the fact that risk assessment within this organisation is not a function of product costing, therefore non-applicable; hence the consistent 'Low' rating's for this knowledge type. In such instances other experts within other industries (such as software vendors), or within the same industries, were asked to provide additional opinions. This was in order for the researcher to gain a wider perspective on the knowledge weighting; thus drawing a broader assessment of the particular training requirements, for the originally subjective knowledge type.

5.2 Knowledge Transfer and Grouping

The subsequent grouping of the knowledge types further determined the modules of training. This was achieved again with the aid of expert opinion, as to which specific knowledge was related to any one or more of the other knowledge types and in what manner (see Figure 6). As mentioned previously more the one fundamental knowledge type has been identified as being essential for use within CE^2, (see Table 2). Thus the need for a lateral transfer of both knowledge types, between the disciplines within the overall domain of 'costing' was made apparent, (Mishra et al, 2002). This was further validated by the fact that the same-knowledge types did not, as a rule, get grouped together. For instance a large minority of experts linked process knowledge and risk knowledge. Traditionally process knowledge is classified as engineering; and risk, as commercial. However when assessing the suitability of a new process, the engineering cost experts in one organisation, explained how they were responsible for estimating the risks associated with the process, and relaying this assessment to the commercial cost experts. A decision on the usage of such a process would then be made by the commercial-cost experts, based on the engineering-cost information bestowed. However, it must be noted that knowledge of risk is more commonly identified with the commercial aspects of costing. This is an example of how both engineering and commercial costing knowledge is required by both disciplines. Such requirements were considered in the outlined CE[2] training (Table 6).

Table 4. An *example of the DIF analysis that was performed on each of the knowledge types identified (aerospace).*

Costing Process Knowledge:	Difficulty	Importance	Frequency	Training
Direct Costs	LOW -usually given in BoM (industry dependent), so determined early	HIGH -high effect on cost	HIGH -required for every phase of product / project	TRAIN
Indirect Costs	HIGH -can be different per project	HIGH -big effect on the overall project	LOW -only needed for overall project cost (Not done per component i.e. for material costs, not needed, etc.)	OVERTRAIN
Supplier cost breakdown	HIGH Difficulty in gaining access to supplier information	HIGH Costly if incorrect	LOW At beginning of project	OVERTRAIN
Overhead Allocation	HIGH Can vary per project	HIGH Large effect on costs	LOW Usually once throughout project	OVERTRAIN
Logistics -overseas or not – difference in costs	LOW Simple checks	LOW Not always applicable	LOW No required often, usually determined early in project	NO TRAINING
Legislation	LOW Documentation available	HIGH Potential cost implications	LOW Once per project	TRAIN
Annual cost breakdown	LOW Company will provide	HIGH High effects on costs	LOW Done annually	TRAIN
Depreciation	LOW Can be calculated with the given information	HIGH Can have great effect on cost	LOW Conducted once throughout project	TRAIN

5.3 Knowledge Grouping Translating into Training Areas

One of the most frequently grouped knowledge sets was as illustrated in Figure 6. Thus Manufacturing knowledge' encompasses process knowledge and material knowledge, as well as overall product knowledge and knowledge of design. These four knowledge types can be grouped into one comprehensive module for training: Manufacturing'. The ten knowledge types were grouped by the experts. Table 6 shows the results of this grouping. The author has outlined the resultant training modules, and briefly highlighted how these modules will be developed (Table 6). The CBT will be developed in conjunction with the lecture-based material; as a support. This will aid in the reinforcing of knowledge bestowed within the lectures, along with workbooks and interactive expert workshops.

A minority of the training modules will be more designed towards either one of the disciplines or may be industry focused. For example, it may be aimed at the commercial aspects of costing, and relevant for both aerospace and automotive industries; or focused at commercial and engineering, with more relevance for one industry, then the other. For instance the process and material modules may appeal more to the commercial experts (consisting essentially of cost-engineering knowledge). However it will also serve to broaden the current engineering expert's knowledge-base even further: Or to act as a refresher course. Thus although it will have relevance for the engineering cost expert, it will be primarily aimed towards the commercial-cost discipline. Workshops will also be developed as specified (Table 6). This will aid in the interaction between the relevant cost-disciplines. The aim of such interactive modules (i.e. No. 4, Table 6) is to promote a change in the traditional culture of the working practices, to eliminate role ambiguity; and to thus promote communication and interaction between the engineering and commercial costing disciplines (predetermined content, ICOST 2001). This will involve mixed disciplines and industries, and will help develop a common language (and thus improve comprehension) within CE^2

Table 5. *Aerospace and Automotive Industrial Validation of DIF*

Knowledge Type:	DIFFICULTY:		IMPORTANCE		FREQUENCY		TRAINING:	
	Aerospace	Automotive	Aero-	Auto	Aero	Auto	Aero	Auto-
Process Knowledge	HIGH	LOW	HIGH	HIGH	HIGH	HIGH	Train	Train
Supplier Knowledge	HIGH (Low)	HIGH	HIGH	LOW	LOW	HIGH	Over Train (train)	Train
Risk Knowledge	HIGH	LOW	HIGH	LOW	HIGH	LOW	Train	No Train
Material knowledge	LOW	HIGH	HIGH	HIGH	LOW	HIGH	Train	Train
Costing Process Knowledge	LOW (High)	HIGH (Low)	HIGH	HIGH	HIGH	HIGH	Train (train)	Train (Train)
Product knowledge	HIGH	HIGH	HIGH	HIGH	HIGH	HIGH	Train	Train
Knowledge of company strategy	LOW	HIGH	HIGH	LOW	LOW	LOW	Train	No Train
Design Knowledge	HIGH	HIGH	HIGH	HIGH	HIGH	HIGH	Train	Train
Market Trend knowledge	LOW (High)	HIGH	HIGH (Low)	LOW	LOW	LOW	Train (No train)	No Train
Contact knowledge	LOW	HIGH	HIGH (Low)	HIGH (Low)	HIGH	HIGH	Train (No Train)	Train (train)

5.4 Limitations of the Research

A high level of the knowledge analysis and training assessment was focused on expert judgement. The drawback to this approach is that it is exposed to expert bias, or personal-interpretation. For instance the level of experience an expert has can effect their judgement within these areas. Also the expert's background could create bias, (i.e. a greater emphasis can be placed on engineering aspects, if that is where their knowledge and experience is). This can thus create an inconsistency within the results. Subsequently, the knowledge engineer must be aware of such factors went interpreting the results. A high level of expert interaction can help to account for genuine irregularities within the findings; and determine consistent commonalities: It can expose /reduce individual expert bias.

5.5 Training Focus

It must be noted that the knowledge within this research was identified and elicited from CE^2 experts, within a selection of industries, (Table 1). This specific costing knowledge has thus been used to develop training material. The training development has subsequently been scoped to focus on the aerospace and automotive industries, aimed at CE^2 novices within; and to transfer expert costing knowledge back into the profession. The training is also focused at cross-costing discipline experts. Namely, the relevant commercial knowledge transfer, to the engineering cost expert, and vice versa (refer to Figure 2).

As the knowledge identified originally has been complied from CE^2 experts within different industries, this has allowed the manifestation of the commonalities of costing knowledge requirements across industries. It has also highlighted the costing practices which are special to each industry, and which are particular to specific organisations. This industrial cross-validation of knowledge requirements has enabled the training development to have more of a generic CE^2 focus; as opposed to the current costing training within this profession, which is highly organisational-focused. Thus the intent of the outlined training is to create transferable CE^2 knowledge and skills: Of which will be relevant within different organisations and potentially, different industries.

6 Conclusions

This paper presents a methodology to identify a training programme in CE^2, based on knowledge required within the domain, (aerospace and automotive focus of costing). Through the use of DIF analysis, industrial cost-experts rated the knowledge types required for costing. The method utilised allowed these knowledge areas to be classified into training type (of formal or informal). The grouping of the knowledge types, (which were identified as the formal-training requirements'), dictated the specific modules of cost-training. This expert knowledge elicitation and reuse, ensures that the knowledge currently held within CE^2, is managed and will be held and reused within the profession. The methodology used to elicit and re-use knowledge within the research contributes directly to the enhancement and containment of knowledge within the overall costing profession.

Table 6. An outline of the training module –development for the CE^2 profession

Training Modules	Overview of Training
1. Manufacturing Module: 1a) Process and Materials	A CBT on a section of Process Workbook on Materials and lecture based material
1.b) Product and Design	It Is recommended that companies undergo this training through regular provider-such as university courses. (Though identified as a training area, is recognised as being not feasible for detailed training development within the duration of this research project.)
2. Supplier Knowledge and Contact Management	Lecture based material on Supply Chain Management
3. Costing Process and Risk	Lecture based and CBT plus case studies on both. Separate training for engineers and training for commercial will be developed.
4. Lateral Transfer of Costing knowledge (to promote communication between the engineers and commercial people involved in cost estimating):	An interactive training course: involving lecture based / workshop /visual aids. This will encompass a comprehensive overview of the major aspects within CE2, and will cover the issue of cultural needs of the profession. The course will raise the awareness of engineers about what commercial people do and vice versa.

7 Future Work

The training development outlined in Table 6 is in the process of being developed fully. The prototypes will be validated within industry, modified as required, and then implemented in industries. For the future, it would be beneficial to further develop the diversity of this type of training i.e. Training can be developed and validated, in-depth across a greater number of industries, in addition to aerospace and automotive. This applies to comparative practices on a wider, international scale; and would aid in the promotion of the lateral transfer of costing practices across the CE^2 profession. Comparisons could be made, with commonalities of costing best-practice between industries, being made apparent. This would also serve to help modify the inconsistencies within costing terminology, across and within industries.

Acknowledgements. The authors would like to thank the industrial sponsors of ICOST: BAE SYSTEMS, Ford Motor Company, XR Training and Consultancy, Price Systems, for their continued support and contributions; and the Decision Engineering Research group (Cranfield University), for comments on the draft paper. The ICOST project is jointly funded by industry and EPSRC (Grant No: GR/N 21321).

References

1. Beardwell, I.; Holden L. (Ed.) *Human Resource Management, A contemporary perspective*, 2nd edition, (1997) Financial Times
2. Buckley, R. & Caple, J. (2000) *The Theory and Practice of Training*. 4th Edition. London; Kogan Page.
3. Carayannis E.G., Jorge, J., *Bridging government –university-industry technological learning disconnects: a comparative study of training and development policies and practices in the U.S., Japan, Germany, and France*. Pub. Pergamon, Journal:Technovation Vol.8 No.s6/7 pp383-407 (1998)
4. Clark, R. E., Estes, F., *Cognitive Task Analysis For Training* Journal: Training in Organization, pp403-417 Elsevier Science Ltd (1997)
5. Fairbarns, J. Pluggin *The Gap in Training needs analysis* (1991) Personnel Management, February pp43-45
6. Gael, S. *The job analysis handbook for business, industry, and government* Gael (ed)Vol. 1 pp71-86) New York: Wiley (1988)
7. Goldstein, I.L.; Ford J.K., *Training in Organisations*, Forth edition, Pub. Wadsworth ISBN 0-534-34554-9 (2002)
8. Hall, D.T. *Human resource development and organisational effectiveness,* Fomburun, C., Tichy, N., Devanna, M. (ed.s) Strategic Human Resource Management. (1984) New Yourk, John Wiley
9. Miles, J., Moore, L., Cadogan J., *Matching computational strategies to task complexity and user requirements*. Elsevier Science Ltd, Journal: Advanced Engineering Informatics, 16, pp41-52 (2002)
10. Mishra, K., Roy, R., Souchoroukov, P., (2001) *Knowledge within commercial and engineering activities within cost estimating*. CE2002, Concurrent Engineering conference, Cranfield, UK July 2002
11. ICOST Internal Report (Oct.2001) Cranfield University
12. Odiorne, G., Rummler, G., *Training and Development : A Guide for professionals*. (1988) Commerce Clearing House Inc.
13. Roy, R., Mishra, K., Souchoroukov, P., ICOST Internal Report, (April 2001), *Commercial and Engineering Activities within Cost Estimating: Industry Practice AS-IS*. ICOST01/ April 2001. Cranfield University.
14. Roy, R., Mishra, K., Souchoroukov, P. *Interface between Commercial and Engineering Activities in Cost Estimating: Industry Practice* Third Joint Annual ISPA / SCEA International Conference, USA (12th -15th June 2001)
15. Rye, J.A., *Enhancing Teachers Use of Technology Through Professional Development on electronic Concept Mapping*. Plenum Publishing Corporation, Journal of Science and Technology, Vol.10 No.3, pp223-235, (2001)
16. Tharenou, P., The *relationship of training motivation to participation in training and development*. Journal of Occupational and Organisational Psychology, 74, pp599-621 (2001)
17. Veldenz, H.C., Edwards, F.H., *Computer-Based Training Initiatives for Education in Surgical Decision Making*. Elsevier Science Inc., Journal: Current Surgery, pp165-168 (1999)

Management of Intellectual Capital by Optimal Portfolio Selection

Hennie Daniels[1,2] and Henk Noordhuis[3]

[1]University of Tilburg
Department of Information Systems
PO BOX 90153
5000 LE Tilburg
daniels@kub.nl
[2]Rotterdam School of Management / Faculteit Bedrijfskunde

[3]Financial Analyst
QOMPETENCE B.V.
Almere
henk.noordhuis@hetnet.nl

Abstract. An important issue for the management team of R&D departments is the selection of a portfolio of projects in periods of excess demand. Standard methods mostly focus on project selection on the basis of expected returns. In many cases other strategic aspects are important e.g. at the department level the development of intellectual capital or at the company level achieving comparative advantage.
In this paper we develop a tool for portfolio selection, explicitly taking into account the measurement and balancing of these strategic factors. The indicators of an intellectual capital scorecard are periodically measured against a target and constitute the input of a linear programming model. From the optimal portfolio computed by the model, clear objectives for management can be derived. Our method is illustrated in an industrial case study.

1 Introduction

"Knowledge is power." Yet, managers still determine their strategies mostly on the basis of financial indicators and measurement tools. It is not hard to imaging why. The future investments of shareholders are mainly determined by the short-term profitability of their shares. Apart from this fact there is simply a lack of tools that enable managers to implement a knowledge-based management strategy.

This is especially a problem for R&D departments, since their performance is not reflected in profit figures. Outputs from R&D departments vary widely, ranging from patents in the case of research laboratories to advanced components in the case of development laboratories. However, R&D departments share common characteristics that distinguish them from other departments and business units. R&D laboratories are mainly knowledge-driven rather than profit-driven. Typical characteristics are a

D. Karagiannis and U. Reimer (Eds.): PAKM 2002, LNAI 2569, pp. 613-619, 2002.

highly invariable capacity, a zero-profit target, and constant need to develop new valuable knowledge.

R&D departments have a *highly invariable capacity*, especially in the short run. New employees must acquire specific knowledge during their first period of employment, before they become productive. Knowledge workers in R&D departments have a high level of education, but due to the complexity of their work it may take up to a few years before a new employee becomes fully productive. In a sense this shows that (tacit) knowledge is one of the sustainable competitive advantages in today's world; it cannot be bought or hired like buildings, machinery and production workers. A downside of the invariable nature of the capacity is that in times of increasing demand a shortage of capacity can easily arise. This implies that not all the projects of the (internal) customers can be realized and a project selection tool is needed. A general set up for such a tool, based on a score card approach is presented in this paper.

Another common trait of R&D departments is that they usually have a *zero-profit target*, because the majority of customers are internal. The task of the R&D department is to support business units with the realization of new products. As consequence it is irrelevant to the R&D department itself, whether the projects they work on are profitable or not, as long as they stay satisfy budget constraints. So profitability at the department level is not the key variable in a project selection tool.

The core business of R&D departments is the *development of new knowledge*, efficiently and effectively. New knowledge is mainly developed by conducting new projects in the front line of technology, so-called projects of the first generation rather than projects of the second or third generation. An R&D department that focuses too much on the latter will undermine the future potential of its knowledge base. Not only do R&D departments need to focus on developing *new* knowledge, it has to be done effectively and efficiently. In many branches the time-to-market is the most important indicator for future profitability of a new product [Smith e.a, 1991].

It is clear from the arguments above that effective tools for projection selection in R&D departments are highly needed in periods of excess demand. The method should not be based on (expected) profitability of projects, like the traditional R&D project selection tools [Martino, 1995], but should take into account other factors like development of new knowledge, customer satisfaction etc..However in order to incorporate knowledge as a factor into a model for project selection, we first need to find a way to measure it. In the next section we shortly discuss methods for measuring knowledge or, in a broader sense, intellectual capital.

2 Measurement of Intellectual Capital

Intellectual capital encompasses more than just knowledge. Many researchers have formulated definitions of Intellectual capital', but they all boil down to the same principle: intellectual capital is the difference between the market value and the net book value of a company. In other words, it is the additional value the market wants to pay for the company on top of its equity capital. The next step is to subdivide the intellectual capital into components. Different terminology is in use, here we adopt Edvinsson's terminology [Edvinsson, 1997], which became widely accepted in the field.

The first distinction one can make is between human capital and structural capital. *Human capital* is the tacit knowledge within the heads of the employees'. This includes skills, knowledge and attitudes. Human capital is the part of the intellectual capital that leaves the company after working hours. The remainder is the *structural capital*, the part of the intellectual capital that is structurally present in the company. The structural capital can be subdivided into customer capital and organizational capital. Customer capital encompasses the value of customer relationships, often referred to as goodwill. Since supplier relations also are of great value to most companies, we prefer to speak of *relational capital*, which includes both. The remainder of the structural capital finds is in the organizational structure, called *organizational capital*. The first component of the organizational capital is the process capital, which is the part of the organization capital connected to the way (groups) of people within the organization cooperate. This includes procedures and regulations. The second component of the organizational capital is the *innovation capital*, which consists of codified knowledge. Part of this codified knowledge is legally protected, such as patents and trademarks. This part is the *intellectual property* of the company. The remainder of the innovation capital the *intangible assets*, is not legally protected. Over the last decade a number of methods have been proposed to measure components of intellectual capital. A comprehensive overview of the measurement models can be found in[Sveiby, 2001a]. He draws a distinction between *monetary intellectual capital measuring models*, which express the value of intellectual capital in money, and *non-monetary intellectual capital measuring models*, which measure the intellectual capital in non-monetary ways. Examples of monetary intellectual capital measuring models are Human Resource Accounting (HRA) and the Value Explorer. *HRA* combines methods that estimate the value of the human capital based on costs, market prices or discounted estimates of future earnings of the human resources [King e.a., 1999]. Andriessen and Tissen's Value Explorer® toolkit calculates the value of a company's core-competences [Andriessen e.a., 2000]. The problem with monetary intellectual capital measuring models is that they may provide unreliable results. This is due to fact that all parameters have to be quantified in monetary indicators.

Non-monetary *intellectual capital scorecards*, may yield more reliable results because they use the more natural measurement scales for each indicator, instead of converting everything into monetary figures. An intellectual capital scorecard will group indicators in a consistent and coherent framework, based on the components of intellectual capital that we described previously. Well-known intellectual capital scorecards are Sveiby's *Intangibles Assets Monitor* [Sveiby, 1997] and the *Skandia Navigator* of Edvisson and Malone [Edvinsson e.a., 1997].

Intellectual capital scorecards are very similar to Kaplan and Norton's *balanced scorecard* [Kaplan e.a., 1996]. The difference is mainly in the business process that is being assessed. The balanced scorecard (BSC) is based on the value chain concept, while intellectual capital scorecards are based on the components of intellectual capital [Sveiby, 2001b]. The BSC groups its indicators in four perspectives (Financial, Customer, Internal Business, and Learning & Growth), the Skandia Navigator consists of five components (Financial, Customer, Process, Human, and Renewal & Development).

The *Financial Focus* contains indicators related to the net book value. An example of a financial indicator is the revenues per employee (€)'. The *Customer Focus* consists of indicators related to the customer capital. If a company also likes to measure indicators related to suppliers, it can choose to use the term Relational Focus' instead, and place all indicators related to its relational capital in this perspective. An example of a Relational Focus indicator is ćustomers lost (#)'. Indicators measuring the process capital are placed in the *Process Focus*. Change in IT inventory (€)' is an example of such an indicator. The *Human Focus* encompasses all indicators related to the human capital. An example of a Human Focus indicator is åverage years of service with company (#)'. Finally, the Renewal & Development Focus lists all indicators regarding the innovation capital and the renewal of all other factors. Share of employees under age 40 (%)' would be a typical indicator for this factor.

Companies are free to choose which indicators they want to put on their scorecard. Indicators are periodically (e.g. every month) measured against a target. The *target* is the desired value of the indicator at the end of the timeframe (e.g. a year). If the periodically measured *actual value* is (much) below the target, management should take measures to improve performance. Both, indicators and targets should be derived from the strategy of the department or business unit in our case the R&D department. Examples are: reputation, project size, new competence development, customer satisfaction and risk.
Intellectual capital scorecards serve as a starting-point for the development of a model for project selection. The model assigns a score to each project that depends on the degree in which this project can contribute to the realization of the targets on the scorecard. Of course management would like to carry out all projects that contribute to the main targets. In the cases we have studied (and are working on) there are many capacity constraints on several area's of human expertise. These restrictions due to limited capacities are incorporated into the framework that is described in the next section.

3 Model for Optimal Portfolio Description

For the remainder we assume that an intellectual scorecard has been designed and implemented. As pointed out above the indicators targets and so on will be different in each case. However the model for project selection described here is basically the same. It is described in 9 subsequent steps:

Step 1. *Select relevant indicators from the scorecard.* Restrict the scorecard to include only indicators that are relevant to project selection. Number the remaining indicators from 1 to *m*.

Step 2. *Convert all values on the scorecard to values between 1 and 5.*

Step 3. *Determine the weight of each indicator on the scorecard.* The weight should depend on two factors. Indicators you really want to be at their target at the end of the time frame should get high weight factor. The second factor that should be taken into account is the difference between the target of the indicator and its actual value. If this difference is bigger than acceptable, the weight could be raised in an attempt to improve performance of this indicator in the future. The weight of indicator I_i is denoted by α_i .

Step 4. *Estimate for each project to which extent it contributes to each indicator..* In our case we took values between 1 and 5. For example, if you expect project p_1 to score very well on indicator I_5, that results in $I_5(p_1) = 5$.

Step 5. *Determine the value of each project.* This is done by adding up the invidual score son each indicator:

$$V(p) = \sum_{i=1}^{m} \alpha_i I_i(p)$$

The higher this value, the more the project will contribute to realizing your targets at the end of the timeframe.

Step 6. *Define the overall objective function.* This is :

$$PV = \beta_1 V(p_1) + \ldots + \beta_n V(p_n)$$

Here PV is the *portfolio value*, *n* is the number of projects, $\beta_1 \ldots \beta_n$ are the decision variables in the Linear Programming(LP) model that can take only values 0,1. The values $V(p_1) \ldots V(p_n)$ are calculated in the previous step.

Step 7. *Compute the capacities in the period of consideration.* Suppose the time frame considerd is 6 months and assume that there are only two different types of capacities A and B. In 6 months there are still *TC* =75,000 man-hours to divide; 40,000 of capacity A and 35,000 of capacity B. In that case TC_A = 40,000 and TC_B = 35,000. (*TC* is total capacity.)

Step 8. *Determine the required capacities for each project.* For example:

$C_A(p_1) = 8{,}000$ $\qquad$ $C_B(p_1) = 6{,}000$

$C_A(p_2) = 5{,}000$ $\qquad$ $C_B(p_2) = 7{,}000$

... $\qquad$ ...

$C_A(p_n) = 6{,}000 \qquad C_B(p_n) = 0$

$C_A(p_1)$ is the required capacity of type A for project p_1 and $C_B(p_1)$ is the required capacity of type B for project p_1, etc.

Step 9. *Formulate the constraints of the LP model.* The number of constraints depends on the number of capacities. In this case there are 2 capacity constraints:

$$\beta_1 C_A(p_1) + \ldots + \beta_n C_A(p_n) \leq 40{,}000$$

$$\beta_1 C_B(p_1) + \ldots + \beta_n C_B(p_n) \leq 35{,}000$$

Add the following constraints:

$$\beta_1 \ldots \beta_n = 0 \text{ or } 1$$

This completes the LP model. After solving this model we obtain a value 0 or 1 for each of the β_x $. If the value of β_x is 1, the project p_x is part of the optimal portfolio. The *optimal portfolio* is the selection of projects that come closest to the realization of the targets at the end of the timeframe.

A detailed study based on this model has been conducted in an industrial research laboratory. The LP model was implemented in Microsoft Excel 2000. It is now used by management for project selection. The parameters in the model are estimated by management and experienced experts in the lab. They are frequently changed when different scenario's or what if studies are carried out We are currently working on a similar set up for two other research laboratories in the Netherlands.

Acknowledgement. This research was partially conducted in the framework of the METIS project. The managerial and financial support of Janine Swaak and the Telematika institute are kindly acknowledged

References

1. Andriessen, D.; Tissen, R. (2000). *Weightless Wealth; Finding your real value in a future of intangible assets.* Prentice Hall, Londen.
2. Edvinsson, L. (1997). Developing Intellectual Capital at Skandia. *Long Range Planning*, 30(3), p.320-321+366-373.
3. Edvinsson, L.; Malone, M.S. (1997). *Intellectual Capital; Realizing Your Company's True Value By Finding Its Hidden Brainpower.* HarperBusiness, New York.
4. Kaplan, R.S.; Norton, D.P. (1996). *The Balanced Scorecard; Translating strategy into action.* Harvard Business School Press, Boston.
5. King, A.F.; Henry, J.M. (1999). Valuing Intangible Assets Through Appraisals. *Strategic Finance*, 80(10), p.33-37.
6. Martino, J.P. (1995). *Research and Development Project Selection.* John Wiley & Sons, New York.
7. Smith, P.G.; Reinertsen, D.G. (1991). *Developing products in half the time.* Van Nostrand Reinhold, New York.

8. Sveiby, K.E. (1997). *The New Organizational Wealth.* Berrett-Koehler Publishers, San Francisco.
9. Sveiby, K.E. (2001a). Methods for Measuring Intangible Assets. *http://www.sveiby.com.au/IntangibleMethods.htm*, 18-5-2001.
10. Sveiby, K.E. (2001b). The Balanced Score Card (BSC) and the Intangible Assets Monitor – a comparison. *http://www.sveiby.com.au/IntangAss/BSCandIAM.html*, 18-5-2001.

Integrating Knowledge Management, Learning Mechanisms, and Company Performance

James A. Sena[1] and Abraham B. (Rami) Shani[2]

[1]College of Business, California Polytechnic State University,San Luis Obispo, CA 93407, jsena@calpoly.edu

[2]College of Business, California Polytechnic State University, San Luis Obispo, CA 93407, ashani@calpoly.edu

Abstract. This paper addresses some of the characteristics of learning in knowledge-based work environments. The role that learning mechanisms play in the firm's ability to create, transfer and enhance knowledge is discussed as well as sustaining learning and competitiveness. The work involves a field study of a software development firm [SDF] that utilizes agent-based technologies and other "cooperative decision making" tools, a platform architecture, and "extreme programming".

1 Introduction

In the late 1990s the limited computer-assistance capabilities reflective of Decision Support-based Software [DSS] software were being replaced by integrated, multi-agent, cooperative systems. These signaled the emergence of a new generation of DSS software in which the contributions of several components are coordinated through an inter-process communication facility. The components, commonly referred to as agents, are separate modules depicting one or more processes. They are rule-based expert systems, procedural programs, neural networks, or even sensing devices. They reflect learning on the part of the individual, the team or the organization. Increasingly, these agents have the ability to explain their actions and proposals, as they interact spontaneously with each other either directly or through coordination facilities.

Notions about the dynamic nature of the relationship between knowledge management processes and organizational learning have a relatively short tradition in organizational sciences [1][2]. One emerging challenge to organizations and management is to understand the nature of the knowledge management processes. Specifically, what are those processes that facilitate knowledge creation, knowledge production and knowledge transfer within and between teams and sub units.

At the foundation of these knowledge management process models, conceptualizations, and implementation practices is an organizational learning cycle and process orientation. In this context organizational learning is the ability of the system to continuously improve the way it creates, manages transfers and exploits organizational knowledge. Organizational learning mechanisms are a formal configuration consisting of structures, processes, procedures, rules, tools, methods

D. Karagiannis and U. Reimer (Eds.): PAKM 2002, LNAI 2569, pp. 620-631, 2002.

and physical configurations which are created within the firm for the purpose of developing, enhancing and sustaining performance and learning [3]. Thus, in the context of knowledge management process, organizational learning mechanisms are the formal configuration created within the firm for the purpose of continuously improving the way that the organization creates, transfers, exploits and manages knowledge. By focusing on the organization as a unit for learning, we argue that while individuals are important agents of learning, organizational structures and processes, rules and standard operating procedures influence the organization's ability to manage learning and influence the knowledge management process. As will be seen in the case that follows, in the context of intense information technology workplace, different learning mechanisms were developed within a software development firm (SDF) around knowledge management processes.

1.1 Setting the Context

Software development is by its nature an intensive work situation due to cyclical development, pressure to reduce development time, competitive global market, keeping abreast of ongoing technological innovations, and increasing personnel turnover rates. At the micro level there are pressures to get the product to market that may not be complete or that do not meet all of the specifications. Re-usable code, modules and agents are all assisting mechanisms.

Work intensity is viewed as a socially constructed phenomenon that is embedded in the increasing rate of change in the nature of software development work. In this context, changes in the software development industry seem to occur at many levels: increasing rate of technological hardware development and new software products are being introduced into the market place; individuals are required to put forth a continuous effort at acquiring new knowledge and skills; expectations and pressure to reduce development cycle times are increasing; individuals are pressured to integrate variety of knowledge bases into the process; and last, organizational members are pressured to integrate customers (and at time suppliers) into the process. Two major causes of work intensity are scope creep (unplanned changes to the scope of work as the product development progresses) and the actual delivery of the finished product to the customer (time-to-market). Another negative consequence of the increasing work intensity seems to center on the difficulty in retaining talented software development engineers and management information system specialists. As turnover increases, it is accompanied by a loss of knowledge and understanding of core processes. At the same time, as information technology becomes a critical success factor, especially within firms whose product is the actual development of a software product, loss of key personnel has a major impact.

Based on these characteristics the development of software products can be categorized as an information intensive activity that depends for its success largely on the availability of information resources and, in particular, the experience and reasoning skills of the managers and staff's learning environment. It follows that the quality of the solutions will vary significantly as a function of the problem solving skills, wisdom, knowledge, development solution process. This clearly presents an opportunity for the useful employment of learning mechanisms in which the capabilities of the human decision maker are complemented with knowledge bases, expert agents, and self-activating conflict identification and monitoring capabilities. Agent technologies, with respect to the software industry, are self-contained, intelligent, adaptive software modules that are used as building blocks to construct complex software products. Through the use of collaborating expert agents product development provides the flexibility and range needed for product design sustainability. Heterogeneous, semiautonomous knowledge-based software components are integrated into coordinated applications. Through the use of interoperability standards and methods information can flow seamlessly through an application across heterogeneous machines, computing platforms, programming languages, and data and process representations. [4].

In the broadest sense an agent may be described as a computer-based program or module of a program that has communication capabilities to external entities and can perform some useful tasks in at least a semi-autonomous fashion. These aspects exhibit learned behavior. According to this definition agent software can range from simple, stand-alone, predetermined applications to the most intelligent, integrated, multi-agent decision-support system that advanced technology can produce today. The objective of multi-agent software is not to automate the decision making activity, but to create an effective partnership between the human decision maker and the computer-based agents. In this partnership the human agent must be able to communicate with the computer-based agents in terms of the same real world objects that are used so effectively in all human reasoning endeavors. In their role as active collaborators the computer-based agents will have information needs that cannot be totally predetermined. Therefore, similar to the human agent, they will require the capability to dynamically generate database queries and initiate user interactions. At least some of the information sources accessed by the agents will be prototypical in nature (i.e., standard practices, case studies, and other typical knowledge pertaining to the problem situation) consistent with the notion of knowledge-based systems.

This paper discusses systems wherein software developers and computer-based agents assist each other in the exploration, analysis and creation of software products in which there are many variables with complex relationships and dynamic information changes. The software firm under study, that we term SDF, has developed a framework for generating computer-supported decision aides consisting of an overall architecture, an object model, an agent engine, and an object browser interface. Most of the applications developed were military-related.

2 The Organization

SDF is in the business of building, implementing, and supporting agent-based "Cooperative Decision Making" tools for distributed problem solving. Application areas include: facilities management, transportation planning, military logistics and control, and engineering design. SDF began as a university-based research facility and evolved into a private R&D organization. SDF's differentiating factor has been the development of an agent-based methodology to deal with spatial problems for organizing engineering design with respect to space management, space constraints, and storage priorities from an architectural perspective. Their approach used a series of agents to assist human decision-making.

2.1 Resource Capabilities: Expertise and Longevity

SDF describes their resources very succinctly – the expertise of their employees and longevity. Combining this expertise with a set of re-usable code and software agents is a process called "extreme programming." The management team size is restricted to a small set of long-term employees. With respect to longevity most of the core team members have been together somewhere between four and seven years.

SDF has created a generic set of agents designed to respond to changes in the problem state spontaneously, through their ability to monitor information changes and respond opportunistically. Information may be passed to them in some chronological order based on time-stamped events or predefined priorities. The various agents are able to generate queries dynamically and access databases automatically whenever the need arises. In other words, these service-agents have similar data search initiation capabilities as the user and are not be dependent solely on the user for access to external information sources.

The foundation of a knowledge-based organization may be characterized in terms of three kinds of capital, namely, human capital; organizational capital; and, relational capital. Within the continuous interactions among these spheres the human capital constitutes the source of knowledge that is responsible for generating the capabilities of the organization. The organizational capital generalizes these capabilities through a distributed framework of leadership that communicates the organization's collective intent to all parts of the organizational web-network. The relational capital leverages the capabilities of the organization to generate products.

Human capital plays a vital role in knowledge-based organizations and is receiving considerable attention in both government and corporate organizations. Since knowledge management involves the effective acquisition, development, and utilization of the human capital in an organization, as in the case of SDF, is in the best interest of the organization to maximize the contributions of the individual for the collective benefit of the organization. At SDF knowledge management is viewed as a facilitating vehicle – with the object of enabling (via Agent technologies) the human and organizational capabilities.

In SDF's application designs a distributed framework of leadership and communication is assumed. Here the framework is to utilize the organizational capital and knowledge management capabilities of the client to execute their enabling role in several ways. First, SDF recognizes that every member of the client organization is a contributor and a potential decision maker. They provide methods via a knowledge-about-knowledge approach to emphasize the encouragement, cultivation, and motivation of the individual. Second, SDF recognizes that knowledge management relies on local autonomy and concurrent activities. Their principal tools of leadership are the continuous analysis of feedback, the meticulous explanation and justification of intent and direction, and the maintenance of effective self-development opportunities. Third, SDF believes that knowledge management must foster the formation of internal and external relationships, because the relationship capital of the organization becomes one of the most important catalysts for increasing productivity.

2.2 Learning Mechanisms

Any useful representation of information in the computer must be capable of capturing the relationships among the entities (i.e., objects) in the problem system. While some of these associations are fairly static many of the associations are governed by current conditions and are therefore highly dynamic. They depend on a wide range of factors that relate to both environmental and personal circumstances and dispositions. These factors can be only partially accounted for through embedded knowledge and rules, and therefore become largely the purview of the human members of the collaborative human-computer partnership.

SDF adopted a modular approach to their product development, aligning their structure, processes and product architecture. This work design is characterized as a "platform architecture". At the most basic level, platforms provide a basic core that is altered and enhanced to produce product variants with different features [5].A product platform may be defined as the set of parts, subsystems, interfaces, manufacturing and operational processes that are shared among a set of products and that facilitate the development of derivative products with cost and time savings [6][7][8]. Sharing common software architecture across a product line brings a core set of knowledge and assets to the development process. Complexity, development and maintenance costs are reduced and the production of documentation, training materials, and product literature are streamlined. This approach means that the firm would need to undertake certain knowledge-based activities including identification of core competencies and might even consider such alternatives as outsourcing of some of its tasks.

Foremost though, SDF prides itself on "learning from each other". There is very little outside training. Where the need exists, such as new employees needing orientation, they create in house training, "the school house" where experts give lectures, relate software concepts, and programming styles for their product suite. At the team level "extreme programming" was adopted –very short iterative cycles. They did "not read a book and implement" but instead "learned from their mistakes." The overriding ability of a developer is "eagerness to learn". Responsibility is based on eagerness to work and the amount of work that a developer is willing to do. SDF realized that "most problems are human not technology".

Within the team everyone has to be aware of the domain (realm of the project). Everyone has to know how to use every piece of software. ("Although mangers only know about half of what the developers are doing"). Learning takes place starting with technical expertise in a broad field – everyone looks at the actual data – sharing information with support groups. Most of the developers learn in a narrow architecture – they teach themselves to become experts.

Conceptually SDF employs a common project across the company. Building on their original successes they have created a Tool Kit. The Tool Kit has been used in all of their projects, and in turn, each project has contributed to the Tool Kit and the Knowledge Data Management. The tools consist of components that support each other. These components are set of routines, procedures, methods for combining words, codes, and rules which together allow work to be completed quickly. Every project is cohesive yet restrictive in that the product is proprietary. In any event cross-learning takes place from product development to development. One key to their success is that the tool kit belongs to SDF and is furnished to the clients at no charge. The code belongs to the client but the ten percent ingredient resident in the basic tools is not transferred.

The procedure for handling and adopting new hardware and software products is a team decision. Generally a demo version with full capabilities and limited time usage is obtained. A team member "plays with it", the decision to actually adopt is a multi-team decision influenced by the primary group. Most of the project staff are "so young that they have the drive to want to look at something new – what's really cool and neat!"

2.3 Strategy & Design

The organization of SDF, on the surface, does not appear to be untypical for a software development firm. However, the various departmental units function with a minimum of supervision behaving in a manner that resembles an internal form of outsourcing. A good infrastructure of networks and electronic communications, and a well-thought through layout of workspace facilitate the firm's operation. There is a dual overlapping organizational mapping of departments and project teams – the firm is not unlike many product-based organizations. Much of the product work is conducted by cooperative supporting groups existing within the department structure. It has a flat organizational hierarchy divided along product and support entities. The leadership of each the product team is divided between a product leader and a technical leader. The dual leadership is intended to address these problems by assigning external and internal direction and as a check-and-balance control mechanism.

Within the product structure responsibility and direction of the support groups are divided and/or shared between these two leaders and the various departments (e.g. testing, customer support and training). Disputes or differences have to be resolved through discussion or are brought to senior management for resolution. This has not been a significant problem because the work content and work constituency is relatively homogeneous. New products evolve from existing products and involve technology transfer and adherence to grounded technologies that utilize SDF's spatial agent approach.

The approach, used by SDF, for achieving their application development objective is to represent information in the computer as objects with behavioral characteristics and relationships to other objects [9]. SDF's approach allows real world objects (buildings, products, networks) to be represented symbolically so that computer software modules can reason about them. It is important to note that the relationships among these objects are often far more important than the characteristics that describe the individual behavior of each object. The main idea is to design software components – to make them "generic – plug-and-play". As the team becomes more mature more components are being developed and enhanced – thus reducing the time to market for a product.

Most of the teams have worked together for three to seven years. They termed what they were doing as they evolved – extreme programming. The software development process is very open. Control is readily shared by all team members – roles, parts are only partially planned. The teams are divided into layers, all of which are software architecture-related such as the model, façade, graphical user interface, data base, and agent groups. Experts in each area perform research and dialog/share the results with the team. This design split enables team members to work on several projects simultaneously – enabling re-use and fostering enhancements.

At SDF agents are programmed to serve different purposes. Mentor agents have been designed to serve as guardian angels to look after the welfare and represent the interests of particular objects within the application system. For example, in a typical SDF application a Mentor agent would be designed to simply monitor the fuel consumption of a car or performs more complex tasks such as helping a tourist driver to find a particular hotel in an unfamiliar city. Service agents may perform expert advisory tasks on the request of human users or other agents. At the same time, Planning agents can utilize the results of tasks performed by Service and Mentor agents to devise alternative courses of action or project the likely outcome of particular strategies. Facilitator agents can monitor the information exchanged among agents and detect apparent conflicts. Such facilitator agents could detect a potential non-convergence condition involving two or more agents, and apply one of several procedures for promoting consensus or to merely notify the user of the conflict situation.

SDF looks upon knowledge management and decision-support systems as partnerships between users and computers. The ability of the computer-based components to interact with the user overcomes many of the difficulties, such as representation and the validation of knowledge, that continue to plague the field of machine learning [10][11]. Human and computer capabilities are in many respects complementary. Human capabilities are particularly strong in areas such as communication, symbolic reasoning, conceptualization, learning, and intuition.

All of this aside, work on new project starts with a very small management team, more dollars are put up front – there is an in-depth report analysis, data gathering, and ontology building. This process could take six months without forming a development team. A very large project may need only one or two people to do the design. All during this time there is very close coordination with the customer. The data collection is thoroughly documented and analyzed. Key to the project is an ontology relating data, people and processes; and a clear, precise definition of the user interface.

Looking at the case the following are a few of the design requirements that seem to have been utilized: legitimate formal and informal arenas for exchange of ideas were created; the continuity of support and improvement efforts for the products was maintained over a long period of time; the composition of the team reflected the totality of the business functional areas of expertise; goals, scope and purpose for the teams were defined and refined on an ongoing basis, and; there were effective processes for implementing continuous improvements during the software development process. At the team level coordination is not necessarily the role of the project manager. In many aspects the team is shielded – they are not aware of cost issues – but they are deadline driven.

The design dimensions represent different possible ways to respond to the design requirements. Design dimensions can be conceived on a continuum. Following are a few examples: The team members from one -- to -- several functional areas; the team members from same -- to -- different levels in the firm and; goal setting made centrally -- to -- in the team. Along each design dimensions there would be a range of choices that the organization designer needs to make. This is especially true in the configuration of the specific platform for product launching. The potential cause-and-effect relationships among the designed requirements, design dimensions, platform architecture and sustainability are an area that requires significant research efforts in the future.

2.4 Performance: Sustainability

Platform-based work design provided the foundation for sustainability at both the team and organizational levels. SDF's modular-based design allowed for simultaneous autonomy and scope boundary for work at different levels and phases. The iterative cycles and extreme programming enhanced ongoing knowledge acquisition, the flow of information and continuous improvement of the software development process. Scope creep was reduced by adhering to the modules and boundaries defined in the platform architecture. The time to market for the product was insured through the use of the agent structure.

One of the key findings from the case is that SDF established some type of a legitimate forum for exchange of ideas and actions. From an organization design perspective, the forum is seen as a mechanism with a structural configuration and processes that are devoted to improvements and learning. The iterative cycles approach coupled with the deliberation mechanisms for information-sharing and view typified by the product architecture provides an ongoing opportunity to improve and sustain business results and a way to foster learning at all levels and across all levels of the firm [12]. Our case suggests that not only is a learning mechanism (such as mentoring and face-to-face dialogues) an integral part of sustainability but that the type of learning mechanism is a clear managerial choice that has a significant influence on the organization's ability to develop and nurture sustainability. The very way that the firm chooses to lay out the work environment and the support patterns facilitates and establishes the ongoing learning environment.

Learning mechanisms seems to have played a critical part in sustainability at SDF. As we have seen, the establishment of mechanisms for information-sharing and deliberations at SDF provided an ongoing opportunity to improve and sustain business results and a way to foster learning at all levels and across all levels of the firm. Managers at SDF made choices about the design and deployment of specific learning mechanism. The platform-based architecture for software development work seems to provide a context that has the potential of fostering work environment that can increase the organization's ability to develop and nurture sustainability.

One of the foremost elements is the focus on the team. The team process mandates that "everyone has to work with everyone else." Any new hire or layoff consideration is discussed openly with the team. All interviews for new employees are conducted at the team level and hires are based on team consensus. One interesting observation is that 100% of the software developers and staff all came from the same university. Many of the present employees started out as part-time workers – in support functions such as testing, quality assurance, hardware configuring, etc.

2.5 Performance: Competitiveness

SDF attributes their success to several reasons. As a R&D organization they sold an "intellectual concept" that required a long period of time to analyze. Their goal was not to make money but to instead make change. Management felt that if they had to make money they would have to sell to the most common demands. Instead they choose to only sell what they wanted to sell. They have been in business for fifteen years without having to be "successful" – money was never a factor. SDF has no debt, has always operated at a profit, and has a sustained growth in business and staff. Their tactics were to start slow and only grew once a client gave them a contract. Their success centered not only as a niche player but also because they maintained a lower pricing structure than the large R&D concerns. Their core competency was the ability to develop a "rapid" prototype that "is bullet proof, has intelligence, and has a completely scalable architecture." In effect their products are not really prototypes but something that the client can build from.

They choose to stay within a narrow domain, a niche with limited competition. This was purposeful – "to survive as a small business you go with a knowledge area – an umbrella which they can control – stay within their area of expertise." They realized that for most software R&D firms that it was inevitable that they most likely would be taken over by a large company. However, with no debt, no ambitions to "grow" and a steady clientele it was difficult to be bought out. The production software business was of no real interest to SDF. However, unlike most R&D organizations employed by the military they always provided a tangible product. In most cases this product was a working prototype software system – a proof of concept. SDF's Tool Kit, inherent in each product, provides the nucleus that insures that no other contractor can take over their work. The client must agree to data rights protecting SDF's object schema, library of code, information searches, agent engine and the user interface components.

3 Discussions and Reflections

The SDF case involves a company that attempts to create, transfer and exploit its knowledge in a very competitive market. The organizational learning mechanisms that were implemented at SDF were an integral part of the strategy to achieve success. The intentional design of organizational learning mechanisms around knowledge management processes, while using advanced information technology infrastructure raises a number of challenges. Table 1 provides a summary of the learning requirements, design dimensions, and learning mechanisms that were implemented at SDF. In the discussion that follows we address: the characteristics of learning mechanisms in a knowledge-based work environment; the causal relationship between organizational learning mechanisms and the firm's ability to continuously improve the way the organization creates, transfers, exploits and manages knowledge, and; the relationship between organizational learning mechanisms, knowledge management processes and sustainability.

Software development organizations are viewed as workplaces that are characterized as knowledge intensive – their major emphasis is on knowledge.

Knowledge work is a complex process requiring multidisciplinary expertise in order to achieve a complex synthesis of highly specialized state-of-the-art technologies and knowledge domains. In knowledge-intensive work environments competitive advantage and product success are a result of collaborative, ongoing learning [13].

At SDF learning mechanisms centered on teams and the enhancement of knowledge management processes. The different teams and units, regardless of whether they are the software developers, quality control, user interface specialists, network engineers, or other specialized computer technologists all must keep abreast of technologies within their specific areas of specialization. The advanced information technology infrastructure provided an opportunity to facilitate knowledge creation, knowledge sharing and knowledge transfer within and between units.

However, this quest for knowledge is not restricted to specializations but moreover to understanding the needs and interest of the other team members and other teams. At SDF learning was encouraged and fostered by self-study and sharing of "best practices". As we have seen in the case , the creation of the platform-based work design, code modules and generic agent technologies provided the learning mechanisms and building blocks wherein the developers built on existing knowledge and practices to create a "better, improved agent" and contributed to an ever-expanding repertory of code.

The SDF company case identified few formal organizational learning mechanisms that were designed and implemented by the company for the purpose of continuously improving how the firm was creating, transferring and exploiting knowledge. More specifically, the flexible architecture design of the workspace created the space and facilitated human interaction for the purpose of learning and knowledge creation; the continuous mapping of expert and expertise via the multi-agent mechanism and the direct linkages to them allowed for knowledge transfer, and; the platform-based work arrangement allowed for knowledge transfer and exploitation between the different new product development projects.

At SDF management was there when they were needed but provided the project teams with leeway to make mistakes learn from each other, and to build on what others had done. The survival of the organization hinged on the reputation of their work. New business was generated based on the quality of prior projects. As was describe earlier, there were both formal and informal dialogue mechanisms at the organizational level. The physical work environment that was created encouraged the exchange of ideas to a point where one individual stated the following: "one wonders how anything can get done given the way we are all clustered together, but surprisingly things get done even though it appears to be chaotic at times." The network and software development infrastructure provided a template for new and developing staff to learn by merely using the system mechanisms. Finally, all team members had a common development interface and access to the complete library of software and all past and existent project work – "the design of the developers pod is intended to facilitate the development of the product."

SDF developed learning mechanisms that facilitate sustainable growth and knowledge management of the firm. Being a knowledge intensive firm, the development of information technology infrastructure, the multi agent system, the platform-based work design mechanisms, the iterative cycles of product development process and the formal and informal dialogue mechanisms all fostered sustainable growth. The result was a workplace that contributed to the well-being and development of employees while the system promoted creativity, motivation, commitment, interpersonal skills, learning, and resources for long-term coping, knowledge creation and knowledge exploitation.

Table 1. Learning by Design at the Software Development Firm (SDF)

Software Developers Learning Requirements	Learning Design Dimensions	Learning Mechanisms
Continuous improvement and enhancement of software development skills	* Support for self-learning * Explicit path for progression of task and skill development * Explicit assessment and reward process for skill development	* Recruitment process for highly skilled and already trained individuals * Formal and informal dialogues among team members and teams about continuous enhancement of skill development * "School house" – on-the-job training for new employees
A work environment that fostered and facilitated software development and learning	* Cluster-based workplace design * Open workplace architecture design	* Flexible architecture design that facilitates human interaction for the purpose of learning, knowledge creation and knowledge transfer among and between teams * Platform-based work design * Clear mapping and direct linkages to individual experts and expertise
Access to knowledge bases and best practice software modules	* Information technology infrastructure * Access to external knowledge bases (MSDN) * Re-usable software component library	* Formal and informal dialogue mechanisms * Search and discovery process IT routines - portals * Agent technology assistance

With each project or new product development SDF believed that they were continuously improving on their work. They were building, not only a knowledge repository, but also a better mousetrap. Their toolkit with restrictive code content affords them the protection from competitors to "steal" their code modules. The unique knowledge of the principals affords the organization the luxury of true specialists from the top down. Foremost though their main performance indicator is their desire to excel "without just making money" and to create a product that "they are proud of".

References

1. Ingelgard, A., Roth J., Shani, A.B. (Rami) and Styhre, A. Dynamic Learning Capability and Actionable Knowledge Creation: Clinical R&D in a Pharmaceutical Company. The Learning Organization, 9 (2), 65-77. (2002)

2. Schulz, M., The uncertain relevance of newness: Organizational learning and knowledge flow. Academy of Management Journal, 44 (4), 661-681. (2001)
3. Shani, A.B. (Rami), and Docherty, P , 2002, Learning by Design: Building Sustainable Organizations Blackwell Publications (forthcoming)
4. Lander, S. 1997: Issues in Multi-agent design systems, IEEE Expert, March/April Zhang, Q., and Doll, W. The fuzzy front end and success of new product development: A causal model, European Journal of Innovation Management, 4,2,95-112. (2001)
5. Ebrahimpur, G., and Jacob, M., Restructuring for agility at Volvo Car Technical Services, European Journal of Innovation Management, 4, 2, 64-72. (2001)
6. Krishnan, V., and Gupta, S. Appropriateness and impact of platform-based product development, Management Science, 47,1, 52-68. (2001)
7. Muffatto, M. Introducing a platform strategy in product development, International Journal of Production Economics, 60/61, 145-163. (1999)
8. Myers, L.J., Pohl, J., Cotton, J., Snyder, K., Pohl, S., Chien, S., and Rodriguez, T. Object Representation and the ICADS-Kernel Design, San Luis Obispo, California: CAD Center technical report (CADRU-08-93). (1993)
9. Thornton, C. Techniques in Computational Learning, London, England: Chapman and Hall. (1992)
10. Johnson-Laird, P. Human and Machine Thinking, Hillsdale, New Jersey: Erlbaum. (1993)
11. Sena, J., and Shani, A.B. (Rami), Intellectual capital and knowledge creation: Towards and alternative framework, in Liebowitz, J. (Ed.) Handbook of Knowledge Management, New York: CRC Press, 8-1 – 8-16. (1999)
12. Shani, A.B. (Rami), and Sena, J., Integrating product and personal development, in Docherty, P., Forslin, J., and Shani, A.B. (Rami), (Eds.), Creating Sustainable Work Systems: Emerging Perspective and Practice, London: Routledge (2001)

The Value of Knowledge Doesn't Exist

A Framework for Valuing the Potential of Knowledge

Paul Iske and Thijs Boekhoff

A great deal of work has been done in the past that seeks to identify how best to measure the value of knowledge and indeed the added value of knowledge management. **Paul Iske** and **Thijs Boekhoff** believe however that the real value of knowledge lies in its potential which is in turn dependent on the context in which that knowledge is used.

In the so-called knowledge economy intellectual assets have become the most important factor in determining the value of an organisation. Many activities nowadays focus on discovering the Holy Grail of knowledge management: the value of knowledge and the added value of knowledge management. Prominent work in this area includes that done by Sveiby and Edvinsson. However so far it has been difficult to develop quantitative measures that relate knowledge to the economic value of an organisation.

In fact the subject of valuing knowledge can be considered from a more general point of view in which the value assigned is not necessarily a financial one. The 'balanced scorecard' and the Skandia Navigator are examples of measurement methodologies that could be a starting point for developing non-financial measures that help to determine the value of knowledge.

However one question should be considered: why bother measuring at all? Many of the attempts especially in the US to develop a framework to measure the intellectual assets of an organisation are driven by the need to develop accountancy standards that will be the equivalent of those applicable for tangible assets. Such approaches would lead to the formation of a value for knowledge as being the intrinsic property of the organisation. However in general this cannot be the case.

Consider the process involved in the acquisition of a company for example. An important stage is the valuation of the target to arrive at a fair price. The target might have knowledge that is complementary to that of the buying party and thus of strategic importance. In this case the knowledge has a high value which will be reflected in the take-over price. Yet if the knowledge is already present in the acquirer's organisation or it is of no strategic importance the same knowledge has little or no value. This example demonstrates that the value of knowledge is context-dependent. We can therefore already formulate the main hypothesis of this paper: the value of knowledge is not an intrinsic property but depends on context.

In the remainder of this article we will attempt to narrow this statement down and indicate how one could come as close as possible to a workable definition of the value of knowledge. The valuation of intellectual assets remains important in the strategic

D. Karagiannis and U. Reimer (Eds.): PAKM 2002, LNAI 2569, pp. 632-638, 2002.

(management) processes of every organisation. Research from Gartner for example revealed that companies that pay explicit attention to the management of intellectual assets achieve anything up to a 30 per cent improvement in bottomline performance.

A Framework for Valuing Knowledge

Knowledge management is a prominent management subject and many books and articles on KM have been published. Some consensus on the basic concepts in the field is evident but in general the discipline lacks an adequate and accepted language that would allow us to formulate the necessary concepts in an unambiguous way and help us establish a link between theory and practice. Our opinion is that – as stated in the title – knowledge does not have value in itself but rather in its potential. Instead of the 'value of knowledge' we suggest focusing on valuing knowledge potential.

In this article we first offer you a mathematical drill down with which we hope to provoke a lively discussion among those of you who are struggling – as we are – with the question of measurability and the expectation that surrounds it. In the second part we will attempt to bring the discussion back down to earth by exploring the issue in the context of a well-known tool a PeopleFinder (a yellow pages or expert directory) and a new generation of tools that aim to connect workers with experts. So far the potential of these tools is in our opinion undervalued although this is partly because they are so difficult to implement.

A Mathematical Formulation for Knowledge Management

"Whereof one cannot speak one should be silent." These famous words spoken by Wittgenstein are seldom put into practice. Sometimes however we cannot speak simply because we lack the right words or even the right language. In science we see many examples of words or languages that have had to be invented before further progress in a field could be made. For example in mathematics complex numbers have been introduced as solutions to algebraic equations with some non-real solutions. Complex numbers have proved extremely useful in solving and simplifying various kinds of mathematical and scientific problems.

Though knowledge management is not and should not be quite as theoretical and sophisticated from a conceptual point of view we would probably benefit from the development of a formal language to describe the various stages in the generation distribution (re)usage and evaluation of knowledge.

Obviously we have to start with a definition of knowledge that can be used as a basis for developing the framework. Currently there are probably as many definitions as there are authors lecturers practitioners and so on. For the purpose of this opinion piece we will use the following definition: knowledge is the combination of facts experiences and perceptions that are being used to make a decision or to select an action by which a situation is changed into a more valuable situation.

There is an implicit value statement included in this definition: the value of knowledge is (part of) the difference between the value of the end-state and that of the original state. In the following we will refer to context as being the original situation the transition process and the (desired) end-situation. The context also includes the person(s) systems and organisations that are involved in the related decisions and/or actions. Notice that according to this definition knowledge can only add value within a context in particular in the decision-taking step and/or during the action selection. In other words talking about knowledge is only relevant within a certain context (ie when it is being used).

To be able to discuss the value of knowledge potential it has to be stripped from the context where it was generated or used. This is the opposite to some approaches that consider the replacement costs or the cost of generation to be determinant of the value.

Knowledge can be seen as input in a process context. Often it will be available in the form of information embedded in databases procedures best practices frequently asked questions (FAQs) handbooks personal memory people's behaviour etc. The added value can only be obtained if the knowledge is actually used in context. For discussion purposes we propose a formula (see figure 1) that captures the essential features of the knowledge value chain. At the end it enables us to categorise and prioritise properties of organisations knowledge management activities and even the value of it all.

$$V_P(K(\Omega)) = \sum_{\Gamma} \Big\{ \pi(K(\Omega),\Gamma)\,\rho(K(\Omega),\Gamma)\,\alpha(K(\Omega),\Gamma)\,V(K,\Gamma) + \sum_i \Big[V_P(L_i^{\Gamma}(K(\Omega),\Omega_i)) - I(L_i^{\Gamma}(K(\Omega),\Omega_i)) \Big] \Big\}$$

Fig. 1. Formula for the valuation of knowledge potential

The formula in figure 1 thus reads: the total potential value of the knowledge that is stored in the environment equals the sum over all contexts of the probability that this knowledge is related to the context multiplied by the connectivity that indicates how easy it is to transport the knowledge from the environment to the context multiplied by the activation coefficient that indicates how easy it is to activate the knowledge (to use it) in the context multiplied by the added value that is achieved within the context. Furthermore added value is obtained by learning which means generating new knowledge in context (as a consequence of the knowledge that has been used in this context) that can be stored in environment at the expense of an investment.

The total value of all knowledge potential in the organisation is then represented by the equation shown in figure 2.

$$V_P(K) = \sum_{\Omega} V_P(K(\Omega))$$

Fig. 2. The value of knowledge potential

We can summarise the elements in the first formula that need to be discussed in more detail as:

- Knowledge relevance indicator – the level to which knowledge is considered relevant for the business (processes) and the level to which business issues lead to new knowledge;
- Knowledge connectivity factor – the level to which it is possible to transport knowledge from an environment (source) to the context (work situation business process);
- Knowledge activation factor – the level to which it is possible to activate knowledge (to use it) in a specific context;
- Added value in context – the level to which knowledge has added value (has been useful) in a specific context;
- Knowledge capturing and learning – the level to which new knowledge is generated in a specific context (as a consequence of the knowledge that has been used in this context) which can be stored in a specific environment at the expense of a specific investment.

Note that it is clear from the first formula that if one of the factors is zero there is no value added irrespective of the value of the other parameters. Quantitative insights into the environmental parameters that determine the value of the factors in the formula will help to optimise the return on investment of knowledge-related projects. In general one should focus on the smallest parameter (the weakest link) to achieve optimal improvement.

For the purposes of this article we will describe our experience in the case of a PeopleFinder [1] implementation to indicate how these elements can help us to structure discussions as to the value of knowledge and in particular the added value of knowledge management.

The end result in many KM system implementation projects is usually an infrastructure or ICT-environment through which information is pushed to the user. The internal debate is always about the best way to attract the user to the system in order to encourage people-to-machine interaction and thus value to the business.

Knowledge Relevance Indicator

The great advantage of PeopleFinder-type systems is that the link between knowledge and the originating context is clear. In other words the relevance factor between knowledge and the specific context can be quite large. This will be even more evident in the next generation tools in this area which are expert-locating systems based on questions and answers. A good example of a Q&A-based tool is the website www.askme.com. Currently there are several suppliers of askme-type applications for use within organisations and within networks of organisations and their partners/customers. We believe these tools can add a great deal of value and we have seen some interesting business cases for the implementation of such systems with a reasonably well-justified ROI calculation. Also the use of advanced personalised tools such as portals and applications like Autonomy helps to increase the probability that relevant knowledge is transferred to the context.

Some case examples demonstrate the importance of the knowledge relevance indicator in the past. For instance 3M initially invented glue that could have been dismissed as 'useless' but a newly created context allowed the hugely successful Post-It notes to be invented.

Knowledge Connectivity Factor

Standard KM solutions hardly seem to solve the problem of how to transform information push into information pull through the detailed analysis of people's preferences and needs in knowledge-based working processes. It is our opinion that this issue directly relates to the connectivity factor: the exchange between two (or more) persons as well as the exchange between these workers and the system. Regarding the former certain fundamental questions need to be answered: what is the organisational (physical) distance? Are there any language barriers or differences? Do they have a relationship (do they know each other? Is there a networking effect)? Are there cultural including time and compensation scheme constraints?

Research result from the Delphi Group has shown that up to 20 per cent of an employee's time is spent on re-discovering knowledge that was already present somewhere else in the organisation. This is an indication that in most organisations the product of the knowledge relevance indicator and the knowledge connectivity factor is small.

Knowledge Activation Factor

ICT can be of great value to an organisation in particular web-based technologies. But the main objective of ICT should in our opinion always be to strengthen the interaction between people. The effective and efficient exchange of knowledge depends not only on the ability to transfer exchange and communicate but also on the ability to understand accept and leverage. This latter ability is reflected in the knowledge activation factor.

The effective exchange between two persons must be measured according to the presence of trust communication skills language (barriers) motivation (to send and to receive) the prevalence of Not-Invented-Here syndrome and (shared) mental models. The success of a PeopleFinder depends heavily on these issues. This seems to be an unmanageable set of factors but explicit (peer or management) attention increases the activation factor. Also the effective and efficient interaction between systems and individuals can be measured: the way you develop a user-interface the context-suitable formulation (including language) and the way you introduce the application will lead to measurable increased motivation and usage.

Added Value in Context

Search results and actions taken upon those results indicate the way knowledge has been of use in the business process. The PeopleFinder allows professionals to locate colleagues with relevant expertise and experience for a given project. The level to which knowledge has had added value (has been useful) in a specific context should be derived from the experiences of these users. The result of the evaluation of the PeopleFinder and its effect on the project team and thus on the business is called added value in context. In practice this means that the added value of a PeopleFinder tool is often measured on an anecdotal basis.

Knowledge Capturing and Learning

Humans possess a great deal of tacit knowledge – we know more than we can say and share. The organisational challenge is to remove the barriers and train people to tap into this knowledge in order to create stronger more innovative companies. It requires leadership skills to attract train and retain talented and motivated people. It requires vision to guide and coach talent towards collaboration and teamwork. Most learning programmes in companies address content structure and procedures but neglect the context in which these programmes reside. Competence and learning depend on knowing where to find and how to reuse the right resources to get the job done. The PeopleFinder facilitates serendipity and by offering the opportunity to be lucky it is possible to facilitate action learning.

Summary Conclusion and Next Steps

Value does not lie in knowledge itself. The real value lies in the potential of that knowledge and thus in:

- The ability to identify and remove blockages between individuals and in the system that hinder interaction;
- The ability of knowledge workers to find what they are looking for and indeed through serendipity what they do not know they are looking for;
- The ability to reuse the knowledge through smart 'packaging';
- -The courage and pride of workers to show communicate and sell their knowledge via personal and digital channels;
- The creativity to identify new contexts in which knowledge is relevant together with the ability to realise these contexts in the organisation – these are in fact the essentials in the innovation process.

The main conclusion of this article is that one should speak of the value of knowledge potential rather than the value of knowledge. The value added is dependent on the identification of the transfer to and the activation of knowledge in the various contexts where that knowledge is being used. The value of knowledge therefore is not the intrinsic property of an organisation but is dependent on the environment and the objectives of the measurement.

Most organisations focus their KM (ICT) programmes on knowledge transfer and thus on the knowledge connectivity factor. We believe that more emphasis should be put on the knowledge relevance indicator which is directly related to choosing a 'pull' strategy rather than a 'push' strategy. Finally the knowledge activation factor deserves closer attention since this determines the actual realisation of the value and is influenced by complicated environmental parameters which are often related to human and cultural influences.

- We the authors of this article are working on making the qualitative relationships described above between the elements in the formula and the environmental parameters more quantitative. This will help in the assessment of the key value drivers and the most efficient and effective ways to realise the potential value of knowledge. We hope that this article will spark interaction with our peers so that together we will be able to take the next step in demystifying the true value of knowledge and make more transparent the return on investments knowledge management activities have to offer.

References

1. A PeopleFinder is an automated system to search for and locate colleagues with expertise and experience relevant to a given project (competency profiles)
2. Paul Iske is senior vice president and chief knowledge officer at ABN AMRO Corporate Finance. He is also a freelance consultant on KM issues. He can be contacted at: paul.iske@knocom.com

Thijs Boekhoff is co-founder of Squarewise (http://www.squarewise.com). He can be contacted at: boekhoff@squarewise.com

Author Index